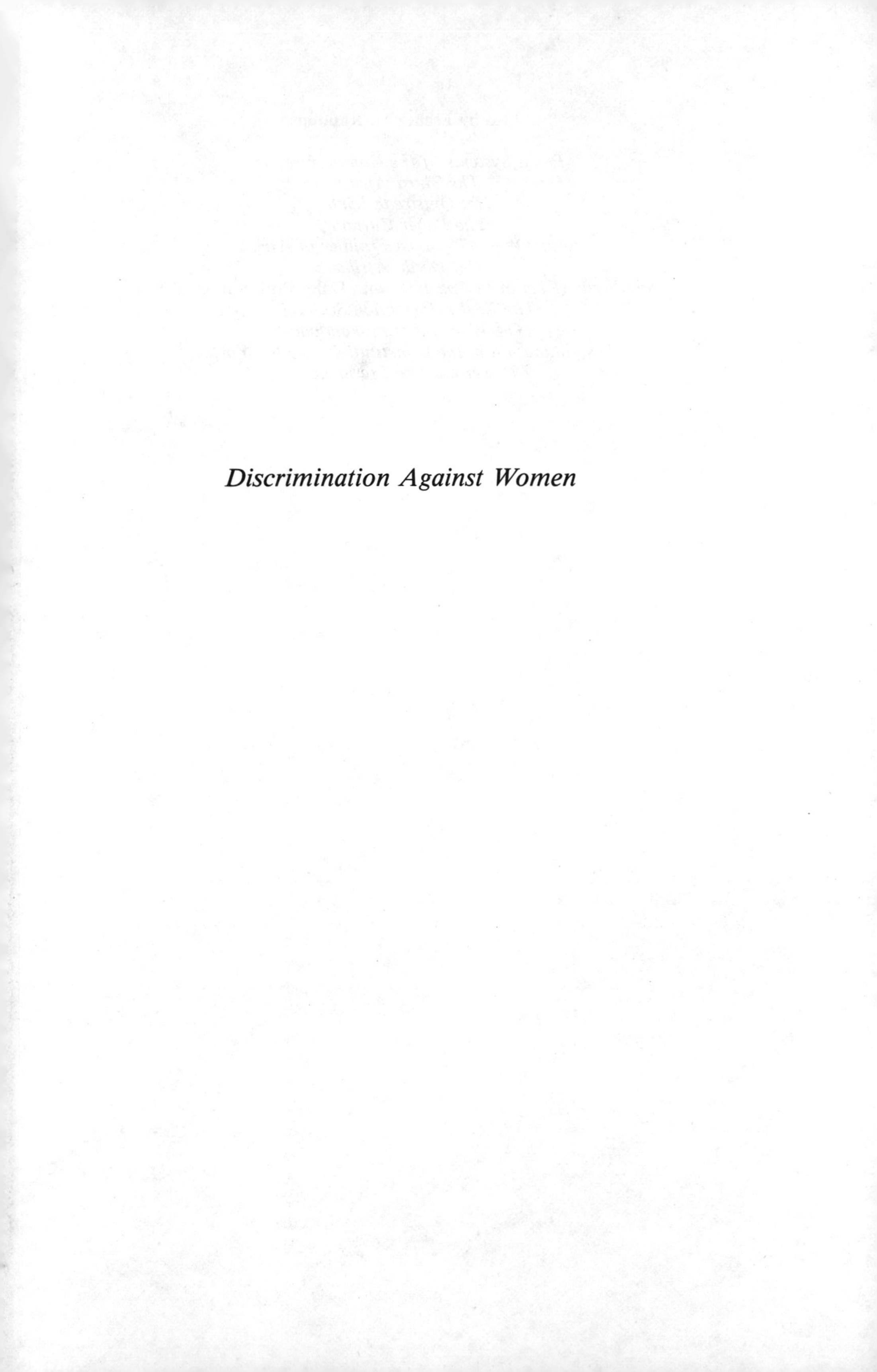

Discrimination Against Women

Also by Eschel M. Rhoodie

Penal Systems of the Commonwealth
The Third Africa
Het Omstrede Land
The Paper Curtain
South West: The Last Frontier in Africa
Het Derde Afrika
Southern Africa in Perspective (with Dale, Potholm, et al.)
The Real Information Scandal
Die Ware Inligtingskandaal
Discrimination in the Constitutions of the World
Power and the Presidency

Discrimination Against Women

A Global Survey of the Economic, Educational, Social and Political Status of Women

by

Eschel M. Rhoodie

with a foreword by

ALBERT P. BLAUSTEIN

McFarland & Company, Inc., Publishers
Jefferson, North Carolina, and London

British Library Cataloguing-in-Publication data available

Library of Congress Cataloguing-in-Publication Data

Rhoodie, Eschel M. (Eschel Mostert)
Discrimination against women.

Bibliography: p. 587.
Includes index.
1. Sex discrimination against women—Law and legislation. 2. Sex discrimination against women. 3. Women's rights. I. Title.
K3243.R48 1989 342'.0878 89-42748
342.2878

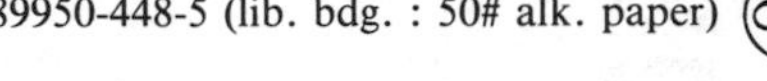
ISBN 0-89950-448-5 (lib. bdg. : 50# alk. paper)

Printed in the United States of America

McFarland & Company, Inc., Publishers
Box 611, Jefferson, North Carolina 28640

To Katy who inspired me

Contents

Foreword

• Women represent half of the world's population and perform nearly 66 percent of all working hours but receive only one-tenth of the income generated and own less than 1 percent of the property.

• Only 5 percent of 160 members of the International Labor Organization have ratified the I.L.O. conventions of 1981 and 1982 protecting women with family responsibilities against unfair termination of employment.

• In the United States some 77 percent of poverty is borne by single, divorced, or widowed women. In New York City, zookeepers (usually men) who did not finish high school are paid more than schoolteachers (usually women) with four years of college education.

• In the Soviet Union, Communist ideology is constitutionally wedded to the principle of sexual equality; yet women comprise 88 percent of the ditch-diggers at any typical hydro-electric project while constituting less than 1 percent of the Soviet Academy of Science.

• In Indonesia, a boy aged 15 is considered the legal head of the family, in his father's absence, even though his mother may be a lawyer or the boy's teacher in high school.

The foregoing are but a few vivid illustrations of the worldwide denial of the rights of women. These examples provided some impetus for this comprehensive analysis of the continuing subordinate status of women. This topic is as important as any in the study of discrimination. Of all deprived groups in the world today, women seem to have suffered the most throughout history. Racial, ethnic, and religious discrimination has produced numerous victims, but women, members of a majority group, have suffered even more than members of these minority groups.

The study of comparative human rights began in a serious fashion only within the past two decades. But the denial of the rights of women around the world has not been seen as a major feature of human rights. A comprehensive and comparative analysis of the rights of women, and of the abuse of those rights, meets as important a need as any in a full consideration of human rights. The time has come to provide a broad-based study of women's rights—a topic at least as important as discrimination based upon race, religion or ethnicity. In compiling such a study, the author of this book has undertaken a pioneering venture.

Until recently, scholarly attention to women's rights and related subjects has been limited, and generally national (one nation) in scope. The most ambitious undertaking has been Rita Falk Taubenfeld and Howard J.

Taubenfeld's multivolume collection *Sex-Based Discrimination,* an excellent collection of treaties, declarations and other legislation concerned with the rights of women in international law. The book in hand goes beyond the examination of international law, to examine the effect of national legislation on such important topics as education, employment, property, marriage and divorce, and the personal autonomy of women.

Governments and international organizations have begun to delve more actively into this heretofore neglected subject during the past two decades. True, the International Labor Office has been concerned with maternity protection since 1919, night work since 1921, and equal remuneration since 1951, but this activity has had little impact. The United Nations itself has called repeatedly for greater progress in the protection and enhancement of the rights of women, but with limited success, in spite of such documents as the Convention on the Elimination of All Forms of Discrimination Against Women (1979) and the earlier Convention on the Political Rights of Women (1953).

The year 1975 was declared by the United Nations to be the start of International Women's Year. In 1985, ten years later, delegates from over 140 nations met in Nairobi, Kenya, to examine the progress of women's rights in the previous decade. Women, it was found, rarely own land in their own right, yet they till the land more frequently than men. Women are concentrated in the lowest paid occupations and are more vulnerable to unemployment than are men. Women do as well as men when admitted to school, but few have been allowed the privilege in many nations. Women's illiteracy is greater than men's on a three-to-two basis worldwide, while in some nations real rates of female literacy are only 6 to 10 percent. Politically, women are dramatically underrepresented in nearly all countries, in spite of legislative or constitutional provisions guaranteeing them the right to participate in politics. Women's health is, on the whole, worse than men's, and women are more subject to physical abuse and other forms of degradation.

Some of this news came to public attention as a result of the vigilance of women's rights groups in various regions of the world. While the activity of women's rights groups is obviously a social development of great significance, this is not a focus of this book. The struggle for women's rights is more than the task of feminists. It is part of a greater struggle for human rights, embracing a majority of the members of the human race.

As a starting point in that struggle there must be a thorough study of the legal situation in which women find themselves in the various nations of the world. This means more than an examination of the international documents concerning women's rights; it means a careful survey of the legal environment in which women live their lives. In the area of women's rights there is a heightened awareness that equality of treatment is virtually unattainable in most countries at present. The elimination of discrimination against women still has a long way to go. Marriage, divorce, and family planning remain special issues for women. Education, employment, property rights and personal autonomy are more general concerns with special salience for women.

In this book a well-reasoned effort to survey the remaining legal barriers to the advancement of women's rights is attempted. The book is a comprehensive, comparative study that up till now has not been available in any language. It is intended not only for women, but for all those who can do the most good in improving the status of women—which often means men, especially those who are informed and enlightened enough to understand that civilized societies cannot continue to neglect their female majorities. Sadly, without the support of men greater equality for women cannot be attained. This book is written in such a fashion that all concerned and well-educated persons may make use of it, not only scholars and specialists. The topic is of such importance that it will interest all those who are concerned with decency and justice.

The research for this book produced surprising features of women's rights, some of which are little known. For example, female slavery still can be found in some not-so-remote areas of the world. The physical abuse of women is another notable example of a topic neglected in many nations. The sexual mutilation of young women is still a customary practice in many nations in Africa, the Middle East and Asia. Women's health is a major issue. Abortion practices in many nations are responsible for more deaths of women of childbearing age than any other cause. In Latin America, in which medically safe abortions are denied women as a result of legal provisions, many unnecessary deaths are caused by illegal abortions. It also appears that there is a linkage between the low literacy of many Third World women and high infant mortality rates.

Even in the industrialized world women lag behind men. In the United States, women's wages are still far less than men's, in spite of recent legislation. Women in Muslim countries are even worse off, since many are denied essential social and economic rights for cultural reasons. Discriminatory treatment of women, especially in wage rates, persists even when the laws seem to protect them.

An analysis of the status of women, emphasizing a comparison of legal and constitutional rights, is a revealing source of information. Although there is a considerable gap between law and reality, one must begin by understanding the state of law. Even though by the 1990s nearly every nation will have ratified the various international conventions protecting and promoting the rights of women, equal treatment of the sexes will not be at hand. Nonetheless, the comparison of the domestic existing laws from one nation to another will provide reformers with basic information, indicating the extent of the gap between international versions of women's rights and the prevailing domestic laws.

Implementation of women's rights and the attainment of equal opportunity is a much more complex topic, in which facts and rumor intermingle. The author of this book has chosen to keep his distance from speculation, and to pay respect to the views of other experienced research teams and scholars. Although considerable attention is paid to implementation issues (including several recommendations), the thrust of this book is directed at revealing the persistence of social, economic and political discrimination against women in the domestic law of their own nations and in their economic status as workers. It is hoped that, armed with the information provided in this book, a more reasonable approach to topics as controversial as "affirmative action" and "comparable worth" will be available to policy makers.

This book should provide a realistic means of measuring the progress of women's rights against legal and statutory provisions while, at the same time, helping to highlight the most serious abuses to the dignity of women. It is an international axiom, embodied in scores of constitutions, that political platforms advocating discrimination based on race, religion and gender have been shunned by the "civilized" world. But the author has shown that, in fact, discrimination against women still exists on a massive scale, even in advanced nations. While there are legal, administrative and economic measures which society can, and should, take to overcome and eliminate this kind of discrimination, perceptions and attitudes of both men and women worldwide must change before any real progress can be made.

ALBERT P. BLAUSTEIN
Professor of Law, Rutgers University
Co-Editor of *Constitutions of the World*
President, Human Rights Advocates International, New York

Part One
Introduction

Maori men in New Zealand were defined by society as "tapu," or sacred, while women were seen as "noa," or common. Similarly, in Hawaii, perceived differences in sanctity made it impossible for men and women to dine together. — From Margot Duley and Mary Edwards, *The Cross Cultural Study of Women.*

1. The Evaluation and Presentation of Data

What began as a comprehensive analysis of the legal environment of women, worldwide, slowly evolved into a broad-based evaluation of the status of women in general with emphasis on the legal environment. Ultimately four themes were dealt with: *firstly,* a profile of women internationally and by region; *secondly,* the status of women vis-à-vis men in respect of education, employment, occupation, and income; *thirdly,* visible discrimination in various fields such as education, religion, wages and employment opportunities; and *fourthly,* the legal world of women: constitutional provisions, statutory differentiation (or discrimination), and traditional or customary law in respect of political rights, family rights (to assets, to divorce, to guardianship of children, etc.), property rights, employment rights and rights of personal autonomy, highlighted by case studies of 20 different countries.

In studying the legal environment of women it soon became evident that for the study to have both academic and practical value, a background canvass on women, a frame of reference, was both desirable and necessary to facilitate the evaluation of the content and effect of legislation in respect of the rights of women. In short, the legal worlds of women should not and indeed cannot be evaluated in a vacuum. Evaluation, appreciation or condemnation is not possible without, at least, a background of women's status in respect of education, employment, income and other factors. At the same time, the United Nations' pronouncements and constitutional formulations which decry the existence of any disabilities against women are not sufficient on their own to evaluate society's attitude towards women. These international formulations, couched in governmental language, are more often than not merely hortatory. This work is more concerned with what national governments, and not the United Nations, have promulgated, enacted and decreed as law. But the United Nations cannot be ignored as an international agency because so many of the laws and regulations which have seen the light during the past decade (to eliminate discrimination against women and promote their general welfare) came about as the result of United Nations resolutions, actions and conventions.

Without a study of the legal worlds of women, the work would have been merely descriptive of the status of women and what people, organizations, governments and international agencies believe the reality should be. But reality is found in a juxtaposition of the dynamics of women's progress and the legal order; in adherence to legal precepts, or in their denial; in legal procedures to compel enforcement; and in the search for new laws to achieve equal opportunities and rights for women, and questions about which laws are most effective.

Anyone who is at all concerned about the rights of women will soon realize that to achieve meaningful equality for women requires first of all a thorough knowledge of the legal environment. Rhetoric and emotion have so far produced unspectacular, even disappointing progress. (See Chapter 29.)

In any debate on women's rights, those who come armed with the facts are going to find the resistance less formidable mainly because both opinion-formers and the decision-makers have already conceded, at least in the West, the fact that women are discriminated against. They have also accepted that such discrimination is wrong and that equal opportunities are necessary. But women themselves are often short on facts as to the severity of the problem, the gap between policy and practice and the legal remedies available to achieve equal opportunities, for example, in employment. The differences which arise are related to targets, tactics, resources and ways to enforce equality where there is willful and persistent discrimination. This subject is dealt with in Chapter 30.

Given the serious nature of the subject of women's rights and the heat which this has generated among so many local and international organizations, it comes somewhat as a surprise that, excepting the United States and a few other Western nations, the women's movement itself, or its supporters, have not taken a closer look at what is already available to them in the many legal worlds of women's rights: in constitutions, national and state laws, regulations, judicial decisions and customary law. These five legal worlds form the bulk of the subject matter of this book insofar as it pertains to political rights, the family, property, employment and personal autonomy. It is possible to add other areas which are also of concern to women, but the aforementioned are the areas where discrimination all over the world is still causing the greatest deprivation. Studying the legal barriers also provides the bonus of knowing what laws already exist to protect women and to ensure their rights.

Women's Views

How do women themselves—those who are recognized experts in the fields of law, economics, political science, labor, education, anthropology, and sociology—perceive the status of women, the reasons for the discrimination against women, and their struggle to win equal opportunities with men? During the past 15 years these women, and women's organizations, as well as research institutes and international agencies, have produced an impressive range of work—some of it highly subjective, most of it balanced, and some of it of excellent quality. The author has gone to extraordinary lengths in his effort to select the highest quality works for this survey, based on depth of research, currency, and objectivity, as well as the relevance of the data. The views of these women deserve wide recognition and this analysis has depended heavily on their findings, also for purposes of comparison.

It was impossible to review the work, objectives, achievements and claims of all women's groups worldwide. That has been (largely) covered in numerous other works as *Empowerment and the Law,* edited by Margaret Schueler; *The Cross Cultural Study of Women,* edited by Margot Duley and Mary Edwards; and in United Nations publications such as *World Survey on the Role of Women in Development.*

Care has also been taken to select only the latest studies. Women's rights is a fast-changing field. The introduction of a single anti-discriminatory law, or the ratification of a United Nations convention to eliminate discrimination against women, can bring significant change in certain countries over a short period. Almost all the source material used for the compilation of this book was published after 1980. Most of the work was researched during the years 1983–1987. A few books are from the period 1975–1980, but their excellence, as in the Lapidus work on women in Soviet society (1978), will be of great value well into the next decade.

Statistical Data

Because the study went beyond the superficial charges of discrimination, the use of statistics and tables became imperative. Where special factors were involved, such as discrimination against women in the Muslim-Arab world, care was taken to examine the basic philosophy and extent of the Muslim religion and concomitant Islamic Law as it affects women.

Statistical data in the United States was not only readily available but also up to date, usually not more than one to three years old. That of Europe was less recent, but in the case of other major powers, such as the Soviet Union and China, even Japan, statistical material was anywhere from five to eight years old. In the rest of the world, notably Latin America and Asia, the situation was much worse, while in Africa, except for the Republic of South Africa, statistics on women, whether as a group or in comparison with men, were so outdated as to be largely useless, some of them anywhere from 15 to 25 years old. Certain statistics were simply non-existent. In 1978 the Center for International Research of the United States Bureau for Census established a special data base, to provide source material for the United States Office of Women in Development (US Agency for International Development), of worldwide demographic and socio-economic statistics disaggregated by sex. With all the resources available to this powerful United States agency, the statistics for West and Central Africa available for publication in 1984 in *Women of the World: Sub-Saharan Africa* (United States Department of Commerce, Bureau of Census, Washington, WID-2) appeared as shown on page 6. ("NA means "not available.")

It should be noted that included in the group in Table 1 are Ghana, Africa's oldest independent state after Ethiopia, Liberia and South Africa, as well as Nigeria, Africa's most populous state. Figures for 41 other African countries were as bad. Only Senegal, the Ivory Coast, Mali, Upper Volta, Cameroon and Malawi provided statistics covering the mid-'70s.

The 1985 study (WID-4) on women in Asia and the Pacific revealed only a slightly better pattern. Statistics for countries such as South Korea, Hong Kong, Pakistan, Burma, Malaysia, the Philippines, and Thailand, to mention just a few countries, were all for the period 1970–1972. When it came to labor force statistics and distribution by sex and occupation, even countries such as India could do no better than 1971. The Latin American study (WID-1 published in 1984) had to use 1970 statistics from Argentina and Brazil, the economic powerhouses of South America, even for such basic material as the literacy rate of men and women. For Jamaica the only available statistic was for 1960. To determine the percentage of boys and girls enrolled in primary school, the best that Mexico, Panama, Chile, and Paraguay could produce was also 1970. Even trying to determine the number of women at university was difficult. The statistics for Costa Rica were for 1970; for Mexico, 1969; for Bolivia and Peru, 1968; and for Chile, 1964. To indicate how many women were at work, Cuba, Panama, Mexico, Argentina, Brazil, Chile, and Guyana could do no better than 1970.

It is highly unlikely that recent statistics produced by many African, Latin American, and Asian governments are anywhere near reliable. In particular, a question mark should be put behind the statistical data which many Third World governments suddenly produced for the international conference in Nairobi in 1985 to mark the end of the United Nations Decade on Women. In *Atlas: Women in the World* (Simon and Schuster, New York, 1986), authors Joni Seager and Ann Olson also observed: "Throughout the research for this atlas we have been hampered by the inadequacy and inaccessibility of international data on women. *Some* information exists on almost all topics but, with the exception of a few standard indicators, information on women is conspicuously absent from conventional sources. . . . The official invisibility of women perpetuates the myth that what women do is less important, less noteworthy, less significant. Women are *made* invisible by policies and priorities that discount the importance of collecting information about them. Although the United Nations Decade for Women (1975–85) resulted in a considerable increase in international information on women, women are still not generally included in the information mainstream. Largely as a result of these data constraints, there are a number of topics that we consider important but could not include. Readers will notice that large areas of interest . . . are missing."

The Countries Selected

Since it was impossible to provide a comprehensive nation-by-nation study of each of the world's 160 nation-states, it was decided to divide the world into various regions, most of which defined themselves automatically in several respects, namely: the European Community, the Latin American World, the Arab-Muslim World, the African World, the Asian World, the Communist World, and North America.

There is also a section on the international community. As far as the latter is concerned there are several important covenants and resolutions of the U.N., decisions of the European Court at Strasbourg, stipulations of the Treaty of Rome and of other international instruments and organizations affecting the rights of women which are important.

Region and country	Literacy	Enrollment	Internal migration	Economic activity	Marital status	Head of household	Fertility	Life expectancy at birth
Coastal West Africa								
Benin	1961	1961	1961	1961	1961	1961	1961	(NA)
Ghana	1971	1970	1970	1970	1971	1970	1970	1970
Guinea	(NA)	1954–55	(NA)	1954–55	1954–55	1954–55	(NA)	(NA)
Ivory Coast	1975	(NA)	1975	1975	(NA)	(NA)	(NA)	(NA)
Liberia	1974	1974	(NA)	1974	1974	1974	1970–71	1970–71
Nigeria	1971-73	(NA)	(NA)	(NA)	(NA)	(NA)	1971–73	1971-73
Sierra Leone	1963	1963	1963	1963	(NA)	(NA)	1974	1974
Togo	1970	1970	1970	1970	1970	(NA)	1970	1961
Central Africa								
Burundi	1970–71	1970–71	(NA)	1970–71	1970–71	(NA)	1970–71	1970–71
Cameroon	1976	1976	(NA)	1976	1976	(NA)	1976	1976
Rwanda	1970	(NA)	1970	1970	1970	(NA)	1970	1970
Sao Tome and Principe	(NA)	(NA)	(NA)	(NA)	(NA)	(NA)	1973–79	(NA)
Zaire	1955–57	1955–57	(NA)	1955–57	1955–57	(NA)	1955–57	(NA)

Note: NA indicates data are not available.

Grouping of the states into geographical regions was on the basis of industrial development, tradition, legal systems, religion, political affiliations, trade blocs and proximity.

It was more difficult to select the various countries within each region to be covered by the research. The reasons that more countries were included in some sections than in others were the availability of information, more recent statistical data, easier access to official records and other source material, and the extent of organized activity on behalf of women.

Only five countries were chosen among the more than 40 Muslim states of the world. Those five were chosen for inavailability of information and willingness of the women's movement, and of men, to express themselves publicly on the subject of women's rights. Talking to the Pakistanis or Saudi Arabians about women is viewed by men in those countries as some sort of sexual or moral aberration on the part of the interviewer.

In the African world there is one country from each of the so-called four Africas: Nigeria in West Africa with its largely Negroid population; Kenya in East Africa with its Bantu-speaking peoples whose customs, cultures and history are very much different from those of West African blacks; South Africa with its dual economy and its multi-racial and multi-cultural population structure; and North Africa. Egypt was included under the section dealing with the Arab-Muslim world.

Though China is indisputably a Communist state, it has been slotted with other countries in Asia, principally because of geography and the fact that, almost invariably, data collected and provided by private and official sources, both nationally and internationally, including the United Nations and the International Labor Organization, all include China with other Asian states. Thus the section on the Communist Bloc (Part Six) is concerned primarily with the Soviet Union and other Communist states of the so-called East Bloc in Europe.

Case Studies

To give detailed information on the strictly legal environment, case studies were completed for fifteen countries. Most of the states elected themselves. Britain is the mother of parliamentary government, a modern state with typical Western values. In Europe, France and Germany are the two dominant states, politically and economically speaking. In the Communist world the Soviet Union is dominant. In the African sphere Nigeria is Africa's most populous state while Kenya is the state currently most concerned among black African countries with women's rights. In Latin America, Brazil is the region's largest and most populous state. In the Arab-Muslim world, Iran is a fundamentalist state, Egypt and Tunisia less so. In Asia no study would be complete without an analysis of the situation in both China and India, the world's most populous states.

The 15 countries received detailed attention in respect of specific laws

Table 1. Lack of statistical data for Africa: 1975–1985

affecting the daily existence of women. Several other states received a general as well as a detailed examination, for example the United States and Japan, both giants in terms of population and industry, yet culturally poles apart.

In the chapters concerning conclusions and recommendations (Chapters 29 and 30) more attention was paid to certain countries because of the peculiarities of women's problems in those states – for example South Africa, with a dual economy and dual legal system, and the United States, political leader of the West with the most organized and public-supported women's movements.

It is assumed that not everyone who is going to read this book, or who would want to interest himself or herself in the rights of women, has sufficient depth of knowledge on the subject of the plight of women to be able to judge the various legal worlds covered in this study, either for necessity, scope, effectiveness, thrust or relevancy. For this reason a special chapter, a general international survey on women's struggle for equality, entitled *The Environment of Discrimination,* has been included (Chapter 3). This international overview should help to place the need for this book in sharp perspective. This book should therefore be seen not only as a source for determining the rights which women already enjoy in law or the rights denied, but also as a source to define the depth of discrimination against women and the extent thereof.

Taking stock of and utilizing the existing legal remedies in the struggle to improve women's lot should be the first task of any concerned individual or organization. In fact, it would be irresponsible and self-defeating not to assess what the legal arsenal holds before firing any other rounds in the battle.

Presentation

In presenting the data compiled for this work it was decided to provide a global introduction for the purpose of orientation (Chapter 2) and this together with *The Environment of Discrimination* constitutes the general frame of reference. In addition, at the beginning of each part of the book there is a chapter (*General Survey of the Status of Women*) providing details of women's status, education, employment, income, wage discrimination, occupational segregation, political representation and other facts to serve as a more detailed background for analyzing and evaluating the world of women in that particular region. Where a country is the subject of a special case study (in terms of its laws) this has been done under the country's property laws, political rights, family law, personal rights and autonomy.

The recommendations made in Chapter 30 are neither global nor aimed at any specific region or country, except for the United States and the Republic of South Africa, which are two special cases. Of all of the world's 26 industrially developed countries, they have the worst record in wage discrimination and occupational segregation, and both lack national policies, and legislation, aimed at providing for working women during pregnancy and after childbirth and for working women with small children at home. The recommendations, even in the case of South Africa and the United States, should therefore not be seen as totally comprehensive. The first part of Chapter 30 will offer certain general recommendations, based on the decisions taken during the world conference of women in Nairobi in 1985, followed by some regional suggestions and then by the two special cases of South Africa and the United States. Affirmative action and comparable worth are analyzed as recommended lines of action.

Research

Because the need for further research is axiomatic, and since this work was written also as an introduction and guide to the study of women's rights (at college and university level), a review of principal, relevant and easily available sources of information was considered necessary (Chapter 31). This was obviously a selective process concerned more with national and regional comparisons. A complete and up-to-date guide for research on the status of women in general would have entailed compiling a massive tome on its own. Some existing individual anthologies and bibliographies already contain as many as 3,000 entries. What is provided here are the names of books and existing sources which, in the opinion of the writer, should be the starting point for anyone who wishes to undertake further research on women in respect of the following topics: their political status; educational problems; wage discrimination; segregation in the market place; social status; economic contribution; activities in the industrial, agricultural or services areas; constitutional and legal problems in respect of education, marriage, the family, or labor; representation in legislative and governmental councils; *regional studies* on the foregoing subjects or *comparative analysis*, either by grouping of countries (e.g. rich, poor, developed or undeveloped, Communist, Western or non-aligned), by religion (e.g. Muslim or Christian), by economic system (e.g. Capitalist or Marxist), or by legal system.

The last chapter of this book contains specific suggestions as to the structure of further research including one complete outline.

There is a bonus to other students of the same subject: Most women will have two fundamental objectives outside their home, namely, to be able to vote (to have a voice in the government) and to secure employment with adequate income. There is a complete analysis of both employment and voting rights, extracted from constitutions and other statutory instruments, fully footnoted, ready to be fleshed in by interested students of the subject.

To facilitate further research on discrimination against women there are a selected bibliography, an examination of the most important sources of data, and an index to this work so that particular subjects and countries can be easily located.

In researching, assembling and interpreting the data used for this study, five subjects emerged, each ideal as a topic for a doctoral dissertation.

Thesis One: Attitudes of men in general determine the pace and extent of women's advance, and not so much constitutional or other legal provisions.

Thesis Two: Women are hampered in their quest for equality by cultural, religious and social tradition in the Western world, far more than by legal impediments.

Thesis Three: Discrimination against women on grounds of gender, in respect of wages, class of employment, birth control, family size, property ownership, marital rights, freedom of speech and freedom of movement and association, is worse in most African and Muslim states than discrimination against blacks on grounds of race in Western countries with a multi-racial population structure.

Thesis Four: Laws passed to protect the position of women have not always had the desired effect; in fact, in certain areas laws have worked to the detriment of women's position.

Thesis Five: Constitutional and statutory provisions for the rights of women and laws promulgated to implement ratification of the United Nations' convention to eliminate all discrimination against persons on grounds of gender are not a guarantee that the laws are applied or the objectives vigorously pursued; in fact, behind the facade of these laws, discrimination against women not only persists but also, in some countries, has broadened.

Hopefully this work will spur further research, particularly to expose, in so many states, the yawning gap between equality on paper and equality in the street. A special report concentrating solely on this subject should be available in every country at least every three years. By constantly hammering away at the problem of policy and practice, women's advocates can accelerate progress towards equality.

One hopes someone will tackle the thesis that discrimination against women in some countries, notably the Muslim-Arab world and Africa, is worse than discrimination on grounds of race in Britain, the United States, or South Africa. The male-dominated Afro-Asian governments, ironically, are the most active in the United Nations and other international forums when it comes to attacking the evil of racial discrimination, but they have forgotten, or they have cynically ignored the fact, that the United Nations decries discrimination on grounds of race, religion *and* sex, not only of race, just as their own constitutions do. Even in the media in Africa sexual stereotypes are permitted to flourish. In the columns of the *Harare Herald* of Zimbabwe the title "comrade" is reserved strictly for men. In Uganda, women journalists may contribute only to the women's page. In Nigeria (Muslim) politicians may not even be interviewed by a female journalist.

There was a time during the period 1960–1980 when the intellectual debate on discrimination centered exclusively on discrimination on grounds of race. This, plus the growth of independent black states in Africa, led to thousands of colleges, all over the world, instituting programs and courses in African studies and racial discrimination. Perhaps during the '90s more attention will be paid to the other two elements of the United Nations triad: discrimination based on sex and discrimination based on religion. At present about 350 colleges in the United States have organized women's study programs and 600 other institutions offer at least some courses in the field. The establishment of these programs and courses is an investment of incalculable value. Expansion and growth will pay important dividends in the future to both men and women.

In the Western world education is the key to long-term success in fighting discrimination against women, for it is at home, and in the classrooms, that boys and girls should be taught that anyone, not only a boy, can become an astronaut, a pilot, an engineer, an architect, a senator, a doctor or a judge. It is everyone's perception of what women are, and what they can do, as well as what women are entitled to, that requires sculpture. Here is a primary target for the women's movement: to change the curriculum in school to bridge the existing gap in perception. One can understand the reason that 99.9 percent of all firefighters in the United States are men. Carrying and handling heavy equipment requires brute strength. But anyone who has heard such intelligent women as Clare Booth Luce, Sandra Day O'Connor, Patricia Shroeder, Elizabeth Dole, Jeanne Kirkpatrick or Sally Ride, to name only a few, will find it impossible to understand why in the year 1986 some 98 percent of all airline pilots, 96 percent of all F.B.I. agents, 94 percent of all dentists, 94 percent of all engineers, 93 percent of all optometrists and more than 90 percent of federal judges, congressmen, senators and professors at university with tenure should all be men. The lopsidedness has nothing to do with the law or with the strength, will, intelligence, education or availability of women. It is a problem of perception, custom and tradition.

There are many other questions which Western women themselves ought to address and to research. Are there sufficient resources to give women what they want? Are there enough jobs to go around? What does the law provide for, what has it done and what has it not done? How can religious obstacles be overcome, in Islam and Catholicism? In the demand for tools to achieve equality, what should be acquired first? The logical answer seems to indicate a greater say in the legislative decision-making process where laws originate and are approved. And in the daily press.

There are also special classes of women whose plight requires preferential study and action, for example, women in slavery and forced marriage (the Arab world), women suffering from sexual mutilation (Africa), women suffering after childbirth because of lack of health care (Asia), and women who have no power in the reproductive choice and who are denied a proper education simply because they are women, such as in India.

In seeking solutions special attention should be paid to the interrelationship between education and law and what educated women can accomplish not only in law but in extralegal efforts. Perhaps there should be a quest for a United Nations covenant on minimum educational standards for women. The United Nations have approved binding resolutions detailing the minimum standards for the treatment of convicted criminals, passed more than two decades ago. Why should the subject of education for women be any more difficult? Gradualism must be fought. Gradualism and slow incremental reforms and improvement, the philosophy of the '50s and '60s, produced stagnation, token progress, which did not really serve the legitimate aspirations of women as a group at all.

Evaluation

In any worldwide analysis of the status of women and the legal, religious, cultural or constitutional obstacles women face in their effort to obtain, enjoy or enforce equal treatment with men, there must, necessarily, be a point of departure: a basic value by which legal, social, political and economic structures as well as attitudes and actions by other states and people can be evaluated—whether this be in education, the workplace, the political arena or some other sphere. From the point of view of strict Muslim societies, and this applies to certain non-Muslim societies in Africa and Asia as much as it applies to Iran or Pakistan, all efforts in the West to enforce equal treatment for men and women, whether instigated by the government or private sector, are fundamentally flawed because of the indelible status already assigned to women in their society in terms of religion or religious laws. Like objectivity, human rights and women's rights are rights only in the eyes of the beholder. President George Bush of the United States and the Ayatollah Khomeini of Iran will approach women's rights from totally different points of departure.

Since a reasoned choice had to be exercised in establishing a point of departure for compiling and evaluating the materials in this work, Anglo-Saxon law and custom was elected as it exists in the leading Western democracies such as the United States, England, Canada, France, West Germany and other states in this group. All value judgments in respect of the status and treatment of women in democracies or non-democracies in Africa, Asia, Europe and Latin America were made in this context.

Finally, a point of departure was also necessary to evaluate actions, trends and attitudes in Western democracies in so far as they concern the rights and status of women. That point of departure is simply that fundamental rights of women, whether implied or in law, are no less, no more, than those of men. This applies in equal degree to everything which flows from that point, whether in education, employment opportunities, wages or political power. True, women may and should be treated differently in their role as mothers of infants, since men do not bear children, but not unfairly because they are women. Women may be exempted from combat duty for physical or biological reasons but should not be denied military service on grounds of gender. Not all men who serve in the military are combat troops. Women may be granted temporary preferential treatment, to redress glaring injustices and imbalances, but not because they are women. Any disadvantage which a woman may suffer on grounds of gender, whether in the economic, political or religious sphere, should be attributed to personal deficiencies, physical, biological, mental or intellectual, but never to lesser rights or fewer and lesser opportunities because of her gender. Thus equal rights, equal opportunity, and equal treatment for men and women is the only basis for any value judgment.

2. The Status of Women: A Global View

Some 1,500 years separate the date of birth of Hypatia, a remarkable woman who lived and studied in the city of Alexandria, and that of Sandra Day O'Connor, the first woman to be appointed to the Supreme Court of the United States. Still virtually unknown to most men and women, Hypatia, astronomer, mathematician and mechanical genius, is now mentioned by leading scientists and historians in the same breath as Archimedes, Ptolemy, Euclid, Eratosthenes, and the other great men whose genius flourished in the city founded by Alexander the Great in 332 B.C. Considered by many as the single greatest center of learning and creative genius in history, the *Bibliotheca Alexandriana* eventually contained some 700,000 works. Hypatia, who developed the process of distilling fluids, was one of many women who were outstanding scientists during the past 3,000 years but whose names and achievements are only now beginning to emerge in the wake of new historical research.[1]

As a woman, Hypatia had her share of enemies. In *Cosmos* Carl Sagan wrote that Cyril, the Archbishop of Alexandria, despised her because of her close friendship with the Roman governor and because she was a symbol of learning and science. Unfortunately for her, any learning and science not wholly controlled by the church was tagged as paganism. In the year 415 Hypatia was ambushed by a mob of Cyril's parishioners. They dragged her from her chariot, tore off her clothes and flayed her flesh from her bones. Hypatia's remains were burned and her documents, writings and other works destroyed. Cyril was made a saint.[2] On the order of the Christian Emperor Theodosius the entire library of books in Alexandria was also subsequently destroyed. The Emperor considered the library and its scientists, where Eratosthenes some 600 years earlier had first accurately determined the circumference of the earth, a nest of paganism. In 1988, President Hosni Mubarak of Egypt laid the cornerstone for the reconstruction of the great library.

There is nothing new about battered women. When Dr. Monique Fouant of the Medical College of Virginia studied Chilean mummies from the Azapa culture (circa 1000 B.C.) she found that 36 percent of the women, but only 9 percent of the men, had broken bones and over half were skull fractures. The nature of the fractures indicated that in 45 percent of the mummies examined, death had been inflicted by lethal blows. It was the same story 750 years later, in the Alto-Ramirez culture. Of the women, 50 percent had fractures; of the men, only 20 percent.[3]

Kidnapping or the sale of younger women for prostitution, cruelty towards women in certain African and Asian countries, slavery, female infanticide, and bride killings in dowry disputes remain problems long after man has reached and walked on the moon.

Between 1985 and 1986 alone, more than 2,300 Indian brides were killed in dowry disputes. The killing of brides, usually by burning, as an expression of dissatisfaction with the dowry, has become one of the scourges of modern India. "Bride Burning, the Horror Spreads" is how these acts were described in a special survey in *India Today* of June 30, 1988. These are only the official figures, mostly from urban areas, and police admit that many more dowry murders take place in the rural areas. India has already passed a Dowry Prohibition Act, the Suppression of Immoral Traffic in Women and Girls Act (1978) and the Cruelty to Women Deterrent Punishment Ordinance (1983), yet the problem continues due to lack of enforcement.

The trafficking in women remains a problem in mainland China. "It is strictly forbidden to kidnap and sell women and girls: This activity [*sic*] will be strictly prosecuted," is a sign put up by Chinese provincial authorities in many cities, particularly on hotel walls, such as the one quoted above which appeared on a hotel in Aigong in the province of Sichuan, China.[4]

Somewhere in between the death of Hypatia and circa 1960, the idea perished that women could be mothers, teachers, nurses, clerks and shopping assistants, as well as scientists, justices of the Supreme Court, astronauts, mathematicians, astronomers, engineers, business managers, newspaper editors, doctors, professors, lawyers, and airline pilots. There is nothing of specific importance about 1960 but, as Margaret Freivogel observed, it is only during the past 25 years that one can speak of any significant gains made by women in their struggle for equal rights.[5] Recognition that in speaking of "human rights" one should also include women's rights, and not only cultural and language rights of ethnic minorities, is something which gained ground only during the '70s.

Insofar as it affects women, a definition of gender discrimination is necessary since there will be many references in this book to discrimination, segregation, and differentiation. The best definition seems that of Constantina Safilios-Rothschild: "Sex discrimination refers to the differential treatment of women and men on the basis of their gender, and without consideration of individual differences, in terms of ability, competence, inclination and commitment."[6]

Is discrimination against women in some countries truly worse than discrimination based on race, such as in South Africa? The answer is "yes" when it comes to women and the laws of God according to fundamentalist regimes in Islamic countries. For example, in Pakistan a blind girl who had been raped and was pregnant was sentenced to be stoned to death. She could not identify the rapist, but according to Islamic law since she was pregnant she was held to be guilty of illegal sex.[7] In South Africa, irrespective of her color or religion, she would have been seen purely as the victim of a crime carrying a statutory penalty of imprisonment.

Perhaps the foregoing was a case of one in a million, but then consider the following: the Islamic states have signed the United Nations convention forbidding any form of political, social or economic discrimination on grounds of gender, yet in most states a woman is forbidden to attend law school; may not visit a public theatre or cafeteria; may not purchase bread or milk at a shop without her husband's or father's permission; is considered to be worth only half the value of a man and must be fired by her employer if her husband so requests. In divorce, the man automatically receives custody of all children older than two years; automatically receives twice as much as the woman in any inheritance; and may legally kill his wife as punishment for adultery, but not the other way around. (See Chapters 21 and 25.) In South Africa, which is not a signatory to the U.N. convention, not a single one of these laws applies, and in every case mentioned above a black woman's legal rights are not only equal to those of her husband (Marriage and Matrimonial Property Law Amendment Act of 1988) but also equal to those of any white person.[8] Since 1979 some 23 laws restricting the rights of black people have been abrogated in South Africa, providing a black woman with opportunity to enter any university, open a business of her choice in any area, join a labor union for women with the right to strike, join any political party—black, white, or integrated; obtain business loans, travel anywhere, study anything from law to gynecology, own property, divorce her husband, eat at any restaurant, stay at any hotel, visit any theatre, all without the need of approval from family or authority.[9]

Assessing the progress made by women during the period 1975–1985 (the U.N. Decade for Women), most qualified observers are agreed that the changes have been extremely uneven and, on the whole, modest. As pointed out by Ruth Sivard in her *World Survey,* in no major field of activity can it be said that women have attained equality with men. The influx of women into the paid labor force has not significantly narrowed the gap between men's and women's pay nor has it stemmed the rising tide of poverty among women worldwide. "Throughout the world women are still disproportionately represented among the poor, the illiterate, the unemployed and underemployed. They remain a very small minority at the centers of political power."[10]

Examples cited by Sivard: Although women are 50 percent of the teachers in primary schools and 31 percent of the total in secondary schools, there were 80 million more boys than girls in primary and secondary schools. Educated women rank higher than educated men in verbal skills but worldwide (excluding China) there are 130 million more adult women than men who cannot read or write. Finally, although they comprise 50 percent of the world's enfranchised population, women hold no more than 10 percent of the seats in the national legislatures. Faith in equal rights for men and women formed part of the Charter of the United Nations. Today, more than 40 years later, it is evident that progress has been mostly promise. There are U.N. members states where nine out of ten women over the age of 25 still have not had any schooling whatsoever.[11]

The wage labor market still discriminates actively and persistently against women, and salary, social security, pensions and working conditions are often less favorable for women than for men. The world averages do, of course, conceal very great regional differences. Working women in manufacturing industries—in Japan and the Republic of Korea, for instance—take home less than half the wages earned by men, while women in Denmark, Norway, Sweden, El Salvador, Burma and Sri Lanka fare best, with average earnings 80 percent of those of men. In Afghanistan only 4 percent of girls are enrolled in secondary schools as against 88 percent in Australia. In Angola only 1 percent of women have access to contraceptives; in Belgium 76 percent do.[12] Comparing women's status in the highest and lowest ranked countries in the world reveals a terrifying gap. The following comparison was provided by the Washington-based Population Crisis Committee in a study which it aptly-named "Country Rankings of the Status of Women: Poor, Powerless and Pregnant."[13]

In Sweden...
(Population: 8.4 million, Area: 173,730 square miles)

- Female life expectancy is 81 years.
- One in 167 girls dies before her fifth birthday.
- One in 53 15-year olds will not survive her childbearing years. (One percent of these deaths relates to pregnancy and childbirth.)
- Fewer than 1 percent of 15–19 year old women have already been married.
- Women bear one to two children on average.
- Over three fourths of married women use contraception.
- Virtually all school-aged girls are in school.
- Female university enrollment is 37 percent of women aged 20–24.
- About half the secondary school teachers are women.
- Three out of five women are in the paid labor force.
- Two out of five women are professionals.
- Women live an average of seven years longer than men.
- Women and men have similar literacy rates.
- About half of the paid workforce is female.
- In 1988 women held 113 seats in Sweden's 349-member parliament.

In Bangladesh...
(Population: 109.5 million, Area: 55,598 square miles)

- Female life expectancy is 49 years.
- One in five girls dies before her fifth birthday.
- One in six 15-year olds will not survive her childbearing years. (About one-third of these deaths relate to pregnancy and childbirth.)
- Almost 70 percent of 15–19 year old women have already been married.
- Women bear five to six children on average.
- One fourth of married women use contraception.
- One in three school-aged girls is in school.
- Female university enrollment is less than 2 percent of women aged 20–24.
- One in 10 secondary school teachers is a woman.
- One in 15 women is in the paid labor force.
- Only 3 out of 1,000 women are professionals.
- Women live an average of two years less than men.
- Some 24 percent more women are illiterate than men.
- Only 14 percent of the paid workforce is female.
- In 1988 women held four seats in Bangladesh's 302-member parliament, out of 30 reserved for them.

In most countries women are less protected by social legislation than men, even in countries that have enacted such legislation. While legislation that guarantees equal pay for equal work (or work of equal value) has been adopted in an increasing number of countries, women's vertical job segregation has not decreased significantly the past decade and, in many countries, is reported to have increased.[14]

Women's single best performance was in gaining full voting powers so that by 1985 voteless women could be found only in the so-called Gulf States, Saudi Arabia and the Republic of South Africa where colored and Indian women gained a vote for their own representatives in the central Parliament (as a result of the new constitution of 1983), which still left blacks out in the cold. Gaining voting rights worldwide is a major development over the 19th century, when the attitude towards women was most blatantly expressed in France's Napoleonic Civil Code, which stated that "those persons without rights at law are minors, married women, criminals and the mentally deficient."

The right of women to hold political office has now also been achieved in virtually all countries, at least on paper. The U.N. Convention on equal political rights (1954) ensured women's right to vote and eligibility for election to public office on equal terms with men, but has not really been translated into tangible results. The convention was passed in 1954 but 30 years later has been ratified by only 90 countries out of a total of over 160 member states.

In effect some 70 countries pay only lip service to the U.N. Convention outlawing sexual discrimination and there is a wide gap between constitutional rights and reality. According to United Nations and United States Department of State sources, women's representation in the highest councils of government in most countries is still less than 10 percent. Considering that women are generally 50 percent or more of the electorate this is a very lopsided situation and women retain the dubious distinction of being the most under-represented major population group in the countries of the world, both in terms of official appointments to the executive and of elected representatives. In the United States women were only 9 percent of all county governing boards in 1987 and only 4 percent were mayors or members of municipal governing boards.[15] Over the past 10 years, the number of women who were cabinet members of United States administrations or ambassadors was so small as to be statistically insignificant. In Africa's most prosperous, richest, and technologically most developed country, the Republic of South Africa, there were 50 cabinet and deputy cabinet ministers in 1987, all of them men. Not one woman was to be found among the 50-odd heads of civil service departments and agencies, either. The major exception in the world to this pattern of deliberate exclusion is the Nordic countries, where women occupy between 18 to 25 percent of the cabinet posts—in particular Norway, where the figure in 1987 exceeded 30 percent. In Sweden one-third of all Parliamentary seats are held by women.[16]

Women in the West seeking divorce from unfaithful, drunken, idle and brutal husbands, men who gamble or recklessly spend the wife's income or inheritance, are still finding the Catholic Church standing in their way. The threat of damnation is powerful. In September 1988 the Vatican also reconfirmed the church's decision that women are forbidden the priesthood.[17]

In 1986 nearly 50,000 protesters led by priests marched through the streets of Buenos Aires to oppose parliamentary moves to allow divorce in Argentina. The Argentinian Republic, with a large Roman Catholic population (85 percent), is one of seven countries in the world that do not sanction divorce. In 1987 the legislature indicated its willingness to pass a law legalizing divorce, but the church threatened legislators who voted for the divorce bill with excommunication.

In July 1986 the Church of England's policy-making General Synod refused for the eleventh time in 11 years to allow women priests ordained outside England to conduct services within Britain. Since 1976 about 600 women have been ordained in the United States Episcopal Church and were invited to conduct services in English churches by vicars who support women priests. The Church of England made it clear that, if further services are held by women priests, the offending vicar will be facing penalties including dismissal from his parish.[18]

In August 1988, however, Anglican bishops from around the world adopted a resolution recognizing the right of national branches of the church to have women as bishops. Thus, female bishops will be accepted in the United States, Brazil, Hong Kong and New Zealand (four states in which the church had already ordained about 1,000 women as priests), but the church will not permit women in England to become bishops. In September 1988, the Episcopal Diocese of Massachusetts finally elected the first female bishop in the 450-year-old history of the Anglican church. In contrast to this painstaking progress in the Anglo-Saxon world, women in Sweden have been priests in the Lutheran Church since the 1950s. The bishop of Stockholm is a woman, and nearly half of the 481 priests are women. In fact, some 20 percent of the total of 4,913 priests in Sweden in 1988 were women. In 1987, the female enrollment at the Theological Institute of Uppsala University was 53 percent, up from 38 percent in 1977.[19]

Little enough had been achieved by those who strove to give women an equal opportunity to advancement in the economic, cultural, religious, political and judicial fields between 1960 and 1975, so that when the United Nations, itself a fortress of male dominance, finally got around to declaring 1975-1985 the Decade for Women, it created a wave of expectancy among educated women and women's organizations around the world.

Ten years is not a long time in the history of any country, or of most governments, but it must seem an eternity for a qualified, experienced woman newspaper reporter to wait for the day when she would be paid the same salary as a fellow male reporter for doing the same work, on the same news desk, and during the same hours of day.

The first world conference dealing with the rights of women and launching the Decade for Women was held in Mexico City in 1975. Considering the generally backward status of women in Mexico in terms of education, employment opportunities, income and career prospects, no better location could have been found in the Western Hemisphere. Only about 19 percent of the active labor force and only 26 percent of all students at university were women.[20]

The U.N.-sponsored conference was almost a disaster because contentious political issues, rather than the advancement of women's rights, became the subject of discussion. To a great extent this was due to the fact that the Communist, Asian, Latin American and African states, with some exceptions, appeared to have instructed their delegations to engage solely in politics. Had the politics included the human rights of women, something might have been achieved; unfortunately the conference was more often than not a mere reflection of ideological disputes in the General Assembly of the United Nations.

The mid-point conclave of the Decade for Women held in Copenhagen in 1980 suffered the same fate as the conference in Mexico. More heat was generated about "Zionism," "racism," and "Western imperialism" than about the basic rights of women and their legally deprived status in over 75 of the 118 countries attending.

According to Jessie Bernard, delegates representing the U.S.S.R. and East European Bloc stated that women in their countries were already "liberated" so world peace and disarmament should be the major focus of the conference. Other delegates insisted that the redistribution of the world's wealth and power was a prerequisite for female equality.[21] A proposal for a new international economic order, requiring the West to give up part of its wealth to the Third World, became a major issue. The United States delegation refused to sign the so-called World Plan of Action because it would not endorse statements that Zionism equalled racism and that the terrorist Palestine Liberation Organization should be recognized. Arab women, shepherded by a group of men and wearing the colors of the P.L.O., had packed the conference hall for three days running, turning the conference into a political debate on the Middle East and issuing statements like: "The only good Jew is a dead Jew."[22]

No attempt was made at Copenhagen to launch a comparative analysis of the failure of more than 100 governments to implement their own constitutional provisions and other laws protecting and advancing the rights of women, the one area where male-dominated administration was so obviously vulnerable to exposure and counteraction. A major finding of the research for this book is that a vast gap still exists between what countries profess their policies to be and what happens in practice. This was true not only of the Communist East Bloc but also of the West, Latin America, Africa and Asia.

In 1985 the Decade for Women ended with a 12-day U.N.-sponsored conference in Nairobi, Kenya, attended by more than 2,000 delegates from 140 countries. Some 13,000 delegates also arrived for Forum 85, a loosely confederated group of 157 non-governmental organizations.

Both meetings were again marred by politics. Once again, political cliches and ideological harangues, associated with East-West and North-South disputes in the General Assembly of the U.N., dominated proceedings. When Israel's chief delegate rose to speak in the U.N.-sponsored meeting, representatives of Third World, Arab, and Communist nations marched out, shouting, "Zionist terrorists go home!" How this demonstration could serve to advance the cause of women in Israel or in the Third World (and the situation of women in the Arab states cries out for improvement) no one ventured to say. Not women, but men, negotiated the wording of many important items, some with heavy political overtones. According to United Press International, men of

Egypt, Syria and the Palestine Liberation Organization dominated the conference proceedings at times and engaged in most debates and rights of reply.[23]

The women's decade could have—should have—ended on a note of massive cooperation and a reordering of strategies and priorities to achieve even more gains for women during the next decade. Sadly, the largest-ever international gathering by women of official and non-governmental status to have taken place so far became what Maureen Reagan, leader of the United States delegation, called "an orgy of [political and ideological] hypocrisy" causing her to recommend that the United States reconsider future participation because of politics and gamesmanship at such conferences.

The same political rhetoric and polemics also defaced Forum 85. The arms race, the refusal of the rich Western countries to acquiesce in a redistribution of the world's wealth, and other East-West ideological disputes received more attention than those areas where a concerted push on the part of delegates could have produced meaningful results in the next decade. Elimination of the existing legal discrimination in the laws and regulations of cities, churches, provinces, states and countries received no concerted, unanimous attention.

Both conferences in Nairobi failed to produce adequate, specific, concerted proposals on how to break down existing cultural, religious and traditional discrimination against women. Even the subject of the right of women to choose when and how many children to have did not make the grade. Yet this issue is one of the most important ones to be addressed by women's organizations and governments in the Third World. It failed to become a central rallying point in Kenya, the venue of the conference, the capital of a country where men's blind and irresponsible resistance to birth control has produced the highest birthrate in the world, creating catastrophic social and economic problems and condemning women to remain in a centuries-old stereotype. At the end of the Decade for Women, and despite Kenya's high profile at the United Nations, 50 percent of all road construction workers in Kenya were still women. Worse, women were being relegated by laws, so-called reform laws, into a landless class dependent on their men for subsistence.

There is a positive side. The United Nations Decade for Women (1975–1985) did more to bring the inequality suffered by women to the attention of the media and the governments of the world than anything else during the past 50 years. It also spurred more research on the status of women, their unequal social status, handicaps, legal disabilities, poor economic status and under-representation in the governments and councils of cities, provinces, states and international organizations than anything else this century. As Maria Riley observed, "One of the most important outcomes . . . has been the development of statistical and sociological information about women that was never available before. . . ."[25] Three-fourths of all the non-governmental organizations questioned on the subject said that the decade succeeded in bringing "a greater awareness of the vital role of women in development, a higher level of consciousness and progress in the legislative field."[26] The so-called Female Bill of Rights which the U.N.'s Nairobi conference adopted was also an important step, even if it took voting on 350 items to include all the difficulties of women that had to be addressed. *The Washington Post* said in its summary of the Nairobi conference that this final document "was a manifesto of 350 feminist proposals demanding that the world's women be given their fair share of power in government, commerce and in their families.... True, the U.N. ... cannot force governments to implement any of the proposals that their delegations agreed to. But approving them constitutes a 'moral commitment' buttressed by international consensus."[27]

But what of the road ahead?

Much was made of women's gains during the Decade for Women, in politics, education, employment and health care; but given the worldwide plight of women in comparison to men, there was really no reason to celebrate the conclusion of the decade by congratulatory resolutions at the two conferences in Nairobi.

There has been a strong tendency, notably among United States writers, to hail achievements of individual women, or progress in specific areas or in certain professions, as a wave of progress for women in general. This is not only untrue but also misleading and can be dangerous for women's objectives, breeding complacency. For example, in the epilogue to her well-publicized work *The Sisterhood* on "women who changed the world," Marcia Cohen commits a fundamental error by seeing regional gains in the United States, substantial and impressive as they may be, as a universal trend. "And the glory was that the world [*sic*] was transformed," she writes. The women she praises deserve that praise. The statistics she quotes are also impressive, for example: "For the first time in history the pay gap between men and women has narrowed to 30 percent; the number of women graduating with engineering degrees increased thirteenfold since 1975; approximately 18,000 women hold elected office."[28] But all this praise and "the world" to which she refers primarily embraces only the United States. It is not the world outside the United States. The world outside the United States, Canada, Western Europe, Australia, and a handful of other countries (about 29 out of 157 countries) is more properly described in the Washington-based Population Crisis Committee's country rankings of the status of women as "Poor, Powerless and Pregnant."[29]

The "transformation" to which Marcia Cohen refers is not even true for the United States. There was improvement but not a transformation. In the past few years important and more authoritative voices—writers such as Mary Mason, Karen Morello, Sylvia Hewlett, Gilda Berger, Barbara Bergmann, Ruth Hubbard, and Helen Remic, to name a few—have been raised against the notion that women's progress (and the women's movement) in the United States is now on track and self-sustaining.[30] If one examines the statistics quoted by Cohen, one will realize that these statistics fail to hide the fact that there are still enormous discrepancies in the status of men and women in the United States in terms of income, quality of occupation, and political and commercial management. For example, although women with engineering degrees did increase thirteenfold since 1975, the increase was from a virtually nonexistent base, so that in 1985 only 4.8 percent of engineers in the United States were women. By 1987 the figure was down to 3 percent.[31]

The existence of a pay gap of 30 percent gains another perspective if one realizes that 30 years ago the gap was 40 percent and that a true sign of progress would have been a gap of only 5 or, at most, 10 percent.[32] As to the 18,000 women in elected office, while this may sound impressive, only 1,176 were represented in state legislatures in 1988, as against almost 7,500 men. In Congress, in the House and Senate combined, there were only 25 women in 1988. To put this in better perspective, in 1961 and 1962, there were 20 women. So after almost 30 years, a gain of five! As stated in *The American Woman 1988–1989: A Status Report,* "Significant progress notwithstanding women occupy proportionately few positions throughout the hierarchy of elected politics and the rate of change has been quite slow."[33] In an interview with *USA Today,* Ruth Hubbard also said that as far as real liberation is concerned women still have a long way to go.[34]

The Decade for Women did not produce fundamental changes in societies' attitudes towards women, or the attitude of men in general. The improvements were statistical, but in limited areas and in a limited number of countries, and the same statistics often revealed new or accentuated existing discrimination. And other issues have come to the fore: the election of more women to Congress; day care; pay equity; abortion rights; and the feminization of poverty.

In judging and evaluating continued discrimination against women some qualified and independent researchers no longer mince their words. "Discrimination . . . is a profound and subtle sickness that has lodged itself deep in the subconscious of both men and women as well as in the structure of our societies," is how editor Debbie Taylor begins the preface to *Women: A World Report.* "This," she continued, "makes it one of the hardest sources of inequality to fight because it grips women from within and without."[35] The National Academy of Sciences, evaluating sex segregation in United States employment, said that this segregation "is a deeply rooted social and cultural phenomenon. It is perpetuated not only by barriers and constraints, but also by habits and perceptions."[36]

How do governments view the problem?

The United Nations document prepared for the World Conference on the Decade for Women (Nairobi, Kenya, 1985) stated as follows: "The overriding obstacle [to eliminating discrimination against women] identified by virtually all governments, irrespective of economic or regional groupings, is the deeply rooted traditional value system and attitudes which subordinate women and establish stereotyped sex divisions of roles in society."[37]

Very often men hardly stop to think of the extent to which male symbolism dominates the world. Nowhere is this more dramatically visible than in the field of religion. Christianity and Islam, the two religions which, together, regulate the moral and spiritual lives of over half of the world's population, both have a ruling male deity (God the Father and Allah), male prophets and male priests. While the other two major religions, Hinduism and Buddhism, which influence the lives of 25 percent of the people on the globe, do not have a single mighty masculine deity, women are denied a place in the priesthood and may even have to be reincarnated as men before being considered fit to achieve ultimate spiritual fulfillment.[38]

That there is a greater awareness among governments of the world of women's rights is evident from the fact that at the end of 1985 more than 90 percent of the U.N. member states had official bodies dedicated to the advancement of women. While some of these state bodies are minor government departments, perhaps just window-dressing, at least 37 countries have full-fledged departments while in 20 countries they are considered major agencies of influence. Of all member states of the United Nations, 66 now have incorporated specific programs for women and their development in parliamentary-approved so-called National Development Plans, often referred to as five- or ten-year programs. Regrettably, many of these programs have shown from early years that they have value and impact only on paper.[39]

There are other "plus" points for women. For instance, there is no doubt that the past ten years have seen a myriad of publications—books, monographs, maps, articles in newspapers, articles in scientific journals, doctoral dissertations and other research—on women. Some of these works are dealt with in Chapter 31 as a guide to existing data, sources of information and further research. There is also no doubt that women have become more and better organized and determined in their effort to promote research. They also show more readiness to assist each other across international boundaries in the common cause of fighting discrimination. The result is a cross-fertilization of ideas. I.S.I.S., short for the Women's International Information and Communication Service, is one example. In the mid-80s, I.S.I.S. had over 10,000 contacts in 130 countries, published a news bulletin, answered questions, produced a resource guide, mobilized international support for women persecuted solely on grounds of sex and provided technical assistance on organizational issues.

Another example is the Women's Institute for Freedom of the Press, which was founded in Washington in 1972 and which became an international organization in 1982, emphasizing news about health and safety as well as economic, political, and international information, an indispensable basis for a mutual support network for women. The Institute stimulates diffusions of news not only among women and women's organizations but also among the general public.[40] At the first World Feminist Media Conference in 1979, more than 31 countries attended. In 1985 the W.I.F.P. published *Media Reports to Women,* listing the channels and resources then available to women. These included 462 periodicals, 116 women's publishing companies, 80 women's bookstores, 31 film groups, and 26 video and cable groups, to mention a few.

There is also *Women's International Network News,* a quarterly established in 1975 as a worldwide open communication system for women, which disseminates information about women and women's groups. In addition, there are special publication projects which serve to keep women in contact, stimulate research, and publicize reports on women. For example, the Feminist Press in the United States publishes both *Women's Studies International* and international supplements to the *Women's Studies Quarterly,* including news and reports from more than 60 countries. It is probably the best source on international conferences on teaching and research about women. The Feminist Press, based at the City University of New York, also publishes *International Monographs on Women's Studies,* presenting details of women's studies in other countries.

It is largely due to individual researchers among women, to women's organizations, and to the women's network that so much more is known today about the status of women all over the globe. True, there are many male-dominated organizations, universities, foundations and institutes, news media, and individual corporations which have both supported and contributed to the financing of this research. Nonetheless, it is the publication of studies by women and women's organizations, not by governments or, with a few exceptions, by men, which have brought the real plight of women to light and which illustrate how much is still to be done before equal rights between men and women, and equal treatment in respect of education, vocational and economic opportunities, and co-responsibility in public administration, law and government, become tangible and more than well-meaning objectives.

The overwhelming impression gained from a worldwide analysis of the status of women and of discrimination against them on grounds of gender is that the so-called pink ghetto (women's occupation of low-paying jobs with low social status) is still characteristic of all countries examined. There is no country in the world in which women do not predominate in low-status and low-paid occupations. (See Table 2, page 25, and 3, page 26).

It is true that there are vast regional variations in the high-status professions. Women are 80 percent of medical doctors in the Soviet Union, 20 percent in West Germany and less than 10 in the United States. Some 40 percent of the engineers in the U.S.S.R. are women as against less than 2 percent in Britain and some 5 percent in the United States.[41] But in countries such as the Soviet Union it was economic and political factors, combined with labor shortages, which motivated the state to upgrade the skills of the female labor force. Consider the fact that the Soviet Union lost 20 million men during World War II, which at one point after the war left a ratio in that country of 147 women to every 100 males. Nonetheless, in the U.S.S.R., as in every other country, women are poorly represented at higher managerial levels and in high social, cultural, scientific, economic and particularly, political decision-making levels.[42]

Even in the most developed areas of the world, such as the E.C.E. (European Market Economy) Countries, women's earnings in manufacturing and all other sectors of the economy were on the average well below those of men, as Table 2 clearly illustrates.

The pink ghetto is not found only in the developing world, such as Africa, Asia and Latin America, but is widespread and persistent in the industrially developed countries of Europe and Scandinavia, as Table 3 indicates.

Equal access to education and enrollment at university level and in technical schools did not spring from concern for equal opportunities for women, but because of industrial, economic and scientific requirements of the state concerned. Where there is an abundance of labor women are still more likely to study humanities and the arts or end up in such traditional vocations as secretaries, nurses, shop assistants, while men pursue the more lucrative scientific, engineering and technical skills. In some of the poorer nations of the East Bloc there are higher rates of women at universities, in technical vocations and in political positions than in some of the richer Western states.

It is almost axiomatic that political consideration, not moral ones, are at

	All sectors			Manufacturing	
Country	*Total*	*Manual*	*Non-manual*	*Manual*	*Non-manual*
Austria, 1983	77.6	72.1	75.7	..	..
Belgium, 1982	..	..	..	72.6	59.3
Denmark, 1983	..	..	73.8	88.6	71.4
Finland, 1981	..	..	..	76.8	76.1
France, 1982	75.0	75.5	83.1	77.7	61.7
Germany, Fed. Rep. of 1982	..	..	64.8	72.7	66.7
Greece, 1980	..	..	..	67.4	57.0
Ireland, 1982	..	..	..	68.5	..
Italy, 1982	..	..	..	86.7	..
Netherlands, 1981	76.8	75.5	..	74.7	..
Norway, 1982	..	..	..	83.2	65.3
Portugal, 1980	75.6	..	..	72.0	74.6
Sweden, 1982	80.7	..	..	90.3	72.7
Switzerland, 1980	..	..	66.9	67.7	66.4
United Kindom, 1980	65.7	61.9	61.2	60.3	53.2

Table 2. Women's earnings as a percentage of those of men in 15 market-economy countries. Source: United Nations, *The Economic Role of Women in the ECE Region,* Geneva, 1985, table V.1., p. 89.

the basis of most government actions to improve the status of women or to remove discriminatory legislation. To disagree with this axiom is to argue that 20 or 50 years ago men in power had fewer scruples than those of today. Most sociologists, historians and political scientists would argue that the opposite is true. Principled politics and high political morality are not easily found among the 160 nations of the world today.

In Africa, Asia and Latin America governments have moved with great reluctance to introduce legislation providing for equality. Most of it came with a rush during the past 15 years under pressure from women's organizations and the United Nations. Many are still dragging their feet in the implementation of these laws. Jessie Bernard cites "improvements in verbal recognition of women's problems in the laws and constitutions, but deeply flawed implementation."[43]

Though women often constitute 50 percent of the voters, the vast majority of governments and legislative assemblies throughout the world are constituted with merely token representation by women. In Africa, Julius Nyerere has been hailed for two decades now as one of the outstanding statesmen of Africa, an honor also bestowed upon him by successive American and British governments, not to mention the media. Yet, in Neyrere's Tanzania women may aspire to only 15 seats in Parliament or 10 percent of the elected representatives.

Country (year)	Prof., technical & related workers	Admin., and managerial workers	Clerical and related workers	Sales workers	Service workers	Agricultural Animal husb. & forestry workers	Production related workers
Austria (1982)	5.7	- 49.8	-	58.0	68.8	47.4	15.9
Finland (1980)	2.8	1.60	85.3	57.1	78.7	39.9	21.5
Germany Fed. Rep. (1982)	39.3	17.0	59.6	56.9	56.2	47.2	15.3
Ireland (1979)	46.6	12.1	70.9	34.3	56.0	8.9	12.8
Netherlands (1979)	34.9	5.8	46.0	37.4	64.3	14.3	6.2
Norway (1982)	53.3	18.0	77.5	56.2	77.3	29.2	13.6
Portugal (1981)	54.2	9.4	47.8	45.3	65.2	53.1	24.1
Spain (1982)	38.1	4.6	39.7	41.5	59.7	25.6	13.1
Sweden (1982)	54.0	19.3	80.6	46.6	75.1	24.6	17.4
Averages	36.5	12.8	63.4	48.1	66.8	32.2	15.6

The western world has not done much better.

In the late '70s in Australia, women formed 50 percent of active party members, but only about 7 percent ended up nominated as candidates for office. In Britain women were between 35 to 50 percent of party members, but only about 20 percent were nominated as candidates. In fact, during the early 1980s Britain's female head of government, Margaret Thatcher, formed a cabinet with less female representation than at any time during the past 20 years. In 1983 the West German electorate of 23.4 million women and only 19.8 million men elected a Bundestag (Parliament) of which 90.3 percent of the members were men. In the United States, the figure for 1988 was 95 percent men, up 1 percent since 1975.[44] During the general election in Britain in June 1987, altogether 41 women were elected to Parliament by the parties involved as against only 19 in 1979.

Generally speaking, women are hopelessly under-represented in the legislatures of states or the cabinets of modern governments. The higher representation of women in the Communist East Bloc countries should be considered in the light that those representative bodies are largely ceremonial rubber stamps and that it is the Communist Party which wields the real power. Qualified observers have dubbed women in politics as "the second electorate."[45]

The other side of the coin is that there has been a marked change in the attitude of people towards women's role in politics and society in the past five years. In Western Europe, for example, 66 percent of people questioned by a series of surveys by the European Community said they believed it was time to break down the strict stereotypes of women's and men's social roles. And between 1975 and 1983 attitudes changed markedly in terms of how people perceive women and politics. In 1975 some 59 percent believed politics should be left to men. In 1983 only 29 percent still held this view.[46] As of the beginning of the '80s, more than before, women were also finding growing awareness and support from men and male-dominated institutions.

When women are better informed and educated, the evidence shows that the family's health and income benefit. When women are given training and skills, the nation's productivity gains and the economy grows. Men in business, health affairs, economics, education, and government are beginning to show that they are not blind to the advantages of a better deal for women. The American economist Barbara Bergmann said in her excellent work *The Economic Emergence of Women* that what we are witnessing is a breakup of the (ancient) sex-role caste system.

Though only just at its onset, one of today's most important debates is the proposal that women's work at home should not be judged in a vacuum but as part of the gross national product. There are two assumptions. The first is that domestic work makes the labor of others possible and that women are, in any case, also forced to work. In fact, it is a rare family in Africa or Asia, and

Table 3. Women's Share of the Labor Force by Occupational Groups, in Percentage, 1979–1982. Source: International Labor Organization, *Yearbook of Labour Statistics,* Geneva, 1982, 1983, Table 2B.

even in the United States, which can manage on the proceeds of just one person's labor. In Italy 85 percent of mothers who hold full-time jobs outside the home stated that their husbands do no domestic work at all. In Europe as a whole, a working women has, on average, only two-thirds of the free time her husband enjoys.

Secondly, women's work in the informal sector, notably in Asia, Latin America and Africa, is a significant factor in production and sales. This contribution is often totally ignored in the system of national accounts because of lack of definition as to what output would qualify as part of the gross national product, and because of lack of records and control. But the contribution is important enough for economists and social scientists to argue that the United Nations itself should revise its system of national accounts. In October 1986, an expert group of the United Nations met in Santo Domingo to determine how to measure women's income and their participation and production in the informal sector. The experts agreed that additional sectoral disaggregation in the system of national accounts is necessary. Women's work at home is therefore rightly described as an enormous contribution to the economy.

An accompanying factor, with strong sociological overtones, is patriarchy and women's labor. In most Third World countries, women's production is not taken into account simply because custom, law, or religion permits the husband to consider everything that she produces or earns as his own and he alone decides on the allocation of her time and their joint resources. There is a case to be made that some families would be far more productive if there were a better distribution of so-called manhours between husband and wife. In *A Lesser Life: The Myth of Women's Liberation in America,* Sylvia Hewlett cites a scientific study which found that the average married working woman in the United States performs 84 hours more work per month than her husband.[48]

In a special study of patriarchy and women's labor, Judith Heath and David Ciskel conclude:

> There are significant policy implications of studying family power and income distribution because the family's power relationships mirror society's stratification system [Lipman-Blumen 1975]. Although women's participation in the labor force has increased significantly over the past two decades, they are still effectively denied equal access to the upper echelons of society and they fail to achieve equality in the division of labor in the unpaid household sector. Women's access to and attainment of top positions in the hierarchy of society's economic, political, educational, and legal institutions will lead to a more egalitarian society, but also to drastic changes in family structure unless patriarchal institutions are radically reformed toward a more egalitarian household economy.[49]

Injustice to women is seen less in the extra work women must do than in the assumption that it is their role, and theirs alone, to do all the work inside the home. This assumption, said Hewlett, is a triple injustice because women end up working twice as many hours as men, are not paid for those extra hours of work, and their domestic work is looked down on because it is unpaid. The chief injustice is that a woman is expected, required, even forced, to hold down a job and also be a mother to her infant children while receiving no assistance from society, or the state, to carry this dual burden.

The question of women's work at home and the evaluation of that work becomes even more important as female-headed households increase. One study of 74 developing countries conducted in the early 1970s found that in 20 percent of all households the woman is *de jure* the head of the family.[50] The figure is now much higher and in Ghana and Malawi, for example, it is close to 30 percent.[51] A study published in 1987 states that, *de jure,* about 25 percent of all households in the developing countries are now headed by women.[52] In addition the *de facto* position also reveals a higher percentage of women as head of the household. Because of mass migration of male labor, women become *de facto* heads of households in many countries in Latin America and Africa. In Kenya, Botswana, and Sierra Leone more than 40 percent of the households are left in the care of women.[53] Increasing divorce rates in Europe (in most west European countries the rate has doubled and even trebled since 1960) and Latin America and Asia have contributed to single-parent households of which the vast majority are headed by women.[54] In 1987, female-headed households in the United States were 10.4 million, up 89 percent over 1970.[55]

Where a woman has become *de jure* or *de facto* the head of the household her difficulties are also often made even worse by the attitude of male-dominated governments. This is particularly true of Africa. In Sierra Leone, for example, an estimated 40 percent of rural households are without an adult male, but the tribal chief will allocate to those women a plot of land only 30 to 50 percent of that usually allocated to a man. In Ghana one study found that 59 percent of women in one part of the country had to forfeit their land because they had lost their husbands, either through death, divorce, or migration.[56] The irony of this is that, in Africa, women farmers tend to be as good as or better than men. In Kenya, 38 percent of the farms are run by women, and they manage to harvest the same crop per hectare as men despite men's greater access to fertilizer, seed and insecticide. Where women received the same amount of assistance they outperformed the male farmers.[57] To add to women's difficulties, their income is often taxed at a higher rate than men's, such as in Zambia, on the assumption that men will meet most of the family expenses.[58] Such unequal treatment is not reserved for African women alone. In West Germany retired women receive, on the average, only half the pension that men enjoy.[59]

This is where law and its application becomes so important.

In the legal world itself, a massive amount of work remains to be tackled—for example, property rights for women in Africa, political representation in the Muslim world, etc. The right to seek and have an abortion remains a major moral and legal issue throughout the world. The policy and political ramifications are manifest, but until the mid-'80s the legal aspect has been largely neglected. Even the subject of women as a force in law requires attention. In the West German Federal Department of Justice there were only nine female lawyers in 1984 or 5.7 percent of the total work force.[60] In all of Italy only 10 percent of the lawyers are women and in India's leading state, Tamil Nadu (Madras), 97.13 percent of persons in the legal profession are men.[61]

In almost all of Asia and Africa the woman continues to have no say whatsoever in the matter of family planning. These women live in states which are among the 89 nations which have so far ratified the U.N. Convention on the Elimination of All Forms of Discrimination Against Women. The covenant, unlike many other U.N. resolutions, is a legally binding document that commits countries to achieving equal political, social and economic rights for women. (Equal pay laws have now also been signed by 94 countries, up from 28 in 1978.) Countries which have signed the U.N. covenant include Muslim, black African, Asian and Latin American states, where equality, as generally understood, is either not applied or not at all promoted by the state; consequently the gap between policy and practice remains wide and deep.

According to World Bank statistics there are more illiterates among blacks in the world than among any other race, but 75 percent of all illiterate people in the world are women. In the so-called Third World (overwhelmingly non-white) the number of women unable to read and write actually increased by 65 million between 1960 and 1980, as compared to only a 13 million increase of illiterate men. There are member states of the United Nations where nine out of 10 women over the age of 25 have never been to school, any school.[62] And in the Soviet Union, that vociferous opponent of gender and racial discrimination, women make up 88 percent of the ditch-diggers at any typical hydro-electric project while constituting less than 1 percent of the Soviet Academy of Science.[63]

In the world at large nothing gives cause for greater concern than the fact that more and more women are falling into poverty. There are many reasons for this, reasons which will become clear in this study. But the situation is serious enough for the 616 delegates from 46 countries who attended the 1984 Second International Inter-Disciplinary Congress on Women, held in Groningen, the Netherlands, to express concern about the rise of the so-called Fourth World, or women in poverty. In many countries of the world—Malaysia, Sudan, Iran, Bangladesh, Ghana, Tanzania, Java, Brazil, Morocco and India, to name but a few—ideologies still define female labor as the property of men, and their income is taken by men in what Haleh Afshar called the "process of proletarization of women."[64]

Even in the world's richest country, the United States, the growing poverty of women may soon become a first-rate crisis.[65] As of 1985, some 87 percent of all single-parent households were headed by women, and over one-third of them were poor.[66] In 1970, families with a female as householder formed 37 percent of all poor families. By 1985, the percentage was up to 48. So 48 percent of all families living below the poverty line were headed by women.[67] The Bureau of Census also reported that, in 1984, 43 percent of females (as against only 20 percent of males) aged 21 to 64 years had no earnings at the time of the survey.[68] And even if these women all were suddenly to find employment, at the rate at which the gap between men's and women's wages has decreased the past decade, women workers will not have parity with men until the year 2020.[69]

What women should beware of most of all is complacency, the belief that the impetus of the period 1975–1985 will become self-sustaining. Such complacency is fed by "tokenism" and the way the progress and achievements of individual women are trumpeted in the media of the West, notably the United States, as if they were the rule rather than the exception.

Indira Ghandi became Prime Minister of India because she was part of a political dynasty; but in her country, women, in terms of income, health, education, employment, political representation, and social equality, are at the bottom end of the scale in any international comparison. Her election was no more representative of women's progress in politics in India than Golda Meir's government in patriarchal Israel (1969–1974). Publicity about the political victory of Benazir Bhuto in Pakistan, a country where women's status is determined by Islamic law, is threatening to fall into the same trap of appearance *vs.* reality. The position of women in Pakistan is among the worst in the world (see Chapter 25), and Benazir Bhuto's achievement would have been virtually impossible had she not been the daughter of a previous Prime Minister who was overthrown in a *coup d'etat* in 1977 and then hanged. She has become the first political head of a Muslim country, but her achievement does not signify any trend in women's politics in Pakistan or in the Muslim world.

Similarly, the 1987 election of Stella Sigcau as Prime Minister of the Republic of Transkei (a black state on the east coast of South Africa whose independence is recognized only by the Republic of South Africa) was an aberration in politics among the male-dominated Sotho society. Sigcau stayed in power for only 86 days before she was ousted on December 30, 1987, by major General Bantu Holomisa in a bloodless coup, ostensibly on grounds that she had received large sums of money for ensuring that gambling rights were given to certain casino owners. Corazon Aquino was inspired to run for President of the Philippines in 1983 because her husband was assassinated—not because she was a career politician riding a wave of political progress by women. In fact, women's representation in the Philippine Congress of 165 representatives had dropped from 12 in 1970 to only seven in 1980.

There are only three countries in the world, Norway, Sweden and Iceland, where there is a constantly expanding and sustained high level of participation by women in representative politics. In 1988 Vigdis Finnbogadottir swept to her third term as Iceland's President. The final vote count showed that she gained 94 percent of the 74 percent votes cast.[70]

Tokenism is visible in many areas and many countries. Rita Suessmuth was elected President of the West German Parliament in November 1988 to preside over a Parliament where less than 10 percent of the representatives are women, even though women form more than half of the West German electorate and also vote in greater numbers than men. When Elizabeth Butler-Sloss became Britain's first woman appeals court judge in June 1988, there was a major problem of protocol since there was no provision in British law or custom for a woman to be a judge of the High Court. She could not be called "Lord Justice Butler-Sloss" and had to settle the ensuing confusion herself. Barristers at the court will now have to address her as "My Lady, Lord Justice Butler-Sloss" or, in short, as "My Lady." In France, Jacqueline de Romilly was elected in November 1988 to the French Academy, the most prestigious academic institution in France. The 40 members are known as "the immortals." Normally they are all men. In the 353-year history of the Academy she was only the second woman elected. (Novelist Marguerite Yourcenar was the only other woman ever given the honor.) Mme. de Romilly could hardly be overlooked. On her election, at age 75, she was a full professor at the College de France, founder of the chair in Greek civilization and the author of 15 works on philosophy and literature.[71] But France has produced many great women scientists, writers, and philosophers and Mme. de Romilly's appointment does not signify a trend.

In the United States, Dr. Johnetta B. Cole became President of Spellman College in Georgia in November 1988. She was not the first woman to head a college in the United States, but Spellman College is a school founded 107 years ago for the sole purpose of educating black women. So after a century Dr. Cole was the first woman to be appointed to this post. Nationwide, her appointment is statistically insignificant. Only 10 percent of the presidents of American colleges and universities are women.[72] In similar vein, when Sandra Day O'Connor was appointed to the United States Supreme Court, her appointment overshadowed the fact that only 5.4 percent of all federal judges were women and, as Karen Morello points out in her excellent book *The Invisible Bar,* of 20,000 judicial positions in the United States only 900 are held by women. Ms. Morello writes in the conclusion to her book that "the entry of substantial numbers of women in law will not necessarily mean that women will move on to the higher levels of the profession. Women are likely to be relegated to a second tier.... The forces that once kept women out of law altogether simply have shifted now to keeping them out of powerful positions within the law."[73]

Often newspapers and magazines in the United States devote considerable attention to the individual stars of media who are women. Though women now comprise 50 percent of all journalists, their presence as editors is statistically insignificant.

Men are still overwhelmingly in control of the media of the United States. At a Washington conference on "Women, Men and Media," sponsored by the Gannett Foundation and the University of Southern California, it was shown that women held only 6 percent of the top jobs in the news media and only 25 percent of middle management. A survey of the front pages of ten major newspapers by a media consultant revealed that women also have little presence, either as makers or reporters of major news. More disturbing was the results of a five year study of media wages by Jean Gaddy Willson of the University of Missouri which proved that women on average earn only 64 cents for every dollar men earn. There was also substantial average wage gaps between women and men, despite equal experience in comparable jobs: a difference of more than $3,000 in radio, nearly $8,000 in newspapers and more than $9,000 a year in television. The study also revealed that in this respect even the foremost newspapers of the world are not above rank hypocrisy. Of the major newspapers surveyed *The New York Times,* champion of racial and sexual equality, had the worst record in terms of payment and employment of women while the much criticized *USA Today* fared the best.[74] It is the same elsewhere in the world. In the print media—newspapers and news magazines—women are represented less than 1 percent in Japan and less than 15 percent in Norway and Denmark. The best performances elsewhere are in countries such as Israel and Austria, where women constitute 20 and 27 percent respectively of editors and reporters.[75]

The global outlook for women is far from good, and in all of the countries of the world except the United States, Canada, Western Europe, Australia, New Zealand, and a few of the Communist states in Europe, conditions are in fact still dismal. There is no country where women enjoy equal status with men, although the Scandinavian states are heading that way. An analysis of the state of equality for women in Scandinavia in 1989 found that women had achieved a percentage share in political power unequaled in the West. Women occupied more than 30 percent of the parliamentary constituencies in Sweden, Norway and Denmark. Eight of the 18 cabinet posts in the Norwegian and eight of the 21 in the Swedish government in 1989 were held by women. Where direct elections are involved women fared exceptionally well. For example, in the regional council of Varmland in central Sweden, 41 of the 81 seats were won by women. The Labor Party in Norway and the opposition Social Democrats in Denmark both apply a quota system whereby 40 percent of all candidates for parliamentary elections must be women.

Nonetheless, a Swedish Cabinet Minister, Maj-Lis Loow, said that though a foundation for equality now exists, behind these sunny statistics there was still an elementary inequality, pointing to the fact that the 40 percent quota system effectively bars women from achieving 50 percent or more. When it comes to the real political power in Scandinavia, such as influential parliamentary committees, the percentages suddenly take a plunge. The 35 percent women in the Swedish parliament provided only 16 percent of the members of all standing committees. As in the case of France and other Western countries, women are also concentrated in the so-called soft areas of power, in cabinet posts such as health, social affairs, pensions and the environment. Scandinavia has never had a woman as Minister of Finance. Outside parliament the labor unions and management in business and industry in Scandinavia remain bulwarks of male domination. This may change in time. Currently 50 percent of all students in business and economics at Swedish universities are women while in Norway they now constitute a 54 percent majority.[76] In Africa, Asia, and Latin America, crushing poverty, worsened by widespread discrimination on grounds of custom or religion, have left most women in a state so dismal as to be difficult for women in Western industrial countries to comprehend. In the final analysis the aspirations of women do not differ that much in rich or poor countries, Islamic or Christian, Western or Marxist: all seek equality under the law; equal educational opportunities; better health services and access to birth control measures; equal wages and equal opportunities in vocation.

Governments in most of the countries of the world could and should have translated these aspirations by legal reform and by stringent implementation. Unfortunately, it has happened in fewer than 25 of the 157 countries of the world. Even in those countries where some individual women have come to be symbols of women's capabilities and where the law has been structured to provide for equal status and opportunity, progress has been either painfully slow or patchy. In most societies, ingrained inequalities are still easy to find.

3. The Environment of Discrimination

Political Power and Participation in the Legislature

The political environment of women is one which subjects them to as much discrimination as the job market. Perhaps "exclusion" is a better word; nonetheless, women's position in freely elected legislatures, as opposed to nominated ones such as are found in the Communist countries, is still extremely unrepresentative. Even in the Communist Bloc, women's representation in top civil service posts and in the policy-making organs such as the politburos is glaringly out of proportion to the number of women who are qualified voters.

In April 1946, just after World War II and under the watchful eyes of the American occupation forces, the Japanese elected 39 women to their parliament. Thirty-four years later, in 1980, they elected only nine.[1]

In Western liberal democracies, with the exception of Nordic countries such as Finland, Norway and Sweden, the situation is just as bad. At times during the 1970s Australia had no women in the national legislature. In the late '70s there were 3 percent women in the British Parliament, 5 percent in Canada and Spain, and 7 percent in West Germany. The pattern has remained unchanged during the '80s. A French delegate to the World Congress of Women in Moscow in June 1986 observed that during the last decade women in the French National Assembly had increased by more than 80 percent. Statistically this is true, but in 1975 there were only five women in the Assembly as against 28 in 1985, which really means that out of the 491 deputies to the French Assembly fewer than 6 percent were women. Even in municipal affairs, women in France constituted only 14 percent of the elected officials.[2]

In Latin America, Asia, and Africa, the political environment gets progressively worse. In Taiwan, women, who gained equal political rights with the 1947 constitution, are limited to a handful of reserved seats which are set by the governing party. After the 1985 elections women comprised less than 17 percent of the provincial assembly members and less than 18 percent of the Taipei City Councillors.[3]

On mainland China the 1954 Constitution of the People's Republic had proclaimed that women and men were equal and that women had equal rights with men in the political, economic, and social life. But after 30 years of equality what has China really achieved in the political representation for women? During the life of the six National People's Congresses (the legislative organ of China and the supreme authority of the country) since the constitution of

1954, women's active participation never exceeded 23 percent. In the standing committee of the Congress, which ranks just below the Politburo in influence and power, the percentage actually had dropped more than 50 percent, from 25 percent in 1975 to 9 percent in 1983. (See Table 4.) In evaluating the emerging women's studies in China, Wan Shanping observed that compared to the conditions which existed prior to 1949 women are, in a sense, "liberated" in China, but that it is only the first step "and women's liberation in China has a long way to go."[4]

The progress in the Nordic countries has been one of sustained growth, rather than a spectacular leap during the women's decade. The diagram in Table 5 indicates that women's representation in Denmark, Finland, Iceland, Norway, and Sweden had been in an upswing 20 years before the U.N.'s declaration of the Decade for Women. What is also significant is that ever since 1973 the growth in women's representation has shown a constant increase, unlike many Western and other countries where the percentages often slipped back and in some cases were worse than at the advent of the women's decade. Yet even in the semi-utopia of the Nordic states all is far from being well. Studies show that the proportion of women in positions of political power decreases as the power of the office or position increases.[5]

Women's political party membership figures are still much lower than those of men. In Norway only 12 percent are party members as against 20 percent men. Only the Christian parties in Denmark, Finland, and Norway have a majority of women among their members. In the Nordic countries in general, women constitute about 35 percent of membership. According to Ingunn Norderval, the political structures themselves are a hindrance to women. "Men are the gatekeepers to the political system. They have defined the entry rules, and they send out the invitations and screen the recruits. Male gatekeepers perceive women as threats to their position in a system with limited rewards. And throughout, the iron law of power prevails: the more power the more men."[6] Several parties are attempting to address the inequality of women's representation by adopting a quota policy system; for example, in Norway both the Labor and Liberal party, as well as the Socialist Left party, have set in motion rules that require at least 40 percent women's representation in all party organs and on the ballots for Parliament.

Lovenduski and Hills observed that there is no state in which parties elect female candidates to stand for election to national legislative office anything like in proportion to their membership in the population. In Australia women formed as much as 50 percent of party members yet only some 7 percent were nominated as candidates for office. In Britain, where women at various times also constituted up to 50 percent of party members, only some 20 percent were nominated. Only in the Communist states, such as the Soviet Union, Hungary or Czechoslovakia, and in the Nordic states do parties select women candidates for state office in any proportion to party membership. Indeed in the three aforementioned Communist states there are sometimes more nominations of women than men, but this, Lovenduski and Hills point out, must be seen in the light of the purely symbolic nature for "legislatures" in Communist states.[7] And nowhere does women's representation at parliamentary level lead to

Year	Women Representatives	%	Women on Standing Committee	%
1954	147	11.9	4	5.0
1959	150	12.3	5	6.3
1964	542	17.8	20	17.4
1975	653	22.6	42	25.1
1978	742	21.2	33	21.0
1983	632	21.2	14	9.0

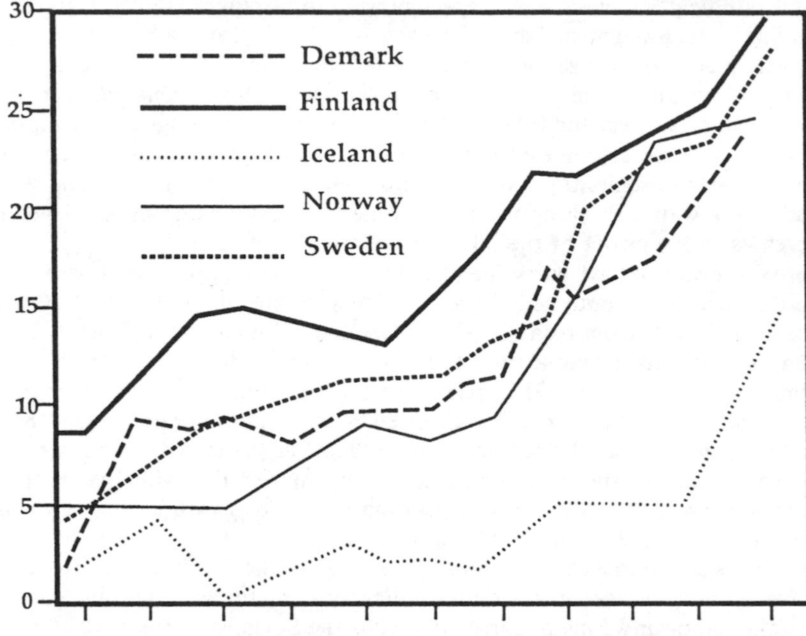

***Top:* Table 4. Women in the National People's Congress of China. Source: United Nations, International Research and Training Institute for the Advancement of women. *Bottom:* Chart 1. Women's Representation in the Scandinavian Parliaments 1945–1985. Source: *The International Social Science Journal,* Vol. 35, N.Y. ©U.N.E.S.C.O. 1983. Reproduced by permission of U.N.E.S.C.O.**

similar representation, proportionately, in the cabinet. The cabinet of Margaret Thatcher (end of the 1970s and beginning of the 1980s) is the most male-dominated of the past two decades. There were no women in the cabinet formed after her 1987 election victory. In the Muslim-Arab states of the world the matter of women's representation in the legislative assembly, where it does exist, is taken care of by the simple process of allocating 10 percent of the seats to women, as for example in Iran. But men, not women, nominate the representatives. In Bahrain, Kuwait, Oman, Qatar, Saudi Arabia and the United Arab Emirates women are not eligible to vote or to stand for election.[8] (See Table 5.)

There are many reasons why women are so woefully under-represented in policy-making bodies such as the cabinet, legislative assemblies or as heads of government departments and other state agencies. For most women the translation of public activity from the economic to the political sphere is impeded by domestic responsibilities. Men also see women as having less of a chance to succeed in politics. There are also many developed countries, notably Australia, Japan, South Africa, where the public's perception of women is that they have no place in politics and that their responsibilities lie elsewhere. Some countries have, unintentionally, signaled their male-rooted perceptions in blunt terms. For example in a report furnished to the United Nations by Bulgaria, the government, in approval, quotes the Chairperson of the Committee of the Movement for Bulgarian Women (a senior Communist Party functionary) that "the supreme moral duty of a woman is to bear and raise children with the help of society."[9] This is a very traditional view, the same attitude that permeates thinking elsewhere in the world. One can read this view in Markowitz's study of power and class in Africa.[10] In *World Affairs,* Asunction Lavrin reports on the "traditional values" which continue to obstruct women's role in politics in South America.[11] In Ireland, where anger at women's continued exclusion from real political participation is simmering just below the surface, Mary Robinson (an Irish Senator) asked herself whether it is significant for women in Ireland in 1986 that men are still dominant as lawmakers and replied: "I believe the answer is *yes,* and that the significance is greater than many women appreciate. It is not simply a question of wanting more women *per se* involved in the various bodies. It is because the male domination at all levels affects the very ethos and culture of our society. It reinforces sex stereotyping and role conditioning. Those with control over the levers of power have little reason to want to change the establishment. At the moment it is male perceptions and male priorities which predominate. Are they necessarily the same as the perceptions and the priorities of women?"[12]

There is also a reluctance among political parties to promote women as candidates for high office, again a decision that is made largely by a male-dominated inner leadership. Rather than change the party structure so that more women possibly could be elected, many political parties in power, or in opposition, include women's rights issues in the party platform, thereby heading off pressure to include more women and running little risk of alienating the female electorate. In their survey of women in the world, Joni Seager and Ann Olson rightly conclude:

> There are few instances where men in authority have shared power with women voluntarily. Women have not automatically gained through national struggles or under "revolutionary" governments: a rising tide does not necessarily raise all boats, and women have frequently been left behind even when broad social advances have been made. The attitudes of men in power to women seem to be remarkably similar across a wide geographic and political spectrum. Within one month in the autumn of 1985 the newspapers reported the words of a high ranking

COUNTRY	1970 M	1970 F	1980 M	1980 F
Australia	187	4	170	19
Austria	213	23	206	30
Barbados	23	1	26	1
Belgium	368	26	360	34
Bulgaria	322	78	317	83
Burundi			59	6
Byelorussia	271	159	305	130
Canada	360	15	343	39
Chile	185	15	77	3
China	2232	853	2346	632
Costa Rica	55	5	55	4
Cuba	376	105	386	113
Cyprus	35	0	34	1
Czechoslovakia	251	99	251	99
Denmark	149	30	137	42
Dominica	20	1	20	1
Dominican Rep.	103	15	139	8
Ecuador			134	4
Egypt			615	43
El Salvador			50	10
Eq. Guinea			58	2
Finland	154	46	138	62
France			770	38
German Dem. Rep.	332	168	338	162
Germany, F.R.	480	38	469	51
Greece	293	7	286	14
Guyana	44	9	55	16
Honduras			76	6
Hungary	251	101	243	109
Iceland	57	3	51	9
India	523	19	514	28
Indonesia	429	31	418	42
Ireland	197	11	206	20
Israel	112	8	112	8
Italy	828	23	886	86
Ivory Coast	99	11	139	8
Japan	701	25	733	26
Kenya	168	4	169	3
Korea Rep.	213	8	268	8
Luxembourg	56	3	53	6
Malawi	83	4	96	10
Malaysia	148	6	146	8
Mauritius	67	3	96	4

Continued on next page.

Table 5. Women's Membership of National Legislative Bodies. Source: *Women: A World Report,* Debbie Taylor (ed.) Oxford University Press, New York, 1985, pp. 375–376. Used with permission of Oxford University Press.

COUNTRY	1970 M	1970 F	1980 M	1980 F
Mexico			110	54
Mongolia			77	23
Nepal			128	7
Netherlands	202	23	182	43
New Zealand	83	4	84	8
Norway	131	24	115	40
Philippines	166	12	165	7
Poland	365	95	346	114
Portugal	230	20	232	18
Romania	275	66	247	122
Rwanda			61	9
Saint Lucia	18	2	26	2
Samoa	46	1	46	1
Senegal	92	8	107	13
Spain	600	27	571	32
Sri Lanka	161	6	147	7
Sweden	274	75	251	98
Switzerland	229	15	221	25
Turkey	627	7	387	12
UK	1715	75	1762	87
Ukraine SSR			416	234
Uruguay	96	3		
USA	516	19	511	23
USSR	1025	475	1008	492
Venezuela			219	12
Vietnam	358	132	389	108
Yugoslavia	86	13	83	17
Zambia	127	8	131	4
Zimbabwe			122	11

Table 5 continued.

American official: "women don't understand the issues at the peace summit . . . or what is happening in human rights"; the Greek president exhorting women to have more babies to help bolster military manpower to face a future threat from Turkey; and President Marcos of the Philippines saying that he was "embarrassed" to be running in a political campaign against a woman."[13]

Cabinet and Executive Government Posts

The only region in the free world where women have made notable progress in the executive and top administrative field of government is in the five Nordic countries, Sweden, Norway, Finland, Denmark and Iceland, where, in 1984, there was a total of 94 women either serving in the cabinet or as heads of major government departments. Sweden, with 28, had the best record. Iceland had 10, including a woman as President. In Norway, with 22, the Prime Minister was a woman. By comparison the rest of Europe shows women woefully under-represented at cabinet level or as heads of government departments with executive powers. Austria, with six women ministers in a cabinet of 23, was still far behind the Nordic countries. In the Netherlands women were almost 20 percent of the deputies to the States General in 1984, but only two ended up in the cabinet and of the 17 secretaries of state only three were women. In Belgium (1983) only 4 of the 25 cabinet posts went to women. In the more recently reestablished democracies of Europe, Spain, Portugal and Greece, the pattern was much the same.[14]

Women's perception of their roles in society is still far removed from the stage where they feel strong enough to make women's representation in parliament or in the cabinet a collective issue. One of the best books written the past two decades on women voters and women's role in politics since Unesco published M. Dverger's book *The Political Role of Women* (1955) is that of Joni Lovenduski and Jill Hills: *The Politics of the Second Electorate* (1981). It and Lovenduski's latest work *Women and European Politics* (1986) represent together the most comprehensive work on the subject of women and politics.[15]

The political pattern in the democracies is repeated in other large organizations such as trade unions which, generally speaking, are still male-dominated today, despite the enormous rise in female membership. In fact, in most countries the growth of the trade unions during the last decade was largely the recruitment of women members. This is true of Ecuador, Fiji, India, the Netherlands, Spain, and the United Kingdom and of almost all countries. The Labor Organization in Sweden reported that more than 90 percent of the total membership increase from 1977–1987 was women. In the Federal Republic of Germany women accounted for 80 percent of the new members in 1985.[16] In China, where women account for 37 percent of the workforce, there are 60,000 full-time women's trade union representatives. Yet, looking at women's roles at the executive level, the picture changes. Women account for only 29 percent of the Executive Committee of the All-China Federation of Trade Union.[17] Surveying the participation of women in trade union positions of power and responsibilities worldwide, the International Labor Organization (I.L.O.) concluded: "Despite the increase in union membership, women remain very much in the minority on decision-making bodies."[18]

Labor Segregation

According to estimates, worldwide, by the I.L.O. women numbered some 676 million out of a total of 1,955.1 million workers in 1985, or about 34.6 percent of the total labor force. There are wide variations according to age group, country and geographical regions. In all regions, the I.L.O. reported, the female share of the market has continued to increase. In many cases, in all regions, female employment has declined less or increased more than that of males during the period 1980–1985.[19] There are 500 million women in China of which some 200 million are working women. Thus China alone has nearly 30 percent of the world's female labor force. The majority, some 150 million, account for nearly 50 percent of the Chinese rural labor force, a crucial asset to this eminently agricultural country. With the recent economic reforms, industrialization is speeding up and out of every 100 women workers 12 are now employed in industry, mining or manufacturing. Over 40 percent of the workers and researchers in China's developing electronics industry are women. But at managerial and executive levels only 10 percent of the positions are held by women. In 1949 there were only 600,000 women working as full-time, salaried employees, or 7.5 percent of all salaried workers. In 1986 the total was 46.88 million, or almost 37 percent of all full-time workers.[20] In the world's richest country, the United States, women comprised 45 percent of the total labor force in 1987.[21]

The statistics and projections indicate that in most areas of the world more women have entered the market in the past two decades (1965–1985) than during any other period and that more and more were seeking employment. In addition to historical and political events, and the changing nature of economic and technological progress, the single most important factor seems to be the educational opportunities which opened up for women during this period.

The projection for female labor for the period 1985–2000 and on is upward and is expected to show a higher rate of increase than the male labor force in Europe, North America, Oceania and temperate South America, and about the same rate as the male labor force in Japan and East Asia. In the developing world, the economically active female population is expected to remain stagnant for the next 15 years while in Africa the male labor force is expected to increase far more rapidly.[22] (See Chart 2.)

With the exception of the public service market, whether in the government or private sector, there has been no real, significant change in market segregation. (See Table 6.) Women are still clustered in so-called feminine occupations, or "pink ghettos," and in less skilled, poorly paid jobs compared to men. In the higher echelons, even in government service, the discrepancies of 1985 are basically the same, sometimes worse, than in 1965. In the United States, for example, women accounted for 37.4 percent of the federal civil service in 1985, yet held only 6 percent of the upper-grade posts.[23] The situation is worse in Germany and, among the 26 industrialized nations of the world, at its worst South Africa.[24]

In Africa the need for an increase in the production of food has led to modernization and mechanism in agriculture. These factors have had, and many continue to have, a devastating impact on women in large parts of the continent. With modernization the factors of production and capital become more important. Yet in most African societies, there are severe limitations on the ability of women to secure capital. Both inheritance and the retention of surplus income are made difficult for women. Rights of inheritance are often restricted, sometimes severely so. Sometimes women have no right to own or inherit property. According to the United Nations survey of women in development, "Women's rights are often eroded by legislation. . . . Women's property rights are withdrawn as property becomes more valuable."[25]

In Latin America labor segregation is also rife. At the first United Nations tripartite seminar on non-discriminatory practices held in Lima, Peru, in 1983 it was pointed out that not only was the female participation rate in labor the lowest in the world, but that women were clearly segregated, concentrated in sectors such as food processing, textiles, garment making, and educational and

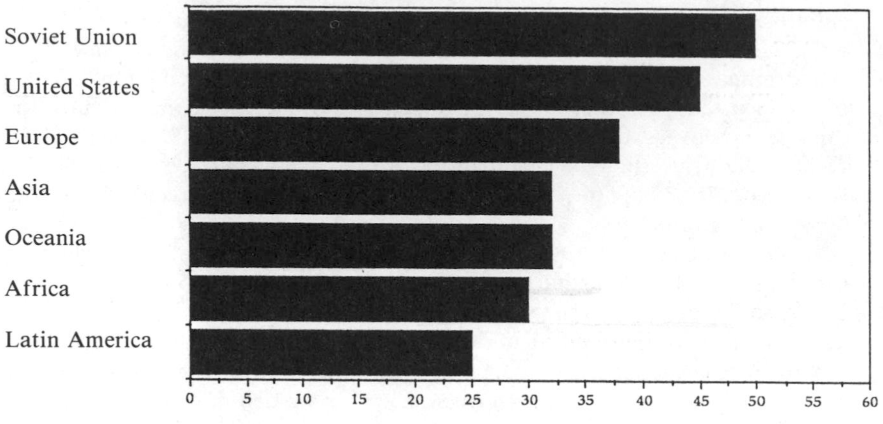

Country	BOSSES Women	BOSSES Men	SECRETARIES Women	SECRETARIES Men
GERMANY (Fed.Rep.)	1.3	4.2	34.0	9.6
HUNGARY	0.1	0.2	16.4	3.5
NORWAY	2.0	6.6	26.0	2.5
UNITED STATES	3.8	10.4	27.9	5.5
JAPAN	0.4	6.4	18.2	9.4
EGYPT	0.8	0.9	25.0	6.5
BAHRAIN	0.4	1.1	46.0	5.8
SINGAPORE	1.2	8.2	14.9	5.7
VENEZUELA	1.6	9.2	16.7	7.6

***Top:* Chart 2. Estimated Percentage of Women in the World's Labor Force by Major Regions: 1987. Sources: International Labor Organization, Bureau of Statistics, Geneva, 1988; United States Bureau of Labor Statistics, 1988; European Commission, Strasbourg, 1988. *Bottom:* Table 6. Occupational Segregation by Gender: Managers and Secretaries. Source: International Labor Organization, 1983 *Yearbook of Labour Statistics,* Geneva, 1984.**

health services. "While technological progress has widened women's employment opportunities, it has also displaced them to less skilled occupations at lower salaries. Occupational segregation is not only due to the structure of the labor market but also to the absence of social infrastructure." Other problems identified included the increasing number of professional and technically trained women workers who are discriminated against in obtaining managerial and executive posts, even though they are suitably qualified.[26]

In the industrial world of North America, Europe and Japan, industrial and economic growth was of statistical significance in that more women obtained employment. But generally speaking, the benefits which women derived from such growth and development were considerably smaller than those derived by men. The main causes are women's lack of training, labor discrimination policies and practices, and occupational segregation, rather than skill differentiation. Women are also paid less even when their seniority, experience, and training are comparable, and they nearly always have fewer opportunities to acquire that seniority. When change occurs in the international economy, women are affected far more than men.[27]

Employment Patterns

One important and positive development for women has been the increase of women in the purely professional occupations. In the United States women exceeded 50 percent of the professional occupations in 1987, and in the E.C.E. region of Europe the increase has also been significant. The rate has been slower in the developing nations, and there are major regional differences. For example, the countries of Latin America now have higher participation rates in the professional categories than other developing regions, although there are some countries in Asia, notably the Philippines, where women are very well represented.[28]

Though the statistical calculations of the I.L.O. show that more and more women are to enter the market as workers, this may increase the concentration of women in the "pink ghettos." Technological change is sometimes at the heart of this problem. In the Federal Republic of Germany it was calculated that 25 percent of office jobs in the private sector and 36 percent in the public sector will become superfluous because of the introduction of micro-electronics, i.e, computers. In the United Kingdom it has been estimated that by 1990 some 170,000 secretarial jobs will be lost in this way.[29]

Employment patterns of women are now definitely related to education, family size, family health, family structure, literacy, per capita income, and demographic issues of which migration is the most important, along with female life expectancy.

There has been an increase in the number of households headed only by women. In the West this has been due mostly to socio-religious considerations, economic factors, and social (federal) support for single-parent households where there are three or more children, as in the United States. In South, West and East Africa the single most important factor has been migration of male workers. Surveys in Ghana, Botswana and Kenya indicates that in areas of male migration up to 50 percent of households are headed by women.[30]

There has been at least one quiet yet successful revolution in employment for women. Throughout the industrial world, women have been increasing their share of jobs, while, in the same industrial field, the numbers of male steel and car workers have declined. Between 1978–1987 some 70 percent of new jobs created in the United States have been filled by women. Unfortunately, many of these jobs have been part-time, low paid and in a narrow range of services. There are surveys which indicate that 81 percent of clerical workers in the United States are women, or one out of three working women compared to one out of seventeen men. Within the clerical profession over 95 percent of the secretaries, typists and stenographers are women. Of all data entry keyers, 91 percent are women. Almost 100 percent of all dental assistants are women and 94 percent of all registered nurses. Of all waiters, telephone operators, librarians and elementary school teachers, more than 85 percent are women.[31]

Behind the surge in women's employment is the growing importance of service industries such as banking, insurance, public relations, accounting and tourism. Between 1975 and 1985 women filled 50 to 80 percent of all new service jobs in the 24 nations belonging to the European-based Organization for Economic Cooperation and Development (O.E.C.D.). Although self-employed workers are still likely to be male, the proportion of women is rising everywhere, ranging from a high of 45 percent in the United States to 26 percent in Japan.[32] From 1973 to 1986 the share of women who received masters' degrees in business administration (M.B.A.) in the United States grew from 6.6 percent to 31 percent.[33]

Two key factors are prompting women to start their own firms. According to Robert Goffee of the London Business School, co-author of *Women in Charge,* these factors are (1) the growing importance of the service sector, and (2) frustrated career ambitions, notably in public relations, finance and computer services.[34]

Entry into paid employment in the marketplace brings millions of women into the mainstream of economic activity for the first time and thus, also, the political attention accorded to their needs. This serves to destroy the isolation of women.

If greater economic visibility through work outside the home is a measure of progress, then the available statistics are encouraging. The I.L.O. projections for 1985 put women at 41 percent of the total labor force in developed states and 32 percent in developing states. The highest percentages are found in the Communist Bloc of Eastern Europe, followed by the New World (North America), the Far East, Western Europe and Africa, with substantially lower figures in Asia (China excepted), Latin America and the Muslim states. (See Table 7.)

Exactly how misleading statistics can be, however, is evident from the fact that the share of women in manufacturing employment of the industrial export zones is known to exceed 80 percent. But companies have shown a decided preference for employing very young women who, in addition to being docile, dexterous and adaptable, are willing to work for low wages. Employers prefer young workers with no seniority because they represent cheap labor, while the absence of family ties makes them more adaptable as far as shift work is concerned. Many firms refuse outright to employ married women and insist that they leave when they get married.[35]

The basic difficulties and inequalities confronting women in the 1960s have shown no substantial change in the 1980s. In most countries official records show women's unemployment rates significantly above men's. Even in Europe, unemployment rates in 1982 compared with men's ranged from 13 percent higher in Sweden to over 100 percent higher in France, Italy, and Japan.

Wage Discrimination

There is also a persistent, substantial gap in earnings between men and women, as can be seen in the case studies in this book. Nowhere, in not a single country, are women even close to reaching a broad parity with men in wages and salaries.

Surveying trends and policies in the world economy, the United Nations reported as follows:

> Data on the occupations filled by women, and the salaries they earn, show that, although the situation is changing in many respects, there are significant differences *vis-à-vis* men. . . . It can be seen that a smaller percentage of the economically active female population occupy . . . [high] positions [in administration and management] than is the case for men. The estimates are based on a limited number of countries; because of a lack of comparable data, they do not include the centrally planned economies. Yet they do reveal that, while the differences have narrowed since the early 1970s, the shares of men and women are still significantly different.
>
> When figures for professional and technical workers are examined, they show that women occupy proportionally more of these positions than do men: nearly 12 percent of economically active women are in this category at the present time, compared with 8 percent of men. This reflects in part the major role that women play in the services sector, which includes many of the occupations that they fill such as teacher or nurse. It also reflects the fact that the higher a person's educational attainment, the more likely will be his or her participation in the labor force. As women are generally a smaller percentage of the economically active population than men, the average educational level of women workers is therefore likely to be higher than that of men.
>
> Examining the ratio between the wages of men and women in non-agricultural activities for a limited number of countries it can be see that, in every country, on average women earned less than men. Data do not permit an assessment of the extent to which this is due to actual differences in responsibilities. Often, within an occupational group, women tend to fill lower-paid jobs than men—teachers, rather than principals in schools, for instance. A comparison between countries is not possible, and conclusions drawn from this limited sample must be tentative. However, the figures, on the whole, show that the difference between men's and women's earnings, as measured, has not narrowed appreciably during the past decade.[36] [See Tables 8 and 9.]

According to Ruth Sivard the increasing employment of women has had little impact in reducing the occupational segregation which is at the base of the inequality of pay between the sexes. Within all three major fields, agriculture, industry and services, women are clustered in unskilled, dead-end jobs with low pay or little potential for training and advancement. The pattern reveals not only lower wages but lower status, longer working hours, fewer or no fringe benefits and less security. In this respect, she wrote, labor patterns and job segregation reflect cultural patterns and stereotypes which have shown equally little change the past 20 years. In terms of poverty (unemployment, low pay, unskilled work) women are still caught in a spreading blot of impoverishment. Rural women in Third World countries are the poorest among the poor, said Sivard. They are the most numerous and the most disadvantaged. Yet in Africa they provide 90 percent of the family food supply.[37]

Region or country grouping	1970				1980			
	T	Agr	Ind	Ser	T	Agr	Ind	Ser
World	35.1	37.4	27.3	37.4	34.8	37.0	27.8	37.8
Developed countries	39.7	44.4	28.8	47.2	40.2	43.3	29.2	48.7
Developing countries	32.9	36.5	25.7	25.9	32.4	36.4	26.5	26.9
North America	36.5	10.8	22.4	46.1	38.1	11.4	23.4	47.3
Western Europe	32.1	28.0	22.4	42.6	33.3	28.5	23.0	43.9
Eastern Europe and USSR	48.1	51.5	38.3	56.0	47.0	49.6	36.9	57.0
Japan	39.1	52.8	29.7	40.4	40.3	53.7	31.6	42.9
Other developed countries	31.7	29.7	15.3	44.1	33.4	29.6	15.5	46.8
Africa (developing)	32.7	34.8	19.7	31.5	32.0	34.4	19.7	31.6
Middle-income countries	29.3	29.9	19.4	34.0	28.7	28.9	19.0	34.3
Low-income countries	36.0	38.4	20.3	26.0	35.3	38.3	20.9	25.7
Latin America and the Caribbean	21.2	8.1	16.7	38.4	23.0	9.3	15.8	38.8
Middle-income countries	20.8	6.8	16.2	37.8	22.8	8.2	15.3	38.3
Low-income countries	23.8	14.6	21.7	44.5	24.6	14.3	20.6	43.8
Asia (developing)	34.2	38.7	27.6	21.8	33.6	38.5	28.8	23.2
Middle-income countries	38.7	41.1	31.7	37.5	38.3	40.7	31.8	38.2
Low-income countries	27.7	28.0	27.6	26.7	27.3	27.6	27.2	26.5
China	37.9	34.8	28.7	20.5	37.6	44.1	30.6	22.7
India	32.6	37.9	26.1	16.2	31.7	37.7	27.1	17.4
Middle East	22.3	28.1	14.3	13.9	22.9	30.3	14.5	15.8

Abbreviations: T = total labor force; Agr = agriculture, forestry, hunting and fishing; Ind = industry such as mining and quarrying, manufacturing, public utilities and constructing; Ser = services.

Areas and Countries	1977	1980	Latest year
Developing countries or areas			
Africa			
Kenya	1.07	1.26	1.17
Swaziland	1.84	2.25	1.50
United Republic of Tanzania	1.49	1.18	...
Asia			
Hong Kong	...	...	1.32
Republic of Korea	2.27	2.25	2.01
Singapore	...	1.59	1.45
Sri Lanka	1.01	1.09	1.35
Industrialized countries			
Europe			
Belgium	1.42	1.44	1.34
Czechoslovakia	1.46	1.46	1.46
Denmark	1.17	1.18	1.22
France	1.28	1.26	1.22
Germany, Federal Republic of	1.38	1.38	1.37
Iceland	1.25	1.17	1.12
Luxembourg	1.54	1.55	1.57
Netherlands	1.25	1.28	1.31
Switzerland	1.50	1.48	1.48
United Kingdom	1.39	1.43	1.44
Japan	1.79	1.86	1.92
Australia	1.15	1.16	1.15
New Zealand	1.30	1.30	1.27

Table 8. Male/female wage ratio in non-agricultural activities 1977, 1980, latest year. Source: Department of International Economic and Social Affairs of the United Nations Secretariat, based on International Labor Office, *Yearbook of Labor Statistics 1987* (Geneva).

Gains in Education

Women have made their greatest gains in the past decade in education. According to United Nations data, 161 of 194 countries and territories with autonomous school systems had compulsory schooling by 1980. Of these, 94 required 8 to 10 years of schooling, 55 required 7 years or fewer, and 12 called for 10 years or more. U.N.E.S.C.O. records show that in 1985 about 300 million more girls were enrolled in the world's schools and universities than in 1950.

Table 7. Women's Share of the Total Labor Force, by Sector and Region, 1970 and 1980. Source: United Nations, *World Survey of the Role of Women in Development,* Geneva, 1985, p.70.

Country	Wage differentials 1975	Wage differentials 1982	Changes in wage differentials (1975–82)
Australia	78.5	78.2	-0.3
Belgium	71.3	73.5	2.2
Burma	88.5	88.8	0.3
Cyprus	45.9	56.3	10.4
Denmark	84.3	85.1	0.8
Egypt	67.8	91.8	24.8
El Salvador	90.4	85.9	-4.5
Finland	72.6	77.2	-0.4
France	76.4	78.1	1.7
Fed. Rep. of Germany	72.1	73.0	0.9
Greece	69.5	73.1	3.6
Ireland	60.9	68.5	7.6
Japan	47.9	43.1	-4.8
Kenya	66.1	75.8	9.7
Rep. of Korea	47.4	45.1	-2.3
Luxemburg	60.9	60.0	-0.9
Netherlands	74.7	74.0	-0.7
New Zealand	65.6	71.1	5.5
Norway	78.0	83.2	5.2
Switzerland	68.0	67.5	-0.5
Sweden	85.2	90.3	5.1
Tanzania	70.7	78.5	7.8
United Kingdom	66.5	68.8	2.3

Table 9. Changes in Wage Differentials Among Men and Women in the Manufacturing Industries of Selected Countries, 1975–1982. Source: International Labor Organization, *1983 Yearbook of Labor Statistics,* Geneva, 1984.

Education influences women's economic participation and earning powers, and leads to a reduction in the number of children and to an improvement in health in the family. Yet in developing countries, national priorities are still so inverted that almost 60 percent of girls in the age group 5 to 19 are not in school. The increase in girls' enrollment since 1950 has in fact failed to eliminate a broad disparity between the sexes. At all levels of occupation boys still represent a majority of students; however, in terms of literacy, the rate for women, not including China, is now 68 percent compared to 59 percent in 1960. Currently over a billion women out of a total population of 2.5 billion women are literate.

There is an almost direct relation between literacy and per capita income. Some 60 percent of the illiterate women live in countries where the per capita income is less than $300, and in 1980 four out of five women over 25 years of age in Africa and South Asia had never attended school.[38]

In the educational structure itself, inequalities between men and women are still rife. Women teachers vastly outnumber men, but women are a small minority among school principals and heads of departments. Within university systems vertical segregation is equally pronounced. In France, West Germany and Britain less than 10 percent of all professors at universities are women.

In the field of education, U.N.E.S.C.O. stresses that it is the quality of education, not the quantity, that prevents girls from becoming better qualified for the workplace. This is a worldwide problem. As an example, take Denmark and Ghana, countries which are culturally and geographically poles apart. In 1982 some 66 percent of girls at Danish technical schools were being trained in the clothing trade, in textile design and in the hotel industry. In Ghana, where girls form 20 percent of the students at technical schools, the vast majority were also studying dressmaking, embroidery and catering.[39]

According to the United Nations, a third of all developing countries (or more than 40 countries) still do not have school systems adequate to educate all their children. In its study of country rankings on the status of women, the Washington Population Crisis Committee said:

> The educational bias against girls observed in some countries and the lower earning power of adult women form a vicious circle. Parents may prefer to educate sons in part because their job prospects are better. Parents may also pull daughters out of school because girls are expected to help in the home. Even where daughters are allowed to stay in school, they may have less time to study than their brothers. Parents may also pull girls out of school when they reach puberty, either because they are considered ready for marriage or because parents want to ensure their chastity. Most countries still make inadequate efforts to get and keep girls in secondary schools.[40]

Women, Science and Technology

Given the vast developments in technology in the world, and given that science and technology are the main source of innovation as well as the driving force behind economic growth, women's role in this relatively new field will become the subject of increasing concern in the future.

Women have traditionally played a smaller role than men in scientific and technological activities. In the nineteenth century there were virtually no female students at universities, and most universities had either legal or *de facto* barriers to the admission of women. Owing to cultural stereotypes, women were assigned non-scientific and non-technical work. It was generally assumed that women were not suited or not as smart as men when it came to science. Psychometric evidence has proven that such an assumption is false. This is supported by the fact that in some countries, such as the Philippines and Russia, women and men graduate in equal numbers in science and technology fields, and also by Favag Moussa's survey of contemporary women inventors in 26 countries.[41] In fact, as Caroline Herzenberg has pointed out, women have been involved in practicing science for 3,000 years and among these women are many world-class scientists.[42] In her study of women scientists in the past, Margaret Alic shows that women's contributions to science have been vastly underrated.[43] Clearly a male-oriented society never took any notice or gave much credence to what women had been doing. It is an interesting fact that the

Region	% adults literate male/female	In school aged 12–17 male/female	% women aged 15–19 married	Average number of children per woman	Infant mortality rate male/female
World	67/54	55/46	30	3.8	103/92
Developed	98/97	84/85	8	2.0	24/18
Developing	52/32	42/28	39	4.4	116/104
Africa	33/15	39/24	44	6.4	151/129
Northern	44/18	42/43	34	6.2	128/114
Western	20/6	29/16	70	6.8	171/145
Eastern	29/14	33/20	32	6.6	142/121
Middle	35/9	52/26	49	6.0	181/153
Southern	55/56	74/70	2	5.2	109/92
North America	99/99	95/95	11	1.8	16/12
Latin America	76/70	58/54	16	4.5	90/80
Middle	75/67	58/46	21	5.3	76/67
Caribbean	67/66	60/59	19	3.8	78/68
Tropical South	74/67	56/54	15	4.6	104/92
Temperate South	93/91	70/73	10	2.9	47/41
Asia	56/34	43/28	42	3.9	108/99
South-West	58/31	54/32	25	5.8	123/99
Middle South	44/17	35/17	54	5.5	138/135
South-East	75/53	43/35	24	4.7	105/87
East	97/92	85/80	2	2.3	57/45
Europe	96/93	81/80	7	2.0	25/19
Northern	99/99	82/83	9	1.8	15/11
Western	98/98	87/89	5	1.6	17/13
Eastern	97/92	80/81	9	2.3	30/21
Southern	93/85	73/66	7	2.3	31/25
USSR	100/100	72/82	10	2.4	35/27
Oceania	90/88	75/71	10	2.8	48/39

School Level	1975		1985	
	GIRLS	BOYS	GIRLS	BOYS
Primary School				
Rich World	92.9	92.6	93.1	92.9
Poor World	54.1	70.6	65.1	78.4
World Average	64.0	76.3	71.2	81.6
Secondary School				
Rich World	83.6	80.5	89.9	87.3
Poor World	28.5	41.5	37.1	48.1
World Average	45.0	53.3	49.8	57.5
Higher Education				
Rich World	28.0	32.8	31.9	34.7
Poor World	6.2	12.4	9.8	16.1
World Average	13.6	19.3	16.0	21.3

Table 11. School Enrollment, Boys and Girls: 1975–1985. Source: *Women: A World Report,* Debbie Taylor (ed.), Oxford University Press, New York, 1985, p. 71, table 4.Used with permission of Oxford University Press.

highest intelligence ever measured in any person up to 1985 belongs to a woman, Marilyn Vos Savant.

There is, however, a vast difference in the number of male and female students studying science and technology in most countries of the world. Women are least represented in engineering throughout the world with the highest percentage found in the Communist East Bloc of Europe, *viz.* 25 percent. In some of the most industrialized countries, such as Japan, Italy, Germany and Switzerland, the representation of women in engineering studies is extremely low. In fact, developing countries such as Burma, Egypt and Paraguay show figures for female enrollment well above those of the industrialized West.[44]

Feminist writers have argued, correctly, that technology in itself has been male-oriented. "The palace-temple-army-technology complex was operated by men, and the kitchen-garden-homecraft-children-bearing complex was operated by women. Technological advance seems never to have deviated from this road and little conscious effort has been made to put science and technology in the hands of women as well."[45]

Despite a 300 percent increase in female enrollment in engineering schools in the United States between 1970 and 1980, women filled less than 3 percent of the technical energy-related jobs in 1985; in fact only 8 percent of all engineers are women. Major corporations have now started a "Women's Careers in Energy Program" to attract more women to technical education

Table 10. Male-Female Literacy, Infant Mortality, Secondary School Enrollment and Average Number of Children per Woman, World Wide, by Region. Source: World Health Organization, U.N.E.S.C.O. and I.L.O., Geneva, 1985.

related to energy and for jobs expected to become available in energy-related areas.[46] But in the most authoritative survey of women's progress in science in the United States in the late '80s, Betty Vetter found that, despite progress, there is persistent inequality of opportunity for women in science and engineering, both in education and employment. The numbers are tapering off, she writes, and the gains of 1975–1985 may not endure. Referring to the increase in science and engineering degree awards to women, she says that this appears to have been related primarily to women's increased participation in higher education. "The rapid increases in number and proportion of these degree awards to women that have marked the past decade appear to be ending well before women's participation in these fields matches their proportions of the population. Bachelors' degree awards to women in several science and engineering fields already are leveling off. . . ." She found that the professional community of scientists and engineers had made little effort to welcome women in the fraternity and projected that the number of women graduates in mathematics and computer-science fields could drop by more than 50 percent in the next few years. Table 12, prepared by Betty Vetter, shows that when it comes to unemployment in the science and engineering fields it is women who suffer most.[47]

Stereotyping: A Principal Cause of Discrimination

Certain preliminary conclusions can be drawn, based on the information in the foregoing pages and tables, as to the scope and reasons for the environment of discrimination which women face all over the world. It is possible that not all women will agree with the conclusions. This should surprise no one. One of the problems men have in trying to understand women's struggle against gender discrimination is precisely that they tend to herd most, if not all, women into the same camp, much the way many whites tend to judge black individuals, no matter their mother tongue, motherland or individual aptitude.

Just as racial discrimination is viewed in different lights by different communities, so discrimination against women is viewed differently by Western women, by Muslim women, by black African, Asian and Latin American women. But the overall impression of discrimination against women being as much of a problem as discrimination against blacks in white society is difficult to question if one's point of reference lies in the Western world.

Not all women support the women's rights movement, nor are they all activists—members of organizations fighting discrimination against women on grounds of gender in every conceivable sphere. Yet discrimination against women and lack of women's rights should be viewed in the same light as race and racial discrimination, or religion and religious discrimination. The facts show that women do not constitute a single caste, class, religious group, race, estate or group without distinction. But many women from different countries and different races have associated to form women's groups which are active in the international sphere. Women of one country and of the same or different color, religion and economic background have duplicated the effort, but on a

	All S'ES 1984 M/F	Doctoral S'ES 1985 M/F	Recent B.S. Grads* 1984 M/F	Recent M.S. Grads* 1984 M/F
All S'ES	1.3/3.4	0.7/1.9	4.8/6.8	3.4/3.7
All Scientists	1.6/3.5	0.7/1.9		
Physical	1.6/3.8	0.6/1.9	9.0/7.8	2.0/•
Mathematical	2.0/2.8	0.4/0.9	2.3/4.4	1.5/5.5
Computer	0.5/0.8	0.2/0.7	2.2/2.3	1.1/1.3
Environmental	2.6/7.1	0.7/1.5	7.7/4.4	4.4/•
Life	1.5/4.4	1.0/2.0	6.8/8.1	4.7/3.6
Psychologist	2.1/3.1	0.5/1.4	10.2/7.1	2.7/2.8
Social	2.5/5.9	0.6/2.7	5.7/7.2	5.6/5.6
Engineers	1.2/2.9	0.6/1.1	3.3/6.8	3.3/6.8

Table 12. Unemployment Rates among U.S. Scientists. •Fewer than 1,500 in the labor force. *Graduates of 1982 and 1983 combined.

national or regional scale. Though women do not form a single group, except in purely biological terms, the problems they face, the discrimination and exclusion based on gender, transcends racial, national, and religious barriers.

A 1985 report by the World Health Organization dealt objectively and lucidly with the problem of stereotyping, as summarized in the following paragraphs:

•Women do not constitute a caste, for the caste system, as known in India, is a closed group of hereditary nature and excludes any meaningful contact or relationship with other castes, particularly marriage. Women do not constitute an estate either, like royalty or the press, because women can lay no claim to all negative and positive privileges suffered or enjoyed by women of all social strata. Neither do they form a social class because they cannot all, homogeneously, be considered to have a relationship based on the availability or unavailability of goods and services. Finally, it is axiomatic that they do not constitute a nominal category.

•By a process of elimination of these fairly common misconceptions, women should simply be seen as individuals defined by the class to which they belong in a particular country and the roles assigned to them in this class. Discrimination against a woman should be seen as no more, no less, than discrimination against any male person, for example, on grounds of color.

•Discrimination against the mass of women, or all women in a particular country, state or city, is thus discrimination against a mass of individuals who are forced, on purely sexual grounds, to suffer the fate of a mostly inferior stereotyping. This is also what makes the battle against sexual discrimination so difficult. With only sex as a basis, women, individually or collectively, become victims of a distorted social (and male) perception. The recognition given in school books to man as the farmer and cultivator is factually incorrect. It may be true in some countries but it is not true of the world in general. United Nations' estimates reveal that, globally, women are responsible for at least 50 percent of food production.

•Sexual stereotypes are molds, produced by cultural and religious patterns, such as in Muslim society, or sometimes calculated, such as in Latin American or black African society. The products of these molds are often unconsciously transmitted, acquired or applied but on these molds are structured patterns, values and beliefs which underlie attitudes towards and behavior by one sex or the other.

•Stereotyping, ignorance, male intransigence and social perceptions (definitions of male and female) are at the root of discrimination against women, not the reinforcements which stereotyping finds in tradition, culture, norms, publicity and the mass media.

•The root of the differences in the development of women's activities as opposed to men's lies in the social division of labor, with its specific allocation of tasks by sex and the different value which society attaches to such tasks. This problem can be overcome only by a transformation of the social division of labor by males, which means altering one of the foundations of the economic organization of society, namely domination by males. It requires little knowledge of the nature of society to understand that this would require probably the most radical peaceful revolution in the history of mankind and that the chances of this taking place over the short term, no matter the weight governments may lend to such a revolution, are almost nil. Hence most observers agree that for the coming decade, at least, the problem would be better tackled by seeking to change the value society accords to given tasks.[48]

Of course the foregoing diagnosis does not apply in equal degree to every society. The Nordic countries could argue that their revolution to real equality between men and women is well under way. Other countries could point to the fact that all of the major legislation is in place to eliminate discrimination on grounds of gender, or that affirmative action is being taken to redress the imbalance. But women in the Nordic countries constitute only a fraction of 1 percent of the world's female population and the concern with women's rights can never be bound to region, race, ideology or economic status. As will be shown in several chapters of this book, the mere presence of legislation is no guarantee that social attitudes will change, or that the law would be vigorously enforced.

There are no national boundaries for women's problems; they are generally the same the world over. The difference is only one of degree. Whether women live and work in South Africa, the Soviet Union, Japan, Nigeria, Israel, India, Brazil or the United States, the greater majority of them face sex discrimination, lack of employment opportunities, exploitation, social taboos and stereotyping. The vast gap between the status of women in the Third World and that of women in the 26 industrialized nations of the world, notably North America and Europe, is one of intensity of problems (of recognition, income and education) and the ways in which they are manifested.

At the non-govermental world meeting for women in Nairobi, attended by some 14,000 women from 150 countries, special attention was called to the fact that women perform two-thirds of the world's work, but receive only 5 percent of the income and own less than 1 percent of the assets.[49]

There is also a vast difference in women's perceptions of their problems and how they should go about solving these problems. As Caroline Pezzullo pointed out, the Communist Bloc women's organizations see women's rights as part of the Marxist struggle against capitalism; African women see the issue of equality as part of other overriding issues such as drought, hunger, illiteracy and political strife; Asian women point to extreme poverty of women in rural areas and non-ownership of productive land as reasons why village women move to the cities where many are eventually forced into prostitution by men; Latin American women view sexual discrimination as a heritage of colonialism and slavery that continues to affect women adversely in political, economic and social aspects of their lives; women in the Muslim-Arab world feel engulfed by political and religious strife as well as by sexual discrimination.[50]

In the United States there is concern about the fact that so many black children live in homes headed by women, a majority of them unwedded. Pezzullo points out that 30 percent of the world's households are headed by women, but that among the poor, female-headed households predominate. These women, carrying a triple work load of income-generation, childcare and housework, work up to 20 hours per day. The volume of abandoned children is growing rapidly and is estimated at between 70 and 170 million.[51]

Defining Women's Needs

Trying to define women's most urgent need is like trying to define a single set of objectives to cure racism and religious intolerance. The priorities of women in Africa, Asia, or Europe are also clearly different. But reduced to basics, women's needs in the Western world and Latin America are first of all a question of a greater voice in politics and legislatures. Almost every aspect of women's struggle for equal rights and equal opportunities can be fought more effectively in the political arena. Decisions about new laws, decisions about law enforcement, decisions about the execution of programs aimed at assisting women, decisions about birth control and women's role in the community in general, decisions affecting wage discrimination, occupational segregation or abortion, all flow from decisions and actions taken by the legislature, and in every Western country the attitude of the legislature is the reflection of political attitudes shaped, overwhelmingly, by men.

Women all over the world are the most unrepresented group in the legislatures and governments of their countries; they are effectively excluded from the vital policy-making and decision-making levels. At the same time they are also vastly under-represented in international councils, in higher education, in the media, in the judiciary and in other important opinion-forming circles.

Educating men to accept women's full political participation is not an easy process. It is a serious problem even in those countries where there is a vast reservoir of sympathy for women in the media, the legislature and political circles in general. A case in point is the United States, where women, who make up half of all the voters, face a national legislature (Congress) where only 4.5 percent of the members are women. Less than 16 percent of state legislators are women. Less than 14 percent of elected county officials are women, and among the mayors of towns and cities only some 10 percent are women.[52] In Africa's industrially most developed state, the Republic of South Africa, there are 15 million women, of whom not one is a head of a government department, a cabinet minister or a deputy minister.[53] The first woman to be appointed as ambassador took up her duties only in 1988.

The reason why the Nordic countries offer a more equal society for women is easy to understand. Norway, which has a higher proportion of females in top government positions, both elected and appointed, than any other country in the world, has a better political climate for women. In 1987 the Prime Minister was Gro Brundtland, and her 18-member cabinet included eight women. Inger Pedersen chaired the Justice Committee of Norway's parliament and was working on a constitutional proposal to amend the constitution so that Norway could also be ruled by a queen. Since 1981 Brundtland's Labor Party has led a drive for equality for women, and by 1990 maternity leave for women will be increased from 18 to 26 weeks. In 1986 almost 34 percent of the 157 members of Norway's parliament (the Storting) were women.[54]

Because outside the Nordic countries women are so under-represented, governments and institutions also continue to define women's needs for them, without women having a say and thereby often leaving the real needs of women unanswered.

The second most important need is for a change in men's perception of women's role and women's work. Still more fundamental than the real absence of mechanisms for drawing women into representative politics and decision-making is the apparent lack of desire of many men to bring women into the mainstream at all. In this respect social attitudes were and remain the key obstacle to progress. And it is remarkable how consistent these attitudes can be. In a major study of sex inequalities in the Third World (showing *inter alia* that women's position in the labor market is a major determinant of their overall status in society), Anker and Hein found that despite the diversity of cultural and constitutional contexts all studies show remarkable similarities in the discrimination women face in the labor market, tracing it to the sexual division of labor within the household.[55]

The attitude of men towards women often varies from the one extreme, such as that of the Nordic countries where women are generally held in the same regard as men, to the other, as in Asian countries where sex differentials in morbidity and mortality in infants prove that a much lower value is placed on girls. In one country a study of intrafamilial sex bias in the allocation of food has shown that for children under five the calorific consumption was on the average 16 percent higher for boys than for girls. The result was that 14 percent of the girls were severely malnourished compared to only 5 percent of the boys.[56] No statistics on infanticide are available for mainland China but since a law was passed regulating the size of the family, deaths of female infants, most of them unreported, have tripled.[57]

China is very much a case unto itself, as will be described in Chapter 28 of this book. One of the foremost Chinese scholars of our time, Phyllis Andors, wrote that the realities of Chinese society remain extremely complex and uneven. In her book *The Unfinished Liberation of Chinese Women (1949–1980)* she said that in comparison with the position of women in pre-1949 China there have been tremendous and positive changes. From a traditional agrarian society in which women were commodities and the predominant female roles were those of housewife and mother, Chinese women have emerged to play important roles in an increasingly diverse and sophisticated economy.[58] On the other hand, although women's status has changed dramatically, economic development and social change have not brought equality. Women, she said, are no longer making gains under the current more open regime; in fact, she states that during Mao's Cultural Revolution women's lot improved as they were massively drawn into the economy, thus breaking the stereotype of women as housewife and childbearer. Because of the threat which uncontrolled population growth posed to economic growth, birth control suddenly was no longer a women's issue but a national issue.[59] Other observers have found that women are now being pushed back into the role of housekeeper but with the additional burden of also having to work outside the home in more restricted areas of the labor market.

The third most important need applies more directly to the Third World, particularly Africa and Asia, and that is the need for birth control, by whatever means. In fact, in those areas of the world, a dramatic decrease in the number of children women bear is perhaps a greater need than more political power, though an increase in political power does go hand in hand with the other major need, a change in men's perception of women's role.

The religious credo on which the Roman Catholic Church bases its opposition to all forms of birth control except for the natural rhythm method has been set by men who do not become pregnant, do not suffer morning sickness, and do not die in childbirth, and whose bodies are not ravaged by having to bear 9 to 10 children before they reach age 30. It is set by men who do not bear and try to rear children in poverty-stricken, desert wastelands without sufficient food and medical assistance. Perhaps if women had as much voice in the church as men, even to being elected as Pope, the issue of birth control and God's will would be open to new interpretation.

Former United States Secretary of State George Schulz has said that rampant population growth underlies the Third World's poverty and poses a major long-term threat to political stability and the planet's resource base. Robert McNamara, President of the World Bank, has said that short of thermonuclear war itself, unchecked population growth is the gravest issue the world faces during the decades immediately ahead. (See Chart 3.)

This huge population increase, primarily in the Third World, has had the result that hard-won economic gains are dissipated by ever more people to feed, clothe, house and educate. More than 40 percent of the Third World's labor force is currently unemployed or underemployed. Many countries can no longer combat a sudden spell of drought, particularly in Africa, and famine stalks the continent. The Population Crisis Committee in Washington observed that grave environmental damage is done by overgrazing, overcropping, deforestation, and other desperate efforts of expanding populations to survive. Millions of rural poor stream into already overcrowded Third World cities in search of nonexistent jobs.

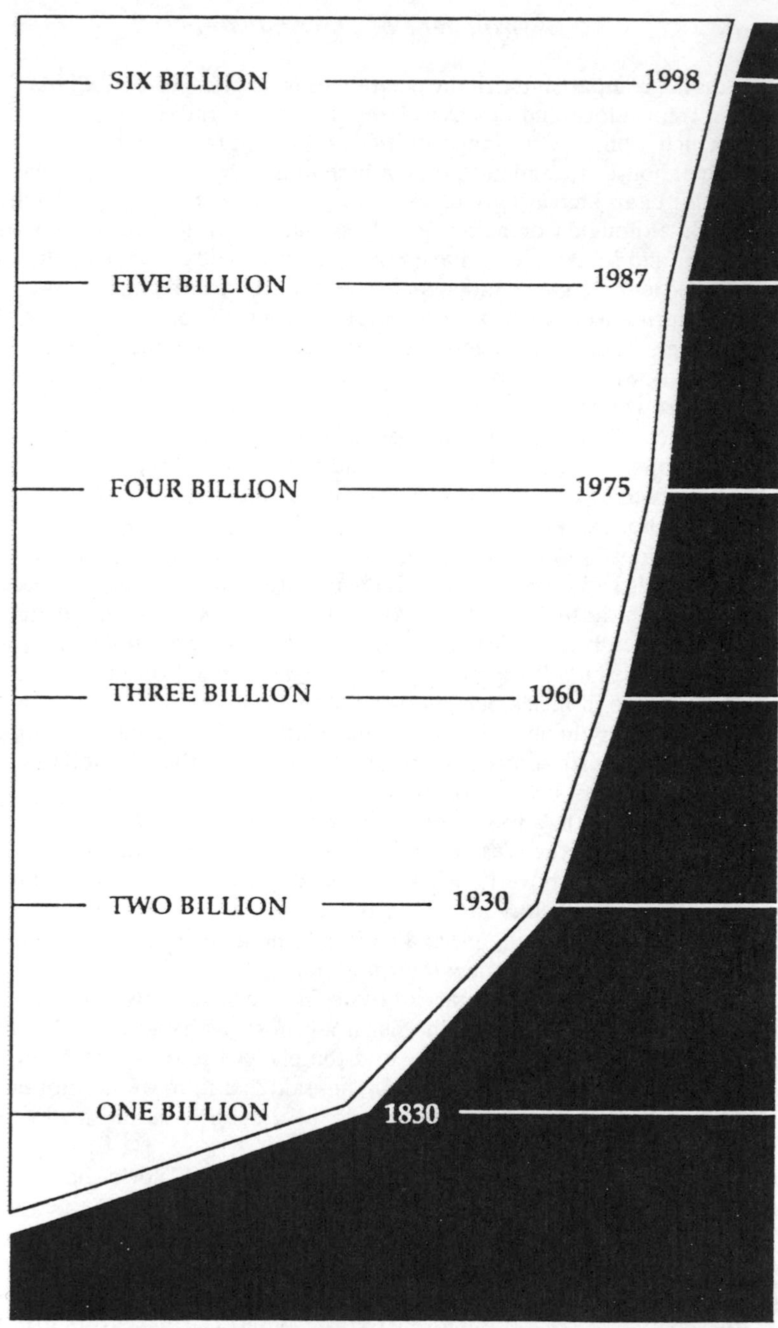

Chart 3. World Population Growth 1650–1998. Source: Population Crisis Committee, Washington DC, 1988.

Country	Fertility Rate	Illiteracy	Life Expectancy
Afghanistan	6.9	94%	41
Chad	5.9	92%	42
Ethiopia	6.7	95%[1]	43
Gambia	6.4	88%	44
Nepal	6.2	94%	44
Yemen[2]	6.8	98%	45

Table 13. Countries With the Lowest Female Life Expectancy. Source: U.N.E.S.C.O., World Health Organization and *INSTRAW* News, Santo Domingo.

Notes: (1) Figures from the Office of Women in Development, U.S. Agency for International Development show a more than 99 percent rate. (2) The following countries all have a female life expectancy rate of 45 years: Upper Volta, Somalia, Senegal, Niger, Mauritania, Mali, Burundi and Angola.

The facts show that the countries with the easiest access to birth control are also the countries with the least population growth and the highest income. There is also the least malnutrition and the least human misery. The countries with little or no birth control are the countries with the highest population growth and the worst economic situation.[60] That this could be a vicious circle for underdeveloped countries is not denied. But the facts also show that those same Third World governments which claim not to have the necessary capital to fund an encompassing birth control program, with free access to contraceptives for all women of childbearing age, are also those which, percentage-wise, spend the most money on weapons and grandiose political projects—countries such as Ethiopia, Kenya, Zambia, Tanzania, the Sudan, Chad, Somalia, to name but a few.

India, which presently adds more humans to the world's population every day than any other single country, spends roughly $550 million per year for its health and family planning[61]; yet, despite its political posture as a pacifist neutral country which threatens no one, India has spent a hundred times that amount in developing nuclear weapons.

There are 250 million women in developing countries who need effective contraception. Data from a world fertility survey indicate that almost 50 percent of all women of reproductive age want no more children. It costs $20 for a full year's family protection against pregnancy in the Third World.[62] But most Third World countries spend 10 times that amount per family, per annum, on purchasing weapons, building palaces for their rulers or constructing grandiose buildings and sports stadiums.

Often society's attitudes towards women reveal a glaring inconsistency. Consider the value generally attached to the women's maternal role. (This is one of the crucial arguments raised by those who are not in favor of seeing more women in the workplace.) How high can that value be if women are allowed to die needlessly in childbirth? Maternal mortality accounts for the largest or near-largest proportion of deaths among women of reproductive age in most of the developing world, perhaps as many as 500,000 every year. Maternal mortality rates in some Third World countries are as much as 200 times higher than the lowest rate in the industrialized countries. In North America the rate is six deaths per 100,000 live births (lowest rate) against 108 per 100,000 in Africa.[63]

Finally, a major constraint to progress for women in many fields has simply been a lack of awareness of the extent and seriousness of the problem, and it is hoped that this work will contribute to a better understanding of the obstacles women face. It is true that there has been enactment of a great deal of anti-discriminatory legislation in many countries. Yet in many countries, notably Africa, parts of Asia and Latin America, grown women remain children in the eyes of the law, prohibited from signing contracts or of practicing family planning (birth control) without their husbands' permission. Even where political commitment to change is strong and important legislative provisions have been made for equality between the sexes, major gaps exist between the spirit of the law and its implementation. The World Health Organization concluded: "Many governments, while professing to support the United Nations Decade for Women, have done little to provide resources to that end."[64]

Part Two: Legal and International Aspects

Those persons without rights at law are minors, married women, criminals and the mentally deficient.—*Napoleonic Civil Code,* France, early twentieth century.

4. The International World

Often the status and plight of women transcend national boundaries: for example, the fates of refugees from war, famine, or political and religious oppression. Thus the economic status of women, their political rights and discrimination against women in general have also become the subject of international scrutiny, international conventions, and agreements which involve international law and international instruments of legal enforcement, such as the European Court whose findings have legal consequences for members of the E.E.C.

Much of the international impetus to improve the status of women came from the United Nations, where equality between the sexes has been a fundamental tenet of the United Nations charter. The charter (1946) specifically affirmed its faith in fundamental human rights and "...in the equal rights of men and women." A year later the United Nations Commission on the Status of Women was established.

From there on, the male-dominated organization dragged its feet. In the first place, the newly established commission was just a subsidiary of the large Economic and Social Council (U.N.E.S.C.O.) and had to compete for attention with a dozen other commissions. It took five years before Helvi Sippila, a Finnish lawyer on the Commission, became Assistant Secretary General for Social Humanitarian Affairs, the first woman to be named to such a high post in the United Nations. It was almost another decade before Lucille Mair became the first Under-Secretary General, one step up the ladder. She retired in 1982 and it was not until 1987 that two women were again named among the 26 Under-Secretaries of the United Nations. Secondly, after the Convention on Political Rights for Women came into force in 1954, it was not until 1976, with the Covenant on Civil and Political Rights, that the United Nations added to the core of women's rights under international law.

The International Labor Organization also adopted a small number of conventions and resolutions but otherwise the United Nations, preoccupied with racial discrimination and East-West, North-South ideological conflict, paid scant attention to the rights of women. When the United Nations finally proclaimed 1975 to be the International Women's Year, it did so "almost absent-mindedly," according to Jessie Bernard.[1]

The International Year was to be devoted to promoting equality between men and women; to integrating women in the international development effort; and to recognizing women's increasing contribution to the development of friendly relations and cooperation among states and to the strengthening of world peace. "But their heart was not in it," Bernard later wrote. "Half of the member states did not even ratify the idea. And 16 out of 138 did not pay their part of the expenses."[2]

It was only after the subsequent United Nations-sponsored international conferences in Mexico in 1975 and in Copenhagen in 1980 that the United Nations adopted the all-important Convention on the Elimination of All Forms of Discrimination Against Women, which became a legally binding instrument after ratification. Prior to this, both the United Nations and the International Labor Organization had adopted several important declarations and resolutions, but in terms of international law only the conventions carried any legal weight.

Following the forward-looking strategy adopted at the Nairobi conference in 1985 at the close of the women's decade and signed by the 140 government delegations which attended, the United Nation's Commission on the Status of Women at last also had a worldwide undertaking which it could monitor for implementation. The thirty-second session of the Commission was held in Vienna in March 1988.

Since only conventions adopted by the United Nations and ratified by the legislature of each member state can convert that convention into international law, it is the conventions which require closer scrutiny. United Nations declarations and resolutions have never been presented for ratification as legally binding instruments. Those conventions which were focused specifically for women are, in chronological order:

1) I.L.O., Convention No. 3 (1919), Maternity Protection.

2) I.L.O., Convention No. 4 (1919), Night Work (Women).

3) I.L.O., Convention No. 42 (1934), Night Work (Women). (This convention was superseded by Convention No.89.)

4) I.L.O., Convention No. 45 (1935), Underground Work (Women).

5) General Assembly, resolution 126 (II) (1947), Transfer to the United Nations of the Functions under the International Convention of 30 September 1921 on Traffic in Women and Children; the Convention of 11 October 1933 on Traffic in Women of Full Age, and the Convention of 12 September 1923 on Traffic in Obscene Publicataions.

6) I.L.O., Convention No. 89 (1948), Night Work (Women).

7)General Assembly, resolution 317 (IV) (1949), Convention for the Suppression of the Traffic in Persons and of the Exploitation of the Prostitution of Others.

8) I.L.O., Convention No. 100 (1951), Equal Remuneration.

9) I.L.O., Convention No. 100 (1952), Maternity Protection.

10) General Assembly, resolution 640 (VII) (1952), Convention on the Political Rights of Women.

11) General Assembly, resolution 1040 (XI) (1957), Convention on the Nationality of Married Women.

12) General Assembly, resolution 1763 (XVII) (1962), Convention and Recommendation on Consent to Marriage, Minimum Age for Marriage and Registration of Marriages.[3]

The remaining 16 conventions and agreements referred to the situation of women as part of more general topics. The important ones will be discussed in the following pages, but among the more general ones the following should be mentioned: Supplementary Convention on the Abolition of Slavery, the

Slave Trade and Institutions and Practices Similar to Slavery; U.N.E.S.C.O. Convention Against Discrimination in Education (1960); and a group of I.L.O. conventions and agreements which went from general topics, such as the elimination of all discrimination in employment and occupation, social, and employment policies and social security to specific topics such as pensions, work on plantations, and dangerous working conditions. The instruments in the second group had a common feature in that discrimination against women was indicated as part of a set of discriminations, on the basis of sex, religion, race, nationality, and political opinion, or, in that women were merely a subgroup within the entire group affected by the convention; for example, women within a convention intended for plantation workers, women within a convention on social security intended for all workers, etc.[4] Besides the above-mentioned classification of focal and non-focal conventions and agreements, two other categories were established for the instruments: those which protected women (protective legislation) and those which promoted women (promotional legislation).

In terms of international law member states of the United Nations whose parliaments or legislative controlling bodies have ratified a United Nations convention must give effect to the objective and stipulations of that convention. As far as women are concerned there are seven conventions which are of particular importance to them, as follows:

(i) Equal Pay for Equal Value (1953) to appraise jobs objectively and set rates of remuneration without regard to sex for work of equal value. By 1986 ratified by 107 countries.

(ii) Equal Political Rights (1954) to ensure women's right to vote and eligibility for election to public office on equal terms with men. By 1984 ratified by 90 countries.

(iii) Maternity Protection (1955) to provide maternity leave before and after confinement, with cash and medical benefits. By 1986 ratified by only 25 countries.

(iv) Equality and Employment (1960) to promote equality of opportunity and treatment in employment in order to eliminate any discrimination. By 1986 ratified by 108 countries.

(v) Equality in Education (1962) to develop national policies for free and compulsory primary education and widely available secondary and higher education. By 1984 ratified by only 71 countries.

(vi) Equal Marriage Rights (1964) to ensure free consent to marriage by both parties, minimum age for marriage and official registration of marriages. By 1984 ratified by only 33 countries.

(vii) Elimination of All Forms of Discrimination Against Women (1980) to enact laws embodying principles of equality and modify those based on stereotyped sex roles, with special reference to rural women. By 1984 this key convention was ratified by only 54 countries.[5]

Of all the above conventions the most important is obviously the 1980 convention which aimed specifically at outlawing discrimination against women in all forms. In Ruth Sivard's view, the highlights from this convention are the following:

General Principles

—Discrimination against women continues and hampers the growth and prosperity of society and of the family.

—Change in the traditional role of men as well as of women is needed to achieve full equality.
—Governments shall take measures necessary to ensure rights for women on equal terms with men.

Rights to Be Ensured

Civil

—to be equal before the law including with respect to property and contracts.
—to have equal rights to family benefits and bank credit.

Political

—to vote in all elections and be eligible for election to all levels of government.
—to participate in the formulation of government policy.
—to represent their governments at the international level.

Education

—to have the same conditions as men for vocational guidance, scholarships, and diplomas at all levels.
—to have textbooks free of stereotypes about sex roles.
—to have information about family health and planning.

Employment

—to have equal pay for work of equal value.
—to have maternity leave with pay, without loss of seniority.
—to have social services that permit parents to combine family obligations with work.

Health

—to have equality with men in health services.
—to have free health services during pregnancy, where needed, and adequate nutrition.

Marriage

—to enter marriage and choose spouse with free consent.
—to have same rights and responsibilities during marriage and its dissolution; also as parents.
—to decide on number and spacing of children.
—to have right to choose a family name and occupation.[6]

When 108 countries have ratified a convention, it seems an impressive figure; yet one should stop and consider that these conventions are *fundamental* instruments in fighting discrimination against women, as fundamental as the conventions on the elimination of all forms of racial discrimination. Seen in that light the member states of the United Nations have no reason to be proud of their record. U.N. General Assembly records and those of the I.L.O. show that resolutions and conventions concerning discrimination on grounds of race or gender usually passed with perhaps one or two objections or abstentions. There are a large number of states who therefore voted for the conventions but whose governments never submitted the same for ratification by their own legislatures. In effect, their vote at the United Nations is more often than not only window dressing. In 1986 ratification of certain key conventions, as a percentage of total U.N. membership, was far from praiseworthy and, in some cases, scandalous. The convention on night work (No. 41 of 1951) was ratified by only 39 percent of member states. No. 44 of 1937, on underground work was ratified by only 55 percent. No. 100 of 1953, on equal remuneration, was ratified by 67 percent; No. 103 of 1955, concerning maternity protection, by only 16 percent; No. 11 of 1960, to prevent discrimination against employment and in occupations, by 108 countries or 67.5 percent; No. 156 of 1983 concerning women workers with family responsibilities, by only 5 percent; No. 158 of 1985, concerning unfair termination of employment, by only eight countries or 5 percent of the total U.N. membership.[7]

Recognizing that progress the past 10 years has not been up to expectations, the United Nations has now pushed its timetable forward, adopting strategies for the period from 1986 to the year 2000.

In 1985 the report of the World Conference to Renew and Appraise the Achievements of the United Nations Decade for Women concluded that "by the year 2000, all governments should have adequate comprehensive and coherent national women's policies to abolish all obstacles to the full and equal participation of women in all spheres of society."[8]

Full equality for women is a goal which, internationally, has been elusive and difficult to implement. The principle of equality was first expressed on an international basis in the 1948 Universal Declaration of Human Rights. Article 2 states that "everyone is entitled to all the rights and freedoms set forth in this Declaration, without distinction of any kind, such as race, color, sex, language, religion . . . or other status."[9]

There have been several subsequent United Nations efforts to define the terms of sexual equality with greater precision. Regional organizations such as the European Community and the Organization of American States have also made bold efforts to construct standards for women's rights. Yet there is no single, clear-cut set of guidelines which is universally accepted. In spite of the efforts of women's rights advocates around the world no pattern has emerged to promote the practical implementation of the laudable goal set forth in the U.N. Universal Declaration.

In fact, the United Nations itself has been a poor model for the equal treatment of women. Within a decade after its creation, the organization had become completely dominated by men. Women were largely confined to secretarial and clerical positions in the U.N. Secretariat. Even those few who emerged to responsible positions were usually found in jobs deemed suitable for women—for example, in areas of social welfare and humanitarian concern. The organization is almost a closed shop as far as any influential position for women is concerned. This is true not only of the functionaries of the General Assembly but of the Security Council, the other councils, the Judiciary, the Commissions, the Secretariat and the specialized agencies of the entire United Nations system.

There is not one woman among the 15 lawyers at the International Court of Justice in the Hague. Not one among the 25 members of the International Law Commission. Not one on the Human Rights Commission, which is, somehow, even worse.

There is one woman among the 15 men who make up the International Civil Service Commission. Out of the 26 Under-Secretaries General only two are women, both appointed in 1987. Prior to that only one other woman, Lucille Mair, former Secretary General of the 1980 Copenhagen Women's Conference, held this post, and only for a brief period of two years. Of the 22 Assistant Secretaries General only three are women and of the 316 Division Directors only 16 are women.[10]

When it comes to the general services, secretarial and clerical work, women outnumber men by far. As pointed out in *Sisterhood Is Global,* the United Nations, in fact, has its own "pink ghetto." Women are concentrated in the usual female-intensive jobs as typists, clerks, guides, etc. In categories of field service, security, dispatching, etc., men form almost 90 percent of the staff. The U.N., like the rest of the world, also displays its own wage differential policy. At the U.N. headquarters in New York the average male salary in the professional and general services category is $44,000 per year compared to $27,000 for women in the same category.[11]

Small wonder that the 1985 Report of the World Conference to Renew and Appraise the Achievements of the United Nations Decade for Women urged greater efforts by U.N. bodies to "achieve an equitable balance between women and men staff members at managerial and professional levels in all substantive areas." In a 1987 report (the second report) of the Steering Committee for the Improvement of the Status of Women in the Secretariat it was also pointed out that the organizational climate at the United Nations favored men when it came to the integration of family life and work. In the professional category, says the report, only 48 percent of the women are married compared with 85 percent of the men in the same category. It is clear that for women to work for the United Nations also means making a choice between career and family life.[12]

It is not only at the United Nations but elsewhere in the international world that a bad example is being set the nations of the world. Lovenduski pointed out that in 1983 only 17 percent of the members of the European Parliament were women. Women are not present in the more important posts at commission level. The European Community administration reflects the same pink ghetto as the United Nations. Women are concentrated at the routine levels of administration and men predominate in the senior posts.[13]

The United Nations is not the first international agency to deal with questions affecting the status of women. In 1902, international conventions were adopted at the Hague dealing with conflicts of national laws concerning marriage, divorce and the guardianship of minors. In 1904 and 1910 conventions were adopted dealing with the suppression of traffic in women and children. The Covenant of the League of Nations included articles calling for humane working conditions for all, irrespective of sex or age, and for the suppression of traffic in women and children. However, the League never completed a survey which had been established to deal with public law, private law, and penal law. Only the private law portion had been completed when the work of the experts was interrupted by the outbreak of World War II.[14] And efforts were never resumed.

The U.N. Charter enunciated a norm of non-discrimination on the basis of sex. The preamble directly affirms "faith in . . . the equal rights of men and women" and other articles pledge members of the organization to take separate and cooperative action to promote universal respect for the human rights and fundamental freedoms of all without regard to sex or other distinctions.[15] The Charter also made possible the Commission on the Status of Women, which was established by the Economic and Social Council in June 1946. This commission has been in a leadership position ever since.[16]

The Universal Declaration of Human Rights, referred to earlier, is actually a resolution of the General Assembly, rather than a binding treaty. It may be regarded as evidence of customary international law or as an elaboration of the general human rights provisions of the Charter. The treatment of women's rights seems to fall into the latter category, since international customary law has not been clear on the topic. Yet there is language in the Declaration which still goes beyond the domestic law of most nations. The Declaration states that men and women are entitled to "equal rights as to marriage, during marriage and at its dissolution."[17] Work is to be provided on a non-discriminatory basis in that everyone "has the right to equal pay for equal work."[18] Furthermore, motherhood is "entitled to special care and assistance."[19] These ideals still remain beyond the reach of most women and are not fully a part of the obligations of nations under international law because they were not subscribed to by the nations of the world through a ratification process.

One international organization which has had success in promoting and monitoring a joint approach to the problem of discrimination against women is the 12-nation European Community. The Community was set up in 1957 by the Treaty of Rome between six European countries: Belgium, France, Germany, Italy, Luxembourg and the Netherlands. Later the six were joined by Denmark, Ireland and the United Kingdom. Greece joined in 1981, and Spain and Portugal became members in 1986 although their actual entry date is four years later.

At the summit meeting of heads of states of the European Community in Paris in 1972 it was agreed to charter a European social policy. In 1974 the European Community's Council of Ministers agreed to take steps to ensure equality in terms of job training, working conditions and pay.

The series of laws which subsequently came into force during the seventies and the early '80s in Europe were partly inspired by these pressures for the development of a European Community law on women aimed at stimulating a common pattern of laws on women's employment and employment opportunities. Essentially there were two models; the negative one, which simply set out to ban discriminatory laws and practices based on gender, and the active model, in which the ban on discrimination against women in employment was to be complemented by positive action and a duty on the part of the employers to work actively for equality in the market. All 12 nations now have comprehensive laws forbidding discrimination against women in almost every sphere.

The laws of the European Community represent an independent legal system, i.e, independent of the legal systems of individual member states. Its source are written (treaties and related legislation), unwritten (general legal principles and tradition) and the decisions adopted by the governments of member states meeting within the Council of the European Community.

The principal written source of Community Law is the contents of the Treaties which established the European Community, including the annexes, protocols and acts concerning the accession of new members, for example Spain and Portugal. The second written source is the laws, regulations, decisions and directives created and adopted by the Community's various institutions.

Article 119 of the Treaty of Rome which established the European Economic Community stipulated that "each member state shall . . . ensure and subsequently maintain the principle that men and women should receive equal pay for equal work. . . ." Because the community formed by the Treaty of Rome was essentially a common market it accounts for the emphasis on equal pay. The objective was to avoid competition between members based on a lower-paid female work force. It did not really stem from a desire to uphold the principle of equality between men and women *per se.* Nonetheless, later directives and legislation were almost invariably based on this article.

Because there was difficulty encountered in applying Article 119 of the Treaty of Rome the Council of Ministers of the Community adopted a resolution in 1972 reminding member states of their obligations to take appropriate action to implement Article 119. Following this the Council adopted a further resolution on 21 January 1974 for a four-year action program to achieve "equality between men and women as regards access to employment and vocational training and advancements and as regards working conditions, including pay." By broadening the principle of Article 119 the Council of Ministers held the view that economic expansion is not an end in itself and should result in an improvement in the quality of life as well as the standards of living of all people in the community.

In order to implement this program, the Council of Ministers adopted a series of specific directives:[20]

• Directive 117 of 1975 on the approximation of the laws of the member states relating to the application of the principle of equal pay for men and women. This was the instrument for harmonizing the laws of member states as provided for in Article 100 of the E.E.C. Treaty of Rome. The directive asserted, *inter alia,* that job classification systems had to be drawn up using criteria shared by male and female workers and that all measures contrary to this principle had to disappear from collective bargaining agreements and individual employment contracts.

• Directive 207 of 1976 on the implementation of the principle of equal treatment for men and women. The various articles in the directive define the principle of equal treatment (article 2.1) and direct how equal treatment should be implemented, e.g. any laws, regulations and administrative provisions contrary to the principle must be abolished. It was intended to eradicate all forms of discrimination, including those called "indirect." Exceptions were accepted when sex was a "determining condition," as, for example, for actors and models, to protect pregnancies and in the event of affirmative action to correct *de facto* inequality.

- Directive 7 of 1979 on the progressive implementation of the principle of equal treatment for men and women in matters of social security.
- Directive 378 of 1986 on the implementation of the principle of equal treatment for men and women in occupational social security schemes. This directive applies only to statutory social security systems and not to private insurance contracts. The basic distinguishing feature is that affiliation to an occupational social security system forms part of the conditions of employment. Article 6 lists a number of provisions which are contrary to the principle, e.g. where a pension scheme is compulsory for men but not for women, lower retirement ages for women, differing rates of contribution to the pension system and systems which bar women altogether.
- Directive 613 of 1986 on the application of the principle of equal treatment between men and women engaged in an activity, including agriculture, in a self-employed capacity, and or the protection of self-employed women during pregnancy and motherhood. It should be noted that in this 12-nation community, with a population of 88 million women between the ages of 15 and 65, a directive is a legal instrument because it has been adopted by the Council of Ministers which facilitates the implementation of community law in terms of the founding treaty. A directive imposes an obligation on member states to take national measures to achieve the objectives laid down in the directive, and within a certain period of time.

In this way an entire set of legal instruments has been established between the 12 nations to promote equal treatment of men and women as regards employment. Of the 88 million women in the E.E.C. some 32 million are in regular paid employment, while the number of women in part-time employment ranges from 46 percent in Britain to 17 percent in Italy and Luxembourg.[21]

One of the fundamental characteristics of the European Community is that Community Law is an autonomous legal system, with its own institutions which have sovereign rights, and in relevant cases Community Law enjoys precedence over the domestic laws of member states. Article 119 of the Treaty of Rome, for example, is part of a treaty among nations, not a directive of the Ministers Council, and thus supersedes domestic law of the countries bound by the treaty. Any domestic legislation which is incompatible with Community Law is considered inapplicable, as made clear in articles 117 and 189[2] of the E.E.C. Treaty. Member states may not adopt or maintain measures which are likely to jeopardize the functioning of treaties.

Not only can the Commission of the European Community and its Council of Ministers bring action against a member state for failing to honor a treaty but, in terms of Article 173 (second paragraph) of the E.E.C. Treaty, an individual may bring an action to have a decision by any organization, corporation or institution in the state of which he or she is a citizen annulled if it infringes upon his or her rights in terms of the E.E.C. Treaty and subsequent directives. An individual may bring an action before a local court in his or her own country. In turn the court may ask the European Court for a ruling on the validity of or interpretation of Community legislation. The judgment of the European Court is binding only on the local court which heard the dispute arising under the national laws of the state in which the court operates.

The European Court itself was set up in terms of the E.E.C. Treaty of 1957 with the task of ensuring that "in the interpretation and application of Treaties the law is observed." Based in Luxembourg, the court consists of 13 judges who are appointed by common accord of the governments of member states. (The first woman to be appointed was Simon Rozes of France, who was appointed in March 1981, exactly 24 years after the Treaty of Rome set up the Community). The European Court is now indisputably the E.E.C.'s supreme judicial authority.

To keep the momentum of equal treatment for women going, the European Commission also launched two so-called action programs, the first covering the period 1982–1985 and the second the period 1986–1990. The programs covered two types of action, one aimed at strengthening the rights of the individual, the other at the practical achievement of equal opportunities, for example, providing better guidance to girls and their parents as to available educational opportunities and, eventually, promoting a wider range of job choices. The E.C. has set up various specialized services to tackle women's problems, for example the European Center for Vocational Training in Berlin which plays a central and motivating role in E.C. activity on wages, social security, family policy and financial grants. In fact the center monitors and promotes the application of E.C. directives listed on the previous pages.[22]

The European Commission's effort has been one of the most successful attempts, internationally, to come to grips with the legal and practical problem of discrimination against women. Its bi-monthly publication *Women of Europe,* published in nine languages, provides women all over Europe with vital information about their rights and opportunities. One of the supplements which the periodical published is *Community and the Law,* explaining what the laws mean to achieve, what the various directives of the Council of Ministers mean, the problems in application, the progress made in each country and how the European Court of Justice works, together with a mass of case histories applicable to women. Other supplements have dealt with women and voting, women in agriculture, the equal opportunities action programs of the period 1982–1985, and women and employment.

The levels of development achieved by the European Community's policy-making powers during 1984 sometimes ran into a stone wall, as in the question of abortion. But as Lovenduski pointed out, though the European Parliament's resolutions are not binding the Parliament has become a powerful and important lobby for women's rights and the improvement of their status. After the 1984 elections the European Parliament established a permanent committee of inquiry into the situation of women in Europe.

Community sex-equality policy has provided tangible benefits for certain women. According to Lovenduski:

> ...organized women have paid increasing attention to Community legislation, which has become an important source of change in national policy. In countries in which governments had been unsympathetic to legislation on women's rights, the E.E.C. has in the absence, often, of an organized women's movement, been the only source of legal reform. Its role has been both formal, in the sense of the impact of particular directives on national law, and informal, in that it has been an important filter for the diffusions of innovation. In Greece, for example, the conjuncture of E.E.C. entry and the election of a Socialist government heralded important changes for women. As well as implementing E.E.C. equality directives, laws on rape, on sexist advertising, on the harmonisation of pensions and the promotion of women's cooperatives were all planned by the new government.... Until membership in the E.E.C. was gained, the Greek government had seen no need for laws on equality. And despite constitutional provision for equal rights, other laws were not brought into line. Similar effects are to be observed in Spain and Portugal, both of whom were aspirant E.E.C. members in 1984. In both countries constitutional provisions for equal rights were followed by laws compatible with Community directives on equal pay and opportunities.[23]

Let us now examine how the international community has dealt with four key aspects of women's rights: firstly, political rights; secondly, the rights of women in the context of the family; thirdly, the rights of women to own property; and, lastly, general employment rights.

Political Rights

One convention proposed by the U.N. General Assembly deals directly with political rights. In 1946 the General Assembly proposed that member states adopt legislation providing women with the same political rights as men. The Convention on the Political Rights of Women was adopted by the General Assembly on December 20, 1952,[24] and came into force on July 7, 1954. The International Covenant on Civil and Political Rights, which came into effect on January 3, 1976, added few important political rights to the list established in 1954. These two documents provide the core of women's political rights under international law.

The Convention on the Political Rights of Women is a treaty which provides that women are entitled to vote in all elections on an equal footing with men. Women are likewise entitled to stand for election and hold public office on such equal terms. Most of the member states have ratified the treaty. Implementation is based upon a voluntary reporting system to the Economic and Social Council of the United Nations. In 1972 the procedure, which applies to both ratifying and nonratifying states, was merged with a reporting system established by the Declaration on the Elimination of Discrimination Against Women.[25]

The Covenant on Civil and Political Rights extends the right of women to "take part in the conduct of public affairs" and "to have access, on general terms of equality, to public service in his country."[26] (The use of the masculine pronoun, "his," is meant to include women, since the article extends these rights to "every citizen.") These rights, of course, are difficult to implement. The Council of Europe has frequently supported the resolutions of the U.N. General Assembly concerning women's rights and has urged members of the European Community to ratify international conventions concerning the prohibition of discrimination based upon sex. In the area of political rights the Parliamentary Assembly of the Council of Europe has urged political parties in member states to encourage women to take an active part in political life, to propose more women candidates for office and to make room for women in party executive positions.[27] If pursued, these recommendations would go a long way towards creating equality between the sexes in political participation.

The Family

A great deal of attention has been given in international law to the role of the woman in the family context. The Universal Declaration of Human Rights declares that men and women of full age have "the right to marry and found a family."[28] They also should have equal rights "during marriage and at its dissolution," since the "family is the natural and fundamental group unit of society."[29]

The Convention Concerning Maternity Protection antedates the Universal Declaration, having been adopted by the International Labor Organization in 1919. A revised version was proposed by the I.L.O. in 1952 and adopted as a convention. In 1955, after the second ratification, the treaty came into force. Although the convention deals mostly with the working conditions of women, a topic to be treated below, it is important to note that the treaty extends to agricultural and administrative work, as well as industrial work. Women working at home are also covered. Unmarried women are covered by maternity leave and other protections.[30]

The Convention on the Nationality of Married Women, adopted in 1956, went into force in 1958. This treaty emphasizes the independence of the nationality of the wife from that of the husband, rather than the traditional principle of family unity. The contracting states accept, with respect to their nationals, that the celebration or dissolution of a marriage or a change of nationality affects the nationality of the wife. Special naturalization procedures must be established to allow a wife to acquire the nationality of her husband if she so desires.[31] Most member states have ratified this convention, thus eliminating the problem of women's loss of nationality upon divorce. The automatic extension of citizenship at marriage also had deprived women of the right of their own nationality.

Marriage law itself is addressed by the Convention on Consent to Marriage, Minimum Age for Marriage, and Legislation of Marriages. This convention, adopted by the U.N. General Assembly in 1962, requires public announcement of marriages, the personal consent of the parties, and a minimum marriage age. Also specific minimum age of consent is proposed.[32] The convention is based upon the principles of the Universal Declaration of Human Rights, which gives men and women "the right to marry and found a family"[33] upon a basis of equality in marriage. These principles are reiterated in the Covenant on Civil and Political Rights, which also obligates signatories to "take appropriate steps to ensure equality of rights and responsibilities of spouses as to marriage, during marriage and at its dissolution."[34]

The most detailed provisions regarding the rights of married women are to be found in the Declaration on the Elimination of Discrimination Against Women. This declaration attempts to consolidate and expand the fundamental principles found in earlier U.N. documents. The declaration was unanimously adopted in 1967 by the General Assembly, but it is not, in itself, a legally-binding instrument. The declaration may be regarded as the fullest extension of women's rights within the family to be found in international instruments.

Women are to have rights to "acquire, administer, enjoy, dispose of and inherit property on the same basis as men, including property acquired during marriage."[35] Child marriage and the betrothal of young girls before puberty are to be prohibited.[36] These specific measures have become part of the domestic law of many enlightened nations, but they are not yet part of international law.

The European Commission on Human Rights has made significant contributions to the development of international law on women's rights. In particular, the Commission has determined the United Kingdom to be in violation of Articles 8 and 14 of the European Convention on Human Rights in the application of its immigration laws. Those laws had made it impossible for women's husbands and fiances who were not United Kingdom citizens to enter the U.K. to join their mates. On the other hand, men who lawfully reside in the United Kingdom may be joined by their foreign wives and fiancees. The Commission concluded that this unequal treatment of men and women was discriminatory and injured family life.[37] This 1980 decision was a test case drawn from over 80 cases brought to the complaint stage. The European Court of Human Rights has not yet resolved the matter fully, but it is evident that members of the European Community are concerned with regional development of women's rights within the family.[38]

Property

The property rights of women have received little attention in international law. The 1985 Report of the World Conference to Review and Appraise the Achievements of the United Nations Decade for Women did state that "the legal capacity of married women should be reviewed in order to grant them equal rights and duties."[39] The Declaration on the Elimination of Discrimination Against Women does make mention of the right of women "married or unmarried" to "acquire, administer, enjoy, dispose of and inherit property, including property acquired during marriage."[40] Since this declaration is merely a resolution of the General Assembly, however, it is not, in itself, legally binding. Article 15 of the Convention on the Elimination of All Forms of Discrimination does accord women equal rights to enter into contracts and to administer property, important principles to establish in international law.

Employment

Protective legislation on behalf of women workers was encouraged by developments in the International Labor Organization during the period between World War I and World War II. In 1937 the Convention Concerning the Employment of Women in Underground Work in Mines of All Kinds came into force, launching a series of measures which have been taken to expand women's rights in employment. Today the direction of these rights is towards the principle of equal pay for equal work, although this principle is not yet firmly established in international law.

The 1937 treaty prohibits all women (with minor exceptions for certain kinds of work) from laboring in underground mines. This treaty has been ratified by 88 countries,[41] and is one of the most accepted aspects of women's rights at international law; night work for women is the subject of a treaty which came into effect in 1936 but was revised in 1948, coming into force in 1951.[42] This treaty has been ratified by 62 nations, and is directed at women employed in factories, mines, quarries, power plants and other "public or private industrial undertakings."[43] The convention does not apply to women "holding responsible positions of a managerial or technical character" and "women employed in health and welfare services."[44] Night labor for women engaged in industrial employment is prohibited by this treaty, meaning work after ten o'clock in the evening and prior to seven o'clock in the morning, although there is some flexibility about exact times. Interestingly, the treaty allows members to renounce ratification at the end of every 10-year period after 1951.[45]

This kind of protective measure is no longer popular among advocates of women's rights, despite the necessity of being vigilant about the exploitation of women in dangerous and unhealthy conditions. For example, the International Labor Organization shifted its emphasis in the 1950s, urging the goal of equal remuneration for men and women workers for work of equal value. A convention based on this principle was proposed in 1951[46] and was followed by a convention on social security and women's rights.[47]

The 1951 Convention Concerning Equal Remuneration for Men and Women Workers for Work of Equal Value has been ratified by 107 nations. It is today the principal legal document in the drive to eliminate wage discrimination based upon sex, under principles of international law. The treaty obliges members to promote the principle of equal remuneration for work of equal value. This is not the same as equal pay for equal work, a more contentious principle. Further, the obligation of members to find "means appropriate to the methods in operation for determining rates of remuneration, and promote, insofar as is consistent with such methods" the principle of "equal remuneration for men and women workers for work of equal value" shall be honored in laws, regulations, and collective agreements.[48] This qualifying language seems to limit the general principle.

The principle of "equal remuneration for work of equal value" is restated in the Covenant on Economic, Social, and Cultural Rights.[49] But an additional two features appear: equal pay for equal work and equal opportunity for everyone to be promoted in his or her employment to an appropriate higher level. The specific language of the first right is important: "in particular, women being guaranteed conditions of work not inferior to those enjoyed by men, with equal pay for equal work."[50] This principle is much broader than the idea of equal remuneration for work of equal value which immediately precedes it in the language of this covenant. Eight nations have ratified this covenant, giving it widespread significance in international law, although there is some confusion concerning the meaning of the operative principles.

Substantial clarification of the principle has been provided to member states of the European Community. The implementation of the principle of equal pay for men and women has been the subject of a Council Directive of the Commission of the European Communities. In 1975 the principle of equal pay of the European Social Charter[51] was given specific content. The principle requires that a job classification system used for determining pay must be based upon the same criteria for men and women. Member states are obligated to "introduce into their national legal systems such measures as are necessary to enable all employees who consider themselves wronged by failure to apply the principle of equal pay to pursue their claims by judicial process."[52]

Under decisions of the European Commission on Human Rights certain national laws of the United Kingdom have been invalidated for failure to honor the principle of equal pay.[53] The conflict between U.K. and E.E.C. law is still not over, and the European Court of Justice has become involved in setting the boundaries for the principle for equal pay.[54]

Disparities between the pay of women and men still exist. Whether these disparities rest upon sex discrimination and a violation of the principle of equal pay remains to be resolved by courts and political bodies around the world. Suffice it to say that such rights as leave with pay, family allowances, paid maternity leave, vocational education and equal remuneration with men in respect of work of equal value are still uncertain claims at international law. These are all addressed in the Declaration on the Elimination of Discrimination Against Women passed by the General Assembly of the United Nations in 1967,[55] but they are not yet part of international law because they have not been presented for ratification in a legally binding instrument. On the other hand, the Convention on the Elimination of All Forms of Discrimination Against Women, which came into force in 1981, does construct certain important rights, most notably "the right to equal remuneration, including benefits," and "to equality of work."[56] The meaning of this language remains for future determination.

For certain countries in the Arab-Muslim world, Africa, and Asia—for example, Iraq, Muscat, Oman, Saudi Arabia, India, the Sudan, and Mauritania—the subject of slavery also affects women. As recently as 1980, women were still being sold on the open market in Mauritania (in the desert town of Atar) and in 1981 the London-based Anti-Slavery Society presented to the United Nations several reports on Mauritanian chattel slavery. The Society estimated that in Mauritania alone there may be as many as 100,000 chattel slaves out of a total population of 1.5 million.[57]

Slavery was abolished in Mauritania by the French colonial authorities in the 1930s and in 1960 in terms of the Mauritanian Constitution. In 1980 it was also abolished, this time by a Mauritanian government decree. The persistence of the practice, 50 years after being outlawed, is simply evidence that legislation alone is not sufficient to ensure women's emancipation in the Third World.

Though India was a co-signatory and sponsor of the United Nations declaration in 1948 which outlawed slavery and the slave trade in all its forms,[58] girls are still being sold into slavery for prostitution in the state of Madhya Pradesh today. The media in India declare this to be "a social evil," yet, simultaneously, shrug it off as a tradition that compels such prostitution among the Bancharas in Madhya. A leading English-language journal in India quoted the leader of a government committee who investigated the problems as stating: "Since selling the body is considered neither derogatory nor detestable, the *khilawadis* (prostitutes) command respect and affection in the family and the community."[59] In terms of its international legal obligations, the Indian government should have put an end to this practice 40 years ago, but in India, as in most Third World countries, the gap between the public profile of its government at world conferences, notably the United Nations, and what that government condones at home is as wide as the Pacific Ocean. Most women who attended the Nairobi conference to mark the end of the United Nations Decade for Women were treated to numerous diatribes against the apartheid system in South Africa. Traditional apartheid denied black women fundamental economic, social and political rights, and was an affront to their dignity as human beings. However, more than a hundred key laws and regulations which defined and structured the racial segregationist system in South Africa were officially scrapped during 1981–1988 leaving only four of real significance, such as the Group Areas Act which legalizes separate residential areas for black and white. But even this act was being modified in 1989 and may disappear in another year. Integrated residential areas has already become a fact of life in South Africa. A visit to South Africa in 1988 showed that in the urban areas universities, business organizations, sports, police and army, hotels, banks, churches, restaurants and theatres represent a face of integration not much different from that of Atlanta, San Francisco, Dallas, Sydney, London, Ottawa, Paris and other major world centers.

Just as the Soviet Union under Mikhail Gorbachev is different to the U.S.S.R. under Leonid Bhrezhnev, so apartheid, circa 1989, bears very little resemblance to apartheid, circa 1949. The fact is that during the past decade black women in South Africa have booked significant gains in business, marriage rights, personal autonomy, and in education. In urban South Africa black women now enjoy a higher rate of literacy (72 percent) than black men, a percentage which dwarfs anything else in Africa. The situation in South Africa has become very fluid since the majority of whites began to support the government's attempt to structure political power sharing between black and white. With the departure of President Pieter W. Botha in September 1989 the new President designate, Frederik F. de Klerk is expected to hasten the demise of the last segregationist laws.[60]

There also seems to be a fundamental lack of knowledge, or concern, among women's movements as to the political fate of black people (male and female) elsewhere in Africa. This attitude is so pervasive, a mirror image of the attitude of the General Assembly of the United Nations, that it has created the unfortunate impression that, in Africa, women's rights, black women's rights, are only of concern when viewed in a black-white relationship, such as in the United States or South Africa. When those same rights are violated by black governments there is no moral outrage.

The truth of the matter is that there is massive and widespread suppression of black people's liberties, which includes women's rights, in the overwhelming majority of African states. Details about oppression and tyranny in black Africa, about political murders, even genocide, which affects women as much as men, are well documented. The hated pass-book system in South Africa (abolished in 1986) still operates elsewhere in Africa, for example under the Tutsi government in Burundi and in Ethiopia. Also, the murder of hundreds of thousands of Lango and Acholi people in Uganda and of hundreds of thousands of Hutu in Burundi are hardly secrets.[61]

It is not only in white South Africa where black women are denied the vote. Free elections in a multi-party system, such as enjoyed by woman voters of the United States, is virtually non-existent elsewhere in Africa. There are only a handful of black African countries where women have a free right to vote and to chose their leaders, for example in Botswana and Senegal. Almost all of black Africa has been effectively disenfranchised. More than 90 percent of African states are farcical democracies with one party state systems and presidents for life. In 1988 there were no less than 22 military dictatorships. Since 1957 there have been more than 150 African presidents yet only six relinquished power voluntarily. As Ghanian born professor George B. Ayittey of the Hoover Institute at Stanford University wrote in his forthcoming book, *Africa Betrayed* (Cato Institute) the freedom black Africans have fought for has perfidiously been betrayed.

One of the reasons why the suppression of human rights and that of black women in South Africa is so well known in the United States and Europe is because there are more privately owned newspapers and news magazines in South Africa than in the rest of the African continent put together. The majority of newspapers in black Africa are owned by the government. In South Africa there are excellent communications with the rest of the world and more permanently based foreign correspondents than in the rest of Africa combined. Another reason is the existence of excellent research facilities at private foundations and institutes at the country's many universities. There are other reasons but the mere fact that there is so little said and published by the United Nations on oppression of blacks (and black women) in other African states does not mean that such oppression is non-existent, or that it is of little consequence to black women. Oppression and denial of economic and political rights is oppression, regardless of color. So is exploitation. In 1988 a gold tax, of two gold coins, was imposed on all the working women of Chad. The official reason was that it was to help pay for the war against Libya. In fact the income was not used for any war effort (Chad and Libya signed a peace agreement in October 1988) but filled the pockets of the president's wife, Fatima Bouteille Habre.[62]

5. Constitutional and Statutory Differentiation

Legal differentiation between men and women, i.e, distinctions which may contain prescriptions discriminating against women, or protecting the other sex, are found on many levels. There are, first of all, the provisions of the constitution of a state. In more than 96 constitutions of the world, provisions are made either to assist, protect, or to provide for women. The effect, however, often ends up as *de facto* discrimination, limiting women's political representation or their right to equal opportunity.

On another level are measures which many governments have promulgated, enacted and decreed as law and which do discriminate against women and inhibit their social, political and economic advancement. In this regard one can also refer to the *absence* of laws to protect women or to provide for equal opportunities with men.

On a third level there are the laws passed by autonomous regions within a federal structure, for example in India, the United States, Australia or Canada, enabling one state to pass discriminatory measures not existing either in the state right next door or in federal legislation.

Finally there is the vast field of *de facto* discrimination and the gap which exists between the objectives stated in the constitution, or in national legislation, and the conditions which exist in the marketplace.

Equality on Paper

There are now 166 recognized nation-states in the world, of which 159 have traditional, one-document, or entrenched constitutions. The United Kingdom, New Zealand, and Israel have a number of basic, organic acts and laws which, collectively, serve as their constitutions. Some countries have no consititutions, such as Bhutan.[1]

Constitutions provide a basic expression of the values and goals of society. They are extremely important documents fulfilling important functions. A conventional definition is that they are the framework which structures the assemblage of laws, institutions and customs which govern a nation. But a constitution is also an ideological manifesto, indicating national purpose, the formulation of the rights of its citizens. The general function of a constitution is to contain important legal pronouncements converting power into law, setting up state institutions and providing indications of how legal and political problems should be solved.[2]

An examination by Gail Cairns and Nancy Heckel, (of the Development Law and Policy Program of Columbia University) of more than 150 constitutions currently enforced has revealed that over the past decade many nations have incorporated statements concerning women's rights in their constitutions.[3] It is the opinion of almost all observers that this means that the state has advanced, at the highest level, an important social policy.

Judging by the number of key United Nations conventions which have been ratified by states, the majority of the world's countries have now formally instituted constitutional and legal equality between women and men, and 45 countries offer free legal advice to help women to fight for these rights. Interestingly enough, 30 of these countries are in the developing world. By 1985, some 65 countries are said to have ratified or acceded to the United Nations convention which eliminated all forms of discrimination against women, thus becoming legally bound by the convention's provisions to achieve equal rights for women, regardless of their marital status, in all fields. In fact, the convention calls for national legislation to ban discrimination.[4]

Cairns and Heckel rightly observed that, apart from the constitution, a nation's criminal, civil, family, labor and health laws may also contain important statements of women's legal rights. The two researchers have identified five principal types of provisions in the 150 constitutions which they examined:

(i) General equal protection provisions

(ii) Equality and non-discrimination provisions which specifically mention sex;

(iii) Provisions for sexual equality in civil, political, economic, social and cultural affairs;

(iv) Articles mandating equality of the spouses in the marriage and the family; and

(v) Provisions requiring equal pay for equal work or sexual equality in employment.[5]

More than 70 constitutions contain general equal protection clauses. An example is that of Tunisia, in which article 6 states that "all citizens have the same rights and the same duties. They are equal before the law." According to legal experts a woman could successfully argue in court that this provision outlaws discrimination on the basis of sex.

Yet, even where the constitution is clear on the question of equality on a *de jure* basis, other factors serve to weaken its provisions and intent. An example is the constitution of the Republic of China, Taiwan. Both the 1947 Constitution and the 1929 General Principles of the Civil Code granted women "equal status" with men. The 1985 Family Law also sought equality for women. But related laws and legal tradition serve to destroy these provisions. Thus a husband's decision takes precedence over his wife's regarding place of residence.[6] In most cases the child must carry the patrilineal surname.[7] The right to manage the joint property belongs to the husband, who may also collect and dispose of the wife's income at will, including joint property.[8] In the case of consent or a judicial divorce court, rulings follow the tradition of favoring the father with the child's custody. In representation in Parliament, the constitution provides that the number of women elected shall be fixed at 10 percent and measures thereto shall be prescribed by law.[9] However, the ruling political party, overwhelmingly men, may restrict the number of women to be nominated as candidates, making more seats available for males. Thus the constitution may have had the intent to ensure a minimum representation for women in Parliament but ended up creating a *de facto* ceiling to women's representation. This pattern of laws and legal tradition running counter to the provisions of the constitution and resulting in *de facto* discrimination against women is common in most Asian countries.[10]

There are constitutions with other provisions where there is no room for doubt, requiring equality before the law regardless of sex and directly prohibiting discrimination on the basis of sex. Some constitutions combine the two provisions and actually mandate the availability of fundamental rights and freedoms, irrespective of sex. Cairns and Heckel cite the following examples:

"Men and women shall have equal rights" from article 3(2) of the West German Constitution. "Men and women are equal before the law," from the Mexican Constitution, article 4. "The law severely punishes prejudicial discrimination of the citizens by sex, religious affiliation or nationality," from article 6(2) of Hungary. "The republic shall guarantee to all equality before the law, regardless of origin, race, sex, religion or opinion," from article I.3 of the constitution of Burkina Faso, and ". . . every person . . . is entitled to the fundamental rights and freedoms of the individual, that is to say, the rights, whatever his race, tribe, place of origin or other local connection, political opinions, colour, creed or sex. . ." from the constitution of Kenya, article 70.[11]

Provisions on sexual equality in civil, political, economic, social and cultural affairs are more specific than the sexual equality provisions because they mandate sexual equality or prohibit sexual discrimination specifically with respect to the areas mentioned.[12] Civil rights of special importance to women include the right to own property, enter into contracts and maintain or change their nationality. Political rights include the right not only to vote but to hold elected office, while among economic and social rights are equal pay for equal work and equal opportunities for promotion in employment.

An example cited by Cairns and Heckel of a constitution which mandates equal rights for women in all five areas (mentioned in the previous paragraph) is that of Equatorial Guinea. Article 20 states: "A woman, whatever her marital status, has the same rights as a man in the civil, political, economic, social and cultural aspects of public, private and family life." Another example is that of Italy. Article 3 of the Italian constitution states that "all citizens are invested with equal social status and equal rights before the law . . . as to sex, race, language, religion, political opinions and personal or social conditions."[13] In fact the Italian constitution goes much further than merely providing these safeguards against discrimination on the basis of sex by stating that it is the responsibility of the state, not the individual citizen, to remove all obstacles which limit the freedom and equality of citizens in the five areas.

A number of constitutions provide specifically for judicial equality of women and men in marriage, for example Japan (article 24), as do various provisions passed in Switzerland, Britain, South Africa, Canada, New Zealand,

Australia and other countries the past five years. Judicial equality in marriage means that the wife has equal rights to acquire, own, manage and dispose of property as well as such personal rights as choice of name, domicile and occupation. The United Nations Convention on the Elimination of All Forms of Discrimination Against Women further provides that women have a right to choose a spouse, to space their children and to have access to contraceptives. This provision was specifically introduced to assist the married women of many countries in Africa.

One of the newer provisions is that of mandating equal pay for equal work or sexual equality in employment. Part of the good news of the decade for women is that, while in 1978 only 28 countries had passed equal pay legislation, by 1983 the number was an impressive 90.[14] One other way of looking at this is that despite U.N. conventions and the decade for women, some 70 U.N. member states have *not* yet passed such legislation. But on balance the trend is positive.

Most existing law providing for equality in employment is found in a nation's labor codes. An example of a constitution that provides for equality in employment is that of Malta (article 15), which states: "The state shall aim at ensuring that women workers enjoy equal rights and the same wages for the same work as males." A similar provision but one which specifically mentions equal chances at applications and promotions is contained in article 12(1) of the constitution of Suriname. The Communist nations almost all have provisions which clearly state that there must be equal pay for equal work, for example, article 18 of the Romanian Constitution: "For equal work there shall be equal remuneration." A few refer specifically to equal pay for women.[15]

Several constitutions specifically provide for pregnancy leave without loss of employment or wages, such as article 128(11) of the Republic of Honduras.

A detailed survey of labor laws in Europe, Asia and Latin America by David Ziskind, associate editor of *Comparative Labor Law,* published by the University of California, Los Angeles, provides a veritable cornucopia of constitutional provisions against sexual discrimination.[16]

Asia

After analyzing the provisions of constitutions Ziskind wrote:

> The desire for *equality and nondiscrimination* receives constitutional expression throughout Asia, both in general terms and in the detailed specification of unacceptable grounds for discriminatory behavior. "Equality before the law" has been supplemented in a few constitutions (Afghanistan, Bangladesh, Burma, Papua New Guinea) by provisions for equality of opportunity or the elimination of inequality. The prohibition of discrimination is not only addressed to the more commonly mentioned grounds of race, sex and place of origin but also to grounds apparently found particularly troublesome in the countries involved. Caste, class, tribe and status are singled out in Afghanistan, Bangladesh, Burma, India, Japan, Kampuchea, South Korea, Malaysia, Mongolia, Nauru, Nepal, Pakistan, Philippines, Russian Asian Republics, Singapore, Solomon Islands, Sri Lanka, Taiwan,

Tonga and Western Samoa. Language or culture is specified in Afghanistan, India, Russian Asian Republics and Sri Lanka. Political opinion receives special mention for protection against discriminatory treatment in Fiji, Laos, Nauru, Papua New Guinea, Solomon Islands, Sri Lanka, and Western Samoa; and even party affiliation is so treated in Taiwan.

Practically no exceptions to the principle of nondiscrimination are mentioned in Asian constitutions. Special provisions relate to "personal law" and the "affairs of any religion" in Malaysia and Singapore and to advantages for natives in Western Samoa and Malaysia. Several island countries expressly preserve "respect for the rights of others" and the "public interest": Fiji, Nauru, Papua New Guinea and Solomon Islands.[17]

Sweeping provisions for equality of all persons or all citizens are found in the following language which can be applied to women:

1. **"Equal before the law"** Bangladesh Art. 27, Burma Art. 147, 22, China Art. 33, Taiwan Art. 7, Fiji Art. 15(1), India Art. 14, Indonesia Art. 27(1), Japan Art. 14, People's Republic of Kampuchea Art. 13, 81, South Korea Art. 10, Laos Art. 2, Malaysia Art. 8(1), Maldives Art. 5, Pakistan Art. 25, Singapore Art. 12(1), Sri Lanka Art. 12(1), Thailand Art. 23, Russian Asian Republics Art. 32, Vietnam Art. 22, 55, Western Samoa Art. 15(1), Tonga Art. 4.
2. **"Equal protection of the law"** Bangladesh Art. 27, India Art. 14, Malaysia Art. 8(1), Pakistan Art. 24, 4(1), Singapore Art. 12(1), Sri Lanka Art. 12(1), Thailand Art. 23, Western Samoa Art. 15(1).
3. **"Equality of rights"** Afghanistan Art. 28.
4. **"Equality of opportunity"** Bangladesh Art. 19, Burma Art. 22(b), Papua New Guinea Preamble sec. 5(c).
5. **"Eliminate" or "remove inequality"** Afghanistan Art. 7, Bangladesh Art. 19(2).

Constitutional prohibitions *against* "discrimination" are at times inclusive, but more often they are directed to the following specific grounds of discrimination:

1. **"All forms of discrimination."** Sri Lanka Art. 12(2).
2. **"Sex."** Sex discrimination is proscribed in the following constitutions: Afghanistan Art. 28, Bangladesh Art. 29(2), Burma Art. 22, 154, 147, China Art. 48, Fiji Art. 3, India Art. 16, 39(a), 15(1), Japan Art. 14, Dem. Kampuchea Art. 12, 13, Peo. Rep. of Kampuchea Art. 30, 81, South Korea Art. 10(1), Laos Art. 2, 6, Mongolia Art. 76, 84, Nauru Art. 3, Nepal Art. 10(2) (3), Pakistan Art. 55(1), Philippines Art. II Sec. 9, Russian Asian Republics Art. 32, 33, Solomon Islands Art. 3, 15(3), Sri Lanka Art. 12(2) (3), 27(6), Vietnam Art. 63, Western Samoa Art. 15(2).

In addition, some constitutions provide that the nondiscrimination clauses shall not prevent special provision "in favor of women or children" Bangladesh Art. 28(4), for the protection of women and children Laos Sec. 6, Pakistan Art. 25, 26(2), or the protection of mother and child Mongolia Art. 84.

Insofar as women at work are concerned, Ziskind wrote that "the Asian constitutional provisions relating to female labor assert essentially equality with male workers, and special protection for women as needed to meet problems peculiar to their sex at work or in the home. The latter are usually coupled with provisions dealing also with children."[18]

Provisions for equal rights accorded to women and men are followed by a specific commitment to the protection of women (Bangladesh Art. 28[4], South Korea Art. 30[4], Laos Sec. 6, Pakistan Art. 25[3], 26[2], Russian Asian Republics Art. 33, Sri Lanka Art. 12[4], Vanuatu Art. 5[1] [k], Vietnam Art. 47, Western Samoa Art. 15[3b]), or by a designation of the assistance to be granted, namely, "the creation of broad conditions for women's education and creating work" (Afghanistan Art. 26) ensuring "participation of women in all spheres of public life" (Bangladesh Art. 10), enjoying "those rights prescribed by law" (Burma Art. 154[b]); protecting motherhood and promoting welfare of women and children (Taiwan Art. 156); improving "the life of working women" (Laos Sec. 6); "ensuring that children and women are not employed in vocations unsuited to their age and sex" (Pakistan Art. 37[e], 34).

Several constitutions contain a more detailed specification of provisions for the protection of working women. Pakistan provides "maternity benefits for women in employment" (Art. 34). Others provide for paid maternity leave and "an expanding network of maternity hospitals, nurseries and kindergartens (Peo. Rep. of Kampuchea Art. 27, North Korea Art. 62, Mongolia Art. 84); and "creches . . . community dining halls and other social amenities (Vietnam Art. 63). Peo. Rep. of Kampuchea provides that the "State and society . . . take other measures to alleviate the burden of housewives" (Art. 27); North Korea "frees women from the heavy burdens and household chores" (Art. 62); and both provide conditions necessary to participate in public life. The state in Communist China also "trains and selects cadres from among women" (Art.48).

According to Ziskind, maternity and child care are given special attention in several constitutions as follows:[19]

1. **General care.** In Peo. Rep. of Kampuchea, "The State cares for mothers and children" (Art. 27); in Mongolia, the state grants "protection in the interests of mother and child," and assistance to mothers with many children" (Art. 84); in Burma, "Mothers, children and expectant mothers shall enjoy . . . rights prescribed by law" (Art. 154[5]; in Afghanistan, "Family, mother and child will be given special protection by the state" (Art. 26), and in the Russian Asian Republics material and moral support are given to mother and child (Art. 33).

2. **Leave.** The state assures or provides "maternity leave" in India (Art. 42) and North Korea (Art. 62), "paid maternity leave and postnatal leave" in Mongolia (Art. 84), "a 90-day maternity leave with pay," Peo. Rep. of Kampuchea (Art. 27), "maternity benefits for women in employment" in Pakistan (Art. 37[e]), "paid leave and other benefits to pregnant women and mothers" in Russian Asian Republics (Art. 33), post-natal paid leave if they are workers or office employees, and "maternity allowances if they are cooperative members" in Vietnam (Art. 63).

3. **Maternity and child care** are provided for generally (Afghanistan, Burma, Peo. Rep. of Kampuchea, Russian Asian Republics, and Mongolia, or

with specific provisions for maternity leave (India, Peo. Rep. of Kampuchea, North Korea, Mongolia, Pakistan, Russian Asian Republics, and Vietnam) or for creches, nurseries, kindergartens and similar facilities (Peo. Rep. of Kampuchea, North Korea, Mongolia, and Vietnam).

Europe

In his work *Labor Provisions in Constitutions of Europe,* David Ziskind highlighted several areas where women are directly affected by various provisions, notably in terms of protection provided by general provisions of equality for *all* citizens, the explicit prohibition of discrimination on grounds of sex, female labor, and maternity benefits.[20]

1. **Nondiscrimination Provisions.** Nearly all European constitutions declare that all citizens are equal (Albania, Art. 40; Belgium, Art. 6; Bulgaria, Art. 35; Cyprus, Art. 28; Czechoslovakia, Art. 20[1], [4]; F.R.G., Art. 3[1], 33[2]; Finland, Art. 5; France, Art. 1, 77; G.D.R., Art. 20 [1]; Greece, Art. 4[1]; Hungary, Art. 61; Ireland, Art. 40[1]; Lichtenstein, Art. 31; Luxembourg, Art. 11[2]; Monaco, Art. 17; Netherlands, Art. 1; Poland, Art. 67[2], 81[1]; Portugal, Art. 13; Spain, Art. 14, 139[1]; Switzerland, Art. 4; Turkey, Art. 10; T.F.S.C., Art. 7, 58; U.S.S.R., Art. 34; Russ. Rep. Art. 32; Yugoslavia, Art. 140, 145.

2. **Special privileges or discrimination on grounds of sex are specifically prohibited** in Albania, Art. 40, 41; Austria, Art. 7(1); Bulgaria, Art. 36; Cyprus, Art. 28(2); Czechoslovakia, Art. 20(3); F.R.G., Art. 3(2) (3); France, Pre.; G.D.R., Art. 20(2); Greece, Art. 2; Hungary, Art. 61(2), 62; Italy, Art. 3, 37; Malta, Art. 15; Netherlands, Art. 1; Poland, Art. 78(1), 67(2); Portugal, Art. 13, 59(3); 60(1); Romania, Art. 17, 23; Spain, Art. 14, 35(2); Sweden Ch. 1, Art. 8; Switzerland, Art. 4(2); Turkey, Art. 10; U.S.S.R., Art. 34, 35; Russ. Rep., Art. 32, 33; Yugoslavia, Art. 154.

3. **Provisions Regarding Women's Labor.**[21] The concept of equal rights for women is spelled out only in the Italian constitution (Art. 37 para. 1) and in Communist constitutions (Czechoslovakia, Art. 27; G.D.R., Art. 20[2]; Hungary, Art. 62[2]; Romania, Art. 23; Russian Rep., Art. 33; U.S.S.R., Art. 35). The Russian constitution enumerates several specific measures to ensure that equality. Other constitutions, as will be set forth below, pledge similar measures without the general blanket of equality.

A general provision of special protection for women is found in several countries (Albania, Art. 48; Bulgaria, Art. 37; France, Pre. para. 3; F.R.G., Art. 6[4]; G.D.R., Art. 38[1] [2]; Greece, Art. 21[1]; Italy, Art. 37 para. 1; Lichtenstein, Art. 19 para. 1; Poland, Art. 79[1]; Portugal, Art. 60[2] [c]; Turkey, Art. 50; T.F.S.C., Art. 30; Yugoslavia, Art. 162 para. 6, 188). Women are prohibited from working at jobs that do not suit their age, capacity and sex (Ireland, Art. 45[4] [2]; Turkey, Art. 50; T.F.S.C., Art. 40[1] [2]).

The household chores of a mother are given some special attention. Ireland "recognizes that by her life within the home, woman gives to the State a support without which the common good cannot be achieved," and therefore the State shall endeavor "that mothers shall not be obliged by economic necessity to engage in labor to the neglect of their duties in the home" (Art. 41[2]). Italy "facilitates the formation of the family and the fulfillment of the tasks connected therewith, with particular consideration for large families" (Art. 31), and declares that "conditions of work must make it possible for (women) to fulfill their essential family duties" (Art. 37 para. 1). Bulgaria, in elaborating special protection and care for mothers, refers to "alleviation in her work" (Art. 37).

The participation of women in society is also mentioned in two constitutions. Czechoslovakia states their equal status shall be secured by special adjustments in "facilities and services which will enable women fully to participate in the life of society" (Art. 27). Poland states it "shall consolidate the position of women in society, especially gainfully employed mothers and women" (Art. 78[3]).

In a special provision pertaining to a state of defense, West Germany provides that women between the ages of 18 and 55 may be required to work in hospitals, but not in service involving the use of arms (Art. 120[4]).

Women workers are recognized as a special class of workers in only a few constitutions; maternal and household functions appear to be of greater concern.

4. **Maternity Benefits.**[22] Several constitutions provide for paid leave prior to and after childbirth (Albania, Art. 48; Hungary, Art. 62[2]; Poland, Art. 78[2] [2]; Portugal, Art. 69[3], 60[2c]; Romania, Art. 20 para. 3; U.S.S.R., Art. 35; Russ. Rep., Art. 33). Austria provides for "maternity and infant welfare" (Art. 12[2]); Czechoslovakia provides for "health care during pregnancy and maternity" (Art. 27); Bulgaria for "insurance and assistance in maternity" (Art. 39[1]); and Monaco for "assistance" (Art. 26). The Swiss constitution requires that cantonal laws must cover maternity insurance and the law "may require persons to contribute financially who are not eligible for insurance benefits" (Art. 34).

Several constitutions specify facilities for maternity care—maternity homes, creches, nursery schools, kindergartens, child care centers, or a network of institutions (Albania, Art. 48; Hungary, Art. 62[2]; Italy, Art. 31; Poland, Art. 78[2] [2]; Portugal, Art. 67[2]). Austria calls for legislation on "maternity and infant welfare" (Art. 12[1] [2]).

Latin America

In *Labor Law in Latin American Constitutions,* Ziskind states that Latin American constitutions generally proclaim equality of all inhabitants in similar terms. "Equal before the law" is the common designation. He cites the following examples:

> Nicaragua elaborates, "It is the duty of the State to remove . . . any obstacles which impede the real equality of citizens and their participation in the political, economic and social life of the country." Uruguay states, "All persons are equal before the law, no other distinction being recognized among them save those of talent and virtue." Cuba provides, "Women have the same rights as men in the economic, political and social fields as well as in the family."

> A few constitutions refer more specifically to equality in employment. "Work in its various forms is the object of protection by the State without any discrimination and within a system of equal treatment" (Peru). All inhabitants are equal and "admissible for employment without any other requisite than fitness" (Argentina). There shall be "Equal opportunity for all to be promoted to the appropriate job classification, with no limitations other than those of service and capability" (Nicaragua). In filling public employee positions, "only ability and honesty shall be taken into account" (Guatemala)."
>
> These proclamations of equality are usually accompanied by provisions against discriminations.[23]

As far as the prohibition of discrimination in general is concerned—which would, legally, also prohibit discrimination against women—Ziskind notes that all Latin American constitutions specifically prohibit various bases of discrimination. He quotes the example of Ecuador, which has gone one step further, adding: "Women, regardless of their marital status, have the rights and opportunities equal to those of men."[24]

Most Latin American constitutions also provide constitutionally for the needs of motherhood. Vacation leave, before and after childbirth, without prejudice to employment, is specifically provided for by Brazil, Cuba, El Salvador, Honduras, Mexico, Nicaragua and Panama. The period of paid maternity leave varies from 30 days before childbirth and 45 days after birth (Guatemala) to six weeks before and eight weeks after birth in the case of Panama. In several constitutions additional care is provided for such things as food, housing, education, recreation and exercise for the mother [Honduras] and the right of the working mother to have her minor children cared for by the state while she is at work [Nicaragua]. The Dominican Republic provides, furthermore, that maternity benefits shall be given regardless of the status (married or deserted) of the mother and Guatemala added that no distinctions may be made between married and single women.[25]

While the legal status of women was enormously improved during the 1980s by constitutional provisions, there is still a gap between policy mandated by the constitution and practice. As Cairns and Heckel observed: ". . . laws and practices still exist which limit women's participation in social and economic development. . . . In some countries, statutes and regulations are not in compliance with the provisions of the constitution guaranteeing equality. . ." and they cite as an example of achieving this objective Decree No. 1482 of Equador (1977), which simply revoked all statutes and regulations that did not recognize married women's full legal capacity as expressed in the constitution.[26]

The Gap Between Policy and Practice

The law on paper and the law in practice, unfortunately for women, are often two different things, and there are many factors which hinder the application of the law. Some are complex, some are rooted in custom and traditions, and sometimes the law is badly written and presented. Even well-written laws can end up being whittled away or diluted so as to have little practical effect or public impact.

Sometimes laws are passed in Third World countries to comply with United Nations conventions with the legislators knowing that there is little hope of those laws ever being applied in their country to such extent that they would have a visible effect in improving women's status. There is a great deal of intellectual dishonesty in the way laws are passed and then buried in many African, Asian and Latin American countries in order to protect male dominance. Sometimes judicial equality ends up in confusion. The 1975 Laws of Mexico recognize but do not guarantee judicial equality of men and women. Adaljiza Riddell cites Carlos Monsivais in stating that women occupy a worse situation than second-class citizenship in Mexico. Women must be controlled, she writes, "in order to maintain the patriarchal social order . . . the only conclusion one can come to is that there is a huge gap between what is legal and what is the reality of life."[27]

In 1967 when the first Brazilian constitution was promulgated after the affirmation of the U.N.'s Universal Declaration of Rigts, the constitution expressly recognized the equality of all before the law. Nevertheless, Brazilian law, attitudes and custom have not always respected the constitutional imperative. There is still flagrant unequal treatment of men and women by civil law. The husband is the head of the household. He, not the couple, has the right to choose the family residence, to administer the property of the couple and to seek divorce. Reforms on the drawing board will, if passed, eliminate the existing inequality.

Sometimes a written law, such as those of Bangladesh, is defective and vague. In addition corrupt law enforcement agencies and complicated and cumbersome legal procedures place legal remedies out of the reach of poor or uneducated women, observed Margaret Schuler. An enormous gap also exists between the provisions of the constitution and general legislation on the one hand and Muslim and Hindu personal law on the other. Similarly, in India, a progressive philosophy in the constitution in respect of women's rights is diluted by a parallel regime of personal law which affects inheritance, custody and succession rights of women. Section 10 of the Indian Divorce Act makes divorce among Christians almost impossible for women. The Hindu Minority and Guardianship Act of 1956, which provides that the natural guardian of a minor can only be the father, not only dilutes but contradicts article 14 of the constitution and its provision of equality.[28]

Muslim women's inferior status in India was actually formally legislated by the passage of the Muslim Women's Protection of Rights on Divorce Act of 1986. Under the Hindu Succession Act of 1956 the interest in joint family property or coparcenary property is acquired on birth only by male offspring. Tribal laws in Bihar, protected under the Chhotta Nagpur Tenancy Act, prevent inheritance of land by females. Similar laws can be found in other states, for example the U.P. Zamindari Abolition and Land Reform Act of 1950, the Delhi Land Reform Act and other laws in Punjab and Madhaya Pradesh. In this way the grand provisions in the Indian constitution to protect women are whittled away or effectively diluted.

In other parts of the world, notably Latin America, the problem is not so much the dilution of the constitution as the absence of enforcement measures.

In the case of Colombia, whose legal structure is examined in detail in this book (Chapter 20), a review of legislation on paper and of the constitution makes Colombia look like a paradise for women. But as legal historian Magdala Velasquez Toro observed: "The essential problem centers on the absence of effective enforcement mechanisms. Because the progressive legislation has not been accompanied by an educational campaign aimed at the masses of women and men, in general, the laws are no longer observed or enforced."[29]

In evaluating women's legal status in Latin America, a United Nations report stated in 1988: "There is no doubt that the *de juris* and the *de facto* treatment of women are two different matters. In general the legislative process achieved in the region has been made in the search to establish equitable relations between men and women. However, experience shows that the laws are inadequate except as a means of expressing an ideal."[30] The full integration of women in development, the United Nations found, is a process in which legal equality is a basic condition but is a task still to be accomplished.[31]

In Africa and elsewhere in the Third World it is a recognized political strategy that in order not to antagonize donor states, all U.N. conventions, resolutions and declarations affecting individual rights are automatically endorsed and set into law. Thereafter the law, or the endorsement, is hidden in the closet. There are nearly 40 states in Africa with restrictive one-party systems, military governments or a self-anointed President-for-Life.[32] It is not an exaggeration to say that the first thing new heads of states in these dictatorships do is to hide the constitution from their own people. Ethiopia, the Sudan, Liberia, Angola and Uganda are good examples.

Unless inequality is vigorously challenged in court, where the legal system permits such action, most women in the Third World never get to know what their rights are, while at international meetings the African and Asian states can effectively defend their household (and criticize other states) by trotting out copies of their constitution. Sigma Huda, who is the secretary of the Bangladesh National Women Lawyers Association, wrote that though existing laws in her country, on paper, are adequate and comprehensive, they remain pure legal theory. "For the majority of the people, over 80 percent of whom are illiterate and poor, the legal system is totally meaningless."[33] In November 1988, the Republic of Zaire announced with some fanfare a new code of family laws which banned polygamy and limited prices men pay for brides. The code, to take effect only some three years after proclamation (in January 1991), aimed to remove "written colonial law" from family life and to return to ancient custom. At the same time, the law also eliminated alimony because it was "unknown by African tradition." The net effect will make it easier for men to acquire wives and easier to divorce them, without having to pay for their upkeep or the children which the women may have borne.[34]

Even where legislation was introduced with the intention to safeguard the conditions of women at work, the same law was sometimes used as shield to discriminate against them, said Margaret Rogers. As the Chairman of the British Equal Opportunities Commission (E.O.C.) observed, the law had prohibited night work, shift work, early starts and late finishes and prevented women from working with lead or where radiation is involved. Pointing out the thin line which existed between protection and discrimination, he observed that shift work and overtime represent the main methods of maintaining a large differential between men's and women's pay. He accused British management of manipulating legislation to oust women from jobs, or to stop their getting jobs, or to keep them on low pay, all without any legal remedy.[35]

The gap between a government's public attitude, adopted in the forums of the world, and what it actually does in practice is most notable at the United Nations. A great many countries of the world which are member states have not ratified a single one of the several important international conventions on discrimination against women, even though their representatives cast a vote in favor of the convention when it was brought up in the U.N. General Assembly and even though it was signed by their respective governments. For example, in 1982 the convention eliminating all discrimination against women had been signed by 88 states but ratified by only 37 (a bare 44 percent) of member states.[36] There is, therefore, no legal obligation on these states to enact the necessary laws or to modify existing legislation. The only obligation is a moral and a political one which, in most countries, does not carry much weight to begin with. At present there is also no worldwide systematic reporting available on legislation which had been passed to implement ratification.

Inequalities also remain because new laws are slowly implemented. They are often overridden by customs and because old laws have not yet been repealed. There are, for example, 12 countries, member states of the United Nations, in which a woman must legally still seek her husband's approval if she wishes to take a job.[37] There are many more where it is demanded by custom, for example in the 30 Muslim states of the world.

The conflict between constitutional law and Muslim law remains unsolved. This has resulted in some extraordinary absurdities. Pakistan's Office of Zina (Enforcement of Hadd) Ordinance of 1979 for the first time made adultery and fornication a crime. But this law contradicts the injunctions of Islamic Law, which is also recognized in Pakistan. According to the *Holy Qur'an* and *Sunnah* of the Holy Prophet, zina (adultery and fornication) can be punished only if proved by the evidence of four adults, who must have witnessed the actual penetration. It seems too absurd to consider that someone discreetly bent on adultery or fornication will ever find himself committing the act of penetration under the watchful eyes of one adult witness, much less four!

Margot Duley and Mary Edwards pointed out one other factor which makes the provision of constitutional equality often appear as only a paper equality, namely, the enormous influence of personal and customary law. In Africa this is a matter of grave concern to women. Section 82 of the Kenyan Constitution of 1969 prohibits discriminatory legislation. But this prohibition does not apply to laws about matters of personal law, e.g. marriage, divorce, division of property, burial, etc. Under the constitution, therefore, many existing or newly established tribal, religious and common laws that discriminate against women are legal. The Sudan is another example. Despite constitutional provisions, customary law dominates the private and public lives of women. Despite the law certain practices are observed which completely ignore women's legal rights. "Where sexual stratification has been imbedded in the structure of the family there has been a particular reluctance (on the part of governments) to intervene."[38]

Thus women find themselves almost completely excluded from the decision-making process in both the political and social realms. The same is true of Arab-Muslim countries.

It is not only in the Muslim states that women are discriminated against because of religious prescriptions. This is also true of society in Israel. The woman is certainly the principal victim of theocratic legislation. In archaic Jewish (as well as Islamic) law she is considered not only an unequal, but the property of her husband.[39] In Israel it is explicitly laid down that the Law of Equality of Women (1953) does not apply to marriage and divorce. Israeli women cannot obtain divorce without their husband's consent. A man may remarry if his wife is declared insane, but the wife remains forever chained to an insane husband. The offspring of adulterous relations of a married woman will be barred for 10 generations from marrying pure Jews but the offspring of a married man with an unmarried female are pure Jews.[40] In reality, women's equality in Israel is still reason for great concern, and some observers have described women's liberation there as a myth.[41]

In a comparative study of legislation in Arab and Mediterranean countries (Egypt, Iraq, Jordan, Kuwait, Lebanon, Libya, Syria, Tunisia, Spain, Italy, France, Portugal and Turkey) concerning so-called "crimes of honor," attorney Laure Moghaizel states that persons who are guilty of homicide or inflicting serious bodily harm where a woman is surprised in the act of illicit sexual relations by an "aggrieved party" (which can only be a husband, brother or male relative), the perpetrator usually obtains partial or full pardon. An excuse may be obtained even in cases where it is suspected that a sexual act is about to occur.[42]

Legislation which thus provides for partial or full excuse in crime of honor discriminates against women because the victim is always female, Moghaizel pointed out. The term "husband" is used in all laws providing for so-called crimes of honor, except for the Lebanese or Syrian penal codes which use the term "spouse"; nonetheless, the intent of the law is that only the husband can benefit from the excuse. The law does not apply where a woman catches the man, even if it is a case of adultery and the man is caught *in flagrante delicto*. Almost needless to say, statutes which provide for excuses to males who commit bodily injury, even causing the death of the victim, openly contradict the individual liberties guaranteed by articles 3, 12, and 28 of the Universal Declaration of the Rights of Man and even the Arab constitutions themselves since they expressly guarantee the equality of women, for example Egypt, Iraq, Jordan and Kuwait.[43]

The laws of God in Muslim states can often result in absurdly discriminatory judgments, seen from both a Muslim woman's point of view and from that of Westerners. Take Pakistan. Though the law is still basically British, Islamization has created a parallel system. Laws passed in 1979 prescribe Islamic punishment for certain "hadod" offenses: stoning to death for fornication, amputation for theft, the lash for drinking and so on. In one instance (in Pakistan) a blind girl who had been raped and was pregnant was sentenced to be stoned to death. She could not identify the rapist, but since she was pregnant she was held to be guilty of illegal sex. That was the law of God, in Muslim eyes, but on appeal, thanks to the remnants of Western law, the sentence was commuted.[44]

Problem Areas

In four of the seven regions which are the subject of analysis in this book, there has been a growing awareness of how the law functions as an instrument of control by promoting or inhibiting access to certain resources while supporting attitudes and behavior that maintain oppressive social structures and relations. Essentially, it is claimed by investigators such as Schuler that the law regulates access to economic and social resources such as land, jobs, credit and other goods and services and, ultimately, to political power which controls the allocation or administration of these resources. This regulation is accomplished by the formulation of laws and policies that favor some but not all, by the arbitrary or selective application of laws or policies and by attitudes and behavior that reinforce and condone the existence of inequitable laws and inconsistent application of the law. "The outcome in most Third World countries is a pattern of legally sanctioned and, in some instances, constitutionally guaranteed, subordination of women."[45]

The subordination, says Schuler, is manifest in several key areas, particularly labor law, penal law and civil law which governs legal capacity, rights and obligations in marriage, guardianship, inheritance, income, land rights and participation in public affairs. Latin America, Asia and Africa are the worst culprits. In some instances women's inferior status is formally legislated. Investigators say that the very concept of legal rights is conditioned.

According to Schuler, the public sphere versus private sphere ideology as expressed in law is a key measure of society's perception of women's rights. The public sphere, work and politics, is accepted as the domain of men. The private sphere, domestic life, home and family are considered the domain of women. This dichotomy is deeply ingrained in the laws of some countries and thus the law plays a critical role in maintaining sexual stratification.[46]

Although Australia was not included in this study, constitutional and statutory provisions and discrimination of its various states reveal the same pattern as elsewhere.

In *A Decade of Women and the Law,* Margaret Rogers discloses many interesting trends in the (British) Commonwealth. There is no doubt, for example, that Australia is in the forefront in legislation to enhance the status of women, more so than Canada or Britain. That significant statutory discrimination still exists, despite the working of the various constitutions and the ratification of various United Nations conventions, is also evident from the Rogers survey. That it continues to exist in Australia, despite the Australian (federal) government's commendable legislative efforts, is equally true. In fact, one of the most recent studies shows that Australia has one of the highest degrees of sex segregation in the work force of any of the industrially developed countries.

The predominantly female occupations are characterized by poor conditions and low pay; furthermore, such conditions cannot easily be challenged by women, who face great problems with the procedures involved in any challenge in court.[47]

According to Margaret Thornton, affirmative action measures are unable to deal with the manifestation of structural discrimination. Examining wage-setting in Australia, she points out that the principle of equal pay for equal work has been accepted and passed into law. But it has had little to no practical effect on the female occupations in the male-dominated arbitration arena. All that the laws have demonstrated is their limited capacity in affecting change where the ideology of patriarchy operates in its many ways.[48]

In the Australian state of Tasmania the latter's Law Reform Commission published a report in 1978, "Discrimination on Grounds of Sex," which contained an appendix of provisions of Tasmanian statutes which discriminate against women solely on grounds of sex. The appendix showed that discrimination occurred in employment, retirement and pensions, family matters, property and protection of women and girls by criminal law. The Commission felt that the most pervasive discrimination was found in legislation which gives men and women different rights in employment and retirement. Discriminatory legislation is found in other states of the Australian union as well.[49]

Conditions elsewhere in the Commonwealth still leave much to be desired. In a *Commonwealth Law Bulletin* report dated January 1984, it is revealed that sexual discrimination in New Zealand still exists within the law profession itself. The report by the Committee on Women in the Profession, established by the Auckland District Law Society, observed that: "For some reason discrimination on the basis of race or religion is much less readily condoned than discrimination on the grounds of sex."[50] In England law students are also embarrassed by the prevailing sexism which exists in the British legal profession.[51]

A major issue facing women in Asia and Africa is the problem of custom, religion, ethnicity and the law.

Ethnic revivalism and religious fundamentalism have played as much a role as politics and the public-private dichotomy to circumscribe the status of women. The two most relevant aspects of custom and ethnicity are customary law and religion, which are dealt with in further detail in the chapters on Africa and the Muslim-Arab world.

Women also face violence and exploitation in the Third World. The law generally condones domestic violence in many Muslim and African states by protecting the patriarchal family from intervention by outside forces. Victims, which include sufferers of genital mutilation, battering and rape, are often further victimized by legal systems that treat the perpetrator with leniency.[52] In Muslim states an unmarried blind woman raped by unseen assailants becomes the criminal in the eyes of both community and Muslim law for getting herself raped.[53]

In its extreme form, male dominance finds expression in horrifying customs imposed on women, such as circumcision, the most extreme way men have of ensuring virginity and fidelity. This is particularly true of Africa. In

Mali, Sudan and Somalia the majority of women are infibulated.[54] At least 74 million women and girl-children are circumcised in Africa, not counting the continent's six Muslim states.[55] At a seminar on traditional practices affecting the health of women and children in Africa, held in Dakar, Senegal, 1984, there was consensus that changing traditional practices such as female circumcision will be slow and difficult process and, despite legislation, perhaps best addressed by the women of the countries in which these practices occur.[56]

Legal Trends

During the past five years, far more so than during the '70s, most states have reacted positively to assert the equality of the sexes and to guarantee equal rights, some by administrative action, some by legislation. By 1985 some 90 percent of U.N. member states had official government bodies dedicated to the advancement of women while 66 countries have incorporated specific programs and and provisions for women in their national development plans.[57]

The general principle of sexual equality now seems to be broadly accepted by all, except for the Muslim states, notably the Arab Gulf States. Ruth Sivard reports that the emphasis in the nineties will most likely shift to the translation of principle and acceptance into programs that can redress the imbalance caused by centuries of discrimination.[58] The objective, in most Western states, seems to be to correct laws and practices which are discriminatory and to promote equality by some sort of affirmative action. A notable example is the United States Supreme Court's ruling of March 1987 that employers may give preferential appointment and promotion to women to redress the imbalance in the marketplace. Another example is the Swedish Act on Equality of 1980 which states that whenever vacant posts are to be filled, the employer must ensure that candidates of both sexes apply and must take whatever steps may be necessary, in particular by organizing vocational training, to ensure that men and women are equally represented in various occupations and categories of workers.

Whereas headway is being made in legislation to ensure that women receive equal chances in the employment field, wrote Sivard, very few national legislative programs have begun to provide support to women's insistence that emphasis should be laid on the following: more training in technical skills for women; more training to broaden their work options; child care provisions to both parents; equal access to credit facilities and equal participation in government councils where priorities are set.[59]

Women's increased participation in the economy, the vast increase in numbers employed, have brought legal action on job protection and compensation during pregnancy in many countries. Legislation applicable to maternity leave is now fairly generally available, at least as far as salaried workers are concerned. Though only 21 countries have ratified the 1955 United Nations convention on maternity leave, by 1985 some 123 countries had passed legislation for maternity leave. While most countries have passed legislation for equal pay for equal work, very few have moved beyond that to address the vexing questions of equal pay for work of equal value.[60]

According to Sivard, modification of laws to provide equal rights for women is the slowest in those countries in which traditional social and religious practices have enforced women's subordinate status. Very often these states, notably in Asia, Africa and Latin America, have sex-equality provisions in their constitutions but still recognize customary (native) law which severely limits women's rights. Kenya, for example, exempted inheritance of property from its constitutional provision on equality. Somalia has an equal rights clause in its constitution but does not prosecute, under any statute, the dehumanizing practice of female circumcision. Burundi's family code invalidated the dowry system but allowed the wife to work only with the consent of the husband.[61]

In much of Africa there is still a deliberate effort to legally or *de facto* exclude women from benefiting from agrarian reform policies, or to relegate them to secondary activities and options. Because there are so many female-headed households this has contributed to an increase in the core of the rural poor, according to the I.L.O. In Kenya and the United Republic of Tanzania, women have traditionally had usufructuary rights to some of their husband's, brother's or father's lands, but recent land reform laws and programs have ignored these rights and established exclusive male ownership.[62] In Kenya the reform laws transferred land to an almost exclusively male-individualized tenure system and relegated women to the inferior position of landless agricultural laborers, dependent for their subsistence on men. Widowed women, despite customary usufructuary rights, became dependent on inheriting sons. If they had only daughters they ended up virtually landless. Divorced and separated women suffered the same fate.[63]

The trend in most of the Muslim states is for traditional holy law to take precedent over secular law. In a few others, such as Tunisia and Turkey, legislation passed as a consequence of the various U.N. conventions supersedes religious laws and custom. Of the 30 Muslim states of the world (states in which Moslems represent the vast majority of the population and in which the *Qur'an* is the official religion and virtually the state's constitution) only six have signed the U.N. convention on the elimination of discrimination against women (Afghanistan, Gambia, Indonesia, Jordan, Senegal and Tunisia); only Egypt has ratified the convention.

Even where the law of the land is clearly against discrimination, and where no religious conflict is involved, social tradition may still affect its implementation or effectiveness, creating a gap between policy and practice. Little effort is made to rigorously prosecute those who break the law. China, for example, has ratified the convention outlawing discrimination against women but has been hugely reluctant to do anything about the traditional preference for sons. When a law was passed to restrict families to only one child, there was a sharp corresponding rise in female infanticide but not a parallel rise in prosecutions for murder. Similarly, India's constitution prohibits payment of money or goods (dowry) by the bride's father to the husband for taking the daughter off his hands, yet the pernicious custom persists.

Some Western countries seem to be fighting worldwide trends. In 1986 Irish voters defeated by 63 to 36 percent a proposal to legalize divorce. The majority has spoken. No doubt the majority are also from happily married families for the decision left an estimated 70,000 couples saddled with untenable marriages. Under Ireland's current law, a manifestation of the strength of the Catholic Church, husband and wife must either endure their life together, however unpleasant, or unofficially separate. The amendment to the 49-year-old law prohibiting divorces would have permitted couples to divorce after five years of separation.[64] Ireland's record in law reform has been poor, particularly with regard to rape and women's status in the family area, unlike the trend elsewhere in Europe. If it had not been for the activity of women's organizations in Ireland, the record probably would be worse. In a paper given as a keynote address to the plenary session on Women in Ireland at the Third International Disciplinary Congress on Women (Dublin, 1987), Senator Mary Robinson of Ireland observed that her country had inherited a common law system which had been compiled by male judges, and that most of the current crop of judges who interpret the constitution were men. She pointed out that the constitution recognizes that the wife in the model (married) family of husband, wife, and children, ". . . by her life within the home . . . gives to the State a support without which the common good cannot be achieved." But, she asked, what sort of limbo does this create for other families in the state, such as single mothers and their children, women not singled out by the constitution? "This approach of confining family rights only to the family based on a valid subsisting marriage," she observed, "is contrary to the European Convention for the Protection of Human Rights and Fundamental Freedoms, and is contrary to the rights of a significant number of women and their children."[65]

What is so intractable about the situation in Ireland is that the constitution itself bans the introduction of legislation for divorce.[66] Thus no matter whether a political party enjoys a vast majority in Parliament and wants to introduce such legislation, it can be done only through a costly referendum to amend the constitution. The situation in Ireland is complex, as some observers have pointed out, but divorce is no longer a matter which concerns only the Church: it has become a civil rights issue, certainly a basic right of citizens in developed Western cultures.[67]

Elsewhere, in the United States, the Christian concept of marriage is increasingly being abandoned with many couples choosing to live together and to have children without formalizing their union by a form of marriage. This has spurred new legislation and a spate of high court decisions on the rights and duties of the partners and the rights of children from such a union. There is no doubt that in the United States the trend of legislation and rulings of the US Supreme Court has been substantially in favor of recognizing that women should be treated differently because they are women and because only women bear children. The Court, in fact, has responded positively to almost all the major issues which have been brought forward by women lawyers, women legislators, and women's organizations. This is clearly set out in Leslie Goldstein's excellent book *The Constitutional Rights of Women,* concerning cases in law and social change.[68]

The trend in the United States is also a constant refining of existing laws. During the 1988 elections, a referendum in the state of Maine even approved the rewriting of the state constitution in "gender neutral language."[69] But the most significant trend which has emerged in the late '80s is a redefinition of legal theory, reflecting the distinctive perspectives of women. According to an article in *The New York Times,* there has been a flood of essays in legal journals in which feminist legal scholars, many of them prominent law professors, are proposing a basic rethinking of everything in law, from the doctrine of negligence to the criminal laws about rape.[70]

Women lawyers are challenging what they, rightly, see as a male bias in the legal system. The general objective of feminist scholars is to eradicate the sexism and inequality which they believe are inherent in Western legal thought. They argue, again with reason, that the law was written with men in mind and that when most Western laws were drafted it was simply assumed that a "person" was a male and that "people" were men. That was certainly how it was reflected in the very wording of legal practice. Even today, Anglo-Saxon countries still refer to the "Master of the Supreme Court." No one ever dreamt that there could be a "Mistress" of the Supreme Court just as no one ever dreamt that in 1988 there would be a woman on the British High Court where the judges have always been addressed as "My Lord." When legal draftsmen of Roman-Dutch law wrote that the court must consider what a reasonable person would have done under particular circumstances, they used the phrase: "A reasonable man."

Feminist scholars such as Professor Catharine MacKinnon of Yale University Law School believe pornography should not be attacked primarily as an obscenity, but for reflecting sexual discrimination which hurts women and violates their civil rights. Others, such as Georgetown University Law Professor Wendy Williams, insist that biological differences between men and women must be considered in law—for example, only women can become pregnant; since pregnancy leads to an inability to work, it should be treated by employers as any other temporary physical disability. Laws which give pregnant women specific privileges in fact imply an unequal status, detrimental to women in the long run. Others, such as Professor Barbara Babcock of Stanford University Law School, believe that the law should also consider psychological distinctions between men and women.[71]

These are highly controversial areas in jurisprudence, even sacrosanct, yet the theoretical ferment which began in the early 1970s is unlikely to subside as the number of women lawyers continue to increase. In 1988 more than 40 percent of all law students in the United States and 20 percent of all lawyers were women. Their influence is bound to grow. The 20th National Conference on Women and the Law in Oakland, California, drew more than a thousand lawyers.

Part Three: The African World

Black women in South Africa suffer triple discrimination: firstly, because they are black; secondly, because they are women; and, thirdly, because they are black women. — Helen Suzman.

6. General Survey

Constitutional and Legal Provisions

The constitutions of almost all African states contain declarations of liberty, equality, freedom and democracy based on race, religion and sex. But African tribal law is frequently given legal recognition, even in the most industrially developed African states, such as South Africa. Tribal law and tribal customs subject most black women to social and legal disabilities. Among the Bantu-speaking nations of East and Southern Africa a woman does not inherit her husband's property when he dies. The inheritance goes to a male descendant. A widowed African woman is always subjected to a man's guardianship. If she wishes to travel overseas, she may have to ask written permission from her own sons.[1]

There are a number of classless societies in Africa in which women not only bring up the children and do all the housework but also are responsible for almost the total production of society, such as the Somali in East Africa. The Somali once regarded their female children as capital and sold them as slaves in time of famine.[2] Somalia is also the country with the highest percentage of circumcised women in the world and has the world's fourth highest infant mortality rate. A 1984 United Nations Children's Fund report said that 50 percent of Somali children do not live past the age of five. Women cannot campaign openly against circumcision, an extremely unhealthy and medically condemned practice, because custom forbids the discussion of any sexual matter in public. Female circumcision in Africa is practiced in 23 different countries, stretching from Mauritania on the west coast to Tanzania on the east coast.[3]

Among the Masai of East Africa it is common for the wife to be thrashed, and the courts are reluctant to act against tribal custom and law. For many years the same custom could be found among the Zulu, Xhosa and Sotho in South Africa and where the accused has the right to be heard according to tribal law.[4] In 1988 Botswana's Attorney General drafted legislation to allow women to be flogged, a law proposed not only by tribal chiefs but also by certain Parliamentarians.[5] In Zimbabwe the country's Marxist President, Dr. Robert Mugabe, became involved in a dispute with tribal chiefs in determining how much a wife was worth. In 1988 the President finally declared that $1,700 and 10 cows was too high.[6] According to the Johannesburg *Star's* Africa News Service, the status of women has been central to a number of clashes between tribal traditions and the socialist ideals espoused by the government of Dr. Mugabe. Several laws to improve women's rights have been passed against a chorus of outrage from male traditionalists. For example, the Legal Age of Majority Act gave women adult status at 18 years, the same as men. Previous laws regarded women as perpetual minors under the guardianship of their husbands or fathers. As a result, fathers of these girls can no longer sue for damages if their daughters become pregnant, an issue which caused an uproar in tribal society. Some 80 percent of Zimbabwe's population of eight million live in tribal areas where traditional beliefs hold almost universal sway.[7] On the other hand, in Zaire, the ruling Zaire State Party recently informed women in the South-Kivu region to switch from Western dress to traditional African dress. Bar owners were instructed by the government not to admit women in Western dress into restaurants and bars. Failure to get out of Western dress and into traditional African attire now means facing prosecution in court. President Mobuto SeseSeko banned Western dress and Christian names as far back as 1970; however, the government has issued no instructions or decrees against Zairean men in European suits.[8]

One of the most difficult tasks for any researcher would be to try to establish how many African governments have actually introduced legislation to implement the various international conventions prohibiting discrimination against women in all forms which they had either signed or ratified. If such a study were to provide the basic data, the next step would be even more difficult: to determine whether or not these laws were being vigorously applied and to what extent the various governments were ensuring that all women knew of their rights under the new laws. In the absence of these facts and other reliable statistics from most African nations it must be accepted that, beyond the principal urban areas, sometimes only the capital city, the well-documented facts about entrenched traditions of male domination leave one with no option but to believe that during the '80s tribal traditions in respect of women's status and rights were still far more powerful than the stipulations of the constitution or Parliamentary legislation. Enforcement of new sophisticated legislation in the vast rural areas of Africa among people of whom the vast majority cannot read or write, particularly among women, and where there is a lack of radio and television, or public debate on the issue, is for the moment an almost insurmountable task.

The International Labor Organization has long established that it is the rural women in Africa who suffer the greatest deprivation and discrimination. In a study of rural development and women in Africa, the I.L.O. rapporteur said these women were caught in a squeeze between their responsibilities to themselves and their families, the resources available to them, and their limited freedom to undertake new activities in order to survive. Under increasing poverty the informal social security system is breaking down, "leaving women without any barrier to utter deprivation."[9] In the Ivory Coast, Senegal, and other countries these women are now denied access to the lands of relatives after new land reform laws were passed in which only men received legal grant. There is a lack of extension services and training for women. In most areas the programs do not even reach women, concentrating only on men. Women, even those with access to farming technology, are refused credit. "Again, most credit that is available in rural Africa is channelled towards men.... Everywhere in Africa, women are restricted by the remnants of the traditional perceptions of women's role and the sexual division of labour."[10] Stratification has increased and has made the situation of women in the rural areas even worse. Women in Libya were taught knitting, a craft useless to women living in the hot Sahara.[11] In such circumstances only a true miracle, or a massive change in male perceptions, can possibly bring equal opportunities and equal rights to these women, a process which may take another century.

Constitutional and legal provisions for equality and women's rights may exist in all of Africa, but, except for six or eight countries they are largely symbolic, instruments known to and available only to the educated African women living in the major urban centers.

The Population Explosion

According to I.L.O. estimates the female population in Africa in 1980 was 237 million, about 56 million more than in Latin America. Also in 1980 about 55 million women were engaged in some economic activity. Of economically active women, the highest ratios to the total population were in Burundi (60.4 percent), Rwanda (55.3 percent), and the Seychelles (51.9 percent). The lowest were in Burkina Faso (1.7 percent), Mauritania (2.6 percent), and Mali (11.8 percent).[12]

While some of the most important factors contributing to discrimination against women in Africa and the inequality of the sexes are traditional male roles, poverty, lack of opportunity, lack of willingness on the part of African governments to vigorously implement the laws which they have passed to satisfy the United Nations, illiteracy of women and migratory labor, the high birth rate and the population factor may be at the heart of the problem.

The population of sub-Saharan Africa, currently about 470 million, will exceed 700 million by the year 2000. At no time in history has any group of nations faced the challenge of development in a situation of such rapid growth. The number of children being borne by black women in almost all areas of Africa is four to five times that of, for example, the United States or Western Europe, despite the very high infant mortality rates.

Explosive population growth impedes any effort to raise living standards, yet in Africa the governments do not appreciate (or understand) this problem. As the World Bank rightly noted in its latest study of population growth and policies in sub-Saharan Africa, family planning in Africa is absolutely essential.[13]

There has long been a fear that the population explosion in Africa will not permit the various countries to maintain even the living standards of several years ago. In 1974 at the World Population Conference in Bucharest only three African governments agreed with the urgency of the problem. By 1984 some 36 of the 47 countries had changed their minds, and now they officially support family planning as embodied in the so-called Kilimanjaro Programme, adopted at the second African population conference sponsored by the United Nations in Tanzania in January 1984.

According to the World Bank's study referred to above, it has been pointed out, time and again, that a rapidly growing population means a drop

Country	Infant mortality rate (deaths per 1,000 live births)	Total fertility rate
Zimbabwe	69	7.0
Kenya	81	8.0
Congo	83	6.0
Tanzania	97	7.0
Zaire	106	6.3
Uganda	108	7.0
Mozambique	109	6.5
Sudan	117	6.6
Ethiopia	121	5.5
Malawi	164	7.6
Ghana	66	7.0
Nigeria	113	6.9
Cameroon	116	6.5
Còte d'Tvoire	121	6.6
Senegal	140	6.6
Sierra Leone	198	6.5

Table 14. Estimated Infant Mortality Rates and Total Fertility Rates in Selected Sub-Saharan African Countries for 1983. Source: International Bank for Reconstruction and Development, *Population Growth and Policies in Sub-Saharan Africa,* Washington DC, August 1986, pp.8–9.

in per capita income, loss of potential for higher economic growth and higher maternal and child mortality and morbidity, tighter constraints on expenditure for education and falling wages as the labor force expands too rapidly. The net result is to erode what little gain women have made and to exacerbate the existing differentials between the sexes. In fact, the employment and wage situation for Africa can only be described as grim.

There is no doubt that failure to institute a massive birth control program is going to produce disastrous results in the medium to long term. Within the time it takes for a child to be born and the time of his entry to a university, i.e., an average of 20 years in Africa, the health and economic problems, even the basic necessity of feeding the living, is going to make the famine and related problems in Ethiopia, the Sudan, and other areas of Africa during the mid-1980s appear to be mild. A mere glance at the massive growth of the black African population and the declining food production placed in juxtaposition with the use of contraceptives in Africa (see Table 15) should make the inevitability of such a scenario clear.

The tragedy brought about by the failure of African governments to do something about the problem, the World Bank wrote, is that the high infant mortality creates a vicious circle, strengthening the demand by African fathers for larger families to ensure that at least the sons will survive. Total fertility rates exceed six children on average in most countries and in some the desired family exceeds seven children. The fact is that in Africa black women marry

Country	Year	Contraceptive prevalence rate (percent)
Cameroon	1977–78	3
Ethiopia	1982	2
Ghana	1979–80	10
Kenya	1977–78	8
Lesotho	1977	5
Nigeria	1983	6
Senegal	1978	4
Sierra Leone	1982	4
Zaire	1982	3
Zimbabwe	1984	27
West Africa	1983	4
East Africa	1983	3

Table 15. Use of Contraception among Women Aged 15–49 in Selected Countries in Sub-Saharan Africa. Source: International Bank for Reconstruction and Development, *Population Growth and Policies in Sub-Saharan Africa,* Washington DC, August 1986, p.50.

early and their status in traditional society is closely tied to their fertility. "Women may recognize the cost of high fertility to their own and their children's health; men, less involved in the care of children, may not."[14] Women in Benin and Lesotho will finish their childbearing at age 38 on average and can expect to live another 27 years. Women in Panama and Jamaica, however, will bear their last child at age 33 on average and live another 44 years.[15]

In a recent study of the causes of Africa's poverty, W. Harding le Riche also singles out the population explosion. In Africa, he writes, the population is doubling every 24 years, but in some areas, like Kenya, it is taking only 17 years. As the numbers increase, soil erosion and the destruction of forests increase. "What is happening in Africa, quite apart from lack of rain, is that productive land is being made into waste land by human mismanagement."[16] The blight of Africa is its rate of population growth, says le Riche. The entire agricultural system is on the verge of collapse and, indeed, in many parts of Africa it has already collapsed. He points out that in 1950 Africa had 219 million people and a livestock population of 295 million. In 1983 the human population was 513 million and the livestock numbered 521 million. (From a margin of more than 35 percent livestock in 1950, the situation had therefore deteriorated in less than one life span to a margin of less than 2 percent.) The future is grim. In most African societies, le Riche points out, children under the age of 15 constitute almost 50 percent of the population. He contrasts this figure with 22 percent under the age of 15 in the United States. "The present theory that increasing the standard of living in Africa will decrease the birthrate is a pleasant theory. . . . Africa is an essentially male dominated society and the value of a woman is stated mainly in terms of the number of children she can produce.... Population growth is not to be looked at as a separate issue.... It is part of the issue of the need for education and it is part of the issue for all sorts of social services. If there are too many people these services cannot be provided."[17] W. Harding le Riche's views are shared by other observers such as Timberlake and Wolf.[18]

An equally grim picture of Africa's economic decline over the past 30 years since the end of colonialism and the bleak future that faces the continent is contained in a final draft of a new report by the World Bank to be published in 1989. It is very likely that, after the various leaders of Africa have used their blue pencils, the final, printed version may sound a more hopeful note, but the major findings indicate almost insurmountable problems:

- At current growth rates, the population will double in the next 20–25 years, accelerating the loss of precious woodland and hastening desertification. By 1984 more than 80 percent of Africa's dry lands, with a population of 92 million, was already classified as moderately desert.
- Two thirds of Africa's land areas are likely to suffer a prolonged drought every decade, similar to that which caused widespread famine in Sudan and Ethiopia.
- The economic situation is going from bad to worse. Africa is poorer today, measured in terms of per capita income, that it was some 30 years ago.
- Life expectancy has declined in nine countries and school enrollment in 12.

Education

The results of education speak for themselves. In 10 African countries studied by the World Bank, desired family sizes among women with seven or more years of education was only five, compared to almost eight among women with no education. Of women with some seven years of education, 11 percent are using modern contraception methods; among those without any education the figure is less than 1 percent.[19]

Primary and secondary education in Africa is illustrated statistically by means of Table 16.

In its study of women in sub-Saharan Africa, the Office of Women in Development of the United States Agency for International Development said that women's disadvantaged position in the economic sphere is not because of a lack of policy on the part of African governments aimed at narrowing the educational gap between boys and girls; "rather it is in large part the consequency of beliefs and attitudes ... that women's activities are primarily domestic and of secondary importance."[20] On the other hand, the agency said that, despite a national policy commitment to provide formal schooling for both sexes on an equal basis, in most countries female educational opportunities continued to lag behind those for males and in 1980 girls constituted only 43 percent of all those enrolled in primary schools. At secondary school girls have fared even worse and form less than 5 percent of secondary school enrollment (South Africa excluded; there the rate is close to 45 percent.) U.N.E.S.C.O. estimates are that less than 1 percent of total enrollment in

Country	Number enrolled in primary school as percentage of age group						Number enrolled in secondary school as percentage of age group	
	Total		Male		Female			
	1965	1982	1965	1982	1965	1982	1965	1982
1 Mali	24	27	32	35	16	20	4	9
2 Burkina	12	28	16	28	8	16	1	3
3 Niger	11	23	15	29	7	17	1	5
4 Somalia	10	30	16	38	4	21	2	11
5 Gambia, The	21	56	29	71	12	41	6	16
6 Chad	34	..	56	..	13	..	1	3
7 Ethiopia	11	46	16	60	6	33	2	12
8 Zaire	70	90	95	104	45	75	5	23
9 Guinea-Bissau	26	88	38	119	13	57	2	15
10 Malawi	44	62	55	73	32	51	2	4
11 Uganda	67	60	83	69	50	51	4	8
12 Burundi	26	33	36	41	15	25	1	3
13 Tanzania	32	98	40	101	25	95	2	3
14 Rwanda	53	70	64	72	43	67	2	2
15 Central African Rep.	56	70	84	92	28	50	2	14
16 Togo	55	106	78	129	32	84	5	27
17 Benin	34	65	48	87	21	42	3	21
18 Guinea	31	33	44	44	19	22	5	16
19 Ghana	69	76	82	85	57	66	13	34
20 Madagascar	65	100	70	..	59	..	8	14
21 Sierra Leone	29	40	37	..	21	..	5	12
22 Kenya	54	104	69	114	40	94	4	20
23 Sudan	29	52	37	61	21	43	4	18
24 Mozambique	37	104	48	119	26	72	3	6
25 Senegal	40	48	52	58	29	38	7	12
26 Lesotho	94	112	74	95	114	129	4	20
27 Liberia	41	66	59	82	23	50	5	20
28 Mauritania	13	33	19	43	6	23	1	10
29 Zambia	53	96	59	102	46	90	7	16
30 Cote d'Ivoire	60	76	80	92	41	60	6	17
31 Zimbabwe	110	130	128	134	92	125	6	23
32 Swaziland	74	111	76	111	71	111	8	42
33 Botswana	65	102	59	94	71	110	3	23
34 Mauritius	101	106	105	107	97	105	26	51
35 Namibia	..	..	..	..	..	..	..	..
36 Nigeria	32	98	39	..	24	..	5	16
37 Cameroon	94	107	114	117	75	97	5	19
38 Congo, People's Rep.	114	..	134	..	94	..	10	69
39 Gabon	134	..	146	..	122	..	11	..
40 Angola	39	..	53	..	26	..	5	..
41 South Africa	90	..	91	..	88	..	15	65

Table 16. Primary and Secondary Education in African States with Populations Exceeding 500,000 Persons. Source: International Bank for Reconstruction and Development, *Population Growth and Policies in Sub-Saharan Africa*, Washington DC, August 1986, p.50; Central Statistical Service, Pretoria.

African educational institutions was at post-secondary education level and of this figure a little more than one-fourth were women.[21]

School enrollments in general may have increased dramatically in Africa but in terms of educational attainments the figures are very discouraging. In 1982 U.N.E.S.C.O. reported that (South Africa excepted) there are only five countries among the 40 states of sub-Saharan Africa in which the fraction of adults age 25 years and over who have completed primary school is 9 percent or more. Women form a small percentage of this group. There is also a high degree of educational wastage in the area. Only 35 percent of females over age five had ever been to school; 26 percent of the total had attended but dropped out after completing only four years and another 8 percent had attended but dropped out before secondary school level. Fewer than 1 percent attended but failed to reach the final year of secondary school. Thus in Kenya the female share of total enrollment decreased from 47 percent in Standard 1 (third year of school following on Grades 1 and 2) to 40 percent in Standard VII, to 26 percent in the last year of high school, and to only 18 percent of first-year enrollment at university.[22]

Single-sex institutions and separate tracking at the secondary and post-secondary level of education are common, and scientific and technical subjects are often found only in educational institutions for boys and adult men. For example, in the Sudan there were no technical schools at all for girls but 11 for boys. Of agricultural higher technical schools there were 282 for females but 692 for men. Of general secondary schools there were 250 for girls and 609 for boys. In Kenya in 1978 none of the secondary vocational and technical schools admitted any girls. Despite the fact that women were engaged on a large scale in rural areas in producing and marketing food, there were only 30 openings for girls at the Bukura Institute of Agriculture compared to 270 for boys.[23] (Elsewhere in this book it has been indicated that women in most of West and East Africa are, in fact, better farmers than men.)

The pattern of separate tracking on gender grounds continues at university. In Ghana women comprise only 7 percent of the enrollment at the University of Science and Technology at Kumasi. Most Ghanian women are concentrated in the faculty of arts. The pattern of sex-bias in program and curriculum is widespread in Africa, causing the Economic Commission for Africa to suggest that secondary education may even depress women's options and that new school programs have introduced even more gender differentiation.[24]

Western-style education is considered a key to wealth and power in Africa; generally, however, women simply have not had the access to proper education and training.[25] Professional women in the business and governmental sectors face far more obstacles than men. Far fewer school spaces are available for girls, and they are increasingly channeled into primary school teaching, nursing and other lower-status fields.[26] Black business women are not helped by the fact that there is discrimination against them in the techniques and activities of the international development agencies.[27] Since independence, the definition of "head of household" as exclusively male in census data and for planning projects has largely excluded women from participating in many national development programs.[28]

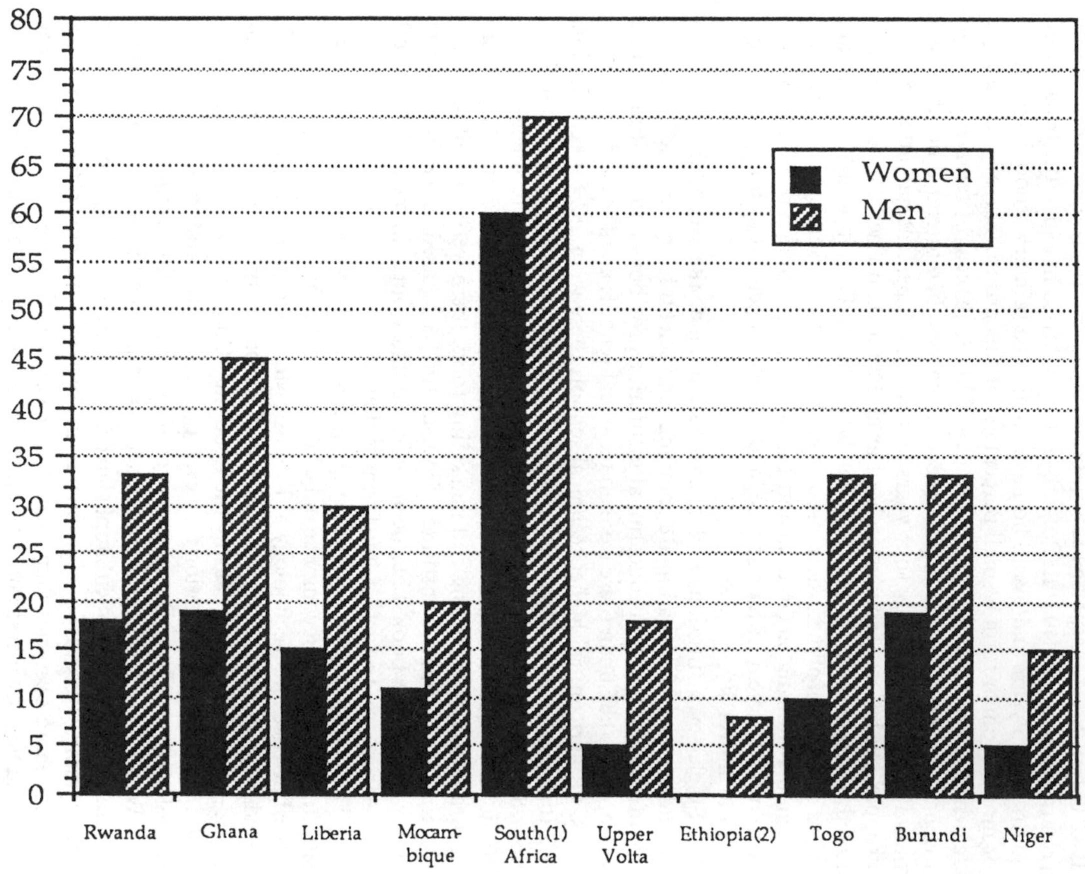
80
75
70
65
60
55
50
45
40
35
30
25
20
15
10
5
0
Women
Men
Rwanda
Ghana
Liberia
Mocam-bique
South(1) Africa
Upper Volta
Ethiopia(2)
Togo
Burundi
Niger

Political Attitudes

In her report on the world conference for women in Nairobi in 1985, Caroline Pezzullo states that in no other area of the world is the traditional pronatalist attitude as strong as in Africa. It has remained strong because the political elites in Africa have developed priorities which have little bearing on the real problems facing their societies. Central planning has been an almost disastrous failure. At the non-governmental meeting most African women delegates pointed out that the "externally oriented development model," i.e., a mindless duplication of what the developing states were doing, adopted by so many African countries during the 1960s, is now recognized as having depleted human and material resources, undermined local knowledge and skills and contributed to the critical food, water and energy shortages on the continent.[29] This is what the liberal French agro-economist Rene Dumas referred to as the false start in Africa, also the title of his famous book.

Political kingdoms and powerful armies to sustain one-party regimes and presidents-for-life have been sought before the development of education, sufficient water water supplies and food production, and a rail and road infrastructure, to say nothing of long-term planning in respect of population growth and health services. Consequently there is needless death of tens of thousands of women. In the Danfa area in Ghana 400 mothers die for each 100,000 births. In Swaziland it is 370. In some areas of Africa it is as high as 600.

The politicizing of even the most fundamental programs to uplift the status of women is evident in, for example, Ethiopia. The Revolutionary Ethiopian Women's Association in Ethiopia now claims to have over 5 million members, 21,000 basic associations, 541 district associations, 110 provincial associations, 15 regional and one national association.[30] In any other country such an organization would be a powerful independent voice for women. In Ethiopia it is, in fact, just an extension of the Marxist party which governs the country, and the executives take their orders from the State. According to US State Department sources, the speech read by the chairperson of the Ethiopian Women's Association at the Nairobi conference where the Decade for Women came to an end was written by the Ethiopian foreign office and personally ap-

***Opposite:* Chart 4. Literacy Among Men and Women, 10 Years and Older, in Select African States. Source: United States Department of Commerce, *Women of the World,* Washington DC, May 1984, p.58; and South African Department of Sociolinguistics, Institute for Research on Language and Art, Human Sciences Research Council, Pretoria. Cf. C.S. Ellis, *Literacy Statistics in the R.S.A., 1980,* Human Sciences Research Council, Pretoria, 1987; and Central Statistical Services, *Population Census 1985,* Report No. 02-85-06, Pretoria, 1986.**

Notes: (1.) Estimated 1988 for all black people, 15 years and older. In urban areas women's literacy [1985] was 72.30 percent against 68.15 percent for men. (2.) Ethiopian women: 0.2 percent. (3.) Percentages for all other countries circa 1975.

proved by the country's Marxist president before it was duplicated for distribution to the press.

Employment and Economic Factors

According to an I.L.O. report, Africa as a region has been affected the worst by the world economic crisis of the 1970s and early 1980s. This has further deteriorated the economic and social conditions of the majority of the workers and, even more so, female workers. As a percentage of the total labor force, fewer African women were employed in 1985 than in 1950. (See Table 17.) There has been increasing evidence of women also migrating in search of employment. For example, in cities such as Addis Ababa, capital of Ethiopia, and Abidjan, capital of the Ivory Coast, there are more female than male migrants. Of the total of 12.7 million refugees in Africa, the majority are women and children. "Employment opportunities in both the modern and traditional sectors are rapidly decreasing and unemployment and underemployment rates in Africa are estimated to be the highest among all the developing regions, ranging between 50 and 70 percent, and in some cases up to 90 percent in rural areas."[31]

According to the International Labor Organization and the United Nations Research and Training Institute for the Advancement of Women there is widespread imbalance between the sexes in the modern sector of urban employment in which higher levels of training and schooling are required.[32] Girls continue to have less access to schooling than boys, especially in the higher grades.[33] Girls drop out of school more frequently, often due to economic reasons. Several recent surveys have shown that women form only a small proportion of workers in the private and semi-public sectors. Even in the public sector they hold only 10 or 20 percent of the jobs and then mainly in the lower levels as primary school teachers, nurses and clerical workers.[34]

There is a widespread job segregation in almost all of black Africa, with women concentrated in the agricultural, service, teaching and nursing professions, and secretarial services. Job opportunities are for men, and whatever is left is for women, including hard labor on the roads. Surveys in Africa indicate that women do three-quarters of the farm work in rural Africa. A considerable number of women are involved in micro-enterprises, small-scale trading or production activities, but, as in the case of unpaid agricultural labor, statistics on these activities are almost never reflected in government data. The smallest percentage of women in the official paid labor force in the world was found in Africa. In countries such as Cameroon, Liberia, Malawi, Mali, Rwanda, and the Sudan, only 2 percent of women are reflected in the paid labor force, but in West Africa and Tanzania substantial numbers of women are recognized as traders.[35]

Political Disabilities

The gap between policy and reality, or between constitutional and statutory dispensation and practice, was a formidable negative factor for women in Africa in the 1970s and has remained so during the decade of the 1980s.

Lopis Adams looked at the situation in Zaire and found that despite the constitutional provisions on equality, women are forced into subordinate roles and economic dependence on men by limited educational and economic opportunities. During most of the '70s, in the city of Lubumbashi, she wrote, only 3 percent of the women in the city were classified as employed. The legal code required married women to have their husbands' permission to work.[36] "With courts and legal practice a predominantly male sphere, the legal rights which women do possess are frequently not enforced."[37]

One of the few women who became a judge in the state of Togo observed that both custom and law treat the woman as inferior: "...in all areas of endeavour rules and customs have been developed to insure the dominant position of the male."[38]

The gap between policy and practice covers almost every field, including ideological commitment. Even where governments have committed themselves in revolutionary fervor to equality between men and women during the struggle for liberation and even where women had initially been appointed to high level posts in the government, such as the cabinet, there has been little noteworthy change in the overall status of women. Zimbabwe, again, is a case in point. Women had played a major role in the war against the white-controlled government of Ian Smith (Rhodesia) and often commanded guerrilla units in the field. In war they were fully equal. They were all referred to as "comrade." Once the Marxist forces of Robert Mugabe achieved victory, things changed. Women were no longer referred to as "comrade" in speeches or in the newspapers—only men. As Jessie Bernard wrote, there was a brief honeymoon but then a great let-down and, in 1984, a massive male backlash. Two women were appointed to head the Ministry of Community Development and Women's Affairs in the newly independent Zimbabwe. The government promised equitable integration and accelerated development for women. Then, Bernard writes, the women discovered that it was easier to put words on paper than to plant new ideas about women's status. Suddenly women were politically downgraded. Finally, a Women's Action Group came to the conclusion that there was a hard struggle ahead in which their major task would be to educate men and to teach women about their rights. As Bernard says, "It was likely to be a long struggle."[39]

Writing in *The Cross Cultural Study of Women,* Lance Morrow points out that women's public recognition, policy influence and direct access to political office and power within African independence movements and national governments "have been severely limited by cultural traditions of public deference, erosion of women's relative economic position, and colonial biases in favour of male African leaders." Morrow also writes that women have been handicapped by disproportionately heavy subsistence production and child care. The black nationalist political movement also heavily emphasizes male roles, and male political leaders have sometimes publicly attacked and resisted efforts to eliminate discrimination against women. Where male military regimes have been established (there are several in Africa) women's influence

Female labor force

Year	*Total female population (thousands)*	*Women in Labor Force (thousands)*	*As percentage of Female population:*		*As percentage of total labor force*	*As percentage of world total*
			Total	*15 years of age and older*		
1950	111,254	31,165	28.0	44.3	32.9	9.1
1975	202,374	49,366	24.4	40.2	32.4	8.6
1980	232,472	54,883	23.6	39.3	32.2	8.8
1985	268,127	61,321	22.9	38.4	32.0	9.1

has been further reduced in the political sphere. These structures and political obstacles "have deprived women of participation and leadership in the development of the rights, services and programs that are defining current opportunities and the future social and political order."[40]

Studies of individual countries indicate that Morrow's assessment is correct. Despite extensive official rhetoric about the importance of ending the subordination and the oppression of women in Tanzania, government programs have failed to address the unequal social structure of gender differentiation or to improve the conditions of women's lives, particularly in the rural areas. Economic and social programs for women continue to be impeded by many constraints such as the granting of land title only to men and traditional male claims to most of the profits from women's agricultural production.[41] History repeated itself in Kenya.[42]

Morrow's conclusion is that women's political disabilities in black Africa are largely a product of discriminatory social values, structural inequalities and institutionalized male privileges. The adoption of socialist and other egalitarian ideologies has made little difference in women's actual political opportunities and benefits.[43]

The Law and Religion

Nigeria (one of the case studies included in this book) is an exceptionally interesting case because it is caught in a growing conflict between Nigerian common law and the Laws of Islam. The northern region of Nigeria (the Hausa) is rapidly being Islaminized, and the vast majority of women in the capital, Kano, are unaware that the Nigerian constitution (when it is not suspended by the military) grants them a legal status that is quite different from the status provided by the *Qur'an.* As stated by Barbara Callaway and Enid Schildkroud, "What an outsider might consider *prima facie* evidence of inferior status is perceived (in northern Nigeria) as a divinely ordained differentiation in sex roles."[44]

Secular law in Nigeria, as provided for by the constitution or crafted by the elected representatives of the people in the legislature, confronts an insurmountable obstacle when it comes face to face with Islamic Law. The reason for this is that the word of God, according to Islamic injunction, is that the rights which have been sanctioned by God are permanent, perpetual and eternal. "They are not subject to any alterations or modifications, and there is no scope for any change or abrogation." Any challenge to the Sharia (traditional Islamic Law) is seen as a challenge to Islam itself; and since the Sharia is sacred (the Word of God, according to the Prophet Muhammad) laws cannot be used as an instrument of social change. The laws of Islam prescribe religion, morals,

***Opposite:* Table 17. Women's Percentage of Participation in the Labor Force in Africa between 1950 and 1985. Source: International Labor Organization, *Labour Force Estimates and Projections 1950–2000,* 2nd ed., Vol. V, *World Summary,* Geneva, 1977; and International Labor Organization Bureau of Statistics, Geneva, 1984.**

politics, commerce, criminal law, law of evidence and procedure.[45] In fact, like Judaism, it is a religion of laws so comprehensive that it has rules for all human activity, including whom not to marry, what to eat, how to govern, and even how to engage in war. There being no area of activity not covered by law, there is no accommodation for a separate secular, as against religious, jurisdiction.[46]

Hausa women are deliberately taught to be submissive and deferential to men and boys are taught that they are innately superior to girls. There are many Hausa maxims specifying women's inferior status, but it is passages from the *Qur'an* which are most frequently cited to sanctify the superior position of men. The fact that the 1979 constitution, Nigeria's latest, protected the position of Sharia law in the Muslim regions of Nigeria is an added factor. Those who drafted the new constitution, though providing for equal rights for women in the constitution, never challenged the systematic sexual inequality inherent in Islamic law.

Examining the status of women in Kano, Callaway and Schildkroud observed that in the prevailing scheme of life women are defined as the minor wards of their fathers and husbands, they are induced to marry by the onset of puberty (the traditional age of marriage among the Muslim Hausa is between 11 and 12 years), to confine their activities to the domestic sphere of social relationships and functions, "and to observe postures of deference and service toward men."[47]

Education is one means by which Hausa women may be less inclined to marry by age 12, but, to counteract this influence, Muslim society has seen to it that fewer women end up in the university. In 1977 women formed 14 percent of the students at Bayero University in Kano. In 1982 the figure was down to 8 percent.[48]

Thus there is no guarantee that sexual inequality, even open discrimination against women, such as among the Hausa, will be successfully combatted through legal reform, whether constitutional or in statute law.

7. Case Study: Nigeria

Introduction

The position of women in Nigerian society is not easy to analyze. Many aspects of Nigerian society today still retain the effects of the colonial period. One of the residual effects is the existence of two systems of law in Nigeria—customary (tribal) law and the general (English) law. In considering the status of women in society one must understand that it may differ relative to the system of law governing the woman's given situation (i.e. marriage, divorce, employment, etc.).[1] Besides the existence of two systems of law, another aspect of Nigerian society today is the result of colonial rule. In pre-colonial tribal Nigeria, women were active in political, community, and economic matters. English rule considerably diminished that activity.

A number of West African traditional societies have political systems which can be described as "dual-sex." In these societies, the major interest groups are defined and represented by sex; each sex manages its own affairs and women's interests are represented at every level.[2] Pre-colonial Nigeria was such a dual-sex system. "Women have a very high status under customary law; and in the political field, women exerted great influence. The Aba Riots in Eastern Nigeria in 1929 showed the resentment of the women over the issue of taxes."[3] In 1929, Nigerian women were actually political activists on that issue! Things are different today.

In Nigerian society in general, women's lack of interest in political matters—or more accurately their invisibility in present-day politics—is a legacy of the colonial period.[4] With English rule came the sexist Victorian values which were to pervade all aspects of life. To understand the status of Nigerian women today, it is important first to understand their role in pre-colonial society and the changes wrought by colonial rule.

In the traditional Ibo society two local monarchs ruled—the male *obi* and the unrelated, female *omu*. Each of the monarchs had a cabinet of dignitaries and councillors. The *obi* ruled the men and the *omu* the women. According to Hafkin and Bay, "the dual nature of the system aimed at a harmonious and effective division of labor by which both sexes would receive adequate attention to their needs."[5] While the *omu* and the *obi* were unrelated, they worked both separately and together to provide effective rule for the whole of society.

The *omu* (and her cabinet) had various functions and responsibilities. One of her major functions was to oversee the community market, held every four days. The *omu* determined the rules and regulations of the market, including price-fixing and disciplining those who broke market rules. She handled family disputes when the family circle was incompetent to do so. And, when the *omu* could not handle a husband's complaint against his wife, she sought advice of the *obi* in council. The *omu* and her cabinet also served as representatives of the women in any important town gatherings and deliberations.[6] Thus, the women had representation parallel to that of the male members, not subservient.

Through the *omu* and the *ikporo ani,* women were represented in traditional Ibo society. While the duty of the *omu* was to represent all the women of her community, the *ikporo ani* was a representative body of women chosen from each section of the town or village. Sometimes representation was on the basis of lineage, but selection was always based on achievement; the representatives were those who had previously demonstrated logic and ability to "talk well."[7] With the advent of colonial rule in Nigeria, wrote Hafkin and Bay, women suffered a great loss of power. "Colonial rule in Nigeria in the first decade of this century marked the beginning of the end of equality of the sexes in village as well as in national politics."[8]

Where the dual-sex system existed, the British acknowledged only the male *obi;* no mention was made of the *omu* when the British instituted local government reforms in the 1930s. The *omu* lost her prestige as well as her clientele. Cases that had formerly been brought before her now went to the British-appointed colonial magistrate. The introduction of imported goods into the marketplace ruined her system of price-fixing. The system of title-taking over which she had presided was displaced as Christian converts took the new title of *mississi* (Mrs.) when they married in the church and achieved higher status in the new social order.[9]

Colonial rule in Nigeria took from women both their political representation and their economic regulatory powers. However, Nigeria's achievement of independence and the urbanization of areas of Nigeria have also affected the position of women today. Women have recently won voting rights, and urbanization has allowed women access to new educational and career opportunities. The mixture of tribal customs and English law makes for difficult analysis, but perhaps, eventually, a more progressive society with the best of both.

The Family

In Nigeria, there are three types of marriage: marriage according to customary law, marriage under Islamic law, and marriage under the marriage laws similar to the English type. We will concern ourselves here with customary law marriage and English (general) law marriage. Certain legal consequences arise according to whether the parties have contracted a polygamous[10] (customary law) marriage or monogamous (English law) marriage. If the parties contract monogamous marriage they are deemed to have agreed that their rights and duties in respect of the marriage shall be governed not by customary law, but by the English law. While the marriage lasts, neither party to a monogamous marriage can contract a polygamous marriage with a third party and vice versa.[11]

A contract to marry under English law is the legal obligation between a man and a woman to take each other as husband and wife, while in a betrothal under customary law the formal agreement is between the woman's family and the man's family. Under the customary law, a woman has no legal capacity to marry without her parents' consent, although in a Christian marriage adult females do not require parental consent.[12] Under the general (English) law, an infant of either sex requires parental consent to his or her Christian marriage in accordance with the provisions of §18 of the Marriage Act of the Federal Republic. Under customary law in the Eastern region, no person may now be betrothed or otherwise promised in marriage while below the age of 16.[13]

In a marriage under the customary law, bride price (or marriage consideration) is an essential part of the contract of marriage. Payment may be made in livestock, other goods, money, or services. It is variously interpreted as being primarily in the mode of (a) compensation to the woman's family for her loss; (b) formation of an alliance between the two kinship groups; (c) as a species of marriage insurance designed to stabilize the marriage, or (d) as a symbol marking the formal conclusion of the marriage contract.[14]

Once a betrothal has been effected, the woman loses her sexual freedom and is now required to have sexual relations with her husband-to-be. The woman is entitled to periodic gifts from her husband-to-be and if he falls short of her expectations, she has a right to break off the betrothal on the ground that he is mean. If the woman has sexual relations with another man, her husband-to-be has grounds for repudiation of the agreement and may recover any amounts he paid in consideration of the proposed marriage.[15]

At the termination of a betrothal within customary law, a breach of agreement action may be brought under customary law. In this type of action, there are no general damages. The only remedies are that the would-be husband can maintain an action for recovery of any betrothal payments or bride price paid, and either party can bring an action to recover any gifts made to the other party. There are no defenses to a claim, because the purpose of the action is not recovery of damages for wounded feelings or lost chances, but restitution of gifts or property transferred for a consideration that has failed.[16]

If the marriage was contracted under English law, a breach of promise action may be brought. The object of this type of action is to award damages to the innocent party as recompense for any mental injury (including ordinary wounded feelings) and for any social, material, or pecuniary loss arising as a direct consequence of the breach of contract, and to punish the guilty party.[17] Thus, the rights and remedies of the parties vary depending upon the type of marriage to which they had agreed.

Under strict customary law, Nigerian women are treated as respected and cherished members of society—mothers of the rising generation, counselors to their husbands behind the scenes, and above all, people who never quite lost their membership of their maiden families and could always count on active intervention from the latter in cases of dispute with their husbands.[18] However, the husband is the domestic authority or the head of the household,[19] and a woman must first obtain her husband's consent to any major transaction or enterprise she wishes to undertake.[20]

Rights of husband and wife in Nigeria include the following: the husband picks the matrimonial home subject to local custom; the husband has a claim to his wife's obedience and respect; a husband has the privilege of chastising the wife moderately; the husband is not obliged to consult the wife in domestic affairs (although he does so in a number of instances); in certain cases a husband may be liable for his wife's torts; the husband acquires exclusive sexual right over his wife (while the wife has no such claim on the husband where polyandry is permissible); and, the husband must maintain his wife (or wives) and children.[21]

A husband is under a legal obligation to provide his wife with the necessities of life according to his means and station in life. According to customary law, this includes food, clothing, medical attention, and also fees for membership of social and recreational societies.[22] Such a right may continue during a separation. The woman has the right to receive support during a pregnancy even if she is separated from her husband if he claims the child. The man must also pay maintenance during separation for a nursing baby.[23] Under the general law, this duty is *prima facie* complied with if he provides a home for his wife.[24]

Even in marriages in which no legal duty of cohabitation exists between spouses apart, there is the husband's legal obligation to provide his wife (or wives) with living accommodation commensurate with his means and station in life, having regard to the normal residential arrangements between spouses in the locality. (This is the rule under both systems of law, customary and English.) This also means that a wife is legally entitled to live in the matrimonial home for the duration of her status as a married woman.[25]

Desertion by a wife is a common feature of domestic life under customary law. A husband has no right or power to recover his deserting wife by force under customary law. A man is relieved of his duty to maintain his wife if she deserts him.[26] As regards Christian marriage spouses, the English law in Nigeria says that a husband has no right to compel his run-away wife by physical force to return to the matrimonial home. He does, however, have an action against her for restitution of conjugal rights.[27]

A husband cannot be guilty of rape as against his wife unless a separation agreement or judicial separation is in effect. However, a husband can be charged with common assault upon his wife, i.e., restraining her by force in order to enforce his right to her consortium.[28]

The consequences of divorce may be seen as the completion of a circle which began with the completion of a marriage contract or betrothal, the resemblance being to contract damages or restitution. The bride price paid by the husband to the wife's family may have to be refunded. If there are issues of the marriage, the amount to be refunded may be reduced. Certain gifts exchanged by the parties may have to be returned. Custody of the children is not categorically given to one parent or the other. Instead, custody may be given to either spouse with the child's welfare being the paramount consideration.[29] Under the general law, a woman may be entitled to alimony and other support payments per the Matrimonial Causes Act, 1965.[30] The same Act provides that in specific circumstances a wife may be required to make alimony payments to her husband (*viz.*, where the husband is insane, where the woman has committed adultery, or where the cause of action is for restitution of conjugal rights).[31]

Property

According to a Nigerian legal expert, S. N. Chinwuba Obi, there is an "air of mystery and confusion which surrounds the question whether or not women have legal capacity to acquire and own property under customary law."[32] Property which a woman acquired before her marriage remains in her separate and exclusive ownership under both customary and general law.[33] However, under the customary law, the mystery and confusion remains as to the question of a woman's ability to acquire and own land once she has married. Basden, researching in 1921, stated that "The only possessions that can really be labelled as the property of a wife are her waterpot, market basket and calabash, together with her cooking utensils, and all the vegetable called *koko (ede)*."[34] However, Obi submits that "a married woman has legal capacity to acquire, own, and dispose of property in her own right and in her own name under customary law."[35]

Studies of various tribes have revealed that women often acquire title to land by providing money for purchase, obtaining it by gift, or receiving a plot from one's husband on which to plant crops. A woman's *koko* yams and her money are her own property over which her husband has no rights or control; the profits from her trade are her own and she spends it mostly on her children, her personal needs, and in helping her own relatives.[36] Talbot[37] concludes that "Among all tribes, the wife's property is exclusively under her own control and can never be touched by her husband; she leaves it to whom she likes, usually to her daughters or sons, but sometimes to her own relatives."[38]

A woman's property rights under general law are governed by the Married Women's Property Act, 1983, which applies as a statute of general application and which has been re-enacted as the Married Women's Property Law, 1958, by the Western Regional parliament. Section 3 indicates that ". . . a married woman shall (a) be capable of acquiring, holding and disposing of any property . . . in all respects as if she were a *femme sole.*" Section 4(1) (b) provides that all property belonging to a married woman before marriage shall be hers as if she were a *femme sole,* and Section 6 provides that all stocks, deposits, annuities and the like which stand in a married woman's name shall be deemed to be her separate property.[39] When a married woman dies leaving children, her property goes to her eldest daughter, who should provide out of it for the younger daughters. When a married woman dies without issue, her property is inherited by her sister.[40]

Inheritance rights of women under customary law do not exist. Nowhere in Southern Nigeria does the customary law give a widow the right to inherit or to share in the intestate estate of her husband. Even where a husband during his life allots a farm, a house, or other form of landed property to his wife for her use and enjoyment, the woman does not thereby acquire inheritance rights in it.[41] However, she does have the legal right to retain the use and possession of the matrimonial home, whoever the new owner of the title may be and even if the matrimonial home is part of the family property. A widow is entitled to make use of as much of her late husband's farm land as she requires. She has this right, whether or not she has any children surviving, and for as long as she wishes to remain in residence among her late husband's people. The widow's rights supersede those of the legal heir, and the legal heir's right to possession is postponed until the widow remarries, dies, or leaves the family.[42]

Inheritance rights of a widow under the general law are more complex and vary from region to region. The law may require a widow to share her husband's intestate estate with her husband's immediate relations. In cases in which the estate exceeds a stated amount, certain portions of the estate may be held in trust for the widow. An intestate estate is distributed differently if there are surviving issue.[43]

Employment

Women produce nearly 80 percent of sub-Saharan Africa's food.[44] In Nigeria, almost all women both farm and trade in the marketplace.[45] The 1979 constitution (suspended twice during the '80s because of military takeovers) sets forth the policy governing employment, including that applicable to women.

Article 17, Section 3, provides that "the State shall direct its policy towards ensuring that . . . all citizens without discrimination on any ground whatsoever have the opportunity for securing adequate means of livelihood as well as adequate opportunities to secure suitable employment." The non-discrimination requirement of the provision provides for women the right to an adequate means of livelihood, but the term "suitable" may be seen as a loophole through which women may be restricted to particular types of employment. However, whatever disabilities this loophole does not create, surely the limited education available to women in Nigeria does. "In the professions, there is seldom any legal discrimination against women, but lack of educational opportunities has limited the number of them who could acquire professional qualifications."[46] The education available in urban areas is more advanced than that of the villages, but fear, tradition, and societal pressures may be disincentives to sending young women to urban areas to take advantage of the educational opportunities available there.[47]

The 1979 constitution also includes an "equal pay for equal work" provision which prohibits discrimination on the basis of sex: "The State shall direct its policy towards ensuring that . . . there is equal pay for equal work without discrimination on account of sex, or any other ground whatsoever . . ." (Constitution, Art. 17[3] [e] [1979]). Whereas women in other countries may be crying out for such constitutional protection, Nigerian women have (on paper) achieved this right. Once again, one must not make the assumption that women will automatically have the access to professional careers and the higher rate of pay accompanying those careers; many Nigerian women do not have the proper educational background to accede to these professions. However, this is significant protection for those women in professional fields in that they will be constitutionally guaranteed equal pay with their male counterparts.

Nigeria's constitution guarantees the protection of all workers' health, safety and welfare, without restricting employment opportunities for women on that basis. "The State shall direct its policy towards ensuring that . . . (c) the health, safety and welfare of all persons in employment are safeguarded and not endangered or abused . . ." (Constitution, Art. 17[3] [1979]). However, there are other provisions which may be seen as restricting opportunities because of the concern for health, safety and welfare. Such provisions prohibit women from engaging in night work and allow the imposition of other restrictive regulations. Labour Decree §54 (1974) states that no woman shall be employed on night work in a public or private industrial undertaking or in any agricultural undertaking. Some categories of women, mainly professionals and top management staff, are excluded from this prohibition. Labour Decree §56 (1974) empowers the Commissioner to make regulations restricting or prohibiting the employment of women in any particular type or types of industrial or other undertakings.

Thus, while women are constitutionally guaranteed the right to an adequate means of livelihood, the question must be "what is adequate?" And who is to determine what is "suitable" employment? While Nigerian women are in a better position by virtue of the "equal pay for equal work" provision, the primary objective must now be to ensure that Nigerian women have educational opportunities equal to those of their male counterparts so that they are qualified for employment in a wider range of fields. A further proviso is that the constitution actually be in place instead of being regularly suspended, sometimes for years, by every new military power.

Political Rights

Nigerian women have not yet fully recovered from the serious deprivation of political power and representation which resulted from the elimination of the *omu* during colonial rule. However, since Nigeria achieved independence in 1960, the institution of the *omu* has achieved some of its earlier importance. Today, the *omu* and her cabinet are involved in the building of improved market stalls, and the formation of weaving cooperatives. She has regained some of her responsibility from the government in that she fixes the prices of agricultural goods and handles minor cases in the market.[48] Hafkin and Bay point out that "since independence there has been a visible and deliberate move to resuscitate those roles that women traditionally played in public life. . . . Though women have been making progress on the village and community level in regaining much of the position they held in the pre-colonial dual-sex system, the national political level remains exclusively single sex. . . . Few women have been appointed to positions of importance by the military government in Nigeria."[49]

Although women have lost the personal representation and political power which they held through the institution of the *omu,* with the 1979 constitution, women gained a new and very important right—the right to vote.

The 1979 constitution says:

39.—(1) A citizen of Nigeria of a particular community, ethnic group, place of origin, sex, religion or political opinion shall not by reason only that he is such a person—(a) be subjected either expressly by, or in the practical application of, any law in force in Nigeria or any executive or administrative action of the government to disabilities or restrictions to which citizens of Nigeria or other communities, ethnic groups, places of origin, sex, religions, or political opinions are not made subject; or (b) be accorded either expressly by, or in the practical application of, any law in force in Nigeria or any such executive or administrative action, any privilege or advantage that is not accorded to citizens of Nigeria or other communities, ethnic groups, places of origin, sex, religions or political opinions.

The Nigerian constitutional expert Jadesola Akande comments that this is an important new development in women's rights because previous constitutions did not include the classification of sex as a forbidden distinction. Nonetheless, he is skeptical of the importance of this non-discrimination provision: "In present day Nigeria, women are still excluded from serving on the jury; they are regarded as chattels to be inherited by men under customary family law; they require their husband's permission to obtain a passport. However, they are now allowed to vote."[50] While we may say that women are "invisible in present-day politics,"[51] perhaps the impact of women's suffrage is merely yet to be seen.

Personal Autonomy

In Nigeria as elsewhere, the ability of a woman to acquire an abortion is a controversial matter. Women in Nigeria have no right of personal autonomy such that they may obtain an abortion in the case of an unwanted pregnancy. And, perhaps, as in the realm of political rights, this is a carry-over of the Victorian principles accompanying colonial rule and reflected in the remaining English law in Nigeria.

The model of abortion law which governs in Nigeria is reflective of English law; §58 of the Offences Against the Person Act, 1861, is applied as follows: "Every woman, being with child, who, with intent to procure her own miscarriage, shall unlawfully administer to herself any poison or other noxious thing, or shall unlawfully use any instrument or other means whatsoever with the like intent, and whosoever, with intent to procure the miscarriage of any woman, whether she be or be not with child shall unlawfully administer to her or cause to be taken by her any poison or other noxious thing, or shall unlawfully use any instrument or other means whatsoever with the like intent, shall be guilty of felony. . . ."[52]

The question of when such action was not unlawful was addressed in the 1938 case of *R.* v. *Bourne* (1939) 1 K. B. 687; (1983) 3 All E. R. 615, which concluded that abortion was lawful under §58 of the 1861 Act only when performed in good faith to preserve a woman's life or health, including mental health.[53] The West African Court of Appeal approved the *Bourne* decision and adopted the same approach in *R.* v. *Edgal, Idike and Ojogwu* (1938) 4 W.A.C.A. 133, an appeal from the Southern States, Nigeria.[54]

Thus, for Nigerian women, a right to personal autonomy (as generally understood in the Western world) in deciding whether to bear a child does not exist; that is, the doctor (determining risks to physical or mental health), not the woman, makes the decision. The results are tragic. The rate of population growth in Africa as a whole is higher than the world average; Africa contributes eight million to the world's population increase of over 60 million per year.[55] In urban areas of Nigeria, the crime of babies being killed or abandoned by their mothers at birth has been going on for the past 30 years.[56] Women in urban areas often have neither the resources nor the inclination to start families. Raising a child is often thought of as a threat to the potential career of a woman or a burden on the education of young girls sent to the cities for that purpose. The alternatives available to Nigerian women today seem to be two—either an illegal abortion, or desertion of the child at birth.

Recently, there has been heavy migration from the villages to urban areas, with a larger migration by men than women. Women make the change either to seek educational opportunities unavailable in their villages or to become members of the working force. The inequality of numbers places a special premium on females' domestic and sexual services. Women and men form working arrangements whereby the woman provides a sexual outlet for the man and the man satisfies the financial needs of the woman: clothes, residence, food, etc. In the event of pregnancy, the man is expected to pay for the performance of an illegal abortion. Women do not become pregnant with the hope of establishing a more permanent relationship with the man. Women are reluctant to exchange their freedom for formal marriage—the woman's price as a mistress is much higher than it would be as a housewife.[57] Because abortions are not legal, women who are unable to obtain illegal abortions or for whom the procedure is ineffective make the decision either to kill or abandon the infants at birth. A woman does this to prevent any unwelcome interference with her life and aspirations.

A dilemma which Nigerian women faced in the past but which has lessened today concerns the right to marry a partner of her choosing. In traditional customary law society, infant betrothal was the norm. Today, while infant betrothal is still lawful in some societies, betrothal in the vast majority of cases is done with the active cooperation of the prospective spouses.[58] However, under customary law, a woman has no legal capacity to marry without her parents' consent, although under the general (English) law, only an infant (male as well as female) requires parental consent;[59] the general law being the Marriage Act of the Federal Republic, §18.

Beyond the requirement under customary law of parental consent to marriage, there is the idea that "[Women] are regarded as chattels to be inherited by men under customary family law."[60] Such a thing can still happen in Nigeria today under the customary law. The practice is called "widow inheritance." Obi points out that where an affianced man has made bride price payments to his fiancee's family, and then dies, "another member of his family has a right, if otherwise acceptable, to step into his shoes and carry on from where the deceased left off, any payments made so far being credited to the new suitor's account."[61] The girl's family may have already spent the payments and she might marry the man in order that her family not have to raise the amount to be refunded. It is also widely held that in the traditional society, "a woman was inherited as a form of property by her husband's sons or heirs, with the one exception that no son could inherit his own mother."[62]

On her husband's death, a woman must choose between two major courses of action—she may leave her husband's family or remain. She must go out on her own or back to her maiden family, or remain with her husband's family either by marrying one of the members chosen by local rule and mutual agreement or remaining on her own and raising children to her husband's name wherever possible.[63] If she chooses to remain with her husband's family, the woman is essentially property which her late husband's family has inherited. Either she becomes an asset as a wife to one of the other family members or she produces or raises children to the name of her late husband, and thus, his family.

8. Case Study: Kenya

Introduction

A careful undertaking to ascertain the status of women in Kenya must necessarily begin with an introduction to the several systems of law co-existent in Kenya today and their effect on the status of women. Kenya, like other former British colonial possessions, has several different systems of laws regulating various aspects of life. Dependent upon the aspect of life at issue (marriage, divorce, etc.), the applicable law may differ. There exist today four different legal systems governing the lives of men and women in Kenya. The multiplicity and overlap of the four different legal systems complicate the task of ascertaining the precise status of women in Kenya.

The systems of law existing in Kenya today are as follows: first, there is the imported law which Kenya inherited as an English colony—such is statutory law; second is the customary (tribal) law which regulates the lives of the various ethnic groups where no legislation has altered or displaced such; and finally, there are the religious laws, primarily Hindu and Islamic.[1] Often the customary or religious laws have been eliminated in attempts to make the law on a particular subject uniform, as in the areas of devolution of property. But the uniformity may apply only to restricted elements of such areas of law, leaving particular topics to the prior law of the different ethnic groups.

A further difficulty in analyzing the situation for women in Kenya today lies in separating the Kenyan cultural traits from those left from the colonial period. As discussed below, many areas regulated by laws "left-over" from the colonial period necessarily reflect the Victorian values of the England of that time. Though Kenya achieved independence in 1963, the Kenyan laws reflective of English legislation remain very much intact in areas such as marriage, divorce, abortion, and employment.

The primary consideration of this case study is an overview of the legal and social status of women in Kenya. Rather than a complete study of every law of every ethnic group, the author will try to give the reader a general understanding of the four major systems of laws in Kenya today in the following areas: marriage, divorce, child custody, property ownership, inheritance rights, employment, political rights, and personal autonomy.

Family

Within marriage, the woman is the humble party—the marriage has been arranged by, and continues to be, a relationship between the families of the man and woman.[2] In support of this contention, one need only look to the practices of *levirate* and *sororate.* Under levirate, the woman may be inherited by her husband's brother.[3] Or, in the event of the earlier death of the woman, her family may give up her sister in the practice of sororate. Another possibility is the custom of "ghost marriage" in which the woman who lost her original husband marries a kinsman of the deceased who would then produce children who are legally the children of the deceased although biologically children of the living kinsman.[4]

One further example of how a marriage is really a relationship between two families is the continued parental control; the parties having been joined through the negotiations of two families cannot separate without the concurrence of the families.[5]

There are two marriage systems legally recognized in Kenya: polygamous[6] and monogamous. Marriages contracted under statutory law (Marriage Act, Christian Marriage and Divorce Act, Hindu Marriage and Divorce Act) are monogamous. Under the Penal Code, it is an offense to contract for another marriage when one is still existent. However, under Islamic and customary law, polygamy is not a crime.[7]

Under the Marriage Act, both men and women must be 18 years of age before they may legally marry. Hindu law requires that the male be at least 18 and the female 16, with the additional requirement that a female between the ages of 16 and 18 acquire the consent of her guardian or the High Court. Further, each party to a marriage must give free consent to such marriage, the lack of which nullifies a monogamous marriage under the Matrimonial Causes Act.[8]

As a result of the colonial period, Kenyan law embodies the English common law notion that women were chattel and had no proprietary capacity. However, a paradox is that such notions afford women "agency of necessity" and "presumed agency." "Agency of necessity" legally empowers a married woman to pledge her husband's credit for the necessities of life commensurate with their normal standard of living. Any married woman automatically possesses this power whenever she is separated from her husband prior to the issuance of a court order for maintenance.[9] "Presumed agency" vests in a woman upon cohabitation (whether legally married or a mistress) the power to bind her husband or lover to a contract for necessities which are commensurate with their current household standards.[10]

During the duration of a marriage, the woman has the right to be maintained or provided with necessities by her husband. Where the husband fails to discharge his duty, the wife has an automatic right to sue for separation and a maintenance order, which includes a provision of a home as a necessity of life. The husband may be prosecuted under Penal Code, Chapter 63 §239, for failure to provide maintenance, and may be imprisoned for a maximum of three years.[11]

In Kenya, the law of divorce is as pluralistic as the law of marriage. Each system of marriage tends to be governed by its own law. Only the High Court can dissolve a monogamous marriage. Section 3 of the Matrimonial Causes Act reads: "subject to the provisions of the African Christian Marriage and

Divorce Act, jurisdiction under this Act shall only be exercised by the High Court . . . and such jurisdiction shall, subject to the provisions of this Act, be exercised in accordance with the law applied in matrimonial proceedings in the High Court of Justice in England."[12] Women, however, are given the exclusive right to seek judicial separation and maintenance in a speedier, less expensive manner in Magistrates' Courts and under the Subordinate Courts (Separation and Maintenance) Act.[13]

The following grounds for separation are available only to women: her husband is a habitual drunkard or drug-taker; he has contracted venereal disease; he has subjected her to prostitution; he has been convicted of a crime under the Penal Code for having caused her bodily harm by causing her to take noxious substances, by unlawfully wounding her, or by assaulting her; or, he has failed to provide the necessities of life to her or her children.[14]

A woman may, in the alternative, petition under the Matrimonial Causes Act where her husband is found guilty of rape, sodomy,or bestiality. Note, however, that none of these grounds is available to a husband if his wife is so convicted.[15]

Polygamous marriages based on Islamic law can be unilaterally repudiated by the husband merely by saying three *talkas* ("I divorce thee, I divorce thee, I divorce thee"). But the wife lacks this power.[16] Polygamous marriages based on customary law cannot be unilaterally terminated and provisions for divorce are not discriminatory. Because the marriage was negotiated between the families, though, divorce is normally a matter for families and clan elders to work out.[17]

In the case of a marriage under customary law, a woman is not normally entitled to maintenance upon divorce or separation. Islamic law provides maintenance for the woman upon divorce or separation, but only for the duration of three months. Statutory law[18] indicates that the court may order support payments from husband to wife, but no provision is made allowing the court to order payments from wife to husband.[19]

Custody and guardianship are governed by the Guardianship of Infants Act, which applies to all unmarried minors below age of 18.[20] The Act treats the mother and father as equals concerning the question of custody. Furthermore, the welfare of the child is to be given paramount consideration. Thus, neither parent will be given custody if neither is fit. In practice, however, courts have established a policy (in accord with customary and Islamic practice) of granting care of children of tender years to the mother, unless she is clearly unfit. To the contrary, though, some judges follow the traditional notion of the father as "owner" of a child unless he has repudiated the child.[21]

Property

Section 82 of the Kenya constitution of 1969 prohibits discriminatory legislation. However, the effectiveness of this provision as a protection of women's rights is illusory for two reasons. First, "discriminatory" distinctions include only "race, tribe, place of origin or residence or other local connection, political opinions, colour or creed."[22] Second, this prohibition of discriminatory legislation does not apply to laws made with respect to adoption, marriage, divorce, devolution of property, death, or other matters of personal law.[23] As a result of the limited application of this prohibition, discrimination against women is constitutional in laws respecting adoption, marriage, divorce, burial, or devolution of property upon death.[24] As such, many existing or newly established tribal, religious and common laws and practices discriminating against women *qua* women are legal in Kenya.[25]

As to ability to own property, Kenyan women have been protected since 1970 by the 1897 British version of the Married Women's Property Act. Under §12, the Act provides full proprietary capacity to married women. Under the Act a married woman is to be considered a *femme sole* in matters affecting her property and is *sui juris,* meaning that she has the capacity to sue in order to protect the property she possesses. However, she can maintain actions only against those other than her husband.[26] Another important law in this area is the Law of Succession Act (1972)of which §5(2) provides that "any female person, whether married or unmarried, has the same capacity to make a will as does a male person."[27] The total effect of these laws is that a single woman can own property and a married woman is to be considered as a single woman in matters affecting her property; single and married women both have the capacity to make wills to dispose of the property they own.

The law on succession rights of women *vis à vis* their husband's property is a bit more complicated. The Law of Succession Act which was enacted in 1972 was to make uniform all laws in succession, but excludes specific items from its coverage. Section 32 excludes agricultural land and crops thereon, and livestock, situated in such areas as the Attorney-General may by notice in the gazette specify. Section 33 states that those items listed in §32 shall be governed by the "law or custom applicable to the deceased's community, tribe, religion or sect as the case may be."[28] Thus, agricultural land and crops and some livestock are subject to laws of succession from the four systems of family law—customary, Islamic, Hindu and statutory.[29]

Under customary law, only sons can inherit property. Wives and unmarried daughters have only a maintenance right; married daughters do not even have such a right to maintenance, since such is the responsibility of their respective husbands. A widow's right to maintenance is lost once she enters into a levirate union (that is, if she marries a relative of her husband) or returns to her family.[30]

Islamic law provides that a widow receive one-eighth of her husband's property if she has children. If she is childless, she will receive a larger portion—one-fourth. Again, "property" refers only to agricultural land or livestock; other types of property are governed by the Law of Succession Act of 1972. Daughters receive only one-half the amount a son obtains through inheritance.[31]

Under Hindu law a widow has rights only to maintenance and, in some cases, a life interest. Thus, Hindu women inherit no property of their husbands.

Statutory law in the form of the Law of Succession Act makes provision for the devolution of all property other than agricultural land and livestock. Section 11 gives a woman security of tenure in the matrimonial home and the right to benefit from the husband's assets, but only if he lists such in an insurance policy as for the benefit of his wife or children. Once the policy has been executed, no outsider can claim against such property if the right claimed arises after the execution. Thus, if the assets have not been named as for the benefit of the woman, she may be evicted by third-party creditors upon her husband's death, regardless of her contribution to the marital assets.[32]

Statutory law places the widow on the same footing as children in terms of inheritance—both are treated as "dependents." Where the intestate has no children, the Act provides certain minimum protections to the widow—she is entitled to all personal and household possessions of the intestate; she is given a certain monetary amount from the estate; and she is given a life interest in the remainder.[33]

Although customary law relating to succession and inheritance discriminates heavily against women in favor of male children, the Law of Succession Act of 1972 has started a trend which in time will lead to the ultimate eradication of such traditional practices in the law of succession. Clearly, the Law of Succession Act has taken significant steps to achieve equality for women in this area of the law. In fact, the Act has provided for more "equal" treatment than the Kenyan constitution. However, the provisions exempting agricultural land and livestock from the Act indicate that women may end up as a landless class.[34]

Employment

Kenya has no constitutional provision relating to the right to work, freedom to choose one's occupation, etc. In particular, Kenya has no constitutional provision concerning economic rights and employment opportunities for women. There exists protective legislation which prohibits women, with some exceptions, from working during certain hours. Although this may be viewed as protective legislation for women, it may also be seen as limiting employment opportunities open to women. The Employment Act, no. 2/1976, §7 (1976), states that no woman (or juvenile) can be employed in any industrial capacity between the hours of 6:30 P.M. and 6:30 A.M. There are several exceptions to this rule. Section 7(1) provides that women or young men may be employed in cases of unforeseen emergencies which interfere with normal undertakings and which are not of a recurring nature. Women may also be employed where they work with raw materials which are subject to rapid deterioration if their work is necessary for the preservation of the materials from certain loss. Another exception to the prohibition applies to women who hold responsible positions of a managerial or technical nature or who are employed in the medical or paramedical professions. Women are generally prohibited from working in mines at any times, with exceptions for those who are supervisors and those who perform medical duties.[35]

The year 1976 brought significant legislation which entitles working mothers to two months' paid maternity leave. However, such leave comes at the expense of the woman's annual leave for the given year.[36] That many mothers do work and that there is a need for such legislation might be evidenced by the fact that as of 1975 there were 5,000 day care centers in Kenya—certainly more exist today.

The humble status of women *vis à vis* men, as well as demographics, prevents women from acquiring the education needed to attain and hold the elite managerial or technical jobs available in a growing industrial society. Kenyan women have limited employment opportunities because of cultural norms and demographics. Most Kenyan women reside in rural regions and lack the educational advantages enjoyed by their male counterparts. Generally, women remain under the authority of their fathers or husbands. Although urbanization has wrought radical changes in the status of a fraction of women, it has had little impact on the vast majority of Kenyan women.[37]

Political Rights

Although on several occasions, the women of Kenya have sprung into political activity,[38] it would seem that more than an actual political presence in Kenya, women are only potential political participants. One factor contributing to this phenomenon is that, for various reasons, women in Kenya do not play an active role in government although they do have the right to vote. Another example of this "potentiality" phenomenon is the activity of Muslim women in *lelemama* in the past (see below) and the failure to utilize the associations which grew out of *lelemama* to achieve political status for women today.

Much of the political activity of Muslim women resulted from cultural differences and the discrimination against Muslim women as compared to Asian, African, and European women.[39] Kenya's coastal Muslim women entered into politics in 1958. During the struggle for coastal autonomy in the late 1950s, 100 Arab women from Mombasa successfully petitioned the colonial government in Kenya to protest discriminatory legislation that denied them the vote but gave it to women of other ethnic communities. Having succeeded with their petition for women's suffrage, the women began a registration campaign that lasted a full year and involved house-to-house visits by Arab women to explain to their neighbors what voting was and why Arab women should vote just like Asian, African, and European women.[40]

Although political activity like the 1958 suffrage campaign has been infrequent, both dance associations and later organizations have mobilized women in pursuit of goals important to the Muslim community. In the 1930s and 1940s dance associations provided entertainment and the mechanism for women to achieve high status; later groups directed their attention to social welfare and education. From the dance associations (Ibinaal Watan and Banu Saada) women learned organizational and leadership experience, and they brought those skills when they joined the Muslim Women's Institution or the Cultural Association.[41]

There have existed over 40 women's associations devoted to dancing *lelemama,* a style brought from Zanzibar to Mombasa at the end of the nineteenth century.[42] The women of the associations worked together to make costumes and to perfect their routines in time for competitions. Dancing sedately, dancers sang only favorites or newly composed songs that revealed the misdeeds of people in the community, publicly shamed individuals, or challenged rival *lelemama* associations by ridiculing their dancing abilities. Associations usually formed competing pairs, and success was measured according to dancing ability and the originality of the songs. Success lay also in the size of the audience and the lavishness of picnics and officers' installations.[43] The extravagances and the sizes of the audiences attending were indications of the prestige of the association "putting on" the *ngoma* (dance).

A primary purpose of *lelemama* was the acquisition of prestige by the women involved. Although participation brought prestige, not all dance associations were equally prestigious. In all associations, however, the leader had to be able to afford an elaborate investiture ceremony.[44] There were two sets of titles which could be held simultaneously and for life, one reflecting Arab social concepts, and the second reflecting British colonial influence. To receive either type of title, one had to spend lavishly.[45] Also, any member who paid the customary fee could demand *heshima* ("rank," "honor," "respect") from the entire community as well as from the association members. According to Strobel, this was one way in which a woman of slave descent might mitigate the stigma of her ancestry. "The *lelemama* ranks offered prestige to women who had few other sources of dignity and honor."[46]

Because of the competition between rival groups, women looked for security and solidarity within their respective dance associations. The women helped each other by contributing money and preparing foods for expensive affairs such as weddings and funerals. In return, by custom, the recipient was to reciprocate with double the gift when the gift-giver needed.[47]

It is obvious that the *lelemama,* or dance associations, did not begin as political associations and did not operate as such. However, the effects of the associations were, in fact, sometimes political—social control, acquisition of organizational skills, expression of rebellion, and promotion of change through competition.[48]

Moreover, the demise of the dance associations served as something of a catalyst for the formation of two current Muslim women's associations—the Muslim Women's Cultural Association and the Muslim Women's Institute.[49] These two groups were to become the new focus for the energies of the women and today have the potential to foster more significant political activity and involvement for the Muslim women of Kenya.

Competition for prestige within the colonial framework was the immediate cause of the formation of both the Arab Women's Institute and the Arab Women's Cultural Association. The impetus for the establishment of a formal women's group came with the announcement in 1956 that Princess Margaret should receive dignitaries on behalf of Mombasa's Arab women.[50] Thus, the initial motivation for the formation of these women's associations was not political, however, the activities of the groups may be seen as contributing to the potential political power of women through education.

The best indication of the gradually, but constantly, growing concern about the position of women among Mombasa's Muslims in general, and among its Muslim women in particular, lies in enrollment figures for the government's Arab Girls' School. Upon establishment in 1938 the school had 14 students; and, after a decade, enrollment stood at 168. But, by 1955, the school had 500 students. Thus, without abstract discussions of sexual equality, women and men were working to erase a basic educational imbalance in Muslim society.[51] The hope is that a better educated population of women will exploit the potential of the Muslim women's associations to become women's rights activists or at the very least, political participants.

Today, both associations serve the needs of women in particular and of society in general. The Muslim Women's Institute has, at different times, offered classes in adult education, religion, child care, and sewing. Beyond the commitment to raising the educational level of Muslim women, the organization has also supported community projects, aid to mosques, religious classes for children, fund-raising for the Coast Institute of Technology, and scholarships for students pursuing university studies abroad. The Muslim Women's Cultural Association at first offered courses in child care, hygiene, reading and writing, religion, sewing, and embroidery, but then concentrated on building and running a private nursery school now called Mbaraki Nursery School.[52]

In her extensive study of *lelemama* and the women's associations of today, Strobel praises the work undertaken and completed by the Muslim women's associations. However, she criticizes the associations for their lack of political activity. In an area of particular importance to Muslim women, the association failed to lobby for or against the passage of any of the bills revising the laws of marriage, divorce or succession which were before the Kenya National Assembly. Because the *Qur'an* addresses the issue of succession, one might understand the women's failure to address the issues of women's property rights and succession on religious grounds. However, there are no such orthodox religious objections (based on Qur'anic injunction) to changing divorce laws. Male religious leaders have supported a bill expanding a Muslim woman's grounds for divorce, but the women's organizations did not rally to the cause.[53]

Strobel feels that an explanation for the lack of political activity by the Muslim women's organizations is the underlying philosophy of the two organizations. Both groups have developed as self-help and community-oriented, rather than as feminist, organizations; and, "until their priorities are rearranged, they will remain organizations *of,* rather than specifically *for,* women."[54]

Besides Muslim women, other women in Kenya also remain potential rather than actual elements of the political (governmental) structure of Kenya. Although every person over the age of 18 has the right to vote, this does not necessarily mean political equality for women. Because of population demographics and an educational disadvantage, few women occupy important official positions in Kenya's government.[55] One would hope that urbanization and the passage of time will provide expanding educational opportunities for women and a growing desire by Kenyan women to become more politically active.

Personal Autonomy

A woman in Kenya is restricted in her personal autonomy by the inability to obtain an abortion legally, except in certain limited circumstances. This prohibition probably stems from the pro-natalist sentiment of customary law in Kenya as well as the influence of laws enacted in Victorian England while Kenya was an English colony. Another restriction on a woman's personal autonomy is the traditional notion concerning the chastity of women, and the common practice of female circumcision in conjunction with such notions.

That the customary law of Kenya is pro-natalist is evident from the practice of polygamy, the involvement of the parties' families in the arrangement of marriages, and the payment of marriage consideration.[56] The pro-natalist ideology is prevalent in many agrarian societies—there are the common beliefs that more children mean more wealth, a source of labor on the farm, and a future old age insurance; and, that the man who has many children is wealthy, powerful, and the head of a strong lineage whose future is assured. High infant mortality rates also help perpetuate the myth that more children mean more wealth—families desire high numbers of children as insurance against the possibility of some dying before maturity. However, the pro-natalist ideology seems to be modified with a shift from an agrarian to an industrial economy,[57] and with the decreased infant mortality rate which will, hopefully, accompany a more industrialized society.

The pro-natalist trend does not necessarily mean there is no family planning. Intercourse is traditionally abstained from during breast feeding, which can last up to two years,[58] and there is no law in Kenya which prohibits the use of artificial or other contraceptive methods.[59] Today, with a population of 21 million and a record-high growth rate of 4.2 percent, the government's objective of decreasing the rate of population growth may be beneficial to women. The desired number of children has dropped by one—from 7.2 to 6.1—and the number of married women using contraceptives has increased since 1978 from 7 to 17 percent.[60] However, the present level of contraceptive use is very low and will not contribute significantly to a decrease in population growth rate. Any substantial change must come from increased use of the family planning devices available to the men and women of Kenya.

Voluntary family planning clinics were established in Nairobi and Mombasa in 1952, after the 1948 census revealed a high rate of population growth.[61] As a result, Kenya has the oldest government-sponsored family planning program in the sub-Sahara region, backed by international aid and a network of 650 clinics. Despite these programs, growth will continue because of several factors—bureaucracy, shortages of supplies and trained personnel, inconvenient hours and locations of the clinics in rural areas, and most importantly, the attitude of the people. The Women's International Network News reports that Kenyans want large families.[62] It might be more correct to state that Kenyan males want large families.

Besides the pro-natalist sentiment of the Kenyan people, legislation prohibiting abortion also seems in direct conflict with government objectives of reducing population growth. Section 158 of the Penal Code makes it an offense for any person, acting with intent to procure the miscarriage of a woman whether she is or is not with child, to unlawfully administer to her or cause her to take any poison or other noxious thing, or use any force of any kind, or use any other means whatever. Section 159 covers cases where a woman takes steps with intent to procure her own abortion, while Section 160 deals with suppliers of abortifacients. Section 228 goes one step further in that it creates the offense of child-killing which is made a felony and punishable with life imprisonment. Section 240, however, permits the lawful interruption of pregnancy where the operation is performed in good faith to save the life of the pregnant woman.[63]

In spite of the statutory position on abortion there is still a rather limited judicial recognition of abortion in Kenya based entirely on the practice in England before the passage of the Abortion Act, 1967 (England). The position itself was reached through the case *R.* v. *Bourne* (1939) 1 K.B. 687; (1983) 3 All E. R. 615, which was decided under Section 58 of the Offences Against the Person Act, 1861 (England). The decision stated that a surgeon need not wait until the patient was in peril of imminent death before performing an abortion if, on reasonable grounds and with adequate knowledge, he was of the opinion that the continuance of the pregnancy would probably be harmful to the patient's physical and mental health.[64] Consistent with Kenya's adoption of the English judicial doctrine, the approach toward abortion in Kenya is that of English practice before 1967; two medical opinions must be obtained—one from the general practitioner who has treated the pregnant woman and a second from a psychiatrist. When the two opinions and the consent of the woman (as well as the consent of the husband of married patients) were obtained, then a gynecologist could perform the operation in a hospital.[65]

A further obstacle to the personal autonomy of Kenyan women is the still-prevalent practice of female circumcision. This may be the result of the widely held traditional notion that a woman who has free sexual relationships is "loose," and thus, that a good woman is one who is chaste, one who has retained her virginity until marriage. Such belief may also be a side-effect of colonial rule, but whatever the source, it has been met internationally with the opposition of various human rights groups, women's rights organizations, and other organizations such as the United Nations.

Surgical destruction of female genital organs is largely practiced in black African countries south of the Sahara where women are much more economically active, especially in agricultural work. This practice of excision is prevalent in Kenya, where it was long supported by President Jomo Kenyatta.[66] Today, authorities in Kenya have begun to speak out against the practice; "while it is true that this is a long standing practice in many communities . . . the health authorities do not support the practice for many reasons although it is a very difficult practice to have done away with."[67] The current President, Daniel Arap Moi, has also come out in support of abandonment of this cruel practice.[68] History indicates that most of this opposition to female circumcision is mere talk, window dressing for the benefit of other countries and the United Nations. The very nature of the act should fill any educated Kenyan with revulsion.

Female circumcision is a form of genital mutilation used to ensure chastity in which the primary source of female eroticism, the clitoris, is surgically removed by a midwife, priest, or doctor. According to Kathleen Barry, the ritual usually is performed on girls between the ages of 7 and 13, and may lead to psychological as well as physical injury. In many cases, the young girls develop fear of adult members of society and often suffer severe physical trauma as well. The operation causes urinary infections, kidney damage leading to high blood pressure and renal failure or cardiovascular accident. Another effect of the procedure is dyspareunia (pain during intercourse because of remaining scar tissue), and the woman must be opened for sexual intercourse and childbirth after marriage. Obstruction during labor leads to severe bleeding, and babies may be stillborn because of the difficult passage during delivery. Thus, not only does the girl suffer the pain of the surgery, but most often, as a woman, she continues to suffer excessive pain during sexual intercourse. An unpleasant paradox is that the male's pleasurable sensations are increased by virtue of the same surgical procedure which causes the woman such physical and mental trauma.[69]

9. Case Study: South Africa

The situation of women in South Africa calls for special examination. Although South Africa, which became indepedent in 1926, is geographically part of Africa with a black population exceeding 25 million, it also has a white population of nearly five million. Many of those whites, whose forebears landed in 1652, look upon themselves, with considerable geographic and historic justification, as a permanent part of Africa,[1] its only white tribe. The country's legal structure is that of a Western nation. More British than almost any other state in Africa, and with its Dutch roots expressed in criminal law which is largely Roman-Dutch, South Africa nonetheless also provides for customary, tribal (traditional) or so-called Bantu Law. Even the economy is marked by duality. Part of the economic structure is Western (South Africa is one of the 26 industrialized nations of the world) and part is a typical African subsistence economy.[2]

Because of three centuries of cultural, educational, social and residential segregation from the black community, most white women in South Africa find themselves in a Western society, with Western norms no different from those of most other Western states, which include discrimination against women. The average white female office worker in Johannesburg faces problems of discrimination no different from those of the average female office worker in the United States or Australia.

Black women, on the other hand, are much worse off, first of all because they are black and therefore have less political freedom, fewer economic opportunities and greater social obstacles to overcome; second, because they are black women, victims of a family and tribal structure which relegates them to an inferior position, subservient to the husband or family; and, third, because they are women. (Much the same can be said of Asian women in South Africa and, to a lesser extent, colored women, women of mixed racial descent.) Despite these handicaps, the facts show that except for the right to vote, a right no longer denied to Asian, Indian, or colored women—only to blacks—these women are better off than women in any other state in Africa in terms of education, particularly university and technical education, in freedom to elect the subjects they wish to study, in job seeking, in employment in general (employment for black women in South Africa has increased rapidly as opposed to a decline elsewhere in Africa), in professional occupations such as medicine, management and teaching, in business organizations and business undertakings, in income, in terms of equal salaries, in terms of mobility and land and home ownership.

The laws protecting white and black women from discrimination in South

Africa, particularly the Labor Relations Amendment Act, the Marriage and Matrimonial Property Law Amendment Act, are different from others in Africa because they have teeth for enforcement, and the availability of legal counsel to women is such that the road to the courthouse is no longer the 100-mile walk it used to be.

Unlike the rest of Africa, black women's presence in business in general is now taken for granted, and there are a host of examples of black women who have made it to the top in business, in the academic world, in medicine, in television, in entertainment, public relations, advertising, and the law. Black women are being nominated now in leading newspapers as business-women-of-the-year. There is no shortage of female, black role models in South Africa.[3] Where black women in South Africa find themselves in the same boat as their sisters elsewhere in Africa is in the number of children they must bear, often against their will, and in the status of women in rural areas. It is the latter who suffer great deprivations.[4]

Statistical Profile of Working Women

During the period 1965 to 1985 the number of women in employment increased by 113 percent compared to 49 percent for men. Women in 1985 formed 34.3 percent of all workers in the country, a higher figure than Western Europe and the Far East, or any other world region outside the Communist East Bloc and the United States. (See Chapter 3, Table 5.) Therefore more than one in every three white adults in urban areas in employment now is a woman. With part-time workers included, four out of every ten workers is female, according to Market Research Africa's Employment Index.[5] Altogether, 49 percent of all women between the ages of 16 and 56 are employed outside the home. Nearly two-thirds of all working women are married, and some 45 percent of women in the work force have children at home. The stereotyped, traditional housewife at home accounts for only 23 percent of all women.[6]

Graduate women in South Africa have made the most significant inroads in the labor market, and during 1985 some 60 percent of all white women, 74 percent of all Asian and 82 percent of all colored women with university degrees were economically active.[7] One by one, barriers to women in higher education have fallen by the wayside. In 1988 the University of Pretoria announced that, as of 1989 women will have an equal opportunity to enter the faculties of medicine, dentistry and veterinary science. Until then, women were subject to a quota system limiting them to 25 percent of the total enrollment in these faculties.[8]

The profile of working women in South Africa is remarkably similar to that of their counterparts in the United States in that the feminization of certain professions has increased while the market segregation, in terms of occupation, has remained basically similar to the segregation which existed 20 years ago. At the same time wage differentiation has not narrowed in any significant way.

The Extent of Discrimination Against Women

In a speech to schools in East London, Margaret Lessing, Director of the Women's Bureau, listed the following points:

• women are not given the same opportunities for in-service training as men;

• in certain fields of study like dentistry, medicine and veterinary science, the number of women students is limited, with the result that women must obtain higher marks than men to be accepted into these professions (a limitation the University of Pretoria removed in 1989);

• in many cases of medical aid benefits, including state and state-supported medical aid schemes, the female member of a scheme is not entitled to maternity benefits;

• women are denied equal salary for the same work;

• women are denied fringe benefits such as housing and study benefits, which their male counterparts automatically receive;

• women advocates admitted to the bar of the Supreme Court on similar terms and qualifications as male advocates do not obtain briefings from male attorneys, who elect to go to their male counterparts;

• women doctors are refused permission to specialize part time even when the majority of doctors in lowly government-paid posts are women doctors;

• when the position of headmaster of a high school becomes vacant, women can apply, but men receive preference.[9]

To Margaret Lessing's list can be added the fact that women are hopelessly under-represented in parliament; that the country has never had a woman in the cabinet since its founding in 1910; that professional women earn, on average, one-quarter less than men for doing the same work; that in education and vocational preparation girls still end up largely in stereotyped positions; and that men are so favored in general administration that the Director General of Manpower personally concedes that many men in senior administrative and executive positions did not get there on grounds of proficiency or talent, but because they were male.[10] At the 1984 National Convention of Women in Johannesburg, Professor J. D. van der Vyver of the School of Law at Witwatersrand University said a recent inquiry of the Women's Legal Status Committee into the composition of 40 statutory administrative bodies in South Africa showed blatant discrimination against women by the male-dominated bureaucracy. Thirty-four statutory bodies, including some of the most important administrative organs of the executive branch of government, were made up of males only.[11]

This chapter will examine discrimination against women subject by subject and also pinpoint the problems and the underlying reasons for this discrimination.

Wage Discrimination

There are still enormous disparities in wages being paid for men and women doing equal work. The concept of equal pay for work of comparable worth is as alien to commerce, industry, politics and the civil service as the idea that a woman could one day become head of state. The operating theater nurses in the famous Groote Schuur cardiac unit will find that the same businessman whose heart is saved with their skill and input will later cheerfully pay a male insurance clerk in his company a higher salary than any of the nursing team.

Except for the United States, no other industrially developed country exhibits worse discriminatory trends between male and female workers than the Republic of South Africa. Should a law have been proposed in South Africa in 1981 mandating equal pay for equal work for teachers, irrespective of sex, the average woman teacher would have had to receive a pay increase of some 25 percent. If a law were passed mandating equal pay for equal work for university graduates, the average female graduate in the workplace would be paid 26 percent more.[12]

It is interesting to note that the differences in wages, income, employment figures and unemployment between black and white females in South Africa reveal a pattern not much different from that found in the United States. In 1986 in the state of Georgia white people had an unemployment rate of 3.6 percent against 11.7 percent for blacks. Among women the rate of unemployment was 4.2 percent for whites and 15 percent for blacks.[13]

The wage gap between men and women doing the same work is far from being solved in South Africa, largely because of a piecemeal approach. In 1986 the government announced that it was to introduce pay parity for nurses of all races as well as for people in complementary careers in the field of health.[14] There is some difference of opinion as to how the elimination of discrimination in other occupations should be tackled even though the concept of comparable worth has proven that it has merit.[15] There have been other positive developments. In July 1987 the government announced that women in education posts from certain levels would be paid the same salaries as their male colleagues, but this still leaves wage discrimination among the vast majority of male and female teachers.[16]

Government regulations issued in terms of new legislation passed in 1988 have put an end to much of the discrimination against women at work. As of September 1, 1988, it became an unfair labor practice to discriminate against women in the workplace in terms of the Labor Relations Amendment Act. The government spokesman, Minister of Manpower Pieter du Plessis, said that pay discrimination had existed and persisted "largely because it has so often been taken for granted that women's salaries would be lower than those of men."[17]

Despite the government's assurance and the stipulations of the various laws, there are still loopholes. Certain categories of women are excluded from the Labor Relations Act, a number that may well be as high as 1.5 million. According to statistics supplied by *South African Barometer,* a journal of current affairs statistics, those excluded are women in the farming and domestic service, and persons employed by the state, including transport, medical and educational institutions and local authorities. The vast majority of these are black women.[18]

Occupational Segregation

Women are more confined to a narrow range of employment opportunities in South Africa than in any of the other 26 industrialized countries of the world. Women in South Africa also find themselves in the so-called pink ghetto when it comes to categories of employment. The overwhelming majority end up as typists, secretaries, shop assistants, clerks, factory workers, cashiers, teachers, and civil servants. Even in the professional field the pink ghetto remains starkly visible.

The relegation of women to stereotyped "female" jobs has become even more prevalent during the past 20 years. The percentages of male and female sales workers show that between 1965 and 1981 twice as many women as men entered this field. The number of male clerical workers actually decreased by 20,000 between 1965 and 1981, while the number of women increased from roughly 290,000 to almost 410,000. Of women in the professional fields a total of 61 percent were either in teaching or the nursing profession.[19] Teaching on the primary and secondary level is fast becoming solely the domain of women.

Using the Manpower Surveys 8, 14, and 15 as a source, Truida Prekel of the School of Business Leadership at the University of South Africa compiled the table on page 142 in which the concentration of women in the fields of teaching and nursing is clearly visible.

No other country in the free world has a worse record than South Africa when it comes to women in decision-making positions, as top executives of the administration or as members of the political hierarchy. During the entire 67-year history of South Africa, from the formation of union on May 31, 1910, until April 1988, not a single woman has ever made it into the cabinet, as a deputy cabinet minister, as a commissioner general, as head of a government department or as ambassador to a foreign country,[20] though a few women made it to become a judge. The 1987 election of Stella Margaret Sicgau by the ruling National Independence Party as Prime Minister of the black state of Transkei (on South Africa's east coast and formerly part of the Republic of South Africa), is as much an exception in black and white politics in southern Africa as the election of Golda Meir as Prime Minister of Israel or that of Benazir Bhuto to lead Pakistan. Politically both Israel and Pakistan are male-dominated societies, as is the Transkei with its strongly enforced *Sotho* traditions. Sicgau, daughter of Transkei's first president, Paramount Chief Botha Sicgau, came to power after evidence of massive financial corruption in the Transkei surfaced, destroying virtually the entire top of the male political structure, including Prime Minister George Matanzima. She was deposed in a coup d'etat barely two months later.[21]

Even though in 1985 29 percent of all lecturers at institutions for higher education were women, only a small percentage (less than 3 percent of all staff) achieved a tenured professorship at one of the 18 universities.[22] Male-dominated professions remained unchallenged, more or less maintaining the profile of 1977, when men formed 87.4 percent of all natural scientists, 96.6 percent of all engineers and metallurgists, 96.8 percent of engineering technical staff, 88.4 percent of all executives and managers and 96.4 percent of all qualified artisans and artisan apprentices.[23] Between 1970 and 1980 a mere 56 degrees in engineering were obtained by women. This represents only 0.7 percent of all engineering degrees issued by South African universities,[24] giving the country the doubtful distinction of being outclassed in this field by every major country in Latin America and the vast majority of countries in Asia and the Communist Bloc. But in most other respects the status of women in South Africa and their problems most closely parallel that of the United States.

It is true that there has been a marked, even a dramatic, shift in the career orientation of South Africans, notably white women studying at universities. For example, in 1963 more than 92 percent of all female students enrolled at the University of Pretoria chose education as their field of study. Only 23 percent of women students enrolled in courses for physics and mathematics. That figure went up to 50 percent in 1983. Enrollment in medicine, which included studies in apothecary, rose from 19 to 42 percent. Economics and political science went up from 7 percent to 30 percent, while enrollment in law courses increased from 4 to 29 percent.[25] Similar changes in enrollment have occurred at other universities, but it will be another decade before these statistics translate into meaningful figures in the elimination of occupational segregation—provided, of course, that other factors which play a role in the way occupational segregation develops are also eliminated or, at least, diluted.

One important piece of data which came to light in 1986 in a novel study, which has not yet been duplicated in most other Western countries, is an indication that women may be better and more reliable workers than men. Using 3,000 professional women as a base for its research, the Professional Provident Society revealed that professional female workers not only live longer than men but are getting healthier and do not take sick leave as much as men do. As a result of its findings, the society stopped loading income protection premiums against women. (Most major insurance companies still charge women more than men, and often the cover ceases on marriage.) Women not only are getting healthier and taking fewer days off for illness, the Professional Provident Society found, but also are less accident-prone, down from 48 to 26 percent, while the percentages for men rose from 30 to 36 percent.[26]

Traditional Forms of Discrimination and Male Attitudes

Role models for white women are easy to find, except in the political field. In the academic field there are outstanding women. At the University of Witwatersrand there are several women at the head of important faculties. The Dean of the Law Faculty is a woman. So was her predecessor. Various departments at Rand Afrikaans University are also headed by women. In 1988 Karen Blum was appointed a judge of the Transvaal division of the Supreme Court. One of the judges of the highest court, the Appeal Court, is a woman. There are women who head highly successful publications both as publishers and editors. There are women with excellent achievements in business, on the stock exchange as well as in the production and management field. There are women

Profession	Black Women[1]			Colored and Asian Women			White Women		
	1969	1981	1983	1969	1981	1983	1969	1981	1983
Medical, dental technicians	-	17	50	26	54	103	467	501	1062
Chemical technician	9	16	6	6	28	94	365	419	363
Technical assistants	29	170	230	44	504	747	1987	5230	5886
Medical, dental practitioners	6	17	39	17	153	85	373	1500	1512
Nurses & Midwives	7132	19720	21888	1351	6607	7699	11516	19373	21518
Pharmacist	-	17	17	-	31	33	272	1486	1216
Home economist/dietician	-	13	10	-	3	18	148	307	336
Therapists & Medical auxiliaries	123	217	540	60	251	356	1754	3623	3493
University & College professors & lecturers	23	89	329	19	162	771	1187	3002	3371
School teacher	18532	41303	59279	9432	22818	22622	24582	43246	44390
Legal profession	0	13	40	7	26	20	79	624	592
Market researcher	1	7	173	1	-	3	64	178	133
Librarian/archivist	15	34	28	14	103	173	639	1694	1769
Psychologist	2	12	13	-	6	13	109	421	330
Sociologist	198	249	458	93	421	532	854	1207	1639
Public relations officer	-	149	19	3	5	24	108	742	795
Programmer/systems analyst	-	37	14	5	35	42	305	2021	2207
Total professionals[2]	33613	75503	95251	13059	34918	37743	54799	107513	112958
Percentage increase in total professionals 69–83 (81–83)		183.4	(26.2)		189	(8.1)		106.1	(5.1)

who are pilots of South African passenger jets. The first woman has been elected by the South African Air Force for training as a pilot. Yet, as in the United States, the very publicity accorded these high achievers has obscured the rest of the field and the influence of male-instituted traditions.

Writing in *Rooi Rose,* Karin Brynard observed that traditions in South Africa die very slowly and that traditional perceptions about women in South Africa have still not changed. There is still a disbelief about her presence in the workplace, almost as if she did not belong there. "Look, this is no place for you. Your place is in the kitchen. It doesn't matter how clever and educated you are," is an attitude which one observes when analyzing the wage packet for working women and comparing it to that for males. Brynard cites a case of a working woman who lost her existing housing subsidy the moment she got married. Though she earned more than her husband, she was no longer considered the "breadwinner." Her husband earned less than she did, had no medical fund, no pension system where he worked, and no housing subsidy. But tradition dictated that he was the "breadwinner." The only way the woman could regain her previous status would be through divorce or the death of her husband.

Brynard cites Dr. Rene Uys, head of the research unit at the post-graduate school for business administration at Potchefstroom University, who found through an in-depth research that 50 percent of companies harbor rules in company policy which discriminate against women simply because they are women, particularly married women. Uys found that 70 percent of the companies discriminate against women *de facto* even though it is not contained in company policy. Evidence of this is the fact that a working woman's pay packet changes after she becomes married. She pays more income tax than her married male colleagues, but less to the company pension fund, with the result that she is much worse off than her male colleagues on the day of retirement.[27]

The central government relies on women for 40 percent of all civil service occupations, but even there inequalities are visible. Two-thirds of all working women in the civil service are married, but they are not considered to be breadwinners, even if they earn more than their husbands. They are therefore not entitled to any housing subsidy. Traditional policies cited by Uys are unlikely to be changed easily through legislation; a complete change of attitude is needed. She said that few South African women are members of labor unions

Table 18. Employment Trends of Women of Different Races in South Africa, 1969, 1981, and 1983. Source: Truida Prekel, in *South Africa: The Road Ahead,* G.F. Jacobs (ed.), Jonathan Ball Publishers, Johannesburg, 1986, p. 215.

Notes: (1). Statistics for black women understate the increase in the number of professionals since statistics for black women in Namibia, Transkei, Bobhutha, Tswana, Ciskei and Venda were excluded from recent surveys on grounds of political autonomy granted to these territories between 1969 and 1983. (2). The totals of professionals in the various race and sex groups are larger than those listed in the table since only those occupational categories in which black women produced significant trends were included in the table.

or militant personnel associations; in fact, only between 10 and 20 percent of South African women are members of unions or similar organizations. Thus, not much pressure for change is coming from that group.[28]

Brynard also cites as an example the case of a woman who is a lecturer at one of the leading universities. After she married she lost a housing subsidy of R550 per month. She contributes 6 percent of her salary to a pension scheme of the university to which the university adds 12 percent. In the case of her male colleagues, the respective percentages are 8 and 16 percent. This means that on retirement, no matter the fact that they may be equal in seniority, her male colleagues obviously will receive a higher income. When she became pregnant she received no maternity leave. But male colleagues called up for army camp receive special leave and full payment. The discrimination in this situation is obvious.[29]

Often there is no need to go to court or to introduce legislation to eliminate discrimination. Brynard points out that the giant Electricity Supply Commission (ESCOM), a parastatal mass employer, has made its own arrangements that from January 1, 1987, married women will receive the same pension and housing packet as men. Women merely had to submit evidence that their husbands were not also receiving a housing subsidy. What changed was not the law, Brynard wrote, but the attitude of ESCOM's management.[30]

In some cases of discrimination the twisted logic of the decision-makers is mind-boggling. One case on file with the Women's Bureau and made available for this research deals with the case of a female medical doctor, aged 26, who was pregnant. She was the only wage earner in her family since her husband was a fifth-year medical student (in 1986). On getting a Transvaal provincial authority post, she was compelled to join the Public Service Medical Aid Association (PSMAA); however, the association refused to accept her husband as her dependent. PSMAA would pay nothing at all towards her maternity expenses but, incredible as it may sound, would willingly have paid all expenses if she and her husband were not married but merely living together.[31]

White women may have entered the field of management in South Africa in much larger numbers the past decade, but they still have a long way to go. There is a tremendous shortage of managerial skills in South Africa, to the point where it has become a structural problem, which helps to sustain high inflation and hampers economic growth. Women do have managerial skills and do exceptionally well at schools of business administration all over the country. Yet the number of women who sit on the boards of the 100 largest companies in South Africa can be counted on the fingers of one hand.

The absence of women from the executive levels is largely a question of the patriarchal nature of South African society, reflected in deep-seated male chauvinism combined with a disbelief in women's capabilities in so-called male areas. Men in South Africa have come to accept women in the medical field. They still find it difficult to envision women as engineers. They are still years away from seeing women as project engineers. Their attitude extends past South African women to all women. White males in South Africa, even most white women, will find it difficult to adjust to the idea, even express disbelief, that the project engineer of the high-speed aerodynamics division of the United

States National Aeronautical and Space Administration in Hampton, Virginia, is a woman—a black woman.[32]

A substantial section of Part V of the Wiehahn Commissions report concerned itself with the role of women in employment. The Commission found that many instances of discrimination against women existed in South Africa. Some of the discrimination had its origin in legislation and consequential regulations and practices, while a substantial part was the result of tradition, prejudice or a genuine effort to provide women with protection against exploitation.[33] Since publication of the report not much has changed. Nor has there been a real effort to train South African women as artisans; instead, expensive advertisements continue to be placed overseas and large expenses incurred with foreign missions to obtain qualified artisans from other countries.

A study of 2,336 women working in traditionally male occupations in the industrial sector has indicated that women could easily handle and be happy in male occupations. Cilliers and Hirschowitz rightfully concluded that "division of labour on grounds of sex differences just cannot be justified. Even at the level of factory worker, women and men can hold down similar jobs." They also pointed out (despite their conclusion) that the training of women as artisans and as technicians is still in its infancy. "Yet our research among 50 (major) employers has shown that they are willing to accept women in these positions."[34]

Stereotyping of Women

The stereotyping of women in South Africa is extremely negative. The saying among men is that politics and business are a man's world, not "suitable" for women, and that women are not temperamentally qualified for this area. Women are not considered "tough" enough for the hurly-burly of politics and decision-making at cabinet level. The examples of Golda Meir of Israel and Margaret Thatcher of Britain usually evoke the response that South African women are "different." Arguments that women all over the world have shown themselves capable of mental and political toughness, astute in finance, smart in business, good at administration and even tougher and better at arduous physical tests, such as the dog sled race through the Alaskan Arctic wilderness (which has twice been won by a woman the past three years) is shrugged off by the argument that South African (white) women have always had it too easy. Perhaps if things were made less easy for white women, by letting them compete on equal footing with men in business, education and politics, the white women of South Africa might also win a race or two. According to Professor J. D. van der Vyver of the law school at Wits, women's absence in high political and legal professions is the result of traditional, social and religious prejudice. In 74 years only Leonara van der Heever was considered good enough to be confirmed as a judge of the highest court.[35]

The stereotyping, absurd though it may be, has for decades set back the progress of women, not only in politics but also in business. Elizabeth Bradley became the first woman ever to be appointed to the main board of a South

African bank. In 1986 there were only two women in all of South Africa who were managing directors of companies listed on the Stock Exchange.[36] The past decade in South Africa, during which the shortage of managers became notably acute (as economic integration between black and white mushroomed), has been kind to women in terms of opportunities. The number of women holding managerial positions has increased from 5,376 in 1969 to 24,705 in 1983.[37] But their progress has been one of economic necessity and is not due to men's intellectual acceptance of women's capabilities or the principle of giving women an equal chance.

Hanneli Bendemann stated that according to her research South African men's negative attitude to women in the workplace is one of the worst problems to be faced by women in employment. Men frequently refuse to accept a woman's authority. They don't respond seriously, refuse to report to her and consider her a threat. Men also had all kinds of prejudices against women's capabilities, management potential, expertise, and decision-making prowess and even questioned their intelligence.[38]

The real liberation of women needs to come not from a struggle against or competition with men, but from a new kind of partnership with them, according to Dr. Jopie van Rooyen, deputy director of the National Institute for Personnel. In a lecture "Women: Facilitators for Change" at the Congress of the SA Federation of Business and Professional Women in 1986, she said that both women and men need to break away from gender stereotypes. Adherence to traditional roles had created a sharp division of labor around sex-linked behavior.[39]

The recent report of the National Manpower Commission on high-level manpower indicated that professional personnel was the most important single scarcity factor in the South African labor market. The obvious question, therefore, is whether females cannot make a contribution in this respect? Yet male perceptions of women stand in the way even when women have already proved at the various schools of business leadership across the country that they can manage as well as men.

Newspapers which support the present South African government waxed enthusiastic about the fact that the 1987 general election (for whites only) produced four women members of parliament. In fact this was no better than the situation in 1953, when there were also four women in parliament. Though the largest number of women (24) stood as candidates since the franchise was extended to women in 1930, the fact remains that this number barely exceeded 5 percent of all candidates.[40]

Most women realize that women's issues cannot be dealt with in politics only by women, and that women's rights should be the concern not only of women but also of men. "We do need support from male colleagues," observed Helen Suzman, a 35-year veteran of South African Parliament.[41] She said that women's role in government should be encouraged. "There are so many competent women who don't get the opportunity they deserve because of discrimination."[42]

Some women believe that the time has come for women to exert political pressure in their bargain for a better deal. Dr. Trysie Grobler, a tax expert of

Womanpower, believes that married women are tired of paying for the privilege to work, referring to the double tax paid by married couples. She feels that while the government is bending over backwards to accomodate the farming community, the burden of married working women is being neglected. "The time has come for political parties to take account of married working women as a pressure group," she said. "With our current tax position we are treated like second class citizens."[43]

Stereotypes in South Africa begin at school. In both secondary and high school education there is a conscious effort to provide boys and girls with subjects considered more fitting to a "man's" or a "woman's" career, the exception being made only for the bright scholars. The teaching of science at school, particularly girls' schools, is poor, said Dr. Gail Galasko. Social conditioning (stereotyping) influences women's attitudes towards certain careers which are still considered by many women as secondary. Poor salaries and few opportunities coupled with job dissatisfaction have resulted in few women qualifying as scientists.[44]

Prejudice and false beliefs had led to an educational system which tried to keep women in a subordinate position, said Dr. Franklin Sonn, President of the Technikon in Cape Town. "School books and material showed men doing interesting jobs, and women in reproductive child-rearing roles. The humanity of both sexes is distorted by portraying only men in dominant, positive roles and women in negative or passive roles."[45] Dr. Sonn's views were later echoed by Dr. Anna-Mart Schwerdtfeger of the University of South Africa, who pointed out that if research was confined to library books the impression is gained that 95 percent of the human race consists of men living and doing interesting things while the balance, women, drift around aimlessly somewhere in the background. Referring to school books on grammar, she shows how easily sexist stereotypes are created.[46]

Motherhood and Employment

As in the United States, employed women are confronted by the dual burden of motherhood and career. Cilliers and Hirschowitz cite in an analysis of the views of 5,000 women graduates in South Africa that 20 percent gave preference to motherhood and family at the cost of a full-time career. More than 75 percent were unprepared to accept the challenge of combining a full-time career with family responsibilities.[47] Women face agonizing choices when it comes to children.[48]

As in the United States the number of single-parent families has increased as the result of the higher divorce rate. But the figure of 6 percent of South African women who are divorced or widowed with dependent children is significantly below the 23 percent for the United States. There are other similarities to the United States. Women's participation in the labor force is at the lowest in the age group 20–34 because of childbirth. Disruption of career means that women with children overwhelmingly end up with part-time work such as typing, clerical, administrative duties, receptionist, bookkeeper, social worker and freelancing in certain professions. Research also reveals that, as in the United States, graduate women usually have their children at a later stage, have fewer children, and remain in a full-time occupation after marriage. But all women who have pre-school children, irrespective of level of qualifications, find it difficult to obtain part-time work.[49]

South Africa has no statutory law protecting pregnant women against dismissal. In this respect South Africa now stands alone in the industrialized world. The only chance a woman dismissed on grounds of pregnancy enjoys is to seek relief and reinstatement in terms of the Labor Relations Act under the law on unfair labor practice. During 1985 a number of labor unions in South Africa have started to consider the question of maternity rights for their women members, and some have successfully negotiated such rights with employers.

Not only are working women not protected against dismissal, but they may not even be employed one month before and two months after birth. The intention of the law here is good, but it is less important than the woman's need to keep her job. During their period of unemployment of three months, women are neither protected from dismissal nor fully compensated. The right of working women to have children has never been legally recognized by parliament. In fact it can be argued that women's right to work has not been guaranteed, because without maternity rights a woman's employment is always in jeopardy. It is true that some pregnant women are covered by the Unemployment Insurance Fund, but the benefits are available only to certain segments of the working population. In order to earn the maximum benefits under the Unemployment Insurance Fund, a woman can have a child only once every four years. The fact is that many women do not wish to space their children that far apart.

The Wiehahn Commission studied the situation of working mothers and recommended that various acts be modified in order to provide for preconfinement leave, increased remuneration during pregnancy leave, the prohibition of termination of employment on grounds of pregnancy, and requirements to reinstate women at the end of approved absences from work.[50] This was refused by the South African government although a precedent had already been created by section 4 of the Defense Act (Act 44 of 1957) which makes it an offense for employees to be dismissed or penalized for enrolling for military camps and service.

The Wiehahn Commission accepted the argument that the needs of women and of society in general were being severely impaired by the present lack of maternity protection. The government, replying through a white paper, refused to legislate maternity protection because it thought purely in terms of production losses. It was completely blind, perhaps deliberately so, to the critical needs of working women. Economic considerations were given priority over human ones.[51]

There is growing awareness in South Africa that something will have to be done about child care in support of working women. Dr. Michael Ewart Smith of Witwatersrand University medical school (lecturer in psychiatry) observed that South African society is not adapting to the changing roles of women. There is a higher incidence of depression among women as they try to cope with the explosive social change taking place in South Africa. Drastic changes are necessary to support women and prevent their becoming the first victims of change in South Africa. The pressures on women to fulfill their careers outside the home are more extreme now than ever before. Smith states that, as women continue to play a greater role in the marketplace, attention must be given to who is going to care for the children if stress on women, because of their double burden as mothers and workers, is to be reduced.[52]

Women entering the paid labor market while continuing to perform the same duties as wives and mothers results in "overload" rather than "liberation," observed sociologist Professor Sylvia Viljoen of the University of Pretoria. What is needed is a more egalitarian dispensation where men and women share roles instead of adhering to the traditional male-female patterns. For this to happen, she added, fundamental changes are needed to educational systems, so that children are no longer conditioned to think in a stereotyped way.[53]

Women's Pensions

In a well-researched analysis on staff pension schemes in South Africa, D. M. Potter, editor of *Law Reports of South Africa,* stated that sex discrimination is a real factor in the labor scene when it comes to the determination of wage packets. Belonging to a pension scheme is an important part of any wage package. Fiscal statutes provide encouragement to companies for employee retirement and other benefit schemes. In South Africa, the Tax Act provides tax deductions for employers' contributions to pension provisions and benefit funds and of pensions to former employees and their dependents. In short, Potter states, pension schemes are part of the standard pay package. In some pension schemes the retirement age for women is five years earlier than men, and given the formula for calculating years of service, these women therefore have their years of pensionable service shortened by ten years. In other schemes women's contribution is at a different rate. The rationale for this discrimination is that men are the breadwinners. Some companies said that the rationale for discrepancy in retirement ages was a "historical thing," while others said it was "government policy." In some cases, Potter stated, no reasons could be given. He found several pension schemes where women and men were equally treated and companies admitted that males were no longer considered the sole breadwinner. Potter concluded: "The problem of discrimination in pension funds is an important issue and one that urgently needs rectification. Fair treatment in labor relations is always in the public interest."[54]

There are other aspects of the pension scheme which require attention. A woman who marries a man just after his retirement and who may have been married to him for 10 years at the time of his death will discover that the vast majority of pension funds will, after his death, make no further payments.

Legal and Administrative Aspects

In the legal world women are much better off in South Africa compared to a decade ago, though several areas of inequality and friction remain. The

Matrimonial Property Bill of 1984, considered by the Women's Bureau to be a positive and progressive step to legal and economic equality of married women,[55] still left women with some major disadvantages. The act abolished marital power for weddings enacted after its passing, but retains the anachronisms in marriages concluded prior to the act such as inheritance and succession, which could leave some women worse off than minors under guardianship. Under the new act husbands are still considered the head of the family. Wives cannot acquire their own domiciles and they occupy a subordinate position in respect of the guardianship of children. Equal rights between men and women in marriage are not yet complete.

When the Law Commission in 1983 recommended the new laws to parliament, its proposals were not enthusiastically endorsed by everyone. Some newspapers suggested editorially that it was doubtful the Commission's recommendations were the real answer to the problems faced by women.[56] Others considered it a giant step and said that a woman's charter had become a matter of urgency.[57] Though a married woman may have contributed substantially to family income over a period of many years and though the new Matrimonial Property Act provides for a share in accumulated wealth, the fact is that a court divorce order does not entitle the woman to receive the proceeds or an equal share of the proceeds of annuities or insurance policies.

There are positive developments as well.

A divorced woman in South Africa may now be able to ask for rehabilitative maintenance payments to allow her to undergo further education until she is able to support herself on her own income, similar to the French system. According to a spokesman of the SA Law Society, the courts have always had the discretion but have rarely used it.

In 1977 a study group on women in employment was established in South Africa to investigate the working conditions and legal status of women and to make recommendations to a government commission of inquiry into labor legislation. The group found that women already represented 32 percent of the working force in South Africa and that they were subject to various forms of discrimination in employment: (a) traditional discrimination by employers, (b) lack of mobility, and (c) discrimination through education and training. Job advertisements were often worded to deter women from applying. The group also believed that the danger of "the rate for the job" without fair employment legislation could lead to the retrenchment and discharge of many women. Given the choice most employers would give preference to employing men, and given the choice would discharge women before men. Seniority and equal performance would be ignored. "Only legislative sanctions against discrimination could avoid malpractice." Female agricultural workers were in particularly bad circumstances. They were covered by the Workmen's Compensation Act but have had no standards of pay, working conditions or housing laid down for them. Black pregnant women almost invariably lose their jobs. Maternity benefits are only 45 percent of the worker's salary compared to full pay in Australia and 90 percent of salary in Great Britain.[58]

In general women are paid much less than men in South Africa, the professional division in the public service being a major exception. The South African

Wage and Industrial Conciliation Acts make no explicit provision for the abolishment of wage discrimination based on sex. Childless professional women, married career women and highly qualified employed married women with children are the subjects of massive legal tax discrimination. The government's argument that their income is jointly taxed with that of their husbands' because they are working only to supplement the family income is belied by the tens of thousands of married career women in South Africa whose husbands make more than enough for the entire family. In fact, a thorough study by the J. Walter Thompson advertising agency revealed that most working women came from households with a higher than average income. One in four South African women now regard their job as a career, and nearly six in 10 working women are married.[59]

In 1986 the Minister of Finance announced that in the future R1,800 or 20 percent of a married woman's income will be exempted from tax. There was a euphoric response in newspapers which support the government. In fact, thousands of women who are in the service of their husbands' companies, or in partnership with their husbands, or working for private companies of which their husbands are directors, or important shareholders, were excluded from this handout. The 1986 concession (*sic*) in fact still made it more attractive for professional men and women not to marry but simply to live together.[60]

In 1988 the government tried again to grasp the nettle of married women's taxation but only succeeded in painting a picture of even more blatant discrimination against women. It rejected the recommendations of the Margo Commission, which proposed separate tax for working married women, and announced that the first R20,000 earned by a married woman would not be added to that of the husband for tax purposes. If she earned more than R20,000, her income, less 22.5 percent, would be added to her husband's. This amounted to punitive discriminatiion against women and sent a message to women that it would be better for them to remain in a subordinate position. Families where the woman, and not the man, was the high earner would be taxed more heavily than families where the man earned the most. In a family where the woman earned R1,000 more than her husband (taking R40,000 as their joint income), the tax would be 67 percent higher than one in which the husband earned R1,000 more than the wife. There is no escaping the conclusion that the higher tax was because it was the woman who was the principal wage earner. Thus, women are penalized if they make financial gains in the labor market.

The Law and a Bill of Rights

Many prominent and educated women in South Africa are convinced that a Bill of Rights with specific provisions for the entrenchment of women's rights would go a long way to ensure that women are not overlooked when major change takes place in South Africa. The issue of women's rights has to be specifically addressed if the status quo regarding women is to change.

The Women's Legal Status Committee (W.L.S.C.) has submitted a memorandum to the SA Law Commission investigating the feasibility of a Bill of Rights, calling for the specific inclusion of provisions to protect women's rights. So far, 23 organizations have supported this proposal. W.L.S.C. states in its memorandum that the Bill must embody the principle of equality of men and women and ensure the realization of this principle by Act of Parliament. It should eliminate discrimination against women by any person, organization or enterprise; protect women in pregnancy and maternity; and establish all appropriate measures to ensure the equality of women with men in marriage, parenthood, and political, social and economic life. The memorandum stated that women currently suffer prejudice in hiring, advancement and retirement. There is no equal access to education for women and men. There is a different emphasis in education for boys and girls, with boys benefiting from those subjects which lead to better opportunities for higher education and bursaries.

In a different memorandum to the SA Law Commission, Gretchen Carpenter, Associate Professor of Constitutional Law at the University of South Africa, argues that it is essential that a clause prohibiting discrimination based solely on sex should be incorporated into any bill of rights. Although she said that it is not relevant to refer to discrimination against women in the context of constitutional law, discrimination against women is often hidden and occurs, not in the formal statutes and regulations, but in the implementation and in the mind-set of the officials. Furthermore, there is the possibility that discrimination of the hidden variety may manifest itself in administrative law situations. Administrative law occurs within not only the central government but also in the affairs of semi-government organizations, parastatals, city councils, clubs, churches, and even sports clubs.

Carpenter argues that if the test of objective reasonableness were to be adopted by the South African courts, the courts would examine the effect or consequences of discrimination, not whether the administration had any discrimination in mind when the act of discrimination occurred. For example, is it objectively reasonable to refuse a license to a woman for no other reason than that she is a woman? In the same context, if young women with superior academic qualifications are refused acceptance to a medical school because the policy is to restrict women students, such discrimination would be unauthorized under common law. She also argues that thus far the principle of manifest injustice or oppression has been applied by courts only to racial discrimination. But this rule, that discrimination between persons or classes of persons may not be manifestly unjust or oppressive, could also find application in many cases which have upset women: admission to studies, service benefits, salary, leave privileges, access to senior positions, etc.[61]

The Women's Bureau of South Africa also submitted a memorandum to the Law Commission and stated that discrimination exists because there is no Act which stipulates that discrimination against women on grounds of gender is unlawful. The memorandum cited four fields of discrimination: (a) access to academic training, (b) medical aid to women, (c) the absence of equal salaries and opportunities for promotion in the private sector as well as in the educational profession, and (d) inequality in benefits such as housing subsidies. A general clause outlawing discrimination, the Bureau argued, would serve as a mechanism not only to have discrimination tested in court but also to prevent discrimination on grounds of gender.[62]

Women and Religion

One area where women have quietly made progress is in the church. Enormous controversy raged in Britain during 1988 over the ordaining of women; in Canada, over the possibility of a female Bishop; in Israel, because the conservative Jews in the United States have permitted women to be certified as cantors. But in South Africa the breakthrough happened with little fanfare. In Methodist, Presbyterian, Congregational and Nederduits Hervormde Churches, women have become fully ordained ministers. In 1986 several women were in training at various seminaries; the Nederduits Hervormde Church had no fewer than 17 trainees, a figure unthinkable 10 years before.[63] In 1988 the Nederduits Gereformeerde Kerk (N.G.K.) of Western Transvaal voted overwhelmingly to admit women to holy orders and said that there should also be women elders. The decision is to be ratified by the General Synod of the Church in 1990.[64]

White women may benefit both spiritually and financially from entry into the ministry, but non-white women may, down the road, have to face the inherent discrimination in Islamic Law if the state permits a further encroachment of Islamic Law on the terrain of common, secular, law.

Considering the conflict in Nigeria with regard to secular law versus Islamic law, a problem which has repeated itself in every country where recognition has been given to Muslim laws, it is interesting to note that the Islamic community in South Africa now totals 318,000 persons among Asians and coloreds. In addition, there are 40,000 Malays, also followers of Islam, commonly referred to as the Muslims of the Cape province. Their numbers are increasing.[65] A serious effort is being made by the Islamic community to spread the religion among the black population of South Africa. In the near future, South Africa, like India, Nigeria, Egypt and other countries, will be faced with the conflict between secular and religious laws.

The Muslim community in the Cape province has already successfully applied and received permission to establish its own bank in the Islamic Corporation Limited. The new institution allows for the fact (and this formed part of the submission to the Registrar of Financial Institutions) that Muslims are not allowed under Islamic law to receive or pay interest and as such were forbidden from operating traditional bank or building society accounts.[66] Thus a deviation from existing law and regulation was permitted *on grounds of Islamic Law*. The Muslim community in South Africa, mostly of the Sunni strain, or orthodox section, will no doubt in the future be asking for other deviations now that the precedent has been established. The spread of Islam in South Africa is significant. Equally significant was the new translation into Afrikaans of the *Qur'an* by the Department of Semitic Languages and Islamic Studies at the Rand Afrikaans University in 1987.[67]

Black Women

Discrimination against black, Indian and colored women in the urban marketplace, in rural areas, and at home is particularly harsh and unreasonable.[68] African tribal tradition regards women as perpetual minors, which means that they have to get male permission even to travel or to take a job. Until recently, in terms of South African law, a black woman could not remain in an urban area, not even a black urban area, unless she had lived there for at least 10 years, was married to a man resident in the area, or was living with a male relative already legally in the area. In June 1983 the government decided that blacks permanently resident outside the so-called black homelands (or national states as the homelands are officially designated) could purchase homes in black townships. That put a spotlight on the legal status of women. At the time 90 percent of all married black women in South Africa were legally minors and could not purchase any property on their own. Whether married under civil or traditional (tribal) law, their husbands had marital power over them.

In recognition of the inferior status of black women, the Department of Community Development agreed to let these legal minors purchase houses, but in a Catch-22 situation they were not entitled, as legal minors, to obtain any building society loans. Even single black women with long-term employment records and substantial salaries found it difficult to obtain housing loans. The situation was particularly difficult for black women considering that in tens of thousands of homes, the woman was *de facto* the head of household or brought in a higher salary, or the only salary, to keep the family going.

In 1985 the South African government tried to remove the roadblocks for women who were anxious and able to purchase a house by proposing a bill which stated that women, whether married under tribal or civil law, are entitled to buy or sell leasehold; however, an accompanying white paper stated that "a woman who enters into a customary union becomes subject to customary law with regard to her status." The woman's capacity to engage in, for example, leasehold transactions might thus be affected by her being subject to customary law. Another Catch-22. Because of the problems that arose from the interrelationship of principles of civil law and African customary law, the government announced in 1986 that a new law was being considered to take care of the status of black women in marriage.[69]

Following on further proposals by the South African Law Commission, the government submitted new legislation which was passed by Parliament in February 1988. The benefits for black married women were enormous. The Marriage and Matrimonial Property Law Amendment Bill made black women legal and equal partners in marriage and abolished the marital powers which husbands had enjoyed. The new laws put the marriage of black women on an equal basis with that of white women, who were covered by the 1984 Matrimonial Property Act. This meant that any marriage entered into by blacks, without an anti-nuptial contract, will be automatically in community of property and that the principle of joint accrual will also be applicable in the case of black women married with an ante-nuptial contract. The new law will not apply retroactively, so a generation of marriages will have to pass before the new law could be of general application. The new legislation also radically altered the status of customary (i.e., tribal) unions. It sees a customary union as an impediment to a civil marriage and the equality which it represents.[70]

Truida Prekel, like most other qualified observers, believes that something needs to be done to reverse the vicious cycle black women find themselves in: a cycle of poverty, high birth rates, high infant mortality, low educational levels and under-employment or unemployment. Citing a recent survey by the Human Sciences Research Council, she pointed to a positive correlation between educational level and the use of contraceptives.[71] Many whites in South Africa are anxious about the explosive black birth rate. A better education for black women is part of the answer to that problem—that and legislation for black family planning in South Africa, giving a woman legal say in the number of children she wishes to have. Elsewhere in this book there are several references to World Bank, United Nations and other investigations proving that with higher education the birthrate falls, often dramatically.

According to Professor Francis Bosman, Director of Development of the South African Law Association, it is a constant struggle for women to obtain equality and to improve their status generally. Women still suffer under various disabilities, but black women suffer more disabilities. The government and the S A Law Commission had looked at these problems, said Professor Bosman, and she cited the following important changes of recent years: (1) A 1986 law amendment that made it possible for black women to buy their own property on leasehold. Prior to the new law black women could not do this. Furthermore, black women may buy property irrespective of whether they are married. (2) A law of 1986 pertaining only to black women in Natal and Transvaal, who previously had to obtain their fathers' permissions to marry even if they were past the legally independent age of 21 years. This parental restriction has now been outlawed, and a black woman may marry at will past the age of 21. In addition, said Professor Bosman, the marriage laws of black women had been brought in line with those of other race groups in South Africa whose position was vastly improved with the so-called Marriage Act of 1984. Black women should therefore be encouraged to step away from marriages under customary (black) law and rather enter into marriage under civil law.[72]

Under customary or tribal marriage the law of the land protects women only in three respects: the husband must pay maintenance to the wife and children after divorce; should the husband die in an accident due to someone else's negligence the widow may claim compensation from the guilty party; and, should the husband be killed in the course of employment, the wife could institute a claim according to the existing Workman's Compensation Act. But nothing else.

Black Women in the Labor Market

The picture for black women is not all gloom and doom. Black women are said to be winning a quiet revolution against the factor of double discrimination. Between 1969 and 1985 black women had increased their share in the South African labor market by 212 percent, to 497,985.[73]

In 1985 the new Congress of the South African Trade Unions (C.O.S.A.T.U.) adopted a strong feminist position, rejecting exploitation of and discrimination against all women, at work and in society. One of the resolutions passed was for equal pay for work of equal value (comparable worth) while the Congress would also fight for childcare and family facilities "to meet workers needs and make it easier for workers to combine work and family responsibilities." The Congress also proposed maternity rights, including paid maternity and paternity leave, similar to that provided in Scandinavian countries. The C.O.S.A.T.U. stand on women's rights is the most outspoken position ever taken before in South Africa by a black representative, and predominantly male, body.[76]

In contrast, the elected black government of the self-governing state of KwaNdebele defends its stand as the only one of the self-governing black states (forming a part of the Republic of South Africa) where women may not vote. A spokesman of the KwaNdebele Department of the Interior told the black newspaper *City Press* that the cabinet is adamant that women would not be permitted to enter the KwaNdebele Parliament. In 1988 the women of this tiny state therefore brought legal action against the State President of South Africa and the government of KwaNdebele on grounds of discrimination against them on the basis of sex. The KwaNdebele government stated in its defense that votes for women were in conflict with customary law, but the Pretoria Supreme Court ruled in December 1988 that women have the right to vote and declared the government of KwaNdebele illegal and the previous election null and void.[77]

Black women also will benefit from the fact that advancement of black people in general in the management field has become an economic necessity. Sheryl Raine examined the medium-term trends and found that by the year 2000 South Africa will need to produce 210,000 executives and more than one million skilled managers and white collar workers. But there are simply not enough skilled white candidates graduating from white high schools to make this even remotely possible, she said. In 1985 there were 56,000 white matriculants and 37,000 blacks who finished high school. Fifteen years down the road, white matriculants are projected to be down to 54,000, while blacks will number almost 187,000. Omitting the public sector, the current ratio of workers to managers is about 50 to 1, or six times higher than in Europe and about nine times higher than in the United States. At present only 10,802 blacks are listed as managers or administrators, less than 4 percent of all workers. When all these figures are combined, experts agree that of sheer economic necessity the race for black advancement is on.[78]

According to Truida Prekel, manpower surveys conducted over the last three years have shown that black women are the only group (grouped by race and sex) whose employment in listed occupations has actually increased. She describes their steady move into technical, professional, managerial, clerical and sales fields as a quiet revolution. This has happened despite the fact that they are most often treated as fourth-class citizens, ranked after white men, white women and black men. Economic necessity has forced many black women to establish their own businesses and network of support organizations. "As a result, they have valuable leadership experience and a helpful professional network."

Prekel cites the following factors as the key obstacles to black women's progress: they are traditionally subordinate to men, regardless of age, education and marital status; they are at the bottom end of the pay scales; they cannot afford day care for their children, domestic help or futher education; they seldom have maternity benefits; their time and energy are sapped by hours of traveling to and from their workplaces.[79]

Black Professional Women

While their numbers are small, black women, despite huge legal, political and social obstacles, are also beginning to enter the professional fields. During the period 1982–1983 the number of black women who had entered the professional sector rose by 13 percent to 93,000 compared to a 2.5 percent increase for white women during the same period. With the cancellation of the so-called "pass laws" and the relaxation of influx controls, this percentage is expected to increase.[80] By 1985 more than 30 percent of the members of the black National African Federated Chamber of Commerce (N.A.F.C.O.C.) were women entrepreneurs. Black female clerical workers increased by 35 percent during 1982 and 1983, compared to a drop of 5 percent in male workers. In the service industries there was a 4 percent increase of black women, compared to a 6 percent drop for white women. Black women in industry increased by 3 percent, while male black workers declined by 8 percent. As supervisors black women showed the most important gains of all, increasing by 24 percent.[81] When the 1981 Manpower Survey is compared with the 1969 survey the increase in some categories can only be described as remarkable. In 1969 there were only 29 black female technical assistants. In 1981 the figure rose to 170, and the estimated figure for 1989 at the current rate of increase is over a thousand.

One positive outcome of black women's entry into the professional workplace was the appearance of high achievers who quickly became role models. The board of directors of most major companies in South Africa is traditionally composed of men. When a woman is appointed it is still something unusual. When a black woman is appointed, such as the 1988 appointment of Beatrice Khubeka to the board of Bates Wells Advertising, it is a major event. In an article in *Southern Africa Today* in 1988, Leslie Dellatolla presented an impressive list of black women who had achieved fame and prominence in South African society: Ester Chinkanda, deputy head of the Social Section of the Human Science Research Council, Marina Maponya, director of Pace College and of the Manpower and Management Foundation and Business Woman of the Year for 1982; Pauline Matshete, TV3 presenter; Olivia Kwatsha, winner of the 1987 Altech Production Management Institute trophy; Gcina Mhlophe, screen and stage actress, playwright and film producer; Nomvuyo Mdladcamba who runs a Johannesburg Stock Exchange investment game for South African high schools of all races; Professor Themba Mashaba, head of the Department of Nursing Science at the University of Zululand—to name just a handful. At the 1987 graduation ceremony of the Medical University of South Africa, 42 of the 60 black doctors who qualified were women. Of *Fair Lady* magazine's *Who's Who of South African Women,* 27 are black, their careers spanning management, trade unions, fashion, performing arts, medicine, nursing, community service, academics, and television.[82]

On the other hand, black women generally suffer discrimination not only because they are black, but also because they are black women. Their discrimination stems from white, as well as from black society.

In South Africa's society, women's status is subordinate to men's, regardless of age, education or marital status. In tribal areas women are regarded as minors, regardless of age. A mature woman must obtain permission from a male if she wishes to enter employment. The tradition of subordination has been reinforced by racial laws in South Africa which in the past (until as recently as 1986) stipulated that a black woman may not live or work in an urban area unless she is married to a man working there or has been living there uninterruptedly for more than 10 years. Laws restricting the movement of black people in South Africa were completely abolished in 1986.[83]

The attitude of black men does not make life any easier for black women, just as the attitude of white and black men in the United States often makes life difficult for black and white women in that country. When a black woman in the urban areas of South Africa is paid the same as a black man, the man feels that he is being discriminated against. In fact, black men's perception of the role and status of women is much worse than that of their white male counterparts.[84]

Asian women in South Africa suffer the same discrimination as black women at the hands of white society. So do colored (mixed blood) and Chinese women. But major changes in South African government policy as regards coloreds and Asians (blacks excluded) have provided unexpected opportunities to Indian and colored women.[85] For example, those joining the defense force have found that they will now be offered the same choice of training open to white women, including training as air traffic controllers, radar operators, signallers, finance administration, nursing, and military police, although their training will still take place at a different venue. In October 1988 Shamshaad Begum Khan became the first Indian woman to be promoted to the rank of captain in the South African Prison Service.[86]

The Women's Movement

Though the various women's organizations in South Africa were much better organized in the '80s than in the '70s (the Women's Bureau of South Africa, the South African Association of University Women, Womanpower and the Business and Professional Women's Federation, to name a few), women in South Africa, like women in most other Western states, lack an overall representative body for women with which all organizations who are interested in promoting the status of women, or in fighting discrimination, are affiliated.

The Women's Bureau of South Africa appears preeminent. The Bureau does not replace other women's groups, said Margaret Lessing, but rather acts as a holding organization for the latter and provides a support system and vast information base through its resource center. The Bureau has nine branches countrywide and 35 working groups. Lessing sees the Women's Bureau as a catalyst working for the benefit of all women but stops short of saying that national presentations to the government and to parliament could be made through the bureau.[87]

Demands have increased for women's organizations to join forces; for example, Dr. Rina Venter, President of the Suid-Afrikaanse Vrouefederasie (South African Women's Federation), said in 1984 that women should not only join their forces but also should draw up a joint constitution in which their common aims were identified. She said that each organization was too preoccupied with its own aims, and there was not one which had developed a well-balanced perspective with regards to the thinking and sentiments of all women in South Africa. "They [women's organizations] have never arrived at a point where they have a vision of a common task." On the chances of such a national organization being established, Dr. Venter is herself skeptical because the various organizations have so many prejudices towards one another stemming from political, religious and cultural viewpoints that it was difficult even to get down to basics with each other.[88]

That view was echoed two years later in a meeting in Bramley, Johannesburg, called the National Assembly of Women. Some 900 delegates and observers of all races from all over South Africa attended what was an intensely political investigation of woman's role in the country, then in a state of emergency as the result of black township riots. The prevailing mood was that women's liberation cannot be fought for separately from political liberation. The conference was dominated by black women. There was enough goodwill going around but also enough Third World liberation political hype to scare off women's organizations representing other groups.[89] To a certain extent the National Assembly acted like Third World delegates at the United Nations Nairobi conference in 1985 when a demand (*sic*) for redistribution of wealth between the rich and the poor nations was also on the table. This all-or-nothing approach holds out little hope for a multi-racial national women's organization with clout.

In the interim other organizations would be better off trying to align themselves behind an established or newer organization with more realistic but equally important objectives, taking the hurdles on the road to women's equality with men one by one. A Woman's Bill of Rights for South Africa is not a far-fetched idea, something along the lines of the Sullivan Principles which forced American companies in South Africa to treat their black and white workers as equals in the marketplace. But without a central organization, with sufficient membership to be able to wield political clout, getting an overwhelmingly male-dominated executive or legislative body to launch a "Sullivan Program for Women" is highly unlikely. Yet it is an indisputable truth that only economic and political pressure brings real reform in South Africa. And 52 percent of all voters in South Africa are women. Only a very small percentage of women have not suffered from some stereotyping or legal, social and economic discrimination. With proper organization and teamwork, it should not be impossible for women to collect 250,000 signatures to petition parliament, or the President, to appoint a blue-ribbon commission of inquiry into discrimination against women with a view to bringing South Africa in line with the rest of the world, at least in terms of legislation.

South Africa is one of the most politicized countries in the world; in fact, short of the Communist states, no industrialized country in the world is so overly governed as South Africa. And the heavy hand of government is controlled by a male chauvinistic party. Anyone who believes that women can rapidly improve their status, narrow the wage gap, force the legislature to pass an equal pay act and put an end to discrimination against women on grounds of sex, without an organized political input on women's part, is simply not being realistic.

Defining Women's Needs

The Women's Bureau of South Africa held an end-of-the-decade conference for women in Cape Town in May 1985, just preceding the end of the United Nations Decade for Women, and identified five key issues and difficulties for women: social problems, job creation, women's advancement, communication and the political problems of the country. Short of communication, all the other issues can be heavily influenced, or regulated, one way or the other, by laws, government regulations, political decisions (by an all-male cabinet), or by the heavily male-dominated parliament. It should be clear to women that the organization of a national women's movement with a narrow, but clearly defined, objective should be a priority. Women elsewhere have proved that this could be done.

Women may be reticent to act because activism of this kind is alien to most women. But injustices against women can be fought in the political arena. Statistically women have the power to reform the political process. Dr. Jacklyn Coch of the University of Witwatersrand told the National Congress of the South African Federation of Business and Professional Women in 1984 that this could happen if women overcame the passivity rooted in women's sense of themselves as powerless victims.[90] In 1987 out of 50 cabinet ministers and deputy cabinet ministers, plus another 32 top civil service positions such as director general of a government department and other state-appointed administrators, not one was female, giving South Africa the worst record of discrimination against women in top administrative and political posts in the entire world outside the Muslim-Arab states.

Again, South African women constitute 52 percent of all voters, yet in areas where it matters most, to the majority of women at least, women's wishes as well as their essential requirements are simply ignored. That South African men, generally speaking, have the wrong idea of how women feel about their role in life was illustrated by Sunette van der Walt following an investigation by the Human Sciences Research Council during 1984 involving more than 5,000 men and women. Only 8 percent of economically active women still believed that having children and caring for her husband is woman's prime responsibility.[91] But unless there is massive input by women in the political arena, either through existing women's organizatioins or the political parties, women's requirements will forever remain on the back burner, if considered at all. During the past three decades, gender equality has not been part of the political platform of any political party.

There are several areas where parliamentary action (legislation) is called for, and if party organizers were to be asked by every second woman whose vote and financial contributions they seek, when legislation in these areas is going to be considered, the same long-ignored issues will suddenly receive priority treatment. As the 1987 general election proved, the lives of prominent cabinet ministers were saved by a mere handful of votes. Lovenduski and Hills rightfully observed that women's massive voting strength, thoughtfully used *or withheld,* could activate even moribund political leaders.[92]

The obvious areas where legislation is inadequate or virtually non-existent are voting rights for all women, equal opportunities in the marketplace, and wage discrimination. If, on the average, women with exactly the same university training and work experience receive 26 percent less than men with the same qualifications and work experience, then it represents a constitutional aberration which should be rectified by law. It is only the uninformed who still believe that women cannot do the same work as men in fields of education, research, aviation, administration, engineering, architecture or medicine. In 1986 some of the most sought-after prizes in the South African academic world went to women for being the top students in engineering, medicine and architecture.[93]

Tax laws require modification. Some of the most brilliant minds in the country end up paying 77.5 percent tax on their personal income because they are women. The result of this economically inane policy, in a country which desperately needs all its highly qualified personnel, is that many of these individuals decide not to work. Considering that the tax payers (who include women) contribute significantly to the costs of putting young women through university, the continued existence of this policy remains a financial mystery.

In 1984 the Human Sciences Research Council investigated which factors influenced women's participation in the marketplace and, specifically, the role of taxation. The women questioned all indicated that a higher living standard, an opportunity to contribute to family income, the opportunity to achieve something, the opportunity to employ their skills and contact with other people were the five most important reasons why married women went to work. This makes a mockery of the government's view that women work mostly because they wish to contribute to the family income. The political truth is simply that the state needs the additional revenue to carry out a costly ideological program but, as politicians are wont to do, will seize on even the most inane excuse to justify an indefensible position. The consequences of this attitude is clear. Of non-working married women, almost 50 percent of all white women and 38 percent of Asian women said that they did not want to work because of the burden imposed by taxation of joint income.[94]

South African companies, like companies elsewhere in the world, either pay lip-service to declared policies of equality in the marketplace between men and women, or simply do not understand the principle involved. A glaring example is the question of medical aid. All major companies in South Africa provide medical aid to their employees and their families, women and children—if the employee is male. A woman, working full time, will find (almost invariably) that her husband is not included. She may earn as much as or more than her husband, but she is denied equal benefits by company policy (and by medical insurance schemes); she cannot list him as a dependent, the way the husband can list his wife, even if she also works. This sexual discrimination has been fought in the courts overseas and every time the courts have ruled that it was an unlawful discriminatory act. The sex of the employee should have nothing to do with who the dependents are. This is one area where the women's organizations in South Africa could join hands.

Another area of dissatisfaction for women is housing loans. Refusing to provide working women with housing loans is discrimination against the individual on grounds of gender. Women's organizations should press that this practice be abolished. As a point of departure their lawyers could argue that, in terms of the South African constitution, all persons, irrespective of their sex, are equal in the eyes of the law. Why should they be unequal in the eyes of business men, insurance companies, building societies, or their elected representatives in parliament? When it is voting time, one woman's vote equals that of one man.

Unlike the rest of the civilized world, South Africa (and the United States) are also the only two industrially developed countries which penalize qualified, tax-paying, working women for having children. The husband is not penalized in any way. In many instances maternity leave of six months also means that the woman's employment is suspended, whereas a man who is called up for army camp does not have his service suspended. (A law was passed for this very purpose.) There is no other country in the West which believes that preparing men to wage war, even if it is in defense of the sovereignty of the state, is more important than creating the lives who will one day have to bear the burden of defense. Men who go in army camps in South Africa are paid their full salaries. Working women who have to take off time for childbirth are denied the same right. If women were not taxpayers and not voters, then this paradox would at least have made some sense. But it makes no sense. That is why a general commission of inquiry into the status of women, particularly in respect of discriminatory practices, is overdue in South Africa. Countries as far apart as India and Canada have appointed such commissions against vehement objection and every time the results have come as a shock to the general public. But women will have to force the issue, and the key to that is simply good organization.

Of all the needs for women to improve their status and achieve equality with men, find better employment, earn higher wages, break out of the cast of stereotyping and subordination to men, and reduce the high fertility rate, none is so important as a proper education. Education of white children in South Africa is at a level which matches the best in the Western world. Black education has shown phenomenal improvement in sheer numbers of schools built, teachers trained and enrollment the past decade. In 1973 there were only 5,500 black students finishing high school. In 1987 there were 151,000. In 1980 there were only 10,000 blacks at university. In 1988 their enrollment was in excess of

50,000 while another 16,000 were studying at Technicons. There were only 700,000 black children at school in 1948. In 1989 there will be 7.2 million.[95]

Despite these figures there is a massive amount of work still to be done. Raising the educational level of women could help to prevent the high rate of unplanned pregnancies among school girls. In some rural areas this represents nearly half of the first pregnancies.[96] Raising the educational level of women could also drastically improve their general status. Professor H. L. Rautenbach of Stellenbosch University, surveying the needs for improving education for blacks at home and improving the status of women, also found that:

> parallel to the efforts at improving the status of women and the self respect of men, it is essential to assist families in need by providing facilities for the care of children of working mothers; educating and training girls for satisfying careers, including that of wife and mother; programs to improve parenting; better housing; increasing opportunities to work in the formal and informal sectors of the economy; increasing productivity and elimination of migratory labour by married people whenever possible, etc. Creating a healthy home environment for the upbringing and education of children therefore requires the building of self-respect of men in their work environment and in the community. On the other hand it is essential that the status of women be improved and that due respect be accorded to the positive roles they are playing in the very difficult transitional situations. This presents a major challenge to all South Africans, especially to people like employers, community leaders, ministers of religion and their congregations, men's and women's organizations, trade unions, and the media.[97]

Research

The study of women's rights has not made much headway at South African universities; some aspects, but not actual courses on women's studies, are taught at a few universities. In 1987, however, the University of South Africa announced the establishment of a fully fledged Center for Women's Studies to be housed within the Department of Sociology, the first of its kind in South Africa and in Africa. The center will carry out long- and short-term research projects related to women; the dissemination of publications and newsworthy items on a regular basis; the establishment of a scientific journal for women's studies; the establishment of a data bank by which information about women can be gathered, stored, retrieved and published; and the organization of lectures, seminars, workshops, exhibitions and courses on topics relating to women.[98]

Professor Sunette van der Walt (University of Bophuthatswana) believes the focus for future research should be solutions surrounding the effects of women's double role, namely role conflict, role overloading, guilt feelings and stress, as well as the increasing number of women entering the marketplace—for example, the implications of retraining necessitated by new technology. She believes that the research field of environmental factors surrounding the working women in South Africa is lying fallow. This includes factors such as the demand for more part-time jobs, the need for child care facilities, flexible working hours and employment opportunities within the informal sector. There also needs to be greater emphasis on various psychological and social aspects such as values and stereotypes that have implicatiions for the utilization of working women. "The lack of effective vocational guidance at school and the implications thereof in terms of incorrect choice of subjects and occupations focus the attention of a further research priority to ensure the full potential of limited human resources."[99]

Dr. Jacklyn Coch, senior lecturer in sociology at Wits University, suggested in her series of lectures on women's studies and issues in 1987 that the following questions be examined:

• What is specific and different about women's experience of wage work? Why do women tend to be concentrated in the lowest paid, least skilled and most vulnerable jobs?

• What is specific and different about women's experience with sexuality? Why and with what consequences are women subject to a rising incidence of rape, wife abuse and battery?

• What is specific and different about women's experience of home? Housework is still widely defined as women's work. What follows from women's dual burden of work inside and outside the home?

• What is specific and different about definitions of femininity and how is it appropriate for women to behave?[100]

Another area which calls for research is to ascertain whether women themselves are aware of the extent of discrimination against them; what changes would recent graduates like to see in the school curriculum and which would better prepare them for studies at institutions of higher learning and for their first occupation; what would be the financial implications of a short-term program to bring women's wages into line with that of men; to what extent would commerce and industry support maternity leave and other forms of assistance to working women with small children; what is the wage differential in parastatal organizations between men and women doing the same work and men and women doing work of comparable worth; finally, to what extent are individual members of the national legislature informed about women's issues?

South Africa has become a society which depends on women's labor as much as it depends on the automobile. A society that depends on vehicles is forced to construct roads. But largely because of male prejudice and gender discrimination, South Africa has not faced up to the fact that though they depend on working women (of whom the majority are married) these women also have and will continue to have children. If one can build roads for cars, one can build structures to support working women with children and to ensure *de facto* equality of treatment between men and women in the labor force. That has not happened in South Africa because the male-dominant society has refused, so far, to face up to statistical and sociological realities.

Part Four: The European Community

Though 54 percent of the West German electorate of 43 million voters are women, the Bundestag (Parliament) is 90 percent male.

10. General Survey

There are 22 countries associated with Western Europe which usually are referred to as the European Market Economy Countries. These include Iceland, all of the Scandinavian states, and Turkey, though the latter is, geographically, part of Asia. But both Iceland and Turkey are members of N.A.T.O. and are joined in various treaties with the others. This study, however, is interested primarily in the 12 European Common Market countries (the E.C.), of which Britain, France, West Germany and Italy are the most important. The total population of the E.C. in 1988 exceeded 322 million.

As outlined in Chapter 4, the E.C. has played a major role in the past decade in the promotion of equal opportunities for men and women. Its legislative activity and the First Action Program 1982–1985 have made a significant contribution to the progress achieved in this area at European level. As a result there has been a shift in public attitudes towards a more equal participation by men and women in economic, social and political life, a shift which has also been measured by major opinion polls. Unfortunately there is frequently a gap between people's intentions and their real life actions. In this context the Commission of the E.C. launched its Second Action Program 1986–1990 also to respond to new economic and social challenges in the area of equal treatment for men and women. The second program deals with an important number of actions concerning women's employment, particularly those which encourages an equal level of participation in employment linked with new technology, and a more equal sharing of family responsibilities.[1]

Equality in education and training, equal pay and equal social security rights are objectives of all the European governments, but in most countries there is still a gap between principle and practice. There is a policy but the results indicate that the policy either is being ignored or is not being implemented with any vigor. Alternatively, the existing laws are not being tested sufficiently. Take Britain as an example. In 1985 British women still earned less than three-quarters of the average hourly earnings of men. From 1970 to 1976 women's hourly earnings increased from 62 percent of that of men to 73 percent. But the progress towards equality stopped after 1977.[2] The average hourly earnings of full-time women workers, aged 18 and over, stalled at just over 73 percent by the end of 1985.[3]

The range of job opportunities for women in Europe, or the lack of them, begins at school. In the classrooms, girls are far too frequently still the victims of prejudices and stereotyping which close off career opportunities. There are also inadequacies in career guidance so that girls often opt for shorter education and training periods, finally offering lower qualifications when they enter

Country	Total female labor force as percent of female population 15–64, 1980	Gross enrollment ratio of female students at third level, 1977/78	Proportion of female students registered in Humanities and arts, 1977/78	Proportion of female students registered in Science engineering medicine, etc. 1977/78
Austria	49	18	34	24
Belgium	48	22	13	37
Denmark	71	28	22	29
Finland	67	21	21	34
France	53	24	-	-
Germany, Fed. Rep. of	49	21	24	37
Ireland	35	15	36	26
Italy	40	23	26	36
Netherlands	35	21	30	21
Norway	63	23	19	30
Sweden	74	34	5	41
Switzerland	50	10	32	25
United Kingdom	58	14	22	22

Table 19. Educational Influences on Female Labor Force Participation in Europe around 1980. Source: L. Praukert, "Personal Preference, Social Change or Economic Necessity? Why Women Work," in *Labour and Society,* Vol. 7, No. 4, 1982, International Institute for Labour Studies, Geneva.

the market, and ending up with poorer job opportunities. Part of the program which the E.C. Ministers had approved in 1982 was to concentrate on these problems in order to improve training and to promote equality of opportunity.[4]

Statistical Profile

In the European Community, 52 percent of the women aged between 14 and 59 had a job or were job hunting during 1983. Out of a total working population of 118 million in the E.C., women account for about 44 million. Of these, 69 percent work in the service industry, 25 percent in industry and only 6 percent in agriculture. There are also more women out of work in proportion to their share of the total workforce. At the same time, women occupy 90 percent of Europe's part-time jobs.[5]

In 1980 the E.C. industrial sector employed more women than the agricultural sector. During the period 1980–1982 the highest proportion of women in the agricultural sector was found in Portugal, namely 53.3 percent. In Germany and Greece the figure exceeded 40 percent. The lowest proportion was in the Netherlands with 15.5 percent.

The percentages of women in the industrial labor force are roughly 22 percent with Portugal 29.4 percent, Germany 25.4, Britain 23.3 and the

Country	Labor force change			Share of women in total labor force change
	Both sexes	*Males*	*Females*	
Austria	2.6	1.0	5.0	77.4
Belgium	5.4	-0.8	17.4	110.1
Denmark	10.1	2.5	20.9	85.6
Finland	13.4	10.7	16.6	57.4
France	5.5	1.2	12.7	85.8
Germany, Fed. Rep. of	1.8	-0.1	5.0	104.8
Ireland	15.2	11.1	26.2	46.2
Italy	10.7	3.5	27.3	76.9
Netherlands	18.7	7.4	47.3	71.6
Norway	16.3	6.5	32.3	75.0
Sweden	6.3	-1.8	17.4	116.4
United Kingdom	5.0	0.4	12.5	94.7

Table 20. Percentage Change of European Labor Force by Sex and the Share of Women in the Total Labor Force 1975–1984. Source: Economic Commission of Europe, Geneva, 1985.

Netherlands only 13.1. Spain, Belgium and Greece all had percentages around 19. Greece and Spain had the highest proportion of independent female workers, representing 18 and 12 percent respectively. In Germany, the Netherlands and Britain, less than 5 percent of women earned their income independently. Women also formed an almost insignificant percentage of administrators and managers. In the Netherlands and Portugal, they were less than 1 percent. In Spain they were 0.2 percent.[6]

Wage Differentials

Wage differentials between men and women working in the manufacturing sector reveal that there is still a significant gap between the sexes and that between 1975 and 1982 no substantial changes occurred. Where the gap narrowed, it was a matter of 2 to 5 percent. In Germany it was virtually unchanged at 73 percent of men's wages. In Luxembourg, the gap widened by almost 1 percent. In the Netherlands there was no change. In England the gap narrowed from 66.5 percent to 68.9 percent. This compares with the far more rapid improvement in the Nordic countries. In Sweden women's hourly wages in 1982 were 90.3 percent those of men. (See Table 22.)

Changing Trends

Since 1975 significant changes have taken place in West European countries which have affected the legal status and economic situation of women. The general economic developments favored women with most obvious repercussions in women's status in the labor market in terms of their wages, levels of employment and degree of integration in the market. There have also been profound alterations in the role and institution of marriage and the family. The number of marriages has dropped significantly during the period 1970–1980. This has an equally significant impact on the distribution of women by marital status, especially in the younger marriage ages. (See Table 23.)

A 1985 United Nations report on the economic role of women observed:

> Some of these changes may be viewed as a continuation of historical trends, while others reflect new developments. Demographic changes, a rising level of education, and sectorial shifts in the economy are among the longer-term trends which have continued to influence women's labor force participation over the past 10 years. Economic developments in the last decade or so are among the more recent factors contributing to new patterns of labor market behavior in many countries of the region. During recent decades, one of the outstanding features of labor market developments in the E.C.E. region has been the dynamics of the participation of women. Whereas, for some time the activity rates of men have been showing a tendency to decline, those of women have generally been rising, very rapidly in a number of countries. As a result, the growth of the female labor force has become a major determinant of the evolution of the work force. General and admittedly rough, estimates of labor force trends for the whole of the E.C.E. region provide evidence to this effect.[7]

And further:

> According to these estimates, women accounted for more than three fifths (63%) of the expansion of the labor force in the region from 1960 to the present. The number of women in the labor force increased by more than 60% over this period, compared with a rise of just over 20% for men. These different growth trends for males and females have resulted in the share of women in the labor force rising from less than 37% in about 1960 to nearly 44% currently. Moreover, the trends show an acceleration over time: while, between 1960 and 1975, the rate of growth of the female labor force growth slowed down somewhat for men and rose further for women, causing a widening of the growth differential. It is thus estimated that, between 1975 and 1985, the rate of increase in the number of women in the labor force was three times that of men, and that women accounted for two thirds of the expansion of the work force during this period.[8]

Occupational Segregation

There is, however, one trend in industrial segregation by sex which is very clear: the female labor force is strongly concentrated in one branch of the tertiary sector, i.e., community, social and private services. In some European countries the proportion exceeds 50 percent. It serves once again to illustrate the important linkage between occupational and industrial segregation by sex. (See Table 24.) Health and social care services were strongest in the countries where these sectors are most publicly run. In the Scandinavian countries this has been running at over 50 percent.[9]

It is estimated that between 23 and 30 percent of the women in Western

Country and year	Manufacturing	Wholesale trade	Retail trade	Banking	Insurance	Public administration
Denmark						
1974	63.9	71.2	72.6	70.0	63.1	..
1983	71.4	74.4	75.5	76.4	68.1	..
Finland						
1970	58.3	57.3	70.0	75.7	58.0	72.0
1981	76.1	69.4	87.3	78.6	68.5	74.0
France						
1974	58.0	66.6	66.1	71.8	67.6	..
1978	61.7	69.7	67.5	74.5	66.1	83.9
Germany						
Fed. Rep. of						
1971	63.5	67.0	60.1	71.6	73.9	..
1982	66.7	68.3	65.9	77.4	76.8	..
Norway						
1970	55.1	61.3	69.9	71.8	59.1	75.5
1982	65.3	70.5	80.6	77.7	65.5	82.9
Sweden						
1970	58.6	60.9	80.3	84.6	82.4	..
1981	72.1	72.3	92.2	92.5	86.1	88.3
Switzerland						
1970	61.8	71.6	63.4	71.7	70.4	..
1982	66.6	74.5	63.9	78.6	73.1	79.6
United Kingdom						
1971	44.3	44.2	47.1	-	46.0 -	56.7
1980	53.2	54.1	56.1	-	49.9 -	60.9

Europe would have to change their occupations with men—i.e., many millions—in order to achieve a proportionate representation of women in each of the major occupational groups. In general, the countries of Western Europe displayed a higher degree of concentration of the female labor force than the Communist Bloc countries. In several countries up to 70 or 80 percent of the female non-farm labor force was concentrated in a group of typically female occupations: nurses, teachers, clerical workers and sales persons.[10]

In an earlier study by the United Nations on the economic role of women in the ECE region (1980) the following conclusion was reached:

> With respect to occupations, the findings indicated increased sex segregation for the major groups. Using the more detailed occupational classification, the results revealed that, even if an increase was observed in the female share of some male-dominated occupations, these changes were more than outweighed by the increase of women in the traditionally female-dominated occupations and the share of these occupations in the total employment structure. In 1971, 52% of female wage-earners worked in 6 out of 75 occupational categories (auxiliary administrative work, trade, cleaning, teaching, bookkeeping and health services). The changes over the period were more positive with respect to the vertical dimension of occupational segregation. Women had increasing access to higher occupational positions, mainly for white-collar working women. As far as occupational categories were concerned, a slight polarization was evident between 1972 and 1980. More women were employed as salaried employees... The share of women among university teachers remained the same: 20%. Their share in administrative and managerial jobs in private firms decreased, not only in the early 1970s, but from the 1960s onwards. The data ... indicate that the decrease of women in administrative work in the private sector is offset at the occupational-category level by an increase of women in administrative work in the public sector. The female share of all administrative work and managerial jobs rose from 15% in 1970 to almost 23% in 1980.[11]

It is commonly recognized that occupational segregation of women, apart from the influence brought about by stereotyping of girls at home and in school, is often the result of outright discrimination. How this discrimination can take place in countries with laws where sex discrimination is constitutionally prohibited is described by the United Nations:

> Labour market segmentation may also be caused by discrimination. Discrimination according to sex can take several forms; discrimination occurs, for instance, where women are paid less than men for the same type of job, or if the job qualifications required for a particular job are higher for women than for men. Direct discrimination may also take the form of restricted promotion possibilities for women or less access to on-the-job investment and training. Discrimination also exists in indirect forms: one is "statistical discrimination," where a woman seeking a job is not evaluated according to her individual qualifications. Rather, it is assumed that she has the characteristics of the "average" woman worker. Statistical discrimination exists, for example, where women are not given access to jobs at

Table 21. Average Monthly Earnings of Full-Time Non-Manual Women Workers, as a Percentage of Those of Men in Selected European Countries, 1970–1980. Source: International Labor Organization, *The Economic Role of Women in the ECE Region, 1985, Table V8.*

Country	*Women's wages compared to men's wages (in percentages)*							
	1975	**1976**	**1977**	**1978**	**1979**	**1980**	**1981**	**1982**
Belgium	71.3	70.5	70.7	70.7	70.2	69.7	72.5	73.5
Denmark	84.3	84.8	86.5	86.2	86.4	86.1	85.8	85.1
Finland	72.6	73.3	74.3	74.8	75.3	75.4	76.3	77.2
France	76.4	75.6	75.8	76.7	76.8	77.0	78.1	-
Germany Fed. Rep. of	72.1	72.2	72.3	72.8	72.8	72.7	73.1	73.0
Greece	69.5	70.3	68.8	69.0	67.9	67.8	67.2	73.1
Ireland	60.9	61.0	61.4	63.7	66.6	68.7	67.6	68.5
Luxembourg	60.9	64.1	62.5	60.4	58.7	61.2	60.0	-
Netherlands	79.2	79.8	80.0	80.4	80.1	80.2	79.3	79.2
Norway	78.0	79.4	79.8	80.2	80.5	81.9	82.6	83.2
Sweden	85.2	86.9	87.4	88.7	89.3	89.9	90.1	90.3
Switzerland	66.0	66.5	65.4	66.1	65.9	66.4	66.9	67.0
United Kingdom	66.5	70.2	70.8	69.1	69.1	68.8	68.8	68.9

Country	Year	Ages 20–24	25–29
Austria	1971	52.8	76.5
	1981	39.6	67.5
Belgium	1970	59.4	86.6
	1981	52.0	81.6
Canada	1971	55.7	82.7
	1981	48.0	76.8
Czechoslovakia	1970	63.2	85.5
	1980	64.5	84.2
Denmark	1970	54.0	82.5
	1981	22.0	58.0
Finland	1970	47.0	75.5
	1981	29.3	63.1
France	1970	53.8	81.2
	1981	43.5	72.6
German Democratic Republic	1970	634	85.6
	1981	54.6	79.1
Germany, Federal Republic of	1970	56.9	82.7
	1981	36.2	70.0
Hungary	1970	65.4	85.2
	1981	66.0	82.5
Netherlands	1970	51.8	84.5
	1981	39.2	74.3
Norway	1970	53.1	81.8
	1981	36.0	71.6
Poland	1970	52.5	83.1
	1978	52.2	82.2
Sweden	1970	39.7	73.9
	1981	14.9	45.4
Switzerland	1970	44.5	75.9
	1980	26.5	63.6
United Kingdom	1970	58.6	84.8
	1980	48.0	78.7

Table 23. Percentage of European Women Aged 20–24 and 25–29 Years Who Are Married. Source: International Labor Organization, *The Economic Role of Women in the ECE Region,* 1985, p. 10.

higher levels of responsibility and the promotion possibilities for which they technically qualify, because it is expected that they will have a low level of job stability in the future. Another type of indirect discrimination on the part of the employer may take the form of sex-role stereotyping with respect to the type of work which women can perform in the labor market. This include an exaggeration of women's comparative advantage in traditionally female work or a prejudice against female

Table 22. Differentials in Hourly Wages Between Men and Women in Manufacturing, 1975–1982. Source: International Labor Organization, *Yearbook of Labor Statistics,* Geneva, 1983, Table 17A.

Country	All sectors	Non-farm sectors	Industry	Services
Austria				
1961	40.3	36.5	32.1	43.4
1971	38.6	37.2	26.6	47.7
1981	38.6	37.5	28.7	49.7
Belgium				
1961	27.0	27.9	18.1	38.3
1970	29.5	30.1	20.0	39.0
1981	37.7	43.4	18.3	45.6
Denmark				
1960	21.2	36.0	20.8	48.5
1970	36.6	38.3	22.9	48.8
1981	44.4	46.5	24.8	57.8
Finland				
1960	39.4	41.7	27.5	55.4
1970	42.4	44.8	29.4	56.6
1980	46.3	47.5	30.8	58.3
France				
1968	34.6	35.1	22.2	46.7
1975	36.6	37.4	24.1	47.4
1982	39.4	34.9	25.1	49.7
Germany, Fed. Rep. of				
1961	37.0	34.3	25.5	45.6
1970	35.8	34.8	26.2	44.1
1981	38.4	38.0	26.4	48.8
Ireland				
1961	25.9	33.6	23.9	38.9
1971	26.3	32.4	21.1	40.3
1979	27.7	31.2	19.4	40.5
Italy				
1961	25.1	24.5	19.7	30.8
1971	27.0	26.6	20.0	34.1
1980	33.2	30.8	23.4	37.2
Netherlands				
1960	22.3	23.9	12.0	34.6
1971	25.9	26.8	12.4	35.9
1979	29.7	30.0	11.4	40.0
Norway				
1960	22.9	27.3	13.9	38.7
1970	27.6	28.9	13.9	39.9
1981	41.7	42.4	18.7	53.9
Sweden				
1960	29.8	33.2	17.9	50.7
1970	35.4	36.7	18.9	50.7
1981	45.9	47.0	22.3	54.3
Switzerland				
1960	30.1	32.8	22.1	47.0
1970	34.4	35.2	23.9	47.7
1980	34.4	..	..	..
United Kingdom				
1961	32.5	33.3	24.3	42.2
1971	36.5	37.1	24.5	47.8
1980	39.1	40.6	23.6	51.5

employees in work which is deemed not "suitable" for them. . . . Women are caught in a vicious circle whenever discrimination in the labor market exists. In such cases of discrimination, women who pursue a career receive relatively low gains, and thus the cost of dropping out is also relatively small. Employers can then point to the labor market behavior of women who do drop out, and continue to discriminate against them.[12]

The Dynamics of Change

According to a worldwide advertising supplement released in 1988 as part of the upcoming 500th celebration of Christopher Columbus's coming to the New World in 1492, the Spanish Minister of Social Welfare, Matilde Fernandez, stated that "nothing has changed so profoundly in Spain during the past 15 years as the role of women." Spain's sexual revolution lagged behind that of the rest of Europe, and it was only in 1981 that divorce was finally legalized. The legal framework to attain equality of opportunity is now in place in Spain, and a 155-page booklet, *Equal Opportunity for Women,* published by the government in 1987, outlines a comprehensive plan of action between 1988 and 1990 to further combat sexist stereotypes, to prevent sexual harassment at work, and to address other matters of importance to women. Women are increasingly entering domains previously held only by men. Two state-run companies are now headed by women, and in September 1988 almost 200 young women entered the military academy near Seville, the first women in history to become members of the Spanish armed forces. Spain's entry into the E.C. in mid-1992 is expected to further improve women's status and opportunities.

Since World War II the status of women in Italy, long the most neglected group in Europe together with women in Greece and Spain, has also undergone enormous changes. June 1946 marked the first election with women's suffrage. The 1948 constitution stated explicitly that women are fully equal with men: "All citizens have equal social dignity and are equal before the law, regardless of sex, race, language, religion, political opinions or personal and social conditions."[13] Subsequent governments have passed equal employment and equal opportunity laws, as well as equal eligibility for public office. Despite these provisions married men could still, legally, beat their wives, a situation which changed in 1975 only with the passing of the Family Laws.

Italian women are covered by special protective statutes as employees, e.g. they cannot do heavy or dangerous work and cannot be fired for marriage or pregnancy. During the 1960s the law that made adultery a crime only for the wife was invalidated by the Italian Supreme Court. The 1970s saw legalization of divorce and birth control, and the court ruled in 1975 that abortion is legal for a woman whose physical or mental health is endangered by her pregnancy.

Table 24. Percentage Share of Women in the Total Labor Force of Europe, by Major Economic Sectors, 1960–1980. Source: International Labor Organization, *The Economic Role of Women in the ECE Region,* Geneva, 1985, p.41, Table IV.2.

Country	Year	Administrators and managerial workers		Proportion of women	
		Men and women (number)	*Women (number)*	*Managers (%)*	*Manufacturing workers (%)*
Germany, Fed. Rep. of	1982	291,000	33,000	11.3	30.3
Hungary	1980	3,000	1,000	33.3	46.5
Norway (a)	1982	22,000	2,000	9.1	24.1
Portugal	1981	22,000	1,000	4.5	40.3
Spain	1982	75,400	2,000	2.7	23.7
Sweden (b)	1982	19,000	1,000	5.3	26.1

Despite all these changes, Italy still has a lower divorce rate than any other European country except Ireland. In 1986 some 16,000 Italian couples divorced, compared with about 160,000 in the United Kingdom. However, the dramatic decrease in the number of marriages in Italy during 1976–1986 suggests that people are not following in their parents' footsteps.[14]

Considering the Italian women's lack of support in the media, the attitude of the Catholic Church, and the late start in the organization of women's rights movements,[15] it can be said that women's progress in Italy between 1973 and 1983 was quite dramatic.[16]

In April 1975 there were further revisions by parliament in the Family Laws of Italy. The wife obtained equal say in where the family lives and how the children should be educated. She may sign the family's electric, gas and telephone contracts, using her maiden name. She may keep her own bank account. At the end of 1977 the Italian Parliament passed an equal opportunities act making it illegal to discriminate on the basis of sex in the marketplace, whether in training, hiring, promotions, dismissals, or pension. The law also abolished previous legally sanctioned differences of treatment on gender basis, e.g. the compulsory retirement age for women, which was five years earlier for women.

The new laws brought a reversal of the long decline of the number of women in the work force, one of the special characteristics of Italy in comparison with other E.C. countries. Between 1972 and 1980 women entered the marketplace at a rate of five women to one man. This paralleled significant changes in women's education together with a massive drop in the fertility rate. Women also entered jobs that had previously been closed to them. For example, after 1977 the Fiat company employed some 10,000 women for the automobile assembly lines. Previously Fiat had never hired women for this work.[17]

Compared to Britain, Italian women are legally and constitutionally in very good shape, but authorities rarely fulfill the promise and the rights held out by legislation. Nonetheless, Italian women have made impressive strides in education and in business. It is only in politics that Italian women have fared less well. During the 1970s, not one made it to the Cabinet. Women have never been considered serious candidates for the post of mayor of any major Italian city. Their strength has been in business and the arts.[18]

In September 1985 the Swiss conducted a national referendum on equal marriage rights for women. The vote in favor was 54.7 percent. The referendum stripped husbands of the right to control their wives' finances, to stop wives from taking outside employment, and to decide such matters as where to live and how to raise the children. The husband is no longer the legal head of the family. Wives are now full and equal marriage partners. Husbands must

Table 25. Proportion of Women in Administrative and Managerial Occupations in Selected European Countries. Source: International Labor Organization, *1983 Yearbook of Labour Statistics,* Geneva, 1984. Notes: (a) mining, quarrying and manufacture; (b) mining, quarrying, manufacturing and public utilities.

now tell their partners about their earnings, debts and properties. Previously, men in Switzerland could legally keep their financial affairs a secret, whereas women had to disclose theirs. A man could sue his wife for divorce because she took a job without his permission. In the event of divorce, savings and debts must now be divided evenly. In the past, husbands were entitled to two-thirds of all assets.[19]

Sexual equality in Switzerland has been advanced enormously by the new referendum in a country where women attained the vote at federal level only in 1971 and where an equal rights amendment (Article 4 of the Constitution) was approved only in 1981. Small wonder that after the referendum on women's marital rights the Geneva daily *La Suisse* banner headlined the result as followed: FROM MALE DOMINATION TO EQUAL PARTNERSHIP.[20]

In Iceland the single most important issue for women has always been the wage disparity issue. Politically women have made great strides, and in 1983 Vigdis Finnbogadottir became Iceland's first female president. Towards the end of 1985 the Icelandic women staged a historic 24-hour general strike against male privilege. Even the President stayed at home to show her support for the women. What made the continuing wage disparity senseless was the fact that Iceland simply cannot do without its female labor. Out of a tiny population of 240,000 women form more than 80 percent of the labor force but, on the average, earn 40 percent less than men.[21]

Upset, and spurred on by the slow progress towards equality for women, the women's movement in Iceland organized the first women's political party. In national elections during May 1987, 10 percent of the voters cast their ballot for the Women's Alliance, thus providing the alliance with six seats in parliament, otherwise known as the *Althing*. More important than the six (out of 63) seats that they won in parliament is the fact that the election gave none of the coalition groups a clear majority. The Women's Alliance party therefore now holds the pivotal role in the formation of the new government. One of the party spokeswomen (Gudrun Agnasdottir) told the press: "Our main emphasis is to improve the condition and status of women. . . . We regard all issues in society as women's issues. We want better wages, better care for children, longer maternity leaves. And we want it as soon as possible."[22] On June 26, 1988, Vigdis Finnbogadottir swept to her third term as Ireland's President, defeating not a man, but another woman for the post.[23]

In the Netherlands, women have forced their way into the highest positions in politics, the media, medicine, and the academic world. The law has been slow to change in a country known (or infamous) for its lengthy deliberations. It was only in 1976 that a clause was introduced in the Civil Code forbidding the state and other employers from firing a woman because of pregnancy.[24] In many other countries of the West, women were not permitted by custom and tradition to occupy certain positions. They were simply excluded, not outlawed. But in the Netherlands in 1910 it was legally forbidden for a woman to occupy the position of judge, lawyer, mayor or civil servant.[25] Although there is no such law or code in existence in later years, it is known that up to 1969 women were simply not accepted as advocates. Even today there are very few women advocates in the Netherlands. In 1983 only 20 percent of all attorneys were women and female notaries were less than 3 percent. The Netherlands is seen as being caught up in a vicious circle, slowing progress for women, because of too much stereotyping; there is still much discrimination in general against women.[26]

Women in France have made remarkable progress in the legal system. In France the judges are civil servants. In 1983 women were almost 42 percent of the legal staff at the lower levels in a city like Paris. Women were 12 percent of the Courts of Appeal, equivalent to the judges of the Supreme Court in South Africa, or federal judges in the United States, and 11.7 percent of the *Cour de Cassation,* which, in most countries, would be the highest court of appeal. (In France there is one higher level, the nine-member Constitutional Council, which rules on matters affecting the Constitution.) As Lovenduski pointed out in *Women and European Politics:* "The feminisation of the French judiciary has been a phenomenon of the 1970's and 1980's and represents a remarkable achievement for French women."[27]

The dynamics of equality have worked best and earliest in Scandinavia, although the suicide rate among women is higher in this part of the world than anywhere else in Europe, with Denmark the highest. The price women have to pay in Scandinavia for achieving an equal status both in terms of the law and in practice appears to be high. Today Finland and Sweden lead the West in their efforts to make the working mother and wife a practical reality. Legal systems have been revamped for this purpose in all Scandinavian countries. Taxes no longer penalize a two-career family as they do in so many countries. The Scandinavian commitment to sexual equality is clear-cut. The abortion laws are "liberal" in that abortion is available to residents until the nineteenth week of pregnancy.

Careerwise the Scandinavian women have done well at an early stage, and up until the end of the 1970s the highest post held by a woman in the United Nations was that occupied by a Finn, Helvi Sipila. According to Shari Steiner, women already controlled the city councils of Norway's largest cities in the '70s. The President of Norwegian Senate during the '70s was a woman. The Vice President of the Swedish Parliament is a woman. Women are Supreme Court judges in both Norway and Denmark. All four Scandinavian countries have women in the Cabinet. Finland and Denmark had the largest female proportion in their work forces of any country outside the Eastern Bloc during 1976.[28]

Steiner found that one area in which Scandinavian women have not made the progress they had hoped for is in business, and female candidates for the post of Prime Minister are taken less seriously than in France and England. But as she quite rightly observed after her study of Scandinavian women: "For the moment Swedish women have the most freedom to develop their individuality of any women on earth."[29]

Women in Government and Politics

In government and politics women have made little significant progress in Western Europe compared to women in Scandinavia. In Britain there was not much difference between the late 1960s and the early 1980s. In fact, in 1963 there were more women in top government positions than 20 years later. (See Table 26.)

By contrast, women comprised 28 percent of the members of the government in Sweden in 1984, 28 percent of legislators and 29 percent of local councillors. A similar pattern was apparent in Norway, where women were 22 percent, 26 percent and 23 percent, respectively, of holders of such positions. In Finland and Denmark women were also well represented at the governmental level, if not to the same extent as in the other two countries. Denmark has a woman Prime Minister. Only in Iceland were women's shares of elected posts below 20 percent and of government posts as low as 10 percent.

Elsewhere in Western Europe Lovenduski found the pattern to be very mixed and, from the women's point of view, very unsatisfactory. Whereas Austria had no fewer than six women cabinet ministers in a 23-person cabinet at the beginning of 1982, there were only 10 percent women among the members of the national legislative assembly. On the other hand, in the Netherlands women are almost 20 percent of the members of the States General (parliament), but only two of those made it to the Cabinet. In Luxembourg almost 15 percent of the members of the national assembly were women; in Ireland it was 8 percent; in Belgium 7.5 percent; and in Switzerland 10.5 percent. The Swiss figure has some significance since women only obtained the vote in 1971.

In 1984 there were only 13 women among the 300 members of the Greek Parliament. In Italy women formed only 7.9 percent of the members of the Chamber of Deputies and less than 5 percent of the Senate. In Spain women were less than 5 percent in both the upper and lower house of the Cortes in 1984, and in Portugal there were 18 women out of a total of 250 members, or slightly more than 7 percent. According to Lovenduski, it is difficult to single out any specific reason for the variations from country to country.[30]

The higher percentage of women in senior government and political positions in France also requires some qualification, wrote Lovenduski. Women usually have oversight of the so-called "soft areas" of government such as family, education and women's questions. When the socialists were in power in the early 1980s, they introduced a quota system so that women received at least 20 percent of places on the various party organs. The socialists, under President Francois Mitterand, also strongly supported women's programs and created several senior posts to deal with women's affairs.

France has also tried to promote a political quota system, the first time, according to Lovenduski, that this has been attempted by an European government so as to increase the proportiion of women candidates in local elections—decreeing in 1981 that the list for municipal elections, which is a highly politicized affair in France, should not contain more than 80 percent men for any party. Before the system could get off the ground, the French Constitutional Court ruled it to be unconstitutional. But women, without the assistance of a quota system, have done well in the French labor unions, better than in any other of the European countries, with 27 percent women serving as executive committee members while forming only 30 percent of the union membership, or close to parity. In contrast (see Table 27), women formed almost 41 percent of the union membership in Sweden but only 12 percent of the council members. Clearly there is a divergence here in Sweden in terms of labor politics and national politics. In the Netherlands there were no women in the labor union executive although almost 15 percent of the union's members were women.

In Britain women formed a substantial percentage of the membership of various political parties but had a very small representation in parliament. The same pattern is noticeable in the labor union movement. Women formed almost 33 percent of the union's membership but had none of their sex in the executive councils. On the Trade Union Council women have six places out of a total of 51, a quota system which the unions somehow defend as democratic. Thus, the pink ghetto has its reflection for women within parliamentary and labor union systems in England.

When it comes to government officials, civil servants, the pink ghetto is equally visible as Table 28 reveals. It would appear as if tokenism is very much part of British policy when it comes to improving the status of women.

The Gap Between Paper Rights and Real Rights

In Europe, as in all other areas of the world, the gap between policy and practice, between legal and constitutional provisions and reality, remains a major headache for women's rights movements, because it is not easy to close. A good example is the election of members to the very prestigious French Academy. Up to January 1989, the 353-year-old organization had elected only two women to become members, and in 1989 Jacqueline de Romilly was the only woman left.

In Switzerland the laws appear to be in place to fight a successful battle against discrimination, but the deeply rooted traditional belief in Switzerland that men and women have different roles remains to be overcome. According to this belief men are the providers and women the wives, mothers, and housekeepers. Ilda Simoma believes that there are two other obstacles. The existence of two distinct labor markets is one; the better remunerated jobs, carrying prestige and responsibility, go to men, while the routine jobs requiring a low level of skills are reserved for women. The second is the widespread resistance to the implementation of the principle of equal pay. "Along with the new legal provisions . . . a change of attitude at all levels of Swiss society . . . is essential to achieve a labor market policy fairer to women and to accelerate an evolution ensuring equal status to men and women." The majority of working women, she wrote, are in jobs that require little education or training, have low pay and present little possibility for promotion. "Employers use every pretext to avoid paying women and men the same wages for work of equal value." On average, she found, the wages of women in the private sector are about 25 to 30 percent lower than men's wages, even where the work performed and the skills required are the same. Even among workers with college degrees the difference between men's and women's wages is about 25 percent. Though the law prohibits wage discrimination, individual arrangements between

Country	Date of Women's Franchise	Percentage in House of Assembly	Boroughs and Town Councillors	Mayors	Ministers and Junior Ministers [a]
Denmark	1915	30.7	21.0	[b]	19.0
Germany	1918	15.4	10.8	21.4	5.9
Netherlands	1919	17.4	19.0	4.0	14.3
Luxembourg	1919	14.0	12.0	[b]	8.3
Ireland	1922	8.4	7.4	[b]	[b]
Britain	1928	6.3	14.4	[b]	8.7
France	1944	5.9	14.0	[b]	12.0
Italy	1945	7.0	8.3	[b]	3.3
Belgium	1948	6.5	13.9	[b]	8.7
Greece	1952	4.0	[b]	1.4	7.5
Portugal	1976	6.0	[b]	1.8	[b]
Spain	1930	7.9	8.0	0.5	5.0

Country	Women as percent of membership	Women as percent of congress	Women as percent of council members
Iceland	46.7	27.0	18.0
Denmark	43.0	14.9	23.8
Sweden	40.9	25.0	12.0
UK	33.3	9.8	13.7
Norway	33.0	19.0	12.0
Belgium	33.0	6.4	5.5
Italy	33.0	15.0	15.0
Austria	30.2	NA	1.9
France	30.0	30.0	24.0
West Germany	21.0	7.5	7.9
Switzerland	11.0	6.0	2.0

Post	Men	Women	Total	Percent of women
Permanent secretary	37	0	37	0
Deputy secretary	129	5	134	3.7
Under secretary	497	26	523	3.7
Assistant secretary	977	66	1,043	6.3
Senior principal	623	12	635	1.9
Principal	3,705	409	4,114	9.9
Senior executive officer	6,820	536	7,356	7.3
Higher executive officer	18,087	4,150	22,237	18.7
Executive officer	26,514	17,807	44,321	40.2
Clerical officer	27,640	57,901	85,505	67.7

employer and employee may not contain a specific provision regarding wages and are therefore exempt from the law.[31]

Top: **Table 27. Women as a Percentage of National Trade Union Councils in Europe Representing All Major Unions, 1981. Source: International Labor Organization, Geneva, 1983.** ***Bottom:*** **Table 28. Percentage Women in the British Civil Service, Selected Posts, 1983. Source: United Kingdom Civil Service Statistics, 1983.**

Opposite: **Table 26. Percentage of Women in Government and Politics in Europe: 1987–1988. Source: Commission of the European Communities,** ***Women of Europe 1978–1988,*** **Supplement No. 27, June 1988, Women's Information Service of the EEC, Brussels; various editions of** ***Women of Europe,*** **bi-monthly, Women's Information Service of the EEC, Brussels, January–December 1988; annd Joni Lovenduski,** ***Women and European Politics,*** **University of Massachusetts Press, Amherst, 1986. Notes: [a] Cabinet Ministers, Deputy Ministers, Secretaries of State or Directors General; [b] not available for 1987–1988.**

The Swiss Constitution was amended in June 1981 to guarantee equal rights to men and women. However, acts contrary to this provision cannot be fought in the courts, observed Rosemary Sarri. The Swiss Federal Court has also refused to control the constitutionality of federal laws said to contain the worst discrimination. Because of different and restrictive interpretation of the meaning of equality where it concerns women, some observers believe the right to equality will remain a paper right for years to come. Because the Swiss parliament is 90 percent male, little hope is expected from that source. The dispersion of women according to class, religion, language or region means women cannot rely on a uniform conception of equality.[32]

In a special article, "Law and the Promotion of Women," in *Women's Studies International Forum,* Jennifer Corcoran points out that the 1975 law forbidding sex discrimination in Britain has also not had the impact it was expected to have. It is being used very infrequently to pursue equal pay cases. Sex discrimination complaints to the tribunals are increasing, but the use of enforcement powers by the Equal Opportunities Commission is diminishing. Once again it shows that the U.K. government has demonstrated a lack of commitment to the principles of equal treatment.[33] On the other hand, the E.O.C. played a major role in arranging with the Engineering Council to designate 1984 as Women into Science and Engineering (W.I.S.E.) Year, and hundreds of projects were undertaken by schools, colleges, universities and other institutions all over the country.[34]

Emma MacLennan and Nickie Fonda wrote that though the past 15 years in Britain have been a period of growth for women's relative employment and earnings and have seen some desegregation of the jobs that most women normally do, "this has occurred largely despite, rather than as result of, government labor market policies aimed at women."[35]

In Italy the Equal Employment Opportunities Law, as in Switzerland and in Britain, not only has certain internal flaws but, as pointed out by Bianca Becalli, there has been an overall failure in its implementation within and beyond the sphere of work. "There have been remarkable continuities in the Italian situation," she wrote. Job segregation by job is not changing and, according to a study by P. Barile and L. Zanuso which Becalli cited, there has even been a slight increase in sex segregation in both manual and nonmanual occupations.[36]

In West Germany there does not appear to be even an implicit provision for affirmative action to eliminate the existing inequalities in the labor market, wrote Hanna Schop-Schilling. In fact, she said, "the Federal Republic of Germany does not have a comprehensive labor market policy designed to protect women from discrimination nor does it have effective individual laws and measures aimed in that direction." In this respect her findings indicate not only the existence of a gap between policy and practice but also the absence of policy as laid down by law.[37]

In France the pattern in the civil service, unlike the pattern in the higher echelons of government and politics, reverted to what seems to be the norm in the E.C. countries, observed Lovenduski. Sex equality in the civil service is official policy, and residual legal discrimination was also removed by statute in 1982. But there is a wide gap between formal and substantive opportunities for women. Women form 50 percent of the civil service staff, but at the senior levels they were less than 12 percent in 1983.

Areas of Significant Progress

One area in which most of Europe has made really significant progress is instituting family support systems for working mothers. The E.C. countries cope with child care in many ways, including generous tax credits, state-funded *ećoles maternelles* for infants, so-called "baby nests," parent-controlled play groups for toddlers and nurseries, all state-funded, -constructed or -supported. A recent report of the European Commission showed that in France, Belgium, Italy, and Denmark more than 80 percent of children aged 3 to 5 enjoy publicly funded child-care facilities. In Spain, Greece, West Germany, Ireland, the Netherlands and Luxembourg, 50 percent or more of three- to five-year-olds enjoy such facilities.[38] Currently the various central governments are trying to decrease their own role by devolving responsibility to local governments, provincial, state and city. The socialist governments of Europe provide more funds and better care for young children, which explains why more three-year-olds and younger in relatively poor Portugal receive state care than toddlers in wealthy Germany. The pressure in Europe to provide, widen, and improve child care services is largely feminist-driven in the capitalist countries and fairly widely supported by the general public in the socialist states. The European Commission, reported *U.S. News and World Report* magazine, concluded that "child care continues to be a major cause of inequality for women."[39]

European men and women did not see women's lack of legal equality as their only handicap—as women's organizations in the United States did. Instead, Hewlett observed, they recognized women's dual burden, their work in the home and as mothers and their labor in the workplace. The objective was to lighten this burden by the only way possible: assisting women with the care of their children to make it easier for them to work, and eliminating disruption to their careers by absence from work as the result of pregnancy.[40]

Hewlett states that in trying to achieve this objective European women and European governments did not consider assistance to working mothers with children as the beginning and the end of women's rights. Most groups in Britain, Italy, France and the Nordic countries fought for concrete rights, benefits and services for women, true, but only in later years. Hewlett writes that in the 1960s and 1970s the women's movement in Italy, and in other countries, worked within the system with issues such as sexual and personal freedom—divorce, abortion, and non-sexist education. Following the advent of the various equality laws passed in Europe under pressure from United Nations conventions and the European Commission itself, most organizations immediately started to emphasize material realities—which the women's movement in the United States failed to do. Several countries—Britain, Sweden, Italy, France and West Germany—made significant progress in one decade. Support policies for divorced mothers, for example, did not remain limited to the social welfare states of Scandinavia. In France, Hewlett continued, newly divorced women receive a special social security payment for a full year after divorce or until the youngest child is three, reimbursement of children's health expenses, a family allowance, a variety of special tax deductions and government retraining programs which pay 90 percent of the minimum wage. West Germany and other countries have also instituted a system whereby the government guarantees the custodial parent, usually the mother, a minimum child support payment.[41]

European maternity policies are indeed generous, though perhaps not as generous as those of the Swedes, who provide parental leave of nine months when the child is born, replace 90 percent of the mother's earnings up to a maximum, protect her seniority on the job, provide other fringe benefits and guarantee that the mother will get her former job back after maternity leave. In Italy a pregnant woman is entitled to five months' paid leave at 80 percent of her salary followed by a further six months at 30 percent. Her job is held for both time periods. Britain's Employment Act also provides women with time off for pregnancy, six weeks' paid maternity leave and re-employment on terms not less favorable than those which applied when she left.[42]

Another area where there has been significant progress is in public attitudes towards women's role in society, notably in respect of politics.

At the request of the European Commission a special opinion poll was conducted in the 12 member states of the E.C. in 1987, carried out by various specialized agencies of these states, and co-ordinated by the market analysis group *Faits et Opinions* of Paris.

Altogether nearly 75 percent of men in Europe disagreed with the notion that politics are men's business. Some 67 percent of men also said that they had confidence in both men and women as parliamentary representatives, while only 14 percent said that things would be worse if there were more women in parliament. The study said that the awareness of women's problems in Europe was very high in 1975, when first measured, but then it declined in all countries in 1983, only to resurge in 1987. It is in Italy, Spain and Portugal that the public is at present most aware of the issue of women's rights. Women are traditionally more aware of the problem than men and over the 12-year period under review, the gap between the sexes has not narrowed. It is at its widest today in Ireland, Greece, Spain and Portugal. The concept of complete equality of husband's and wife's role is still in the minority. It is most advanced in Denmark, while Germany and Luxembourg are the least egalitarian. In nine out of the 12 countries the majority of men are in favor of their wife's working. It is only in Germany, Luxembourg and Ireland that the majority of men are opposed to this situation.[43]

Despite the foregoing, the possibility of massive insincerity cannot be ignored. The survey has shown that men are strongly in favor of women in politics. Yet, as Table 26 indicates, that belief has not been translated into practice. A separate survey conducted in Spain in 1986 for the Ministry of Culture also revealed that 75 percent of those questioned thought that more women should be involved in politics, 75 percent opposed the idea that politics was not for women and 63 percent believed that political activism was compatible with women's family responsibilities.[44] Yet, again, looking at Table 26, women form only 6 percent of the members of parliament in Spain, which hardly coincides with public opinion.

In the European media, newspapers, radio and television, there is a constant reference to discrimination in other countries of the world on the grounds of race and religion. Yet a special study of women in television in Europe in 1988 reveals the insincerity of this attitude. In the first place the proportion of women being recruited to television in 1988 is no higher than it was as far back as the early '70s. The potential of women to influence policy in television is also negligible because women occupy less than 8 percent of the top three grades of management in all of the European television stations surveyed. The reality is that the majority of women in television in Europe, in fact more than 60 percent, are administrative assistants, secretaries and clerks.[45]

The situation in the daily press is not much different. In the Netherlands only 10 percent of the staff of daily newspapers are women. In Greece only 183 out of the 1,060 registered journalists on daily newspapers are women. In Portugal in 1988 only 25 of the 1,508 professional, card-carrying journalists, or 1.6 percent, were women.[46]

A third area in which there has been significant progress is the success in amalgamating the aspirations of various women's movements and in the organization of conferences to discuss the remaining problems facing women in Europe. For example, at the invitation of the British Fawcett Society and the Women's Information Service of the European Commission, women delegates representing 85 European organizations with more than 50 million members met in London in November 1987, *inter alia* to hammer out the concept and details for a European Women's Lobby.[47] A Nordic forum in Denmark in 1988 drew more than 10,000 participants from the various Nordic countries.[48]

What tasks lie ahead for women and the women's movement in Europe? For governments and society? What obstacles remain to be removed on the road to equal treatment and opportunities for men and women?

The following survey of selected problem areas in the 12-nation European Community has been drawn up based on information contained in various 1988 editions of *Women in Europe*. It clearly indicates, above all, that despite the impressive legal apparatus which the E.C. and its member governments have structured, there is still an acute *de facto* discrimination that needs to be overcome.

In Belgium...

- Women pensioners receive only 86 percent of the pension paid to males.
- Sixty percent of the unemployed in Belgium are women.
- After the elections of December 1987 there were five fewer women members of Parliament than after the 1985 elections.

In Britain...

- According to a Labor Research Department Survey of British trade unions with the largest female membership, women account for less than 10 percent of full-time union officials in 60 percent of the unions surveyed.

• Women currently account for only 1 percent of the workers in the offshore gas and oil industries.

• Only 2 percent of technicians in the engineering industry are women.

• Eighty percent of single parent families in Britain in 1986 were women.

• More than 42 percent of undergraduate students in Britain and 37 percent of post-graduate students are women, but in 1985 only 20 percent of the academic staff at British universities were women, and of these 75 percent were research personnel.

• The Equal Opportunities Commission revealed that in 1987 women accounted for only 18 percent of all civil service employees in Northern Ireland, while 50 government employers had not hired even one woman. The Commission also observed that the labor market in the area remained rigidly segregated on the basis of sex. In 1987 women's average weekly earnings were only 73.5 percent of those of men. Only 9 percent of engineering and technical students are women.

In Denmark...

• Studies have shown that since the Equal Pay Act was passed in 1976 the gap between men's and women's salaries, far from narrowing, has actually widened and that the same is true of bonuses.

• The union membership rate among Danish women, currently 81 percent across the board, has topped that of men, but men are still the overwhelming majority among union executives.

• A court case revealed that some companies are still paying women wages 25 percent lower than those of men.

In France...

• Between 1984 and 1987 women's salaries were on average 31 percent below those of men.

• A study of women in politics published in 1988 showed that in 1986 only 6 percent of the members of the House of Assembly were women; only 3 percent of the senators; only 10 percent of regional councillors; only 14 percent district councillors; and only 4 percent county councillors. The study by Marie Sineau of the French National Center for Scientific Research refers to the phenomenon of "enforced specialization" of women in politics.

• Work at home remains a typically female occupation, and studies show that even at home male and female workers do not compete in the same areas of the labor market since men overwhelmingly occupy the most skilled positions.

In Germany...

• According to a 1988 study by the Prognos Institute, at the present time women hold only 3.6 percent of the key positions in the German economy, even though the economy is short of 500,000 managers.

• Part-time work is still mostly carried out by women. In 1986 women held 92.3 percent of part-time jobs.

• Among government civil servants the proportion of women has not improved. At a meeting of the civil servants association in 1987 there were only 36 women with the right to vote out of total of 425 voting delegates.

• Only 16.5 percent of the judges in Germany in 1987 were women. A survey by the Ministry of Justice published in 1988 showed that 75 percent of women with legal training who sought work in industry and 70 percent of those who sought employment with law firms admitted to having been turned away because of their sex.

• Although women constituted 55 percent of all art students they formed only 15 percent of the teaching staff.

• Though 38 percent of all students at German universities are women, the teaching staff is still overwhelmingly a male bastion, with only 5 percent of the professorates occupied by women. At the University of the Ruhr, there are only seven women out of a total of 407 professors.

• Almost 60 percent of all female students are studying languages and more than 57 percent arts.

• Only 1.5 percent of German fathers are taking advantage of the paid leave granted after the birth of a child.

• Less than 3 percent of Germany's ambassadors are women.

• Eighty percent of new trade union members are women; however, even where women now make up more than 33 percent of the membership they hold an average of no more than 3 to 8 percent of the executive board seats.

In Greece...

• In a 1986 study of European community law and women it is revealed that bonuses, which constitute wage increases, are mostly awarded for work mainly performed by men; collective arrangements still exist which provide for different wage levels for men and women doing the same work; quotas are laid down by sex for the training of primary school teachers.

• A meeting of the Hellenic Association of Women Jurists concluded that in the areas of social security and labor law, the status of women remains significantly inferior to that of men.

• A study published by the Women's Rights League in 1988 shows that there is as much sexual harassment in Greece as in the other member states of the E.C.

In Ireland...

• The Irish government, which has already refused to name a cabinet post for women's affairs, in 1988 axed a number of women's services set up by previous governments.

• In 1986 more than 70 percent of all part-time work, generally unskilled and low-paid jobs, was performed by women.

• A 1988 survey indicated that 97 percent of top management jobs in Ireland's leading 100 companies were men.

In Italy...

• Only 5 percent of company directors in Italy in 1987 were women.

• In Milan only 6.5 percent of police officers are women.

• In all of Italy there are only three women who are harbor workers; all three at the Port of Livorno in Tuscany.

In Luxembourg...

• Ten years after the U.N. Convention on the Elimination of All Forms of Discrimination Against Women was signed by Luxembourg's ambassador to the U.N., the convention could not be ratified by the Luxembourg Parliament (House of Deputies) because male heirs of the House of Nassau, the ruling dynasty, have priority in succeeding to the throne, even if they have older sisters, and because the Constitution forbids women to give their children their maiden names.

• According to a regulation dating back to 1915 a waitress can only be employed with special permission of the district council, while no authorization is required to hire a waiter.

In the Netherlands...

• In 1987 only 13 percent of principals at primary schools were women, and at secondary school level, only 5 percent.

In Portugal...

• Studies in Portugal indicate that the feminization of agricultural work is increasing. In 1986 more than 71 percent of all agricultural workers were women, of whom 20.4 percent were defined as "unpaid workers who are family members."

• In all of Portugal only one woman is a listed broker at the Securities Exchange.

• Sixty percent of the unemployed in Portugal are women.

• In spite of the fact that the examination failure rate among girls at school is lower than among boys, girls constitute more than 60 percent of school drop-outs.

In Spain...

• According to a joint study by the Women's Institute in Madrid and the National Center for the Study of Education published in 1988, only 33 percent of students in higher education in Spain are women, and women make up 77 percent of all illiterates.

• Women hold less than 5 percent of all company management posts in Spain.

• More than 82 percent of all persons interviewed on Spanish television in 1986 were men.

• According to a 1988 study by the Ministry of Economic Affairs, Spanish women earn an average of 22.6 percent less than men. In administrative occupations, women earn an average of only 58 percent of that earned by men.

• At the end of 1988 only 1.4 percent of the workers at the Ministry of Foreign Affairs were women. The highest proportion was found at the Ministry of Culture, but even there the figure was only 27 percent.

• In a 1987 report on women at work in Spain it was revealed that 63.2 percent of all women workers were concentrated in only five sectors of economic activity: trade, agriculture, domestic service, education and health.

11. Case Study: United Kingdom

Introduction

Britain's legal commitment to women's rights is unquestioned. The combined verbiage of the much-heralded Equal Pay Act of 1970[1] and the Sex Discrimination Act of 1975[2] probably provide the most comprehensive formulation of the rights of women to be found in any constitution or law in any place in the world. But the effect of these laws has been a disappointment. The British Parliament (and even more so its parliamentary draftsmen) must be blamed for the current situation, where the most important progress in rights for British women is the product of the courts of the European Economic Community and the Council of Europe.

These two Acts, unfortunately, "were clearly intended not to be mutually exclusive."[3] But it does not work in practice. Two of the justices of the House of Lords made appropriate comments on that issue in *Shields* v. *Coomes (Holdings) Ltd.* Wrote Lord Bridge: "The particular provisions designed to prevent overlapping between the two Acts are complex and it may often be difficult to determine whether a particular matter of complaint fails to be redressed under one Act or the other."[4] Wrote Lord Denning: "The task of construing them is like fitting together a jig-saw puzzle. The pieces are all jumbled together, in two boxes."[5] And not only that, the very verbiage tends to be verbose and confusing.

This is in stark contrast to the clarity and simplicity of the laws of the European Community discussed in the previous chapter.

But language infirmities are not the only obstacles to proper enforcement. The Acts themselves lack desirable and desired enforcement procedures. And, in addition, there are too many substantive gaps.

"Some of the gaps," according to J. M. Steiner,[6] "have been filled by the courts arguing by analogy from one Act to the other, as Browne Wilkinson, J., did in *Jenkins* v. *Kingsgate.*"[7] "There is little doubt," concludes Steiner, "that these gaps have been filled with our EEC obligations in mind."[8]

But Steiner is wrong. Significant gaps have not been filled, especially in the areas of personal autonomy. Britain's laws on women's rights say little, for example, about family planning and abortion in the wave of new medical and scientific techniques available for birth control.

There is one more important reason why there are more United Kingdom cases before the Luxembourg and Strasbourg courts than cases from any other country. It is simply because Britain does not have a one-document constitution encompassing a bill of rights.[9] There are no "constitutional" provisions on sexual equality going beyond the parliamentary dictates of the two statutes. As a result, the Luxembourg and Strasbourg courts can take jurisdiction over cases where there are statutory gaps, since national remedies have been exhausted.

The absence of a constitutional bill of rights has also restricted judicial activism in developing a body of law to enforce women's rights. Unlike courts in the United States, which have been able to apply phrases such as "due process" and "equal protection of the laws" to cover a multitude of women's rights issues, the British courts have had to remain silent. Thus, even though the two British statutes are the most detailed of them all, they are just not detailed enough.

There is some indication, however, that as a result of the cases decided in Luxembourg and Strasbourg and as a result of studies of the American and European experiences, more British statutes will always be forthcoming. Before parliament now, for example, is a proposed statute on battered women.

Political Rights

Britain did not need the sexual revolution of this generation to give women equality at the polls, or equality in the quest for political office. Ironically, Prime Minister Margaret Thatcher, the first woman to head a Western government, had no connection with the women's rights movement and is never categorized as a women's rights leader. She emerged as an English political leader who happened to be a woman.

The failure of women to participate in British politics to the same extent as the other women of Western Europe has nothing to do with the law and little to do with male chauvinism or discrimination. From the perspective of the outside observer, it appears that women are just not interested. The female sex numbers only 25 in the 650-member Mother of Parliaments. And women are conspicuous by their absence in local government.

There is some evidence that women vote in approximately the same numbers as men (a much higher percentage, for example, than in the United States), but they do not vote for other women.

The struggle for equal rights at the polls was both protracted and violent since its beginnings in 1866, when John Stuart Mill presented his Woman Suffrage Petition to the House of Commons. The first woman suffrage society was formed in the following year—followed by 51 years of proposed statutes which failed to obtain parliamentary consent.

On February 6, 1918, royal assent was given to the government's "Representation of the People Act"[10] which enfranchised women over 30 who met certain specified qualifications. They had to be householders or wives of householders, occupiers of property having a annual value of £5, or graduates of a British university, or women who had fulfilled the qualifications for graduation but because they were women were not allowed to graduate.[11] Subsequently, but far less dramatically, women acquired voting rights on the same basis as men.

Prior to the British statute, only the Scandinavian nations (except

Sweden), plus the Soviet Union and (to a limited extent) Portugal, had previously granted women the right to vote. And it was more than two years later, with the ratification of the Nineteenth Amendment, that the franchise was given to women in the United States.[12]

The Family

Unlike the other countries of Western Europe, the United Kingdom does not provide family allowances on the basis of parentage; nor is there a system of child support and benefits such as is best exemplified in Scandinavia; nor for the English is there, for example, a system which gives women 80 percent or more of their wages when they are absent from work during pregnancy. Whatever protection pregnant women can receive in English law is largely given by (and limited by) the Equal Pay Act, which permits special treatment to women in connection with pregnancy or childbirth. This is discussed in the section on employment.

The Sex Discrimination Act of 1975 assists family life by prohibiting discrimination against a married person of either sex on grounds of marital status. One goal of this Act is to protect working married women against employment discrimination which could arise because their husbands are the primary breadwinners. Another objective of the Act is to assure that married women, who could be expected to lose some time on the job because of childbearing and child care, will not be subject to invidious discrimination. Obviously, the role of women in the family is protected and enhanced by such legislation.

Women's family rights in the British sense revolve around the breakup of the marital union – from issues involving physical violence to the legal analysis of the woman's share of matrimonial property.

Such rights begin with the Matrimonial Homes Act, 1967,[13] which gives protection (albeit limited) from forced eviction. And there is protection from brutality on the part of husbands ("wife-battering" is the British term) in the Domestic Violence and Matrimonial Proceedings Act, 1976).[14] This statute gives wives the right to speedy injunctions against violent husbands.

Divorce laws also have been changed to advance the position of women. The mechanism has been the Divorce Reform Act, 1969,[15] which was incorporated into the Matrimonial Causes Act, 1973.[16] "The sacramental character of marriage has thus been largely replaced by the notion of marriage as a shared undertaking dissoluble at the instance of either party," conclude Albie Sachs and John Huff Wilson.[17]

As Sachs and Wilson explain it, the concept of matrimonial fault has been replaced by the notion of the irretrievable breakdown of marriage. While "cruelty, adultery and desertion still survive in modified form as facts evidencing breakdown,"[18] the present laws provide for divorce by consent after two years of separation and divorce without consent after five years of separation.

The big issue in divorce – in terms of women's rights – is the distribution of family assets. There are two statutes which deal with the problem: the

Matrimonial Proceedings and Property Act, 1970,[19] and the Matrimonial Causes Act, 1973.[20] There is even a major book on the subject.[21] But understanding the law first requires an understanding of the meaning of "family assets." Master of the Rolls, Lord Denning, has provided the recognized definition in the leading case of *Wachtel* v. *Wachtel:*[22]

> The phrase "family assets" is a convenient short way of expressing an important concept. It refers to those things which are acquired by one or other or both of the parties, with the intention that they should be continuing provision for them and their children during their joint lives, and used for the benefit of the family as a whole. It is a phrase, for want of a better, used by the Law Commission, and is well understood. The family assets can be divided into two parts: (i) those which are of a capital nature such as the matrimonial home and the furniture in it; (ii) those which are of a revenue-producing nature, such as the earning power of husband and wife. When the marriage comes to an end, the capital assets have to be divided: the earning power of each has to be allocated.

But how should assets be divided? How should earning power be allocated? Under the common law, women possessed only such property as was theirs by purchase and inheritance.[23] True, the Married Women's Property Act, 1882,[24] "acknowledged that husbands and wives were separate individuals in the eyes of the law, but because husbands generally had greater earnings, and therefore greater purchasing power, the creation of separate property regimes usually left wives with little or no property at the end of their marriages. The only claim that they had on their [former] husbands was for periodical maintenance payments out of future income."[25]

Under present British legislation, all family assets are first pooled together and then divided between the divorced parties on the basis of what amounts to judicial discretion. The statutory language is long and involved. The present practice stems from Lord Denning's analysis and conclusion in *Wachtel* v. *Wachtel*[26] which—as a "starting point"—awarded one-third of assets to the wife and two-thirds to the husband.

How Lord Denning, a strong proponent of women's rights, reached this conclusion is significant:

> . . . In any calculation the court has to have a starting point. If it is not to be one-third, should it be one-half or one-quarter? A starting point at one-third of the combined resources of the parties is as good and rational a starting point as any other. . . . In these days of rising house prices, she should certainly have a share in the capital assets which she had helped to create. The windfall should not all go to the husband. But we do not think it should be as much as one-half if she is also to get periodical payments for her maintenance and support. Giving it the best consideration we can, we think that the fairest way is to start with one-third of each. If she has one-third of the family assets as her own and one-third of the joint earnings her past contributions are adequately recognized and her future living standards assured as far as may be.[27]

Whether the legal recognition of women's rights in the dissolution of marriage has actually increased divorce is a matter of sociological conjecture. The fact remains, however, that women today are more free to contemplate divorce, and that the divorce rate has been going up at a steady rate. There were

12 decrees of divorce for every 1,000 married couples in England and Wales in 1981, compared with two in 1961.[28]

And there was more cohabitation without benefit of clergy. "Nearly 20 percent of women in Great Britain marrying in the late 1970s where the marriage was the first for both parties had lived with their husbands before marriage (compared with six percent in the early 1970s) and about 13 percent of non-married women aged 18 to 49 were cohabiting during 1982."[29]

Property

There was a time in modern English legal history—a time which extended almost to the eve of World War II—when the widow's portion of her deceased husband's estate was solely determined by his will. In the era of absolute freedom of testation, the property owner could dispose of his property as capriciously after death as he did in life. Even in feudal times, widows had fared better, at least receiving some fixed portion of the estate.

This is no longer the law. Widows (and mistresses as well) are protected now by the Inheritance (Provision for Family and Dependents) Act of 1975.[30]

Now the power to protect the widow's estate is subject to the discretion of the court: for now the division of matrimonial property on death is much like the division upon the dissolution of marriage. The surviving spouse (or, in some cases, the mistress) has a right to approximately one-third of the estate, based on a "reasonable" portion analysis, and not limited to necessities or living expenses. This discretion of the court supersedes the wishes of the testator.

Employment

Employment practices, discrimination in the marketplace and wage differentials dominate the women's rights struggle in Britain. It is in the area of employment that the United Kingdom statutes are most concerned. It is in the area of employment (and the parallel area of retirement) that Britons have instituted litigation in the courts of the E.E.C. and the Council of Europe.

Women comprise roughly two-fifths of the British work force. Sixty-one percent of married women between the ages of 16 and 60 are wage-earners, most of whose income is essential to their families.

If overtime pay is not counted, they earn just less than three-quarters the sum earned by men. (See Table 29.) And in 1970 prior to the passage of the Equal Pay Act (which came into full effect in 1975),[31] hourly wages of women were just under two-thirds of the masculine scale. Further, despite the efforts of parliament and the courts, women's incomes are destined to remain depressed. Women work in the lower paid sectors of the economy; they have fewer opportunities for overtime pay; and the educational structure of British society restricts the access of women to higher paying opportunities in law, medicine, engineering and the other professions.

The Equal Pay Act of 1970 and the Sex Discrimination Act of 1975 (which also incorporated and updated the Equal Pay Act) ostensibly were to provide

Sector	1971 Manual	1971 Non-manual	1980 Manual	1980 Non-manual
Total (weighted average)	52.0	50.6	60.9	58.5
Mining	-	-	-	-
Manufacturing	50.5	44.3	60.3	53.2
Construction	-	41.8	-	51.5
Electricity, gas, water	-	51.2	-	54.0
Transport and communication	67.0	51.5	75.1	58.2
Distributive trades	52.7	44.2	64.4	53.6
Insurance, banking, finance, business services	-	46.0	-	49.9
Professional and scientific services	58.0	58.7	65.1	68.1
Miscellaneous services	54.2	52.7	65.4	64.4
Public administration	66.1	56.7	72.8	60.9

Table 29. Average Gross Weekly Earnings of Full-Time Adult Women Workers in the United Kingdom as a Percentage of those of Men, by Sector, 1971–1980. Source: International Labor Organization, *The Economic Role of Women in the ECE Region,* Geneva, 1985, p. 70.

for sexual equality in wages for the same and similar jobs and the end of discrimination in employment, education, training and service.[32] But the statutes have proved inadequate.[33] The English courts have had to seek additional guidance from the directives of the European Economic Community.[34]

A significant lacuna in these statutes has been the absence of equality of treatment provisions relating to both pension schemes and retirement plans. And in their absence women suffer from discrimination under existing programs. Women are often obliged to retire at an earlier age than men, even though they have a longer life expectancy. In the United Kingdom, the common retirement age for men is 65 and for women 60. Further, since many women interrupt their careers to raise families, these may not build up sufficient years of pensionable service to acquire adequate pensions in retirement.

Such problems remain unresolved. English courts are without guidance. And this at a time when increasing numbers of British women are working more, living longer and increasingly demanding equality in years of work opportunity and more generous and equitable payments at pension time. These concerns have been supported by scholars[35] and have been brought before both parliament and the E.E.C.

Unfortunately, even the necessary law reform will not solve prevailing discrimination patterns. Sadly, the existing acts are little used by women in asserting their legal rights. Moreover, women who have taken cases before the appropriate commissions have had a low success rate—only 11 percent, for example, before industrial tribunals. Procedural red tape and the low rate of success, have not only discouraged proceedings, but have also resulted in a high rate of discontinuances or withdrawals of actions previously pursued.

Implementation of the two basic acts is the responsibility of the Equal Opportunities Commission, established in 1975. Unfortunately, it is a body with limited resources and few casework officers.[36] Commission staff cannot make the necessary visits to applicants. In addition, the complex legal and factual issues involved in equal pay and sex discrimination cases require the collection of a significant amount of data, usually obtainable only from employers, many of whom are resistant to sexual equality in employment. Nor have the unions shown interest in the equality quest. It would be unfair, however, to render a blanket condemnation of the Equal Opportunities Commission. Its legal division, largely female, often provides outstanding support for women claimants.

There is also an Advisory Conciliation and Arbitration Service which has been assigned the task of promoting voluntary settlement of sex discrimination claims in employment. This organization, however, has been criticized for giving inaccurate advice and for pressuring women to drop their complaints. An important recent study reported one woman's statement that "A.C.A.S. talked me into a settlement."[37]

Without positive changes in both E.O.S. and A.C.A.S. budgets and procedures, there is little hope for a comprehensive victory in the quest for sexual equality in employment. For only a very few cases can or should come before the judiciary.

Personal Autonomy

It is in the area of wife abuse (usually termed "battered women") that British law has maintained continuing concern. This dates back to the Matrimonial Causes Act (Magistrates) of 1878[38] and includes the current Domestic Violence and Matrimonial Proceedings Act (D.V.A.)[39] and the Domestic Proceeding and Magistrates' Courts Act (D.P.M.C.A.),[40] passed in 1976.

Such legal developments, according to researcher Kathryn McCann, "provide an example of women being able to define and, to a certain extent, achieve an increase in their legal 'rights.'"[41] However, she continues, legal advances are "being eroded by the implementation of the legislation and by the ambivalent responses of agencies required to enforce the acts."[42]

The D.V.A. authorizes non-molestation and exclusion injunctions, independent of any other judicial proceedings, with relief available to both married and cohabitating couples on an equal basis. Exclusion injunctions may direct the male being charged from entering a premises and surrounding area or many compel him to leave such area. In addition, the county courts have the discretionary power to imprison a husband for breaching an order.

The D.P.M.C.A. grants similar powers to the magistrates' courts. Where the court is satisfied that the husband has used violence, an order may be issued for him to leave the matrimonial home or to prohibit him from entering that home. However, unlike the county courts, the magistrates' courts do not have the authority to restrict husbands from specified areas. Nor do they have power to act under an *ex parte* emergency procedure. Further, the authority under the D.P.M.C.A. can be exercised only on behalf of the married woman against her husband.

Based on a study of three magistrates' courts and interviews with women who had undergone the legal process, it is McCann's conclusion that the promise of these statutes "has not been established in practice. Rather this has been undermined both by case law and in the application of the provision(s) by the courts and the police."[43] "If we are to see a material improvement in the situation of women," she argues, "it is clear that the agencies must take wife abuse seriously."[44]

Conclusions

As in the rest of Europe, progress towards constitutional protection and legal assistance in England to address the imbalance in women's rights had a late start. It was only in 1970 that the British Parliament passed a simple law requiring equal pay for equal work, and even this only became effective in December 1975 and was hastened by the Treaty of Rome after Britain joined the E.C. But the act does not provide for equality of opportunity, leaving room for manipulation of the law.[45] It was only at the end of 1974 that the Wilson government launched a Women's Rights Law.

It would not appear on the surface, constitutionally, that there should or could be discrimination in Britain against women, but such is very much the case. In certain areas such as in medical practice, Steiner observed, women have made incredible strides; elsewhere they still find themselves in the traditional areas of employment of 20 years ago, and wage and legal discrimination remain. The average English woman cannot enter into contract unless she has her husband's signature, even if this is to make a contract with the gas or electric company. Legally, she has no right to see her husband's tax returns, although he is required to sign hers. English law is adamant that man is the breadwinner and owns the home. If a woman does not contribute regularly to the joint account, it is considered to be entirely the husband's. For a loan to start a business, even if she finances and staffs the venture on her own, the woman must obtain her husband's signature on the application form.[46]

British laws on divorce were long enough among the most discriminatory in the world when it comes to the rights of women, but in a protective sense. A woman divorced in her 20s can expect to receive money from her ex-husband for the rest of her life. There is absolutely no need, no provision, no incentive, or discipline in the law that divorced women should make an effort to become financially independent. By 1983 the climate appears to have changed in the British Parliament based on the recommendations of the British Law Commission on the subject. The new laws proposed are designed to promote a clean break between couples and, in some cases, end the so-called meal-ticket-for-life maintenance payments. The Law Commission recommended maintenance to be given only for the time it takes the spouse to adjust to his or her situation and to find a job, with priority given to the needs of children. For women, the compensation is that the courts will have far greater power and discretion to divide the property of spouses.

According to researcher Judith Blake, the past five years have seen women make great strides towards obtaining equal rights and treatment as well as equal opportunity in England, but equality in practice is vitiated by the segmentation of the labor market—by level, by sector and by skill categories. Female labor, she wrote, is still treated as supplementary, while opportunities for upward mobility are limited by lower continuity of employment and indirect, if not outright, discrimination. In political life men and women are educated equally for citizenship and afforded equal rights of participation, though no special effort is made to encourage the exercise of such rights. Despite the role presented by Margaret Thatcher, Prime Minister of Britain, few women are active in politics at the national level.[47]

The degree of emancipation which British women enjoy has come through the economy's demand for labor, rather than through political pressure alone, and legal emancipation has followed rather than preceded economic emancipation, according to Jill Hills, an expert on women and government in Britain.[48]

Originally the franchise for women was extended only to women who were householders over the age of 30 or who were 35 years and older and the wives of householders. It was only in 1924 that the full franchise was extended to women.

Hills points out that women were heavily employed in Britain during both World Wars, but by 1947 only 18 percent of married women were in employment. Thirty years later women formed 41 percent of the labor force, but more than 75 percent were in the pink ghetto: clerical workers, waitresses, cooks, hairdressers, shopworkers, nurses, social workers, teachers and canteen assistants. They competed with each other rather than with men, since 97 percent of canteen workers, 88 percent of hairdressers, 92 percent of nurses and 82 percent of shop assistants were women. Only 4 percent were architects and 6 percent solicitors.[49]

The Equal Pay Act of 1970 gave employers five years in which to ensure that equal pay was granted to women for equal work. Between 1970 and 1980 the difference between women's and men's pay did not decrease, and in some respects the gap became even wider. The Equal Pay Act and Sex Discrimination Act of 1975 outlawed discrimination in terms of job entry, pay, conditions of employment and promotion. This did not do much to decrease the differential in income and in 1980 it was officially admitted that a further decrease in the gap would come about only if women entered male-dominated occupations.[50]

In the field of education not much has changed either. In 1986 the 110,000-strong Assistant Masters and Mistresses Association of England protested the system whereby schools segregated traditional so-called "boy's subjects" from "girl's subjects." Only 37 percent of male teachers were receiving the lowest salary scale for teachers, whereas more than 76 percent of female teachers found themselves on this scale. As for headships of schools, only 7.3

Year	Percentage of Men's Gross Weekly Wages	Percentage of Men's Gross Hourly Wages
1973	55	64
1974	56	65
1975	61	70
1976	64	73
1977	64	73
1978	63	72
1979	62	71
1983	65	72

Table 30. The Wage Gap Between Men and Women in British Industries, 1973–1983. Source: New Earnings Survey Part A, table 15, April 1979, and Department of Employment *Gazette,* October 1983.

percent of women were appointed as heads of primary schools compared with 31 percent of men.[51]

Despite the fact that the E.C. Commission agreed on equal treatment of workers in 1974, it was not until 1986 that women in England received the right to continue working until the same age as men. And the only reason this decision by the British government came in 1986 at all was because of a six-year battle by Helen Marshall, a Hampshire dietician, who waged a campaign in the European Court of Justice (as provided for in the Treaty of Rome) against British authorities who forced her retirement at the age of 62. The European Court ruled in February 1986 that her dismissal was a violation of the Common Market anti–sex discrimination directive to which Britain and the other countries had subscribed. Helen Marshall's success established case law in respect of government and public authority employees but not for those working for private companies.[52]

The barriers to women's political participation on equal terms with men are formidable. In *The Politics of the Second Electorate,* Jill Hills referred to a host of intangible barriers. "A combination of gender stratification at school, low educational achievements, opportunities for marriage, the norms of good motherhood, lack of public child care facilities, low wages and a stratified labor market. . . ." She also found that of the original four demands of the women's movement in Britain – free contraception, equal pay, equal education and job opportunity, 24-hour day nurseries and abortion on demand – only that of free contraception has been achieved.[53]

12. Case Study: France

Introduction

In France, a country with a long and proud human rights tradition, women had to fight a long uphill battle to gain the equality proclaimed in the Human Rights Declaration of 1789. For them equality and the right to work did not yet entail any validity.

After the Revolution it was of more significance that property and ownership had become a constitutionally guaranteed human right. As such it became part of the Code Napoleon 1804 (civil code), where it also resulted in changes to matrimonial law and the law of succession. However, with respect to women, the traditional legal view prevailed. A wife remained under the husband's protection, subject to his authority; without his consent she could not dispose of her own assets.[1] The early women's movement in the first half of the nineteenth century realized very quickly that the Human Rights Declaration of 1789, the "Declaration des droits de l'homme," in fact meant only the rights of *man* (literal translation of "droits de l'homme"). They believed that women's rights must be an integral part of human rights. Thus they pressed for changes in the position of the married woman in the civil code and claimed their rights as workers.

History has shown that until very recently a woman's fortune remained subject to traditional morality and principles, and to males. However, in the battle for improved social rights for men and women, women had some partial successes. These included the introduction of two-month paid maternity leave in 1910, the right of women to dispose of their revenues from a gainful occupation (Act of 13th July 1907), the right to exercise a profession (except if the husband opposed), and, in 1920, the right to join a union without requiring the husband's consent.[2]

In French constitutional history, the preamble of the 1946 Constitution of the Fourth Republic first expressly set out the fundamental principle of equality between men and women. This preamble, as well as the Human Rights Declaration of 1789, is part of the 1958 Constitution of the Fifth Republic.

It was not, however, until the 1960s that the law-making machinery began to move to this end. We can observe a continuous and gradual process of granting women equality with men in all domains as prescribed in the Constitution and the establishment of governmental machinery to safeguard women's rights. The first body to be set up in France in 1965 was the Study and Liaison Committee for Women's Employment. The apparatus for safeguarding women's rights has since expanded. It became increasingly broad in its aims and had more effective resources. In 1974 a State Secretariat for the Status of Women was created. In 1979 the Ministry for Family Affairs became responsible for the status of women. When the socialist government came to power in 1981, it created a Ministry for Women's Rights. Existing bodies of other ministries dealing with women came under the authority of this ministry. The ministry also has a network of regional delegates at its disposal, as well as delegates of the Women's Information Centres which are directly attached to it.[3]

The election of the new rightist government in March 1986 showed that the Ministry for Women's Rights was short-lived. It has been replaced by a Delegate for Women's Issues, under the authority of the Ministry for Social Affairs and Employment. Fifty-two million French francs have been cut in funds allocated in the 1986 budget for special educational and informational programs for women.[4]

However, the present government has created a new Ministry for Human Rights. Whether it will exercise authority in the area of women's rights remains to be seen.

Political Rights

Women in France did not obtain the right to vote until 1945, much later than most other northern European countries. One of the reasons for women's enfranchisement at that time was their active involvement in the Resistance during the occupation of France during World War II.

Women's presence in the political arena was and still is not very impressive. The number of women in the National Assembly dropped steadily from 30 in 1945 to 10 women in 1977. In the period 1945–1974 only three women held the office of Junior Minister. By 1976 five women were in the government, but the most prominent of them had not worked their way up through the party hierarchy.[5] The National Assembly elected in 1981 had 26 and the National Assembly elected in 1986 had 34, equalling 5.89 percent women deputies, distributed as follows: Parti socialiste and left groups: 21; Rasamblement pour la République (RFR), French democrats (UDS) and other right groups: 9; Parti communiste: 3; Front nationale: 1.

Out of 25 persons in the Council of Ministers there is only one woman, assigned to the Ministry for Social Affairs and Employment. Three of the 16 Secretaries of State are women.[6] On the municipal level we find that in 1983, 14 percent of councillors' posts were held by women, and only five towns with populations over 30,000 had a woman as mayor.[7]

The French Constitutional Court has ruled that the Electoral Act of July 1982, which provided that at least 25 percent of the candidates on municipal electoral lists in municipalities with over 3,500 inhabitants should be women, was unconstitutional.[8]

The socialist party has now introduced a quota system for elections; at least 20 percent of candidates must be women. For the elections to the European Parliament, the quota was fixed at 30 percent. This has led to an increase in female French members of the European Parliament. Women in other parties are also making their demands known and protesting against the types of discrimination from which they suffer.[9] Women's low involvement in politics appears to be less due to their reluctance to come forward than to French male chauvinism.[10]

As far as processing of news and media are concerned, women in France are as aware as their counterparts in Germany of their need for greater participation. In the 10 years up to 1982, the number of female journalists has increased from 15 percent to 25 percent. However, they are still kept in low-level positions in "typical" female areas, such as culture. Prestigious areas are reserved for men. *Le Monde* has 8 percent female journalists, only one having a position with political responsibility.[11]

Family

In France the family enjoys the "statut d'ordre public." The preamble of the 1946 Constitution requires that the individual and the family be provided with the necessary conditions for their development. It guarantees all people—in particular, children, mothers and pensioners—health protection, material security, rest and leisure. Prior to the Constitution of 1946 the French state was already very concerned about special family care. It has a long tradition of providing generous family allowances. A population decline which began in the nineteenth century continued until the 1930s. In 1932 a first attempt was made to remedy this, with the institution of family allowances. In the post-war years, child allowances were extended and are now among the highest in Europe, often counting for 30 percent of a worker's income.[12] As we shall see, family allowances are the same regardless of whether the natural parents are married or unmarried. The same is true for maternity assistance and single-parent allowances.

In France matrimonial law is based on the civil code of 1804. Some of the legal duties, obligations and rights set out in the civil code are still operative, while others have been heavily modified. Since 1804 civil marriage has been the only legally accepted form of marriage.

Marriage creates a relation ("alliance") between the spouses and their respective partners. It creates a legal relationship carrying the duties to cohabit, form a life union, show fidelity and be of assistance. Spouses must raise and maintain their children together. Both are liable for the debts arising from the maintenance and education of their children. They must contribute together to charges incurred during marriage, with the contributions depending on their respective abilities. Since the Matrimonial Act of 1964, spouses are on equal footing as far as the rights and duties of the marriage are concerned. The role of the husband as breadwinner was abolished. He can no longer object to his wife's intention to seek gainful employment, nor does she need his permission to open a bank account, run a shop or get a passport. In 1970 the "autorité paternelle" was finally changed to "autorité parentale," so that parents have joint custody.[13]

In the French legal system the obligation of a married woman to give up her maiden name (as used to be the rule in Germany) is unknown. The only legal name is the name acquired at birth. However it is permitted—and this a very common practice—to use the husband's name in daily life. The children of the marriage carry the husband's name. The Act of 23rd of December 1985 now in force authorizes the child to carry both parents' names as surnames.[14]

Unless the spouses make a special arrangement before a notary, they submit themselves to the "régime legal," which imposes "communaute d'acquets," i.e., all the gains accrued during the marriage become common property. Other possible arrangements are separation of property, participation in gains, communal and universal property. Spouses can adopt one of these settlements but are allowed to modify or combine them as seems fit and most appropriate for their situation. It is possible to change the marriage contract in the presence of a notary, with subsequent court approval. If a spouse endangers the other party's interest, the aggrieved party can apply in court for a separation of property.[15]

In France it is the general rule that the family household is taxable in respect of the total income, i.e., joint taxation of husband and wife. The 1982 Finance Act eliminated the notion of head of household, obliging both spouses to sign income tax returns. Tax assessment takes into account the family situation.[16] A married couple, and a single, separated, divorced or widowed parent can, if they are working, be granted a tax deduction up to 5000 FF per year for child care expenses, provided the child is under the age of five.[17]

Both husband and wife, if living under the same roof, are jointly liable for the income tax of one or the other spouse, irrespective of whether they are married under the regime of "communaute des biens" or "séparation des biens."[18]

There are three different procedures for divorce: by mutual consent, by fault, or by rupture of the life union. In every case the assistance of a lawyer is obligatory. The procedure takes place before a court. In the first case, introduced in 1975, the spouses can regulate the consequences of the divorce themselves or ask the judge to make a ruling. Divorce by fault means that there are facts (e.g. violence, injuries, infidelity) which make a life union intolerable. Prior to 1964 courts were still obliged to regard a wife's infidelity more seriously than a husband's. The party at fault loses the right to claim a "préstation compensatois" (compensation paid to the financially weaker party). If the spouses have been separated for at least six years the marriage is considered to have ruptured and a spouse can demand a divorce. A couple can also live under special terms of separation without a dissolution of their marriage. They are still liable for their mutual security, maintenance and fidelity but are no longer obliged to live together. It also leads to a separation of goods. Such a separation must be pronounced by the court.[19]

De Facto Marriage[20]

In France "le concubinage," "union libre" or "vie maritale" (*de facto* marriage) has become very common. For a long time this facet of life and its legal implications were ignored by the legislature and the judiciary. The latter long viewed "le concubinage" as an immoral situation which was *contra bonos mores,* thus no rights could arise from it. Today, however, there is clearly a liberal tendency emerging within the judiciary and the legislature. Without actually defining concubinage, the legislature has specified the rights of *de factos* in the area of social security and in "droit fiscal" (fiscal law). The latter introduced the notion of "concubinage notoire" (evident *de facto* marriage). In such a case Article 3 of the Finance Act 1982 stipulates that for the purpose of capital levy the value of the common assets and the accessible value of both partners is decisive. For other tax purposes *de facto* partners are dealt with separately, which can in fact be advantageous. Tax deductions to pay off housing loans are granted individually, even though the house was purchased in joint name.

As far as social security is concerned, a *de facto* marriage enjoys almost the same advantages as a marriage, especially with respect to health insurance during maternity and to family allowances. The partner who does not benefit from social security in his or her own right can enjoy the benefits (notably health care) through the insured partner. The Act of January 1978 stipulates that such a person must be effectively dependent upon the insured person. Each year they must make an honorary declaration to that respect before the health insurance authorities. However, in some circumstances, e.g. to obtain certain advantages like public transport or housing benefits, it is useful to produce a "certificat de concubinage." The mayor can deliver such a certificate for the *de facto* marriage provided someone testifies that the couple lives in a *de facto* marriage. This certificate has no legal value apart from the above-mentioned use.

As a logical expansion of previous laws, the "code du travail" of 13th July 1983 (labor code) has defined the principle of equality very clearly (Article 123). Accordingly, discrimination on the basis of sex or family status is illegal. The status of *de facto* marriage may in no circumstances lead to any disadvantages in the working world. For example, on the birth of a child to a *de facto* marriage, the father is eligible for a three-day holiday to assist the mother and to maternity leave.

Children born outside marriage have the same legal status as children born inside marriage. In order to establish a legal bond with the child, the natural parents must officially acknowledge parenthood. If only the mother recognizes the child as hers, the child carries her name but if both parents do so, it carries the father's name. The "court de cassation" (court of succession) in its decision 1 re.ch.Civ. 16th November 1982 rejected the right of the child to have a joint name, but the Act of 23rd December 1985 (which entered into force on July 1, 1986) introduced this right.

Even if both parents recognize the child, the mother exercises sole parental custody (Article 374 code civil). However the father may make an application in court to obtain joint custody.

Even though it is still held that a *de facto* marriage creates legal obligations neither between the partners nor with respect to a third party, this principle is subject to exceptions. If a third party causes the death of one partner the other partner can obtain damages. This change in jurisdiction stems from the ruling of the "mixte chamber" of the "court de cassation" in 1970. It ruled that the relationship must have been one of stability and long duration.

To compensate for the non-applicability of the law of succession, *de facto* partners in France must also, as in Germany, resort to legacy, donation, life insurance and other such legally accepted forms. In the event of the dissolution of the *de facto* relationship, property and financial questions are dealt with according to the civil code, either by the rules of co-ownership or *de facto* partnership. Upon the termination of the concubinage—by death or separation—the partner benefiting from the other's social security rights may still enjoy these rights until 12 months after the termination or until the third birthday of the youngest child he or she is in charge of.

Property

Until 1964 much of the joint property of a marriage was legally the husband's property. Even though this law had been subject to change, the husband still remained the sole administrator of property held jointly by the couple or belonging to the children. Only he could, with the wife's consent, use their joint property for the sake of purchasing real estate or constituting mortgages, etc. The Act of 23rd December 1985 provides that each of the spouses can administer their joint property. Acts of great importance require mutual consents. Joint property includes the "biens ordinaire" (goods acquired during marriage by either spouse, gains and salaries and revenues from property acquired prior to marriage) and the "biens réserves" (which constitute a woman's salary and gains). The woman was the sole administrator of the "biens réserves." Prior to the new act, it was held that all of the couple's joint property, "biens ordinaires" and "bien réserves," was liable for the husband's debts arising either from contracts towards the charges of the marriage or from personal obligations. The wife, on the other hand, found it very difficult to obtain a credit since she on her part could guarantee only with her salary, but could not engage the couple's joint property. So in effect she was liable with her salary for all her husband's debts but not vice versa. Under the new act, this inequality has also been changed to the effect that their respective debts equally commit the joint property, with the exception of their salaries. Salaries enjoy protection from the other party's creditors, unless the debts arise from the charges of the marriage.[21]

The law of succession does not provide succession in ownership for the surviving spouse. However the legally prescribed form of succession applies only in the absence of a testament or a donation. According to the law, the widow obtains the right of usufruct to one-fourth of the inheritance if there are no children, but parents, brothers or sisters of the husband. If none of the above-mentioned is alive, she becomes the proper legal heir. In a testament the spouses can determine, depending on the number of the children, to what extent the surviving partner shall obtain a right to full ownership and usufruct.[22]

Employment[23]

The socialist government and its Minister for Women's Rights were highly motivated to improve the situation of women in employment. There was increased legislative and administrative activity, and more funds were made available for professional training of women and for research on the situation of women in all sectors of society. The Ministry for Women's Rights ran several information campaigns to make women aware of their rights as well as to sensitize employers and other specialized agencies dealing with women.

The number of working women has steadily grown to reach 69 percent in 1986 of the female population[24] and 65 percent of mothers between 25 and 55 years of age. In 1983, 52 percent of women aged between 15 and 65 years were working. The wage gap between female and male salaries is gradually shrinking. Average female hourly earnings in non-agricultural occupations were 78.8 percent of male earnings in 1973 and 83 percent in 1984.[25]

In early 1983 new legislation was adopted to strengthen the measures on equality. The new Act, an extension of the labor code, covers both equal pay and equal treatment for men and women and for the first time provides trade unions with the right to lodge claims on behalf of individual workers in case of discrimination. This does not exclude the individual's right to take legal recourse. The burden of proof rests with the employer.

The principle of equal pay had already been set out in Articles 1 and 2 of the Act of 22nd December 1972 (labor code), which specified that pay meant wage or salary including all benefits and supplements paid directly or indirectly in cash or in kind and that the various components of pay must be fixed in accordance with identical rules for all workers. The categories, criteria of classification and occupational advancement and all bases for calculating pay, in particular the methods of job evaluation, must be common to employees of both sexes. The "inspecteur du travail" supervises the application of the labor code. He can draw up a "procès verbal" (report). To ensure equality at work, the 1983 legislation provides for greater involvement of employers, e.g. each year employers with more than 50 employees must prepare a report on the situation of women compared to that of men with respect to salaries, promotion, recruitment and training. In co-operation with the worker's representatives the employer must draw up equality plans which set out the policies on promotion, training and recruitment. The state offers guidance and may also assist financially. Job advertising can no longer refer to the sex of a candidate, except with some legal reservations (1983 Act.).

In the public sector certain jobs in the police, finance and customs have been opened for women by "textes votes" (administrative orders) dated 7.5.1982, 14.7.1983 and 11.7.1984.

Unlike the Electoral Act, the Constitutional Court has not declared the 1983 Act Governing Equality of Treatment for Men and Women in Employment unconstitutional with respect to its positive action measures. The Act expressly provides that social measures and temporary practices introduced with a view to achieving equal opportunities for workers regardless of sex do not infringe on the principle of equality between the sexes. These positive measures are known as remedial measures for the benefit of women.

For the first time there is a legal framework for the development of positive action in private enterprise.[26]

Sex barriers and prejudices do not exist only in the adult world. We find that school books often preserve traditional views and prejudices. In France, as in many other European countries, school textbooks now undergo strict scrunity. The association "pour une education non-sexiste" has been very active to increase public awareness and, especially, awareness of parents, teachers and community workers.[27] The choice of professional training presents the next barrier. Women still hesitate to enter into traditionally male professions, and job and career advisors are reluctant to recommend that young women attempt "male" professions. Private bodies, e.g. Guild Chambers, have launched a campaign to inform young women about "male" occupations. The Ministry of Education has issued a particular circular to career advisors and job guidance centers. They encourage women to enter into male-dominated professions and especially not to miss out on job opportunities in the field of new technology which will create future professions.[28] The last government funded 100 or so pilot vocational training courses for women job seekers aged 25 or over in male trades or new technology. Women were entitled to the minimum wage. The pilot center also provided child care facilities. Most women completed the course and found an appropriate job afterwards.[29] There appears to be an appreciation of the fact that new technology may make a lot of jobs in manufacturing and in the services sector redundant. Therefore, it is very important to provide women with the skills for future professions.

The wider effects of the 1983 legislation and the information campaigns launched by the Ministry for Women's Rights may show only in the long term, though the efforts were certainly very inspiring.

In France we also find that more women than men work in part-time jobs. An order dated March 16, 1986, ensures that part-time workers have individual rights identical to those of full-time employees. The remuneration must be exactly proportional to that of employees working full-time in an equivalent job. However, part-time work must be considered with all due caution. Part-time work must not remain a woman's domain involving only low-skilled jobs.[30]

The Act of 10th July 1982 has improved the status of women who work beside their husbands in a private business. Such a woman can now choose whether to become the assistant, partner or employee of the husband running a business, thus securing effective recognition of her work and the resultant social security benefits. An interesting new development is presented by the associations of assisting wives in husbands' businesses, which have sprung up throughout the country and enable women to support each other in their mutual professional interests. There are separate associations for different professions, but there also exists an all-encompassing national organization.[31]

The 1983 Act on equality does not apply to the public service, whose statutes provide for equality with respect to legal guarantees. In France more than half of the public servants are women (excluding the Ministry of Defense). On the average, however, women earn 19 percent less than men in public service. Women are offered jobs with low qualifications and all too rarely occupy managerial posts. In 1984, 5.6 percent of the staff of major government institutions were women. The Act of 7th May 1982 reduced from 29 to 15 the number of exempted bodies where separate recruitment for women and men were permitted.[32]

Maternity

During maternity and maternity leave, working women enjoy special protection with respect to recruitment and termination of the working contract. In the case of the first and second childbirths, the leave prior to birth is six and after birth 10 weeks. For the third and subsequent children, the leave increases to eight weeks prior to and eighteen weeks after delivery. In addition to maternity leave, parents can choose to take parental leave or part-time work for a maximum of two years. The leave is unpaid, but for its duration the contract of employment is simply suspended, not terminated.

When parental leave to educate a child was first introduced in the private sector in 1977, only women benefited from it. Since 1978 women and men in both the public and private sectors benefit from parental leave. If a private undertaking has fewer than 100 employees (since 1984; in 1977 it was 200), the employer may object to the request under certain conditions.[33] Articles 122–28 of the labor code allow a salaried employee, in order to bring up a child, to terminate a contract at the end of maternity leave without being bound by the rules of prior notification but nevertheless enjoying a prior right to employment for one year.[34]

The common pension schemes honor child-rearing with two years for each child. Parents who brought up at least three children have a right to a 10 percent increase in their pensions.

The pension scheme is also open to voluntary participation of housewives. A widow does not automatically benefit from the deceased pension's scheme, since priority is given in social security schemes and allowances to supporting widows financially.[35]

Personal Autonomy

In France the anti-contraception laws of 1920 remained in force as recently as 1967. These laws prohibited all publicity for birth control, including advisory clinics, and forbade the sale of contraceptives except for some medical purposes. Prior to the early 1960s, birth control and family planning were virtually taboo subjects for public discussion. In 1956 a woman doctor, Marie-Andrée Weil-Halle, founded the "Mouvement Français pour le Planning Familial." It actively sought to bring down the anti-contraception law, and in 1961 it began to open advisory clinics. By 1966 there were 200 throughout France. They were tacitly accepted.[36] Today contraceptives and advice on their use are easily available. The pill requires a doctor's prescription, but not parental approval. There is no formal distinction between married and unmarried women as far as these services are concerned. They can all receive contraceptives free on the health service.

In the early 1970s activists turned their attention to France's legislation on abortion after the hurdle of legalizing birth control had been overcome. The number of clandestine abortions was estimated at 700,000 to 800,000 a year. Abortion was finally legalized in 1975 under the government of Giscard d'Estaing and his Health Minister, Mme. Simone Veil. After a trial period of four years the law was re-enacted in 1979.[37]

Since February 27, 1983, 80 percent of the cost of an abortion is reimbursed by health insurance. Under certain conditions, the Department for "l'Action Sanitaire et Sociale" may assist in paying all costs.[38]

In 1982 a massive information campaign on family planning, birth control and abortion was launched under the authority of the Minister for Women's Rights. It made use of the press, radio, television, schools and government agencies.[39]

Sexism and violence against women remain ongoing concerns in France. In case of rape, an association is allowed to institute civil proceedings, unlike in Germany. Furthermore, any person, including the husband, is liable to be charged with rape. There is discussion on how to improve the machinery for redress in cases of sexism and violence. Associations should be allowed to institute proceedings in all such cases (they are excluded from cases of violence within the family or infringements on the dignity of women in the media) and there should be a better definition of violence against women, including the concept of infringement of dignity, especially in the media. (It is interesting to note that the "Ligue du Droit des Femmes" [League of Women and the Law] has drafted a bill to prevent sexist portrayal of women in the media. The bill has been widely discussed but has not yet been taken up in parliament.)

In the meantime direct measures to improve the reception service for victims in police stations and in hospitals are needed. As of March 1986, the Ministry for Women's Rights was subsidizing 30 associations which run homes for battered women.[40]

Women's personal autonomy—at all levels of society—depends to some extent on their awareness of their rights. In France women can rely on a widespread network of general women's information centers as well as specialized centers. The first centers were opened in 1972 under the patronage of the Prime Minister and worked in close cooperation with authorities with a two-fold objective: to inform women abut all their rights, and, on the basis of their requests, to inform the authorities about women's needs. With the creation of the Ministry for Women's Rights, the centers were made directly responsible to the minister and, furthermore, their number was greatly enlarged. Now there are some 200 centers throughout France.[41]

Summary and Conclusion

An equal rights clause—of the type that at this writing still eludes campaigners in the United States—has been enshrined in the French constitution since 1946: "The law guarantees to women, in all fields, rights equal to those of men." In addition, female employees are formally guaranteed equality of rights by virtue of French membership of the European Common Market. Article 119 of the Treaty of Rome requires equal pay for equal work in all Common Market countries. Consequently career women in France enjoy an acceptance and status that professional women of many other countries envy, helped along by the fact that the most recent polls, conducted in the 1970s, indicate that French men overwhelmingly have no objection to women working, obtaining better jobs or holding more important positions than they do. Almost

70 percent voted that they would accept a woman for a boss.[42] France has a higher percentage of women lawyers and engineers than any other Western country.

The situation has changed dramatically since the 1920s, when France was the only country in Europe where women did not even have the right to vote in municipal elections. The French Napoleonic Code served to restrict women's energies to backstage intrigue for over a hundred years. World War II and particularly the presidency of Valery Giscard D'Estaing changed all of this.[43] There is still a gap between what the law states and what happens in practice, but that gap is less than what it is, for example, in the United States. In 1972 average wages for professional women in France were 93.3 percent of men's.[44] In the United States, they were 58 percent in 1972, and even by 1986 were still only 59 percent.[45] But in certain industries—banking, insurance, commerce and the textile industry—the women's percentage in France compared to men's has dropped sharply, to about 60 percent. Also, in top command positions at universities, the civil service, politics or business, the French society still does not see women in true posts of influence. Women are notably absent from positions of political power in France, particularly in the legislature. In 1980 there were only 20 women among the 491 members of the National Assembly and seven among the 295 senators.

According to Janine Mossuz-Lavau and Mariette Sineau, both French political scientists, important forms of discrimination in education continue in France. In the prestigious *lycées* (state-controlled high schools), 75 percent of the women opt for specialization in philosophy and only 35 percent in science. At the universities women represent 66 percent of the students in humanities and only 20 percent in science and 14 percent of economics and law. "It is therefore understandable that so few women attend the *Grandes Ecoles* from which the country's economic and political elites are recruited. Vocational training is equally segregated. In addition parents still prefer to send their daughters to Catholic schools where they receive an education that often perpetuates a traditional view of women. This . . . is responsible for some of the most serious discrimination in women's working lives."[46]

In 1967 the French government under President Charles de Gaulle was responsible for the Neuwirth Law legalizing contraception. In December 1972 the National Assembly passed a statute embodying the concept of equal pay for equal work. Six years later women's income as a percentage of men's was still significantly lower, and during the following six years (1978 to 1984) the pattern showed very little change. In 1984 the percentage for all workers was just over 78 percent, an increase of only 6 percent. At that rate, equality will be reached by the year 2009.

At the beginning of President Valery Giscard d'Estaing's period of office, wrote Lavau and Sineau, French political elites began to give serious attention to the status of women. In 1975 a series of laws were passed to give equal rights to men and women. One forbade sex discrimination at work. One gave mothers the equivalent rights to fathers in the running of the household. One was a matrimonial equality act. One was a divorce reform law. In the autumn of 1979, an abortion law that had been on a trial period from January 17, 1975,

Sector	All workers	Manual workers	Non-manual workers
All activities	71.9	72.7	62.5
Industry	64.8	72.2	60.7
Coal mining		83.5	62.8
Oil refining		77.8	59.1
Nuclear fuel production		85.4	65.5
Electricity, gas, steam		84.5	71.1
Water distribution		83.2	66.4
Ore extraction		63.6	64.9
Basic metal industry		74.6	58.5
Chemical industry		75.4	60.6
Artificial fibres		76.2	73.2
Machine building (heavy machinery)		77.5	58.7
Computer and office machinery		80.3	61.7
Electrical machinery and electronics		80.3	63.4
Automobile industry		76.1	61.8
Precision instruments		75.5	54.5
Food, drink and tobacco		74.3	56.7
Textile industry		78.9	56.8
Leather industry		79.7	57.0
Footwear and clothing industry		76.6	57.9
Paper, printing and publishing		66.7	58.1
Construction and public works	97.2	78.4	58.6
Transport and communications	80.1	..	..
Distribution	67.0	..	64.6
Wholesale trade	..	..	68.0
Retail trade	..	..	63.1
Banking	..	..	71.9
Insurance	..	..	62.0

Table 31. Average Annual Earnings of Full-Time Manual and Non-Manual Women Workers in France as a Percentage of those of Men, by Sector, 1978. Source: International Labor Organization, *The Economic Role of Women in the ECE Region,* 1985, Table V.3.

was taken up in the statutes, making it possible for women to obtain abortion at either public or private health institutions. On April 11, 1980, the Assembly voted for a redefinition of rape and the penalities to be incurred for this offense.[47] All of this indicated that legally French women were being taken care of. What was not changing, or changing rapidly enough, was the situation in the workplace, in schools, in public affairs and politics.

Legislation calling for affirmative action for women has been largely the responsibility of the Ministry for Women's Rights and very seldom have initiatives been taken by employers, without prompting from either the press or the government. Andrée Michel writes that most people connected to the labor market know that the subordinate position of women is largely due to discrimination against them. She found two types of discrimination in France, overt and covert. Overt is when parents or schools refuse to prepare girls for occupations other than the traditional ones or when a manager promotes only men, never women. Covert is found both within and without the work setting, such as the refusal of working, married women to take certain training courses because they still believe it inappropriate for wives to show interest in advancement. In such a case one can speak of "autodiscrimination," said Michel, since the traditional role of women is being perpetuated by women themselves. But regardless of the weights assigned to overt or covert discrimination, she wrote, both are sufficiently pervasive so that in the eighties French women occupied a distinctly subordinate status to men in the labor force.[48]

13. Case Study: West Germany

Introduction

Historical Background. Three historical factors have played an important role in determining the present legal status of women in Germany. The three factors are:

1. the ideas and the impact of the enlightenment;
2. the industrial revolution (with its resulting change of employment patterns and social structures); and
3. traditional, conservative forces and ideas.

The impact of the French Revolution, the German revolutionary movements early last century and the industrial revolution led to the formation of the early German women's movement. The first women's association, "Alldeutscher Frauenverein," was founded in 1865 by Luise Otto-Peters. It aimed at improving education and employment conditions for women. Very soon two main streams became apparent in the women's movement's fight for equality, a bourgeois line and a proletarian line. The bourgeois line intended changes within the existing structures of society to reduce men's power in state and society and to allow women access to education and professions, but still maintained the notion that the prime role of the married woman was to be wife and mother. The proletariat line regarded women's problems as part of the class struggle against the capitalist economy and claimed for themselves the right to work, since it would mean economic independence. As much as women today they claimed that motherhood was not to exclude employment. The contradictory demands of paid employment and motherhood and therefore all the problems women were faced with had to be overcome, not by the individual woman, but by an overall effort of the whole of society.[1]

Of equal importance to the women's movement was the struggle for political rights. It was Clara Zetkin who at the Second Socialist International in 1907 demanded equal franchise for all people, including women. The Weimar Constitution of 1919 guaranteed women equality with respect to civil rights and duties, as well as to marriage and family. Equality as such was not enshrined in the Constitution. The legislature was obliged to implement equality in family law; however, the civil code was never adjusted.

Women's position in society appeared and still does appear to be strongly determined by the prevailing needs of industry and the moral views of society. The industrialization of the nineteenth century changed the employment pattern of women. Industry required cheap labor and so women began to leave the house, their usual domain. At the same time public administration and public services increased as well. It is then that we find for the first time that women were permitted to take up positions in the public service. Economic demands at the time of World War I once again increased the recruitment of women into the workforce. Although the Weimar Constitution provided for equality between men and women as well as equal access to the civil service, women in the civil service were the first to suffer from demobilization orders (February 23, 1919; January 25, 1920) designed to provide soldiers returning from war with jobs. Therefore, when in 1930 right-wing parties and associations started a campaign against double-wage households, it was not an entirely new development.

The Nazi impact on the position of women in society is still disputed. Nazi ideology promoted only typical female professions, emphasized women's role in the farm household and as childbearer and strongly opposed women's emancipation. This, it is argued, largely reflected the prevailing traditional views on women. However, it is significant that the Nazi regime made great efforts to realize their ideology. As a result, women were not permitted into certain professions and were deprived of qualified positions, access to certain university courses, and the right to be elected to parliament. The war efforts of industry and its demand for labor made a strict implementation of the Nazi policies impossible. Before and during World War II women were increasingly used as the reserve workforce. After World War II they were again attracted back to resuming their traditionally assigned roles and duties.[2] It would be inadequate to make a general assessment of the impact of national socialism on the position of women in society. Nevertheless, it can be said that the Nazi regime suppressed all independent women's movements and helped to keep the prevailing traditional views about women alive.

In the Constitution of the Federal Republic of Germany (FRG) of May 23, 1949, Article 3 GG ("Grundgesetz," Basic Law) is the key to the legal position of women in Germany. Articles 3 S.2 GG stipulates that men and women have equal rights,[3] and it is considered to confer a duty whereby the legislature and the constitutional court are liable to materialize these rights.

The political forces which have developed since the enactment of the Basic Law have failed to fulfill the constitutionally required changes on all levels of the society. A constitutional deadline ("Verwirklichungsgebot") given in Article 117 S.1 GG prescribed that all existing laws had to be brought in line with Article 3 S.2 GG by March 31, 1953. Finally, the "Gleichberechtigungsgesetz" (equality law) of 1957 was passed. This law dealt only with matrimonial and family law. The whole economic area, though debated during the preparation of the law, was excluded from the final act.[4] The "Gleichberechtigungsgesetz" did not achieve full equality even with respect to family law. In a dispute over how to exercise parental care the final decision was reserved for the father. The constitutional court ruled that in this respect the "Gleichberechtigungsgesetz" was unconstitutional.[5]

The main criticism of the legislature is that it undermined the totality of the precept in Article 3 S.2 GG by cohesively regulating matrimonial and family law while the area of employment and social welfare developed largely uncontrolled, allowing discrimination and inequality. The constitutional court contributed to this development by maintaining the basic concept that functional or biological differences between men and women can be connected with different legal consequences. This jurisdiction has been criticized for allowing inequality to manifest itself, rather than eradicating it. The court always argued from the point of view of women's position in the family and not of her socio-economic interests as a person. By treating the question of equality on the basis of marriage and family and enhancing women's position in that context, the conflict between gainful occupation and motherhood is disregarded.[6]

Political Rights

The constitution of the F.R.G. restored the political rights of women: every German has the same civic rights and duties (Article 331 GG). Despite their formal equality women are still under-represented in public life.[7] The proportion of female membership in political parties 1982–1983 is illustrated in Table 32.

The present "Bundestag" (parliament) has 51, or 9.8 percent, female members. On the "Länder" (state) and the community level, the proportion of female deputies and councillors is slightly higher. The parties' women's organizations increasingly demand a more equal participation of women in responsible positions and active policy making. For example, the S.P.D. women aim at a ratio of 30 percent female candidates for the next elections. The ratio should continuously increase until it reaches 50 percent, since women make up half the population. The C.D.U. women want female participation according to the proportion of female members. The Green party aims at a 50:50 ratio between men and women in all party positions and in parliament.

Apart from party women's organizations, the unions and professional societies, among others, actively monitor politics and its effect on women's rights and position in society. Out of 10 million union workers, 2.5 million are women. Recent increase in union membership has mainly been through women. In the unions, as in political parties, women demand a fairer share of the responsible positions and a better deal for promotion. The apparent increase in discussions on the role of women in public life and society may have partly been stimulated by the example of the Green party's progressive politics. Furthermore, great participation and political involvement of women can be observed in groups other than political parties, like peace groups, the anti-nuclear movement, environmental groups and "Burgerinitiativen" (citizen's initiatives).

Since the media play a significant role in politics, in forming public opinion and depicting women's role in society, it is worthwhile noting the level of women's participation in the media. In Germany, broadcasting stations are incorporated under public law. Besides an administrative council and a director general, broadcasting cooperations have a broadcasting council which comprises representatives from the "socially relevant groups." There are no safeguards to ensure that women play an appropriate role in planning, organizing and deciding programs for radio and television. Journalism is largely regarded as a male domain, above all when it involves transmission of political

Party	Member-ship	Party Executive Committee	Members of Parliament	Proportion of the Parliamentary Group
CDU	**21.42%**	**6.3%**	**14**	**7.3%**
SPD	**23.38**	**17.5**	**21**	**10.8**
CSU	**13.5**	**7.0**	**3**	**5.6**
FDP	**24.5**	**12.5**	**3**	**8.8**
Greens	**35.5**	**30.0**	**10**	**37.0**

Year	Number	Percentage(1)
1953	52	10.7
1957	49	9.4
1961	49	9.4
1965	41	7.9
1969	32	6.2
1972	36	6.9
1976	41	7.9
1983	50	9.7
1987	80	15.4

***Top:* Table 32. Percentage of Membership of Women of West German Political Parties, 1983. Source: *Frauen in der Bundesrepublik Deutschland,* Bundesminister für Jugend, Familie and Gesundheit, Summer 1984, p. 43. *Bottom:* Table 33. Women in the West German Parliament. Source: *The Politics of the Second Electorate,* Joni Lovenduski and Jill Hills (eds.), Routledge & Kegan Paul, London, 1981; and *Official Handbook,* West German Republic, 1988. Note: (1) Percentages vary because the number of seats in the Bundestag change as result of regular delimitation. In 1953 there were 410; in 1957, 519; from 1965 to 1983, 518; and in 1987, 519 seats.**

information. Women play hardly any part in the formation of public opinion in Germany. They are assigned to cultural, educational or family programs. The public broadcasting cooperations are run almost exclusively by men and moreover controlled by very many men and few women on the supervisory boards. Out of 170 ArD (broadcasting corporation) foreign correspondents in 1982, only two were women. The ArD has 40 women among 431 members of bodies. Women made up 9 percent of journalists in the political, economical, sports and news sectors for radio and 8 percent for television.[8]

The Family[9]

The present form of civil marriage goes back to 1875, when it was introduced by Chancellor Otto von Bismarck as the only legally accepted form of marriage. In German constitutional history, the Weimar Constitution, Articles 119–122, was the first to deal with the protection of marriage, social support for motherhood and family, parental custody, protection of youth, equality between children inside and outside marriage and equality between men and women. The constitutional support for marriage and family was understood to guarantee the structure of family law as codified in the "Burgerliches Gesetzbuch" (BGB). Article 6 S.I GG follows the German constitutional tradition of protecting the bourgeois marriage and family. At present, women who are mothers enjoy special constitutional protection through the community (Article 6 S.IV GG).

The significance of Article 6 GG is as follows. According to the jurisdiction of the Constitutional Court, Article 6 S.I GG is understood not only to entail the obligation to protect but also to promote marriage and family since the family is the "germ cell" of society.[10] The protection especially prohibits discrimination against married persons with respect to unmarried persons, or against families with children compared to those without children. Article 6 GG not only guarantees marriage and family as individual rights, but is furthermore considered to be an institutionalized guarantee.[11]

Other such institutionalized guarantees are, for example, ownership and the law of succession. It means that the essential structural principles of matrimonial and family law are constitutionally protected and barred from change, because these are moral principles which determine social life.[12] Contemporary family law has evolved within the framework of "institutionalized guarantee." The Constitutional Court has in various decisions called upon the legislature to fulfill the constitutional obligation of Article 3 S.II GG, that is, men and women are equal in matrimonial and family law.

Major legal changes which led to equality between men and women in matrimonial and family law were materialized only by the first "Ehe-und Familienreformgesetz" (reform of matrimonial and family law) in 1976. This law reform introduced the principle of equal partnership in marriage. The "housewife marriage" was abolished. Gainful occupation was no longer conditional upon non-interference with a woman's duty in marriage and family. Both spouses were now mutually obliged to maintain the family (§1360 BGB) and have a free choice in how to achieve this end.

While the legislature basically abstained from regulating conjugal life, the provisions for conjugal property are very detailed. The legally proposed status of property is that of an association with accrued gains ("Zugewinngemeinschaft," §1363 BGB). The property and assets of the spouses prior to marriage do not become common goods. Upon termination of the marriage, assets acquired during marriage are subject to equalization of accrued gains ("Zugewinnsaugleich").

However, it remains open to the spouses whether to adopt the proposed model, which is not legally binding. In a marriage settlement (§1408 BGB), they can also stipulate that they shall live with a joint property ("Gutergemeinschaft," §1415 BGB) or separate property ("Gutertrennung," §1414 GBG) arrangement. Separate property means a complete separation of assets with each spouse administering his or her own assets, except for those obligations arising from conjugal life. In a joint property arrangement all assets, whether acquired prior to marriage or after marriage, automatically become common goods of the spouses. In the absence of any special arrangement, joint administration is required.[13]

For mixed marriages, e.g. a German married to an alien, the property question is regulated according to Article 15 EGBGB, a by-law to the civil code. The Constitutional Court declared Article 15 S.I,II EGBGB unconstitutional because of its infringement of Article 3 S.II GG (decision of the 22.2.83). Article 15 EGBGB rules that conjugal property law applies only for a German husband, not for a German wife, whose property questions are to be decided according to the laws of her husband's nationality. New provisions to the extent that the laws of the country where the spouses have their main residence will be applicable are expected. Article 17 EGBGB contains a similar rule to Article 15 EGBGB for divorce. There is not yet a decision of the Constitutional Court, but the highest civil court ("Bundesgerichtshof fur Zivilsachen") jurisdiction has applied to Article 17 EGBGB the same principle as the Constitutional Court has to Article 15 EGBGB.[14]

Tax law reflects the special protection of marriage and family. Spouses have a choice whether income tax should be collected separately or jointly. The latter—also called income-tax splitting—means that both incomes are added, then divided and taxed. It balances out higher taxes on higher incomes so that progressive tax increase is diminished. All personal allowances are granted twice.

Until 1976 wives were obliged to use the husband's name as family name. Now they can choose either name. The party not providing the family name can use their own name as a suffix to the family name.

To obtain a divorce the marriage has to be deemed irretrievably broken down (§§1565,156 BGB). Since the 1976 reform the principle of guilt is no longer a precondition for divorce. If after the divorce one partner is not capable of financially caring for himself or herself because of child rearing, old age, ill health, unemployment or acquiring professional training missed out on during marriage, or for reasons of fairness, he or she can obtain a maintenance claim against the other, §1569BGB. Prior to the reform the guilty party was denied any right to maintenance. §1585c BGB permits spouses to make maintenance arrangements, either excluding the legal provisions in total or modifying them. An arrangement that would result in one party requiring state social benefits is void. If one partner at the time of the arrangement is obviously in need of maintenance the other cannot clear him- or herself of the responsibility by excluding all maintenance claims.

The 1976 reform also introduced for the first time the principle of statutory pensions equalization ("Versorgungsaugleich"). It aimed at achieving a fair balance between the pension rights acquired by both partners during the time of marriage. The legislature's intention was to improve the position of the housewife and the lower-earning partner. To introduce a general housewife pension did not seem to be feasible. Pensions equalization is open to divergent agreements, but these acquire the approval of the family court.

De facto Marriage ("Nichtehleliche Lebensgemeinschaft")

Even though marriage may still be the dominant form of a union for life there has always been a substantial and increasing number of people who live in a non-conjugal life arrangement. They do not enjoy the same special constitutional protection that married people do according to Article 6 GG. Their mode of life falls within the general protection provided by Article 2 GG for freedom of action ("Handlungsfreiheit"). As yet no special legislation exists to deal with the legal implications of *de facto* marriage, unlike matrimonial law. It has been argued that any such legislation would be impossible, because of the enormous diversity of such unions. Furthermore, it may not be the wish of the people who choose to live in such a union because they reject legal subjugation.

Therefore in a non-married partnership, partners cannot rely on the automatic legal consequences of marriage: equalization of accrued gains and pensions, maintenance in case of separation, legal right to an inheritance, and equalization of accrued gains in case of death. However, a *de facto* marriage does not exist in a legal vacuum. Courts increasingly have to deal with litigation arising from such relationships and it is generally acknowledged that these partners may need the assistance of the court.

Jurists have not agreed on how to legally qualify such unions: contract *sui generis,* which after a long lasting *de facto* marriage should be treated as analogous to marriage; as law of partnership as in the civil code; or as an association with ownership in common. The jurisdiction is very reluctant to make analogies to matrimonial law because equalization between the two life forms could mean a discrimination against marriage. The jurisdiction rather applies other concepts of the civil code when they seem fit, such as the law of partnership to solve questions of ownership and property after separation. Current jurisdiction does not automatically consider contracts of inheritance, excluding the lawful heir, as unethical or *contra bonos mores.* Otherwise analogies to the law of succession as applied to spouses are not made. In individual cases courts have acknowledged a right to succeed the deceased partner as a tenant, as is provided for married partners.[15]

As a general rule, it is safest for non-married partners to have a partnership contract or arrange their affairs in joint name. Children of non-married partners are treated like those of a single mother, i.e., as children born outside marriage. The mother has sole parental custody (§1705 BFB) and she is the legal representative of the minor. She can determine the father's access to the child (§1711 BGB) but the guardianship court can impart authority to the father to have access to the child (§171 II BFB).

There is, however, one law which explicitly mentions *de facto* relationships. Partners who live in a *de facto* relationship may not have advantages over married couples receiving social welfare benefits with respect to conditions and amount (§122 BSHG, "Bundessozialhilfegesetz," Federal Social Welfare Act).

Property

In Germany, a woman's right to own property, to inherit property and to dispense with property assets is equal to that of a man and is unrestricted except if otherwise agreed to in a marriage contract.

Employment and Assistance to Working Women

In the public debate, an increasingly strong emphasis on the issue of women and work can be observed. There appears to be unanimous agreement that discrimination against women still occurs. Women have fewer opportunities, are a minority in higher positions and suffer first from unemployment. However, there is great dispute about the appropriate steps to improve the situation of women. Some figures should help to illustrate the position of women in employment.

In 1984, 38.2 percent of the workforce were women, as opposed to 35.9 percent in 1970. However, 90 percent of working women were employed in only 12 different professions (in 1982). Women also tend to have lower level jobs, e.g. only 5.3 percent of university professors are women. Of the 31 million part-time workers without social security in 1984, 93 percent were women; this was also the case for part-time jobs with social security. In 1984 44 percent of unemployed persons were women, even though they represent only 38.2 percent of the workforce.[16]

The governmental machinery to promote equality between men and women has evolved from a mere administrative unit to, first, a Directorate of Women's Affairs (within the Federal Ministry for Youth, Family and Health—"Bundesminister für Jugend, Familie and Gesundheit")[17] finally in 1986 to an independent Ministry for Women's Affairs joined together with the above-mentioned ministry. The effectiveness of the Ministry for Women's Affairs remains to be determined.

Eight out of the 11 states and some cities have established women's units or offices to deal with all women's issues but especially to promote equal opportunities for women. These states have introduced either a legislative framework or directives for positive action concerning the promotion of women in the public service and their access to the public service. Sanctions for non-compliance are not provided for. On the federal level, a directive of February 24, 1986, calls for promotion of women in the public service. It should be noted that the public service is directly bound in its employment policies by Article 3. S.II GG. Access to the public service may only depend on the qualifications and capabilities of a person. In the past, internal directives unfavorable to women have been disclosed in various sectors of the public service.[18]

As far as equality between men and women in the private sector is concerned the courts have always ruled (a continuous jurisdiction since 1955) that sex discrimination at work is illegal. It was only in 1980, however, that the equal treatment of men and women and in particular the principle of equal pay was enacted into the civil code. This was necessary in order to bring Germany's legislation into line with the European Community's directives on the subject.

These new provisions of the civil code have been criticized as too weak because of the lack of a supervisory machine and effective and adequate sanctions to ensure that parties discriminated against receive appropriate compensation. The European Court in Luxembourg ruled that compensation should have a deterrent effect.[19]

Furthermore, the burden of proof, at least the *prima facie* evidence, rests with the person discriminated against. Job advertising "shall" not specify the sex of the candidates (§611b BGB). A "must" would have been more desirable. The enforcement of equality at work still depends on the individual; he or she has to take legal recourse.[20]

A variety of schemes to promote women in education and employment is now under debate. Some of them suggest strict to flexible quotas for the number of women who have to be allowed access to training and employment.[21] Special attention is given to enforcement procedures and sanctions. There is dispute whether positive actions, e.g. positive discrimination to enforce certain quotas, would be an infringement of the constitution. However, according to basic constitutional principles, the state must ensure social justice and welfare through a balancing and distributive justice. On the basis of these principles, positive action may be employed to eradicate existing injustices.

A most progressive anti-discrimination bill has now been proposed by the Green party. The bill seeks to improve earlier proposals of this kind. It entails the following:[22]

1. obligatory equal access of women to vocational training and employment, quota and enforcement regulations;
2. eradication of sex-oriented education;
3. prohibition of sex discrimination in media and advertising;
4. a women's delegate who will supervise the implementation of the new law; and
5. right of action for associations.

A special act, the "Beschaftigungsforderungsgesetz" of May 1, 1985, with occupational development programs to improve public funding of programs which help women to enter or re-enter the workforce after bringing up children, was passed. Under the new act, part-time workers shall be treated the same as full-time workers unless there is a qualified reason for not doing so.

In 1979, maternity protection was improved. In addition to six weeks leave prior to birth and eight weeks after, any employed woman has a right to four months leave. During pregnancy and six months after birth, a woman enjoys special protection against termination. During the four months leave, a woman can participate in a special state remuneration scheme which pays up to 750 DM per month. The law of December 1985 introduced a scheme whereby a non-working parent who engages in child-rearing will receive 600 DM per month until the child reaches the age of 10 months. On the one hand the law is to be welcomed, for it fills in the gap of maternity protection for non-working mothers, but on the other hand it may serve to induce women not to take up a job at all or resign from their jobs when they become pregnant.

Germany has a well-functioning kindergarten system for children aged three to six. For children under three years of age, it is very difficult to find day care or publicly available creches. Some universities may offer day care centers, but as a general rule it is not common in Germany for big employers to offer day care facilities for their employees.

Personal Autonomy

The July 1976 reform of the penal law legalized abortion within the first three months of pregnancy under limited conditions: medical reasons, social reasons which would amount to great distress and cannot be otherwise resolved, or a pregnancy that has been caused by a criminal offense. Various financial support schemes have been designed to help overcome problems of financial distress. The pregnant woman has to undergo medical examination by two independent doctors and has to see a counseling service. Services for family planning and counseling on contraception are readily available for women in Germany.

The questions of whether rape inside marriage should also be punishable as rape is under continuous discussion. Under the present legislation such a case could invoke a penalty for duress and causing bodily harm. Throughout Germany, there is a network of self-help groups, women's advisory bureaus (for legal, family and health affairs) and houses for battered women, some of which are publicly funded. One of the main aims of these initiatives is to encourage women to report and talk about violence they have been subjected to.

The social and legal implications of the various forms of *in vitro* fertilization have caused much controversial discussion among women and jurists alike. The legal problems still remain to be solved. Among women, one can observe a great deal of skepticism about this male-dominated technology. As far as surrogate motherhood is concerned, the majority opinion among jurists is that such contracts would be void for ethical reasons.

A step towards more financial autonomy was taken in 1972 and 1973 with the reform of the national pension insurance scheme. Non-working women have since then been able to join the insurance scheme: they can determine the monthly contribution themselves. In general, non-working wives benefit from their husbands' insurance. A widow receives 60 percent of the husband's pension. The average worker's pension for men was 1172 DM in 1983 and 42 DM for women. The average salaried employee's pension for men was 1626 DM and for women 767 DM.[23]

The difference is due to women earning lower wages and having fewer working years because of rearing children. Since January 1986, women born after 1921 receive an increase in their pensions for child-rearing. For women born before 1921, the scheme will apply progressively, reaching all women by 1990. This step-by-step introduction is highly disputed in Germany.

Conclusion and Comment

Individual West German women have made an impressive mark in the political and legal professions. In December 1972 West Germany's Bundestag elected Annemarie Renger as President of the Bundestag, the third highest office in the German state after the Federal President and the Chancellor.

Wiltraut von Brunneck became only the fourth woman in the world to become a Supreme Court judge. The other three were all in Scandinavia. In 1982 she was followed by Sandra Day O'Connor of the United States and by Bertha Wilson of the Canadian Supreme Court.

Achievements of individual women have been important, but when one looks past them, the picture in West Germany still leaves much to be desired even insofar as women in law itself are concerned. "Although in the Federal Republic every woman according to the letter of the law, has equal access to any legal profession, the actual facts differ conspicuously," a West German advocate said during a 1984 symposium on women in law.[24] In the early 1950s women formed less than 5 percent of the law students. By 1983 this percentage had grown to 30 percent but, according to the West German Federal Chamber of Lawyers, only 10.8 percent of all lawyers in 1984 were women. According to the *Statistical Yearbook* (1984) of the Federal Republic only 14.69 of all judges on State Courts during 1983 were women. In the same year, only 4.85 percent of judges at the Federal Courts were women. Considering that in 1975 the figure was 4.48 percent, the Decade for Women has not achieved much in this area in West Germany. According to Gisela Wild there were only nine female lawyers, i.e., 5.73 percent, employed by the Federal Department of Justice in 1984.[25]

Women have struggled long and hard in order to enter the legal profession in Germany. Prior to 1900 they could study law only in other countries. The new German Constitution of 1919 stated that "men and women have in principle equal civil rights and duties"[26] but it was only in 1922 that parliament (the German Diet) passed a law permitting women to the judiciary. Considering that more than 60 years have elapsed since then, the current situation of women in law in West Germany leaves much to be desired. Ms. Wild states correctly: ". . . it remains to be seen whether society is prepared to appoint women to a greater extent to leading professions in the legal world."[27]

Article 3 of the West German Constitution, known as the Basic Law, provides for equality between men and women. Court decisions have interpreted this to include equal pay for equal work. Yet women continued for many years, up to 1980, to earn between one-quarter and one-third less than men. Women were also spread over a very narrow range of occupations. At the universities women in 1979 were only 2 percent of university professors, some 17 percent of tenured civil servants and less than 3 percent of top managers.[28]

***Opposite, Top:* Table 34. Percentage of Women Councillors in West German Towns. Source: *The Politics of the Second Electorate,* Joni Lovenduski and Jill Hills (eds.), Routledge & Kegan Paul, London, 1981, pp. 169–170. *Bottom:* Table 35. Average Full-Time Earnings of Manual and Non-Manual Women Workers in West Germany as a Percentage of Those of Men, by Sector, 1982. Source: International Labor Organization, *The Economic Role of Women in the ECE Region,* Geneva, 1985, p. 71.**

Size of town	1 Jan. 1973	4 May 1975	1 Jan. 1977	1 Oct. 1979
1 million and over			11.8	14.0
500,000–1 million	12.3	13.2	13.8	14.7
200,000–500,000	11.6	12.2	12.7	14.7
100,000–200,000	10.7	12.1	12.4	14.5
50,000–100,000	9.1	10.1	11.0	12.0
30,000–50,000		8.3	9.3	
20,000–50,000	6.9	-	-	10.3
Total	8.3	10.0	10.8	11.4

Sector	Manual workers Hourly	Manual workers Weekly	Non-manual workers monthly
Industry, commerce, banking and insurance	..	..	64.8
Industry	72.7	69.2	66.7
Mining	..	..	61.2
Basic materials industry	77.3	74.0	70.6
of which:			
Iron and steel	75.7	73.2	66.0
Oil processing	71.6	70.3	70.3
Chemicals	74.0	71.4	72.0
Artificial fibres	76.6	75.2	72.9
Investment goods industry	75.9	72.6	65.8
of which:			
Machine building	76.5	73.0	65.4
Automobile and vehicle industry	82.8	79.7	65.6
Electro-technical industry	77.9	74.9	67.1
Precision instruments	78.6	77.0	68.2
Office equipment, data-processing equipment	82.9	80.6	65.9
Consumer goods industry	72.6	68.5	66.4
of which:			
Paper and cardboard	72.8	67.2	64.7
Printing and publishing	69.7	67.2	66.1
Footwear	80.6	78.1	63.9
Textiles	81.1	76.2	69.1
Clothing	76.6	73.4	70.3
Food, drink and tobacco	70.3	63.9	69.5
Construction	..	..	62.6
Wholesale trade	..	..	68.3
Retail trade	..	..	65.0
Banking	..	..	77.4
Insurance	..	..	76.8

In politics women remain significantly under-represented both in town councils and in the national legislature, the Bundestag. (See Table 34.)

Observers agree that women play a very subordinate role in politics in West Germany. An important point is the extent to which men in Germany are prepared to give up rights and privileges which they have enjoyed in the past. Jane Hall, an expert on the role of women in German politics, stated that men pay lip service to the idea of more women office bearers as long as the expansion does not take place in their constituencies.[29]

Women play an important role in the labor union movements in Germany. One of the three-member ruling committee of Germany's Amalgamated Workers' Union (the second largest federated union, in membership, in the world after England's Trade Union Congress) was a woman, Maria Weber. But as Shari Steiner observed, "Once one looks past the outstanding examples the picture of women takes on a decidedly less optimistic cast." She pointed out that second-rate status is reflected in wages and that equal pay for equal work remains a major objective for women in West Germany.[30] Thus the Treaty of Rome seems to have had little practical legal impact in Germany.

On the vexing question of abortion, the situation remained fluid at the end of the 1970s. Sterilization was legalized in West Germany in 1973 and in Austria in 1975, and in Swiss law varies from canton to canton. Abortion on demand was legal in East Germany, but is illegal in Switzerland. Abortion on demand was legalized in West Germany and Austria in 1974, but the German Constitutional Court later declared the law unconstitutional. Abortion is now available only for health reasons.[31]

There remains a vast area in which discrimination against women is prevalent and for which a constitutional solution seems difficult to achieve. The fact that it took 100 years for the Berlin Philharmonic Orchestra to admit a woman to membership (in 1983) is a good example, as was the strike threatened by the orchestra when the director, Herbert von Karajan, wanted to bring in a second female.

The increase in women's representation in the paid labor force is one of the most significant developments in most industrialized societies in Europe. But Hanna Schöp-Schilling made the interesting observation that in West Germany, women's 38 percent of the work force in 1980 was only 1 percent higher than their share a hundred years earlier, during the old German Reich. It is the number of married women and mothers in paid employment which has increased disproportionally. In 1980, she pointed out, 45 percent of all married women were employed and of these about 50 percent had children under 15 years of age. She also observed that when it comes to bargaining women are still neglected. Women are vastly under-represented in the labor unions as well as in the works councils which represent employee's interests within firms. Women are also under-represented in terms of membership, representation of the union committees and in higher decision-making positions of labor unions.[32]

14. Case Study: Switzerland

Introduction

Swiss women have only very recently been able to employ the principle of equality as a politically significant instrument in their struggles, even though this principle was first enshrined in the Swiss Constitution in 1798. At that time, Napoleon's invasion led to the Helvetic Confederation's acquiring a new constitution modeled on the French Revolutionary Constitution. The principle of equality thus became a main feature of the Constitution and an integral part of Swiss legal tradition. The early appreciation of the principle was associated mainly with equal political rights rather than with equality in all relevant legal aspects of society.[1] Furthermore, it was not held to apply to women.

The present Swiss Constitution came into force in 1874 but did not introduce political rights for women until 1971.

Progressive political forces have since the late nineteenth century been engaged in a continuous battle to enfranchise women. The "Bund Schweizer Frauenvereine" (Federation of Swiss Women's Associations, founded in 1900) and the "Schweizer Verband für das Frauenwahlrecht" (Swiss Association for Women's Suffrage, founded in 1909) were the first to work towards this goal. Various attempts to enfranchise women, one as early as 1918, failed. In 1959 the Federal Assembly proposed a revision of the Constitution which would guarantee political rights for women. The popular referendum of men on February 1, 1959, rejected this proposed change by a 655,000 to 324,000 majority. Women had suffered an outright defeat. However, there was some hope. In the same referendum, one canton—Waadt—had voted in favor of political rights for women at the canton level. The cantons Neuenburg and Geneva followed this example in fall 1959 and spring 1960, respectively.[2]

Two events helped the women activists to gain momentum and inspiration.

1. In 1965 the U.N. and its specialized agencies sponsored a support program for women. By referring to the special U.N.E.S.C.O. women's program, women successfully demanded that the Swiss commission in U.N.E.S.C.O. should set up a working group to study the position of women in Switzerland. This project eventually received the approval of the Federal Council.

2. In the late 1960s, Switzerland signed the European Convention on Human Rights, but with a reservation concerning the enfranchisement which made manifest a very long-lived injustice. Pressure brought upon the Federal Council forced the latter once more to pay attention to the question of the women's vote. After increased political activity and large women's demonstration in Bern in 1969, women finally obtained the vote in 1971.

At first this success threatened to endanger the all-encompassing U.N.E.S.C.O. study on the position of women in family and society. There were voices which considered this undertaking redundant. However, they proved to be a minority. After its completion in 1974 the sociological analysis of the position of women in family and society by Thomas Held and Rene Levy became the first major sceintific study to prove the inequalities women were subjected to and to point out the underlying sociological patterns. This study has incited further discussions and served as a basis for demanding that complete equality between women and men be achieved.

In 1975, the U.N. International Year for Women, this demand turned into a concrete people's initiative. (The first congress occurred in 1896 and had since convened every 25 years.) A resolution in favor of launching a campaign to revise the Constitution was the most important outcome of the congress. Women had realized that the principle of equality as stated in Article 4, "All Swiss are equal before the law," did not suffice to guarantee equality for women. The principle required specification, notably a clear reference to women.[3] According to the traditional interpretation of the Constitution, women and men had to be treated equally only in areas where they were considered to be equal. These considerations were determined by the traditional understanding of men's and women's role in society. Thus sex could be a legally relevant reason to apply different rules.[4] The old Article 4 of the Constitution was ambiguous and left too much scope for undermining equality.

After over six years of intensive efforts, the revision of Article 4 was accepted by the Swiss people in 1981. Sex alone can no longer be grounds for different treatment. Article 4SS2 now reads as follows: "Men and women are equal before the law. The law provides for their equality, particularly in the domains of the family, education, and work. Men and women are entitled to equal wages for work of equal value." However, the new Article 4 does not fulfill everything women had been striving for. It is only the principle of equal pay which has direct legal implications, e.g. provides a basis for legal recourse. Otherwise, the revised article remains a political imperative requiring the legislature, i.e., the parliament and the people, to physically enact the constitutionally prescribed principle.

In Switzerland there are no means to ensure that legislation is consistent with the Constitution. The Swiss democracy is based upon popular vote, and laws are passed by referendum. Unlike the case in Germany, the Constitutional Court cannot send an unconstitutional law back to the legislature for revision. Federal law and decisions are binding for the Federal Court, which has no power to review them with respect to their constitutionality. With respect to federal legislation, legal action to pursue an equality claim is therefore impossible. The Federal Court can review only cantonal law with respect to its constitutionality.

Political Rights

On February 7, 1971, the Swiss constitution was changed by a majority vote of 65.7 percent. Article 74 of the Constitution now guarantees Swiss women political rights and duties equal to those of men. The revision of the Constitution in favor of the women's vote in referenda and elections was the first major breakthrough in equal rights for women.[6] However, the Constitution guarantees organizational autonomy to cantons. By virtue of this autonomy each of the 22 cantons can decide for itself whether to give women political rights on the canton and community level (Article 74 SS4). The two Appenzell half cantons still deprive women of the right to vote on canton affairs, and in Appenzell Innerhoden, also on community affairs. The National Council has refused all measures to force the two Appenzell half cantons to enfranchise women. A petition to that effect was rejected on October 3, 1985. The petition has sought to lift the reservation in Article 74 SS4.[7] Canton Graubunden was the most recent to grant women the vote, on February 27, 1983.

Since women obtained political rights, they have been elected in increasing numbers to the Federal Assembly, which is made up of two houses: National Council and Council of States. See Tables 36 and 37 for an illustration of the development of the number of women in the National Council.

In considering how recently Switzerland enfranchised women, the trend of an increasing membership in parliament is encouraging. It is worthwhile noting that women in other countries, e.g. France, experienced the reverse process, from 7 percent in 1946 to 5.3 percent in 1981. West Germany saw a very slow increase in the number of women members of parliament, from 6.8 percent in 1946 to 8.2 percent in 1980 and 9.8 percent in 1983. Over this period of time the number of female members of parliament rose significantly only in the Scandinavian countries and the Netherlands.[8] It is also noteworthy that in Switzerland female party membership is increasing.

Some of the smaller parties, e.g. Poch and the Alliance of Independents, have 40 percent and 45 percent female members. The larger parties represented in the National Council also have a fairly high proportion of female members compared to other European countries. Furthermore, the proportion of women candidates standing for elections corresponds in most cases with their proportion in party membership.[9]

The chances of a woman's obtaining a mandate in the National Council largely depend on the structure of the canton she stands for. Small cantons with few seats and cantons with a large workforce in rural and agricultural employment tend not to elect women into the National Council. We find that women are still best represented on the local level: 14.3 percent of councillors' positions are held by women. Women are worst represented in the cantonal parliaments. However, their number rose from 6.4 percent in 1976 to 9.2 percent in 1982.[10]

Despite these positive trends there are other less positive aspects. The Federal Commission for Matters Relating to Women states that women participate to a lesser extent—the average difference is 12 percent—than men in referenda. Only in the case of the referendum on equal rights for men and women (Article 4 of the Constitution) did the gap close to 5 percent. In the 1979 elections for the National Council, women's participation was 16 percent below men's participation. The Commission points out that taking an active political

Year	Candidate	Elected Members
1971	15.8%	5.0%
1975	16.8	7.5
1979	18.8	10.5
1983	-	11.0

Table 36. Swiss Women in the National Council 1971–1983. Source: Swiss Foreign Ministry, Bern, 1985.

interest depends on the level of education, status of occupation and on generally being well informed. These are factors which determine social status and self-confidence. With respect to all of these factors women's position is generally lower than that of men. If they are housewives, they are often completely excluded from outside life. Switzerland does not yet have a long tradition of women's integration in politics, and so it is difficult for women to decide on and gear themselves towards political careers. They have no previous images to model themselves on.[11]

On the other hand, women are confronted with the fact of barely being tolerated in politics. Those who are active have very few chances to work their way up through the party hierarchy. Apart from some isolated exceptions, women are not found in leading party positions. The same is true for the government, the federal administration, the courts and other important public offices. Women are found only in low-level positions. Some of the outstanding exceptions are as follows: For the first time in 1982, a woman became president of the National Council, the highest office in the Federation. Since 1984 the Federal Court has had two female judges, the first being appointed in 1974. In 1984 a woman first became one of the seven members of the Federal Council.[12] In mid-1986 a woman was first appointed ambassador. The current Swiss permanent representative at the U.N. in New York is also a woman; she enjoys ambassador's status. In the whole of the Swiss diplomatic corps women represent 8 percent of the staff.[13]

In order to ameliorate the general position of women in politics and public life, special women's committees have been created in various bodies: in 1980 in the personnel department of the federal administration, in political parties and in local, cantonal and federal parliaments.[14]

Among the politically active women, a very large proportion appears to prefer involvement in non-institutionalized groups, such as various action groups and movements on local and federal levels, environmental groups and parents' organizations. Their common non-hierarchical character in which individuals are not restrained by limited roles seems to appeal to women.[15]

Parallel to the discussion on how women can make full use of their political rights, debate arose on women's civic duties with respect to national defense. So far, national defense and protection of the civilian population has been an exclusively male obligation even though Article 18 of the Constitution obliges all Swiss to defend their country. Women can join voluntary organizations which are active in the framework of national defense. There has not yet been a decision on women's further participation in defense. However, the Federal Council has ruled out a general obligation to serve and is of the view that women's participation in defense should remain voluntary. The scope for voluntary participation should be extended, and some training courses (e.g. first aid) may become obligatory.[16]

Family

In the opinion of the Federal Commission for Matters Relating to Women the family is seen as the pivotal point for the position of women in Switzerland. The family life is interrelated with the areas of work, politics, public life and society in general.[17] The traditional family concepts built up many barriers for women, making it very difficult for them to enter into the above-mentioned areas with the same self-confidence as men. Traditionally, not even a woman herself expected to be involved in any of these areas. Today the legal system in Switzerland no longer wants to give legal support and justification for a traditional socialization of the sexes. A reform of matrimonial and family law is being undertaken in several phases.

The first important change of the civil code was the partial revision of the family law section in 1975. The revision in force since 1978 provides for equality in matters of custodial care and no longer makes a distinction between legitimate and illegitimate descent. For legal purposes the parental relationship between mother and child arises with the child's birth or adoption, no matter whether the mother is married. Paternity is either based on marriage with the mother, recognition or on a court decision. The child of a married couple always obtains the father's surname. If the parents are not married, it will carry the mother's name. Custodial care and parental rights are jointly exercised by married parents. This also applies in relation to a third party. In the case of an unmarried couple, the mother has the sole custodial care. It is not possible for a father to make a court application to obtain the same parental rights as the mother and exercise them jointly, as is the case in France.

In addition to the family law reform, the new provisions of the Nationality Act for the transmission of civic rights are now in force. Prior to July 1, 1985, only a woman of Swiss origin, married to a foreigner, could pass on Swiss civic rights to her child, provided that the child was born in Switzerland. The same now also applies for Swiss men married to foreign women.[18] The existing laws still allow only a foreign woman, but not a man, marrying a Swiss citizen to acquire Swiss nationality. A Swiss woman married to a foreigner may still also lose her nationality, unless she expressly declares her retention of it or if she would become stateless otherwise. For the second phase of the nationality law reform it is suggested to put a foreign wife and husband on equal footing. Neither would automatically obtain Swiss nationality, but there would be favorable conditions for spouses to become naturalized.[19]

Similar inequalities exist for foreign couples. According to the federal law, a husband living in Switzerland has the right to bring his wife and children to Switzerland as well. This does not apply to a wife residing in Switzerland.[20]

Party		**Year**		
	1971	*1975*	*1979*	*1983*
Parties well represented in the National Council				
Socialist Party	14.6	18.6	19.4	25.0
Democratic Socialist Radical Party	16.5	13.0	15.7	16.1
Christian Democrat Party	16.8	14.0	11.6	16.4
Centre Democratic Union	13.9	13.1	13.3	9.7
Parties poorly represented in the National Council				
Labour Party (Communist)	15.3	20.2	30.0	33.3
Progressive Organizations (extreme left)	37.5	26.9	44.7	49.0
Evangelical Party	17.4	18.4	16.1	18.9
Liberal Party	18.2	20.0	20.0	21.2
Parties not represented in the National Council				
Alliance of Independents	18.6	17.4	20.8	25.2
Swiss Republican Movement	6.3	8.7	14.1	20.6
Nazionale Aktion für Volk und Heimat (AN)	19.4	10.9	11.3	
Revolutionary Marxist League	figures not supplied	27.3	25.0	-
SPLGR	17.3	21.5	17.9	27.1

The next step in the family and matrimonial law reform program will be matrimonial law, leaving divorce aside for a third stage. To date, matrimonial law has remained in its entire traditional framework. However, revision was approved by the people in a referendum on September 22, 1985, by 54.7 percent to 45.3 percent. For administrative reasons, the reform only entered into force on January 1, 1988. In order to appreciate the changes, the main features of the intricate old law will be summarized below.

The family had to function according to a clear role model, in which there was no equal division of rights and duties. Upon marriage the husband became the head of the union. He determined the place of residence and maintained wife and children. She acquired her husband's surname and was obliged to perform all house duties. The union was legally represented by the husband. The wife could represent the union only with respect to her home duties or if she was authorized to do so otherwise. Furthermore she was dependent on her husband's permission to exercise a profession. However in case of an emergency she could be forced as part of her matrimonial obligations to work outside the house.[21]

Under the new matrimonial law husband and wife are equal partners. Both can represent the union. Important decisions have to be joint decisions. The husband's name still remains the family name. The wife is allowed to use her maiden name only as a suffix to the family name.[22]

A spouse has the right to institute divorce proceedings for various reasons. The most important are if the other has committed adultery, attempted to take his or her life, caused serious bodily harm, or seriously injured his or her reputation; or if the marriage has broken down. If this breakdown is mainly caused by one party, the other one can demand divorce.

The Swiss taxation law most evidently reflects the traditional concept of matrimonial law. The common federal and cantonal taxation system treats single women and men equally. For a married woman, however, family taxation applies. That means only the husband is liable for income tax on both his and his wife's incomes and for property tax. Husband and wife are an economic entity, with her income being added to the husband's income. Within a progressive tax system, this leads to higher taxes and may make a second income less desirable. The wife has no right to participate in the tax assessment procedure, nor in court proceedings, nor can she sign tax papers. The tax law is also part of the law reform program. However, there is not yet a fixed date. The reform should abolish the obvious disadvantages for families and put married women on equal footing with their husbands.[23] In the Canton Solothurn, a new taxation law has entered into force in 1986. It introduced a special family tariff which balances out the advantages *de facto* partners have previously enjoyed.[24]

Like taxation law, health insurance and pension schemes are based on the marital status of a person. They still make many unjustified differences between

Table 37. Proportion of Women Candidates in Elections to the Swiss National Council, 1971, 1975, 1979, 1983. Source: *Women in the Political World in Europe,* Council of Europe, Strasbourg, 1984, Vol. 2, pp. 16–17.

men and women. The pension scheme distinguishes between unmarried, single, divorced and widowed women. While single and divorced women are entitled to a pension, a married woman whose husband is a pensioner has no individual right to a pension. Couples have a joint pension. A suggestion for the anticipated reform of the pension scheme is a general pension for men and women regardless of their marital status.[25]

Property

Under the most common matrimonial regime of joint property a woman would lose control over property and assets belonging to her prior to marriage. This applied also to property or assets obtained free of charge during marriage, e.g. inheritance. The civil code stipulated that the husband administers the conjugal property, with the sole exception of her salary. Under the revised matrimonial law the new matrimonial regime, "participation in accrued gains," provides that each spouse individually administers and uses his or her property and assets. Despite the basic separation of property there are safeguards which protect common matrimonial interests, e.g. joint property can be disposed of only by consent. A spouse cannot dispose of only his part. A disposition on the conjugal home has to be a joint one regardless of whether it belongs to only one of them. Upon dissolution of the marriage a woman is now entitled to one-half of the husband's accrued gains, and vice-versa. That means a wife's income is no longer a "special asset" but has to be equally shared as well.[26]

Employment

In the whole spectrum of education, professional training and employment, the unequal conditions which the society imposes on women become most obvious. For more than three decades, one-third of the workforce consisted of female employees. On January 1, 1980 (last population census), women made up 35.2 percent of the workforce (Swiss women and foreign women combined). The female Swiss workforce was 33 percent as opposed to 46 percent of foreign women. Since a woman's life is still very much determined by traditional views on her role in the family, we find the highest employment ratio among single women, about 80 to 90 percent, followed by divorced or separated women. Young women with family obligations are least often employed. Among these women there is now a tendency to enter or re-enter the workforce after they have been through their child-rearing phase.

The general worldwide rule that women are most vulnerable to unemployment is just as true in Switzerland. Female unemployment rose from 16.3 percent in 1974 to 43.4 percent in 1982. In the same period, male unemployment fell from 83.7 percent to 56 percent. In 1985 more than two-thirds of the unemployed were women.[27]

Observers of the present situation of women in employment stress that the educational system is one of the root causes. It still entails many inequalities and disadvantages for women. This is true despite formal equality. The Constitution provides for equality between men and women in education and work,

Article SS 2. Previous efforts to that end have not been entirely successful. School textbooks may still transmit traditional role models. School curricula are not always the same for boys and girls. The education for girls is still found to be gender-oriented—lessons in household management, textile work—and geared to prepare them for their traditional roles and professions. In some cantons, the lessons in household management are compulsory.

In Switzerland, it is very difficult to establish a common standard in the educational system. Education falls within the authority of the cantons. It is part of their autonomy. However with respect to their rules on education they are subject to the Federal Court jurisdiction. It is expected that the court will pass a ruling on school regulations in the near future.[28] In an earlier decision, the court had declared impermissible the practice of making access to secondary education for girls dependent upon achieving higher marks than boys.[29]

Of equal concern to women is the fact that the average income of women is 30 percent less than that of men. As far as this is due to unequal pay, women are entitled to take legal recourse, in terms of Article 4 SS 2 of the Constitution. Article 4 is not only binding for the Federation but also for third parties, e.g. in the private sector. However, it has been argued that an individual claimant is in a weak position and too vulnerable to termination of employment. The parliamentary initiative to permit associations to institute legal action in equal pay cases was rejected by the National Council (October 4, 1985), though it will be considered as a postulate.[30] Those workers who work under a collective labor agreement enjoy the protection of Convention No. 100 of the International Labor Organization. Since the Federal Council has ratified that convention it can refuse to approve any collective labor agreement which contradicts the principle of equal pay. However, only a minority of workers fall within the category of collective labor agreements. Thus, it does not have a great impact on equal pay problems.[31]

The 30 percent gap between male and female earnings, it is stressed, is to a greater extent due to causes other than unequal pay. Women generally are less qualified than men. This is largely due to unequal education, professional and vocational training and promotion. It is on this basis that the principle of equal pay as the only directly applicable legal remedy has been questioned. The application of the principle of equal pay alone cannot diminish the gap between men and women in the working world. Other legal and administrative structures are needed. Women in Switzerland are looking across their borders to see how other countries apply positive action programs benefiting women, hoping to spur national discussion.[32] It appears that some of the bigger Swiss employers have become more sensitive to the problems of women at work and have created internal structures to assist and promote women. Examples are Ciba-Geigy, IBM, Migros Genossenschaft, Bund Schweizerischer Bankgesellschaft, and Swissair.[33]

There are also increasingly more back-to-work schemes addressing in particular women who have been out of work. The schemes are run by the private sector and both private and public bodies. Women's associations again play an important role in advancing the cause. The Republic and Canton of Jura, which also has a woman's status bureau, runs information campaigns for young girls seeking work as well as other support programs for women at work.[34] Despite the absence of an overall countrywide approach, the issue of women and employment now receives attention at various levels of society. The barriers in the education system and in professional training are beginning to crumble. Prejudices against women professionals are under attack. Women are beginning to learn typical male trades. There are already some outstanding examples where women have broken into male domains. Recently some women reached high positions in Geneva's finance and banking world.[35]

Women working in the primary sector are faced with some particular problems. A farmer's average wage is assessed in order to determine agricultural prices. When the work and wage of women working in the primary sector is estimated, it counts for only 85 percent of the wage of their male counterparts.

The "Schweizerischer Landfrauenverband" (Swiss Farmer's Wives Association) requested the Federal Agricultural Office to assess women equally to men. This request has been rejected[36] but a revision is anticipated for the next parliamentary term.[37]

Certain provisions of the labor code which are meant to protect and favor women have been under attack. The critics want to see them revised in the near future. One of the provisions is the ban on night work and particularly dangerous work and other such rules. Some of these rules are now considered to be a hindrance for women rather than an advantage. The same is true for the provision that the employer must show respect for a female worker's duties in house and family. In particular, this provision is no longer seen as a privilege but rather a manifestation of female role models. Women would like to see working hours flexible enough so that both men and women can equally take care of domestic charges.[38]

In Switzerland maternity protection and assistance is still very basic. Self-employed or non-working women may be excluded altogether from special assistance. Working women don't enjoy protection against unwarranted termination during their pregnancy.[39] They are entitled to receive wages during maternity leave eight weeks prior to birth and eight weeks afterwards. Only in that period of time do they enjoy special protection against termination. The revision of maternity protection has not yet been accomplished. Some of the bolder proposals, which included nine months paid leave, were rejected. Nor is it planned to revise the health insurance laws which provide for maternity protection.[40]

Personal Autonomy

Since the 1970s the autonomous women's movement throughout Europe has founded women's homes, in particular homes for battered women. Individual women should not remain in isolation with their problems. Switzerland now has eight homes for battered women. Most of the eight homes are struggling with financial problems. They are usually privately run but publicly subsidized. Annual statistics show that women take advantage of these houses and that their existence is certainly needed. In 1985 more than 1,000 women and children sought protection.[41]

In larger cities, women usually can find a whole range of different women's organizations which offer their services in information and counseling. Among those are also special consumer associations to advise on all consumer's interests.

Switzerland is undertaking a revision of the Swiss penal law on sexual offenses. The planned revision was supposed to make rape inside marriage punishable as rape. This, at least, was the recommendation of the expert committee. However, the bill as it is now proposed by the Federal Council does not provide for rape inside marriage as a rape offense.[42]

In Switzerland abortion has not been legalized, except for some limited medical reasons. The initiative to legalize abortion during the first 12 weeks of pregnancy was rejected in a referendum on September 25, 1977. There has now been a people's initiative against the misuse of gene technology. To provide for this, Article 24 of the Constitution, which deals with protection of the human being and his natural environment, is expected to be enlarged. Manipulation of paternity and motherhood shall be made impossible. There should be some control over experiments with human genes.[43]

Conclusion

The long struggle for reform has finally led to a healthy and dynamic political climate which appears to be rather favorable for the realization of the foregoing reforms. The trust placed upon the legislature and the people by Article 4 of the Constitution has not been in vain.

The Swiss democratic system with its plebiscitary democracy allows more scope for interest groups to act and take the political initiative, e.g. starting a people's initiative.

Women's organizations are very involved in the process of making equality a political reality. They have relentlessly revealed inequalities in the legal system and, at the same time, suggested solutions.

The Federal Commission for Matters Relating to Women is of equal importance in this process. It was set up in 1976 according to a decision of the Federal Council. Its 20 members representing political parties, regions, languages, women's organizations, and both sides of industry are appointed by the Federal Council. The Commission serves as an advisory body and has no special other powers, e.g. to remedy cases of discrimination against women.[44] In spite of these shortcomings the Commission is very active in its function as an advisory body both to the government and to women and women's organizations. It has scrutinized both federal and cantonal laws to expose all laws which treat men and women unequally. At the same time it has proposed a legislative program to remedy these inequalities. The prime target is family and matrimonial law. The traditional concept of family law has further ramifications because, for example, the whole social security sector (including the allocation of allowances) and taxation law are based on these traditional matrimonial and family concepts.[45]

Part Five: North America

Based on 1984 median earnings of women who worked full time, a woman in the United States with four years of college education still earns less than a male high school dropout. – Sylvia Hewlett, *A Lesser Life: The Myth of Women's Liberation in the USA*.

15. Case Study: Canada

Voting and Political Rights

S. C. 1918, c. 20 granted Canadian women over the age of 21 the right to vote in federal elections.[1] But this was limited to Euroamerican women and all native peoples were excluded until 1960[2] when S. C. 1960, c. 39 was enacted.[3] The provinces of Alberta, Manitoba and Saskatchewan had already enfranchised women in 1916 but other provinces acted later—Nova Scotia in 1918, New Brunswick and Ontario in 1919, British Columbia in 1920, Prince Edward Island in 1922, Newfoundland in 1925, and Quebec in 1940.[4] Federal voting rights are now guaranteed by the Constitution Act of 1982 and in Section 3 of the Canadian Charter of Rights and Freedoms. "Every citizen of Canada has the right to vote in an election of members of the House of Commons or of a legislative assembly and to be qualified for membership therein."

The final clause of section 3 of the Charter provides women with the right to run for and hold public office in federal and provincial legislatures. Although the right to vote had been granted in 1918, women's right to hold public office was still being debated in the provinces of Canada eight years later. Five women brought the question to the Supreme Court of Canada for the determination of whether women were included in the term "persons" under the British North America Act of 1867 and whether or not they were eligible as members to the Senate.[5] The case was then appealed to the Judicial Committee of the Privy Council in England who overruled the Supreme Court of Canada. The Privy Council held that women are officially persons under the Constitution.[6]

As section 3 of the Charter does not apply to the Senate, the same definition has been included in the Constitutional Act, which uses the term "persons" in setting qualifications for senators.[7] The right to participate in municipal elections is also omitted from section 3.[8] The controversy of whether women are included in "persons" could arise in other contexts due to R.S.C. 1970, c.I-23, the Interpretation Act, which states that a woman is included within the definition "unless a contrary intention appears."[9]

Canadian women are treated differently from Canadian males under the Citizenship Act. A foreign-born wife of a Canadian male can apply for citizenship after one year, while a female's foreign-born husband must wait five years.[10] Children who are born abroad may also be treated differently depending on which parent is a Canadian citizen. The child of a Canadian father automatically becomes a citizen while a Canadian mother's child does not, unless the mother is divorced or unmarried.[11] A provision in the Immigration

Act similarly derogates a woman's position by allowing a woman to be deported under an order deporting her husband.[12]

Property

The Constitution Act of 1867, §92(13), authorized the provincial legislatures to regulate "property and civil rights in the province."[13] This includes the law of real and personal property with all its derivatives as well as the creation of property rights, their transfer and succession.[14]

All of the Canadian provinces currently recognize that a woman has the capacity to enter into a contract. But in Quebec it was not until December 16, 1954, that married women were removed from the list of persons determined to be incompetent under Article 986 of the Civil Code of Lower Canada.[15] Unlike minors and interdicts, married women were determined to have the capacity to contract for the first time.

The traditional legal regime in Canada is separation of property. Under this system whatever a spouse accumulates remains as his or her own property. The result is that a woman who contributes to the support of the family by maintaining the home can be left with nothing when the marriage is dissolved through death, divorce or separation.[16] Legislation has created one safeguard for wives by prohibiting either spouse from disposing of the family residence without the consent of the other.[17] Some provinces have extended women's rights in this area by setting a statutory share of the deceased's property as belonging to the surviving spouse.[18]

Quebec has replaced the separation of property regime with a system known as Partnership of Acquests. Couples have the option of using the separation of property scheme by entering a marriage contract. The traditional system may be favored in marriages where both spouses are employed.

Partnership of Acquests is codified in Quebec Statute chapter 39 (1980), articles 463–524.[19] The Civil Code Revision Office released its Report on Matrimonial Regimes (1968) which outlines the system as follows: "During the marriage, each consort retains the entire control of his patrimony, and remains fully responsible for his debts: the autonomy of each is complete, save for the obvious need that each contribute, according to his means, to the needs of the household."[20] At the time the marriage is dissolved due to death, divorce or separation, all financial earnings and property are split with half going to each spouse.[21] The general rule is refined so that property acquired before marriage or by gratuitous title, as well as the proceeds from such property, is not included in the partition.[22] Also excluded are items of a personal nature and tools or items used in a trade or business.[23]

The new regime retained the feature from the separation of property system requiring the consent of both spouses prior to a sale of the principal family residence. The requirement has been extended somewhat. Article 449 prevents one spouse from pledging, alienating or removing the household furniture from the principal family residence.[24] Article 451 states: "Neither spouse, if the lessee of the principal family residence, may, without the written consent of the other, sublet it, transfer it or terminate the lease where the lessor has been notified, by either of them, that the dwelling is used as the principal residence."[25] Both spouses are protected from an unreasonable refusal or the unobtainability of consent. A court, acting under article 456, can authorize the spouse to act if "consent is unobtainable for any reason, or its refusal is not justified by the interest of the family."[26]

Personal Autonomy

Prior to 1981, when a woman married no law existed which required her to adopt her husband's surname. But laws in other areas made it a legal necessity for her to do so. One example was a passport law which required that she apply for a new passport using her husband's surname.[27] Although the woman was permitted to include her maiden name, her marital status and husband's surname were mandatory.[28] A married woman was not qualified to sign her child's passport, only the father.[29]

The Quebec Civil Code, article 442, strives for female equality in this area.[30] This article states: "In marriage, each spouse retains his surname and given names, and exercises his civil rights under this surname and these given names."

The enactment of this legislation presented the problem of what surname the children would use. Article 56.1 of the Civil Code of Lower Canada provides the answer. "A child is assigned, at the option of his father and mother, one or more given names, and the surname of one parent or a surname consisting of not more than two parts, taken from the surname of his father and mother."[32]

In 1980 Canadian feminists organized a constitutional lobby *inter alia* to fight the country's abortion laws.[32] Their efforts, but largely those of Dr. Henry Morgentaler, a Toronto physician, achieved a major victory in January 1988 when the Canadian Supreme Court struck down Canada's restrictive abortion law, ruling 5-2 that it was unconstitutional and a violation of a woman's right to control her body. Thus ended the 18-year battle in the courts to secure abortion on demand for Canadian women. The Canadian Supreme Court ruled the abortion laws were in violation of Section 7 of the 1982 Charter of Rights and Freedoms which said that everyone had the right to security of his person.[33] The ruling mirrored the United States Supreme Court decision of *Roe* v. *Wade* in 1973, which struck down United States abortion laws. Previously *Borowski v. A.-G. Can.,*[34] the court had held that the rights in section 7 were provided to "everyone" but everyone does not include a fetus.[35]

Section 251 of the Criminal Code decriminalized abortion in 1969 for situations where the mother's life or health is endangered.[36] This determination was not made by the mother and her doctor. The law required that a committee of three physicians be appointed by the hospital board and the committee's approval was necessary before an abortion could be performed.[37] The result was divergent interpretations of the terms "seriously endangered" and "health." Some committees defined health to include social and mental health, while others refused to apply such an expansive scope.[38]

This situation resulted in limited availability of abortion throughout

Canada. Newfoundland presented an example of a province where a woman had problems in finding a doctor willing to perform the operation.[39] Prince Edward Island disbanded its one hospital committee in June of 1986, after four years of continuous denials of approval for abortions.[40] Women in this province were left without any possibility, under any circumstances, of receiving an abortion in their local hospitals. Quebec represented the opposite situation because the law had not been enforced in this province since 1976.[41]

Family

The Constitutional Act of 1867 allocates to the federal parliament in §92(26) the power to make laws in relation to "marriage and divorce."[42] Section 91(12) gives jurisdiction over "the solemnization of marriage in the province" and "property and civil rights in the province" to the provincial legislatures.[43] The boundary between the two powers may be difficult to determine, but in practice the provinces have provided the major bulk of law.[44]

Areas in which the federal power has been upheld include the capacity of the parties to enter marriage and criminal charges arising out of family disputes.[45] Federal laws prescribe the prohibited degree of consanguinity and affinity and also the capacity of divorced people to remarry. But at the same time it has been determined that a requirement of parental consent for the marriage of a minor is properly within the provincial jurisdiction.[46]

The federal Criminal Code includes legislation concerning failure to provide the necessaries of life (§197), assault (§245), and abduction (§250).[47] Marital rape was made illegal under a December 1982 law.[48] A husband may also be charged with assault by his wife but under provincial legislation an application for an injunction must be accompanied by a petition for divorce or separation, or a short-term court order of protection.[49] These laws offer little protection to women when police refuse to arrest husbands, or demands for proof are difficult to meet, or legal problems result in delays.[50]

The age requirement for marriage is provided in provincial legislation. The minimum age varies between provinces but parental consent is required for prospective spouses under the age of 18.[51]

Quebec's Civil Code lists the "Rights and Duties of Spouses."[52] The objective of the Civil Code is to promote equality between spouses. The rights and duties are as follows:

Article 441. The spouses have identical rights and obligations in marriage. They owe each other respect, fidelity, succor and assistance. They must live together.

Article 442. In marriage, each spouse retains his or her surname and given names, and exercises his or her civil rights under this surname and these given names.

Article 443. The spouses together take in hand the moral and material direction of the family, exercise parental authority and assume the tasks resulting therefrom.

Article 444. The spouses choose the family residence together.

Article 445. The spouses contribute towards the expenses of the marriage in proportion to their respective means. Each spouse make his or her contribution by his or her activity within the home.

Article 446. A spouse who enters into a contract for the current needs of the family also commits his or her spouse for the whole, if they are not separated as to bed and board. However, the non-contracting spouse is not responsible for the debt if he or she had previously informed the other contracting party of his or her unwillingness to be committed.

Article 447. Either spouse may give the other a mandate to represent him or her in acts relating to the moral and material direction of the family. This mandate is presumed if one spouse is unable to manifest his or her intention for any reason or is unable to do so within the proper time.

Article 448. If the spouses disagree as to the exercise of their rights and the performance of their duties, they or either of them may apply to the court, which will decide in the interest of the family after fostering the conciliation of the parties.

Under §12(1) (b) of the Indian Act, native women face a form of discrimination not encountered by other Canadian women. Indian status, in accordance with the Act, descends through the male line. The result is that a white woman who marries an Indian man will have Indian status, as will their children.[53] There is a negative result for Indian women who marry non–Indian men. These women lose their status (as do their children) and thus lose their rights to live on reservations and other privileges under the Act.[54] A relieving clause was provided in the Act for widows and women who remarry Indians.[55]

Prior to the enactment of the Charter of Rights and Freedoms, §12(1) (b) was challenged as being inoperative under the "equality before the law" clause of the Canadian Bill of Rights which has never had constitutional status. The court in *A.-G. Can.* v. *Lavell*[56] held that "equality before the law" means "equality in the administration or application of the law by the law enforcement authorities and the ordinary Courts of the land."[57] This means that the law itself may discriminate but no discrimination in its application is permitted and §12(1) (b) of the Indian Act was upheld. Similar provisions in the Act state that upon an Indian man's death his estate passes to his children and not to his wife. Also included is a provision which automatically enfranchises an Indian wife when her husband opts for enfranchisement.[58]

In 1984, Bill C-47 was introduced, which would have amended status under the Indian Act so that it would be determined based upon one-fourth descent from Indians who have status. It also provided a measure which would restore status to those women who had previously lost it through marriage.[59] The effect of the bill would have been to remove the gender-based discrimination, but as of the end of 1984 the bill had not been incorporated into the Indian Act.

Another piece of legislation which may have an effect on the status provision is a Constitution amendment made in 1984 to the Charter of Rights and Freedoms. Section 35(4) was added, which states: "Notwithstanding any other provision of this Act, the aboriginal and treaty rights referred to in subsection (1) are guaranteed equally to male and female persons." Subsection (1) recognizes and affirms the aboriginal and treaty rights of the native peoples.

Divorce is also covered by both federal and provincial legislation. In 1968 the first comprehensive Canada-wide legislation on divorce was passed. This is the Divorce Act, S. C. 1967–68, c.24; now R.S.C. 1970, c.D-8, ss. 10–12.[60] This law provides universal grounds for divorce (excluding Quebec). Grounds include sodomy, rape, adultery, bestiality, homosexual acts, bigamy, mental or physical cruelty, or "marriage breakdown" (separation due to imprisonment, drug addiction, desertion, or no conjugal relations for one year).[61] Federal law does not provide for divorce by mutual consent.[62]

The Divorce Act also confers upon the superior court in each province the jurisdiction to grant divorces.[63] Conflict in divorce orders dealing with custody, maintenance and alimony has arisen because of the power of courts to make orders under either the federal or the provincial legislation covering these areas. Under the federal law both spouses are entitled to apply for custody of the children, and the standards which are used to measure the fitness of the parent are the same for both fathers and mothers.[64] Both spouses are also entitled to apply for maintenance. The federal Divorce Act can help women achieve equal treatment in provinces which may still make distinctions based on stereotyped roles.[65]

Employment

The Charter of Human Rights and Freedoms includes certain provisions which help protect women's equality with respect to federal and provincial legislation. Section 15 reads: "(1) Every individual is equal before and under the law and has the right to the equal protection and equal benefit of the law without discrimination and, in particular, without discrimination based on race, national or ethnic origin, colour, religion, sex, age or mental or physical disability." This section has incorporated various formulations with the purpose of expanding the restrictive interpretation of the Bill of Rights clause, "equality before the law," that was given in *A.-G. Can.* v. *Lavell* (administrative not substantive equal protection).[66] Section 15 is intended to apply to the substance of the law as well as the administration and application of the law.

Another interpretation placed on the Bill of Rights clause which has proved detrimental to women is found in the case of *Bliss* v. *Attorney General of Canada.*[67] This case arose under the Unemployment Insurance Act, which requires an eight-week employment period to be eligible for benefits and a longer employment period for maternity benefits. Stella Bliss had not been working for the necessary time for maternity benefits when her employer dismissed her for maternity-related reasons. Bliss was denied the regular benefits.[68] The court held that the distinction in the law was not discrimination based upon sex but rather discrimination based on pregnancy.[69] This inequality "was not created by legislation but by nature."[70] The opinion in this case also suggested that when legislation was providing benefits it was not subject to the equality standards in the Bill of Rights.[71] Section 15 of the Charter includes the phrase "equal benefit of the law" which may, when interpreted, prevent future holdings from following the Bliss decision.[72]

Section 33 of the Charter derogates the power of §15. It reads:

> (1) Parliament or the legislature of a province may expressly declare in an Act of Parliament or of the legislature, as the case may be, that the Act or a provision thereof shall operate notwithstanding a provision included in section 2 or sections 7 to 15 of this Charter.
>
> (2) An Act or a provision of an Act in respect of which a declaration made under this section is in effect shall have such operation as it would have but for the provision of this Charter referred to in the declaration.
>
> (3) A declaration made under subsection (1) shall cease to have effect five years after it comes into force or on such earlier date as may be specified in the declaration.
>
> (4) Parliament or the legislature of a province may re-enact a declaration made under subsection (1).
>
> (5) Subsection (3) applies in respect of a re-enactment made under subsection (4). Under this override power a legislature can enact discriminatory legislation just by declaring within the law that §15 does not apply.

Section 28 grants equal protection of rights granted under the Charter to male and female persons. All this section seems to require is that the provisions of the Charter be implemented without discrimination but it does not apply to any other legislation.[73]

Affirmative action in the field of sex discrimination is protected under §15(2) (subject to the §33 override) which states: "Subsection (1) does not preclude any law, program or activity that has as its object the amelioration of conditions of disadvantaged individuals or groups including those that are disadvantaged because of race, national or ethnic origin, colour, religion, sex, age or mental or physical disability."

All of the provinces and the federal government have enacted human rights codes and organized commissions to administer these codes. The commissions investigate and arbitrate complaints of violations of code prohibitions against discriminatory practices in hiring and employment.[74]

The provinces have all promulgated at least equal minimum-wage legislation.[75] This, of course, will have little effect on wage discrimination in general, as Table 38 illustrates.

Current legislation in the field of equal pay for equal work includes a Quebec law which allows a woman who believes she is being underpaid because of her sex to bring her case before a provincial human rights tribunal.[76] This right is given to employees in both the public and private sectors. Ottawa has enacted a similar law but it is limited to federal employees.[77] Manitoba has taken a slightly different approach with its Pay Equity Act. The Act allows use of numerical job evaluation formulae to determine if there is gender discrimination in many public jobs.[78] Ontario was formulating a system similar to Manitoba's which would be applied to both the public and private sectors, but as of October 1986, no law had been enacted.[79]

Maternity leave is absent from federal legislation and has been left as a provincial decision. Quebec, Saskatchewan and Alberta allow 18 weeks, but as of 1984 Prince Edward Island and the Territories provide no period for maternity leave. The remainder of the provinces set leave at 17 weeks.[80] Unemploy-

Level of education	Men	Women	Female earnings as percentage of male earnings
All levels	18,537	11,743	63.3
0–8 years	15,704	8,904	56.7
Some high school	17,214	10,797	62.7
Some post-secondary	19,016	11,851	62.3
Post-secondary certificate or diploma	19,602	12,943	66.0
University degree	26,533	17,842	67.2

Table 38. Full-Time Annual Earnings of Male and Female Workers in Canada by Level of Education, 1980, Canadian Dollars. Source: International Labor Organization, *The Economic Role of Women in the ECE Region,* Geneva, 1985, p. 85.

ment insurance is provided for women in unionized jobs with no loss of job security or time accrued for seniority but only 25 percent of the female workforce is employed in unionized jobs.[81] The usual benefits are 60 percent of their normal wage to a maximum of $276 per week for 15 weeks.[82]

Child care has also been left to the provincial governments, which have had various results. Although the Royal Commission on the Status of Women has recommended that an extensive, publicly financed day care system be established, nothing has materialized.[83] There is a shortage of facilities and many of the existing ones have problems, such as being unlicensed or violating existing regulations governing their operation, and some have proved more harmful than beneficial to their wards. This situation has made it more difficult for women to compete on equal terms with men in the job market.

Conclusion

Progress has been made in Canada, but not nearly as much as expected at the beginning of the United Nations Decade for Women in 1975. Even in the legal world itself, few Canadians know what the true state of affairs is. "The role of women in the law remains surprisingly understudied," Sylvia Bashevkin of the University of Toronto said during the 1984 symposium on women in the law.[84] Even after Canadian universities began to admit women to the law schools, Ms. Bashevkin observed, many continued to refuse them post-graduate training.[85] The right of women to practice law across Canada was already established by World War II, but the actual number of women in the law remained low until deep into the '60s. A 1970 Royal Commission found that during the '60s the percentage of women in law in Canada was only 3 percent, against 26 percent in France. The low figure was not confined to women in law. Women physicians formed only 7 percent, dental surgeons 4 percent, and engineers less than 1 percent.[86] In a study by Professor Marie Huxter of the University of Toronto, more than 44 percent of women law graduates cited gender as a key obstacle to their articling or to permanent employment in a legal capacity.[87]

16. Case Study: The United States

The constitutional rights of women, discrimination against women, occupational segregation, disparities in income of men and women, and legal remedies to provide women with equal opportunities to compete against men have received more attention in the U.S., in elected bodies, on the state and national level, in academic circles, in labor unions, and in the media, than in any other country in the world. Yet at this writing the disappointments remain numerous. The slow pace of change in the workplace in respect to wages, occupational segregation, and equal opportunities counterbalances the rapid progress made in the legal field.

It is true that there have been some important victories, important progress, for women in the legal, educational, business, and economic field, but by and large these victories have been patchy and regional. Four fundamental reasons for women's continued disadvantage and subordination have remained largely undisturbed: continued segregation of jobs in the marketplace; the substantial gap in income between men and women doing the same or similar work; women's dual burden of being mothers and workers; and, lastly, but perhaps most importantly, sexist perceptions, the careless attitude of American males concerning the legitimate aspirations, complaints and requirements of women, particularly working women with children.

The Changing Profile of American Women

The profile of women in the United States, notably married women and women in employment, continues to change. In 1986, for the first time, women outnumbered men in the United States (by some six million), and women born on July 1, 1986, had a life expectancy of 78.3 years, compared to 71.3 for men.[1] Some observers are saying that women may lose this lead since more and more are smoking, predicting that their life expectancy in the next few decades will be about the same as men's.[2] However, the United States Bureau of the Census estimates that by 2050 women will outnumber men in the United States by 12.5 million and projects that, in the same year, 28 percent of older women will be 85 years or older, as against 17 percent for men.[3]

Women are pouring into the workplace. In one 12-month period during 1983 and 1984, some 1.8 million more women went to work. By the end of 1987, nearly 68 percent of all women 16 years and older were working. All in all, women comprise 45 percent of the total United States labor force, up from only 29 percent in 1950. Between 1980 and 1985, the number of women working two or more jobs rose by almost 40 percent to 2.2 million and comprised nearly 40

(Percent)

Year	Women 20–64			All women	
	All	*White*	*Black and other*	*20–24*	*25–34*
1890	17.4	14.9	38.4	30.2	16.8
1900	19.3	16.5	41.0	31.7	19.4
1920	22.9	20.7	43.1	37.5	23.7
1930	25.4	23.3	44.1	41.8	27.1
1940	29.4	27.9	42.9	45.6	33.3
1950	33.3	32.2	43.2	43.6	32.0
1960	42.3	40.9	54.0	46.1	36.0
1970	50.0	49.1	57.2	57.7	45.0
1980	60.8	60.5	62.8	68.9	65.5
1986	66.4	66.3	66.4	72.4	71.6

Year	Working part time	Working as temporary help
1987	13,124,000	NA
1986	12,862,000	502,700
1985	12,587,000	440,900
1984	12,441,000	396,300
1983	12,367,000	302,400
1982	12,170,000	255,700
1981	11,664,000	NA
1980	11,271,000	NA
1979	10,990,000	NA
1978	10,658,000	NA
1977	10,213,000	NA
1976	9,799,000	NA

***Top:* Table 39. Labor Force Participation Rates for American Women, by Age, 1890–1986. Source: *Economic Report of the President,* United States Government Printing Office, Washington DC, 1987, p. 210. *Bottom:* Table 40. Part-Time Workers 1976–1987. Source: United States Bureau of Labor Statistics. (NA: Not available.)**

percent of all so-called "moonlighters." In addition, women make up the majority of America's "new work force," part-time employees.[4]

Part-time, temporary and contract jobs now account for more than 25 percent of all jobs, according to the United States Bureau of Labor Statistics. Use of such employees is projected by the Bureau to increase by 10 to 15 percent in the next two years. Women who work part time to help run their husband's businesses have also been given the added advantage, as the result of judgments in court, that they are considered partners-in-fact and thus can claim social security benefits.[5]

In 1970 women held one-third of the professional jobs in the United States. By 1986 they formed the majority, just over 50 percent. This increase was not reflected in salaries, and during the period 1983–1984 professional

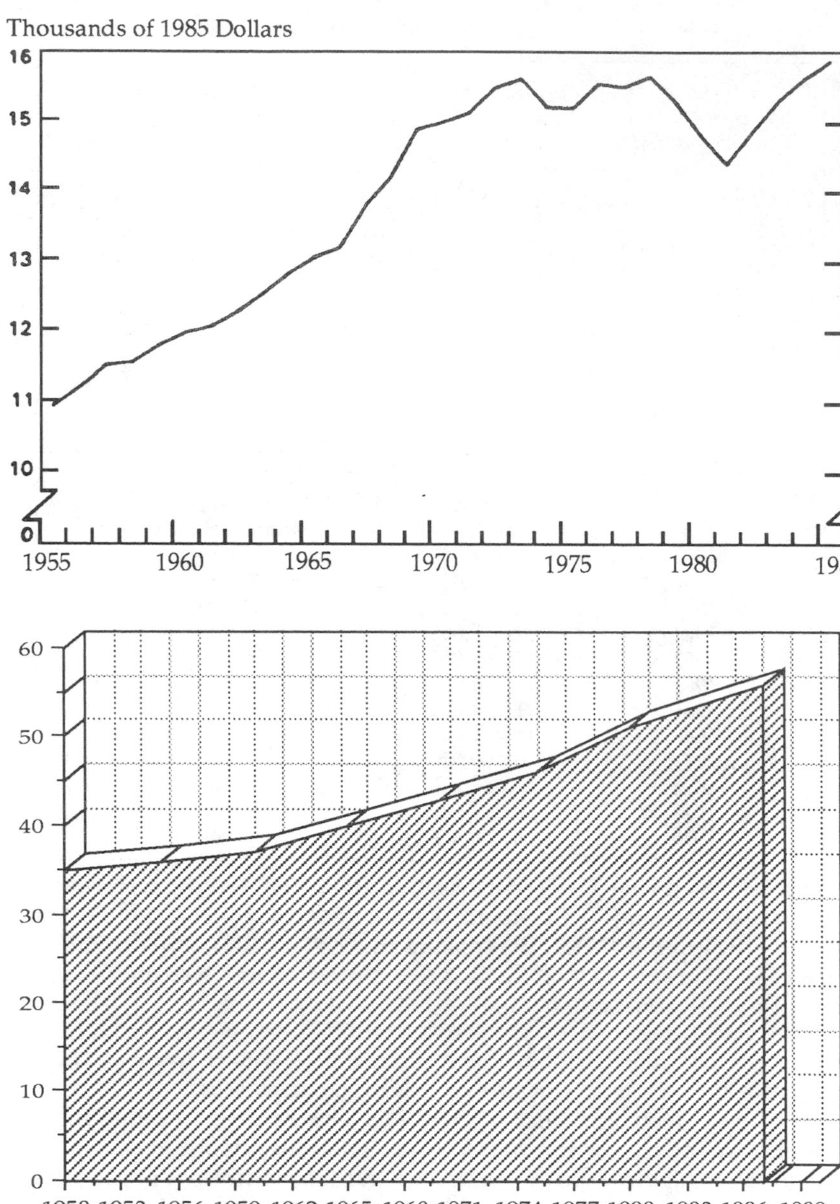

***Top:* Chart 5. United States Women's Real Annual Earnings 1955–1985. Source: *Economic Report of the President to Congress,* United States Government Printing Office, Washington DC, 1987, p. 214. *Bottom:* Chart 6. Percentage of Women in the United States Labor Force with Young Children: 1950–1987. Source: United States Department of Labor.**

women, on the average, had median earnings of only $19,200, compared to $29,550 for men. Elsewhere in this chapter it will be shown that the disparity in some areas is increasing and not decreasing. All women's real earnings have been rising steadily since 1955.

Married-couple families fell from 70.5 percent of all families in 1970 to 53.8 in 1985. Single-family households increased from 30 percent in 1970 to 46.2 in 1985. Single women, with or without children, increased from 21.6 percent in 1969 to almost 30 percent in 1985.[6] The pace has picked up rapidly. Between 1980 and 1984 nearly half of the 2.4 million new households were run by women. There is also a shift in the age of childbearing. Some 22 percent of births in 1984 were to women 30 years of older, compared with 18 percent in 1970.[7]

Working mothers with young children are hitting record numbers. In 1987 some 62 percent of all mothers with children under the age of 18 were at work. Almost ten million had children under the age of six.[8]

The increase in the number of women with children of school-going age has created enormous pressure, social and political, for more child care aid, flexible work hours and other corporate and legislative changes. There are now 10.5 million children under the age of six being cared for by people other than their parents. By 1995 two-thirds of all pre-school children and 80 percent of all school children will have both parents in the work force.[9] A whole new debate has arisen around the subject of working women with children, spurring the proposed Family and Medical Leave Act (1989) *inter alia* to help parents with newborn children to hold their jobs. In June 1988 the Census Bureau declared that, for the first time, more than 50 percent of new mothers remained in the job market. Some states, such as Tennessee, now have laws which provide that companies with a work force of more than 100 must give mothers of newborn children as many as four months' leave (unpaid).[10] An adjunct, but equally important, debate is the question of child care. Should the government help working parents pay for safe, high-quality day care? In 1981 Nyloncraft became the first United States corporation to provide a round the-clock learning center for the children of workers. In 1987, in a Labor Department survey of more than 10,000 United States companies, more than 60 percent reported that they had specific policies and benefits to make child care easier, ranging from flexitime, paternity leave, and work-at-home to help with child care expenses and employer-sponsored day care. Though day care is provided by only 2.1 percent, this translates into more than 1,000 corporations, a significant increase since Nyloncraft introduced the concept in 1981.[11]

More and more women find themselves on the move. According to travel records, women now account for 34 percent of all business travelers compared with only 18 percent in 1979. Female business travelers are increasing at a rate three times that of men and it is estimated that by the turn of the century women will comprise 50 percent of all business travelers.[12]

Women and children have become the two most sought-after marketing segments. The reason is growing buyer power. Women are the buyers, or they influence the purchase decision, in over 80 percent of all cars sold—worth some 50 billion dollars.[13]

The tide of women leaving home for the workplace is the single most important change that has happened in the American labor market in the late twentieth century. In less than a generation, the size of the female labor force has doubled, and by 1987 included the majority of working age women. At the beginning of the twentieth century less than 20 percent of all women worked outside the home.[14]

In the late 1960s unemployment for women was 34 percent higher than for men, but by the beginning of 1987 the jobless rate of men was 6.3 percent and that of women 6.1 percent.[15] In the next decade two out of every three newcomers to the labor force will be women. The sheer pressure of these numbers will bring further and profound change which may not even require Supreme Court blessing. In 1987 the annual report of the President's Council of Economic Advisers devoted its concluding chapter to the phenomenon of women's pressure in the labor force. Professor Barbara Bergmann of the University of Maryland calls this "the greatest economic revolution of our time."[16] Female employment has been aided by the switch from industries producing goods, where men are most heavily employed, to services where women get most of the jobs.

Women's best achievement in the United States, apart from the total numbers coming into the labor force, has been their progress in the professional field. According to the annual report of the President's Council of Economic Advisers, women earned 30 percent of all medical degrees in 1985, compared to only 13 percent 10 years ago. In dentistry women are up from 3 percent to 21 percent and, in the legal field, up from 15 percent in 1975 to 38 percent in 1985. By 1985 some 28 percent of all women entering universities elected business as their major subject, as against only 10 percent who picked education. The number of women earning doctorates as a qualification for a professional career has also increased significantly, except in science and engineering.

In the economic field another improvement for women has been the number of companies now owned by women. Based on 1982 federal tax returns the United States Bureau of Census estimated in 1986 that 24 percent of partnerships, sole proprietorships and other corporations were owned by women, an increase of more than 50 percent since 1977. Most of them are still small businesses. In 1977 there were only 437 businesses owned by women who had more than 100 employees. In 1982 the figure had risen to 668.[17] In 1986 women were starting new enterprises at more than three times the rate of men and seemed to be creating a business world with a style and *modus operandi* all their own. A major financial and management periodical, *INC.*, published monthly, reported that women are the fastest growing segment of its audience.[18] In an article in *SKY,* Elaine Rogers cites a Dun & Bradstreet Corporation report of 1988 that of all new business incorporations and unincorporated ventures of 1987 (totaling 950,000) some 25 percent are owned by women. She also cites Internal Revenue Service figures that between 1980 and 1984 the number of female-owned sole proprietorships increased by 33 percent. In 1987 there were 3.7 million altogether, up from 3.4 million in 1984, and their total sales receipts rose from $56 billion to $65 billion. According to Rogers, the Office of

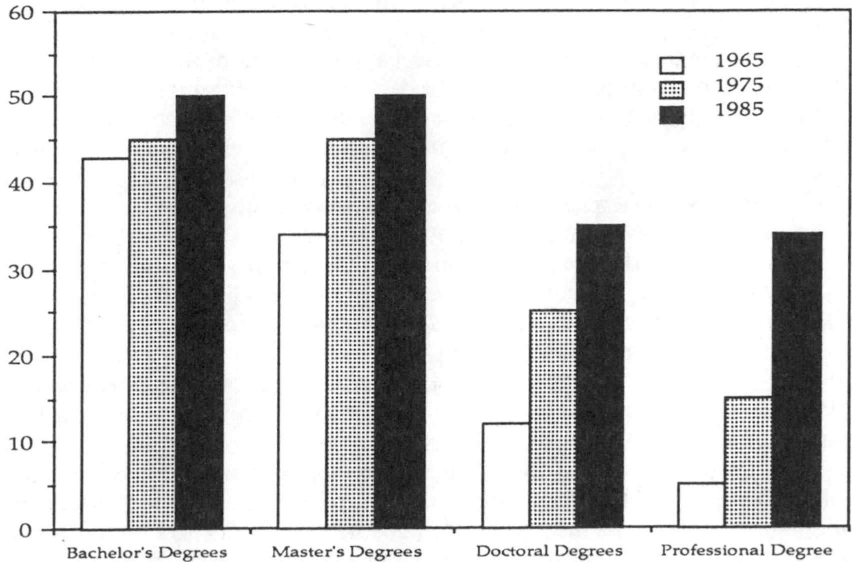

Chart 7. Women's Percentage of Earned Degrees, 1965–1985. Source: *Economic Report of the President to Congress,* United States Government Printing Office, Washington DC, 1987, p. 216.

Women's Business Ownership of the United States Small Business Administration believes that in another 10 years one-half of all sole proprietorships in the United States will be owned by women.[19]

By 1988 total revenue from women-owned enterprises was estimated at $100 billion. These enterprises have an increasingly significant impact on the United States economy. They pay about $50 billion in federal and state tax and local levies. In a report of the House Small Business Committee concerning women in business, the increase in women's enterprises was described as "the most significant economic development of recent years." However, the 1988 report also found that women business owners still face considerable difficulties—for example, in gaining commercial credit and bidding on government contracts. "Women have had to work harder, wait longer, manage with fewer dollars and be content with smaller operations just to maintain their present levels of independence and business success."[20]

The 3,000-member National Association of Women Business Owners who took its case to the House Small Business Committee, insisting on equal treatment when it came to commercial credit and business loans, succeeded when the committee introduced the Women's Business Ownership Act (H.R. 5050) of 1988 to eliminate practices whereby banks (often) expect women to put up collateral *five times* the amount of the business loan applied for, whereas in the case of men an amount equal to the loan is standard. The bill also took sharp aim at United States federal agencies since currently 99 percent of all government contracts valued over $10,000 go to businesses owned or headed by men.[21]

According to economist Barbara Bergmann, the major trends of this century (more women in the labor force, a decline in the birth rate [See Chart 8] and greater instability in marriages) were spurred by a vast improvement in wages. As women had fewer children, more and more decided that it was worth the income to work.

In Bergmann's view, the real increase in the wages of women was the main cause of women leaving home for the marketplace.[22]

The reason for the decline in the birth rate were given by Bergmann as improved methods of birth control, the cost of raising children in terms of lost opportunity for the mother and the fact that having children was getting progressively less economically rewarding. Bergmann's data show that the fewer young children a mother has the more likely she is to participate in paid work. Among married couples, in 69 percent of those with only one child under 18 both parents worked.[23]

The drop of the fertility rate has had many consequences, said Bergmann. It has affected the ratio of working people to retired people, the expenditure of the family, per capita income of families, the demand for schools and more jobs for wives. The number of childless women has increased, and women are having their first children at a much higher age. This has meant that more women can enjoy a fairly continuous career.

According to Bergmann, divorce affects women's labor force participation in several ways. Divorced women seldom receive sufficient alimony and since the vast majority have children, divorced mothers will choose to work at a paying job. Divorced women have high labor force participation. About 80 percent of divorced women with children are working. Unmarried divorcees now constitute 10 percent of all ever-married women.[24]

The second trend which accompanied the growth in women's employment—instability in American marriages—is almost a duplicate of any table indicating female labor force participation for 1900 to 1980, but by 1983 various factors began to play a role in slowing down the breakup of marriages. Among these were the drop in unemployment, the scare brought about by the herpes virus as the result of extra-marital affairs, greater stability in the home brought about by higher income per family, disillusionment with the sexual freedom and no-fault divorce program pushed through by the women's movement, as well as a return to old-fashioned family values promoted by various religious movements and the Reagan administration. The equally massive publicity given to the infectious disease AIDS during the period from 1986 onwards further slowed and slightly reversed the trend. Based on averages from the years 1980–1986 and provided there is no economic recession, marital instability will continue to level off somewhat during the next decade. Using a different yardstick (divorces per thousand Americans) statisticians in the United States Bureau of the Census, Marriage and Family Branch, stated that the rate of 5.3 per thousand in 1981 had declined to 5.0 in 1985. According to the same source, the actual number of divorces decreased from 1.2 million in 1981 to 1.18 million in 1985.

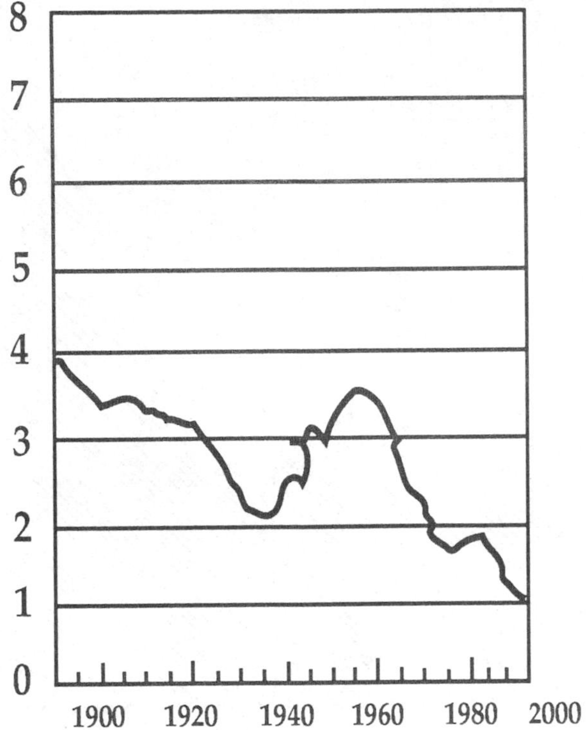

Chart 8. Total Estimated Fertility Rate of White Women in the United States, 1900–2000. Sources: A. Thornton and D. Freedman, "The Changing American Family," ***Population Bulletin,*** **Vol. 38, No. 4, Washington DC, 1983, p. 17; United States Bureau of the Census, "Fertility of American Women,"** ***Current Population Reports,*** **June 1987, No. 427; and** ***Statistical Abstracts of the United States,*** **1988, Table 82.**

All of the evidence demonstrates that in the economic arena divorced women, and their children, have fared badly while divorced men have done considerably better. In her landmark study of the revolution brought on by the so-called no-fault divorce laws, passed ostensibly to eliminate the acrimony and stigma of divorce and to treat men and women equally in divorce settlements, Stanford sociologist Lenore Weitzman concluded.

> Divorce today spells financial disaster for too many women and for the minor children in their custody. The data reveal a dramatic contrast in financial status of divorced men and divorced women at every income level and every level of marital duration. Women of all ages and at all socioeconomic levels experience a precipitous decline in standard of living within one year after divorce, while their former husbands' standard of living improves. Older women and women divorced from men in the higher-income brackets experience the most radical downward mobility.[25]

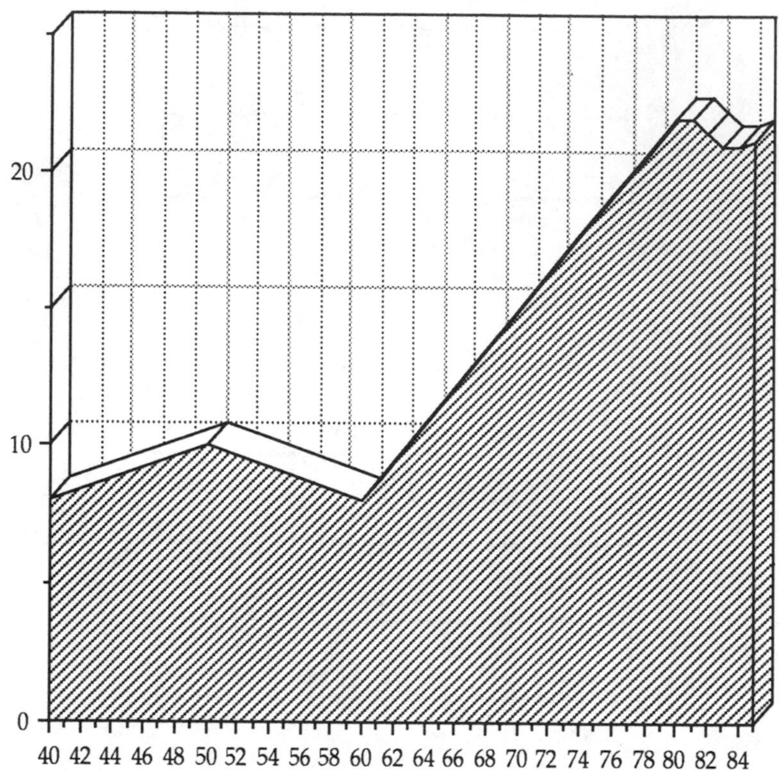

Chart 9. Divorce Rate for Every 1,000 Women over Age 15. Source: United States Bureau of the Census, *Statistical Abstracts of the United States,* 1988, Table 81; and United States Department of Health, *Monthly Vital Statistical Report,* Vol. 37, No. 4, July 1988.

Weitzman revealed that just one year after divorce, the standard of living of the ex-husband had risen 42 percent while that of the ex-wife had fallen 72 percent.

Sylvia Hewlett referred to a finding by the New Jersey Supreme Court that "divorce portends long term, deepening poverty for a large proportion of women and their custodial children." According to Hewlett the impact of divorce in the United States is particularly severe because of the absence of policies designed to lighten the load of single parents. In 1983, Hewlett states, children from households headed by single women constituted almost 25 percent of children in the United States. As in the case of Weitzman, her findings also reveal that divorce can depress a single mother's income by as much as 70 percent. In addition, of the five million women who are legally due child support, only a third receive the full amount. Hewlett cites the 1982 census findings that 41 percent of custodial mothers are not awarded any child support to begin with. Men who must pay alimony are often delinquent in their child support payments but, she pointed out, a study in Denver shows that the same men are current with their car payments. In summary Hewlett said fewer than 14 percent of women nationwide are awarded alimony and fewer than 10 percent of those who are awarded alimony ever collected any payments.[26]

Weitzman, Hewlett, and other researchers such as Mary Ann Mason all agree that a major portion of the blame must fall on the push for equality-or-nothing by the National Organization for Women. "No-fault laws," wrote Mason, "reflect the new egalitarian attitude toward divorce which has effectively replaced moral responsibility. Neither party is at fault; therefore no one is responsible for the end of a marriage. Laws that protect women and children following divorce have been replaced by laws that dictate that women can take care of themselves as well as men can, even when they are also taking care of the children."[27]

Education has had a major and positive effect on women's income and employment opportunities as well as career options. This has been particularly true of those who earned professional degrees. Women with university degrees working full time had a 40 percent higher income on the average than women who only finished high school. Because of the greater opportunities which they enjoy, women who are college graduates are currently 24 percent more likely to be employed than those who only finished high school.[28]

In the Presidential report on economic affairs to Congress in 1987 it is stated:

> Young women are changing their training and initial job plans as they anticipate greater commitment to the labor force. This is evident in the increased proportion going to college.... Women now receive about half of the bachelor's and master's and more than one-third of the doctoral degrees. The sharpest growth in the past decade has been in professional degrees. In 1985, women received 30 percent of the degrees in medicine (up from 13 percent in 1975), 21 percent in dentistry (up from 3 percent in 1975), and 38 percent in law (up from 15 percent in 1975).... Women's college-major choices are converging toward those of men. In 1960, 46 percent of degrees awarded to women were in education. Since then, the increased commitment of women to the labor force has led them to choose a greater variety of college majors. In the fall of 1985, only 10 percent of women beginning college intended to major in education, while 28 percent opted for business, making it the most popular major for women as well as for men.[29]

An ever increasing number of women were earning Ph.D. degrees in the field of science. (See Chart 10.)

Apart from very important laws which have been passed during the past decade and Supreme Court rulings eliminating discrimination against women, or providing for equal opportunities, the foregoing survey of the changing profile of American women in general and of women at work contains almost all the good news. In the sections on occupational and wage discrimination (which follow) a different story unfolds.

The Profile of Women in the Labor Force

Women now constitute 44 percent of the total labor force. By the end of 1986 the majority of adult women were married and worked outside the home.

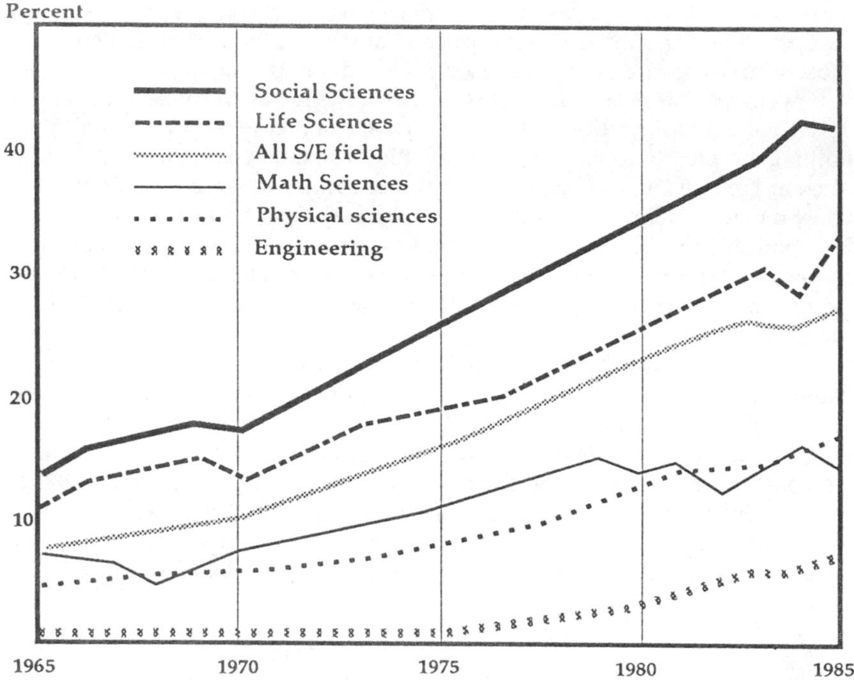

Chart 10. Ph.D's Earned by Women. Source: National Science Foundation, "Education and the Professional Workforce," *Mosaic,* special issue, 1987, Vol. 18, No. 1, p. 3, citing data from the National Center for Educational Statistics and Cooperative Institutional Research Program of University College, Los Angeles.

The actual number of working women rose from only 16 million just after World War II to 49 million the beginning of 1987.[30]

In recent years, a pattern of increased employment of married women with young children has emerged in most industrialized countries. As can be seen in Chart 11, the number of working women with small children, particularly very small children (aged two years and less), has increased considerably during the past decade up to 1988.

Women who maintain families alone have had high rates of market participation throughout the postwar period, and although participation rates for these mothers have grown, the major increase in female employment in recent decades has come from married women. The sharpest increases have been for wives with very young children. About 54 percent of wives with children under the age of six participate in the labor force. The rate for wives with infants is almost 50 percent, more than double the percentage in 1970.[31]

It is somewhat of a fallacy that there is something new, exciting or attractive about women taking on a career in the marketplace. The television and

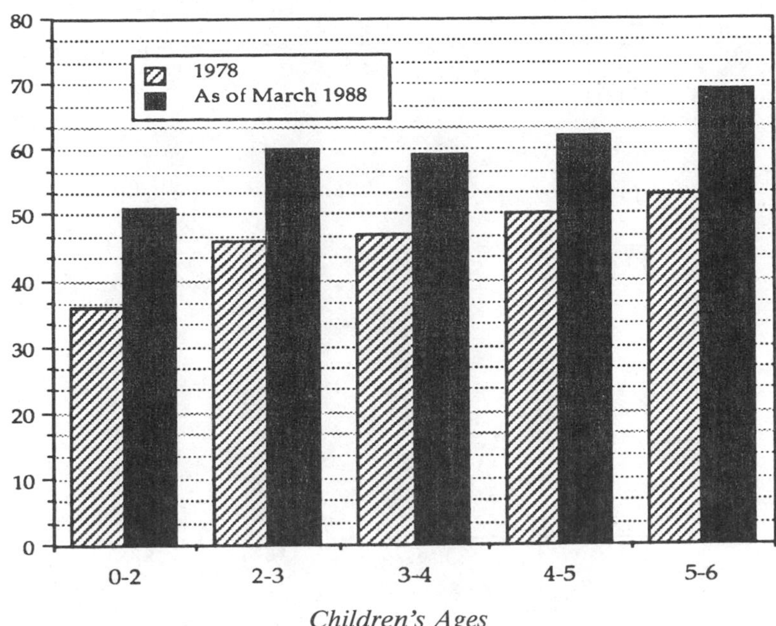

Chart 11. Women in the Labor Force, Age 16 and Older (in Percentages). Source: United States Department of Labor. Note: Labor force includes full- and part-time workers.

glamour magazine image of women storming the bastions of male-dominated executive and management levels, earning high salaries and jet-setting all over the United States, is mostly a myth, a caricature. As Sylvia Hewlett, one of America's foremost experts on the status of modern American women, wrote in 1986: "The plain truth is that modern American women, liberated or not, have little economic security as wives and mothers, or as workers. They are squeezed between the traditional and modern forms of financial security to an extent which is unknown in other societies."[32]

According to Hewlett, only 7 percent of employed women in America work in managerial positions, the vast majority earning 40 percent less than men. Three-quarters of working women spend their time typing letters, filing documents, waiting on tables, cutting hair, teaching the young and emptying bedpans in hospitals. The harsh reality, she wrote, is that 70 percent of women in employment are there because of sheer economic necessity. They are single, widowed, divorced, or married to men who are either unemployed or earn less than $15,000 a year. One out of every four women earns less than $10,000 a year.[33]

In his 1987 economic report to Congress, the American President stated that "the 1980s have brought increases in both women's real earnings and women's earnings relative to men's, changes that further encouraged work in

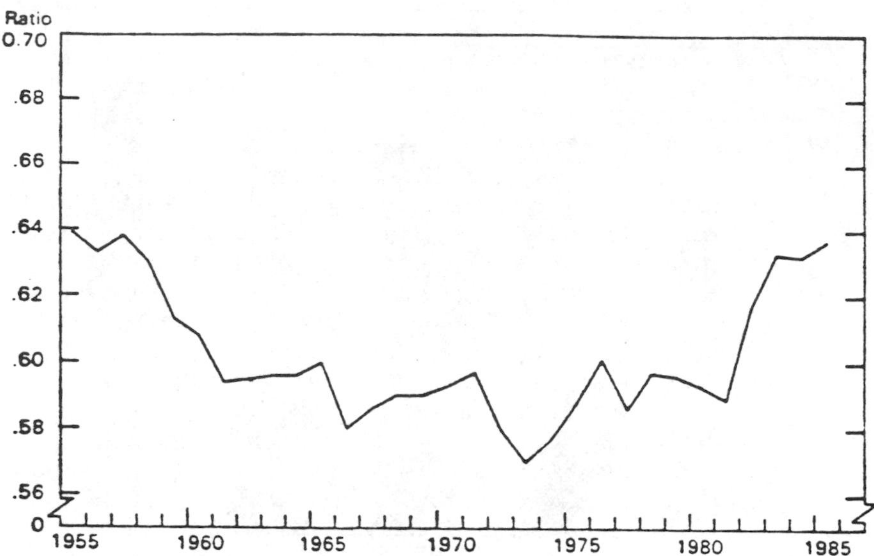

Chart 12. Ratio of Female to Male Earnings for Full-Time Workers 1955–1985. Source: *Economic Report of the President,* United States Government Printing Office, Washington DC, 1987, p. 221. Note: Median wage or salary income of year-round, full-time civilian workers excluding self-employed persons.

the marketplace."[34] [To put these gains in proper perspective, it should be noted that in the same report there is evidence that the wage or salary earnings of full-time workers in 1985 merely reached the point where the ratio stood in 1955, as Chart 12 clearly shows.]

The United States still has one of the largest wage gaps in the industrial world and is one of the few countries where the gap in earnings has not decreased significantly the past two decades, 1986–1987 expected. It is also one of only two countries among the 26 industrialized nations of the world (the other country is the Republic of South Africa) that has no nationwide statutory maternity leave, while in 117 other countries women are guaranteed leave from employment for childbirth, protection of their employment while they are on such leave and the provision of a cash benefit to replace all or most of their earnings during their absences.

In 1985 virtually 50 percent of women in the marketplace worked full time for the entire year and only some 12 percent worked part time for part of the year. Survey estimates indicate that wives employed full time average 25 hours of work in the home and 39 hours of work in the marketplace, each week, while husbands averaged 13 and 47 hours respectively at home and in the workplace.[35]

Occupational Segregation

Occupational segregation is all-prevailing in the United States and can be traced, and scored, either by looking at individual, high-profile professions, by statistical averages, by case studies or by judgments handed down in federal courts all over the United States.

In the United States, the press has often seized the high moral ground in the debate on quality in terms of race, religion, and sex. But in real life, this moral superiority appears to be mere posturing, cynical and misleading. More women than men are currently enrolled in the nation's schools of journalism, but a careful search through the *Editor and Publisher Yearbook* reveals that, of the hundreds of major newspapers with circulation in excess of 100,000, only seven women have reached the upper echelon. And with the resignation of Kay Fanning of *The Christian Science Monitor* at the end of 1988 the small band has decreased to only six in 1989.

In January 1988 the State Farm Insurance Company agreed in San Francisco to pay $100 million to $300 million in a pool to women for damages and back pay because they were refused jobs as insurance sales agents in California over a 13-year period. Among other things, women were told that a university degree was a requirement for appointment although men were hired without degrees.[36] The case was brought under the Civil Rights Act of 1964, which forbids discrimination on the basis of sex. Ironically, in August 1988 the House finally got around to setting up an office to enforce the law it had passed a quarter of a century before. At the end of 1988, almost 80 percent of all committee aides in Congress earning less than $20,000 were women, while 75 percent of those earning $40,000 and more were men.[37]

Spellman College in the state of Georgia was a school founded more than a century ago for the sole purpose of educating black women. In 1988, after 107 years, the trustees finally discovered a woman, Dr. Johnetta Cole, to serve as president. In fact, only 10 percent of presidents of all United States four-year colleges and universities are women.[38] Among the two-year colleges, however, women presidents increased to 109 in 1986, a rise of 56 percent compared to 1981.[39]

As indicated in Table 41, the spread of occupational discrimination is not affected by the size of the city or the region. In most major metropolitan areas only between one-fifth to one-quarter of women are employed in a managerial or professional occupation.

Gilda Berger found that about two-thirds of all women are concentrated in lower-paid white-collar jobs, also referred to as "the pink ghetto," resulting in women earning on the average only about 60 percent of what men earn in this section of the work force. Over half these women are concentrated in teaching, social work and health careers, she said. Women are 99 percent of all secretaries, 97 percent of all dressmakers and seamstresses, and 94 percent of bank tellers.[40]

Catalyst, a New York–based research group, says that only about eight of every 1,000 working women hold high-level executive, administrative or managerial jobs. Women occupy only about 3 percent of the 16,000 seats on

Metropolitan Area	Women Employed	Percentage Managerial/Professional
Atlanta	58.9	25.4
Charlotte	60.8	20.5
Dallas-Fort Worth	62.7	25.8
Dayton	54.4	22.5
Indianapolis	58.8	20.2
Kansas City	60.8	22.6
Louisville	52.4	23.6
Miami	52.9	24.8
Minneapolis-St Paul	64.5	25.4
Norfolk	55.4	21.1

Table 41. Percentage of Women Employed in Ten Major Metropolitan Areas and Percentage of These Women in Managerial and Professional Jobs, 1986. Source: United States Department of Labor Statistics, 1987.

the boards of the 1,000 largest United States corporations listed by *Fortune* magazine. On the other hand Shelley and Crates said men form 98 percent of airline pilots, 94 percent of dentists and engineers, 93 percent of optometrists, 89 percent of architects, 88 percent of surveyors and 86 percent of geophysicists or geologists—all high-paying professions.[41] The figures are born out by the percentages in Table 42.

The foregoing examples are to show not only that occupational segregation in the United States is widespread and severe in the economic field but that change has been painfully slow.

Bergmann considers sex segregation on the job as the root of women's disadvantage and their poor position in the marketplace. She cited studies by Bielby and Barron, who designed a test whereby establishments with totally segregated labor forces scored 100; of the 393 companies investigated by them, 232 had scores of 100 percent. Only 8.5 percent of the 60,950 workers involved worked for establishments that were less than 90 percent segregated. This occupational segregation in the United States marketplace is the oldest of traditions and perpetuates itself through the self-interest of the beneficiaries.[42]

In 1986 a historic milestone was reached when women, for the first time, held the majority of professional jobs in the country—yet only 17 percent were doctors and 18 percent lawyers, indicating that men's traditional dominance in some areas was still enormous and that the milestone was more quantitative than qualitative.[43] "Professional" jobs also included teachers, librarians, nurses and social workers, a huge category long dominated by women. The women continued to be clustered in the low-paid "pink ghetto" or "pink-collar" jobs. It was said that, on the bright side, women now form the majority of statisticians, psychologists, editors and news reporters. An analysis, however, showed that although women outnumber men as "reporters" and "editors," this included editors and reporters of company newsletters, convention reports and industry newsletters. When it comes to the mass media, such as the daily

Occupation	Women as Percent of Total Employed 1975	1986
Airline pilot	-	1.5
Architect	4.3	9.7
Auto mechanic	0.5	1.0
Bartender	35.2	48.8
Bus driver	37.7	50.4
Cab driver, chauffeur	8.7	12.5
Carpenter	0.6	1.4
Child care worker	98.4	97.4
Computer programmer	25.6	34.0
Computer systems analyst	14.8	34.4
Data entry keyer	92.8	91.1
Data-processing equipment repairer	1.8	11.1
Dentist	1.8	4.4
Dental assistant	100.0	99.0
Economist	13.1	39.3
Editor, reporter	44.6	50.5
Elementary school teacher	85.4	85.2
College/university teacher	31.1	36.0
Garage, gas station attendant	4.7	5.8
Lawyer, judge	7.1	18.1
Librarian	81.1	85.9
Mail carrier	8.7	20.6
Office machine repairer	1.7	1.6
Physician	13.0	17.6
Registered nurse	97.0	94.3
Social worker	60.8	65.0
Telephone installer, repairer	4.8	13.3
Telephone operator	93.3	87.9
Waiter/waitress	91.1	85.1
Welder	4.4	5.1

Table 42. Occupational Segregation in the United States. Source: Bureau of Labor Statistics, *Employment and Earnings,* January 1976, Table 2, and January 1987, Table 22.

newspapers, the picture changes dramatically. Women constitute fewer than 40 percent of the reporters on the daily press, less than 12 percent of the managers and less than 3 percent of the editors of the more than 1,700 daily newspapers.[44] Few would argue that the daily press has a much greater impact on public opinion than any other written publication. The implication for women should be clear.

In business and government women also accounted for a majority of the professional work force.[45] But this figure does not include any executive, managerial or administrative positions, where women held only 36 percent of the positions. The fact is also that the average woman in full-time professional employment earns only 72 percent of what a man earns, while in the general category full-time employed women earn only 59 percent of what men do.[46]

In higher education the situation is no better. Of 499 full professors at the University of Georgia in 1986, only 24 were female. Georgia State University had 238 men to 28 women, and Georgia Tech 170 male professors and only 14 women in the same position. At many of the universities the pay gap between men and women is as wide as 30 percent. Even at predominantly female schools, such as Agnes Scott College in Georgia, where most of the faculty is female, male assistant professors two steps up earned almost $36,000 a year to $32,500 for women.[47] Similar disparities existed at all other college faculty ranks according to a 1983 report by the United States Department of Education's National Center for Education Statistics. The report showed that only 38.3 percent of Georgia's female faculty members had tenure or were working with job security, compared to 61.7 percent of men. Full-time male faculty members outnumbered women by three to one despite passage of Title VII of the 1964 Civil Rights Act and Title IX of the Higher Education Act—both of which outlaw sex discrimination.

To further illustrate the occupational segregation in the United States between men and women, consider that only 5 percent of the top executives of the 50 largest American-owned companies are women. On the management level, the situation is as bad.

The most massive occupational disparity in the United States is found in women in public office. The immediate past is a good example. Before 1977 only three women had ever held cabinet rank. By 1977 only 10 women had ever sat in the Senate, and all were filling the unexpired term of another senator, most often a deceased husband.

The Carter administration was the first to include two women in the cabinet. In 1978 there were only two women state governors in the United States, and women comprised just 4 percent of the combined membership of both houses of Congress. Political scientist Judith Evans summarized the situation in the United States at the time as follows: "...there is a striking discrepancy between apparent equality of the sexes at the level of grass roots politics, and the various social, economic and educational gains made by women, and their virtual exclusion from the upper levels of politics, the inner counsels of power."[48]

What was the situation five years later? In 1982 only 19 of the 435 members of the United House of Representatives were female, roughly 4.3 percent. In the Senate it was 1 percent. The exclusion of women continued. A Cox newspaper survey in 1983 discovered the following situation in the citadel of freedom and equality, the United States Senate: In the higher paid ranks of committee staffers in Congress, 77 percent were men. At the other (lower) end of the scale, women made up 79 percent of the staff. In both the House and Senate, regardless of party affiliation, eight of the nine lowest paying job categories contained more women than men. Of all employees of the Senate staff the average male salary was approximately 30 percent higher than that for females in the post of secretary. When comparable positions were taken, such as press secretary, the average male still earned about 18 percent more than the average female.[49] Between 1983 and 1988 there has been little change, as shown earlier in this section.

The absence of women in representative, elected offices in politics has remained enormous. In the 100th Congress, elected in 1987, only 23 representatives in the House were women and only two senators were women. Progress? Twenty-eight years ago there were already 18 women in the House. Thirty-five years ago (1953–1954) there were three women in the Senate, more than today.[50]

Laws can do little to change this situation since almost every opinion poll indicates that the absence of females in politics is due to "cultural resistance," "public prejudice" and "stereotyping of women." The resistance runs highest among Americans, both male and female, aged 50 and up. The result is that women have a difficult time raising the money required for a successful political campaign. There has been a modest improvement in state legislatures, where women increased their presence from 4.5 percent in 1971 to 15.8 percent in 1988. In 1988 there were also two women governors of states, and 15 women were lieutenant governors.[51]

Research by private individuals and organizations in the United States, and elsewhere, has shown that, at any level of human capital, women are concentrated in lower level occupations and at lower ranks within a given occupation. The proportion of the difference in male and female earnings due to human capital or "compositional" variations has been assessed differently by various authors.[52] It has been found that only about 20 percent of the difference in male and female earnings could be ascribed to human variables.[53]

The occupational segregation issue has been the subject of several important and scientific studies by sociologists and economists during the past decade, for example by Treiman, Hartmann, Ferber, Spaeth, Gold and others who have indicated that there are several factors and not just one explainable variable involved in respect of male-female earnings.[54] The findings suggest that job segregation is much more rigid than the global national data indicate. In smaller firms, very few jobs are performed by both men and women. The President's Council of Economic Advisers, in its report of 1987, maintained that women chose occupations which have come to be called "sex-segregated" because these occupations allow work-time flexibility and shorter working hours.[55] On the other hand, the contributors to *Women's Work, Men's Work: Sex Segregation on the Job* consider the concentration of women in a few occupations, not as choices deliberately made, but as the result of discrimination against women in hiring, wages, and promotions. The extent of this segregation, they point out, has not changed much since 1900 even though the number of women in the work force has increased by 200 percent.[56]

One research team in Europe established that "custom and practice played a major role in explaining any existing division of labor and structure of pay and employment." They said managers only introduced changes when forced to do so by a change in product or a new technique. "Thus, women are allocated to particular jobs and excluded from others primarily because this has always been the case, as far as the current management could remember."[57]

United Nations statistics indicate that the continued availability of women for employment at low rate, custom, the intra-family division of labor, lack of opportunities for advancement to women in the market, are all factors which contribute to the creation of a sex pattern, a mold. The mold is nowhere easily broken. In the United Kingdom in 1971 women formed only 9.6 percent of the architects, engineers and related technicians and 9.1 percent of physical and life scientists and related technicians. Ten years later, despite the fact that considerable publicity had been given to the subject of wage discrimination and occupational segregation in England, the percentage actually *dropped* for both categories, to 8.9 percent. Even in Sweden the figure for architects and engineers dropped from 7.4 to 6.3 percent. On the other hand, in the pink ghettos of nurses, stenographers and typists, there was almost no change. In England the percentage for nurses increased from 91.3 to 91.8 percent and for stenographers and typists it "decreased" from 98.9 to 98.1 percent.[58]

New Legal Support for Women in the Workplace

The progress of United States women in the workplace received a major boost in March 1987 when the Supreme Court ruled that women can receive preferential treatment in hiring and promotion, even when there has been no previous record of discrimination. All that was required was evidence of a manifest imbalance of women and men in the positions in question.[59]

Legal experts and women's rights advocates agreed that the ruling will expand job opportunities for women and help shield employers from reverse sex discrimination lawsuits.[60] In effect, the Supreme Court's ruling put into action a quota system for women (and racial minorities) to make affirmative action real. Minnesota's employee relations commissioner, Nina Rothschild, said: "What it does more than anything is clarify that this form of promotion is legal.... It's clear that you can have remedies for disparities in your work force." The Executive Director of the National Organization for Women's Legal Defense and Education Fund said the decision "...sends a strong message to employers that voluntary affirmative action is the way to go to remedy past discrimination against women."[61]

Earlier, in June 1986, the Supreme Court had also ruled that on-the-job sexual harassment is illegal even if the victims are not hurt economically. The Court said that sexual harassment creates a hostile environment. The decision of the Court upheld a standard adopted by the Federal Equal Employment Opportunity Commission. The Court's action was hailed by the women's movement, and attorneys said it will serve to educate women about their rights.[62]

In June 1987 the Massachusetts Supreme Court became the first state court to rule that sexual harassment in the workplace violated the state's anti-discrimination laws. The state's highest court ruled that a clothing manufacturer had violated a woman's employment rights by failing to correct a sexually harassing work environment. The woman had complained that a male supervisor had harassed her. The ruling was considerably stronger than that of the United States Supreme Court, which mandated that such complaints be considered on a case-by-case basis.[63]

In July 1987 the United States District Court in Washington found that the

State Department was guilty of bias against female foreign service officers in job evaluations, job assignments (including assignments to key senior posts), and honor awards.[64] In August the United States Court of Appeals for the District of Columbia upheld a lower court decision that a major corporation had discriminated against a woman on the basis of sex when it denied her a full partnership. According to the ruling, the company allowed "sexual stereotyping" to play a significant role in denying the applicant a partnership.[65]

Whether the Supreme Court's ruling legalizing affirmative action is going to work in the marketplace on sufficient scale to make all women aware of their rights and employers of their freedom to act is another question. And will it change male attitudes? Opening the workplace to all may (should) be the goal also of corporate affirmative action. It is good business. But defining the workplace by skin color, sex and surname, as the Court's ruling could also be interpreted, may be a prescription for future friction.[66]

A United Nations study in 1980 reviewed some research on long term trends in occupational segregation by sex for selected countries, including the United States. The conclusion was that the tendency for female workers to be crowded in a relatively small range of occupations had changed relatively little over the past two generations whether it was in the United States, the Soviet Union or Britain. The study concluded:

> . . . it would appear that the concentration of women in occupations where the labor force is predominantly female is a phenomenon which is largely unrelated to differences in level of economic development, in cultural values, size of country and geographical location, or in economic and social systems. It would seem that . . . a relatively rigid distribution of jobs and economic roles between the sexes came to be adopted in every country and that this has led to a general categorization of "men's jobs" and "women's jobs" although the set of typical male or female jobs often differs from one country to another. This development has *stereotyped* certain fields of work as falling within the sphere of women and this has had a significant effect on their employment status.[67]

So sexually segregated was the American job market in 1982 that 60 percent of all working women would have had to move across occupational categories in order to equalize the distribution of the sexes by job. Two researchers of the University of California, working with data collected by the United States Department of Labor and the Bureau of the Census between 1968 and 1979 found that this pattern has changed very little since 1900. "Economic discrimination against women is not just unequal pay for equal work," the two researchers concluded. "It's rather an issue of not having equal access." So pervasive is sexual segregation in the workplace, they added, that even women's rights groups seem largely unaware of the economic and professional handicap it places upon female workers. Women are accorded fewer training opportunities, narrower advancement possibilities and lower salaries.[68]

The Male/Female Wage Gap

Despite the law, despite all the smoke and thunder of the women's movement in the United States during the 1970s, and despite the enormous publicity

Occupational Group	Men	Women	W/M
Managerial and professional specialty	$583	$399	.68
Executive, administrative, managerial	593	383	.65
Professional specialty	571	408	.71
Technical, sales, and administrative support	420	269	.64
Technicians and related support	472	331	.70
Sales occupations	431	226	.52
Administrative support, including clerical	391	270	.69
Service occupations	272	185	.68
Private household	NA	130	NA
Protective service	391	278	.71
Service, other	230	188	.82
Precision, production, craft, repair	408	268	.66
Mechanics and repairers	400	392	.98
Construction trades	394	265	.67
Other	433	253	.58
Operators, fabricators, and laborers	325	216	.66
Machine operators, assemblers, inspectors	341	216	.63
Transportation and material moving occs.	369	252	.68
Helpers, laborers, others	261	209	.80
Farming, forestry, fishing	216	185	.86

Table 43. Weekly Earnings of American Workers, by Occupational Group and Gender, 1985. Source: United States Bureau of the Census, Current Population Reports, *Money Income of Households, Families and Persons in the United States, 1984,* Washington DC, 1986, Series P-60, No. 151.

generated by discrimination against women, wage discrimination against women in the United States is widespread and persistent.

International comparisons of European and North American countries indicate that on an economywide level, women's earnings lag behind men's least in Sweden and most in the United States. In manufacturing, the earning gaps are again smallest in Sweden and largest in the United States. The male-female wage gap in Sweden is less than 10 percent for manual workers. Sweden is followed by Denmark, Italy and Norway.[69] By the end of 1986 the gap in the United States was still 36 percent.[70]

The following analysis looks at wage discrimination in the United States at the end of the period 1980–1981 (when the pressure from women's organizations was at its height), and the situation five years later (1985–1986).

• **Period 1980–1981.** In 1980 the median salary for managers and administrators was $12, 936 for women and $23,558 for their male counterparts. According to a special survey made by *Time,* following the defeat of the Equal Rights Amendment Act, weekly medians for earnings by occupation in other areas during 1981 revealed that the ratio of men's pay compared to that of women to be the following: clerical workers 3.2 to 2.2; computer specialists 4.8 to 3.5; engineers 5.4 to 3.7; lawyers 5.7 to 4.0; physicians 4.95 to 4.0; sales workers 3.6 to 1.9; teachers 3.7 to 3.1; waiters 2.0 to 1.4 and, among the moral conscience of the nation, the press, 3.8 to 3.2.[71]

There is a popular misconception in the United States that a proper education, specifically a university degree, puts a woman on an equal footing with men and serves to vastly decrease the gap in earnings. The contrary is true. Women's percentage of men's income on the basis of education sometimes reveals that with less education they actually do better. (See Table 44.)

• **Period 1985–1986.** That not much has changed during the past five years is evident from Table 45.

"When all is said and done," observed economist Barbara Bergmann, "we cannot make a precise estimate of the proportion of the wage gap that is due to discrimination, but we can say with considerable confidence that the statistical evidence points strongly to discrimination as an important force in the labor market. No researcher . . . has been able to come forth with credible statistical evidence that the wage gap is substantially accounted for by non-discriminatory factors." She added that two leading exponents of the opposite point of view (Mincer and Polachek) who studied the pay gap ended with 59 percent of the gap unaccounted for. Citing several cases, Bergmann explained that the evidence of direct discrimination is plain and overwhelming.[72]

The American administration has a somewhat different view. "The average employed man has more work experience, fewer interruptions in that work experience, and longer tenure with his current employer than does his female counterpart of a comparable age. However, these differences are now beginning to narrow. For example, in 1963, women's median years of tenure with their current employer were 2.7 years less than men's; 20 years later, in 1983, the difference was 1.4 years. For women 25 to 34 years old, the tenure differences were 1.5 years and 0.6 years respectively in hours worked even for full-time workers. In 1985, full-time women workers averaged 6 percent fewer hours than full-time male workers." In September 1987 the United States Bureau of the Census produced a special analysis to indicate that the wage gap had closed between full-time female and male workers from 62 percent in 1979 to 70 percent in 1986. (In fact 70 percent was only achieved at the end of 1987.) The Census Bureau study also stated that the remaining gap was caused by factors such as education, work experience, seniority, union input and other factors but conceded that 33 to 40 percent of that difference is because of sex discrimination.[73]

The average female worker will be more impressed by the following facts uncovered by Gilda Berger. It takes women nine days to earn what men do in five. Among government workers, women make on the average $15,579 while men earn $30,553. At the present rate in which the wage gap is closing, it will take women until 1995 to earn three-quarters of what men earn on the average. The average annual retirement income for women, including Social Security and pensions, is little more than half of that of men. As for opportunities, fewer than 1 percent of girls in vocational schools are receiving the training which would open the doors to higher-paid occupations. In a two-year study of vocational education programs in five states—Massachusetts, Pennsylvania, Idaho, Iowa and Wisconsin—it was found that sex segregation in training pro-

Level of Education	Men	Women	Female Earnings As Percentage of Male Earnings
All levels	22,220	13,117	59.0
Elementary			
Less than 8 years	13,561	8,133	60.0
8 years	15,800	9,841	62.3
High School			
1-3 years	16,705	9,690	58.0
4 years	19,545	12,023	61.5
College			
1-3 years	22,166	13,765	62.1
4 years	27,737	15,844	57.1
5 years or more	33,913	20,066	59.2

	Annual Earnings		
Educational Level	*Men*	*Women*	**Women's Earnings as a Percent of Men's**
Elementary school			
Under 8 yrs.	$15,272	$ 9,798	64
8 yrs.	17,392	10,976	63
High school			
1-3 yrs.	18,575	11,808	64
4 yrs.	22,312	14,076	63
College			
1-3 yrs.	24,737	16,241	66
4 yrs.	33,086	19,885	60
5 yrs. or more	39,829	25,370	64
Average	$25,884	$16,036	62

***Top:* Table 44. Annual Full Time Earnings of Male and Female Workers in the United States by Level of Education, 1981. Source: International Labor Organization.*The Economic Role of Women in the ECE Region,* Geneva, 1985, p. 85. *Bottom:* Table 45. Annual Earnings of American Men and Women by Educational Level, 1984. Source: United States Bureau of the Census, Current Population Reports, *Money Income of Households, Families and Persons in the United States, 1984,* Washington DC, 1986, Series P-60, No. 151.**

grams parallels that of sex segregation in the marketplace, and this despite the laws and amendments passed during the 1960s and 1970s with the specific objective of eliminating this type of segregation.[74]

Sylvia Hewlett is of the same opinion as Berger. "The advantage in pay that men have over women in the American labor market is really remarkably large. Women's annual pay in full time work averaged 68 percent of men's in

1985. Another fact vividly conveys the extent of men's advantage: A woman with a college degree who works full time takes home little more pay on average than a man with comparable years of experience who failed to graduate from high school."[75] The most important reason that women have such poor position in the labor market, she said, is that they are not allowed to compete on a fair basis and that employers regularly and habitually act to disadvantage women.[76]

Official reports seem to concede that wage discrimination is still widespread but that there are multiple reasons for the earning differences between men and women. In various reports[77] there are references to job tenure, occupational differences, educational differences, interruptions in employment due to childbirth, etc. But the latest report by the Bureau of the Census, which involved 60,000 interviews during 1986, noted that only 35 to 40 percent of the wage gap can be explained by differences in work experience, job tenure and education, field of study, or sex segregation in occupations.[78]

There are other views which seem to indicate that the last five years up to 1989 proved to be not much different from the situation five and even 10 years earlier. In a study for the Women's Research and Education Institute of the Congressional Caucus for Women's Issues, Nancy Barrett observed that what passed for gains of equality between the sexes during the second half of the 1980s is really the result of negative market conditions for male workers.[79]

There are other pointers which indicate that overt and covert discrimination on grounds of gender is still very much alive.

The median salary for United States garbage collectors in 1987 was $14,872 while childcare workers earned $12,800, according to a study by the Child Welfare League of America. Janitors and cleaners also earned several hundred dollars more on average than child care workers.[80]

Perhaps the foregoing is a case of mistaken priorities. Consider, then, Table 46. As can be seen, women earn less than men in every field of science, in every employment sector, at every degree level, and at every level of experience; and, as Table 47 indicates, the salary gap widens with age. There has been no evidence advanced at date of publication of this work that this trend has been reversed. What is significant is that the occupations in these tables represent some of the elite in the professional and scientific field.

At colleges the difference between salaries for men and women at professorial level remains unbridged and, in certain areas, have even widened. At two-year colleges, the average salary for women professors in the period 1985–1986 was $27,294, an increase of 5.9 percent over the period 1984–85; however, the average male salary was $30,490, an increase of 6.5 percent.[81]

In August 1988, the United States Bureau of the Census said that since 1982 the median income of women had risen by 28 percent to $17,504 in 1987. Though men's median income rose only 23 percent, it reached $26,722. Using median income as a base, women in 1987 earned only 65 cents to their male counterparts' dollar. More important, for every dollar earned by a man, women working the *same* full-time hours in the *same* occupation earned 57 cents in the transportation business, 51 cents in sales and, in heavy labor only 78 cents.[82]

Field	1973	1975	1977	1979	1981	1983	1985
All Fields	82.3	80.8	79.6	77.3	75.9	77.8	77.2
Physical Scientists	81.4	79.3	70.1	80.0	78.8	80.1	81.2
Math Scientists	87.8	85.5	84.3	81.3	83.6	87.2	83.0
Computer Scientists	79.4	76.3	79.7	79.2	87.3	97.2	98.0
Environmental Scientists	81.6	80.9	75.8	79.3	83.3	87.3	84.6
Engineers	87.0	82.5	79.8	80.1	81.6	85.0	84.6
Life Scientists	76.6	83.6	83.7	79.6	78.9	80.6	80.5
Psychologists	87.6	86.3	82.7	82.9	79.6	82.6	84.9
Social Scientists	84.4	83.1	81.8	84.3	81.2	84.5	83.0

	Years of Experience						
Ph.D. Field	*0–5*	*6–10*	*11–15*	*16–20*	*21–25*	*26–30*	> *30*
All Fields	85.0	86.0	84.5	83.8	86.9	84.8	85.5
Physics/ Astronomy	91.9	92.3	93.1	91.2	*	*	*
Chemistry	94.8	92.4	86.4	79.2	83.1	83.6	83.3
Mathematics	92.1	87.9	93.6	84.2	92.1	*	*
Computer Sciences	95.7	103.0	102.0	*	*	*	*
Environmental Sciences	94.3	100.5	83.9	90.3	*	*	*
Engineering	96.7	114.5	96.3	*	*	*	*
Agricultural Sciences	95.6	92.4	81.7	*	*	*	*
Medical Sciences	94.1	89.2	82.0	90.2	72.8	90.2	72.8
Biological Sciences	96.3	84.1	90.3	84.7	88.8	89.4	85.7
Psychology	94.9	96.2	91.6	93.8	93.8	92.0	*
Social Sciences	86.1	96.9	88.7	95.7	104.2	89.4	•

***Top:* Table 46. Women's Salaries as a Percentage of Men's for Doctoral Scientists and Engineers. *Bottom:* Table 47. Women's Median Salaries as a Percentage of Men's Median Salaries Among Full-Time Employed Doctoral Scientists and Engineers in 1985, by Fields and Years of Experience. Source for both tables: National Science Foundation, *Mosaic,* Vol. 18, No. 1; (Top) p. 8 and (Bottom) p. 9, citing National Research Council biennial *Profiles of U. S. Doctoral Scientists and Engineers.* Note: Medians in Table 47 were not computed if based on fewer than 20 responses.**

Equal Pay and Comparable Worth

When it comes to the question of improving women's positions by instituting equal pay for work of comparable worth, an entirely new argument is raised. The now-famous question by Nina Rothschild—when a nurse makes a mistake she can kill you while a mistake made by a painter will only annoy you, so why should painters be paid more than nurses—is particularly apt when it is pointed out that a registered nurse in Minnesota in 1984 earned $1,723 a month while a male vocational education teacher made $2,260 per month. A woman working as senior legal secretary in California earned $665 per month while a man at the senior carpenter level got $1,040. According to a study completed by researchers from the State University of New York, these jobs are considered comparable in terms of education.[83] While the researchers said that the jobs were also comparable in terms of "responsibility" this is difficult to accept on rational grounds. According to the Rothschild principle, the carpenter's mistake will result in a financial loss. A nurse's mistake could result in death. The responsibility is not equal.

Fifteen states in the United States have enacted laws requiring that men and women be paid equally when they hold jobs judged to be of equal value. Five others have passed resolutions declaring comparable worth as a goal of state pay plans, while 24 are evaluating their job titles with an eye toward correcting wage disparities between predominantly female-staffed and predominantly male-staffed jobs.[84]

No matter the relative pros and cons of comparable worth (see Chapter 30), the fact is that it is already putting far more into women's pockets than they would have been able to obtain in any other way, or by any other argument or appeal. All over the United States, thousands of dollars in higher income have been earned by secretaries, nurses, data entry operators, municipal workers and others. Though the issue of comparable worth is still to be ruled on by the United States Supreme Court, many counties, cities and states are acting as if it is a foregone conclusion that comparable worth is going to receive the same favorable rulings as those regarding preferential hiring and promotion of women to undo a manifest imbalance in the marketplace.

In Washington State about 35,000 workers, all at the low end of the pay scale, have been receiving pay equity increases averaging 4 to 5 percent through 1991. In Chicago about 3,500 workers in 79 predominantly female-staffed occupations received a 5 percent raise. In both cases, the state and the city agreed to the increases rather than face a court battle with the American Federation of State County and Municipal Employees (A.F.S.C.M.E.) on the question of equal payment for work of comparable worth. In New Jersey, a predominantly female group of about 9,000 workers received a 5 percent wage increase in February 1987. Similar pay equity adjustments are on the way in many states, such as New York, Pennsylvania, Connecticut, Ohio, Wisconsin, and others.[85]

It is anticipated that a major effort will soon be made to bring the weighty arguments of equal pay for work of comparable worth to bear on the education scene, where pay disparity is still widespread. In all of the United States, 60 percent of all teachers are women, but only 19 percent are principals of schools and only 1 percent superintendents. In the state of Georgia, 84 percent of the teachers are women, while only 17 percent are principals and 4 percent superintendents.[86]

Legal Process and Statutory Discrimination

The Constitution of the United States contains no clause which discriminates against women. But there are laws passed by the various states which are discriminatory. There are also federal statutes that contain gender differences. In 1983 there were still 113 such federal statutes—44 to do with the armed forces, 20 with Social Security benefits and 10 dealing with Indian tribal law, e.g. that a white man may not acquire right to Indian tribal property by marrying an Indian woman. A number of American states still have community property laws, and in all the community states, except Texas and Washington, the husband has power of attorney over the community property. There are also discrepancies in criminal law. Several states, such as New Mexico, have statutes which exonerate a husband who kills his wife's lover *in flagrante delicto* but leaves punishable a similar crime committed by a wife against her husband's mistress.[87]

In many states such as Mississippi, Alabama and others women faced inequality because state laws to outlaw unfair discrimination against women are still non-existent. In South Carolina, the state does not have a pay equity policy for women, or laws barring sex discrimination in education, credit, housing, or public accommodation.[88]

Of the fifty states, the state of Washington (West Coast of the United States and not to be confused with the city of Washington, District of Columbia, capital of the United States) has made the most progress in legally addressing the problem of women's inequality. The state has passed an equal rights amendment act to its constitution; has a pay equity policy for state employees; equal pay and equal employment laws; state abortion funding; a model law on enforcing child support payments; laws benefiting displaced homemakers and abused spouses; divorce laws that permit joint child custody and require equal distribution of property; and laws against discrimination in credit, housing and public accommodations.[89]

There are few other states close to achieving what the state of Washington has. The net result is that the status of working women in the United States is still a far cry from that of men. According to the National Association of Working Women, almost 20 million United States mothers, more than 63 percent of all women with children younger than 18, are working outside the home, and half of all women with children younger than one are working. But only about 1 percent of employees in medium and large companies are eligible for any coverage of child care costs. More than 60 percent of the working women get no maternity leave, and just 13 percent are on an alternative work schedule such as flexitime. Almost 40 percent are still in the traditional pink ghettos, the 10 traditional women's occupations of secretary, bookkeeper, retail sales clerk, cashier, waitress, registered nurse, school teacher, domestic help, typist and nurse. Even where men find themselves in the pink ghetto, they still earn more than women for the same work. Annual salaries of male secretaries are 33 percent higher than those of female secretaries. Of all 20 million working mothers, one-third are earning wages below the poverty line. For black women who maintain families alone, 58 percent are below poverty level.[90]

In 1987 no more than 40 percent of United States working women had job-protected, paid maternity leave of six weeks' duration. Only 38 percent of major United States companies guarantee women the same job after childbirth; 43 percent offer a comparable job; 6 percent offer some job; and the rest make no guarantees. On the money side, 40 percent give full salary during the six weeks period, 58 percent give a reduced salary, and the rest provide no payments.[91]

By federal law, companies must give pregnancy leave if time off is granted for other types of "disabilities." In January 1987, the United States Supreme Court gave states the right to grant or deny unemployment benefits to anyone who leaves a job for reasons unrelated to work, including pregnancy. The court upheld a California law requiring employers to grant unpaid leaves of absence of up to four months to women whose pregnancies leave them unable to work, even if leave is not granted for any other liability. The court concluded that the California law does not conflict with a 1978 federal law, The Pregnancy Disability Act, which bans discrimination based on pregnancy.[92] This will undoubtedly bring a massive rethinking of the role of women in the labor force, particularly since 90 percent of the female labor force will end up having children. It is anticipated that small companies will have a difficult time complying.[93]

At present only five states grant women paid maternity leave, but it is expected that more states will follow. Worldwide, most observers agree that the American economy is helped if experienced workers who have lost a job because of pregnancy are brought back into the labor force as soon as possible.[94]

The Equal Rights Amendment Act Proposal

The proposed Equal Rights Amendment to the United States Constitution, which finally failed in 1983 to gather sufficient support from state legislatures (35 instead of the required 38), was supported by 63 percent of the American people at that time, according to a nationwide Harris opinion poll.

Though the fundamental principle was that the federal government and all state and local governments must treat both men and women as individual persons, not as members of a sex, opponents pointed out that there were sufficient laws in existence to cover all contingencies, at federal, state and local level, and since the amendment would apply only to government action, such as equal pay and legal rights, the amendment would miss the real target of reform: private actions and social relationships, i.e. male perceptions of women and the continued existence of female stereotypes. As Gilda Berger wrote in her excellent book on women, work and wages: "Strong enforcement of existing laws and new legal action would help women in their fight for better employment opportunities and more nearly equal pay. But laws alone cannot change employers' perceptions of the working woman."[95]

The proposed Equal Rights Amendment to the Constitution of the United States, which the House approved on October 12, 1971, was the epitome of simplicity: "Equality of rights under the law shall not be denied or abridged by the United States or by any State on account of sex." Perhaps if the proposal had contained the words "on account of sex, race, or religion," it would have stood a better chance of ratification. Perhaps if the words "the United States or any State or person, organization, or institution" were added, it would have been more effective once approved. The E.R.A. failed, after a history of frustration for its proponents ever since it was first raised as a possibility in 1923 at a meeting of the National Woman's Party.[96] The E.R.A. proposal was not something that just fell out of the air during the hey-day of feminism in the 1970s. Back in the 1920s the militant women of the National Women's Party anticipated that giving women the vote would not be enough to achieve equality. In the 1970s the National Organization for Women and others believed that the existence of civil rights laws would not be enough to achieve equality either. The women of the '20s and the women of the '70s were both right. But whereas women's suffrage was a cornerstone, the proposed E.R.A. was not. The cornerstones to protect women against discrimination based on sex are already imbedded in United States law. The E.R.A. would merely have added to the arsenal. The many federal and Supreme Court judgments handed down in favor of women the past decade has proved that women's constitutional rights can be enforced and are thoroughly documented, such as in the N.O.W.'s *State by State Guide to Women's Legal Rights* and Leslie Goldstein's *The Constitutional Rights of Women.*[97] But the dispute continues.

There is still a notion that the passing of an Equal Rights Amendment to the United States Constitution would bring an immediate end to remaining discrimination against women, but the passing of such an act, unfortunately, would be only symbolic, at best a spur. Passing of an E.R.A. in France in 1946 did not eliminate discrimination within a year or two, or rapidly accelerate its decrease. It was a change in the attitude of men and society, a change which paved the way for individual legislative acts on marital rights and improvement of women's share in the marketplace.

The passing of the Equal Credit Opportunity Act in 1974 is different and was one of the turning points in the changing role of women in the national economy of the United States. Bankers could then no longer assume that all women were economically dependent on men. Bankers were forced to deal with an America in which 50 percent of all marriages break up, leaving the women as the heads of the households. The E.C.O. Act forced changes in the way society treated women as earners and borrowers. Some 20 years ago it was extremely difficult for a married woman to obtain a credit card in her own name. Today about 20 percent of American Express cards in circulation belong to women, with 37 percent of new card applications coming from women. In this way, the old profile of the typical American home and the typical American woman has gradually changed in the past decade. Bankers are saying that the law did not change the situation. What has changed are the women. Some sociologists echo this view, stating that "the really important shift has been from jobs to careers."[98] Others say it was a change in the perception of women on the part of the financial world.

There are three reasons why the notion that an Equal Rights Amendment to the United States Constitution would result in a *de facto,* dramatic improvement in occupational segregation, wage discrimination and equal opportunities is unlikely to be realized.

In the first place, existing federal laws outlawing discrimination which have been on the law books for 20 years continue to be violated. Why would the E.R.A. be honored? In July 1983 the United States Supreme Court banned employers from offering retirement plans that provide men and women with unequal benefits, but the law on which the court based its decision was passed in 1964 and is known as Title VII of the Civil Rights Act—which forbids employers to discriminate on the basis of sex, race, religion or ethnic origin. It will therefore take a decade of massive litigation before the *existing* laws are implemented by the vast majority of American companies.

Though laws passed during the 1960s clearly prohibit discrimination in employment against women and other minorities, the Equal Employment Opportunity Commission continues to have to file job-bias suits against major companies. During 1986 more than 500 cases were filed. Of particular interest, in illustrating the matter of attitude, the E.E.O.C. in 1985 filed charges against a major bank for discrimination against minorities and women. Even during the seven-year investigation, the bank's employment of women and minorities *decreased,* though it opened almost 40 new branches.[99] Existing laws were sufficient to bring the bank in question to court. The E.R.A. would have made no difference.

The second reason why the E.R.A. will not bring massive change within a year, or even within 10 years, even if the existing laws were to be vigorously applied, is a subtle (male) discrimination against women that will take much longer to eradicate and which no E.R.A. would be able to assist. It is the sort of discrimination which states that women may not become members of prestigious private clubs. In this and other respects the attitude of the average American male is two decades behind that of the average Frenchman. Again, existing laws and by-laws are being used to pry open the doors to these clubs. In the city of Atlanta the most prestigious clubs are being cracked by the simple process of denying the clubs a liquor license unless blacks and women are also permitted to become members. The famed Cosmos Club in Washington DC saw the writing on the wall and in July 1988 voted to break a 110-year-old tradition to accept women as members. Two days later the United States Supreme Court unanimously upheld a New York City ordinance requiring admission of women to clubs that promote the furtherance of trade or business.[100]

Breaking down perceptions and attitudes is and will be a long process involving many court battles as yet to come. The United States is not alone. Britain has a woman on the throne. The country also has a woman as Prime Minister. One of the judges of Britain's highest court is a woman. Yet women may, as yet, not become members of Britain's M.C.C., the headquarters of the cricket-playing world in London. British tradition has it that (only) men play and watch cricket, and though the redoubtable trio of women mentioned above may be fanatical supporters of the game, they may not enter the hallowed M.C.C. clubhouse as members.

The third reason is that in looking at the E.R.A. care must be taken not to equate sex with race. If the idea is that there must be no law or no rules that establish differentiation between men and women, or boys and girls, and that any differentiation would be a violation of the Constitution, then organizations catering to men or women (and widely supported by both sexes) would be seriously jeopardized, e.g. the Boy and Girl Scout movement; all single-sex private schools and colleges receiving federal aid in any form would have to be sex-integrated; school policies will have to be sex-neutral, e.g. on the length of hair; Catholic seminaries would lose their tax-exempt status unless they admit women for training to the priesthood and so would Jewish universities and seminaries which maintain separate seating for men and women according to their religious beliefs. Women would lose exemption from military draft and combat duty. Separate sleeping huts, toilet facilities and showers for men and women in the United States armed forces could be successfully challenged—by men.

It is a flawed and even a foolish argument that sexual equality in the workplace, in schools and universities, in training, in wages, in social intercourse, or in the United States armed forces can be fought with the same constitutional language as racial discrimination.

Women who once fought for the E.R.A. are beginning to admit that perhaps the energy employed during the 1970s could have been better directed. In the epilogue to *The Sisterhood,* Marcia Cohen wrote that in the mid-'80s, an age labeled "post-feminist" by *The New York Times,* the Supreme Court applied its stamp to a state's compensatory promotions for women; to a guarantee of their jobs after they return from maternity leave; to their acceptance in all-male clubs; to a ruling against sexual harassment. These rulings, she observed, were not ensured by an E.R.A.

> So perhaps that constitutional amendment did not, after all, matter quite so much.

By 1988, the Pentagon itself, the symbolic core of male supremacy, was demanding more jobs for women and an end to sexual harassment in the military.[101]

Indeed, in the year 1987, the army opened an additional 24,000 jobs for women, including Marine Corps guard posts and work on Navy military supply ships. The Army's deputy chief of staff for personnel said 50 percent of the positions in the 1.5 million regular Army, reserves and National Guard could be filled by women but that women were shying away.[102] (United States law prohibits women in the armed services only from serving in jobs that put them at risk of combat.) In July 1988 a woman became the Marine Corps first general and Corps base commander.[103] Both the Navy and the Air Force have allowed their first female pilots and navigators.[104] The Defense Department and the armed forces admit that sexual harassment is a problem and remains a problem, and that women are often restricted in their careers.[105] But an E.R.A.

would have made not the slightest difference to this situation. It is a problem of men, and women's perceptions of what women could and should do.

Perhaps the most useful book on the rights of women to be published in the United States the past decade is that of Susan Ross and Ann Barcher, who adopted the approach that women do have rights not limited to marital status and that their interests are similar to men's. Their book tells women how to cope with discrimination by using existing laws. Instead of merely bewailing the defeat of the E.R.A. the authors state that women should realize that in the same decade that the E.R.A. was defeated, sex discrimination law in the United States was transformed. Under pressure of the women's movement, the United States Supreme Court changed its interpretation of the Constitution and ruled that many of the existing sex-discriminatory laws of states were in fact unconstitutional. Ross and Barcher maintain that the constitutional doctrine which can be effectively used to get rid of sex discrimination is derived from the fourteenth amendment to the Constitution. The key language provides: "No state shall . . . deny to any person within its jurisdiction the equal protection of the laws." This clause can be used to combat both discriminatory laws and practices. Their argument is that technically the equal protection clause prohibits discrimination, i.e. a state legislature may not treat its citizens differently.[106]

Apart from the Constitution there are four major federal laws and a myriad of state and city laws which also forbid discrimination in the important field of employment: the Civil Rights Act of 1964 (Title VII), the Equal Pay Act, the Pregnancy Discrimination Act of 1978 and the Wage Discrimination Act of 1967. Of all, Title VII of the 1964 Civil Rights Act is the most far-reaching and most important law. Teachers have additional relief under the Education Amendment Act of 1972, but in 1982 the Supreme Court also ruled that Title IX prohibits sex-based discrimination against students and employees in federally funded education programs. In addition, there is the Equal Credit Opportunity Act of 1974, which benefits all women who head the household, work or run their own business. (These laws are presented in more detail further on in this chapter.)

Women in the United States are closer to the goal of equality in terms of the Constitution and the laws of Congress, as well as the laws of the states, than even informed members of the women's rights movement seem to realize.

It bears repeating that the major problem in the United States is not a constitutional one; it is the attitude of men towards women in general. It is men's *perception* of women that is stuck in the past. The education of the American male is apparently one of the most important tasks facing United States feminists and it is a much more daunting task than getting the Congress to pass an E.R.A.!

In 1986 the National Committee on Pay Equity found that the pay gaps between men and women and between black and white have continued, despite the Equal Pay Act of 1963 and the Civil Rights Act of 1964. The committee found that in 1986 white women, employed full time, earned 63 cents compared to every dollar earned by white men, while black women earned 56 cents and Hispanic women only 53 cents.[107]

Twenty-three years was not sufficient for the law to take effect. Would an E.R.A. have helped?

The 1984 defeat of the proposed Equal Rights Amendment to the United States Constitution was seen by the women's movement as a devastating setback to years of committed, extensive and expensive campaigning. But in March 1987, with little warning, the United States Supreme Court came out with a ruling (*Johnson* v. *Santa Clara County Transportation Agency)* which turned out to be no less than a momentous victory for those who believe that the inequality in the marketplace (and discrimination as well) can be remedied by affirmative action, better known as the quota system. The Court ruled on March 25, 1987, that women, as well as blacks and other minorities, can receive preferential treatment in hiring and promotion, even when there has been no proven history of discrimination. All that is necessary is evidence of a manifest imbalance in the number of women or minorities involved.

The landmark affirmative action ruling delighted the women's rights movement. According to the Executive Director of the Women's Legal Defense Fund, it vindicated the historic position of the movement that sex discrimination, like race discrimination, can be remedied by legal action. The ruling sent a strong message to employers in the United States that affirmative action is the way to remedy past discrimination against women, added the Executive Director of the Education Fund.[108]

The court's ruling also evoked sharp criticism, some of it on strong legal grounds. Title VII of the Civil Rights Act of 1964 strictly forbids hiring and promoting workers by race or gender. Yet this was precisely the law which the court invoked in its ruling so that a law that forbids sex promotions was in fact used to permit the same action. One of the dissenting judges (Scalia) quite rightly said that Title VII was thereby not merely repealed but actually inverted. The ruling, said Scalia, effectively required employers to engage in intentional discrimination on the basis of race or sex: "... we effectively replace the goal of a discrimination-free society with the quite incompatible goal of proportionate representation by race and sex in the workplace."[109]

The President of the Washington Legal Foundation termed the court's decision one of "social engineering" on a large scale. The Director of the Anti-Defamation League said that the decision represents "exactly what civil rights laws were designed to free us of."[110] No one disputed the fact that (in the United States) race and sex were the most important factors in the segmentation and inequalities of the workplace. Yet in an advanced society with almost a million lawyers, fewer than 18 percent were women or doctors. A 1986 survey of the 600 largest firms in the United States by A. S. Hansen, Inc., found that only 7 percent of all executive positions in those corporations were held by women, and in some 300 there were no female executives at all.[111]

Only a month later there was another major breakthrough for sexual equality when the Supreme Court ruled that states may force Rotary International to admit women as members. The 7-0 equality decision clearly indicated that numerous other male-only (or female-only) "private" organizations, which operate publicly, may have to comply with state laws requiring equal access to "public accomodations." By its decision of May 5, 1987, the Supreme Court broadened the impact of a 1984 ruling that states may force the Jaycees to admit women as full members. Legal experts agreed that the May ruling could have a dramatic impact on breaking down barriers for traditionally male-only groups. The Deputy Attorney General of California, Marian Johnson, told the press: "Symbolically it also has tremendous importance. . . . The ruling shows that just because discrimination is traditional (men-only clubs) does not mean that it is lawful."[112]

Existing Legal Protection

The following laws are the most important acts passed *inter alia,* to eliminate discrimination against women and to provide for fair wages and equal pay where possible, marriage and divorce, maternity rights, child support and the rights of older workers. These laws are considered the most important from women's points of view.

• **Equal Pay for Equal Work.** Wage disparity between men and women who do the same work is the most widely practiced form of discrimination in the workplace. The Equal Pay Act of 1963 requires that men and women receive equal pay for equal work. Title VII of the Civil Rights Act of 1964 orders an end to discrimination in employment practices, including wages. The courts have ruled that the word "equal" does not mean "identical" but only substantially equal. Minor differences in duties cannot be used as an excuse for lower wages. The United States Supreme Court in several landmark cases, e.g. *County of Washington* v. *Gunther* (1981), ruled that wage discrimination based only on sex is unlawful under Title VII of the Civil Rights Act of 1964. In this case, which concerned women prison guards, investigators found that the women did approximately 90 percent of what the men did in guarding inmates but received only 70 percent of the pay; in fact, the highest paid woman received less than the lowest paid man. Subsequently, in other cases, the term "same work" was refined to mean the same place, a single location, same skill, effort and responsibility.

• **Fair Wages.** Three acts are involved. Title VII of the Civil Rights Act of 1964, the Equal Pay Act of 1963 and Executive Order 11246 amended by Executive Order 11375 prohibit government contractors and sub-contractors from discriminating in hiring. The Equal Employment Opportunity Commission (E.E.O.C.) became the federal agency that administers Title VII.

• **Education.** Rights of female students can be enforced under the equal protection clause of the fourteenth amendment to the United States Constitution, the Equal Education Opportunities Act of 1974, Title IV of the 1964 Civil Rights Act and the Education Amendments of 1972 (which include Title IX), 1976 and 1984. These acts cannot and should not be seen as an aid and protection to only one sex. Both sexes are covered. In 1982 the Supreme Court (in a ruling written by Justice Sandra Day O'Connor, the first woman on the United States Supreme Court) ruled in *Mississippi University for Women* v. *Hogan* that the Mississippi University for Women could not exclude men from its school of nursing.

• **Vocational Education.** Several laws now require states to take steps to overcome sex discrimination in federally funded vocational education programs. Title IX of the Education Amendments Act of 1972, in addition to the 1963 Vocational Education Act, prohibits sex discrimination. In 1976 and 1984 amendments were passed to the 1963 act to end occupational segregation in vocational education.

• **Divorce and Marriage Laws.** In 1970 a Uniform Marriage and Divorce Act was approved by the Uniform Law Commission. The new proposals were submitted to the states, which modified and ratified the Uniform Marriage Act so that by 1983 all but three of the old common-law states had adopted some version of the new act. The Uniform Marriage Act gave birth to the concept of equitable distribution and altered the previous laws in several ways. Marriage is now an economic partnership. Property is treated as it is treated in the dissolution of a business. Contributions of each spouse are recognized. (Laws in 31 states now require courts to include in marital assets a wife's contribution as a homemaker.) Valuable property (such as a house or an oil painting) is considered joint property in case of divorce, regardless of who holds title. A spouse may be awarded alimony and fault is largely eliminated. Fault no longer serves as a major bargaining tool, hence the term "equitable distribution" to describe the new act. Elsewhere in this book (see pp. 255–257), there is reference to the fact that the women's movement now considers this change in the law to have been a mistake and that it did not serve the interests of women. In fact, it is considered a national disaster.

• **Maternity Rights.** The Pregnancy Discrimination Act of 1978 forbids discrimination against women because of pregnancy, childbirth or related medical conditions. In June 1983 the Supreme Court ruled that the provisions of the act also applied to the wives of employees. Companies had to provide an employee's wife with pregnancy disability coverage equal to other health-related dependency benefits; otherwise, the companies would be found to be discriminating against male employees.

• **Child Support Enforcement Amendment Act, 1984.** The Act was designed to enable federal and state officials and courts to grapple with the problem of delinquency in child support payments. (In 1984 such unpaid support totaled a staggering $4 billion.) The bill requires states to set up a system for withholding money from paychecks of parents whose support payments are a month or more overdue. The act does not provide for an income for the parent while the state goes after the delinquent, as similar European laws do.

• **Retiring Workers.** The Employee Retirement Income Security Act of 1974 set minimum standards for pension plans. This act was followed in 1984 by the Retirement Equity Act. Instead of the man now electing to receive all his payment during his retirement, the wife must give written permission so that the other option, of lower payments on retirement, but with monies continuing to be paid to the survivor, is more likely to happen. In 1983 the Supreme Court also ruled that it was illegal for women to receive smaller monthly retirement pay than men based on life expectancy and that all retirement benefits must be calculated in a gender-neutral manner.

• **Abortion.** Anti-abortion laws of states were struck down by the Supreme Court in 1973. In November 1988 the Supreme Court refused to give a husband the right to block his wife's abortion, cutting off the argument that a prospective father had rights equal to those of the mother in deciding the fetus's fate.

Conclusion

Should the drive for equality be stepped up? Almost no one can tell with certainty whether the enormous changes in the profile of working women which took place during the past two decades will be followed by equally dramatic improvement in the disappearance of the wage gap, in eliminating occupational segregation and in rendering working mothers the necessary assistance to enable them to compete with men while sustaining themselves and their children.

The views of Barbara Bergmann, Lenore Weitzman, and Helen Remick regarding the status of modern working women serve as a strong background for the claim by Sylvia Hewlett that liberation of women in the United States is largely a myth and that the drive for equality may have made things worse.

According to Remick, nine of every 10 women today will work in paid employment for 25 to 45 years. As heads of households, two of every five women will be responsible for the support of children and others. Over one-third of women who are heads of households have income below the poverty level. The earning ratio of women to men has shown no significant improvement over the past three decades.[113]

Bergmann states that two of every three entrants to the labor market from now to 1990 will be women, and women will fill seven out of every 10 jobs created in that period. Fifty-five percent of all mothers who have children under voting age are in the labor force. Currently more than two out of every three adult women under age 30 work. Over the past 20 years, the number of employed women rose three times faster than that of men. An estimated 75 percent of women work because they need to support themselves or their families, or both. For most women, working is a necessity of life. Employed wives who work full time outside the house contribute more than 40 percent of the average family income.[114]

Against this background, Sylvia Hewlett's book *A Lesser Life: The Myth of Women's Liberation in the United States* outraged a large and prominent sector of the women's movement, such as the National Organization for Women (N.O.W.), but a careful, dispassionate analysis of her findings leaves little doubt that she has made a strong case to justify the title of her book.

Hewlett points out that the United States not only has one of the largest wage gaps between men and women in the free world, but that the gap has not narrowed significantly since the 1950s. Wage gaps in Europe have been closing, slowly, but nonetheless significantly, and women's wages relative to men's are now between 2 to 30 percent higher in Europe than in the United States. American women earn almost a third less than men, despite having as much education as their male counterparts.[115]

The rate of divorce in the United States is now two to 20 times higher than

Presence and age of child	Wives, husband present				Women maintaining families alone
	1970	*1975*	*1980*	*1986*	1986
Total	40.8	44.5	50.2	54.6	62.1
With children under 18 years	39.8	44.9	54.3	61.4	69.5
Under 6 years	30.3	36.8	45.3	53.9	57.9
Under 3 years	25.8	32.6	41.5	51.0	50.9
1 year and under	24.0	30.8	39.0	49.8	44.7
3–5 years	36.9	42.2	51.7	58.5	64.5
6–17 years	49.2	52.4	62.0	68.5	76.8
6–13 years	47.0	51.8	62.6	68.0	74.5

Table 48. Working Women with Teenage Children 1970–1986. Source: *Economic Report of the President to Congress,* United States Government Printing Office, Washington DC, 1987, p. 211.

in the other major powers of the West, double that of Sweden, Britain and Germany, triple that of France, and 20 times higher than that of Italy. According to Hewlett, "The degree of financial insecurity and injury women suffer as a result of divorce is far higher in the United States than anywhere else in the world. Women are forced to work because of low family income, but have little economic security as they are squeezed between the traditional and modern forms of financial security to an extent unknown in other countries." While 90 percent of all women in the United States will have children at some point, more than 60 percent of working mothers have no right to maternity leave; in fact, Hewlett points out that the United States is the only industrialized country in the world that has no statutory maternity leave, something which women enjoy in 117 other countries.[116]

In terms of sex-segregation in the marketplace, Hewlett argues that in 1982, 50 percent of all employed women worked in only 20 occupations out of the 427 occupations detailed by the United States Department of Labor. She admits that there are areas where women have made significant inroads into traditional male areas of employment. Between 1962 and 1982 the proportion of women among engineers rose from 1 to 6 percent, from 3 to 17 percent among mail carriers, from 6 to 15 percent among physicians and from 12 to 47 percent among bus drivers. But these are exceptions, she says. Women still account for 99 percent of secretaries, 97 percent of typists and 96 percent of registered nurses, leaving the pink ghetto of women's employment virtually the same as it was 10, 20 and 30 years ago. According to Hewlett, the ghetto has nothing to do with differences in men's and women's educations. There is no scarcity of women with high academic qualifications in the United States since almost 33 percent of all doctorates are held by women. Yet in its 1982–1983 report from more than 2,500 institutions of higher education, the American Association of University Professors concluded that, after a decade of affirmative action, women have achieved very little. At Harvard, women were only 4.2 percent of full professors, at Princeton 3.2 percent and at Stanford 2.6 percent. And male professors were paid significantly higher salaries than their female counterparts, even where the women had more experience.[117]

These are only some of Hewlett's arguments in her analysis of the status of American women before she concludes that liberation is, as yet, a myth.

The problem, as she sees it, is that everyone believed that once women possessed the same legal rights as men, and could choose not to have children, they would achieve true equality of opportunity and be able to compete for jobs, income and power on the same terms as men. Because of this misconception they also made the gigantic mistake of assuming that modern women wanted nothing to do with children, when the crux of woman's dilemma is not an urge to become a male clone, but the dual burden of home and workforce that leads to her second-class status and the agony of reconciling motherhood with the need to work. At the heart of America's problem, she said, is the fact that, unlike the rest of the Western world, "there have been no cultural or institutional changes in the way children are supposed to be raised." When all is said and done, Hewlett points out, the fact is that motherhood is not going out of style. Women are having fewer children, true enough, but more women are having at least one child than ever before; they only have them later.[118] (For more on this, see the section on the United States in Chapter 30.)

In *The Equality Trap,* a work written a few years after Hewlett's, Mary Ann Mason points out that women in the United States were working harder than ever before but growing poorer while watching their families break up. The feminist drive for equality has actually made things worse, she said. Women work more hours per week in the house and outside than ever before, and a paying job has become a necessity. Because women are the primary care-providers for the children, they must take a flexible and thus relatively low-paying job to be available in case of a problem. "Ironically, the failure to obtain passage of the Equal Rights Amendment, the capstone of the egalitarian crusade, delayed for more than a decade a realization of what was actually happening to women.... The real revolution in the United States has been an economic revolution that requires women to work to maintain a family in the face of declining living wages." Mason points out that the many new jobs which the United States churned out in the 1960s and 1970s had a few things in common: lower pay, lower benefits and less security than those in the declining manufacturing sector. During those years, she writes, mothers rushed into the workplace in order to shore up the family wage or to survive following divorce. Without realizing it, the women's movement supplied an ideology which suited the economy's need for new workers. The crusade for equal rights gave women equal responsibility for supporting the family. But equal rights did not challenge the structure of the economy or the role of the government, which is why America lags even behind some Third World countries in child care, maternity benefits, and health care for women and children. "As the richest nation in the world, we rank an abysmal sixteenth in infant mortality." The maternity-leave debate, she observes, is merely the latest bout in the old and painful conflict between women's rights and an equal-rights strategy.[119]

To answer the question posed at the beginning of this section as to whether the pace of change should be stepped up, it appears that what is required may perhaps not be more pace but a different direction. "This is a critical juncture in the history of women in America," writes Mason, "for the first time the great majority of *married* women are working outside the home and for the first time the divorce rate nearly equals the marriage rate.... It is time for some hard rethinking and reevaluation of the direction of the women's movement.... A return to the flexible, pragmatic concept of women's rights, rather than the rigid ideology of equal rights, is in order."[120]

The United States is the most fertile area for growth of women's rights and has the highest potential for broadly based improvement. The fact that women have rights, that there is discrimination against women, that women are struggling for equal opportunity, is better known to the masses in the United States than to any other people on earth—thanks to the vast media network in that country. This is where the greatest and the most rapid development should be taking place. The data researched revealed that while there has been improvement in some areas, a claim to widespread and substantial progress cannot be substantiated. In fact, in several areas the progress made by women in Scandinavia and Europe is far more impressive. Take personal income. While women in the United States in 1988 earned 70 percent of what men did, three years earlier, in 1985, the percentage for women in France was already 78, in Sweden 81 and in Italy 86. As Hewlett pointed out, at the rate of increase of the period 1975–1985, it will take United States women a quarter of a century to get to the point where the Italian women are today.[121]

The difficulties individual women face in their struggle for equal consideration remain as difficult as 50 years ago. In May 1986 Patricia Ashcraft, who had been trying for five years to get an appointment as a ranger with the Georgia Department of Natural Resources, a post for which she was qualified in every respect, finally had to bring a lawsuit against the Department for not hiring her.[122] The stereotype called for a ranger to be a man, and here a woman had the effrontery to apply for the post when her stereotype cast her as a secretary, a bookkeeper, perhaps an auditor in the department, but not as a ranger. That she was more able, trained and qualified than the male applicants was considered irrelevant, or deliberately ignored.

For real change to take place, and to take place soon, male attitudes must first change and stereotyping must be destroyed.

The important point is not so much that there has been a vast improvement in the legal position of women, but that the progress in the United States (where the legal structure on the national level no longer impedes progress) has been so slow the past 10 years, or confined to a handful of professions. In some areas in the United States the situation is still pre–World War I. In the state of Georgia, for example, more than 54 percent of the voting age population is female; nonetheless, men account for 100 percent of the state's United States senators and representatives, 90 percent of state legislators, 93 percent of mayors, 98 percent of county attorneys, 100 percent of district attorneys, 95 percent of county commissioners, 97 percent of the heads of colleges and 98 percent of superior court judges.[123]

There is some hope that a change in public attitudes towards working women will, one day, translate into tangible benefits. Fortunately the changes taking place in the women's world have been accompanied by a marked shift in public attitudes. In her concise and well-written book *Gender Politics,* Ethel Klein traced these changes over the past 50 years. In 1937, 72 percent of the United States population did not approve of women holding jobs when their husbands could work. Legislators in almost every state introduced bills restricting the employment of women because so many men were unemployed. A Gallup Poll of 1939 showed overwhelming public support for such legislation. When the war came, there was a massive switch in opinion, and by 1942 some 62 percent were in favor of women working. This was a repeat of what happened during World War I, except that when 1945 came, 60 percent of a cross-section of employed women indicated that they planned to continue working after the war. On the other hand, 62 percent of the general population, tested by opinion polls, disapproved of married women being employed. However, as women kept on working and materially improved the conditions of the family, the opposition gradually dropped. By 1967 only 27 percent disapproved. The figure has hovered around this mark ever since, while the approval rate went up from 18 percent in 1945 to 55 in 1967 and to 72 percent in 1978.[124]

Not only do people today recognize that women's lives have changed, but women's entry into the non-traditional roles now also has wide support. Looking at the year 2,000, nearly 75 percent of all men and nearly 85 percent of women believe that by that year all adult women in the United States will be working. Almost half the population believes that marriage as a lifetime commitment will no longer exist, and 65 percent believe the male homemaker will become accepted. More than 70 percent of the public today also support feminists' efforts to ensure stricter enforcement of laws against wife abuse and the banning of discrimination against women in the workplace and in education. Some 63 percent already support the expansion of federal assistance for child care centers.[125]

Will men's perceptions of the role and subordinate status of women change and, if so, how fast?

No one can really tell. Ten years after the decision to erect a memorial monument for the men who served in Vietnam, the male-dominated United States Senate finally got so far as to approve a single statue to honor the 10,000 women who served in the same war.[126]

During the 1980s some individual women did exceptionally, even spectacularly, well in the marketplace. But it means little to women in general to trumpet, as Marcia Cohen did in *The Sisterhood,* that in the Fortune 500 companies 60 percent of women officers are paid $117,000 per year. There is no shortage of such role models in the United States. The fact that Susan Estrich became the first woman to lead a presidential campaign (that of Michael Dukakis, the Democratic Party nominee for the election of 1988) is not going to lead to a sudden upsurge in the number of women in Congress, or in the Senate.[127] What is of more importance than the high salaries earned by senior women executives in the Fortune 500 group is the fact that in the same group 64 percent of personnel managers admitted that there was sexual harassment in their companies; 90 percent of all companies had received formal complaints of sexual harassment; 35 percent have been hit with lawsuits; and nearly 25 percent have been sued repeatedly, despite the guidelines on sexual harassment published in 1980 by the Equal Employment Opportunity Commission and despite the fact that 76 percent of the companies reported that they had written policies banning sexual harassment.[128]

Discrimination and sexual harassment will not go away until American men are educated about women's rights and their roles in a modern economy. And that is a formidable, long-term undertaking. As the National Academy of Sciences reported: "Sex segregation is a deeply rooted social and cultural phenomenon. It is perpetuated not only by barriers and constraints, but also by habits and perceptions."[129] Role models such as Susan Estrich and Justice Sandra Day O'Connor are very important in such a task, but only in their proper perspective. When Justice O'Connor was appointed to the Supreme Court, only 5.4 percent of all federal judges were women, and of over 20,000 judicial positions only 900, or 4.5 percent, were held by women. As Karen Morello, a role model herself in the world of lawyers, wrote: "The forces that once kept women out of law altogether simply have shifted now to keeping them out of powerful positions within the law."[130] American Bar Association statistics show that in 1988 20 percent of all lawyers were women, compared with only 4.7 percent in 1970, but a year-long investigation by the A.B.A. about women in the legal profession led investigation head Hillary Clinton to publicly express her shock as to how much overt discrimination against women still existed.[131]

Women themselves have not been fooled by publicity given to role models. A 1987 Gallup Poll found that *fewer* women today believe that women share equal opportunities with men, particularly for jobs, than was the case in 1975. In addition, 50 percent felt women were denied access to executive positions. On the other hand, men's opinions, according to the same poll, did not change. In both the 1975 and the 1987 polls, the vast majority of men believed that men and women have the same opportunities.[132]

The major event marking the increased awareness of women's issues during the bicentennial year of the United States Constitution was the national conference "Women and the Constitution," which was convened by four former first ladies under the auspices of the Carter Center of Emory University in Atlanta. Summarizing the feelings of participants and other women at the start of the conference, June Schneider reported: "We found that an overwhelming majority of people agreed that although women have made significant strides, they are still unfairly treated. Women do not earn as much as men, their access to power is still obstructed, sexual stereotyping still impedes their progress.... For many the career/family conflict remains burdensome. Personal, social and institutional sexism abounds."[133]

That was the situation in 1988, a state of affairs not that much different from 1978. The chances are that a decade from now widespread meaningful change will still not have taken place.

Part Six: The Communist East Bloc

In terms of the Soviet constitution women enjoy absolute legal equality with men, and ever since the Bolsheviks came to power in 1917 they have also committed themselves, ideologically, to sexual equality in all walks of life. Yet forty years after the Revolution, there were only eight women among the 307 members of the Communist Party Central Committee, not one on the 109 National Council of Ministers or in the all-powerful 13-member Politburo.

17. General Survey

Perspectives on Equality

Communism claims to have emancipated woman and provided her with an equal place in society, not only with equal rights but also with equal opportunities. At the First International Conference for the Decade of Women, held in Mexico City under the auspices of the United Nations, the East Bloc delegates (some of them wives of heads of state) all claimed that women in their countries were already liberated, therefore, not women's rights but world peace and disarmament ought to be the key topics of discussion.[1]

The "achievements" in the Soviet Union and other Communist countries have been noted with admiration in many Western nations, but more so in the Third World, which has accepted Soviet propaganda at face value. The Communist countries have made disinformation into a science, and seeing that the status of women in most Third World countries has been so utterly subordinate and lacking in opportunities (in Ethiopia fewer than 1 percent of women are literate), the position of women in the Soviet Union, relatively speaking, is indeed close to paradise. The same Soviet propaganda, so readily, and naively, accepted by educational institutions and politicians in the Scandinavian and other western states, has also suggested that women in the Soviet Union were better off than women in the West. The reality, for various reasons, has been slow to dawn, though a decade ago prominent Western researchers already debunked the myth of the "glory of Soviet womanhood." As political scientist and Sovietologist Barbara Jancar pointed out in her comparative, interdisciplinary study of women in the Communist world, Westerners have only had carefully selected impressions and incomplete knowledge upon which to base their opinions.

While Communist regimes may be useful vehicles for the emancipation of women in societies in the initial stages of industrialization, said Jancar, severe and permanent ideological and political strictures inhibit women's further advance. She found that sexual stereotyping and all its consequences exist in Communist nations as well. Women are primarily unskilled or semi-skilled workers. Women do become medical doctors in greater percentages than in the West, she said, but she pointed out that medicine in the Communist world enjoys much less prestige and even within the medical profession in the East Bloc there is male-female stratification. Hungarian women doctors, she discovered, could not aspire to become gynecologists or urologists because these carried more prestige and male entrance quotas are much higher than for women. In other branches of society, she said, few women reach positions of executive power. A survey of 16,000 Bulgarian women revealed that there were no women in management positions in finance and credit, agriculture, construction, or forestry. Only .04 of 1 percent identified themselves as managers.[2]

One of the claims made by the Communist country representatives at almost every international conference on the rights of women is that in the Communist Bloc, constitutional and other statutory provisions are such that women's equality is ensured in almost every walk of life; furthermore, the very nature of the Marxist-Leninist system (state socialism politically controlled by the Communist Party) is such that a women's rights movement would be an academic exercise. The problems which women encounter in the West, so the Soviet argument runs, can be traced directly to the nature of capitalism. This refrain is repeated at every opportunity and was advanced by almost every speaker from the Communist Bloc at the international conference of women in Nairobi to mark the end of the United Nations Decade for Women.

In her study of women under Communism, Jancar found a situation which totally contradicts this argument:

> With heavy-handed paternalism, the Communist regime tells each citizen that there is only one way to the future, one meaning of women's liberation, one goal: to work. Neither men nor women have many options in life style. But if men are limited in their choices in Communist societies by the constraints of educational opportunities, influence, and party loyalty, women are even more limited by the dual commandment to work and bear children. What is not allowed either sex is sufficient space to develop according to individual inclination. Women fall into a lower category because they bear the special responsibility of producing the next generation, and every Communist country puts this responsibility ahead of a woman's development as an individual. Thus, while Communist systems have had great success in mobilizing women into the work force, educating them, and moving them into what the West has considered high-status professions, women as a group tend to be more apolitical and less visible in positions of political, economic, and social power in the Communist countries (with the possible exception of China) than in the West or the developing nations.[3]

The image of a state system in which women have no problems with equality, either in terms of the constitution or the law, or in competing on an equal footing with men is pushed in every document dealing with the rights of women submitted by the U.S.S.R. and other East Bloc countries to the United Nations. Taken at face value, these reports show women in the Communist countries to be living in a feminist paradise—not only in the Soviet Union, but in Czechoslovakia and the Communist Republic of Mongolia.

The following are extracts from the Mongolian report to the United Nations of March 1984, which is a masterpiece in extravagant claims by Communist officialdom:[4]

> 70. The representative of Mongolia introduced his country's report by giving a brief summary of the historical, political, socio-economic, cultural and geographical aspects. Since the revolution of 1921, he pointed out, much had been accomplished in the development of Mongolia and one of the most significant achievements was the realization of full equality between men and women in all aspects; any attempt to deny women's rights was punishable by law.
>
> 71. The representative of Mongolia pointed out that the women of Mongolia

were among the first in the Orient to acquire political, economic and civil equality. Mongolian women formed 49 percent of those working in economic and cultural activities.

72. Attention was drawn to the demographic situation and it was pointed out that children under 16 accounted for 47.1 percent of the population and that 65 percent of the population was under the age of 35. The representative of Mongolia pointed out that the Government had given much attention to the question of illiteracy which, before 1921, stood at 98 percent and which was now totally eliminated. Currently, of every 10,000 persons, 2,373 attended general educational schools, 246 attended specialized secondary educational institutions and vocational schools and 130 attended higher educational establishments. In fact, every fourth person was studying.

73. In Mongolia, the representative continued, the basic provisions of the Convention on the Elimination of Discrimination Against Women had become a reality. Women enjoyed all political rights on an equal footing with men; the same rights at all levels of education, which was free; and the same rights in terms of employment and remuneration. Paid maternity leave was granted and special consideration was given to nursing mothers. As a result of systematic all-round socio-economic and health-related measures taken by the Government in the past 65 years, the country's population had increased threefold, and life expectancy had more than doubled and now reached 67.

92. In responding to the questions raised, the representative of Mongolia stressed that equal rights were guaranteed in his country and that the solution of women's problems was inseparable from the general advancement of his Government.

93. With regard to questions raised on employment, the representative pointed out that, under socialism, every citizen has a guaranteed right to work and to receive payment for work in accordance with its quantity and quality. There was no unemployment and there was equal pay for equal work.

94. The representative of Mongolia stressed that all able-bodied women who wish to are permitted to study or are employed in the national economy and culture, and today there is no branch in the economy and culture where women are not employed. Women made up 49.2 percent of the labor force in 1983, 46.6 percent in material production and 57.2 percent in the non-material sphere; he cited some figures for the participation of women in the labor force. In order to protect women from undertaking certain kinds of hazardous work, the Labour Code forbade the employment of women underground at work that was heavy and hazardous to women's health. A woman cannot be dismissed because of pregnancy or because she is nursing a child, nor can her wages be lowered because of these conditions.

95. With regard to questions on pensions, the representative stated that the Pensions Act and the Labour Code gave all citizens the entitlement to an old-age pension: women at the age of 55 and men at the age of 60. Many people, he pointed out, did decide to continue working beyond the retirement age.

96. The representative of Mongolia pointed out that illiteracy had been eliminated long before, and that compulsory eight-year education had been introduced. He also cited some statistics on education and pointed out that female students comprised 55.7 percent of the student population.

97. With regard to the family, he replied that men and women had equal rights in family relations; all members shared in household duties; women had equal property rights; and children born out of wedlock enjoyed the same rights as other children. It was also possible for men to take special paid leave to look after a sick child, spouse or parent.

98. The representative of Mongolia pointed out that motherhood was considered a privilege and an honor. He also informed the Committee that the decision

for the number of children rested with the spouses; medical care and education were free; and creches, education and cultural facilities were also free. Women had benefits of maternity leave and there were additional benefits for nursing mothers. It was pointed out that rural women enjoyed the same social and political rights as urban women.

If these remarks are to be believed, there is no doubt that Mongolia is the most progressive, liberal country in the world insofar as women's rights are concerned. The same would apply to other Communist states. In replying to some probing questions on the status of women in Czechoslovakia during the discussion of that country's report to the United Nations Committee on the Elimination of Discrimination Against Women, the Czech delegate made the following observations, no less extravagant than those of Mongolia—even blaming the world's oldest profession, prostitution, on the tourist trade from the capitalist countries (see paragraph 184).[5]

174. Several mechanisms existed in Czechoslovakia to ensure that equality between men and women was exercised: through law, which unequivocally gave the conceptual foundation of this principal; through the court system, where both sexes had the same rights and duties; by appealing through higher courts if the first judgement was found discriminatory; by independent women's commissions operating in enterprises and plants; through the Czechoslovak Union of Women already mentioned; by the National Committees, which had the right to inform other competent authorities of discovered violations pertaining to the equality between women and men; and by trade unions, through their influence in examining labor norms.

175. He stated that the difference in the wages of women and men could be favorable as well as unfavorable to women. Salaries were determined on the basis of stipulated criteria with a minimum rate and a maximum limit. The criteria included practical experience, educational background and personal capabilities. Though subjective elements could play a part, ultimately the objective factors were the decisive elements in wage classification. The Government, he added, enforced the principle of equal pay for equal work and more printed information would be made available to the Committee.

176. The number of women holding executive, political and public offices was now twice as high as 10 years before. The Chairperson of the Czechoslovak Union of Women was a Secretary of the Central Committee of the Communist Party. Women were fairly represented in senior posts at the medium and lower levels of management. In the trade unions, he stated, women constituted 50.1 percent of functionaries in enterprise committees. In the Central Trade Union Council, 38.5 percent of the membership was made up of women. As to the judicial system, women were 60 percent of the judges. (In fact, "judges" in Communist states are Communist Party officials appointed to the post—author.) Forty to 50 percent of the Socialist Youth Union was made up of women functionaries.

177. The care of children in kindergartens was financially covered by the State while the parents only contributed to the catering by paying 5.50 or 6.5 koruny per child per day. At this time, existing nursery facilities were not fully utilized due to years with lower birth rates. However, the existing facilities were still being used, giving women more spare and leisure time.

184. The Penal Code did not include explicit provisions on prostitution since, in 1961, when the Code had been adopted, the problem did not exist. The representative stated that, with the development of international tourism, prostitution had been brought into Czechoslovakia. Obstacles to this practice were contained in provisions of labour and tax legislation. However, the latter did not apply to foreign nationals and adequate countermeasures were very difficult to formulate.

How true are these answers and statements?

Almost every important student of discrimination against women in the Communist countries has found that sexual inequality is a fact of life despite the aims and pronouncements of state socialism.[6] In Chapter 31 these reports from Czechoslovakia and Mongolia to the United Nations Committee on the Elimination of Discrimination are discussed to indicate to what extent they can be accepted as credible.

A Profile of Working Women in the East Bloc

In 1983 there were nearly 214 million women in the socialist countries of Europe, of which the female population of the Soviet Union alone was more than 145 million. During the decade 1970–1980, the economically active female population increased more rapidly than the female population as a whole in most of the Communist countries, particularly in Czechoslovakia, East Germany, Hungary, the U.S.S.R. and Yugoslavia. In East Germany the percentage rose from 41 in 1971 to 49 in 1982. In the Soviet Union and other East Bloc countries the proportion of women of working age active in the economy ranged from 70 to as high as 90 percent. In Poland the figure was 68 percent, the lowest, but in the Soviet Union more than 93 percent of women were either working or studying at universities or technical schools (Soviet and East Bloc statistics).[7]

The official statement, that in the Soviet Union and other East Bloc countries women work in all economic sectors and in virtually all occupations except those which demand "arduous and hard labor," can be proved to be untrue. (See the next chapter.)

According to what the Soviet Union told the International Labor Organization, there have been major increases of women in the engineering field, in machine construction and in the chemical industry. In the U.S.S.R. women account for 52 percent of the work force engaged in the electronics industry and 67 percent in the manufacture of precision instruments and radio engineering. In Hungary some 53 percent of the labor force in the electronics industry in 1983 were women. In that year, fewer women were engaged in the agricultural than in the industrial sector. With technological progress the structure of female labor in the agricultural sector has changed significantly. Some 55 percent of all experts in animal husbandry and 37.5 percent of all veterinary surgeons are women (all official Soviet and East Bloc statistics).[8]

While in most Communist countries more than 60 percent of all the teachers are women – more than 70 percent of teachers in health, social security and physical education – women are said to have also made heavy inroads in the field of science. In the East Bloc as a whole in 1983 some 40 percent of scientific workers, varying from medicine and biology to physics, genetics and chemistry were women. A steady increase in the number of women with doctorates and master's degrees was also reported between 1975 and 1983, with the number increasing by 70 percent in Hungary and 30 percent in the U.S.S.R.

Country	Labor force change			
	Both sexes	*Males*	*Females*	Share of women in total labor force change
Bulgaria	9.8	4.7	15.7	74.3
Czechoslovakia	5.2	5.1	5.4	46.6
German Democratic Republic	5.3	0.0	10.5	99.0
Romania	18.9	11.8	31.6	60.0
USSR	9.1	10.2	8.1	45.3

Country	Labor force as a percentage of population 15–64 years					
	Both sexes		Males		Females	
	1975	*1984*	*1975*	*1984*	*1975*	*1984*
Czechoslovakia	74.2	75.4	81.9	83.0	66.6	68.0
German Democratic Republic	76.0	76.1	81.0	74.8	71.5	77.5
Hungary	72.0	71.0	82.5	79.3	61.9	63.0
USSR	71.5	71.7	74.8	73.7	68.6	70.0

Top: **Table 49. Percentage Change of the Labor Force in the East Bloc by Gender and Share of Women in the Total Labor Change, 1975–1984. Source: Economic Commission of Europe, Geneva, 1985.** *Bottom:* **Table 50. Labor Force Participation by Sex in the East Bloc, 1975–1984 (Percentages). Source: International Labor Organization,** ***The Economic Role of Women in the ECE Region,*** **Geneva, 1985, p. 14.**

The Pattern of Discrimination in East Bloc Countries

According to Suzanne Korosi's article in *Sisterhood Is Global,* sexual discrimination is a quite banal feature of Hungarian society. She observed that while the proportion of skilled women in industry has decreased during the previous decade, that of unskilled women has increased. Among men just the opposite trend was found. The same is true of agriculture and the service sector. The inequality between men and women is not only by profession and general education, but that all social and economic policy measures that have dealt with the situation of women in Hungary was based on the belief that man is the principal breadwinner and that women's income was merely to supplement the breadwinner's contribution.[9] This attitude is shared by many other governments, even in the industrialized world, such as the Republic of South Africa where joint income is taxed so heavily that almost 50 percent of women not working cite taxes as being one of the prime reasons for staying out of the marketplace.[10]

Poland, with less emphasis on an increase of the population and, thus, the labor pool, reflects the same picture of legal equality and, in practice, obvious

Country	All sectors	Non-farm sectors	Industry	Services
Bulgaria				
1965	44.0	35.5	30.9	42.4
1975	46.8	45.1	40.4	51.0
1980	47.1	47.7	41.6	55.5
Czechoslovakia				
1961	41.0	38.2	32.3	48.2
1970	44.7	44.6	37.4	54.4
1980	46.6	47.4	38.3	59.4
German Democratic Republic				
1964	44.2	43.3	33.8	54.4
1971	46.3	46.5	37.3	57.7
1980	52.4	53.7	38.9	66.6
Hungary				
1960	35.1	33.6	28.5	40.3
1970	41.2	42.1	36.6	50.3
1981	44.9	46.6	39.4	54.4
Poland				
1960	43.3	33.4	26.0	41.6
1970	46.0	40.5	31.5	51.9
1980	42.7	44.4	34.8	54.8
Romania				
1956	45.3	26.4	20.2	33.9
1966	45.2	29.2	21.3	39.9
1970	32.7	33.9	26.7	42.8
1980	38.7	40.2	35.1	46.9
USSR				
1959	51.9	44.2	40.6	47.9
1970	50.4	49.8	41.3	58.7
Yugoslavia				
1961	36.6	27.9	22.3	35.4
1971	36.8	31.2	25.4	39.0
1980	35.5	36.3	28.1	41.2

Table 51. The Share of Women in the Total Labor Force of the East Bloc by Major Economic Sectors, 1960, 1970, 1980 (Percentages). Source *The Economic Role of Women in the ECE Region,* Geneva, 1985, p. 42.

inequalities and discrimination. Sociologist Anna Titkow observed that equality of the sexes in Poland is only a "trite platitude" although it does exist formally in legislation.

> At the same time, however, no women are present in the government, or in the groups of decision makers, or in the authorities of the Polish Workers' Party, or in the leadership of the free trade-union movement, Solidarity. Women do not dominate in low-prestige occupations, but sex equality in occupational prestige in Poland seems to be rather vacuous; power and income are not its correlates. Women's employment does prevail in the worst-paid branches of the national economy: education, health care, administration, and various services. In 1979

women comprised the majority of workers in the service sector (90 percent)—among clerks (76 percent) and salespeople (90.4 percent). About 60 percent of all working women are employed in the above-mentioned branches, and they earn 30 percent less than men. Occupational promotion of women is much more difficult than that of men, even in such "feminized" occupations as, for example, teaching—where women comprise 70 percent of the employees, but only 10 in 100 women hold executive posts. The all-Polish surveys on time-budget show that professionally working women are four times more burdened with housework than men.[11]

Rumania is the best example of how the Communist countries plan their provisions for women, not with the principle of equality in mind, but to bridge the economic shortcomings and achieve the objectives of the state. As pointed out in *Sisterhood Is Global,* the entire thrust of Rumanian Communist Party policy is to enhance the status of the family and to enable women to have more children so as to increase the labor pool. To this end all kinds of advantages are passed on to working mothers. The Constitution states specifically that the state shall protect marriage and the family and shall defend the interests of mothers and children. Nothing is said of the interests of the fathers. In the political arena there is the usual token representation by women in the National Assembly (33 percent) but only some 10 percent in the government. The state does not furnish separate data on wages for men and women, but the concentration of women in agriculture (99 percent of the agricultural labor force according to International Labor Organization figures), in the service sector, in unskilled jobs, in textiles (78 percent of all workers in 1983) and in health care (74.5 percent in 1980) inevitably results in lower wages.[12]

When it comes to legal provisions in the Rumanian state, women appear to be well taken care of.

Article 18.2 of the Constitution supports the principle of protective labor legislation for women. Thus, night employment is restricted for all women and prohibited for those more than 6 months pregnant or nursing children. The Family Code (Article 1) states that "Marriage with full consent of the spouses shall be the basis of family life . . . men and women shall have equal rights in relations between the spouses and with regard to children." Article 42 of the Family Code stipulates that in matters of divorce the courts shall decide custody in the interest of the children.

The state actively encourages women to have four children or more. Beginning with her third child, a mother receives a financial grant. (Also, the Order of Heroine Mother, or the Maternity Medal, is given to women with many children.) Women who care for their children up to age 18 receive a monthly allowance, increasing with each child. Women cannot be fired for pregnancy or during maternity leave, nursing leave, or sick leave, and pregnant women are entitled to various free checkups for pre- and ante-natal care.[13]

As far as the gap between the income of men and women is concerned, available statistics indicate that, although not strictly comparable, disparities in earnings between men and women in the East Bloc countries are about the same as those of the Soviet Union. (See following chapter.)

According to *Women in the World,* Yugoslavia is the only Communist

Year	Country and Labor Force Group	Female Earnings as % of Male Earnings
1969	Czechoslovakia: socialist sector	66.2
1970	Czechoslovakia: socialist sector	67.1
1972	Poland: socialist sector	66.5
1972	Hungary: state sector	72.5

Table 52. Gross Earnings Differentials in the East Bloc Between Men and Women. Source: A. McAuley, *Women's Work and Wages in the Soviet Union,* George Allen and Unwin, London, 1981, p. 23. Reprinted with permission of Unwin Hyman Ltd., London.

country in Eastern Europe where there are significant differences with the Soviet system, principally because the Yugoslavs have partly broken away from the iron grip of the Soviet Union and are pursuing a much more independent course in the economic field. It is the only Communist state whose constitution provides for private farms. Although the farms may not exceed 10 hectares in size and are therefore too small to be really productive, the government has set up co-operatives to assist the independent farmers, of whom half are women, and assisted in the modernization of the farms.[14]

Although the pattern of under-representation at high political levels is the same in Yugoslavia as elsewhere in the Communist world (in 1982 there were only 53 women out of 308 members in the National Assembly and only 273 out of 1,480 members of the six socialist republic assemblies which make up Yugoslavia), nonetheless in 1983 Milka Planinc became the first woman to be appointed as Prime Minister in a Communist state. Early in 1978 the Executive Council of the National Assembly had passed a resolution aimed specifically at the betterment of the social and economic position of women.[15]

The Yugoslav state, as such, has also been extremely active in promoting real public awareness of the concerns of women. Yugoslavia sponsored several international seminars on women during the United Nations Decade for Women, and its official women's association co-operated with women's associations in a hundred other countries. Yugoslavia was also instrumental in calling the Bagdad conference on women in development in 1979 for the non-aligned nations. Finally, it held many public meetings to assist the government in preparing a special report on women to be filed with the United Nations committee monitoring the elimination of discrimination, though the report was not quite the success the Yugoslavs had anticipated.[16]

There is also another substantial difference between Communist Yugoslavia and the Soviet Union. There is a small independent women's movement in Yugoslavia which at times is quite active, and which is not tied to either the state or the Communist party. In any other state in the East Bloc, this group would have been banned or exiled. In *Sisterhood Is Global,* Rada Ivekovic wrote with understated sarcasm:

> It was said that the law had given them equal rights, and that many women were in the work force. Indeed, most women worked, but they were and still are expected to perform household duties as well. In politics or in workers' self-management control of their enterprises, women are usually found in posts of low and local responsibility. Patriarchal mentality remains widespread in Yugoslavia and fosters confusion by repeating a sophism: "Women have all rights *by law*, so they already *are* equal."[17]

While "neofeminism" is permitted to exist, said Ivekovic, this does not mean that it is free from attacks. Most of the criticism directed at these women cites the so-called six mortal sins: (1) Feminism is an imported ideology, from the capitalistic world. (2) It reveals a love for power—the Communist Party complains that neofeminism merely wishes to replace female power for male power. (3) It is guilty of elitism because too many intellectuals among women are involved. (4) It represents an uninstitutional activity and since this cannot be controlled (by state or the Communist Party) it is therefore dangerous. (5) Its activities are apolitical which will dilute women's roles as builders (*sic*) of the socialist society. (6) Finally, the feminist theory excludes women's issues from the class struggle where, in the eyes of the Communist theoreticians, it rightfully belongs.[18]

For the rest, women in Yugoslavia find themselves in the same predicament as in the other East Bloc states. Occupational segregation is widespread.

Agriculture, textiles, education and service sectors form the ghetto of women's occupation. Work segregation had actually increased by 1980. Comparing the statistics of 1970 with 1980 shows that in teaching, textiles and social services the percentage of women workers had increased between 4 and 5 percent.[19] Statistics show there has been little change in occupational segregation in the last three decades. According to Olivera Buric, about 70 percent of all textile workers in the country are women and women constitute about 80 percent of those employed in non-industrial economic activities, for example, as public servants in social work and health care. In her study of women workers in Yugoslavia she wrote that permanent tenure on the job is guaranteed by law to men and women and dismissal occurs only for serious offenses. "However, sex discrimination does occur in hiring. If a man and a woman apply for the same job, his chances of being hired are better than hers . . . because business and industrial organizations are discouraged from hiring women, especially young mothers. . . . The law guarantees long maternity leave to mothers as well as leave to take care of ill children under the age of seven." She also pointed out that the industries where many women are traditionally employed are lagging because technology in female-dominated industries is outmoded.[20]

It is true that women, overall, have increased their participation on the important workers' self-management councils to as much as 29 percent in 1979. But in the controlling bodies they were only about 5 percent. One study indicated that among directors of state enterprises there was only one woman among the 115 men and only eight women were among the directors of schools.[21] When the figures of women in the Workers Councils are analyzed, researchers found that women did best in the small business sector. According to Miroljub Labus in *Women Workers in Fifteen Countries,* in the smallest businesses there are 33,000 council members, of whom 46 percent are women. The large-scale enterprises are run by 9,000 members of Workers Councils, of whom only 14 percent are women. In Yugoslavia business and industrial organizations are grouped into five sections of which small businesses are at the bottom of the scale in importance. In small businesses women are 10 percent of the top managers. In large-scale enterprises there are virtually no women at the top.[22]

While the Yugoslavs have made much of the improvement in women's education, this improvement has not translated into real, tangible benefits to women in higher levels. Sources quoted by Joni Lovenduski indicated that a larger increase in male than in female activity was found as the educational hierarchy was ascended, with the result that in Yugoslavia the gap between men's and women's activity rates was greatest in the best educated segment. Thus education was less beneficial to women than to men in terms of its effect on political activity.[23]

Political Power and Women's Labor

According to Lovenduski, the bottom line is that in the political field the Communist Party controls all the available gateways to political power and sets the terms and describes the forms political activism will take, including the nature and status of women's movements. If it is not political discrimination against women then it is, at best, political exclusion on sexual grounds. In general, she wrote, East European women have greater access to such resources as education and employment than in the West, but this has not led to concomitantly greater economic or political power. Women's presence in politics has been more visible at lower and local levels. East Bloc women have been more active in non-partisan groups such as school boards and friendship societies than in political parties. There has been a steady increase in membership of women of the Communist parties in the East Bloc, but this has not been accompanied by greater representation by women in leadership positions at national level. Thus in East Germany women, who in 1981 were 33 percent of the members of the Socialist United Party (the ruling Communist elite), held only 13 percent of the Central Committee places but no place in the Politburo.[24]

The popular image of the East Bloc, or of almost any Communist state, said Lovenduski, is that workers' organizations, labor unions, are a key element of party power and thus one type of organization which could effectively promote the interests of women at all levels. Lovenduski states that it is true East European labor unions do have specific capacities to defend women's interests but these do not rise from an independent collective bargaining role as they do in the West. "They are rather capacities specifically designed by the state to enable unions to carry out responsibilities for ensuring the implementation of sex equality at work. . . . When assessing the general pattern of women's high visibility in East European unions it should be remembered that the unions there rarely, if ever, involve themselves in an autonomous action. They are concerned with conditions of work, with plant fulfillment. . . ."[25]

Country	Constitutional Provision	No.
Bulgaria	Complete Equality	0
Rumania	Complete Equality	1
China	Complete Equality	1
Soviet Union	Complete Equality	1
Czechoslovakia	Complete Equality	0
East Germany	Complete Equality	0
Poland	Complete Equality	1
Vietnam	Complete Equality	0
Yugoslavia	Complete Equality	1

Table 53. The Communist Bloc: Women in the Politburo. Soviet Union 1988. All others 1985.

The exception can be found in East Germany, where policies on women's employment have been extremely comprehensive, making that country the most regulated of all Communist societies in the East Bloc, even more so than the Soviet Union. East German trade unions run extensive affirmative action programs in which the promotion of women is stipulated and enforced by agreements made with management.[26]

In the state socialist systems of the East Bloc the benefit of the absence of an established powerful structure for collective bargaining is neutralized by the concomitant absence of any independent organizations which might express women's interests. As Lovenduski pointed out, "State policy makers in this respect have a clear field for the formulation and the implementation of measures directed at women." She found that in the U.S.S.R. the high participation rate of women in the economy is also a product of economic and demographic goals. The shortages of male labor have simply made women's employment a vital component of economic strategy. Up to 92 percent of Soviet Union women of working age are in paid employment outside the home. Even when the women's question has been given new recognition, it is posed in terms of the needs of the economy or of population replacement. Similar patterns are to be found in East Germany and Czechoslovakia.[27]

In East Germany the Constitution and the Labor Code both stipulate that the state is required to create the institutions and the conditions whereby a woman may combine a full professional life with roles as a wife and mother of children. Thus in 1980, 92 percent of all children between the ages of three and six years were cared for in state-supported kindergartens and over 60 percent of all infants were cared for in the state-supported nurseries. The state has also set out to train women as productive economic units. By 1980 some 70 percent of all working women had completed some vocational training. Nearly 52 percent of the students in building material technology in 1974 were women.[28]

Women entered the labor force in Eastern Europe much earlier than in the West, and women's participation in paid employment still exceeds the levels in the free world; however, it is a myth that complete equality has been achieved in those areas of importance to women. According to one of the world's leading experts on the Communist East Bloc, Sharon Wolchik, Russian-speaking professor of international affairs at the Institute for Sino-Soviet Studies at George Washington University, reality reflects a less euphoric vision. Wolchik states that it is true that differences between the sexes have not been eliminated in access to either education or the labor force. But in all countries (of the East Bloc) girls continue to follow general education programs rather than vocational, an observation born out by the statistics in Table 54, columns 4 and 5.

In higher education, Wolchik found, most women still tend to specialize in areas such as education and the humanities, considered "appropriate" for women, and in medicine, which has become heavily feminized since the establishment of the Communist systems. Wolchik wrote:

> The effects of continued difference in educational specializations are evident in the area of work, for there is still considerable sex segregation in the labor force in all East European countries.... Most women continue to work in highly feminized branches of the economy, such as education and culture, trade and public catering, health and administrative services. This tendency is also true of women with specialized educations and professional women ... women earn on the average approximately two-thirds the wages that men do. This difference in income, which is also a reflection of the fact that women tend to be assigned and to accept job classifications ... other than those for which they are qualified, outright discrimination and the paucity of women who are trained as skilled or highly skilled manual workers, does not vary greatly from one country to another.[29]

Wolchik also found that women's educational levels have undoubtedly risen in all of the East Bloc countries and that rates of economic activity outside the home have also increased but that there has been no spill-over effect into the decision-making political arena:

> This exception was only partially fulfilled. While women are somewhat more active politically now than in the pre-Communist period in most of these countries, substantial differences persist in the extent of political activism of men and women, particularly at the elite level. Despite the changes noted above and despite the important differences in the organization and nature of political life in Communist states, women's political behaviour in Eastern Europe and the Soviet Union displays many of the same patterns evident in women's participation in politics in western democratic countries.[30]

Women in Eastern Europe play a very small role in the exercise of political power. As observed by Putnam, women's participation in political decision-making circles conforms to "the law of increasing disproportion," i.e., as the importance of the office increases, the number of women declines.[31] What this means, wrote Wolchik, is that they play a greater role in leadership at the local level and are more frequently found in deliberative bodies than in the Politburo or the cabinet. By 1978 two women had been selected for the Romanian Politburo, bringing their total to only eight out of 199 members in all of the East European countries for that year.[32]

In *The Politics of the Second Electorate,* Sharon Wolchik states that, given the small number of women in the political elite of the East Bloc, "there

Country	Total female labor force as percent of female population 15–64, 1980	Gross enrollment ratio of female students at third level 1977/78	Proportion of female students registered in: Humanities and arts 1977/78	Proportion of female students registered in: Science, engineering, medicine, etc., 1977/78
Bulgaria	72	21	17	48
Czechoslovakia	75	14	4	34
German Democratic Republic	74	34	3	43
Hungary	63	13	3	22
Poland	70	20	10	35
Romania	70	9	..	..
USSR	75	23	3	48

Table 54. Educational Factors and Female Labor Force Participation in the East Block, 1980. Source: L. Paukert, "Personal Preference, Social Change or Economic Necessity? Why Women Work," in *Labour and Society,* International Institute for Labor Studies, Geneva, Vol. 7, No. 4, 1982.

is little relationship between the educational and employment levels of women in particular countries and their representation in either government or party elites." She added:

> More important in explaining the limited role which women play in leadership in all of these countries are popular attitudes and the legacy of traditional cultures which view different spheres of activity as appropriate for men and women. The influence of these views is evident in many areas of life and limits both the supply of and demand for women activists. Many men and women in Eastern Europe continue to see politics as a man's sphere. Given the different types of educations men and women receive and the occupations women enter, they do not develop the specialities which would be useful politically. Nor, in most cases, are women employed, in jobs which require high levels of political activism.[33]

18. Case Study: The Soviet Union

Policy and Reality

Since 1920 Soviet law has (ostensibly) provided for total equality between men and women in the Soviet Union. This is the picture which the Soviet Union is currently trying to project, particularly at the United Nations and other international forums. The only occupations closed to women, its officials have declared, are those considered to be too "arduous" for women.

What is the true situation?

In 1965 about 60 percent of the women working at an ore enrichment plant in Eastern Siberia were involved in activities listed as "hard physical labor." At another plant women made up more than 70 percent of steel erectors and concrete workers. They are 55 percent of transport workers, 95 percent of crane operators and 97 percent of motor mechanics. Elderly women chip ice and sweep streets in the bleakest of winter mornings.

The foregoing picture by *Christian Science Monitor* correspondent David Willis, of Soviet women doing the same hard physical work as men, is not confined to one area such as this eastern part of Siberia. In the country as a whole, he wrote, one in every three construction workers is a woman, carrying bricks and mixing cement in sub-zero temperatures. In many factories in Moscow women carry the same heavy loads as men.[1] Gail Lapidus also wrote that in agriculture the overwhelming proportion of women is engaged in heavy manual labor while men move into the newly mechanized jobs. A similar situation, she found, prevailed in industry.[2]

Thus the first lesson to be learned in a study of women in the Soviet Union is not to take any Soviet policy statement or statistic at face value. The same applies to any law or constitutional provision the Soviet Union displays to the world. Article 35 of the Soviet Constitution of 1977 proclaims the equal rights between men and women, but every statistic on women's wages compared to men's and on occupational segregation disclaims this provision.

Whenever a movement has been started, independent of the Communist Party or the state, to promote the rights of women, the organizers have been severely dealt with. The founders of the Leningrad women's paper *Almanac: Women and Russia* were forced into exile in 1980.[3] One of the most incisive recent articles on the problems women face in the Soviet Union and particularly in trying to get some attention for the women's movement in Russia entitled, "It's Time We Began with Ourselves," was written by Tatyana Mamonova, one of those exiled in 1980.[4]

Gail Lapidus wrote in her landmark study of women in the Soviet Union that Russian women were indeed well ahead of their West European counterparts in terms of their access to university education and on par with American women in enrollment at medical schools just on the eve of the 1905 revolution. (After the Bolsheviks came to power in 1917 they publicly committed themselves to sexual equality.) Lapidus believes this was an ideological commitment, founded on principle, but that the real reason has much more to do with the disastrous loss of millions of lives, mostly men, during the forcible collectivization and Stalinist purges of the 1930s, followed by the loss of over 20 million during World War II. Small wonder that in 1946 there were only 59 men for every 100 women in the 35–59 age group. According to Lapidus, by 1959 some 30 percent of all Soviet heads of household were women.[5]

These enormous shortages of men during the post-Stalin era brought 18 million more women into the ranks of the paid employed, and women have formed more than 50 percent of the paid work force since 1970, some 16 years before women in the United States reached that level. Surveying these developments, Joni Lovenduski wrote that in the post-Stalin era, Soviet women benefited by policies "derived largely from economic, military and demographic events. Policy on women and their changing status appears to have been as much a result of the logic of those events as it has to any Marxist-Leninist commitment to feminine emancipation, sex equality or equal opportunity.... Improvement has always been a by-product of policy designed for some other higher purpose.... Soviet women, whether as women or otherwise, have had little say in the determination of those 'higher' purposes."[6]

Women and Political Power

The history of Russian culture shows that traditional Russian society was woman-centered in its divinities, folklore, art, and social organization. The religion of the Great Mother Goddess stems from the Eastern Slavs, carriers of the myth of "mother earth," from which the name "Mother Russia" developed. The introduction of the patriarchal Christian religion was followed by decades of progressive denigration of women, and from the Muscovite to the Imperial period the Russians, who constitute almost 50 percent of the population of the U.S.S.R. today, also grew increasingly patriarchal.[7] After the Imperial period and under the Communist Party, "Mother Russia" became a nationalistic political logo, synonymous to the German "Fatherland." In 1988 Alexandra Biryukova became only the second woman in the history of the Soviet Union to be appointed to the all powerful Politburo of the Communist Party and the first woman since 1961; however, she is a non-voting member.[8]

There are 149 million women in the Soviet Union as against 136 million men.[9] In the Communist Party, which controls all power in the Soviet Union, women comprise 29 percent of the membership. As a reward they have one, non-voting woman member of the Politburo, and fewer than a dozen of their number in the 307-member Central Committee.[10] The percentage of women on the Central Committee is not only small (3.5 percent), noted Genia Browning, but it has not increased during the entire 70-year history of the Soviet Union. The Central Committee meets only twice a year. The work of its various

Year	**Total female population (thousands)**	**Female labor force**				
		Number (thousands)	*As percentage of female population*		*As percentage of total labor force*	*As percentage of world total*
			Total	*15 years and older*		
1950	101,022	48,593	48.1	64.3	51.8	14.1
1975	136,589	63,058	46.2	60.4	49.7	11.0
1980	142,454	65,862	46.2	59.6	48.7	10.6
1985	148,326	66,671	44.9	58.4	47.7	9.9

departments is supervised by the Secretariat, which consists of top male Communist Party officials. Browning wrote that the Communist Party claim, that women in the Soviet Union are more politically active than their Western counterparts, cannot be justified since the women to which the party refers are all at the lower level of the political structure. For example, in the local Soviets (or councils) women participate in almost equal numbers to men.[11]

So much for women's position of influence at the decision-making level of the Communist Party. The situation in the official parliament of the Union of Soviet Republics, the Supreme Soviet, is somewhat better. After the elections of 1979 women formed 32 percent of the deputies to the Supreme Soviet. At the very top, however, in the Praesidium, they constituted only 11 percent. Down at local level, again, they formed 49 percent.

The Soviets have never been able to explain why women, given their high representation at local level, do not seek higher office. General attitudes can best be described by the reply which a Soviet woman physicist gave to the question: that the main acts of equality in 1917 were introduced by men, and since men support equality therefore it is not necessary to have a similar number of women in power positions! On party level, a spokesman for the Communist Party Central Committee said that the committee had people specializing in women's problems and attention is given to the question in party policy adopted at each congress. Hence there is no acute necessity for a woman in the Politburo. Officially, Soviet government explanation for women's unequal representation is threefold. First, the sexual division of labor gives women too much responsibility at home for them to devote time to politics. Second, traditional attitudes toward women still exist and lead to some discrimination. Third, female political consciousness still falls behind that of men.[12]

According to Lovenduski, women's under-representation at policy-making levels has been so startling that "a student of Soviet politics could safely use the *absence* of women in a high party or state organization as an indicator of that organization's importance! That this is the case is one of the ironies in the wake of the first government ever to have produced a policy directed at women's emancipation."[13]

In some areas women's participation in politics even declined between 1944 and 1974. In *Women in Soviet Society,* Gail Lapidus quotes official Soviet statistics to show that in Tadzhikistan women formed 30 percent of the party membership in 1944 and only 18.9 percent in 1974. In primary Communist Party organizations women formed only one-third of the total. Women formed less than four percent of all urban and district party secretaries in the U.S.S.R. in 1973. Despite the new Soviet Constitution and its liberal phraseology, she wrote, the fact is that since 1928 the proportion of women in the Central Committee has never exceeded 4.3 percent.[14]

Table 55. Labor Force Participation of Women in the Soviet Union, 1950, 1975, 1980, 1985. Source: International Labor Organization, "Labor Force Estimates and Projections 1950–2000," *World Summary,* 2nd ed., Vol. 5, Geneva, 1977; and data from the Bureau of Statistics, International Labor Organization, Geneva, 1984.

Other researchers have uncovered similar information. Since World War II only two women have been members of the Soviet Union's Council of Ministers, and only seven of 550 deputy ministers and deputies of ministries and state commissions of the U.S.S.R. have been women.[15]

Wage Discrimination

One of the most important claims which the Soviet Union has made, in its official communications and documents submitted to the United Nations and at international conferences dealing with the rights of women, is sexual equality in work and wages in the U.S.S.R. In fact, writers critical of the subordinate status of women in the West have often held up the Soviet Union as a model of what could be achieved, both in the economy and in society at large. One researcher who successfully destroyed this myth early on is Alastair McCauley. His study *Women's Work and Wages in the Soviet Union* is a landmark analysis. McCauley made the point that those who have praised the Soviet system "have confused Soviet aspirations with Soviet reality, have taken the exception for the rule, have failed to consider the full range of available evidence and explore the shortcomings of Soviet politics along with their successes."[16]

Since earnings differences are one of the most important factors used in evaluating discrimination against women, Tables 56 and 57, prepared by McCauley, are largely self-explanatory.

The disparities in salaries and grade classifications persist despite the fact that women (nationally) equal or surpass men in total completed years of general secondary and higher education. Indeed, Joel Moses wrote, women overall tend to be the least mobile workers in industry.[17] Both Lapidus and Chapman calculated that, at best, women's earnings are a maximum of 87 percent of those of men.[18]

McCauley concluded that the earnings disparities between men and women in the market appear to be substantial although he concedes that the study of this question is made difficult by the fact that the Soviet Union (because it denies the existence of *de jure* or *de facto* discrimination against women) does not publish official data on wages and salaries classified by sex. In McCauley's opinion, the male-female earnings differential was not seen as a pressing political or economic problem in Moscow.[19] He also stated:

> In so far as sexual inequality can be measured by disparities in earnings, Soviet policy must be adjudged to have failed. In the 1970s the gross earnings of women were some 60 to 65 percent of those of men. This disparity is of the same order of magnitude as that observed in an industrial economy like Britain; it is somewhat greater than those found in Eastern Europe or in Scandinavia. Further, although available statistics leave much to be desired, there is little to suggest that differences in the earnings of men and women have diminished in the past two decades.... While segregation may have fallen among white-collar workers, it appears to have increased among manual non-agricultural employees. Further, women still predominate in occupations that elsewhere are regarded as women's work – the textile trades, garment manufacture, and services; they possess fewer industrial skills

Date	Location and Labor Force Group	Male Earnings (R per month)	Female Earnings (R per month)	Female as % of Male Earnings
1960–5	Leningrad: workers	n.a.	n.a.	69.3
1963	Erevan: state employees	114.59	74.29	64.8
1965–8	S. Russian industrial town: workers	131.00	84.00	64.1
1967	Latvia: women who married in 1959	120.89	76.03	62.9
1968	Kiev: divorce petitioners	134.00	88.00	65.7
1965–70	Moldavia: industrial employees	(145–155)	90–100	58–69
1965–70	unspecified	n.a.	n.a.	66.7
1970	Kiev: newlyweds	116.00	84.00	72.4
1972–4	European Russia: urban workers	160.30	96.50	60.2
	urban white-collar	188.90	113.10	59.9

Year	Location and Labor Force Group Covered	Male Earnings (R per month)	Female Earnings (R per month)	Female as % of Male Earnings
1966–67	Moscow; food processing employees	90–93	52–57	61–64
1964	Novosibirsk; machinebuilding:			
	new hires, workers	97.4	74.1	76.0
	quils - lathe operators	89.4	73.6	82.0
	-labourers	94.7	67.8	72.0
	-5 occupations	93.2	73.1	78.0
1968	Ukraine; metallurgy employees	127.0	86.3	67.9
1970	Leningrad; machinebuilding:			
	married workers	149.1	108.1	73.0
	unmarried workers	132.6	98.6	74.0
1973	Kiev; cotton-spinning:			
	basic process workers	n.a.	n.a.	86.0
	auxiliary workers	n.a.	n.a.	57.0
	knitwear:			
	basic process workers	n.a.	n.a.	86.0
	auxiliary workers	n.a.	n.a.	67.0
	confectionary: workers	n.a.	n.a.	90.0

***Top:* Table 56. Gross Differentials in Male-Female Earnings in the Soviet Union, Multisectoral Samples. *Bottom:* Table 57. Gross Differentials in Male-Female Earnings in the Soviet Union, Single-Sector Samples. Source for both tables: A. McCauley, *Women's Work and Wages in the Soviet Union,* George Allen & Unwin, London, 1981, p. 25. Reprinted with permission of Unwin Hyman Ltd., London.**

> than men; they are less likely to work with machines.... Women have penetrated many male occupational preserves. But women are still under-represented in positions in which they might be called upon to exercise managerial authority.[20]

The disparity in earnings cannot be attributed to rate discrimination in any sense, concluded McCauley. It cannot be ascribed to differences in hours worked either. Thus, for the most part, disparities must be the result of occupational segregation. Later studies, such as the comprehensive survey of women in the Soviet Union by *Time* magazine in 1988, found that though women are train conductors, engineers, garbage collectors and construction workers, they more often than not receive less pay than their male colleagues for the same work.[21]

Occupational Segregation

Soviet statistics show that women's percentage of the total Soviet workforce exceeded 50 percent in 1970 for the first time after World War II. (In 1945 women constituted 56 percent of the workforce.) Since 1970 the percentage has remained constant at 51 percent. Today almost 90 percent of able-bodied adult women are either employed or engaged in study, almost all of them full time.[22] Some Soviet professions have become virtual female preserves. Women represent 75 percent of all teachers, 69 percent of all physicians, 87 percent of economists, and 91 percent of the labor force in the service sector, more than 80 percent in the credit and state insurance sector and 84 percent in public health, physical culture and social welfare. In industry, where women represent almost half of all production personnel, they constitute over 80 percent of food and textile workers and over 90 percent of all garment workers. Lapidus found that women predominate in the lower and middle levels of white-collar and technical employment but are very under-represented in supervisory and managerial positions. Moreover, within any given occupation or workplace, women are concentrated at lower levels of the job pyramid. She said that this segregation by economic sector and occupation cannot be ascribed to an older generation of women with limited education and fewer skills. The educational attainments of the female labor force, she pointed out, now match and even exceed those of males. She cited a study of industrial enterprises in Taganrog which found that 40 percent of all female workers with higher or secondary specialized education occupied low-skill industrial positions, compared to only 6 percent of males with comparable educational attainments.[24]

The Soviet Union, like the rest of the Communist East Bloc (like the rest of the world), therefore also harbors a series of pink ghettoes for women.

Women are vastly over-represented in the service level, amongst lower white-collar occupations and in the sub-professions. The only difference is the fairly high proportion of women, about 16 percent, employed in agriculture, which Lovenduski describes as "a symptom of residual backwardness" in the Soviet economy, and a high proportion of women in engineering, about 44 percent at the end of the 1970s. Dodge found that in 1970 certain professions (typical of the pink ghetto) contained between 70 and 90 percent women: primary and secondary school teachers, other lower teaching professions, bookkeepers, technical laboratory assistants, communication workers, midwives and others.[25] McCauley's study revealed that working women had an average of only 19 hours a week of free time, compared to men's 31 hours.[26]

Similarly, another observer (Sachs) found that women predominated among textile workers, garment workers, waitresses, postal workers, orderlies and nurses, varying from almost 85 percent among textile workers to more than 98 percent of orderlies and nurses.[27] Within the Soviets' "pink ghetto" for women, females are considerably less likely to be in the more senior, better paying jobs. According to Gail Lapidus, the percentage of women becomes progressively lower as each higher level is reached in the agricultural, industrial engineering, medical, educational and scientific communities.[28]

As far as vertical segregation in the labor market is concerned, McCauley states that an investigation of the wage differential system already indicates that the Soviets have been unable to guarantee equality of opportunities to women in the labor market.[29]

After a detailed examination of official and private documents and statistics, McCauley came to the following conclusions concerning vertical and administrative segregation:

> The evidence, though far from ideal, has tended to confirm the existence of both. Among female manual workers, there has been little change in the character of mass occupations in the past thirty or forty years; they are still heavily concentrated in semi- or unskilled non-industrial or traditional occupations. This suggests that women possess less industrial training than men. Further, for those women in industry (and, by implication, in other branches of material production) conditions of work are often unpleasant: work is monotonous and frequently involves considerable effort.
>
> Among white-collar workers there has been more change. Again, women are to be found in large numbers in routine clerical occupations and in traditional 'caring' roles. But, in increasing numbers, they have moved into specialist and professional positions demanding considerable prior training. And, if they are still seriously under-represented in areas which call for or permit the exercise of managerial discretion, which confer authority over others . . . both the character of the occupations that women now do in the Soviet Union and the changes that have occurred in the past thirty to forty years imply the existence of extensive occupational segregation between the sexes. And this in turn is consistent with substantial earnings disparities.[30]

The Soviet Union has defended itself against criticism of sex segregation in the marketplace by pointing to the fact that in the judiciary women's position is roughly commensurate with their presence in the legal profession. In 1975 women were 30 percent of the lawyers and 32 percent of the people's judges. There were 27 women judges of the higher courts and 14 of 45 people's assessors were women. In Moscow women were 43 percent of the prosecutors and investigators in the procuracy. Commenting on this, Joni Lovenduski states:

> Aggregate data such as these give no real indication of women's standing in the

judiciary other than demonstrating that men remain in the majority. In the institutions of state administration, women are known to predominate in the routine and clerical posts. However, the fusion of politics and administration is almost total in state socialist societies, where there are no ideological requirements for maintaining political neutrality amongst bureaucrats. Indeed a strong commitment to party goals is an essential qualification for senior positions. Women's share of such positions is not known but is unlikely to be any greater than their share of party membership.[31]

Marriage and Motherhood

A Soviet study published in the Moscow press in 1986 cited housing as the most acute problem confronting young married people. The survey of the City of Minsk found that 50 percent lived with parents (in tiny cramped apartments) and fewer than 3 percent in their own apartments. As a consequence, young people are eager to get married to get their names on the official waiting list for their own accommodations. While people are marrying at a later age in the West, in the Soviet Union, reports *Time* magazine, the age is dropping. A Moscow State University survey, prepared by its Center for Population Studies in 1986, found that 25 percent of Soviet women marry at age 18. *Time* also cites a 1986 study published by the Communist youth newspaper that one-quarter of women who marry are pregnant and another third become pregnant within nine months.[32]

Youthful marriages, crowded living conditions, and heavy drinking on the part of men has led to a massive divorce rate. Soviet divorces are now running at almost one million per year and close to 600,000 children are joining the swelling roster of single-parent households each year, said *Time.*[33]

For the vast majority of women in the Soviet Union, the main means of birth control is abortion. Since 1960 some seven million abortions have been performed each year. Sex education is rarely taught in school. Unhygienic conditions at gynecology clinics are widespread and even officially admitted. This inattention to women's health seems curious, and even contradictory, given the state's emphasis on child bearing. The state actively tries to encourage women to press past the usual two-child-per-family rate, offering a one-time bonus for a third baby and early retirement from employment to those women who have more than five children.[34] Women are also paid money on the birth of the first and second child.

In an attempt to get couples to marry and have children, priority on housing lists is given to couples with children. Increasingly women are being looked upon not as individual human beings but as economic units, human reproductive units. In 1981 it was announced in the Soviet press that the 26th Congress of the Communist Party, in order to make "demographic policy" truly effective, had approved important measures designed to increase the prestige of motherhood. Beginning in 1981 working women were eligible for partially paid leave until a newborn child reached one year of age. They were also given the additional right of leave without pay to take care of the child until it reached age 2. Afterwards the mother could return to work without suffering an interrupted work record. All these measures were introduced to emphasize child care as a purely female domain and to permit working women more time to perform their customary duties inside the home.[35]

There is no indication, whatsoever, that the foregoing measures had anything to do with making Soviet motherhood less drudgery to the individual woman. Writing in *Soviet Sisterhood,* Mary Buckley said:

> Many policy-makers feel that women should be encouraged to have more children in order to diminish future labor shortages and to check the falling birthrate. Russians, Ukrainians, Lithuanians, Latvians and Estonians, in particular, are encouraged to have more children due to consternation about the gap between high birthrates among Soviet Moslems and low birthrates among Slavic and Baltic peoples. It is in the interest of the Soviet state to have more children, and therefore it is the duty of Soviet women to bear them. In short, pro-natalist policies have affected Soviet ideology on women and the family. They have injected it with biological determinism and also fostered references in the press to femininity, to the personality traits of the fair sex and to the rewards of motherhood. . . . Soviet theorists go further than stating the obvious point that women and men have different reproductive functions. . . . They make a leap of inference . . . that . . . women have a duty to the Soviet state not only to produce children (three is the desired number), but also to take proportionally far more responsibility for their upbringing than men.[36]

Soviet leader Mikhail Gorbachev has not deviated from the foregoing policy objective developed during the days of his now much maligned predecessor, Mr. Leonid Brezhnev. Speaking at the opening session of the World Congress on Women in Moscow in June 1987, Gorbachev referred pointedly to women's "inherent functions, those of mother, wife, the person who brings up the children." Later in a television interview, he referred to women's "predestination," that is, "as keeper of the home fires." The Soviet leader has promised to increase child allowances for low-income families and to extend pre-school child care.[37]

Women, Soviet Society and Ideology

One obvious question is why wage disparities between men and women and vertical segregation in the workplace should occur in a Soviet socialist system which has legalized women's equality to an extent no other country outside the Communist Bloc has achieved and then crowned it with a large dose of ideological justification. According to Lovenduski, the answer lies in the fact that (a) the Soviet Union has over the past decades created its own class system, even though it was ideologically dedicated to fighting the stratification of society by class; (b) women's equality was based on biological thinking on the part of the Soviets; and (c) in a system which deliberately maintains male political power, women have become only a utilitarian concern, not a human concern.

In his notable and extremely interesting book, entitled *Klass,* David Willis wrote that Russia is the most class-conscious nation in history, but while even the rural peasants rate as a class, the majority of women, compared to men, "remain the statusless sex." Willis, who had spent more than four years in Moscow as the representative of *The Christian Science Monitor,* said that because of the lack of proper contraceptives for women abortion has become the best legal contraceptive.[38] The highest ranking woman official in the Soviet Union, Alexandra Biryukova, non-voting member of the Politburo, told Western news correspondents in January 1989 that the number of abortions approximately equaled the number of births. She lamented what she called the "abnormally high" abortion rate and the lack of proper birth control measures. An article in *Moscow News* early in 1989 said that nine of every 10 first pregnancies are aborted and that many women have had four or five abortions "because it was nearly impossible to find contraceptives." Mrs. Biryukova conceded that "these complaints were well founded."[39]

Willis also writes that while the Soviet Union has long held itself up as a model for women's liberation movements, liberation has been only partial. "Soviet women have failed to win social equality in a land where traditional Russian sexism is still overwhelming." He added that it was not Soviet society but the Communist Party which reserved for itself the sole right to determine the conditions under which Soviet men and women may live and work. The women's organizations are kept in rein. The attitude is that in the Soviet Union "women are more useful than equal." Willis cited numerous examples of the way men dominated society and enjoyed social and sexual liberties denied to the average Russian woman. He rejected the Soviet argument that the presence of almost 500 female deputies of the Supreme Soviet is a good example of women's political influence and input in the Soviet Union for the simple reason that deputies have no power. "They are selected by the (Communist) party amid stage managed hoopla and transported to Moscow twice a year to ratify decisions already made by the Politburo and Central Committee secretariat." In other words, they form only part of the official rubber stamp. Women do much better in the trade unions, but Soviet labor unions "are merely conveyor belts on which CP discipline and rewards reach the work force and which carry back reports on workers' moods and complaints."[40]

Two Swedish researchers, Carola Hansonn and Karin Liden, have also written extensively about the problems of women in their book *Moscow Women.*[41] According to them, women are also discriminated against in the Soviet Union because of traditional sex-role attitudes:

> The ideology of equality that the Soviet Union embraces is based on "biological" thinking which helps to explain why the myth of equality has become so entrenched. Not only the physical differences between the sexes, but also the psychological ones are considered to be biologically determined.... Soviet sociologists and experts on women's questions believe that the demand for equality must be tempered by the basic differences between the sexes ... that make them less suitable for certain "demanding" assignments. In this way the consequences of biological thinking become a permanent impediment to improving women's place in the work force. Even though the means of production have been taken over by the Soviet state, there hasn't been any change in a work pattern originally set up by men for men.... And we know the consequences: ... Women are more poorly paid and have lower status than men, male competitiveness is allowed to crowd out women.... Today the Soviet Union still talks about expanded social services as the most important

solution to women's problems.... Soviet conception of femininity doesn't have any cultural or social overtones.... Instead the conservative sex-role model is the one that is persistently reinforced in schools, cultural life and the mass media.... The community and the work place are almost exclusively dominated by male standards and ideals....[42]

In *Women in Soviet Society,* Gail Lapidus wrote that despite a deliberate expansion of female political and economical participation in the Soviet society the past decade "the terms on which it occurred both sustained and reinforced a pervasive asymmetry of male and female roles. This ... was not merely a consequence of cultural lag, but reflected, rather, a coherent, mutually reinforcing and systematic pattern of official perceptions, priorities, and institutional arrangements that impinged on every dimension of social structure." Ms. Lapidus presents a strong case, based on Soviet official sources and documents, that "the utilization of women as a major political and economic force ... could not help but transform the very meaning of equality, ultimately draining it of libertarian and humanitarian underpinnings and infusing it with instrumental and utilitarian concerns.... Sexual equality ultimately came to mean an equal liability to mobilise." She pointed out that Soviet patterns of political authority precluded the emergence of a genuine civic culture that would permit the political participation of men and women alike as citizens. "The very recognition accorded women as a collectivity is itself a reflection of a subject political culture in which no autonomous group activity is permitted."[43]

According to Lapidus both classical Marxist theory and Soviet revolutionary ideology were insensitive to the deeper psychological roots of family patterns and sex roles. "By assimilating sexual relationships into Marxist models of stratification, Soviet ideology obscured the ways in which patterns of sexual inequality derived from irrational and indeed unconscious psychological processes.... Soviet ideology thus concentrated on the more superficial economic aspects of women's roles...."[44]

Lapidus' views of Marxism and women are shared by those of the German researcher Marielouise Jannsen-Jureit, who observed that in the few instances where Marx makes special mention of women, it is always to say that the cheaper women's and children's work supplants that of a man.[45]

In the Soviet Union there is a critical distinction between mobilization and liberation. "The fact that women were perceived as a major economic and political resource was compatible with an extreme degree of exploitation," Lapidus observed.[46] The Soviet version of affirmative action was protective labor legislation, public child care institutions, expansion of educational opportunities—all aimed at providing more and educated labor units. Entry to schools and technical institutions was carefully regulated, she said. There was no intention of really opening Soviet economic society to women because they deserved it as fellow Soviet citizens; the aim was to regulate the supply of labor. In support of this she quotes Soviet figures that of 607 students attending a special school for mathematics and physics in Novosibirsk only 11 percent were girls. She also found that even during the 1970s there was substantial evidence that discriminatory admissions policies persisted.[47]

Prospects for Women in the U.S.S.R.

Women are now the most educated class in Russia, even though class is officially denied them.

Between 1970 and 1983 the proportion of female students in higher education is said to have increased from 49 to 53 percent in Russia. The fact that women are the most valuable and trained human asset the Soviets have will unfortunately not lead to freedom from the many other forms of subordination. The U.S.S.R. admits that the professional and technical schools train pupils for 1,498 different occupations, of which women are now trained for only 968.[48] It is necessary to view most of these census statistics from the Soviet Union with considerable skepticism; nonetheless, in view of the legal equality in education to which the Soviet state lays claim, the fact that women are not trained for 530 occupations (nearly 30 percent) is in itself a rather damaging admission.

In his chapter "The Soviet Union in the Women's Decade" in *Women of the World,* Joel Moses described the period 1976–1985 as somewhat of a turning point because women's issues received more attention than at any other time since 1920. Yet real political power remains in the hands of men. And in the Soviet Union it is political decisions, directing the economy, which most affect women. It is at this level, said Moses, that there is no input by women or by independent women's organizations, unlike some Western states, notably the Scandinavian countries.

But the Soviet Union, wrote Moses, in publishing reports citing the low level of political participation by women in trade unions and other organizations, "has now re-activated many women's councils and commissions." They have been re-activated "both to mobilize politically working women and homemakers and to articulate distinct female interests as organizational counterweight to the still male dominant local party and trade union committees."[49]

Joni Lovenduski concluded:

> Clearly in a one-party state the decisive feminine political participation will be that which takes place within the party. Positions of responsibility and effectiveness in the state bureaucracy, the planned economy and the elective assemblies are all closely controlled by the party. That party has been unable, despite considerable efforts, to recruit women to its membership in any proportion to their presence in the society; and it has been apparently unwilling to promote those recruited into positions in its leadership. . . . There are no women making the feminist case in the contemporary Soviet elite and the radicalism of Bolshevik feminism died with socialist democracy in the U.S.S.R. It is therefore unlikely that the kind of thinking necessary to produce a sustained attack on sex-differentiated domestic roles, not to mention the concept of domestic roles itself, will emerge.[50]

Skepticism that all is not necessarily well in the (Soviet-claimed) socialist paradise for women is evident from the rare admission by a state body that Soviet women are losing the battle for equality. In January 1987 the state-sponsored Soviet Women's Council acknowledged that Soviet women, in fact, hold some of the country's most physically demanding and lowest paying jobs and were losing ground in their fight for equality. It was also an admission that the law, which states that women have equal access to all occupations, except those which are physically arduous, is not respected, or simply not applied. The report reflected long-held views that life for Soviet women is very difficult, despite official statements to the contrary and the Soviet Constitution's provision that women must enjoy full equality.[51]

The foregoing admission by the Soviet Women's Council is all the more remarkable given the fact that women have served the Soviet Union well, particularly after the massive loss of male lives during World War II. In addition (as the Russian sociologist Professor Vladimir Shlapentokh observed), sociological studies have shown that Russian women are superior to Russian men in many respects. There is a high degree of alcoholism among Soviet men not found among the women. In 75 percent of divorce cases in Moscow, alcoholism is cited by women as the main cause. Women also reveal much higher moral values than men, and there is an exceptionally high percentage of women at universities where they are doing very well and where intelligence tests have proved them to be as well endowed with intelligence as men.[52] In any event the Soviet government has shown no leniency towards women who became involved in actions "detrimental to the state," whether this included efforts to obtain immigration rights for Jews or efforts to promote religious freedom. One of the worst cases in the Soviet Union is that of Sister Valeriya Makeyeva, who was arrested in 1979 for making belts embroidered with quotations from the Psalms, and placed in a penal psychiatric hospital where she was subjected to forced injections.[53] Another was the banning of the feminist publication *Almanac,* which publicly criticized the patriarchal behavior and approach of the Soviet system.[54]

With a declining birth rate (seven million abortions per year) and a divorce rate in 1988 of 515 divorces for every 1,000 marriages, the Soviet government is now concerned about the labor supply 20 years down the road. The party needs workers and wonders how to push up the birthrate while keeping the women on the job. One answer in 1980 was to ban women from 460 occupations on the grounds that the work is too arduous or too dangerous. Another was to make life easier for women and to boost the birthrate. In this way the entire principle of equal treatment for women in the Soviet Union is made subordinate to economic considerations. The Soviets are also leaning towards the East German model of lending money to newly married couples which is then repaid in children. The first child represents repayment of 40 percent of the loan. A second child pays off the balance.[55] The new practical ideology has constructed femininity as motherhood and child rearing. Thus femininity is politically structured, a decision taken entirely by males and which has little or nothing to do with female self-determination. As women in the West, slowly but at least progressively, become more free to determine their own future as individuals, Soviet women become less so.

In a special introduction to the work of Hansonn and Liden, Sovietologist Gail Lapidus, commenting on the main thrust of their book, said that the potential impact of Western feminist values and perspectives on Soviet women is limited by various factors. Soviet women do not know what the program of women in the West embraces and to the extent that it is perceived as hostile to men, or critical of the family as a social institution (an image enjoyed by the National Organization of Women in the United States) it holds no attraction for the average Soviet woman who values marriage, children and the family.[56]

The Soviet Union's leader, General Secretary Mikhail Gorbachev, has now candidly admitted that past Soviet policy in respect of women was wrong but in advancing his vision of future Soviet policy falls into the same trap. Although he only uses the word "shortcoming" to describe past policy, he proceeds to state in his new book *Perestroika: New Thinking for Our Country and the World* that there are now, in fact, heated debates in the Soviet press, in public organizations, at work and at home about the question of what the Soviet Union needs to do to make it possible for women to return to their purely womanly mission. Thus Hansonn, Liden and Lapidus correctly saw that the U.S.S.R. is now anxious to get women back in their homes for purely economic reasons, namely, to help push up the birthrate, although Gorbachev has phrased this in an almost Western understanding of the problem.[57] Gorbachev admits, for example, that over the years the Soviets have failed to pay attention to women's specific rights and needs arising from their roles as mothers and homemakers. Though he claims the state put an end to the discrimination women suffered under Czarist Russia, and that women gained a legally guaranteed social status equal with men, this is clearly not what happened in practice. Perhaps *de jure,* on paper, but not *de facto* as several researchers have pointed out.

Gorbachev also concedes that with all the work women were doing they no longer had enough time to perform their "everyday duties" at home such as housework, the upbringing of children and the creation of a good family atmosphere. He said that many of the Soviet Union's problems with young people's behavior were caused by the weakening of family ties. This, he wrote, was the paradoxical result of the Soviet's sincere desire to make women equal with men in everything.

Unfortunately, while recognizing the problem, Gorbachev missed the essential point which Hewlett (*A Lesser Life*) and others have made, namely, that it is not only the woman's task to create the right atmosphere at home, to educate the children, to do the housework and to strengthen the family ties, responsibilities specifically mentioned by Gorbachev as falling exclusively on women's shoulders, but also that of men.[58]

Gorbachev indicates that women's future role in the U.S.S.R. should be more that of housewife and mother when, instead, he should have advocated that men also assume more responsibilities at home, and that social and economic policy be structured in such a way that it helps women to fulfill their dual roles as workers and mothers. The new policy will also fail, because the Soviet Union cannot do without women's labor while, at the same time, women are expected to have more children and to be the homemaker. The reality is that no woman can be in two places simultaneously.

Glasnost has given birth to a trickle of articles on male insensitivity and the problems of women.[59] Earlier gushing praises of Soviet socialism for having liberated women have been replaced by more sober appraisals. Soviet sociologists have now admitted that the reality of the women's question is much more complex than Soviet literature had allowed. From an official achievement of socialist construction, solving the women's question has become a distant goal.[60] It is true that when Mikhail Gorbachev addressed the women's international congress in Moscow in June 1987 he enumerated the benefits and legal rights Soviet women enjoy, but he also asked: "Can we draw the conclusion that everything is in good order? Frankly, no."[61]

Yet there may be hope. In March 1989 the Soviet Union announced that it will henceforth accept the authority of the World Court in major human rights treaties, thereby ending 40 years of resistance to the court's jurisdiction. The Soviet Union had signed the treaties but had always added the reservation that it did not accept the World Court's authority in disputes. The Soviet Foreign Minister, Mr. Edward A. Shevardnadze, said that his country would specifically recognize the binding jurisdiction of the court in the 1952 Convention on the Political Rights of Women and the 1979 Convention on the Elimination of All Forms of Discrimination Against Women.[62] The fruits of *perestroika* may yet benefit women, as long as President Mikhail Gorbachev remains in power.

Part Seven: Latin America

In Latin America abortion is responsible for more deaths and health problems of women of childbearing age than any other cause, but even medically safe abortion is forbidden by law in most Latin American countries.

19. General Survey

Trying to obtain up-to-date (1980 or later) reliable and comprehensive statistical material about the status of women in Latin America and the Caribbean, even for elementary topics such as literacy, school education, university attendance, occupational segregation, or wage differentiation, is one of the most vexing tasks facing any researcher. Such data are non-existent, are extremely dated, or have escaped the attention even of the International Labor Organization (to which all states in the region report), the United Nations' specialized agencies (such as the Economic Commission for Latin America), or other, non-governmental, organizations such as the World Bank.

A United Nations study of the status of women in nine Latin American countries in 1983 tried to establish the pattern of female labor by branch of economic activity. The best the research team, working on the spot, could come up with was statistics for the period 1970–1973, i.e., 10 years old or more. Argentina, Mexico, and Brazil could do no better than provide figures for 1970. Ecuador could provide no information.[1] The Office of Women in Development of the U.S. Agency for International Development did not fare much better. In a study issued in 1984, the statistics for female enrollment at university were all for 1970. The only exception was Colombia, which had figures for the mid-1970s. Countries such as Argentina, Venezuela, Brazil, Bolivia, Cuba, and Chile could not tell how many women were enrolled at their universities in the mid-'70s. When it came to indicating which subjects women were studying, Bolivia, Chile, and Venezuela could not say how many women were studying economics at university in 1968, 1964, and 1971 respectively. The larger, richer, and more developed countries, Argentina and Brazil, could provide statistics only for 1972 and 1973, and Mexico for 1969.[2]

As in the case of Africa and Asia, which suffer from the same malaise, this did not prevent the various Latin American and Caribbean states from suddenly producing statistics for 1980 and later, when it came to the 1985 U.N. International Conference for Women in Nairobi. Countries such as Ecuador, Peru, Venezuela, Cuba, Bolivia, Chile, Colombia, Argentina, Brazil and Mexico, which two years earlier had been struggling to get statistics for the years 1970–1972, suddenly produced statistics for 1980.[3] Some countries did indicate that some of their statistics were from the years 1973–1976; nonetheless, the unfortunate impression gained is that most figures for 1980 were, at best, mere window dressing, "guesstimates," at worse artifically created under political pressure to produce something for the Nairobi conference.

The most recent United Nations–sponsored studies on the status of women in Latin America were the result of a decision taken at the 15th session of the Economic Commission for Latin America in Quito, Ecuador, in March 1973. The commission requested recommendations as to the measures to be taken to eliminate discrimination as well as a report on the lack of educational, employment and economic opportunities for women. The 188-page document was published only 10 years later, in June 1983, though it was written as a position paper for the second conference on the Integration of Women into Latin American Economic and Social Development, held in Caracas, Venezuela, November 1979, four years earlier.[4]

A study of Latin American and the Caribbean by the Economic Commission for Latin America said that changes in the status of women from 1975 to 1985, when they have occurred, have been more a reaction to global influences than to policies or actions by governments in the region directed specifically at women. The increased number of women with access to education was part of a global movement set in motion by the U.N. declaration of 1975 as the Year for Women and of 1975–1985 as the Decade for Women. The 1960s and 1970s were also marked by substantial migrations all over Latin America, a flow to the cities but similar to what happened in Africa and Asia. As a consequence, women had easier access to education, the urban labor market and means of communication.[5] In a special article dealing with population growth *The National Geographic Magazine* said in December 1988 that in the decade up to 1950 urban growth in Brazil was 34 percent, but for the decade up to 1988 the growth was 71 percent.

The Economic Commission for Latin America classified most public policies aimed at women as of a focal or "experimental nature." In some countries the laws were changed but mostly in a family context, for example, equality of the woman in the married couple. Policies for the greater integration of women have run up against conceptual and traditional views of the role of women as mothers and housekeepers. What information was available to the Commission indicated that the average rate of participation by women in the labor force remained at about 20 percent. "Furthermore, problems persist concerning discriminatory treatment in the area of wages and types of jobs for women, more in private activity than the public sector, in which, in several countries, women have been holding important supervisory positions for many years."[6]

In 1985 Latin America and the Caribbean had a female population of about 198 million, 115 million of which was aged between 15 and 64 years. The estimated female labor force was about 27 million.[7] A small group of countries—Argentina, Brazil, Colombia and Mexico—accounted for the vast majority of the female population.

The highest percentage of women in economic activity was in the rural sector, especially in areas where the peasant economy predominated. In the cities, 50 percent of the women are normally employed in the service industry, most of them as domestic employees. In Brazil, the percentage was as high as 58.7, and in Costa Rica 59.2 The overall pattern of labor segregation has not undergone any fundamental change.[8]

There has been a constant problem of under-reporting of women's activity in all of the Latin American region particularly in agriculture. In-depth data from Peru and Honduras, as an example, illustrate women's contribution to agriculture production while the countries' national statistics tell the opposite. Peru's national statistics indicate that only about 16 percent of women were active in agricultural work, whereas the in-depth survey showed that women participated in agricultural field work in 86 percent of all households.[9]

The International Labor Organization reports that in Latin America, where land ownership is often concentrated in just a few hands, the ownership pattern has begun to be reshaped by land redistribution and the increasing control by multi-national corporations of large tracts of prime agricultural land. Here the tradition is to employ men as farm laborers, and they far outnumber women in paid agricultural work. In Costa Rica, Guatemala, Honduras, Panama, Chile and Colombia, for example, the ration is 10 to 1.[10] For the most part, women work unpaid on their own family land or migrate to town in search of paid employment. Where land redistribution, mostly limited, has been introduced to cushion Latin America's rural poor against the economic depression of the past decade, the women were still in the most vulnerable position of all. In Chile, for example, land was allocated only to people who had been in continuous employment on an estate for at least three years. Since most women were hired only at harvest time, the majority did not qualify for land.[11]

During the decades 1965–1985, said the International Labor Organization, most of Latin America underwent rapid economic and social change. There was a falling trend in the birthrate for all of the region, but in some states the average size of the family increased. Agricultural modernization gave the rural sector more dynamic growth which, in turn, produced a high rate of internal migration. At the same time industrialization has not generated enough jobs to absorb the increasing supply of labor stemming from natural population growth. But the rapid rate of social and economic change was not accompanied by a similar change in values and attitudes, patterns and lifestyles as regards women, their rights and status within the economy, society in general, or in the family.[12]

The pattern of segregated employment is changing at the pace of a glacier. Table 58 shows the proportion of women in administrative and managerial jobs in the manufacturing sector in selected Latin American countries for the period 1980–1982. In Venezuela the percentage of women who were manufacturing workers in 1960 was 18.2 percent, while in 1981 it was 26.1 percent, or an increase of 8 percent over two decades in one of the region's most prosperous states. The growth in Peru was more or less the same.

At the United Nations conference in Nairobi and at the non-governmental meeting in 1985, according to Caroline Pezzullo, Latin American delegates stressed that women have lost serious ground in their struggle for equality and an improvement in their status because of inflation, their country's crippling external debts, the austerity measures required by the International Monetary Fund and their economic and political relations with the United States.[13] In the continent's largest and most powerful state, Brazil, women were forced to collect a petition to present to the Ministry of Agrarian Reform and Development, begging for women to have the same rights as men to land, property and technology.[14]

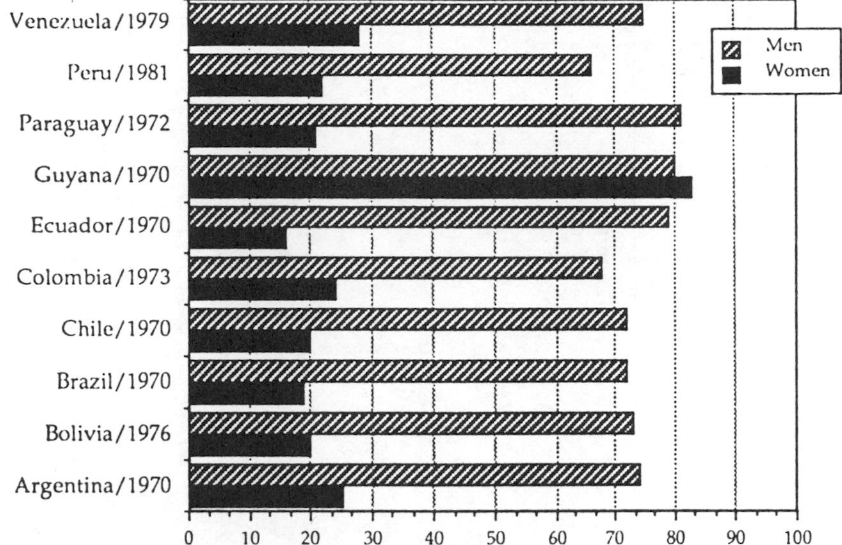

Chart 13. Male and Female Labor Force Participation Rates, South America. Source: *Women in the World,* WID1-4, Office of Women in Development, United States Agency for International Development, United States Department of Commerce, Washington DC, 1984, Figure 5.2, p. 76. Note: Includes females 10 years and older. Guyana includes persons regularly engaged in home duties.

According to the United Nations, education continues to be a matter of concern. In many urban areas primary schools are enrolling both boys and girls on an equal basis, but in rural areas attendance by girls is much lower because their labor is required for subsistence activities. It has been calculated that on average school enrollment for girls aged 10–14 years in rural areas is 60.6 percent as against 86.7 percent for urban areas. This is reflected in literacy rates of 84 percent in cities and 55.6 percent in rural areas.[15] While enrollment of girls at secondary schools is 48 percent of the total, the type of education still contributes to limiting their future, and from the very first year the teaching programs discriminate to a greater or lesser degree between the two sexes.[16] As United Nations observers rightly stated: "In this way the social reproduction role of education has been intensified, i.e., sex divisions in employment are maintained since this educated sector will mainly carry out the traditional functions of mothers and wives."[17]

In particular young women do not acquire the technical qualifications that provide more favorable job prospects. It is true that young women make up some 40 percent of the university student body in most Latin American countries; however, they pursue a very narrow range of university courses that does not improve their prospects for the labor market.[18] The courses preferred by Latin American women in general are social sciences, fine arts, education and nursing.[19]

Country	**Year**	**Administrators and Managerial workers**		**Proportion of women**	
		Men and women (number)	*Women (number)*	*Managers (%)*	*Manufac-turing workers (%)*
Barbados	1982	400	100	25.0	54.3
Chile	1981	19,200	2,000	10.4	23.0
El Salvador	1980	2,910	781	26.8	41.8
Guatemala	1981	3,397	489	14.4	23.9
Panama	1980	3,360	560	16.7	21.8
Peru	1981	15,700	1,315	8.4	24.0
Venezuela	1981	48,152	2,867	6.0	26.1

One other way of looking at the foregoing pattern, however, is that some university education is better than none since studies conducted as far back as 1975 have already indicated that in Latin America women with university education had three times as many chances of being employed as women with fewer than four years of primary education. Higher education becomes even more significant when it is considered that the average wage of a woman with a university education is 6.9 times that of an uneducated woman, whereas the corresponding difference between men is a factor of only 3.7.[20] In fact, in order to compete with men for the same job, women must have *higher* educational achievements, and in the end most women do not even bother to compete with men in the same labor market.[21]

Unlike North America, Australia, South Africa and Western Europe, education in Latin America is not legally compulsory and is consequently directly and negatively affected by deteriorating economic conditions. Only primary education is generally free and, sometimes, legally compulsory, but even where compulsory the legislation is not suitably applied in all countries.

The decade after 1975 produced severe economic recession in large parts of Latin America, particularly as oil prices spiraled down. Because of austerity measures adopted by Latin American governments there has been an interruption in the rapid growth of enrollment in higher education and education has been subordinated to criteria of efficiency and self-financing. The United Nations observed that "... several decades are still needed to achieve the objective that the entire population should complete at least a basic education."[22]

At the time this book was completed (in 1988), one in four adult women in Latin America was unable to read or write. Only 65 percent of girls aged 5–19 were enrolled in first- and second-level schools.[23] It is also the young among the grown women (over 37 million women in Latin America are aged 15–24) who have been particularly hard hit, already the victims of a struggle between tradition and change. Their status was the subject of a special conference in Santiago, Chile, in 1984 held under the auspices of the Economic Commission for Latin America and the Caribbean.[24]

New legislation is still required in several areas in Latin America, particularly as regards the family institution. Joint ownership, parental authority, the duties and rights of spouses to each other and to their children are still based on the Hispanic and Napoleonic legal traditions. But legal reform in Latin America is also a very difficult and sensitive issue because it involved family models with a long history and deep roots. It has often been noted that the problem does not lie so much in the lack of adequate legislation, as in the timeliness of the legislation and the real possibilities of enforcing it. Take Argentina. The proposed law to legalize divorce is being bitterly opposed by the Catholic Church, which has threatened legislators who vote for passage of the law with excommunication, and by vast numbers of women themselves

Table 58. Proportion of Women in Selected Latin American Countries in Administrative and Managerial Occupations in the Manufacturing Sector. Source: International Labor Organization, *Yearbook of Labour Statistics, 1983,* Geneva, 1984.

Country	Year	Total	Agriculture	Economics, commerce	Education	Engineering	Fine arts	Humanities	Law	Medicine, dentistry	Natural sciences	Social sciences
Cuba	1975	35.9	20.1	(NA)	51.2	19.5	(NA)	38.0	(NA)	[1]45.0	49.2	36.0
Costa Rica	1970	37.5	3.6	13.1	64.9	[2]2.7	55.6	40.9	15.9	18.9	(NA)	74.7
El Salvador[3]	1975	33.2	6.8	22.4	[4]52.4	[2]15.3	(NA)	([4])	29.7	51.4	(NA)	([4])
Mexico	1969	22.7	2.9	(NA)	59.8	3.2	[9]9.9	49.8	13.5	[1]24.0	40.6	17.5
Argentina	1972	38.4	16.3	25.5	81.8	6.9	68.6	([4])	40.9	38.7	52.3	66.5
Bolivia	1968	28.3	10.1	(NA)	68.0	1.6	[5]25.5	56.0	21.5	27.8	4.5	21.5
Brazil	1973	42.5	9.1	17.6	[4]81.4	3.0	80.1	([4])	28.3	[1]31.6	55.7	96.5
Chile	1964	46.1	(NA)	(NA)	[4]60.9	0.0	71.7	([4])	23.5	42.5	(NA)	47.5
Colombia	1973	19.0	3.0	12.0	45.0	6.0	(NA)	41.2	21.0	23.6	20.0	73.3
Ecuador	1972	31.8	7.0	31.8	57.2	2.0	25.0	41.6	14.4	19.3	8.6	56.0
Peru	1968	34.3	3.8	17.8	49.7	4.5	43.4	34.3	13.8	15.5	26.8	65.5
Venezuela	1971	46.8	16.5	(NA)	[4]68.3	9.8	(NA)	([4])	48.9	55.3	36.1	52.1

who fear that in these difficult economic times, divorce may cause them to end up in a worse situation. Certainly, the women's rights movement in Argentina cannot hope to muster the 50,000 women who marched through the streets of Buenos Aires in 1987 to protest the proposed legalization of divorce. Perhaps during the boom times of the 1970s there would have been less protest?

Abortion is another example. In most Latin American countries it is either illegal or permitted only to save the mother's life. Studies show that induced abortion accounts for the greatest proportion of maternal deaths and is the most frequent cause of hospital admissions among women. Again the Catholic Church continues to exert great pressure on governments not to bring any change in the abortion laws. Many studies also show that women of all strata, pressured by economic realities and responding to wider opportunities for women, desire to limit their family size so they can educate themselves and work outside the home. With the exception of Chile and Bolivia, almost all Latin American and Caribbean countries do support family planning programs.[25]

Where women have made efforts to enhance their status through business and other economic opportunities, they have run up against a wall of prejudice. The Industrial Bank of Peru credit records show that only 16 percent of their Urban Small Enterprise Development Fund's borrowers were women.[26] Yet, women are often better credit risks than men. For example, the loan portfolio of the Women's World Banking in the Dominican Republic presents a repayment rate of 97 percent. The records of the credit facilities provided in the same country by the Association for the Development of Micro-Enterprises revealed that women had a 100 percent repayment record as compared to repayment records of 75 to 85 percent for men over the same two-year period. Yet in Brazil, 88 percent of the funds distributed in agricultural credit programs went to male operators. In 1980 in St. Lucia, women received only 1 percent of the total loans disbursed by the Agricultural and Industrial Bank. In the Dominican Republic, a study of six major national banks showed that women comprised less than 10 percent of their loan portfolios. In Honduras, this discrimination against women farmers and business entrepreneurs has resulted in only 15 women's co-operatives out of 971.[27]

While Latin America rightly boasts of some of the world's earliest constitutions and statements of human rights (e.g. Venezuela in 1811) and some of the oldest constitutions in continuous existence (e.g. Argentina since 1853 and Colombia since 1886), the legal status of women south of the Rio Grande River lags far behind that of women in Europe and North America.

Table 59. Preferred Courses: Latin American Women at University. Source: *Women of the World,* WID1-4, Office of Women in Development, United States Agency for International Development, United States Department of Commerce, Washington DC, 1984, Table 4.8, p. 64. Notes: (1) Medicine includes pharmacology, medical technology, and other specialties. (2) Engineering includes architecture. (3) Data are for the University of El Salvador only. (4) Education includes the humanities (and, in El Salvador, also the social sciences). (5) Fine arts includes architecture.

Women's rights throughout Latin America make a pattern which can be more clearly understood by exploring the legal framework in particular countries: Bolivia, Brazil, Colombia and Peru – with ancillary references to relevant constitutional provisions in other countries in the region.

Yet, there is a temptation to conclude that the Latin American countries possess sophisticated lawyers and sophisticated legal systems which *appear* in many ways to protect the rights of women – that those rights are denied in practice by an unfortunate combination of poverty, corruption, inefficiency, religion and cultural machismo. But this is not the case. The laws themselves have been discriminatory. For example, voting rights were not given to the women of Paraguay until 1961, Peru until 1955, Colombia until 1954, showing that women's rights have far to go in Latin America.

In Peru, one of the countries of which a case study has been prepared (Chapter 20), 30 percent of the entire population is non-literate, and of this group 70 percent are women. Although the 1979 Constitution (Article 2) specifically forbids discrimination with respect to race, religion or sex, there were only 12 women in the legislature of 240 members, and of all top level public servants only 2.3 percent were women. All over Latin America traditional values continue to obstruct women's role in politics.[28]

There is an angle of official deceitfulness to discrimination and equal rights in Peru. Discrimination is prohibited, but the equal rights provision (Civil Code, Article 5) has a rider to it. The article reads that men and women enjoy the same civil rights except for the restrictions imposed on married women. The same civil code (Article 162) ensures that the husband has the authority to choose the domicile and the wife must follow. Article 173 states that she cannot work outside the home without his permission. He is the family's legal representative (Article 168 of the Code of 1936) and property or profit acquired during marriage falls into the husband's hands (Articles 177–178). Article 180 states that if the wife does not contribute "economically" to the matrimonial duties, the husband has the right to demand that his wife's property fall under his administration, i.e., even property which she brought into the marriage. Articles 391–392 of the 1981 Civil Code give parents equal rights over children, but the father's authority prevails and he is their legal guardian.

The foregoing analysis indicates that no matter what the Constitution may provide for in terms of non-discrimination, when it comes down to statutory rights, in terms of equality, a different mind set applies. The entire situation is a massive contradiction. The Constitution (Article 2) states that "the law does not grant women any fewer rights than men." In practice, however, that is exactly what the law does. It diminishes the rights of women. It legalizes the authority of the husband and dominance over the wife to such an extent that men in Peru frequently resort to violence against women to make their authority felt. It is claimed that between 70 to 80 percent of all crimes of violence reported to the police are cases of women who have been beaten by their husbands.[29]

And the response to women's rights claims has also been old-fashioned. The emphasis has been on family-oriented and protectionist constitutional provisions and laws. Little has been done about property rights, affirmative action in the workplace, the marketplace and the universities or the demands for exclusive control by women of their own lives and bodies.

In both Bolivia and Brazil, husbands may restrain or prohibit their wives from engaging in remunerative occupations for moral reasons or when marriage relationships might be affected. The first article on constitutional rights and obligations of the current 1980 Constitution of Chile (Article 19) dictates that "the law protects the life of those about to be born."

In the following chapter, exploring women's rights in the four nations of Latin America selected for case studies will be done chronologically in the order that their Constitutions were promulgated: Colombia (1886), Bolivia (1967), Brazil (1969) and Peru (1979).

20. Brief Case Studies of Colombia, Bolivia, Brazil and Peru

Colombia

While Colombia's 1886 Constitution—as one would expect—makes adequate provisions for freedom of speech, press, assembly and religion, fair trials, etc., it is completely silent—as one might also expect—on women's rights. It was not until the constitutional reform of 1957 (Decree 247) that the Constitution was amended to provide (in Article 1) that "Women shall have the same political rights as men."

Yes, women had been granted the vote in 1954, but that, admittedly, had done little to affect discriminatory treatment in other areas of Colombian life. However, it did give women a political voice, and it is significant that the provisions of Decree 247 of 1957 contained the preamble that "the military junta of the government of the Republic of Colombia (was) interpreting the national opinion expressed in the subscribed accords by the political parties."

Regrettably, this was still far from adequate. Inequality was ingrained in the Colombian Civil Code which, via the Napoleonic Code, closely followed Roman legal sources. The pressure of change continued and became part of the campaign pledges of Alfonso Lopez Michelsen in the presidential race of 1974. After taking office, the new Chief of State promulgated Decree 2820 of 1974, which caused a virtual legal revolution on behalf of women. By examining the status of women (on paper at least) both before and after this decree, one can assess the disability of women in Colombia a scant decade ago and the scope of attempts to achieve equality.

The state of reform was set by the Declaration of Purpose which was to guide the interpretation of Decree 2820. It read:

> Despite recent laws concerning the family a great disparity still exists between the law and the actual situation. There is a clear discrimination against women. Because of the limitations of the law in solving family conflicts and in doing justice to women, a grave social situation is being tolerated. // In analyzing the spirit of our legislation we find that it incorporates two attitudes which are particularly harmful to the strength and stability of the family. In the first place, this legislation makes it easy for men to neglect their conjugal obligations, and to preserve discrimination. This results in irresponsible procreation, a high number of extramarital unions and the proliferation of children resulting from these. In the second place, the submission and dependency of women has impeded the development of marital relations on a plane of equality, especially with regard to obligations and rights.

Family Relationships

Before 1932 married women had no rights, no legal capacity. The husband represented his wife in all matters and had sole control of the family. The woman could not even represent her own children. Although Law 28 of 1932 did authorize married women to enter into contracts without the legal authorization of their husbands, the father was still the sole representative of children under 21. He had the sole authority, for example, to authorize the marriage of minor children.

The 1974 amendments to Article 62 of the Civil Code created the joint exercise of *patria potestad* over minor children and provided that "if one of the parents is not available, legal representation shall be exercised by the other." In the case of marriage, present law enables either male or female to enter into marriage without parental authorization.

Once married, the woman is no longer legally obliged to follow the husband's choice of residence. According to the new statute, both make such choice jointly. However—and here the Colombia law is unique—if there is a disagreement as to where the couple should reside, the decision will be made for them by a judge.

While extramarital sexual relations of either spouse are grounds for divorce, polygamy and adultery are not crimes, and in Colombia it is common for a man to live with more than one woman. Bigamy, however, is a crime.

Article 177 of the Civil Code, as now amended, provides that both spouses are responsible for the management of the home and, again, in case of a disagreement, disputes are to be judicially determined. This includes, of course, parental authority over non-emancipated children. No longer does the legal system contain such an anachronism as was found in Article 13 of Law 45 of 1936: "[R]ights are to be exercised over legitimate children by the father and in his absence, the mother, as long as she lives decently and does not remarry."

Property

Equality of property rights exists in law if not in fact. Married women have complete legal capacity to enter into contracts and to engage in property transactions, just as if single. Interestingly, married women who are minors are held to be of legal age, enabling them to engage in business activities—a right denied male minors and single female minors.

Colombian law establishes the *sociedad conyugal,* effective at the celebration of marriage. Under this institution, all property acquired after marriage belongs to both spouses as communal property. Theoretically, both husband and wife share control, but in practice the old system is followed, which under the law gave the husband exclusive administrative control over such property. (Property belonging to each spouse before marriage remains in their exclusive control and does not become a part of the *sociedad conyugal.*)

Widows and widowers equally, who wish to remarry, are required to prepare formal inventories of the property of their underage children from their previous marriages before public notaries.

Employment

Title III, Article 17, of Colombia's Constitution provides in a 1936 amendment that "labor is a social obligation and shall enjoy the special protection of the State." But what this means is unclear, and it is certain that this vague language has not greatly aided women in their struggle for equality in the marketplace.

Somewhat more specific is the Labor Code which, in Article 10, recites that all workers are equal under the law, with the same guarantees and protections. There does exist an equal freedom of both sexes to choose their means of livelihood. Further, laws passed as early as 1950 (Decrees 2662 and 3743) established the eight-hour day and 48-hour weekly work schedule. But exceptions were made for agricultural labor, in which so many women are engaged; enforcement has been limited by the infrequency of women's complaints. There is little enforcement of such laws in domestic service because these offenses are rarely reported.

Government attempts to protect women in Articles 236 to 238 of the Labor Code—in Colombia as in all nations—have a negative impact on the ability of women to obtain and retain jobs. There are paid maternity leaves and even leaves in the event of abortion, plus paid time off for nursing. There is even a prohibition against discharging women for either pregnancy or nursing.

This has inevitably resulted in discrimination against married women of childbearing years in hiring and in discharging female employees upon marriage. Whether this type of discrimination can be cured by law is open to question.

Personal Autonomy

While abortion leave is granted under the Labor Code, the act of abortion is a crime under the Penal Code. Articles 386 and 389 provide penalties against a woman who induces her own miscarriage or has an abortion performed upon her with her consent. The same penalty is set forth for the person performing the abortion who acts with the consent of the woman, while a more severe penalty is prescribed for the performance of an abortion without consent.

Machismo enters the picture with the provision that the penalty may be diminished (or judicial pardon granted) if the abortion was performed to "save the honor" of a husband, mother or children.

If a pregnancy exists during marital separation, the law now authorizes the woman to inform her husband's relatives or her closest relatives of legal age about the state of pregnancy, and a doctor must verify the pregnancy. Under prior practice it was possible for the husband to subject the estranged wife to a humiliating examination which did not require a physician in attendance.

Like other Latin American countries—and unlike most European and Asian countries—there are severe penalties for procuring. And the penalties are recited in detail, making the punishment more severe if a "virtuous woman" is induced into prostitution, or if the woman is younger than 18, or if the conduct is habitual, or if procuring is done by a person who has a position or office giving him authority over the victim, or if violence or tricks are employed. A father, husband, brother or son (of legal age) who participates in any way or simply tolerates the prostitution of daughter, wife, sister, or mother is subject to fine or imprisonment.

Bolivia

In spite of having the world's most unstable political history[1] and the lowest gross national product per capita in Latin America,[2] modern Bolivia has made rapid strides in its official recognition of women's rights.

The Constitution of 1967 recites in Article 6 that "every human being has juridical personality and capacity according to the laws." And even more specific is Article 96 of the 1972 Code of the Family: "Art. 96.—In the interest of the family and in accordance with the personal condition of each one, the spouses have equal rights and duties in the direction and management of the affairs of their marriage, such as the raising and education of their children."

Family Relationships

The law of October 11, 1911, was significant for Bolivian men and women in two respects. First, this law liberated urban women from the marital constraints imposed by the Catholic Church. Second, this law gave legal sanction to the various conjugal arrangements of Bolivia's indigenous peoples. This was especially important in a nation where more than half of the population is Indian or "tribal."

Since 1911, "the law recognizes only civil marriage"[3] "performed before an Official of the Civil Register."[4] A canonical or religious marriage may be entered into after the civil marriage, but only the latter has legal status.[5]

The Family Code expresses the view that "free or *de facto* unions that are stable and monogamous produce effects that are similar to those of marriage . . . (and that) the norms that regulate the effects of matrimony can be applied to such unions."[6] Protected are specified pre-marital indigenous relationships and *de facto* unions of aborigines, plus "other unions in urban, industrial or rural centers."[7]

And while women's rights to minimal support are recognized and protected by the Law of April 15, 1932, the remedy is archaic: "Food allowances for a wife and children is [sic] to be enforced by threat or corporal punishment, to be administered immediately and opportunely, whenever the husband or father maliciously avoids this obligation."

Modern Bolivia, in its 1967 Constitution, maintains that "marriage, the family and maternity are under the protection of the State" and "the legal equality of spouses is established."[8] This development was nothing short of revolutionary to a country whose Civil Code, promulgated more than 100 years earlier,[9] contained this language:

> Art. 130. —The husband owes protection to the wife and she owes obedience to the husband. // Art. 131. —The woman is obligated to reside with the husband and follow him wherever he chooses to live. The husband is obliged to receive her in his home and give her everything she needs for living in accordance with his powers and his condition. // Art. 134. —A wife cannot give, alienate or mortgage property or acquire title by gift or otherwise without the permission of the husband, or his subsequent consent in writing. // Art. 137. —If the husband has been condemned to corporal punishment or defamation, even if only for contempt of court, the wife cannot appear in court or enter into contract during the term of the husband's punishment without authorization by judge, who will grant this authorization without summoning or hearing the husband.

The Constitution of 1945 legislated the juridical equality of spouses. Consequently, all of the clauses pertaining to women in a negative way were annulled.[10]

The Constitution currently in effect[11] states the following: "Every human being has juridical personality and capacity according to the laws."[12] Thus, the 1967 Constitution recognizes women's civil and political rights. However, due to prevalent societal prejudices, *de facto* equality cannot be expected to occur overnight.[13] But it is certain that women have come a long way since the days when it was necessary for legislation to give women a legal right to her husband's name.[14]

Property

Bolivia's detailed and complicated 1861 laws on dowry came to an end in 1972 with a provision asserting that "the administration of the familial patrimony is the right of both spouses or only one if the other is absent or disabled."[15]

The prior law, among its other provisions, stated that only the husband could administer the dowry property during the marriage.[16] Even more arresting was that this prior law contained the following archaic provision: "*Arra* is the donation made by the husband to the woman in return for her dowry, her virginity or her youth. It is the possession of the wife or her heirs."[17]

In 1972 the Code of the Family established what can be termed a community property provision. Article 101 provides that "from the moment of its formation, marriage constitutes a communality of property; at the time of dissolution, the property and earnings acquired during the marriage are to be equally divided, except for the judicial separation of property in expressly permitted cases. The communality exists even if one of the spouses owns more property than the other, or if only one of them possesses property."

Employment

With the exception of a law designating May 27 as Mother's Day, providing all working mothers with a half-day of extra vacation time, all of Bolivia's women's rights laws in the labor field are in the nature of protective legislation.

Pregnancy and maternity rights date from the law of August 13, 1943. From 15 days before birth to 45 days after birth (or longer in cases of illness) women retain their employment rights—but for 50 percent of their salaries. After returning to work, they are entitled to rest periods (of not less than an hour) for nursing.[18] Moreover, companies with more than 50 women workers are required to maintain separate rooms for nursing, plus centers to care for the children while the mothers are at work.[19]

In advanced nations, women's rights groups eschew the protections which were so important to women's rights activists in earlier times. However, in Bolivia, these protectionist laws still remain. Regulations decreed on September 21, 1929, prevent the employment of women between 9:00 p.m. and 6:00 a.m. in offices and factories. These same regulations give the Health Ministry the authority to restrict female employment in "industries deemed unhealthy." This is clearly a paternalistic kind of protection.

Mining accidents[20] led to the Supreme Decree of August 4, 1940. This law prohibits the employment of women[21] in mines and subterranean galleries or working with blast or smelting furnaces. Considering the importance of mining to the Bolivian economy, this is a remarkable example of protectionism.

It was also during this early period, on December 8, 1942, that the General Law of Labor was enacted to protect women in domestic service. When the projected term for such work for a single employee is to exceed one year, a written contract is required which must be registered with the Security Police. The Ministerial Resolution of May 19, 1954, added the virtually meaningless requirement that all live-in domestic employees have at least one eight-hour break per day and at least 14 hours of free time per week or a fully paid day once a week. Clearly, domestic service must have been very harsh to have justified such lenient rules.

Personal Autonomy

In the modern sense of the equality treatment for women's rights, Bolivia may be among the most advanced countries in its requirement that women serve in the armed forces.[22] The Law of National Defense Service of August 1, 1966, established a voluntary Women's Auxiliary Service. However, Article 52 of the Organic Law of the Armed Forces requires every Bolivian woman between the ages of 19 and 35 to participate in the Auxiliary Service in time of war or emergency for service which might include combat.[23]

However, lest one be under the impression that Bolivia is a strong bastion of autonomy rights for women, a quick glance at some other laws will dispel that notion. In Bolivia, women are required to hold themselves to a higher degree of comportment than men. In fact the social marginalization of women is such that if a man abducts or rapes, or both, a "notorious" or "vulgar" woman, his guilt is mitigated by her status alone and his punishment is automatically half of that which would be apportioned to him if he had abducted or raped an "honest" woman.[24] The connotation is purely sexual since many "honest" women can be "notoriously" outspoken in expressing political views.

Political Rights

Law No. 03128 of July 21, 1952, conferred the right to vote on all citizens.[25] The Constitution of 1967 gave force to this law by providing for universal suffrage.[26] Moreover, participation in political parties became open to women slowly but surely. This, too, is embodied in the 1967 Constitution.[27]

Brazil

The South American giant, Brazil—sixth most populous country of the world—is the leader in industry and development throughout the Latin American world, except when it comes to women's rights.

True, Article 153, paragraph 1 of the 1969 Constitution provides that "all are equal before the law, without distinction as to sex, race, occupation, religious creed, or political conviction." But Article 175—promulgated at the same time—declares that "marriage is indissoluble." True, again, this is no longer the law and there have been legal (and other) efforts to raise the status of women. Yet the law has been slow to formulate change. Most of the changes have been protectionist and even then, practice has lagged behind the law.

Family Relationships

It was not until the promulgation of the Constitutional Amendment No. 9 on June 28, 1977, that the constitutional prohibition against divorce came to an end. But this reform was far from liberal. The new Article 175, paragraph 1, now reads: "Marriage may be dissolved only in the cases set forth in the law, provided there has been a prior judicial separation for more than three years."

Half a year later, Law 6515 of December 26 was enacted to deal with marriage dissolution, divorce procedures, division of property and alimony. Far from satisfactory is the provision that a separation upon mutual consent is permitted, but only after two years of marriage. If a court so declares, judicial separation can become a divorce after three years. And after five years of *de facto* separation, a divorce proceeding can be initiated by either party.

The new divorce law provides that all property acquired after marriage is held in common and is equally divided upon marital dissolution. Interesting to note, it is the party at fault who must provide the alimony, if needed.

In addition, if separation is the result of the fault of one of the parties, custody of children is given to the innocent spouse. And if both parties are at fault, custody goes to the wife, unless the judge rules that moral damage would result.

If a decree of separation is obtained against a woman, she may no longer use the married name. If she is the innocent party, however, such use is optional. This is important in a country where—pursuant to the strictures and customs of Roman law—the woman must assume the surname of her husband upon marriage. It is so important that Law No. 6216 of June 30, 1975, even makes provision for unmarried women to obtain a similar right: "The single woman, separated woman or widow, who lives with a man who is single, separated or widowed, in exceptional circumstances and having a strong motive, may request a competent judge to have entered in the birth register the patronymic of her companion, without prejudice to her own surname, so long as there is a legal impediment to their marriage and the prior civil state of whichever party or both parties has elapsed."

The family structure receives an added protection by the requirement that social welfare payments – a family salary – be given to large families, in direct proportion to the number of children.

The traditional bride's dowry is now unknown in Brazil, and Article 277 of the Civil Code recites that spouses must meet marriage expenses "in proportion to their incomes" unless they stipulate otherwise in an ante-nuptial contract.

Property

Brazil uses the term "pantial community property" to denominate the communal ownership of property acquired after marriage, without regard to which spouse has obtained title. Property owned by spouses before marriage or inherited individually subsequent to marriage, however, does not become part of the common property. This is set forth in Articles 269 and 271 of the Civil Code.

Ownership is one thing; power and control are others. The husband, under Article 274 of the Civil Code, has the right to administer not only communal assets, but also the property of the wife. Further, the husband may contract debts as head of the marital union which will result in an obligation of the wife proportional to the benefit received.

There is a qualification based on Article 3 of Law No. 4121 of 1962 which, in practice, protects women: "Debt obligations of whatever nature, signed by only one of the spouses, even though the spouses are married under the system of community property, can only touch those particular goods which pertain to the signatory and regarding community goods up to one-half of the goods must respond to the debt."

Employment

The 20-paragraph Article 165 of Brazil's constitution, supplementing and supplemented by the 1968 Consolidation of the Labor Laws (C.L.T.: Law No. 41473 of June 2, 1968) provides a veritable catalog of workers' rights. Many of them relate to women and the family.

Paragraph III establishes a "prohibition of differences in wages and in criteria for employment because of sex, color, or marital status." Article 1 of the C.L.T. declares void any "dispositions and provisions" based on sex in public, private or mixed enterprises. This is folllowed by the C.L.T. Article 5 mandate that work of equal value should be similarly compensated regardless of sex. And Article 372 makes it clear that rules of benefit to male workers are likewise applicable to women.

One chapter of the Consolidation of the Labor Laws, entitled "Protection of the Labor of the Woman," relates specifically to women's rights. Thus, while the Constitution, in Article 165, paragraph VI, limits daily work schedules to eight hours (with a rest interval), the C.L.T. goes further in prescribing conditions of work for women, rest periods during night work, etc.

Under the Constitution (Article 165, paragraph X) women are prohibited from working in "unhealthful industries," and Article 387 of the C.L.T. forbids female labor in subterranean mines and in quarries. The C.L.T. in Article 379 limits night work of women under 18 to employment by the telephone company, or jobs in hotels and restaurants and in educational institutions, a series of reasonable exceptions to the law on woman's night employment.

Women may retire at full pay after 30 years of employment. Article 164, paragraphs XIX and XI, establishes maternity leave both before and after childbirth "without prejudice to employment or wages." Paragraph XVI also establishes "maternity protection, through contributions by the union, by employers, and by employees."

The C.L.T. chapter on Protection for Motherhood (Articles 391–397) forbids the discharging of women workers because of marriage or pregnancy and voids any laws or contractual provisions which might restrict either marriage or the right of pregnancy.

Pregnancy-maternity rights prohibit work four weeks prior to giving birth and eight weeks after, during which a Maternity Salary (equal to full salary) is paid. Until the child is six months old, the nursing mother is given two special one-half hour rest periods daily. And any enterprise employing more that 30 women must have an area set aside for such nursing unless district nurseries are available.

Personal Autonomy

Sterilization is not prohibited under Brazilian law, but abortion may be employed only to save the mother's life or where the pregnancy resulted from rape. Prostitution is legal, and while there are laws against the trafficking of women, they are seldom enforced.

Peru

On July 28, 1974, General Juan Velasio Alvarado, who was the President of Peru and head of its armed forces, announced the so-called "Inca Plan" for governmental reform. Item 23 of the Plan stated that "[t]he Peruvian woman does not exercise in an effective form her rights as a citizen; the access of women to high political and administrative positions and to other activities is very limited; the man disposes of the property of the marriage, without the consent of his spouse; there is discrimination against the woman in employment and in salary; there is unjust and inhuman treatment of the unwed mother; and the low level of culture of the masses exacerbates the abusive treatment of women by men."

This plan called for a greater degree of equality for Peruvian women and signaled the beginning of a remarkable series of paper victories for advocates of women's rights. Eventually the subsequent revised 1979 Constitution of Peru itself was influenced by this drive for women's rights. In fact, the Constitution contains many progressive features in this area, making it one of the most advanced of modern constitutions.

The Preamble to the Peruvian Constitution declares, among other purposes, the desire "to promote the creation of a just society . . . without exploited or exploiters, free from all discrimination by virtue of sex, race, creed or social condition." Article 2 declares that "the law recognizes that the rights of women are no fewer than those of men." This language, in itself, provides at least a paper commitment to the betterment of Peruvian women, and it is amplified by other portions of the Constitution. However, a closer examination of the laws of Peru shows that despite some gains women remain far short of the equality promised in Article 2.

Family Relationships

Chapter II of the Peruvian Constitution is entitled "Concerning the Family," and it is as a member of the monogamous family unit that the Peruvian woman is classified under law. Article 5 provides that "the state protects marriage and the family as a natural society and fundamental institution of the nation." Article 6 proclaims that "the state protects responsible parenthood." At the same time, Article 7 puts mothers in a special category, stating that "the mother is entitled to the protection of the state and to its assistance in case of need." For what it may be worth, Article 10 then claims that "it is the right of the family to enjoy a decent home." These special provisions on the position of the woman in the family give some legal force to the claims of female-headed households, which are becoming more prevalent in Peru.

Yet, the Peruvian Civil Code declares that spouses must live together unless the health, honor or business of either would thereby be gravely endangered. The wife still has the legal duty of "attending the household," while the husband may determine the domicile and decide basic economic questions concerning the family. These decisions must be accepted by the wife unless the husband abuses his rights. The husband's chief legal duty is to supply his wife and family with the necessaries of life as best he can. So, the Civil Code, in spite of the egalitarian language of the Constitution, retains the traditional male-dominant style of Peruvian marriage.

Extra-marital unions are common in Peru. In fact, "concubinage" has a legal status, defined as a union existing between a man and a woman outside marriage who share a permanent and habitual sexual relationship. The origins of "concubinage" can be traced to the indigenous Incas, and the institution is widespread in the Andes region and rural coastal zones. Casual sexual relations do not create concubinage, for such unions require permanence. The children produced are guaranteed food allowances and certain other rights, but their inheritance rights are limited. The mothers retain their own property and inheritance rights but gain none from the union (Civil Code, Article 366).

Property

Peruvian laws concerning marital property discriminate against married women, giving their husbands a primary role over such matters. The Civil Code (Sections 158–246) makes the husband the representative of the marriage partnership, and gives him the power to administer the marital community property unless he is unable to act or his whereabouts are unknown. Marital community property includes all property acquired by the work, industry, or profession of either spouse subsequent to marriage, and all property of the spouses is presumed to be community property unless either can prove the contrary.

The subservient and dependent position of Peruvian women still is evident in the provisions concerning work outside the home. For this she must have the express or implied consent of her husband. If she chooses to contest his decision she may seek the authorization of a judge, and she must show that working outside the home is required for the interest of the marriage partnership or that of the family. The Peruvian Commercial Code and the Civil Code both make this point.

Employment

To the extent that Peruvian women are permitted to join the workforce, they are given ample legal protection. Working Peruvian women enjoy a series of unusual special protections uncommon in Latin America. Moreover, the Constitution declares that "the worker of either sex has the right to equal compensation for equal work performed under identical conditions for the same employer" (Article 43). Equal pay is, of course, not "comparable pay." The work performed by women must be identical in kind to the work of men, and the work output must be similar.

Article 45 of the Constitution declares that "the law determines the means for protecting the working mother." In this sphere Peruvian law has long been innovative. In 1918, Law No. 11321 created an obligatory maternity leave for women employees for 42 days before birth and 42 days after, accompanied by grants for nursing equal to 30 percent of the mother's average salary.

The same 1918 Law No. 2851 also established some rudimentary child care arrangements in factories. However, child care facilities are not generally available after infancy. Nothing like the elaborate Scandinavian child care facilities is available to Peruvian women workers.

The Peruvian Civil Code appears to create equality of working conditions for women, but Peruvian women still perform arduous agricultural and domestic labor. Frequently, they are the chief providers for the family. Although they no longer work in mines and quarries they are often assigned simple, monotonous jobs with low salaries and responsibilities. In spite of the premises of the Constitution, working women have only made slow gains in Peru.

Personal Autonomy

Prostitution in Peru is considered to be just another possible occupation for women and comes under government regulation. When declaring their occupations to the Peruvian census many women cite prostitution, which is officially listed under the column designated "other services."

Although prostitution itself is not punished or condemned, the corruption of a minor with intent to make a profit is subject to criminal penalties. So, too, is pimping, pandering and procuring.

Abortion is prohibited as a means of birth control. Therapeutic abortion is permitted, but only when there is conclusive proof of the danger of death of the fetus or mother, certified by two consulting opinions (Sanitary Code, Decree of Law No. 17505 [1969]).

Thus, Peru shares in the paradoxical treatment of personal autonomy so common in Latin America. Women are permitted to become prostitutes, but they may not have abortions. Yet, the law remains oblivious of the paradox. Consider the General Law of Education, Title 1, Article 11, which states: "Education will be oriented toward the revaluation of the woman, offering her maximum opportunities for full and free personal development, the only authentic base for her decisive function in the family and for her creative participation in Peruvian society."

Part Eight: The Arab-Muslim World

A blind Muslim girl who had been raped and became pregnant as the result of the assault was sentenced to be stoned to death. The rationale in terms of Islamic Law: she could not identify the rapist but since she was pregnant she was automatically held to be guilty of illegal sex and therefore had to be executed. – *The Economist*, London.

21. General Survey

There are nine regions of the world where more than 95 percent of the Muslim peoples live: the Middle East, which is the heartland of Arab culture and includes countries such as Saudi Arabia, Turkey, Iraq and Syria; the Nile River delta; Egypt; the Mediterranean coast of North Africa with, for example, Algeria, Libya, Morocco; the largest portion of the Sudan, Northeast Ethiopia; the East African coast; the central steppes of Asia; the Indo-Iranian area which stretches from Iran to Bengal; and Southeast Asia, which includes Indonesia.

In Muslim countries discrimination against women over a wide spectrum is institutionalized, religiously based (which makes arguing against discrimination like blasphemy) and overlaid by dominant male attitudes. Altogether it totally precludes women's chances to significantly improve their economic and educational status, much less to self-determination and political power. As pointed out earlier in this book, a woman elected to power in a Muslim state is a political aberration, such as Benazir Bhutto in Pakistan. If her father, former President Zulfikar Ali Bhutto, had not been murdered by his political opponents, Benazir Bhutto would not have become the first female ruler in the Muslim world in centuries.

The Muslim religion automatically spawns acts of negative discrimination. Of course, discrimination, like beauty and objectivity, is in the eyes of the beholder. To the African Muslim tribesman or an Iranian Muslim clergyman, these acts may not appear to be discriminatory at all. To a Christian citizen of Britain, France or the United States, they are both discriminatory and abhorrent. On October 2, 1983, a wire service report from Islamabad, Pakistan read as follows: "A widow accused of adultery cried out as she was flogged 15 times before 5,000 onlookers . . . many of those watching were women who broke into sobs."[1] In New York City the average Christian would consider this a brutal, despicable act, but in Pakistan the community was merely observing accepted Islamic (religious) penal law being enacted as the holy *Qur'an* decrees.

A practice which generates severe criticism in the Christian world is female circumcision in the Arab-Muslim world. Although not *per se* a Muslim practice and not required by the *Qur'an* (in fact the practice predates Islam), it is nonetheless widely applied in the Arab-Muslim world.[2]

Other forms of discrimination in the Muslim world are rife.

Political discrimination on the basis of sex is legally entrenched in Muslim countries by the rule that women, no matter their numbers, are entitled to only 10 percent of the representatives in the legislature, the National Assembly. This is the case in Iran, Pakistan and other states. (Morocco is the one exception.) In Bangladesh the 30 women's representatives in the 300-strong elected parliament, for which elections were last held in May 1986, are not even directly elected by women but by the (male) legislators.[3] The only Middle East Arab state with an elected government is Kuwait. But of their entire population only 3.5 percent or about 5,700 men are allowed to vote. Every effort by women to seek the vote has been refused, the last time in 1985.[4]

There are 300 million women in the Muslim world whose status is regulated by Muslim religious laws derived from the *Qur'an.* Many are subject to marriages and adoptions against their will. The modern definition of slavery includes such matters as forced marriage and pseudo-adoptions, both of which are violations of women's rights in the eyes of Westerners, but not in the eyes of the Muslim world.

Let us now look at the overall constitutional and legal situation in the Muslim world insofar as it affects women's fundamental freedoms. (Further on in this chapter the law is examined in more detail.)

To any Christian, the Islamic laws as they apply to women are discriminatory in principle and in practice. The *Qur'an,* the holy Bible of the Muslim world, is the Constitution in many of the world's 40 Muslim states. (There are 30 Arab-Muslim states.) It contains discrimination against women which would be unconstitutional in the United States and illegal in dozens of other countries of the world. A Western woman in Saudi Arabia could be contravening the Moslem laws in ways which appear to us, either as Christians or as Westerners, to be even absurd! She may not drive a car; she may not appear in public in anything less than a floor-length dress with arms covered to the wrist; it is illegal for women to work openly; women who do work face the constant threat of discovery by the religious police who may confiscate their passports and, if they are not Saudi citizens, impose heavy fines or deport them. In her own home, a Muslim woman has to occupy separate quarters from her husband.[5]

The restrictions on women differ from state to state. They are worse in Arab states but elsewhere the laws of Islam are the same. In Pakistan in 1983 there were massive riots with police in Lahore having to use tear gas and batons to break up a women's demonstration against further Islamization of the law such as making the testimony of one man equal to that of two women.[6] The previous year there were demonstrations when the men-only Pakistani contigent flew out to the Asian Games, the Asian equivalent of the Olympic Games.

If ever there was a field in which the effort of the individual should be above discrimination on the basis of race, religion, politics and sex, it is sports, particularly at international levels such as the Olympic and Asian Games. Yet Pakistan could not send a women's hockey or basketball team since men are forbidden to watch teams of women play. The demonstration casts an interesting sidelight on the morality of the International Olympic Committee (I.O.C.) which prohibits South African individual athletes from participating in the Olympic Games, not because the teams are racially segregated—on the contrary, South African athletic teams are all multi-racial (so are the selection committees and the audiences who watch them compete)—but because the South African political system discriminates against blacks.

The Pakistani action (discrimination against women) calls for a similar boycott against Pakistani teams by the I.O.C., but it is not to be. Though there may be no discrimination against athletes on grounds of race, religion or sex, clearly political discrimination on grounds of race is considered to be a greater evil in the eyes of the I.O.C. (This is known as selective indignation.) The counter argument is also that if South Africa is to change its entire political structure to satisfy the I.O.C. (and the United Nations) then Pakistan must change its Islamic legal structure, which it cannot do because the legal structure is their Bible, the *Qur'an*. Similarly, individual athletes in South Africa cannot, single-handedly, change the system just as women hockey players in Pakistan cannot discard the *Qur'an* and replace it with the Christian Bible, no more than individual female gymnasts from the U.S.S.R. can change the Soviet Marxist system.

Islam is to a high degree simply a male-oriented doctrine. The constitutions of most Arab states fail to provide a realistic picture of discrimination against women. In the Islamic law of succession, a woman's portion is equal to half the portion of a man; the daughter of a testator receives under the law only half the share of the brother. This is exemplified in the Civil Code of Morocco, Articles 237–244, and the Civil Code of Syria, Articles 277/2. Article 65 of the Constitution of Pakistan specifies that there shall be 15 seats in the assembly set aside only for women. A majority of women is thus represented by a small minority of delegates in parliament.

The pattern of discrimination is set by the *Qur'an* itself. "Men should be favored above women . . . because they (men) are responsible for them (women)."[7] Here are further examples. Children remain under the father's authority even after a divorce or after "banishment" of the mother. In the case of the father's death, his authority is transferred to his closest male relative. A Muslim woman may not be married to a man of a different faith, either Jew or Christian.[8] The right of banishment of a woman from her home is entirely the man's prerogative.[9]

On May 5, 1985, the Constitutional Court of Egypt officially restored to men their full Islamic legal rights. Men can now take four wives and divorce them at will. In principle the man can dissolve the marriage at any time. If a woman dies childless, half of what the woman leaves belongs to the husband. If the husband dies first in a childless family, the wife receives only one-fourth (the rest goes to the father or mother of the deceased or to the community), and if the man dies leaving children, the woman's part is further reduced and she receives only one-eighth of the man's estate.[10]

Sexism is deeply rooted in the religious and cultural norms of Islam. According to the *Qur'an,* feminine names should not be used for angels.[11] No alimony is due to a woman in case she is imprisoned, even unjustly, or arrested, or raped, or left her husband's house . . . or she was in any condition which rendered her useless as a wife.[12] It should always be kept in mind that Muslim law is an echo of Mosaic law in which women were property.[13]

In the less modernized Muslim societies women also have to contend with a form of quasi-slavery including servile marriage. The Anti-Slavery Society has also directed considerable attention to female circumcision which accompanies service marriage.[14]

From time to time one is struck by oddities in Islamic Law and in customs which seem to contradict the discriminatory pattern.

Article 75 of the 1973 Constitution of Sudan dictates that a pregnant woman may not be executed, but this is not because of the woman, but for the sake of the unborn child. The execution takes place after birth.

In Saudi Arabia the recent opening of a bank for women is seen in the same context as the first all-women bank in New York. Yet there is a world of difference. In Riyadh, where the particular bank is situated behind the National Commercial Bank's Nassiriah Street branch, the women's bank is conspicuous for the fact that an armed guard sits in the foyer to prevent any male from entering. The windows are closed and draped so that no man can see the female clerks at work.[15] In the West this is considered absurd. In Saudi Arabia, it is merely a further response of Islam's restriction on public co-mingling between men and women.

Elsewhere in the Muslim world the situation is much the same.

The Bengali women in Bangladesh, both rural and urban, traditional and modern, live in a social system that sanctifies an unequal and inferior status for women. As Rounaq Jahan wrote: "There has been no serious movement to modify the legal system to give women equal rights of inheritance, guardianship, or marriage and divorce."[16] Several researchers have referred to the fact that in Islam a woman who has been raped is rejected by society. Of an estimated 200,000 cases of rape in Bangladesh one year only 22,500 were reported because the family wanted to keep the rape secret.[17]

A most interesting statistical analysis by Marielouise Jannsen-Jurreit in her book *Sexism* (originally published in German under the title *Seximus: Über Die Abtreibung der Frauenfrage*) shows that whereas in Western society the proportion of women in the population was higher in 1982 than that of men, by the year 1985 the proportion of women was projected to drop to 49.78 percent (which it did). In Arab and Islamic countries, however, the decrease is more significant and visible. In Libya it is already 48 percent, in Iran 46.92, in Kuwait 43.19 and in the United Arab Emirates the figure is down to 38.14 percent. "Either the women are regarded as so insignificant," wrote Jannsen-Jurreit, "that any census of their numbers is inadequate, or they are consciously decimated by negligent hygiene."[18] At the United Nations Arab diplomats deny that either is the case, pointing out that 15 of the 30 Arab-Muslim states have an official, government-sponsored women's movement. But as Nadia Youssef observed, it is not surprising that expanded options for women, such as an increase in education, have not been a response to pressure from these organizations but due to the needs of national development and the degree to which the Arab governments have viewed changes as important to their objectives.[19] For example, in Kuwait, women's college enrollment is as high as 60 percent of the total enrollment, but in Saudi Arabia it is only 7 percent. Women's participation in the labor force is 48 percent in Egypt but 1 percent in Saudi Arabia. As Chart 14 indicates, the pattern is the same in other states.

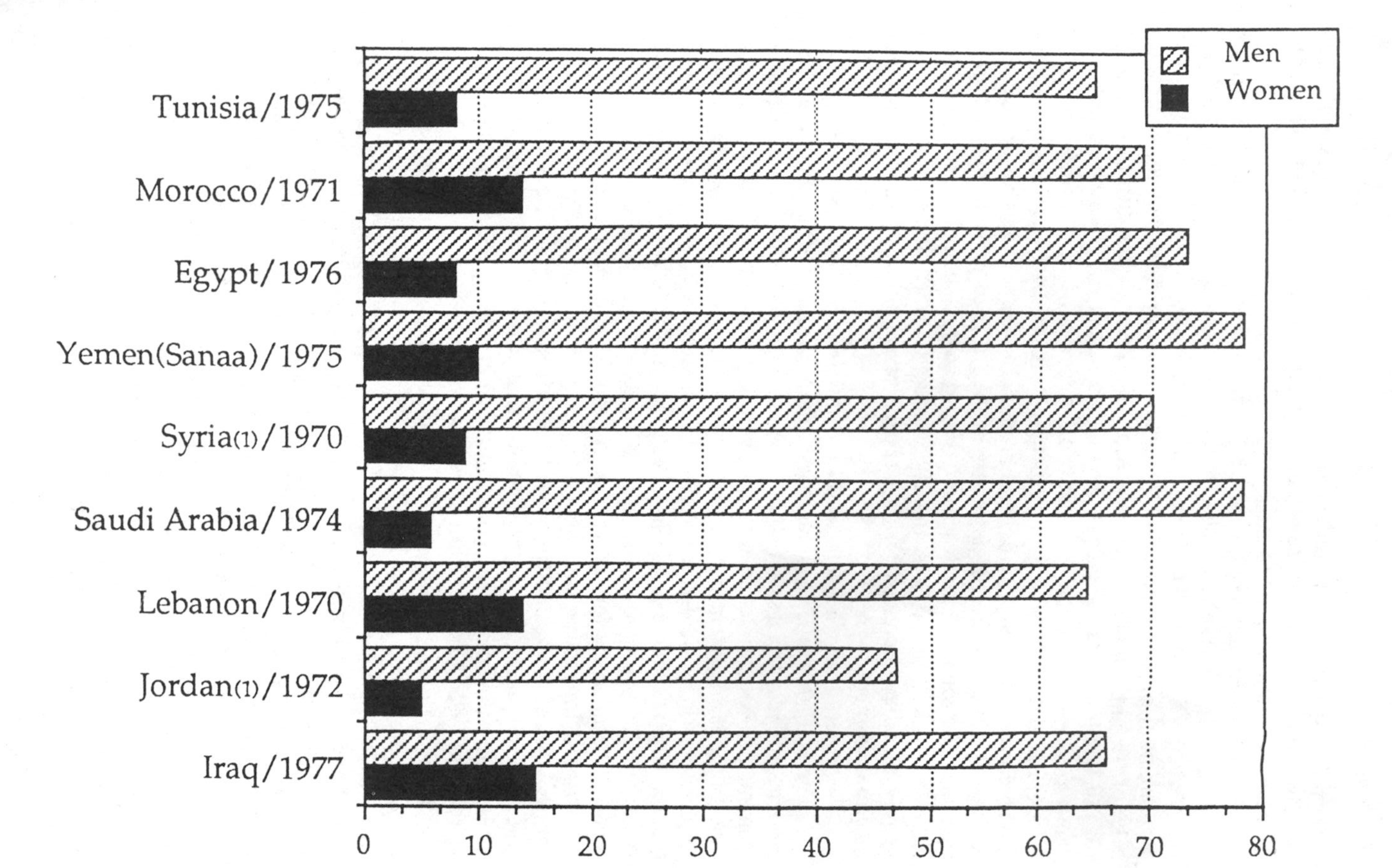
Men
Women
Tunisia/1975
Morocco/1971
Egypt/1976
Yemen(Sanaa)/1975
Syria(1)/1970
Saudi Arabia/1974
Lebanon/1970
Jordan(1)/1972
Iraq/1977
0
10
20
30
40
50
60
70
80

In Saudi Arabia the middle class Arabs who have been educated in the West are chafing under the many restrictions of the closed political system of an Arab kingdom with absolute powers. In addition the kingdom's religious leaders are constantly calling for closer adherence to puritanical Islamic rules. Many of the strictures are directed at women. One recent decree banned them from riding alone in taxis or hotel limousines. In Riyadh and Jidda, women must board buses through the back door and sit separately from men. At King Saud University female students attend class on a separate campus and listen to lectures from male professors over closed circuit television.[20]

According to the International Labor Organization, the proportion of female workers in the Muslim states is very low, notably in the so-called Gulf States. In Bahrain, Jordan, Kuwait, the United Arab Emirates and Democratic Yemen, the figures show fewer than 50,000 women in the official labor force. In Yemen women formed only 5.6 percent of the economically active labor force. Whereas in most other regions, except North America and Europe, women form the bulk of the agricultural labor force, in Iraq, Jordan and Yemen the figure is less than five percent.[21] Even in Muslim countries with large populations women's agricultural contribution remains largely invisible.[22]

Agricultural changes in the Middle East resulted from considerable male emigration from non-oil exporting to oil exporting states. Agriculture in countries such as Jordan, the Syrian Arab Republic, Yemen, Morocco and Egypt is therefore characterized by male labor shortages. The countries reacted differently to this situation. In Syria more women were used as laborers. In Jordan the state reacted by importing Egyptian male labor, leaving the Jordanian female rural reserves in unemployment.[23] It also explains why the percentage of women in the labor force in Egypt is as high as 48 percent.

In other employment sectors the situation is not much different. In Saudi Arabia women account for only 3 percent of the total labor force in the services section. In Kuwait more than 90 percent of the female workers were salaried employees and wage earners. In the Syrian Arab Republic some 50 percent of the female labor force are unpaid family workers.[24]

In Table 60, showing concentration of female workers by occupation, it can be seen that the proportion of women in managerial and administrative positions is extremely low. This is the result of these posts being reserved almost exclusively for males.

The overwhelming number of women in regular paid occupations were nurses, midwives, teachers, secretaries, sales clerks, house servants, and seamstresses. The vast majority were in low-paying and unprestigious jobs. There is also substantial wage discrimination for the same work. A study of Egyptian manufacturing industries revealed that in 1975 female workers (mostly tailors, dressmakers, spinners, weavers, knitters, and clerical workers) received only 375 Egyptian piastres per week as against 556 for men.[25]

Chart 14. Male and Female Participation in the Labor Force. ***Women of the World,*** **WID-3, Office of Women in Development, United States Agency for International Development, United States Department of Commerce, Washington DC, 1985, Figure 4.1, p. 75.**

Country	Total	Professional & Technical	Admin. & Manage-rial	Clerical & Related	Sales	Service Workers	Produc-tion Re-lated	Others
Bahrain,	16.2	5.0	0.1	4.4	0.2	5	0.3	16
1981	100%	30.9%	0.6%	27.2%	1.2%	28.4%	1.8%	9.9%
Iran,	1985.7	188	1.4	64	8	68	659	174
1976	100%	9.5%	0.1%	3.2%	0.4%	3.4%	33.2%	8.8%
Kuwait,	62	24.7	0.1	11	0.5	26	0.4	-
1980	100%	39.8%	0.2%	17%	0.8%	41.4%	0.6%	-
Syria	343	52.7	0.7	24	2.5	6	45	11
1979	100%	15.3%	0.2%	6.9%	0.7%	1.9%	13.2%	33%
United	10	4.3	0.1	2	0.1	3	0.1	0.4
Arab	100%	43%	1.0%	20%	1%	29%	1%	40%
Emirates,								
1975								

In almost all Arab-Muslim states a far greater number of women than men are illiterate. There are also significant gender differences in the literacy rates between rural and urban women. The literacy rate for rural women in Morocco is only 5 percent of the corresponding rate for urban men while for urban women it is 62 percent. In Tunisia among rural women aged 35 years and older, fewer than 1 percent are literate and even in the urban areas fewer than 7 percent are literate. There is a significant increase in literacy among the younger population but the gender difference remains. In Syria, for example, some 36 percent of Syrian women aged 15–24 are literate but among young men of the same age the percentage is 78.[26]

In school enrollment a much lower proportion of women than men is enrolled at school at every age and for every country (see Table 61).

The highest school enrollment is found in Jordan and the Lebanon. The lowest enrollments are in Afghanistan and Morocco. Today literacy and higher levels of education are recognized as prerequisites to entering the labor force, especially the modern sectors. Given the deliberate discrimination against women, particularly against rural women, and the massive rate of illiteracy it will be another three or four generations before there is any significant improvement and then only if Muslim religious prejudices are stowed away, which seems extremely unlikely.

Muslim Law

The legal (or general social) status of women in the Middle East cannot be reported upon or understood without reference to Muslim law. For so pervasive are the Muslim legal restrictions on women's rights that today's feminist struggles in this part of the world have been largely battles for piecemeal secularization.

Only in Turkey, immediately following World War I, has any Middle Eastern nation formally abandoned religious law. What Turkey did was to translate the Swiss Civil Code and adopt it as its own. The rigidity of many Islamic precepts have been somewhat relaxed and modified in several other Muslim nations and this will be understood by examining the law in Egypt, Morocco, Iraq and Iran.

And perhaps the guideline for the future is to be found in the Preamble to the Universal Islamic Declaration of Human Rights, proclaimed by the Islamic Council in 1981. This sets forth the "obligation to establish an Islamic order" (g) (i) "wherein all human beings shall be equal and none shall enjoy a privilege or suffer a disadvantage or discrimination by reason of race, color, sex, origin or language." For the moment, however, the guideline, the only structure, is the *Qur'an*.

Table 60. Distribution of Economically Active Women by Type of Occupation in Selected Muslim-Arab States, in Thousands. Source: International Labor Organization, *Yearbook of Labor Statistics,* Geneva, 1982, 1983, Table 2B. Note: "Others" include workers not classified by occupation and the unemployed. Agricultural and forestry workers not included.

	Rural		Urban	
Measure and age	*Women*	*Men*	*Women*	*Men*
Percent literate				
15 to 24 years	15.6	72.7	68.2	84.8
25 to 34 years	4.5	33.4	41.3	74.0
35 years and over	0.8	13.6	12.4	43.0
Percent enrolled:				
10 to 14 years	34.4	72.8	80.2	90.4
15 to 19 years	19.0	40.4	43.8	59.2
20 to 24 years	2.0	9.5	11.0	19.2

Table 61. Literacy and School Enrollment. Source: *Women of The World,* WID-3, Office of Women in Development, United States Agency for International Development, United States Department of Commerce, Washington DC, 1984 and 1985, p. 3.

The legal status of women in Islam has been conceptualized and outlined by the *Qur'an,* supplemented by the *Hadith* (sayings of the Prophet), developed by *Ada* (local practice), formulated into *Shari'a* (Muslim code), interpreted by the *Mullahs* (religious leaders and teachers) and pronounced by the *Qadis* (religious judges). To complicate matters, there are not only divisions between Shi'ite and Sunni law but also four schools of Sunni law.

Despite the inescapable conclusion that Islamic law is restrictive of women's rights, it was (and is) a basic precept of the *Qur'an* that its rules regarding women are designed to raise their status and position. For the Muslim faith came to Arabia at a time when tribal law dictated the sale of women into marriage—sale by their guardians who kept the purchase price. It came at a time when married women had no property or succession rights and were completely under the rule of their husbands who could break the marital bonds at will.

The *Qur'an* may have raised the social position of women with its teaching that every member of the faithful is equal before Allah, and it certainly removed or at least modified some of the injustices of the then-customary law. But Muslim law is ever within the framework of Surah 4 of the *Qur'an:* "Men have authority over women because Allah has made the one superior to the other.... As for those from whom you fear disobedience, admonish them and send them to beds apart and beat them."

Family Relationships

Under Shi'ite law and three of the four schools of Sunni law, a woman's marriage must be dictated by her guardian, usually her father. A guardian is supposed to give regard to the wishes of his ward, but he is nevertheless empowered to contract her into marriage without her consent. This likewise applies to minors among the Hanafis, but the Hanafi school of Sunni law permits adult women to contract their own marriages.

Since there is no minimum age regulating this marriage contract and since many Muslims believe that a woman is in disgrace if she is not married after reaching puberty, child marriages have been all too common.

Polygamy is authorized under Islamic law, but only for men. Up to four wives are permissible, provided that each is given a separate residence. The only way to protect a woman from her husband's prospective polygamy is a stipulation prohibiting subsequent marriage or marriages in the contract of marriage entered into by her guardian.

A wife may have only one husband, and adultery is punishable by stoning.

Divorce poses very difficult problems for the Muslim woman. It is something which she has been denied under religious law. There does exist the *Faskh,* a judicial dissolution of marriage, but it is quite restrictive. Under Hanafi law, it will be granted only if the husband is impotent. There is also the *Khul'a* or *Ikhula,* in which the husband and wife may agree to a marriage dissolution; but this usually leaves the woman stripped of any property of the marriage.

The husband, on the other hand, may still invoke the *talaq,* the unilateral repudiation of the marriage, at any time, for any reason. This existed as well in Middle East tribal law. It was modified in the *Qur'an* by the introduction of the Iddah, a waiting period of three of the wife's menstrual cycles after the *talaq* pronouncement before the divorce could become effective. During this period the husband may unilaterally revoke the repudiation and reinstate the marriage.

But this is scant protection for the married woman. Alimony does not exist for the divorced wife, nor is there generally any obligation to provide support save, according to some schools, during the waiting periods. Her only protection has been a provision in her marriage contract for a dower payable on divorce.

The matters are covered in two sections of the Universal Islamic Declaration of Human Rights, XX(b) and (c). It provides that every married woman is entitled to "seek and obtain dissolution of marriage [*Khul'a*] in accordance with the terms of the Law. This right is in addition to her right to seek divorce through the courts." In the event of divorce, she is entitled only to "receive during the statutory period of waiting [*Iddah*] means of maintenance commensurate with her husband's resources, for herself as well as for the children she nurses or keeps."

In the event of divorce, the wife has custody only when the children are very young, after which custody is given to the father. Under Hanafi law this change of custody occurs when a boy is 7 and a girl is 9.

Property

What was in tribal law a price paid to the guardian for a woman sold into marriage became under the *Qur'an* the dower (*mahr*) which then belonged (and still belongs) to the wife alone. Frequently this right is minimized by the husband's management rights over the property of his spouse during marriage.

The *Qur'an* (also for the first time) gave the women of then-tribal Arabia the right of intestate succession. It was far from an equal right. The basic *Qur'an* prescription provides that the male takes double the share of the female occupying the same blood relationship with the deceased. Even the newly adopted Universal Islamic Declaration of Human Rights skirts equality on this issue. Article XX(d) merely states that the married woman is entitled to "inherit from her husband, her parents, her children and other relatives according to the law."

While Shi'ite law has the reputation in the West of being more restrictive of women's rights than Sunni law, it is far more equal in the area of intestate succession. The widow or widower or both inherits in all cases. Then all potential heirs are divided into three classes: parents and their descendants and uncles and aunts and their descendants. Those in the first class will take to the exclusion of those in the other two classes. Those in the second class take to the exclusion of those in the third class. Thus a woman in the first class, for example, would inherit property rather than a male in the second or third classes. (A daughter would take to the exclusion of an uncle or grandfather.) However, within the class, the male would get double the share of the female.

Sunni law gives far greater preference to males and to male agnates, i.e., relatives in the male line of the deceased. If the deceased husband had issue, the widow's share is one-eighth; if he had no descendants, the widow's share is one-quarter. Nor can her share be increased by will without the consent of the other heirs.

If a deceased leaves both a son and daughter, the former takes two-thirds and the latter one-third. If the descendant had one daughter she inherits half of the estate; if there are two or more daughters, they share two-thirds. The remaining part of the state goes to the nearest male agnate.

Personal Autonomy

Under Muslim law the woman is restricted to the home, and even there she has few rights. Wifely disobedience is a recognized offense, and punishment by the husband is authorized. It cannot, however, extend to bloodletting or the breaking of a limb.

Having control over his wife's movements, the husband can confine her to the marital domicile and thus preclude her from seeking employment.

Muslim law denies women the right to religious public office; no woman may become a *Qaid,* a municipal officer or judge. Women in some situations are incompetent as witnesses; in other cases the admitted testimony of two women is the equivalent of that of one male witness.

Case Studies

In the following three sections there are broad case studies of the legal worlds of women in Tunisia, Egypt and Iran. Two other countries worth looking at briefly are Morocco, because of its more enlightened attitude toward women in politics (at least legally), and, at the other end of the spectrum, Iraq, which is still extremely backward in the area of women's rights. Morocco is also a good example of an Arab country long exposed to Western influence. Iraq, on the other hand, has had far less exposure.

Morocco

The Constitution of Morocco (1972) declares that all citizens shall be equal before the law (Article 5). It further provides that men and women shall enjoy equal political rights (Article 8). And it does not limit female voting and political participation. However, despite these pronouncements the fact is that few women vote and almost none hold public office. The social customs of this Islamic country still keep women closely tied to the home. True, Moroccan statutes have been somewhat more enlightened than those of many other Islamic countries, but women are still treated by the law as social inferiors.

The Moroccan Family Law was passed the day after independence in 1957. This retains the historical and cultural patterns set by Moslem belief and ideology. The inequality of men and women in the family should be evident from the rights assigned to each. Article 35:

> The rights of the wife in relation to her husband are (1) support ensured by law, such as food, clothing, medical care, housing; (2) equal treatment with other wives, in the case of polygamy; (3) authorization to visit her parents, and to receive visits from them, within the limits of social convention; and (4) full liberty to administer and dispose of her estate without any control by her husband, the latter having no power whatsoever over the estate of the wife." //

Article 36:

> The rights of the husband in relation to his wife are (1) fidelity; (2) obedience; (3) the breast feeding of children issuing from the marriage, if possible; (4) the responsibility of supervising the order and organization of the household; and (5) deference to the father, mother, and close relatives of the husband."

Note that even the rights of married women which are set forth are essentially based upon dependency upon her husband. The exception is the language which provides the wife with full liberty to administer her own estate. This is liberal by Islamic standards. Article 35, item 3, on the other hand, is a sharp curtailment of freedom of movement, since it places limitations upon the right of the woman to visit her own parents or to be visited by them.

Scarcely 20 percent of Moroccan women are in the labor force, a low figure even for a Muslim state. Evidently the weight of custom and tradition is still heavy. For those women who do work outside the home, the law is more in accord with the spirit of the Constitution. Perhaps the most notable achievement for women's rights is the growing numbers of women in the Moroccan civil service. Since 1958 the law (Dahir, February 24, 1958) has stipulated that women should have equal access to public employment. As a result, more and more Moroccan women have gained positions as white-collar government workers. However, apart from agricultural employment, women workers are otherwise not on the increase.

There appears to be a tiny elite of educated Moroccan women who are the chief beneficiaries of enlightened legislation. Apart from governmental employment, this group usually serves as nurses or secretaries. Their numbers are small. As it is, teaching and governmental service are higher prestige positions for Moroccan women.

Rural women generally do not work for a wage. They labor as peasants for only their meals and clothing. Often rural women do perform hard physical labor, such as weeding, harvesting, picking crops, and even carrying loads of firewood. Yet these tasks are little affected by law. The only alternatives are other forms of manual labor or prostitution.

Iraq

Far less exposed to Western influence than Morocco and Egypt, Iraq is sometimes classified among the more backward Middle Eastern states in the area of human rights. This is still the situation in regard to political rights, but great strides have been made in removing disabilities suffered by women.

The Ba'ath government's National Charter of 1971 is generally cited as the cornerstone of women's liberation. It provides *inter alia* for the "liberation of women from feudalist and bourgeois concepts and from the conditions and bondage that had rendered her a mere means of entertainment or second-class citizen."

However, women's rights were legislated long before the 1971 National Charter. It was back in 1959 that the Code of Personal Status was enacted, curtailing the husband's use of *talaq* to nullify the marital union. The practice of polygamy was also eliminated.

It is in employment rights, however, that women in Iraq have made the greatest progress. True, this has been primarily in response to the biological needs of working women. But it is the very recognition of those needs which has encouraged the entry of women into out-of-the-home employment.

Equality in education did not come until the passage of Compulsory Education Act No. 118 of 1976. This made education compulsory for all children between six and ten in free schools. The law also makes intermediate, secondary and university education open to women as well as men.

Prostitution and procuring have been illegal since the passage of Act No. 54 of 1958. And forced marriages and adoptions have been recognized as slavery and prohibited on those grounds.

The right to vote did not come until 1980 in National Assembly Act No. 55, which recognized the right of women to stand as candidates for the National Assembly as well as other elected bodies.

Labor Act No. 151 of 1970, Iraq's basic labor code, provides for both pre- and post-natal care for working mothers and their offspring. Maternity leave is guaranteed and employers are required to maintain free nurseries. The period of maternity leave for government employees is stated with more specificity in Civil Service Act No. 94 of 1977. The proviso is for 72 days, of which 21 may be taken prior to birth.

Two groups of women government employees get special recognition. Female doctors and nurses are given military rank pursuant to the Women's Military Service Act of 1977. Furthermore, women police officers are granted military rank "according to their qualifications" by Revolutionary Command Council Decision No. 550 of 1979.

The Special Case of Iran (Persia)

One of the greatest upheavals in human society since World War II occurred in Iran, where an Islamic identity is now being forced on the population by a state of clergymen, followers of the late Ayatollah Khomeini, who led them to power.

Writing in *Women in the World: A Comparative Study,* Elizabeth Sanasarian traced the major changes brought about by the new regime. First they uprooted the Shah's education system, which was Western in general terms, and substituted an Islamic one. Within the first two years after the Shah's overthrow in 1979 large numbers of teachers, female, and principals of girls' schools were dismissed, many on falsified charges of prostitution and moral misconduct. They were replaced by the clergy or pro-Islamic women. Education opportunities for women were reduced by banning coeducation and disallowing young married women to attend high school. Female students could no longer directly question their tutor. They had to write their questions and hand them to a female inspector who handed them to the professor. A curtain separated male and female students. In 1982 women were also banned from the agricultural faculties.[27] Force-feeding the laws of Islam led to shocking excesses. When a female teacher was found to have books by Flaubert, Zola and Rousseau in her home she was summarily executed.

When Khomeini came to power in February 1979 he drafted a new constitution based on orthodox interpretation of Islamic jurisprudence. Legislation passed in 1983 prevented women from serving as judges or working in the health field or in the military. Segregation laws were passed banning women from public transportation, cafeterias, cinemas and beaches. By 1986 almost all the laws had been converted to the fundamentalist Shi'ite interpretation of Islamic jurisprudence. The minimum age for marriage was reduced to 13 years. The Penal Code licenses a husband to kill his wife if he witnesses her in the act of intercourse with another, but the reverse does not apply.[28]

Absurdities (granted—in Western eyes only) sprouted. Islamic law forbids the execution of a virgin; thus the Ayatollah ruled that any woman condemned by the courts to die must first lose her virginity, through forced temporary marriage or rape. (Thus newspapers were able to report a new type of crime, the official rape of a virgin criminal before she faced the firing squad.) But two women sleeping together naked, after having been warned three times, can be summarily executed.[29] Thus a lesbian virgin can be executed!

By 1981 Khomeini's government had abolished all legislation favoring women's rights. In March 1982 the legal minimum age of execution was set at 10 years for girls, but 16 years for boys.

Khomeini always objected to women having the vote, reported Shireen Mahdavi, and he led the protests in Iran during the reign of Mohammed Shah Pahlavi which resulted in the Shah's proposal to let women vote being dropped. Khomeini did not write specifically on women, Mahdavi said, but he personally set out in writing his views on the rights (*sic*) and duties of a woman in marriage.

For example, "a woman who has entered into a permanent marriage is not allowed to leave the house without her husband's permission. She must submit herself to any pleasure he desires. She may not refuse herself on any ground other than religiously accepted ones. . . . If a woman does not obey her husband according to the manner set out . . . she is then sinful and is not entitled to food, clothes, housing or intercourse. . . ."[30]

Muslim scholars often try to make the point that Islamic Law "protects" women. Whoever can read any protection in Khomeini's interpretation does not understand the meaning of the word or is being intellectually dishonest.

Summarizing the position of women in the hierarchical structure of the Muslim-Arab family, Halim Barakat wrote in *Women and the Family in the Middle East* that women are secluded and segregated; the roles most available to women are those of daughter, sister, wife, mother or mother-in-law; veiling is a must; personal status codes discriminate against women; ownership of property is almost exclusively confined to men; the prevailing standard of morality stresses traditional ideas of femininity, motherhood, wifehood and sexuality; the prevailing religious ideology considers women to be a source of evil, anarchy *(fitna)* and trickery or deception (*kaid)*. Finally, women may still be exposed to such practices as forced marriage, crimes of honor and clitoridectomy.[31]

As far as clitoridectomy (various forms of female circumcision) is concerned, Dr. Nahid F. Toubia wrote in the same book that this aggression against female sexuality is part of the total process of subordination of women to facilitate the use of their reproductive and productive powers by the patriarchal society. The operation reduces women's ability to achieve sexual gratification but not her sexual desire. Thus, Toubia concludes, the physical health of the victim is not the only reason for condemning the act; the psychological cruelty is also to be condemned.[32]

Although Islamic laws cannot easily be dismissed as a religious system designed to serve only the interest of men (though that is the distinct impression it creates for most Westerners), there is also an insincerity and dogmatic inconsistency in the Muslim ideology that is hard to escape. Pro-Muslim scholars admit that, down through the ages, with few exceptions, the consensus of Islamic jurists affirmed, emphasized and praised the "completeness" and "authoritativeness," for all times, of law (*figh)* as found in the (law) books of the four Sunni schools.

As John Esposito, an American professor who writes with understanding and sympathy on Islam, stated: "The law was complete; there was no need for substantive change." Yet the same scholars point to the fact that this situation has been abruptly challenged in the modern period as once-isolated Muslim societies have sought to respond to the challenges of modernization. "While these changes have not affected all of society to the same degree," Esposito wrote, "reforms in Muslim family law have occurred in most Muslim countries. . . . Conflict between the forces of conservatism and modernism has continued. Resistance to change often resulted in indirect, *ad hoc* legal methods of reform. . . ."[33]

If this situation were projected onto the Christian religion, it would be equivalent to dispensing with some of the Ten Commandments simply because the world's economic structure has undergone radical change. Change in laws and change in basic religious principles are two totally different concepts, yet the current conflict among Islamic scholars indicates that religious principles of Islam can be jettisoned if massive income from oil begins to change the economic and financial infrastructure of a Muslim state—and when the need for qualified female labor increases. Thus economic factors would appear stronger than basic laws of God as passed on by the Prophet Muhammad. This point is made in all respect towards true believers in the Muslim faith. But if, as Muslim scholars believe, God laid down certain rules insofar as women are concerned and relayed this via the Prophet, when and where has God's mind changed? And to whom and where has God relayed any changes? Or has God simply been misunderstood all these centuries? By Muhammad himself? And all the clergymen?

A more optimistic note about women in Iran, particularly female employment, has been sounded by Val Moghadam in *The Journal of Middle East Studies.* Moghadam analyzed Iran's ideology regarding women's role and contrasted it with women's employment patterns. She indicated that though labor participation rates for women have declined, they have declined even more for men and government employment for women is actually higher today than before the revolution. She also suggests a discrepancy between ideological prescriptions and economic imperatives. If the statistics of the Islamic regime can be believed (which is extremely doubtful), women's education which received high priority during the years of the last Shah of Iran has not come to a standstill.

Moghadam indicates that there has been an expansion of professional, scientific, and technical workers in the public sector and the higher educational level of women is reflected in the occupation structure of the current female labor force.

In sum, the figures indicate women have not been driven out of the work force. But the conditions have changed. "Stripped of power and status, women work at the pleasure of men and the whim of employers." Nonetheless, Moghadam argues, the mere fact that so many women are still working is a surprise. She said that women's presence suggests a certain resilience and resistance to domination. "Certainly women's activities in Iran exceed the parameters of the orthodox school of Islam." Behind this aberration, said Moghadam, lie the imperatives of economic development; the exigencies of the war with Iraq; resistance by educated women with prior work experience and

Educational Level	1976–1977	%	1982–1983	%
Informal education	7,217	1.6	5,393	1.0
Primary school	51,298	11.2	61,261	11.0
Guidance	4,026	0.9	14,120	2.5
Intermediate	68,126	14.7	33,775	6.0
High school graduate	109,732	23.9	236,028	42.2
Postdiploma	23,395	5.1	43,172	7.7
Bachelor's degree	27,371	6.0	38,797	6.9
Master's degree	3,088	0.7	2,799	0.5
Ph.D.	2,283	0.5	2,985	0.5
NAD[a]	382	0.1	4,777	0.9
Illiterate	163,089	35.5	115,778	20.7
Literate	269,918	64.5	443,107	79.3
TOTAL	406,000	100.0	558,885	100.0

Table 62. Iran: Educational Level of Employed Women Aged 10 Years and Over in Urban Areas: 1976–1977 and 1982–1983. Source: *Statistical Yearbook,* 1363, 1984–1985, p. 64. Note: *a* - not adequately defined.

ambiguities in the discourse and policies of the Islamic political elite. Thus far, educated, Western-oriented, upper-middle-class women have borne the brunt of the Islamic regime's most retrograde policies, concluded Moghadam, and the absence of a coherent state plan for socio-economic development has left some women with some room to maneuver.[34]

22. Case Study: Egypt

Egypt is an Islamic state, if not an Arab society. This explains why Egypt has been a pioneer among the Islamic states of the Middle East in defining and expanding women's rights. Religion and religious law has a less fundamentalist cast. The literal words of the *Qur'an* have been modified and softened, so that the lot of Egyptian women has been improved much more than in surrounding Islamic states. This is also due to the legal heritage of Egypt which also differs from that of its neighbors. Roman law, especially that derived from the Napoleonic Code during Egypt's French occupation, has limited the reach of religious law. And, surprisingly enough, so has the law of the Ottoman Empire of which Egypt was a part.

Modern Egyptian politics has also aided the cause of women's rights. In 1962, in the radical transformation of Egyptian politics brought about by the overthrow of King Farouk by Gamal Abdel Nasser, special attention was paid to women. Nasser's slogan urged that "women must enjoy equal rights with men." In 1956, women were given the right to vote. The education of women advanced greatly, opening more opportunities in universities and in secondary schools. However, in the field of women's personal rights—marriage, divorce, and property—women enjoy less generous treatment. In fact, the substantive laws of Islam still prevail in these areas.

Political Rights

The Egyptian Constitution of 1956 gave women the rights to vote, to run for office in national and local elections, and to hold certain public offices.[1] Although voting is compulsory for men it has never been so for women. This fact, coupled with the traditional Islamic view that women are unequal with men due to their nature (which is inherently unstable and unfit for making important decisions), has resulted in a small percentage of women actually utilizing the franchise.[2] In order to vote the person must be a member of the Arab Socialist Union. Membership has at times been denied to females.[3] Although the government has given the franchise to women it has not provided a legal or institutional framework which would make utilization of a woman's voting rights accessible or practical for a great number of Egyptian women.[4]

Women are limited by Islamic principles from holding all the offices which are open to men. The principle that the testimony of a woman is worth only half that of a man precludes her from seeking judgeships and other high-level positions such as provincial governor.[5] One step which the government has made to facilitate greater representation by women was to change the election laws in order to reserve 30 of the 392 parliamentary seats exclusively for women.[6] But the number of reserved seats for women has remained at 30 while the total number of seats has increased to 448.[7]

The question of equality for women is addressed in the National Charter of 1962 and the Constitution of 1971. The National Charter set out the basic principles which the government hoped to realize and stated: "Women must be regarded as equal to man and must therefore, shed the remaining shackles that impede her free movement so that she might take a constructive and profound part in shaping life."[8] But this broad and encompassing goal was later limited by the Constitution of the Arab Republic of Egypt (1971) in Articles 10 and 11. Although both Articles seem to recognize that both sexes are equal socially, politically, culturally and economically, they confine women's equality to the level set by traditional rules of Islamic jurisprudence. By stressing the importance of the family and obliging the state to ensure that a woman's domestic role and any role she chooses outside of the household are properly coordinated, the Constitution reinforces the belief that women belong in the home rather than the political sphere.[9]

Family Relationships

The Egyptian Constitution makes it evident that women are still primarily regarded as mothers and as members of family units. Article 9 proclaims that "the family is the basis of the society founded on religion, morality and patriotism." A woman's obligations to her family are stressed in Article 11, which says: "The State shall guarantee the proper coordination between the duties of woman towards the family and her work in the society, considering her equal with man in the fields of political, social, cultural and economic life without violations of the rules of Islamic jurisprudence."

In addition, Article 10 says that the state "shall guarantee the protection of motherhood and childhood...."

Article 11 is, however, limited to bestowing political, social, cultural and economic equality upon women which appears to be no "violation" of Islamic law. However, the personal rights of women in marriage, divorce, etc., are separated from her other rights, and are in the care of more traditional Islamic authorities.

The traditional age for marriage under Islamic law is as young as 13 for girls. In 1923, Egypt passed a law which raised the age to 16 for girls and 18 for boys.[10] Two other requirements have been added to the marriage laws since then. They are the requirement that all marriages be registered and that both people consent to the union.[11] Legally, it is impossible to compel an Egyptian girl to marry.[12] The regulation imposed by the *Shari'a* forbidding a Muslim woman from marrying a non-Moslem still remains in effect as does the right of a Muslim man to marry a Jewish or Christian woman.[13] The *Shari'a* does give a Muslim woman the right to retain her birth name after marriage.[14]

As in most Moslem countries, the marriage contract has the ability to provide and protect rights which an Egyptian woman does not automatically possess under Islamic jurisprudence. The future bride has the right to add special clauses to the contract which are legally binding upon the husband.[15] Utilization of this instrument to protect the bride's rights tends to be rare due either to ignorance, romantic notions or the strong desire of the family to have the girl married.[16] Similar problems arise in reference to the *mahr,* which accompanies the marriage contract. Although the dowry traditionally belongs exclusively to the bride it is not uncommon for her to relinquish it to her family or husband.[17] The *Qur'an* sanctions such a practice in Surah 4 (Women) verse 4, which reads: "And give unto the women (whom ye marry) free gift of their marriage portions; but if they of their own accord remit unto you a part thereof, then ye are welcome to absorb it (in your wealth)."[18] Possession of the dowry is legally vested in the wife only upon the actual marriage. In the event that the union is never consummated, half of the *mahr* must be returned to the groom.[19] If the bride is not a virgin at the time of her marriage, she may lose her dowry.

Under Islamic law the wife is to receive full economic support from her husband in exchange for her obedience. The wife's duty to obey was codified in Decree Law 44 (1979) which states that her failure to do so places her in a "legal state of infringement."[20] Under Article 345 she can be forced to submit to his demands.[21] If a woman decides to leave her husband for almost any reason including battery, he can obtain a court decision to force her return and she forfeits her right to his financial support by refusing to live with him.[22]

Decree Law 44 also codifies the Islamic practice of a man's full guardianship rights over his wife and children.[23] Personal Status Amendments were included in this law to temper the customs in the case of child custody upon divorce. Previously the wife retained custody of boys under seven and girls under nine but the amendments increased the ages to 10 and 12.[24] A court may extend her custody period to a maximum of age 15 for males and until marriage for female children.[25]

The Personal Status Amendments of 1979 have also advanced women's positions in reference to divorce in other ways. Islam provides only the dowry and financial support during the *iddah* as maintenance for the divorced wife. The new laws guarantee the wife a home if she has custody of the children whether it is the couple's house or apartment or another which the husband finds for them.[26] The wife will receive 40 percent of the man's salary in alimony for a period of three years, but if they were married for longer than 15 years she will receive alimony for life or until she remarries.[27]

Although men still have the right of *talaq* or unilateral divorce,[28] the Personal Status Laws require that the man register the action before witnesses at the Registrar's Office, and it further demands that his wife be officially and immediately notified of the proceeding.[29] Egyptian law recognizes three types of divorce: revocable, by mutual consent, and by judicial decree. In a revocable divorce the woman is not allowed to remarry during the *iddah* and her husband is permitted to take her back at any time during this period.[30] The husband is allowed three divorces by law, but if his wife remarries after the *iddah* that divorce will not be counted towards the quota.[31]

Law 25 of 1920 and 1924 created the right to divorce by mutual consent and by judicial decree. A woman can obtain a divorce by mutual consent (*khole*) by paying her husband which is usually done by forfeiting her dowry.[32] It may also be granted on the grounds that he is incurably sick or disabled.[33] When seeking a divorce by judicial decree the court will attempt to reconcile the couple, but such attempts are only permitted for nine months, at the end of which the divorce will be final.[34] A woman can bring action on the following grounds: for the husband's failure to provide financial support, if the man physically maltreats or harms her "on moral or social grounds," if the husband has been missing for more than five years, or if he is serving a long prison term.[35] But the woman's and man's rights to attain a divorce remain unequal in that Decree Law 44 maintains in the Islamic tradition that a man's right to divorce is absolute while a woman may sue only on certain grounds.[36]

Polygamy is legal in Egypt and in accordance with the *Qur'an* a man may take up to four wives. Prior to the Personal Status Laws he did not have to inform his wife of any additional marriages, and usually the fact would remain a secret. The new law requires that official notification be sent to the wife of her husband's intent to take a second wife. If she objects she has a basis on which to sue for divorce.[37] When she has not been notified the wife has one year from the time she has knowledge of the marriage to seek divorce.[38]

Recent judgments have struck down a number of the Personal Status Laws on procedural grounds, but some have already been reinstated,[39] and presently the status and rights of Egyptian women in these areas may be questionable.

Property

Egypt retains the Islamic custom of the *mahr*. This means that the husband must make a gift to the wife as part of the marriage contract, which becomes her property. By custom most Egyptian brides use the *mahr* to purchase furniture. Often the *mahr* is paid in installments, but the *mahr* becomes her property only by the act of marriage, not by an engagement. In general, Muslim wives may own property independent of their husbands and marriage does not affect their independent property rights. Neither the husband nor the wife is liable for the debts of the other.

Egyptian women are given the right to own and control their own property at all times, even during and after marriage.[40] The right is granted by the *Shari'a* and includes property the wife gains through her labor, inheritance or dowry. In actual practice this right may not be as beneficial to the majority of Egyptian women as it could be. Only a small number of upper-class women have significant property holdings, and many females feel compelled to turn over their inheritance or dowry to the males of the family.[41] Financial dependence on male kinsmen prior to marriage and in the event of divorce, separation or widowhood induces a woman to relinquish the rights she has.[42]

Inheritance laws allow both men and women to dispose of one-third of their property as they wish, and the remaining portion is divided under Islamic law.[43] Females receive one-half the share of males. A wife receives one-fourth of her spouse's estate unless he has children, and then her share is one-eighth. A wife is also entitled to all of the furnishings in her husband's home.[44]

The *Shari'a* also places strictures based on religion as to who can inherit.

A husband and wife who belong to different religions cannot inherit from each other, and children of a non-Muslim mother cannot inherit from her.[45]

Employment

Egyptian wives may not pursue careers outside the home without the consent of their husbands. If a woman does seek employment without such consent, the husband is relieved of his obligation to support his wife.

Egyptian women have entered the professions, trade, industry, and government in greater numbers than elsewhere in the Islamic Middle East. They receive maternity protection and make financial contributions to the family. Egyptian working women often demand the inclusion of the equal right to divorce as part of their marriage contracts.

There are no government-promulgated laws in Egypt which require that women remain in the home or prohibit their entry into the labor force, but the traditional Islamic practices bar entrance to a large percentage of the female population.[46] Women's role is associated solely with her household, and any outside employment is contingent on the amount of contact she would have with members of the opposite sex.[47] The government has attempted to expand women's freedom to work through the Personal Status Laws which say that the right is no longer contingent upon her husband's approval.[48]

Another factor which limits access to employment is the woman's responsibility towards her family. As mentioned before, the Constitution of 1971 stresses the importance of the woman's familial obligations. This belief has resulted in employment being mostly limited to middle and upper class women who can afford domestic help to relieve the tension and responsibility flowing from their dual role.[49]

For women who do seek employment, there are a number of laws which are designed to protect, but some may also be detrimental in that the cost to the employer of hiring a female may be higher.[50] Equal pay for equal work in the public sector and government is mandated by legislation which was passed in 1933, 1959, and 1978.[51] In 1959, discrimination in employment based on gender was outlawed.[52]

The Labor Code of 1978 provides the present maternity benefits which employers are required to supply. These include three months' fully paid leave which may be utilized twice, and unpaid leave for a period of two years which may be exercised three times.[53] For women who return to work after childbirth, two breaks of a half-hour each are allowed for 18 months in order that the baby may be fed. Any employer who has more than 100 female employees must provide a nursery.[54]

Women are forbidden some types of work which the government believes is physically or morally harmful.[55]

Personal Autonomy

Egypt has been a Middle East pioneer in at least some attempts at family planning as a means of population control. The National Charter of 1962 made family planning a government priority. The upper classes have been responsive to such policies. The lower classes, on the other hand, have been suspicious of these efforts, partly on religious grounds and partly on the basis of the need for the income produced by the labor of their children.

The most striking practice in Islamic countries is seclusion and wearing of a veil by women. This practice is still prevalent in Egypt except to a lesser degree among upper class women. No laws are in force which make any requirements concerning seclusion or veiling.[56] All restrictions stem from Islamic cultural practices. The strong emphasis on family honor which is based on the purity of the female members is protected by keeping women away from men so that they have no opportunity to humiliate the family.[57] Even an adult, unmarried and working woman is restrained by these policies and will continue to live with her parents and limit her social life within a sphere composed entirely of females.[58] The only period in a girl's life when she is allowed to associate freely with men is the time before she reaches puberty.[59] The woman becomes no freer upon her marriage because her husband then gains full authority over her movements so that she even needs his permission to obtain a passport or to travel.[60]

In order to reduce sexual desires in young women many Egyptian families have their daughters circumcised at a young age. This is done despite warnings concerning the safety hazards of the procedure and despite the fact there is no basis in the *Qur'an* for such a practice.[61] In other areas of personal choice, a woman's freedom to make decisions concerning childbirth is limited by Islamic doctrine. Sterilization is one example. Although Egyptian law does not prohibit sterilization, the Moslem religion disallows it except in cases of proven risk of "hereditary disease, physical deformity, or mental illness."[62]

Egyptian law reflects the Islamic prohibition against abortion in the 1937 Penal Code, articles 260, 261 and 263. Islam allows abortion only in the situation where the mother's life is threatened, but the Penal Code expands this to include circumstances of physical deformity and congenital abnormality.[63] If a woman agrees to undergo an illegal abortion she is subject to punishment under Article 262.[64] Other forms of birth control are available, and the Egyptian government promotes their use by sponsoring free family planning clinics.[65]

The criminal codes reflect the traditional attitude of Islam towards women. Prostitution is illegal in Egypt, but punishment when the crime is detected is reserved exclusively for the female who may be imprisoned. The man is only required to testify in order to convict the woman.[66] Although rape is illegal, marital rape is not recognized except if there is an accusation of sexual assault where the male has an infectious (venereal) disease or if he demands anal intercourse.[67] Under Islamic law a woman can charge her husband with battery but if she does she faces the possibility that he will seek a divorce.[68]

Women's rights in Egypt may not be impressive by European or American standards, but they are substantial. The Westernizing influence of French and British colonialism has overcome some of the harsher limitations of Islamic law, and can be seen as a lasting benefit of the much maligned era of colonialism.

23. Case Study: Tunisia

Political Rights

Legislation instituted under President Habib Bourguiba (replaced because of senility in November 1987) gives Tunisian women equal political rights with Tunisian men.[1] This reform began in 1957 when for the first time women were permitted to vote in local elections.[2] The Union Nationale des Femmes de Tunisie (U.N.F.T.) was formed in that year. Bourguiba encouraged this group in its goal to achieve female emancipation.[3] The Tunisian administration believed this goal was a necessary step in their plan to modernize the nation. In order to get women other than the few who were well-educated to exercise the franchise, U.N.F.T. set up conferences to teach women their new rights and duties and also to encourage them to vote.[4]

After the municipal elections of 1957 women voted in all subsequent elections.[5] One failing of the system in its effort to encourage women to participate is the fact that some regions automatically register males over the age of 20 but female voter registration is voluntary.[6] Voting is a duty for a man, and he may be reprimanded for his failure to act, but for a woman to vote is optional.

Legislation was also passed which permits females to run for and hold political office.[7] Many Moslem countries forbid women from becoming judges because of the *Qur'an* statement that a woman's testimony is worth only half that of a man's. Tunisia is one of the few which has opened this important position to women.[8]

The Family

Family law in Tunisia is governed by the 1957 Tunisian Code of Personal Status (Majallet Al-Ahwal Al Al-Shakhsiyah). Book I, Article 5 of this code set the minimum marriage age as the time at which the person reaches puberty and lists the standard as 15 for girls and 18 for boys.[9] With the consent of the potential spouse's guardian and a judge this minimum may be lowered if it is proven that the boy or girl has reached physical maturity.[10] Article 8 requires that the guardian be "the agnatic relative and should be sane, of the male sex and have attained the age of majority."[11] The mother is not legally capable of providing the required consent. The age limits were raised through a 1964 amendment to 17 for females and 20 for males.[12]

Bourguiba's administration was attempting to curtail the practice of selling off young girls by including the minimum age and a mandate that both parties enter into the marriage voluntarily.[13] Traditionally, neither the bride nor groom had any right in the decision of whom they were to marry although the family might heed any objections.[14] Article 3 gives the parties the right of consent or rejection by stating: "Marriage shall not be concluded save with the consent of both spouses."[15] Arranged marriages are still permissible but the spouses must agree.[16]

Polygamy was banned by the Code of Personal Status despite the many Muslim countries which claim that the practice is sanctioned by the *Shari'a*. Tunisia opted to accept an interpretation of the Prophet Mohammed's words as meaning that polygamy is acceptable only in very extreme circumstances such as when there is a large number of war widows who are without any type of support or home. In other circumstances Tunisia believes the Prophet effectively forbids the practice by demanding that all wives be treated with absolute equality. Tunisia has accepted that such an undertaking is humanly impossible.[17] In accordance with this belief, Book I, Article 18 of the code states: "Polygamy is prohibited. Marrying more than one woman shall incur a punishment of one year's imprisonment and a fine of 240,000 francs or either of these."[18] Prior to enactment of the code a man was permitted to take up to four wives.[19]

Another issue faced by Muslim women is the fact that Islam mandates that the husband must have absolute authority over his wife and children. Although the Personal Status Code grants women more guardianship rights in reference to their children it also codifies the Islamic practice of a wife's duty to obey her husband in all family matters. Book I, Article 23 lists the wife's duties as follows: "She shall respect her husband in his capacity as head of the family, and within these prerogatives, obey him in whatever he orders her. . . ."[20] So despite the fact that women are now permitted to shop and generally appear in public, many families still adhere to the Islamic precept that the husband is responsible for all matters outside of the home while the woman's role is limited to matters within the house.[21]

The laws concerning adultery have also been changed in Tunisia from the traditional Islamic practices. In many Muslim countries a man who finds his wife participating in a sexual relationship with another man is excused from punishment if he should murder her. No reciprocal right is given to a woman who finds her husband in such a position. But regulations were added to the Tunisian Penal Code in 1968 which set a maximum of five years' imprisonment for a person of either gender who commits adultery.[22] The Penal Code also provides for a punishment of five years' imprisonment for killing a spouse in these circumstances regardless of the killer's sex.[23]

The Personal Status Code replaced the *Shari'a* with the government's legal system to perform as the sole regulatory authority over all marriages and divorces.[24] The Code represents a great advancement towards equality for Tunisian women, especially in the area of divorce. Traditionally, a husband could obtain a divorce by repudiation simply by stating three times in front of witnesses, "I divorce you."[25] After the final statement he became free to remarry. No reason for his action was needed. This practice was outlawed in Tunisia by Book II, Article 30 which states "[n]o divorce shall take place save before the court."[26]

There are three conditions by which a man or woman can acquire a divorce through the courts. The first, provided in Article 31(1), is by petition of either party.[27] The petition must be made for a reason which is provided within the code.[28] One reason may be that a stipulation in the marriage contract is non-realizable or was violated.[29] Unlike some other Moslem countries, if the husband refuses to pay the dower, a Tunisian woman does not have grounds for divorce.[30] Causes provided in Book IV include failure of an able husband to provide maintenance for his wife (Article 39), or desertion coupled with failure to support (Article 40) except in cases where the wife plans to provide her own support and receive compensation upon his return (Article 41).[31]

Article 31(2) allows the court to grant a divorce if both parties bring the petition and mutually consent to the action.[32] Divorce will also be granted under Article 31(3) when either party sues. This method may act as a form of repudiation in that no specific reason need be given by the party suing[33] but it is available to both men and women. In these circumstances the judge is required to examine the facts of the case and determine which, if either, party must pay damages to the other.[34]

Traditional causes under which a woman may sue for divorce include physical abuse, a husband's impotence, his contraction of an incurable contagious disease, and more recently, mental incompatibility.[35]

The judge is required under Article 32 to attempt to reconcile the couple before granting a divorce.[36] When the marriage has not been consummated the woman has a legal right only to half of the promised dower (Article 33).[37]

Divorced women and widows are required to observe the period of the *iddah* following the termination of the marriage.[38] During this period the woman is not permitted to remarry. Book III of the Personal Status Code designates the time periods which must be adhered to. Under Article 35 a divorcee who is not pregnant is to honor the *iddah* for a duration of three months and a widow must wait four months and 10 complete days.[39] A pregnant woman in either situation must endure the *iddah* until she delivers.[40] If a husband is designated an absentee, his wife must observe the same duration as she would if he had died (Article 36).[41]

Alimony is guaranteed only in the form of maintenance during the period of the *iddah*. Book V, Article 38 is the legal basis for such a claim.[42] The only other regulation under which a divorced woman may be financially indemnified by her husband would be if the judge determines under an Article 31(3) action for divorce that she has been damaged.[43]

If a marriage was consummated prior to divorce, the wife retains ownership of any gifts presented to her by her husband. But if it was not consummated then they belong to him.[44] Article 26 outlines how the home furnishings and other items are to be disposed of. "In the event of a dispute between the spouses over the [ownership] of the furniture of the home and in the absence of proof by either, the husband's word on oath shall be accepted for those items which customarily belong to the man and the wife's word on oath for those items which customarily belong to the woman. Properties of the nature of merchandise shall be attributed, upon oath, to whichever spouse happens to be the merchant. Items which customarily belong to both men and women shall, upon oath by each, be divided between them."[45]

Child custody laws also became more favorable for women under the Personal Status Code. The 1957 Code established a list of preferred guardians, and females were placed at the top of that list.[46] "In the event of dissolution of the marriage, whether by divorce or death, the right of custody shall devolve upon the following in the order stated: the child's mother, maternal grandmother, maternal aunt, the mother's maternal aunt, the mother's paternal aunt, the father's paternal grandfather, the child's maternal grandfather, first cousin, paternal uncle, second cousin."[47]

This law was modified in 1959 to allow the judge to appoint the person he found to be best qualified to act as the child's guardian.[48] The cost of the child's custody is paid first from any property owned by the child, and if there is none, then the father becomes responsible for the expenses.[49]

Custody will last until a boy is seven and a girl is nine for any appointee other than the father. When the child reaches this age the father has the option of taking him or her into his home.[50] His decision can be overruled by a judge if he "considers it in the child's interest to remain with the guardian."[51]

Property

The *Shari'a* grants Muslim women exclusive rights over their property. This religious law is reflected in Tunisia's Personal Status Code in Book I (The Dower), Article 12 and Article 24, The Reciprocal Duties of Spouses. Article 12 states: "The dower is the property of the woman which she may dispose of as she wishes."[52] Although the woman has this right, in many instances her father will retain a portion of the dower.[53] Any other property which a woman owns is also hers to manage and use. Her right is protected from her husband under Article 24, which states: "The husband is not the guardian of his wife's property."[54] Unlike Islamic law, Tunisian regulations place a duty on the wife to use her property to contribute to the support of the family.[55] Thus, her ownership rights are not exclusive or unlimited. It is also customary for a female to hand over her wages to her father or husband who will return what she may need for personal expenses.[56]

In matters of inheritance the Code has not equalized a female's rights with those of a male. The Code allocates a half-share to a husband but only a quarter-share to a wife when dividing the estate of a deceased spouse who has no descendants.[57] Cases where there are descendants result in a quarter-share going to the husband or an eighth-share for the wife.[58] As in the *Shari'a,* the woman receives half of the amount the man inherits. A lone daughter will receive half of the estate, but if there are two or more girls they share a two-thirds portion.[59] A son will receive a share valued at that of two daughters.[60]

Employment

In its effort to modernize Tunisian society the government made education free and available for both sexes.[61] Primary education became mandatory for six-year-old girls and attendance was required for the successive six years.[62] Bourguiba's goal was to provide equal professional opportunities for women including the right of equal pay.[63] Legislation for equal pay and equal rights in procuring employment became effective August 13, 1956. In certain cases an employer may pay a woman less but the minimum is set by law at 85 percent of a man's pay.[64]

This goal was in direct conflict with the Muslim attitude that a woman belongs in the home and that a man gains social prestige by being able to support his wife while she remains secluded from society.[65] Attitudes have been changing as more women have been able to substantially augment their family's incomes and as the need for a larger labor force has grown.[66]

Women's employment in industry, agriculture and commerce is regulated by decrees of April 6, 1950, and February 18, 1954.[67] The laws prohibit women from working in designated fields which are considered dangerous to their health or morals. Female employment between the hours of 10 p.m. and 5 a.m. is also prohibited.[68] Mines, quarries,[69] scrap-salvaging industries, and work involving toxic substances[70] are strictly forbidden to female workers.

Maternity benefits are provided through the National Social Security Fund to women who have been members for at least one year. The Fund was established December 14, 1960, by Laws 60-30 and 60-33.[71] Maternity leave is for a maximum of 12 weeks, during which half-pay can be collected.[72] Subsequent to delivery, a woman may not work for four weeks.[73] Other benefits associated with childbearing are half-hour nursing breaks during working hours (Labor Code of 1966) and nursing rooms built to government standards in every enterprise employing 50 or more women.[74]

Personal Autonomy

Traditionally, the only acceptable behavior for Muslim women is to avoid contact with all men other than family members, and this is accomplished by their seclusion within their homes.[75] Contemporary Tunisia is free of legal bans against women appearing in public places, and the government has gone so far as to encourage female participation in society.[76] Despite government pressure, however, many people have found it difficult to abandon the old customs. This is apparent in many factories where the sexes are strictly segregated, with men and women working in separate rooms and having different working and break hours.[77] Other than in the classrooms, boys and girls avoid contact. A strong taboo still exists, so that a girl who is seen with a boy is considered loose; this attitude results in young women voluntarily remaining in the home.[78]

The government has had to face a similar situation concerning women wearing the veil. Bourguiba did not want to force women to abandon the practice by instituting legislation.[79] School girls were pressured not to wear the veil while attending classes, but many were still required to wear it at home.[80] Eventually wearing of the veil in public was prohibited by the government,[81] but some older women, and some younger women also, have not elected to discard the traditional garb.[82]

Muslim women customarily believe in having many children. Although there is no injunction against birth control in the *Qur'an,* Muslims believe it is God's will to bear many children, and the need for labor within the family and support for aging parents has reinforced these attitudes.[83] Bourguiba and his associates recognized the problem of overpopulation in Tunisia and launched a campaign against it.[84] Their first step was to pass a law in 1960 which limited family allowances to the first four children of salaried employees.[85] Contraceptives had been banned in Tunisia but in January 1961 their import and sale were legalized.[86] The government has also sponsored family planning studies, established the National Office of Family Planning and Research,[87] and instituted a program of mass education in birth control techniques.[88]

In June 1965 abortion was legalized for all women who had five or more children. The service was provided free at all government hospitals.[89] In 1969 this law was amended to remove the five-child limitation.[90] A woman's right to an abortion is limited only by the condition that it be performed by a certified medical doctor.[91] The choice to have an abortion is solely within the woman's discretion. She is not required to have permission from her husband or male guardian.[92]

24. Case Study: Iran

Political Rights

During the rule of Mohammed Reza Shah Pahlavi, women's rights were significantly extended to achieve equality between men and women in social and political activities. On two visits to Tehran, Isfahan and other Iranian cities during the late 1970s, the author observed at first hand, at private, official and public functions, the remarkably high profile of women in society and the ease of communication between men and women. Prior to this time women's rights were defined by the fundamentalist Shi'ite interpretation of Islam[1] which almost completely restricted their roles.

Despite the fact that the national referendum proposing female suffrage was conducted in accordance with the old election laws which excluded women, the franchise was granted in 1963.[2] The Charter of the White Revolution of Shah and People recognized women's full citizenship, and in response the cabinet reformed the election laws to allow for female candidates and electors. Article 10, clause 1 and Article 13, clause 2 of the parliamentary election laws of November 1911 were revoked to allow for female *Majles,* and the male limitations of Articles 6 and 9 of the senate election laws of May 4, 1949, were deleted.[3] By 1979, women were participating in many phases of the government, including acting as judges and running for and being elected to political offices.[4]

When the Ayatollah Ruhollah Khomeini took control of the Iranian government in 1979, he instituted a regime adhering to the orthodox Islamic principles. This meant a reversal of the many rights which women had fought to gain under Pahlavi. Through legislation in 1983 women were permitted government participation only in low-level posts.[5] This retreat from the higher status given to women is best exemplified by the removal of female judges. Article 163 of the Constitution as rewritten by the new fundamentalist regime required that judges be qualified in accordance with Islamic principles.[6] According to the *Qur'an,* Surah 2 (The Cow), verse 282, a woman's testimony is worth only half that of a man's on the witness stand: "...And call to witness from among you men, two witnesses. And if two men be not (at hand) then a man and two women, of such as ye approve as witnesses, so that if the one erreth (through forgetfulness), the other will remember."[7]

Because of the foregoing Qur'anic dictate, women judges were replaced with men, and others in high government positions were removed or placed in lower posts. The regime claimed that it was a woman's religious duty to take care of the family and home and to allow men to run the affairs of the government.[8] The basis for this separation by gender is based on the belief that women are different from men in that females excel in physical beauty but males excel in mental and physical ability. Psychological differences are also recognized which make women unfit to rule. Females are emotional and sensitive so that they cannot make the rational and reasoned decisions which men can.[9] This belief has evolved from the *Qur'an,* in Surah 4 (Women), verse 34, which reads: "Men are in charge of women, because Allah hath made the one of them to excel the other.... So good women are the obedient...."[10] The *Hadith* in interpreting the *Qur'an* strengthens these ideas by noting that women are naturally, morally and religiously defective as well as having weaker intellectual powers.[11] These characteristics make them unfit to rule in the opinion of the present Iranian leaders.

The Family

The Family Protection Law of 1967 (amended 1975) was enacted by the Shah (Pahlavi) in order to allow women greater equality in the areas of marriage, divorce and child custody than they had previously enjoyed under traditional Islamic doctrine. This law restricted the husband's unilateral right to divorce by requiring him to obtain a court ruling, and it also required that he obtain his first wife's consent to any additional wives.[12] Also outlined were broader grounds under which a wife could divorce, and the law allowed the court to award custody of any children to the mother.[13] The 1975 amendment also raised the marriage age for a female from 15 to 18 (the same as that of a male).[14] But the very first act which was repealed under the Khomeini government was the Family Protection Law, and all the Family Protection courts were closed.[15]

Marriage law is now based on the religious law known as the *Shari'a.*[16] In order for a woman to marry she must have the consent of her legal guardian, a male, usually her father or paternal grandfather.[17] This is true regardless of her age. Although her legal guardian can prevent her marriage to someone not of his choice, according to the *Hadith* he cannot force her to marry someone she chooses not to: "None, not even the father or the sovereign, can lawfully contract in marriage an adult woman of sound mind without her permission, whether she be a virgin or not."[18] The freedom to choose whom she will marry is further restricted by the Qur'anic passage Surah 2 (the Cow), verse 221, which states that a Muslim woman may marry only a Muslim man, while Surah 5 (The Table Spread), verse 5, allows a man to marry a Jewish, Christian or Sabian woman.[19] The legal age for marriage is presently 13 for girls and 18 for boys.

When it is decided that a couple will wed, a marriage contract is agreed upon. This contract may be very important for the woman. By imposing specific conditions within the agreement she can attain a variety of rights within the marriage which would otherwise be lacking under the *Shari'a.*[20] But in order for the woman to gain equal rights she must be in a strong bargaining position.[21] In many cases such a position may not exist.

The *mahar* (dowry) accompanies the marriage contract. It belongs to the woman rather than her legal guardian or future husband.[22] The dowry is the woman's only protection in case of divorce or the death of her husband. The *mahar* is based on the woman's virginity.[23] If the bride's virginity is not proven by a blood-stained sheet on the wedding night, her father and brothers are faced with a loss of honor. In some instances they have murdered the woman because of the loss. In such a situation the law punishes the killer with a jail sentence of six months.[24] The groom has the right to repudiate the bride and send her back to her family.

The importance of the wife's sexual activities as a reflection of the man's honor is carried even further in the laws concerning adultery. Article 170 of the Penal Code reads: "If a man witnesses his wife in the act of intercourse or a situation which could be construed as being engaged in intercourse with a man other than her husband and injures or murders one or both of them, he is immune from punishment."[25] The language of this law allows for a broad interpretation which can cover an unlimited number of diverse situations. As such it has been used to exculpate a brother who killed his sister after he saw her get out of a taxi with a stranger. Unlike many heat-of-passion laws, this law does not require the man to have acted at the time he observed the incident.[26] There is no law giving a wife equal protection in a case of her adulterous husband even though the *Qur'an* in Surah 2 (Light), verse 2, requires equal punishment of male and female adulterers and sets the punishment as a "scourge (with) a hundred stripes."[27] Another legal punishment for adultery is stoning.[28]

The lack of such a reciprocal law may be due to the fact that a man is allowed to have up to four wives and as many concubines as he can afford. Polygamy is recognized as a legal right of a man in the *Qur'an,* Surah 4 (Women), verse 3, which states: ". . . marry of the women, who seem good to you, two or three or four."[29] But this passage also requires that the husband take only as many wives as he is able to treat equally in every aspect, which is in all probability humanly impossible.[30] Under the Pahlavi government the law required a man to have his first wife's written consent prior to taking a second, but this was struck down by Khomeini. The only way an Iranian woman can presently prevent her husband from taking another wife is by placing such a condition in the marriage contract.

Although it has been outlawed in most other Muslim countries, another type of marriage, *Mut'a* or temporary marriage, is also sanctioned in Iran. This type of marriage is even more devastating to the woman's rights. It can last from one hour to 99 years,[31] whatever time is specified in the contract. Features of this type of marriage include the man's right to terminate the *Mut'a* any time; he has no obligation to pay maintenance other than the *mahar* at any time; and neither spouse has a right of inheritance from the other.[32]

In all forms of marriage the husband is the legal head of the household. As such he has the authority to beat and admonish a rebellious wife.[33] In exchange for her obedience the wife receives the right to be properly fed and clothed at her husband's expense.[34] As head of the household, he is the sole legal guardian of their children and also of his wife.[35] Because only a male can legally be a head of a household, single women have had problems in obtaining goods in the marketplace. All goods except for fruits and vegetables are rationed and will be given only to the family head.[36] The man is also given the sole power to decide where the family will reside, and the wife must abide by his decisions.[37]

The 1967 Family Protection Act required that marital disputes be filed in court. It also recognized divorce by mutual consent and by judicial decree.[38] But this law was repealed by Khomeini, and the husband's right to unilateral divorce with or without notice to his wife was again made legal. Khomeini said women who wanted the right to divorce could obtain it at the time of their marriage through the contract.[39] The unilateral divorce can be obtained by verbal repudiation (*talaq),*[40] which may be done at will for any reason at all or for no reason at all.[41] All that is necessary for the divorce to be effectuated is for the husband to say three times that he divorces his wife, but the husband can remarry her after the first or second pronouncement.[42]

Under certain circumstances Islam allows a woman to obtain a divorce. These circumstances include a husband's prolonged imprisonment or insanity, his refusal to support his wife or his refusal to perform his marital obligations over a period of two or three years. In return for the divorce the wife is required to return all or part of the dowry and other gifts she received from him.[43]

The Family Protection Law allowed the courts to determine which parent would retain custody of the children. Under *Shari'a* law a man receives custody of any boy over the age of two and any girl older than seven.[44]

After a divorce the woman is required to seclude herself for a period of three months (*iddah*) in order to determine whether she is pregnant.[45] During this time the husband will continue to support her.[46] It is not customary for the husband to pay any alimony other than support during the *iddah* and payment of any balance due on her dowry. Usually the woman is returned to her family, who are then required to support her.[47]

Property

Iranian women have the right to full possession and control of their property. This includes the dowry and all other personal income. She has the right to manage this property during marriage and after divorce. These rights are guaranteed in Surah 4 (Woman), verse 4: "And give of the women (whom you marry) free gift of their marriage portions."[48]

Muslim women also have the right to inherit and bequeath property. The *Qur'an* states: ". . . and unto women a share of that which parents and near kindred leave, whether it be little or much—a legal share."[49] She can dispose of one-third of her property as she wishes, but the remaining two-thirds must be disposed of according to Islamic law. The same rule applies to Muslim men.[50] Surah 4 (Women), verse 11, sets the percentages at which a woman will inherit. It requires that a male receive two times that of a female.[51] A widow will receive one-fourth of her husband's estate unless he has children, in which case she is awarded one-eighth.[52] When the father has no sons, an only daughter will receive one-half of the estate but if there is more than one daughter they will share two-thirds.[53] If there are sons and daughters, the daughters will receive one-half of the amount of the sons' share.[54] Islamic law also disallows married couples of different religions from inheriting from each other.[55]

Personal Autonomy

In April of 1983 Khomeini made the wearing of the veil compulsory for all women. The penalty for not wearing a veil is one month to one year imprisonment.[56] In different areas of the country the extent of veiling is varied. In Yazd, any Jewish or Baha'i women of Muslim origins must wear the *chadur*.[57] This is a black cloth which covers the body from head to toe with either the face or, in the strictest practice, only one eye showing.[58] The regime requires only the *hijab* to be worn in public. *Hijab* is modest dress including a headscarf, long sleeves and a long hemmed skirt.[59] Women who are seen in public with a lock of hair showing or stockings which are too thin are sent to camps for up to three months for instruction on the proper way to dress.[60]

Another law which affects an Iranian woman's freedom of movement is legislation requiring segregation of the sexes in public.[61] Mandatory public segregation has been reinforced by forbidding anything which can lead to promiscuity, such as pop music, discos and alcohol.[62] Presently, the only morally acceptable diversion outside the home for a woman is a visit to the doctor or the cemetery.[63] Women are also prevented from utilizing public transportation, cinemas, cafeterias and beaches by the segregation laws.[64]

These laws also have an important impact on female education. No schools are coeducational.[65] The regime insists that only females teach females, but in cases where public outcry has been strong enough some male teachers are allowed. These men must be married and middle-aged.[66] Some schools have placed a curtain between the students and the teacher.[67] Segregation in the villages results in the discontinuance of classes for girls because of shortages of female teachers.[68] Certain fields of study, especially the sciences, mathematics and sports, may be unattainable for a female because of the lack of instructors.[69]

A woman's control over her own actions is limited by the government in a number of other areas. The Passport Law requires that a woman have her husband's permission to travel.[70] It is impossible to obtain a passport without it. She is confined to her home unless her husband gives permission to leave.[71] Legislation allows the use of birth control if it is a type which does not act by aborting the fetus; if it does not have an adverse effect on health; and if both spouses consent to its use.[72] The Penal Code, Article 182, makes abortion under all circumstances illegal.[73]

The government leaders' belief that women are inferior beings is again exemplified in Iran's Law of Retribution (the Ghissas Bill, 1981). Article 5 of this bill makes the life of a woman who is murdered worth only half that of a man's.[74] There are no laws against sexual harassment of women.[75] Rape is illegal under the Penal Code, Article 207, but marital rape is not recognized.[76]

Much of Pahlavi's legislation in the 1970s allowing a woman to sue her husband for personal injuries resulting from battery was repealed under Khomeini.[77] Any virgin who is condemned to die must first lose her virginity because Islam forbids the execution of virgins. The present regime requires that the woman be raped or forced into a temporary marriage in order that the execution may be carried out.[78]

Employment

Prior to Khomeini's regime, women were employed in a wide variety of fields from service positions such as teachers, white collar workers and sales girls to professional positions as lawyers, doctors and members of parliament.[79] During this period, legislation was instituted to facilitate women's employment opportunities. These included the opening of day care centers,[80] equal pay for equal work and anti-female discrimination laws.[81] Legislation also required maternity benefits of seven months' leave with full pay and made provisions so that a mother who worked half time for three years would be considered as full time when computing seniority and retirement benefits.[82]

The present regime believes woman's proper role is that of housewife and mother. It is her religious duty to remain in the home and leave the public sphere to the men of her family.[83] This goal is reflected in the preamble to the Constitution, which reads:

> The family is the cornerstone of society and the primary institution for the growth and improvement of the individual; consensus and ideological belief in the principle that the formation of family is fundamental for the future development of the individual is one of the main aims of the Islamic government. According to this line of thinking regarding the family, women will no longer be regarded as mere objects (instruments) in the service of consumerism; but while being restored to the worthwhile and responsible task of motherhood, they will be primarily responsible for the raising of committed individuals."[84]

The Constitution further guarantees that "everyone has the right to choose their desired job..." but this is only on the condition that such a job "is not against Islam."[85]

Effectuation of this goal is achieved through the segregation laws and others which work to persuade or coerce women to leave the labor force and return to the home.[86] Legislation provides that women who work only 15 years can retire with full benefits, and another allows the female of a working couple to remain at home while they still receive the full benefits of her salary.[87]

Measures such as these have resulted in an enormous decline of career opportunities for women, which has led to a reduction in the amount of education which they are receiving. A female who is to spend her life taking care of her home and family has no need for more than the basic primary education. Promoting such an ideology, the law bars married girls from attending secondary schools.[88] All women are forbidden entry to any law programs at universities.[89] Vocational training for females is limited to the domestic arts and sciences, teaching and clerical.[90] Women are also prohibited from serving in the military, police corps, any positions during the night, or any heavy or dangerous work.[91] The equal pay for equal work policy has also been obliterated under the present regime.[92]

Maternity benefits have been revised. All day care centers have been closed. A woman is forbidden to work six weeks prior to delivery and four weeks after birth but she is paid her full salary for this period and her position is guaranteed upon her return.[93] Every three hours the mother is given nursing breaks. All maternity benefits apply only to married women.[94]

A female's choice of employment depends on the husband, who has absolute authority in determining whether she will take a job and what type of job she may procure. If he does not approve of her occupation, the law requires the employer to fire her upon her husband's request.[95]

Part Nine: The Asian World

During the past 80 years less than 25 percent of the women of India were taught the basics of reading and writing, and that in a country which, for nearly 16 of those years, had a woman as its Prime Minister.

In Indonesia a boy, aged 15, is considered *de jure* head of the family in his father's absence, even if his mother is a lawyer or, perhaps, his teacher at school. —From *Sisterhood Is Global*

25. General Survey

Between 1950 and 1980 the female population of the world grew from 957 million to 1,251 million, and nearly two-thirds of this growth occurred in Asia. By the year 2,000 the International Labor Organization projects there will be 500 million women workers in Asia. In India alone there will be an additional 50 million workers.[1]

According to the International Labor Organization, economically active women in Asia number about 380 million, or more than half the world's economically active female population. Over the past 20 to 25 years, this group of women in Asia has grown more rapidly than the male population. The proportion of women in each of the three major economic sectors has also increased. In most countries in Asia the percentage of women in the total labor force is higher in agriculture than in industry or the services sector. Of all economically active women, more than 82 percent in India, 90 percent in Nepal, 77 percent in China, and more than 73 percent in Thailand are employed in agriculture. The participation of women in the industrial sector is higher only in a small number of countries: Hong Kong, Japan, Taiwan and India.[2]

The International Labor Organization reports that in the industrial sector there has been a significant shift from the earlier patterns of employment. In China the total number of women in the industrial sector has risen from some 31 million in 1978 to nearly 41 million in 1982. Women are in textiles, light industries, educational services and increasingly in heavy industry, electronics and research.[3] At the same time, women's participation in agricultural work continues to be significant quantitatively and qualitatively.[4] In the developing countries of Asia considered as a whole, only 8.3 percent of the female workforce was employed in industry in 1960. By the year 1980, this had risen to 17.5 percent.[5]

A major and recent study of women's economic participation in Asia and the Pacific, conducted by the United Nations Economic and Social Commission for the region, revealed the extremely important role which women now play in the economies of most countries. But the study also revealed that women's work generally has a much lower status than men's; that women are clustered in low-paying jobs; and that they have less education than men and earn less, even with equivalent qualifications. This was true even of the more industrialized, high-income countries. The study proved how diverse social and institutional barriers hamper women's participation in the general workforce as well as in particular trades and occupations.[6]

One of the major economic successes in Asia has been the drive for export-led industrialization through the use of export processing zones, also known as free trade zones. Located on or near export harbors, the zones are basically duty-free areas so that raw material can be freely imported from abroad and freely exported from the free trade zone in manufactured form. By use of cheap labor and a control over the workforce (by severely limiting the activities of unions), an attractive package is created for industrialists to set up world market factories in these areas, particularly for textiles, garments, and electronics. From just three major free trade zones in 1970, the system has mushroomed to more than 27 in 1988. In 1977 there were already 92 major manufacturing concerns in the Asian export processing zones, ranging from textiles to electronics, metal products, precision instruments, and machinery.[7] The key element has been the abundant supply of cheap labor for these zones, in every instance young women, the majority migrants from the rural areas. Concluding her survey of the relocation of women and the textile industry in Asia, Noeleen Heyzer said that, though these women gain more personal freedom, earn a salary and are therefore no longer drains on their families, and have access to a wider range of life experiences, they remain at the lowest end of the wage structure, work in poor conditions with little hope of any vertical mobility, and are encased in a male-dominated environment over which they have little control.[8]

Not only young, single women but also single women with children, married, divorced, and widowed women have joined the migration to urban areas in Asia. For many, migration and work are a matter of survival. They enter readily into any subsistence production and are hugely exploited by unscrupulous employers.

Migration is brought on by many factors, and national situations differ far too greatly for there to be any single conclusion. But rural change has negatively affected the status of women in most countries. Landless women have fewer work opportunities while women in landed families now face more intensive farm work. Unequal land inheritance has weakened women's access to credit. In her excellent study on working women in Southeast Asia, Noeleen Heyzer said that bureaucracies created for rural women have not been successful in carrying out their task. Their concerns are too narrow and do not reflect the realities facing women. There is little hope for women's emancipation, she said, unless there is a structural change in the labor market, technology, access to land, and effective rural organizations for women. Also of importance is the need for change in perceptions of women's role and work.[9]

Even in Asia's most industrialized countries, the International Labor Organization reported that the international developments of the past decade have led to grave economic difficulties seriously affecting the employment of women. Concentration in land ownership and population growth have increased landlessness and, consequently, dependence on wage labor. Commercialization of farming and introduction of new technologies have affected the self-employment of women in farming on substantial scale, causing rural wages to fall as well as the value of assets. In India more and more women are becoming agricultural wage laborers because of growing landlessness in rural areas.[10]

Year	Total female population (thousands)	Female labor force: Number (thousands)	Female labor force: As percentage of female population — *Total*	Female labor force: As percentage of female population — *15 years of age and older*	Female labor force: As percentage of total labor force	Female labor force: As percentage of world total
1950	665,196	172,894	26.0	37.7	29.0	50.2
1975	1,106,094	322,466	29.2	44.8	34.3	56.0
1980	1,233,556	350,085	28.4	43.6	34.0	56.1
1985	1,369,350	382,144	27.9	42.6	33.8	56.5

In a special survey, *The State of the World's Women,* prepared for the 1985 World Conference of Women in Nairobi, it is reported that in Asia, China excepted, a pattern of development packages has been superimposed on a picture of land scarcity and increasing landlessness. "Between a quarter and half of the rural population of Pakistan, India and Bangladesh are without land and their numbers are growing."[11]

In most Asian countries, the International Labor Organization reported, agriculture is the principal source of employment for women. In some countries like India, Nepal and Thailand over 50 percent of the economically active women are in agriculture. In Japan, which is the most highly industrialized country in Asia, the percentage declined from 36.5 in 1970 to less than 12 percent in 1982.[12]

Women also participate in agriculture production in Asia mostly as unpaid family workers or agricultural laborers, depending on the size of the land and availability of employment. When farm employment is available it is mostly unskilled and therefore vulnerable to the introduction of agricultural technology. Women are rarely independent farmers since prevailing inheritance and divorce laws usually render them landless even when they are heads of rural households.[13] An in-depth study of Nepal reports that women perform from two-thirds to virtually all of the labor in a wide variety of agricultural activities.[14]

Wage differentials between men and women in Asia are more pronounced than anywhere else in the world's major regions except for Africa. Even in the manufacturing industry the gap is considerable. In some states, such as Korea and Japan, women earn less than half of what men earn. In some countries female earnings are incredibly low for the same work. In Japan and the Republic of Korea, for example, women's earnings in 1982 in the manufacturing sector were 43 and 45 percent respectively of men's income, as Table 64 indicates.[15]

There is widespread occupational segregation in almost all of Asia, some of it voluntarily, some of it by need, some of it for economic reasons (low pay) and some enforced for profit. Structural segregation of male and female workers is found in most sectors of the economy. The vast majority of Thai women, for example, are relegated to sales, service, spinning, and weaving. Women constitute roughly 60 percent of sales workers in the Philippines. Sex segregation is most severe among young, unmarried females, particularly recent migrants to the major urban areas. In Thailand the vast majority of these young single female migrants were employed as cooks and maids.[16] (See Table 65.)

Of particular interest are legal restraints of female labor force participation, even in those countries which have constitutionally ended structural

Table 63. Changes in Labor Force Participation by Women in Asia, 1950, 1975, 1980, 1985. Source: International Labor Office, Labor Force Estimates and Projections, 1950–2000. 2nd ed., vol. V. *World Summary,* Geneva, 1977. Also recent information compiled by the International Labor Organization, Bureau of Statistics, 1984.

Country	Year	Non-agricultural activities[1]	Manufacturing[2]
Cyprus	1975	54.9	46.9
	1982	58.2	56.2
Japan	1975	55.8	47.9
	1982	52.7	43.0
Burma	1975	-	88.5
	1982	-	88.8
Korea, Rep. of	1976	47.0	47.4
	1982	45.0	45.0
Singapore	1980	62.9	61.4
	1982	63.6	63.2
Sri Lanka	1980	92.0	80.8
	1982	80.0	81.9

Table 64. Wage Differentials Between Men and Women in Selected Asian Countries, Expressed in Percentages. Source: United Nations, *World Survey on the Role ofWomen in Development,* E. 86. IV. 3., New York, 1985, p. 84; and International Labor Organization, *Yearbook of Labour Statistics,* Geneva, 1983, Tables 16 and 17A. Notes: (1) Includes mining and quarrying, manufacturing, construction, transport, storage, etc. (2) Manufacturing covers all industries according to the International Labor Organization's International Standard Industrial Classification.

discrimination. While both the 1972 and 1978 Constitutions of Sri Lanka endorsed legal equality between the sexes, subtle provisos within these documents permitted the imposition of discriminatory regulations and quotas regarding the access of women to important segments of the public service.[17]

Two extremely important supervisory levels in Asia are staffed almost exclusively by men, namely administrative and managerial. In Hong Kong, Japan, the Philippines and Singapore these posts account for about 1 percent of the female labor force. In most other Asian countries, only one woman in a thousand holds a post classified as administrative or managerial. (See Table 66.)

An analysis of the situation in individual countries indicates how enormous the problem of discrimination against women still is, and how injurious the so-called spinoff to individuals. In 1982 the South Korean government signed the U.N. convention banning all forms of discrimination against women. It came as an enormous surprise to members of the Korean Women's Development Institute, since there is hardly a country in the world, as they explained to the press, with as many forms of discrimination against women as South Korea. Most of this discrimination is by custom, but, in the case of family relationships, it is also by law. Worst of all is the male-dominant Confucian ethic that pervades all of Korea. More than 40 percent of the labor force consists of women, the Director of the Korean Women's Development Institute said, but they are employed only as temporary labor. "The problem of women in Korea is not one of potential," she said, "it's that we simply don't have the opportunity." Only in offices of foreign banks in Korea are women permitted to remain at work after they marry, she said. "Elsewhere an unwritten law forces women to quit." Finally, for middle and upper class families to have a working daughter is considered very shameful, she said, "but the daughters of poor families who do work, work like dogs."[18]

Indonesia, the third most populous state in Asia and fifth most populous in the world, did not reveal any information which could lead one to the conclusion that the plight of women in that community is significantly different from that of women elsewhere in Asia. The pattern of low level of education, low income and poverty, double burdens for women, social and cultural taboos that restrict women, poor health of women, high infant mortality rates and lack of opportunity is as prevalent in Indonesia as anywhere in Asia.

In 1980 there were 78 million women in Indonesia (50.3 percent of the population) and as of 1976 fewer than 10 percent of girls over the age of 10 completed primary school. Only 1 percent completed vocational school and only 0.2 percent university.[19] The Indonesian government claims that the literacy rate for the country is 60 percent and that of women 49 percent but this figure for women seems highly doubtful in the light of school performance. (According to figures in Indonesia's annual report of the Central Bureau of Statistics for 1978, some 20 million women were employed and of these 60 percent had never been exposed to any formal education.)

Indonesian women suffer the same fate as women elsewhere in terms of lower wages and in their concentration in low paid, low status employment. Though sex discrimination in implementing the General Labor Law was prohibited by Act 14 of 1969, lack of minimum wage provision and inadequate enforcement of other stipulations render equal pay laws ineffectual in all sectors except the civil service. But though women formed 32 percent of the civil service in 1983, only some 5 percent were in any position of authority.[20] Again, as in India, in most of Black Africa and in the Muslim states of the world, men are the *de facto* and *de jure* heads of the family. In Indonesia a son age 15 is considered *de jure* head of the family in his father's absence.[21]

Writing in *Sisterhood Is Global,* Titi Sumbung, an Indonesian lawyer, states that life for women in Indonesia is controlled by norms based on *adat* (customary law) and on religious and indigenous belief. These norms govern the relationship of an individual to the family and the community. They also define the roles and status of women, both in the community and in marriage. *Adat* is part of the Indonesian legal system, in much the same way as Bantu traditional law forms part of the South African system and Islamic laws forms part of the legal system of Nigeria. *Adat* regulates ownership of assets, inheritance rights, marriage and family kinship.[22]

The majority of the population is Muslim and this, added to the male dominance which emerges from a study of *adat,* puts women in a very unequal position. For example, in polygamous marriages, legal among Muslims, women can be punished for adultery but men can be prosecuted only as accomplices (*sic*) to adultery.[23] Yet, paradoxically, the Indonesian Constitution guarantees "equal rights" for men and women.[24]

Country	Professional & Technical	Admin. & Man.	Clerical	Sales	Service	Agri-cult.	Produc-tion	Others
Indonesia	3.2	-	1.4	18.4	6.6	53.0	14.8	2.6
S. Korea	3.6	0.1	8.3	17.6	14.4	34.8	18.7	2.5
Philippines	10.7	0.7	5.3	20.1	14.1	37.0	12.1	-
Singapore	10.1	2.3	29.1	11.6	14.9	1.1	29.9	1.0
Sri Lanka	8.4	0.2	3.2	3.7	4.7	42.2	16.6	21.0
Thailand	2.4	0.5	1.6	10.4	2.8	73.6	7.9	0.8
Malaysia	8.6	-	-	4.7	8.1	54.4	10.3	13.7
Bangladesh	2.9	-	-	1.3	10.2	69.8	12.2	3.6
India	3.6	-	-	1.4	3.1	82.6	9.0	0.2
Nepal	3.7	-	-	0.6	0.2	92.6	3.0	0.0
China	5.5	-	-	1.9	2.4	77.1	12.9	0.1

Motherhood contributes strongly to the status of women in most Asian countries. A woman gains prestige by bearing sons, but the value of a daughter is very low. A daughter's birth does not bring rejoicing and the traditional distribution of sweets as in the case of a son's birth. Boys represent future income and care for the mother and father in old age. Girls represent only increased parental responsibility and another mouth to feed.[25] These attitudes are often transformed into differential treatment accorded boys and girls and explain the higher female mortality rates, higher school enrollment for boys, and the higher rate of literacy of males in almost all Asian countries. A study of hospital records in a major Indian city reveals that an overwhelming proportion of women, told that they were expecting a girl, decided to abort the fetus. The study concludes that the selective abortion of female fetuses represents a continuation of earlier social practices of female infanticide.[26]

In Asia, as anywhere else, education provides women with greater access to political, economic, legal, social, and cultural resources. It also provides women with a higher status and a better opportunity to realize some measure of self-determination in a male-dominated society. Yet, a massive proportion of women in Asia, particularly in Bangladesh, Nepal, India, Pakistan, Malaysia, Indonesia, and mainland China, are still illiterate. (See Chart 15.)

The massive illiteracy of women can be traced to ancient traditions about the role of women, the low value accorded to daughters, and outright discrimination on grounds of gender. The mirror image of Chart 15 can be found in tables indicating school enrollment of boys and girls. The exceptions are Sri Lanka, South Korea, Taiwan, Thailand, Hong Kong, and the Philippines, where high school enrollment of boys and girls in the age group 10–14 years is now about equal and reflected in higher and more equal rates of literacy. In both Taiwan and South Korea the estimated figures for 1988 show a rate of school enrollment equal to that of the United States but a higher rate of literacy. In 1981 Sri Lanka listed 82 percent of its women as being literate. On the other end of the scale, only 5 percent of Nepalese and 12 percent of Pakistani women were reported to have the ability to read and write. The corresponding figures for men in these countries were 33 and 30 percent, respectively.[27]

At the World Conference of Women in Nairobi in 1985 Asian women reported to Caroline Pezzullo that they were deeply concerned about the rise in unemployment and "re-domestication" as well as increases in prostitution and rural-urban migration. Indian women saw development as actually reinforcing class and gender inequalities. Although women's liberation in China benefited from its link with class liberation, women still face problems related to their comparatively low education levels and must struggle against a new move to get them out of the wider society and back into the home. Japanese

Table 65. Percentage of All Economically Active Women by Type of Occupation in Major Asian Countries, 1980–1982. Source: International Labor Organization, *Yearbook of Labour Statistics,* Geneva, 1982, 1983, Table 2B; and WID1-4, United States Agency for International Development, United States Department of Commerce, Washington DC, 1985, Table 4.7, p. 72.

		Administrators and managerial workers		**Proportion of women**	
Country	**Year**	*Men and women (number)*	*Women (number)*	*Managers (%)*	*Manufacturing workers (%)*
Bangladesh	1974	5,740	39	0.7	3.8
Indonesia	1978	15,449	0	0	49.8
Japan	1982	570,000	20,000	3.5	38.8
Republic of Korea	1982	89,000	3,000	3.4	38.6
Kuwait	1980	787	2	(0.3)	1.7
Singapore	1982	17,455	1,766	10.1	43.5
Sri Lanka	1981	7,867	895	11.4	32.7

Table 66. Proportion of Women in Administrative and Managerial Occupations in Selected Asian Countries. Source: International Labor Organization, *Yearbook of Labour Statistics, 1983,* Geneva, 1983.

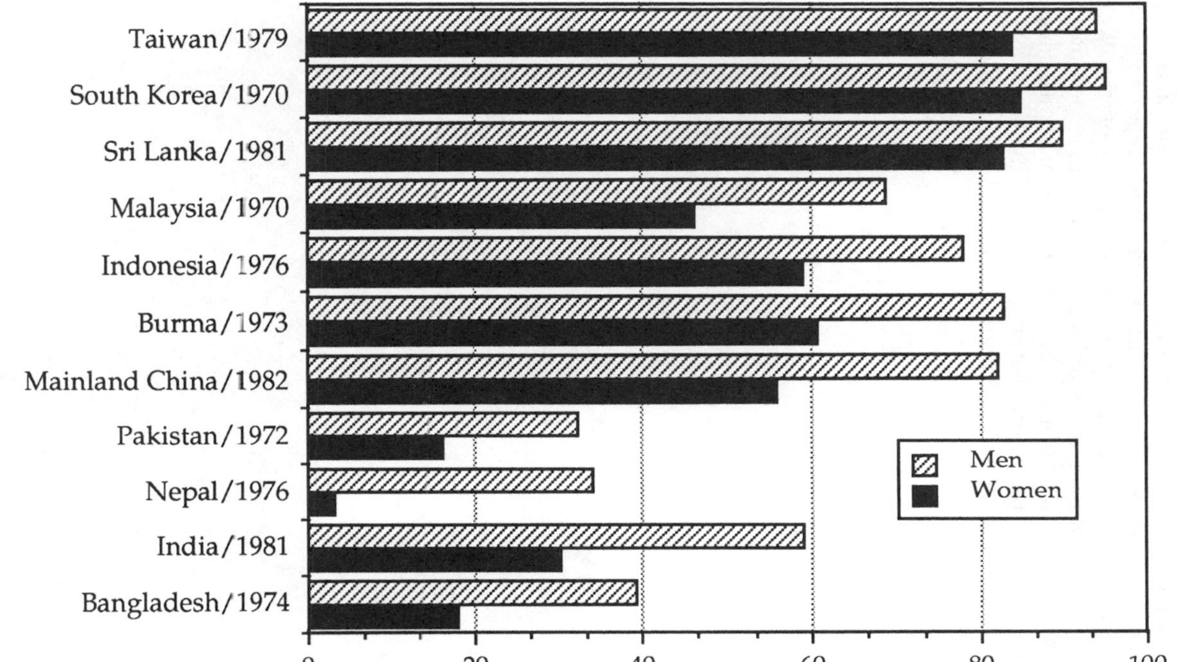

Chart 15. Asia: Literacy Gap Between Males and Females Age 10 Years or Over. Source: *Women of the World,* WID1-4, United States Agency for International Development, United States Department of Commerce, Washington DC, 1984 and 1985, p. 36, Table 3.1.

women noted that while it is important to value housework, that value should not be an excuse for freezing traditional sex roles.[28]

Almost no one who attended the Nairobi meeting, except for the Communist states, lauded the progress made in their own countries in the eradication of sexual discrimination. This is a pattern which has repeated itself also at other international conferences. Jaya Arunachalam of the Working Women's Forum in Madras, India, is quoted as follows in respect of women in her state: "The women are victims of harsh working conditions, unemployment and lack of legal protection because of ineffective laws and male alcoholism leading to family neglect and oppression."[29]

26. Case Study: India

In almost all countries of the world the number of women per thousand of the population is always greater than men. In almost all countries women have a higher life expectancy. But not in India. The 1981 census produced a ratio of 1,000 males per 935 females, and the proportional representation of women has been declining since 1901.[1]

In their revealing article "Women in India: The Reality," Neela d' Souza and Ramani Nataranjan said:

> Behind the figures and charts, dismal in themselves, is the grim reality of neglect of female children, for the intense desire and preference for sons is linked to the often fatal neglect of daughters. If the practice of female infanticide belongs to history, the legacy of discrimination and the neglect of female children is validated in infant mortality rates, nutritional surveys, and hospital registers, which show that medical attention is sought much later for girls in case of illness—a delay with grave consequences. The male child is a potential source of economic support and so gets the major share of parental attention, better nutrition, and preferential treatment in all matters.[2]

Female infanticide in India is something which everyone is aware of, but not much is being done from the official side to put a stop to what the weekly news magazine *India Today* termed "a murderous tradition." Recently the magazine reported that the killing of female babies "is still a widespread phenomenon," pointing to the fact that among the Bhati people there are only 550 girls for every 1,000 boys. In one school there was only one girl among the 175 children.[3] The development of amniocentesis, a genetic technique to determine both the condition and the sex of an unborn child, has worsened the situation. According to Abha Pandya, an estimated 78,000 fetuses were legally aborted in India over the period 1978–1983 because of "birth defects" in the unborn. "This misuse of genetic testing . . . is a flourishing business, mainly in northern India where a daughter's birth may be considered a near calamity." A son is perceived as an economic asset to the family: to capture wealth in the form of a dowry when he is married, to provide productive labor, and to perform the religious rituals after the death of the parents. Protests have arisen in the media and by women's and civil rights groups against the misuse of amniocentesis for what some see as a technological aid to female feticide. It is essentially an urban problem, reported Abha Pandya in *The Christian Science Monitor,* confined primarily to the middle classes, but the amniocentesis clinics are spreading in rural areas, indicating that this discrimination has widespread sociological roots. Women's rights groups have asked the government to ban the use of amniocentesis as an instrument of selective abortion.[4]

Year	Total Pop.	Male Pop.	Female Pop.	Females Per 1,000 Males
1901	238	121	117	972
1911	252	128	124	964
1921	251	128	123	955
1931	279	143	136	950
1941	319	164	155	945
1951	361	186	175	946
1961	439	226	213	941
1971	548	284	264	930
1981	684	354	330	935

Table 67. Female Population Decline in India in Millions, 1901–1981. Source: Census of India, 1981.

Another prevalent practice is the abuse of the bodies of young girls for financial gain. In parts of India there is an economically useful, male-inspired custom which determines that the eldest girl born to a family must become a prostitute in order to support the rest of the family. The matter first came to public attention towards the end of the 1970s, in the midst of the U.N. Decade for Women, and in February 1983 the State Assembly of Western Madhya Pradesh unanimously adopted a resolution urging the Indian government to make a special effort to eradicate this social evil. Five years later a team of investigators from the news magazine *India Today* found the practice flourishing, with nothing changed. In fact, they discovered that prostitution in the community is "socially sanctioned," and that every fifth woman in the community is a *khilawadi,* the local vernacular for "someone who plays." Most parents introduce their daughters to prostitution at the age of 13 or 14, and the girls' initiation is celebrated as a social event.[5]

Women's occupational segregation is substantial. Almost 80 percent of all employed women are in agriculture. More than 70 percent of women teachers are in the primary schools and only 8 percent in higher education.[6]

In 1980 there were only 23 women in the Indian Council of States (9.2 percent) and 22 women in the House of People (4 percent), the two chambers of India's legislature. Women have never constituted more than 17 percent of the candidates for a general election.[7]

Article 14 of India's new Constitution is a fundamental guarantee to women that they would receive equal protection of the law and (Article 16-1) equal opportunity in employment, but as observed in *The Cross Cultural Study of Women:* "Real legal equality has remained a distant reality for most women. Many are either unaware of or unable to secure the enforcement of their theoretical rights. Further, the law contains gaps and inequities that stand in the way of legal equality even for those . . . who are in a position to appeal to the judicial system."[8]

Not much has remained of the high hopes women had after the introduction of India's new Constitution. The overall deterioration of women's status remained largely ignored until the publication in 1974 of a report by a blue ribbon committee appointed to investigate the status of women. The 500-page report was hailed for its eloquence as much as for its real candor and depth of research.[9] Shortly thereafter the United Nations announced the Decade for Women. The combination produced, ever since, a flood of research and publications, conferences and workshops on women's rights. There is now an Indian Association for Women's Studies which publishes a bulletin and a journal of women's studies.[10] One indispensable source of information is *Manushi: A Journal about Women and Society,* published in New Delhi.

Legislative enactments have had only a limited impact as a method of social engineering in India. This is evident in an examination of the provisions, and actual effects, of the Special Marriage Act, the Hindu Marriage Act, the Hindu Succession Act and the Dowry Act.[11]

The equal pay policy is mandated by the Indian Constitution (Article 39.d), and the Equal Remuneration Act of 1975 was passed to reinforce the equal pay provision and to ban discrimination against women. But between 1978 and 1980 not a single charge was brought to court under these acts. The government itself, which legislates equal-pay policies, has set sex differential wages for the same job, e.g. female sowers at 69.8 percent of men's wages in Madhya and 62.2 percent in Tamil Nadu. In the mining industry women earn only 33 percent of men's minimum and 20 percent of their maximum total pay.[12]

In all of India, Muslim women have suffered even more discrimination than the predominantly Hindu community and remained even more isolated from legal and social and economic progress. They have an even lower rate of literacy than Hindu women and an even smaller participation in the workforce or politics.[13]

Indian women, notably the Hindu community, are all concerned about the persistence of a widespread and often vicious form of public harassment of women by young men, which often turns violent. They consider it an expression of a broad pattern of oppression of women in India. The so-called "Eve-teasing" is part of *Holi,* the Hindu festival, but in recent years this has turned so perverse at universities that women are often terrorized.[14]

The Hindu code of marriage outlined in religious texts is, in some respects, worse than the passages from the *Qur'an* which certify women's subordination in Muslim society. According to one of the texts from the *Padmapurana,* even if a woman's husband "is offensive in his manners, is choleric, debauched or immoral; if he is a drunkard or a gambler; if he raves like a lunatic ... whatever his defects may be, a wife should always look upon him as her god and should lavish on him all her attention and care. . . ." The same text then instructs the wife that when her husband dies she should "allow herself to be burnt alive on the same funeral pyre; then everyone will praise her virtue. . . ." Which is exactly what some Hindu women are still doing. On September 4, 1987, in the Indian village of Deorala in the Sikar district of the state of Rajastan, a widow (Ms. Ranwar) climbed atop the funeral pyre for her dead husband, whose brother-in-law then lighted the pyre. Twelve days later more than

100,000 people gathered in the same village for the concluding act of the *sati* ritual. Though outlawed by the British 160 years earlier, and outlawed 20 years ago by the Indian government and by the state of Rajastan, the religious execution of the young widow (officially termed a suicide) and the gathering 12 days later to consecrate the crime, by draping a special cloth over the funeral pyre, was carried out without interruption, either by Hindu leaders or Indian or Rajastan officials.[15]

Laws against dowry and women's harassment have been strengthened in India during the past five years. Giving and taking dowry is a criminal offense carrying a prison sentence of up to two years. Cruelty to women, including coercion for dowry, is also a criminal offense. Yet, the total figures of young brides murdered and then burned for failing to come up with a suitable dowry has risen from 990 in 1985 (the number officially reported) to 1,319 in 1986. Long considered an aberration of the northern Indian states, the murderous practice has now spread to many southern states, to Andhra Pradesh and Tamil Nadu. According to the leading news magazine *India Today,* the (government) figures are most likely only the tip of the iceberg. Dowry-related deaths, the magazine said, have now broken religious, caste, and language barriers. They are a problem for both Hindu and Muslim.[16]

There is no doubt that women are less fortunate as far as the laws or their application is concerned, and there is increasing interest in the legal possibilities of easing women's plight and assuring their rights. Some important conferences have already been held, and important studies launched and published, dealing with this particular approach.[17]

Women's greatest problem comes when laws are in place but are not applied. It is at that point that the presence of sufficient women in the Indian legal world becomes critical. They would be the ones best equipped to bring matters to the attention of the courts and the legislature. Unfortunately in most of the Third World women in law are still a very small and almost impotent minority. India is, again, a classic case. The Indian Constitution guarantees equality before the law and prohibits any state from discrimination on grounds of sex.[18] Yet as a prominent Indian lawyer wrote: "For all that is on paper on the principle of equality, nothing comes to the aid of women in the legal profession."[19] It is not only that women have a tremendous gap to close—in the State of Madras more than 97 percent of all lawyers are men—but that there is no equal opportunity.[20]

India is a good example of a country with an abysmal gap between policy and practice. A fine Constitution, on paper, but which means little to women, even to those in the legal profession. "The odds facing women lawyers in India are tremendous," wrote Phiroza Ankleseria, a lawyer herself. "Any significant change in the status of women in the legal profession is a slow process awaiting a change in society's thinking, difficult to achieve in tradition-bound countries like India.... Hide bound thought and social prejudice hinder the progress of women."[21]

The gap between policy and practice has hurt (and killed) women in many other ways. Infant and maternal mortality in India is among the worst in the world despite the fact that India has had a much-publicized family planning program underway the past 10 years. *India Today* described this program as "the Great Hoax," pointing to the fact that every 1.2 seconds a child is born in India, or 70,000 per day, and that the growth rate of 33 births per thousand people has been unchanged since 1977: "The government's continued bungling has catastrophic implications."[22]

A worse case, perhaps the worst example of the gap between policy and practice, is the way in which the Indian authorities have tiptoed around the forceful implementation of the laws against dowry killings. The law now requires that every unnatural death of a woman in the first seven years of her marriage must be officially investigated both by the police and a magistrate (justice of a lower court). Notoriously amenable to bribes, the police hardly ever investigate a killing which has taken place indoors, pleading that the courts will go by the magisterial inquiry. On the other hand, magistrates see their role as limited to noting a dying declaration, if there is one. Magistrates end up taking the easy way out. They try to get a declaration from the dying person, if she is still alive after being set on fire; failing that, they call her relatives to the office for questioning. If no evidence of foul play turns up this way, the case is closed and, once closed, cannot be reopened by anyone.[23]

Not only have legislative enactments failed to equalize gender stratification in India, Duley and Edwards reported, but so too has the educational system. While the Constitution contains a directive that there should be free and compulsory education for boys and girls up to the age of 14, this objective has never been met. Female literacy was 8 percent in 1951. Thirty years later it was only 25 percent. It is still only half of that of males. (See Table 68.) In formal school enrollment, Duley and Edwards wrote, there are still far more boys being enrolled than girls. Women's unequal access to education is closely linked with the sexual division of labor within the Indian family and cultural attitudes towards women. This attitude has been sustained by the continuing ambivalence about the purpose of female education on the part of the state.[24]

Literacy figures for India's rural women are even more disheartening. Some 214 million out of the total female population of 331 million live in rural areas; the rate of literacy among them is 18 percent as compared to 48 percent for urban women.[25]

In *Women in the World,* d'Souza and Nataranjan wrote:

> The lack of education emphasizes the lower status of women and firmly binds them there. Their work is confined to those areas where skills are not necessary, and it follows that wages will be low. That education is thought unnecessary for a girl only underscores the notion of male superiority; boys are regarded as more able and capable, and naturally they get the better-paid jobs.
>
> Life for a girl is hard. Taking care of her younger siblings, helping her mother gather fuel, cook, clean, wash, and tend the animals. Learning early that her brothers are privileged and she is not, accepting as ordained that men come first in almost every aspect of life, so naturally they should eat first while she and her mother must be content to eat later whatever is left.
>
> Even marriage emphasizes her secondary status. Dressed in her best clothes she is exhibited like any piece of merchandise to the prospective groom's family. She is scrutinized, and if approved the bargaining over her dowry begins.[26]

Year	Percentage of Literate Males to Total Male Population	Percentage of Literate Females to Total Female Population	Number of Literate Females to 1,000 Literate Males
1901	9.83	0.60	68
1911	10.56	1.05	94
1921	12.21	1.81	140
1931	15.59	2.93	132
1941	24.90	7.30	277
1951	24.95	7.93	299
1961	34.44	12.95	354
1971	39.45	18.69	435
1981	46.74	24.88	496

Table 68. Male and Female Literacy Rate in India, 1901–1981. Source: Census of India, 1981.

Future Trends

Over a period of 80 years the Indian authorities, by a combination of fine diplomacy, propaganda and outright deceit, have succeeded in setting a stage on which India plays a major role in striking the moral tone for the human rights of people in many parts of the world. Certainly India is a leader of the debate on human rights at the United Nations. Technologically, India is also poised to manufacture a nuclear weapon and has already constructed nuclear power stations. But in those same 80 years, fewer than 25 percent of the women of India were taught the basics of reading and writing. And that in a country which for nearly 16 years had a woman as its Prime Minister. If India were as committed to eliminating bride killings and the sale of children into prostitution as it is to fighting human rights abuses across the ocean in Africa and in other countries, the situation for women in India would be considerably better.

The lack of education for women in India emphasizes their lower status and why they continue to remain in that status. It is true that in recent years, mostly because of the U.N. spotlight, the Indian government has displayed an increasing sensitivity to women's issues. Colleges have been encouraged to open departments of women's studies, and a university of women's studies has been set up in the south of India. For the first time in the history of India, a separate chapter on "Women and Development" was included in the country's (sixth) Five Year Plan, 1980–1985. The program noted the excessive mortality of female children, low rate of literacy and low economic emancipation of women.[27] Given India's record of grandiose statements, grandiose regal language in laws promoting equality and the harsh reality that achievements have never kept up with promises, it is extremely doubtful that much will have come of the grand objectives of the five-year program.

In *Sisterhood Is Global,* political scientist Devaki Jain writes that women are really powerless in Indian society, and worse, the value accorded them as physical beings is terribly low. "Half as literate as men, the women cluster in monotonous, low-paid occupations. Every statistical trend indicates further deterioration: more women seeking work, more women among the destitute, much more rape and sexual humiliation. . . ." As Jain and many others see it, economic development has become a curse to Indian women, women's worst enemy, because technology is replacing women, leaving families even further impoverished. As many as 35 percent of the poorest families are usually headed by women or have women as sole supporters.[28]

The point that women's real problem in India is not so much the law as abject poverty was also made by Neela d'Souza and Ramani Nataranjan in *Women in the World.* As they see it, the millions of illiterate poor own little beyond the clothes they wear, so that denial of property rights and education affected only the "haves," i.e., the wealthy. The real problems of the masses of women were poverty, insecurity, poor wages. Margot Duley believes that not only has the electoral process failed as a method of equalizing gender stratification in India, but also the educational system has simply failed to make any difference to the vast majority of Indian women.[29] Others, such as Hanna Papanek, believe that women simply face a general injustice.[30] Vina Mazumdar, an outstanding feminist leader in India, perhaps came closest to the heart of the problem when she said that the truth is that even the elite in India, social scientists such as herself, are still ignorant about the real status of women in Indian society, ignorant of the real influence of traditions, customs, cultures, religions and the law relating to women.[31] Without knowledge there can be no cure.

27. Case Study: Japan

Statistical Profile and Women's Status

On the face of things, Japanese women appear to have achieved as much equality as women elsewhere in the West.

There were almost 60 million women in Japan in 1980 enjoying a literacy rate in excess of 97 percent, among the highest in the world and surpassing that of the United States. There were almost as many married women employed in Japan as in the United States at the 1980 census, but the birthrate for Japanese women was 15 percent below that of United States women.[1]

The Japanese Constitution contains a women's equal rights provision from 1947, prohibiting political, economic, or social discrimination on grounds of gender.[2]

Women form 88 percent of all junior college students, receive more schooling than men, and outnumber them as voters. During the 1980 general election in Japan, 75.4 percent of all women voters turned out to cast their ballot compared to only 73.7 percent of male voters.[3]

Yet women are the housekeepers of Japan. They are a minute percentage in the Japanese Diet or parliament. They walk behind the men. They serve the men and they feed a great deal of Japan. In fact, some 62 percent of Japanese farmers are women.[4] True, women have been coming into the labor market in increasing numbers, but as Barbara Bergmann observed, "Japanese women are almost invariably shunted into marginal positions.... Women in Japan remain frankly inferior, their condition an ugly blot on Japan's brilliant economic success."[5]

There has been vast improvement in women's status in Japan in many ways, but only because their position prior to 1947 was so utterly devoid of any status or protection. Japanese women were as much subordinate to men as in any Muslim state. In 1940 the average Japanese woman died at the age of 50. Today she lives to over 80 years—the longest life expectancy for women in the entire world.

In Japan discrimination against women was, and largely remains, a way of life. It took seven years, from 1978 to May 17, 1985, for the Japanese parliament to approve a bill "encouraging" employers (as from April, 1986) to end discrimination on the basis of sex in their hiring, assignment and promotion policies. Today 40 percent of the labor force of Japan is made up of women, and 59 percent of those women are married. Experts point out that "typically ... the woman does the lower status work. Today a mere 6.2 percent are managers or officials."[6] As recently as 1978 about 91 percent of all companies had jobs which were closed to women, 73 percent had different starting salaries for women, 52 percent did not promote women, 77 percent had different retirement systems and only 19.4 percent offered equal training.[7]

Considering where Japanese women found themselves prior to World War II and the defeat of Japan, working women, in comparative international terms, have demonstrated a rate of progress that can easily be termed a miracle equal to the economic recovery of Japan. As Robins-Mowry stated so aptly, prosperity is fundamental to the hastening of Japanese women's continued progress. As long as they produce goods and services for democratic Japan, instead of large families, their economic worth will continue to escalate and this value gives them greater leverage in decision-making in society.[8]

There are three outstanding aspects about the profile of working Japanese women. One, the entry of married women into the work force; two, changes in the age, marital status, and length of service of working women; and three, the upward wage curve for women workers.

During the last two decades all of the industrially developed countries revealed an increase in education for women and in wages for women, a large influx of married women into the labor force and a decline in the fertility rate. The developments in Japan were different. Women's labor force actually decreased until 1976 and the trend only picked up sharply during the 1980s. The fertility rate in Japan also started to decline as early as 1950, stabilized in 1960, and then continued to decline after the mid-'70s, preceding the same movement in the rest of the industrially developed world.[9]

The average age of women workers in Japan has risen from 23.8 years in 1949 to almost 35 in 1980. Whereas in 1950 women worked on the average for only 3.2 years, by 1979 the term had increased to 6.2 years, or 57 percent of the term of men. Whereas in 1952 only 8 percent of women workers (farm workers excluded) were married, by 1979 the figure had grown amazingly to 67 percent.

Finally, women's wages have been rising faster than men's since 1958, although the wage gap, discussed further on in this chapter, is still significant. Wives and mothers are working in Japan, said Dorothy Robins-Mowry in her excellent work on women in modern Japan, (a) because Japan needs their labor to fulfill its economic goals and (b) because 86 percent of working women indicated that they needed the additional income for the family and to pay for the higher education of their children.[10]

Ironically, one of the main barriers to equality in the workplace is the Labor Standards Act passed in 1947 to protect (*sic*) women. According to the act, women are not permitted to work after 10 in the evening and are thus deprived of extra money for night shift work or overtime. The result is that women rarely get anywhere as journalists or in many of the other professions. Women comprise only 6.4 percent of scientists, 2.4 percent of engineers, 9.0 percent of lawyers and 5.5 percent of executive posts. In the civil service women serve on only 5.2 percent of the advisory bodies. Overall, Japanese women make up some 40 percent of the workforce but earn on the average only some 53 percent as much as their male counterparts. In 1983 women made up 21 percent of Japan's civil servants but held a mere 1.7 percent of the managerial posts. Of 2,767 judges and assistant judges in 1982 only 79 were women.[11]

As in Korea the male dominance in Japan, particularly in the business field, is very strong. Discrimination against women is often far more subtle than elsewhere in Asia, but as effective.[12]

While Japanese women were living longer in 1983, depression had become a major problem. Yoshiko Ikeda of the Japanese National Institute of Health stated that a major study had found that Japanese women could expect to live to more than 80 years but that after 40 a great many women will suffer mental depression. This is usually the age when the children start leaving the house. Japanese men can continue to work, but women start to flounder in the absence of the children and other domestic chores. Japanese society also tends to look down on housework.[13] Many Japanese still harbor the image of women as homemakers even though in 1983 working wives by far outnumbered unmarried working women.[14]

The law states and the Constitution dictates that there shall be equality between men and women in Japan. But Japanese women who set out to buy a condominium (apartment) discovered that their fathers still had to guarantee the loan for the purchase price, no matter their own position or income. In 1980 Japan signed a pledge to eliminate discrimination against women so as to fall in with the U.N.'s Decade for Women. Japan also passed an Employment Equality Act in 1985, but there is no provision in the bill, no penalty, to enforce the law. In addition, the pace of change in social attitudes is almost imperceptible.

Japan has ratified Convention No. 100 of the International Labor Organization on equal remuneration for men and women doing the same work, and there has been a significant decrease in the earnings gap between men and women. Some observers say that, nonetheless, at peak salary in 1985, women were still earning only 51.6 percent of men.[15] Others, such as Robins-Mowry and Hiroko Hayashi, set the differential at 54 percent.[16]

There are several reasons for the continued existence of such a large gap in income between men and women in Japan, the greatest among the industrially developed countries. The reasons are both overt and covert. The Japanese wage system is based on strict seniority and since women have worked for shorter periods because of interruptions of marriage and childbirth, their seniority is that much lower. Many women work in the pink ghetto, or for small companies with few fringe benefits, which adds to the difference in income from wages and benefits. The covert reasons are male bias and women's lower status which stems from that bias, resulting in women ending up in the lesser-paying occupations.

As in Korea and Taiwan, Japanese girls find better jobs with better pay and better opportunities in foreign company offices represented in Japan. An estimated 80 percent of Japanese companies will not hire any women university graduates, although they will hire girls coming straight from school. Once employed, women face discrimination in, or outright exclusion from, most training programs. The reason is that most Japanese companies fully expect women to leave work at the age of 25 or 26 to get married.[17]

Occupational Segregation

An indication of the extent of occupational segregation in Japan is evident from the fact that only 6.4 percent of women are scientists, 2.4 percent engineers and 9.3 percent lawyers.[18] In business only 6.2 percent are listed as managers.[19] Of the companies who train their workers, as most do, some 60 percent provide women with different training from that of men.[20] In fact, Cook and Hayashi found that women receive little or no on-the-job training because the employer expects the woman to stay just a short while and to retire between age 27 and 30 to have her first or second child.[21] Long-term careers are still the exception for women. The fact that men in 1981 still held better than 98 percent of jobs as elementary school principals and 99.8 percent of junior high schools is also an indication of male society's biases against women in positions of authority. In her study of women in modern Japan, Robins-Mowry points out that the occupational distribution of women explains why most women are not well-positioned for advance in their career. The bulk of the women (see Table 69) are in sales, service, and office work. Since 1960 women office workers have come to outrank women manufacturing workers.[22] Jane Condon states that today some 150,000 Japanese women work for foreign corporations in Japan, where they get more respect from their employers and better chances at promotion.[23]

Though it is technically illegal to have different retirement ages for men and women, almost 100 percent of Japanese private companies retire men at age 55 or older and 55 percent retire women at age 40 to 55 years.[24] Cook and Hayashi state that "the method of enforcement of the early retirement systems may be by work rule, by collective agreement, by individual contract with an employee, or, more usually, by customary categories. Table 70, page 406, shows the distribution by these categories.

"A distinctive point," Cook and Hayashi said, "is the difference that in fact exists between companies' official retirement rules and the point at which it is 'customary' for women to retire, earlier than the work rules or union agreements may call for. In such cases, the company accomplishes its purpose by 'hinting' to its woman employee at the appropriate time that she is no longer useful to the company and had better retire."[25]

In *Working Women in Fifteen Countries,* Hiroko Hayashi summarized the problem of occupational segregation in Japan. Despite the increase in the number of working women, she said, the opportunities are still unequal to those offered to men. There is no legal prohibition against discrimination in hiring, she pointed out, and legal protection against discrimination exists only after one has been employed. Research by the Ministry of Labor shows that many industries discriminate against women, not only in wages but also in hiring, job assignments, training, and promotion. In 1981, she said, 83 percent of businesses surveyed had positions that were barred to women. "Obviously sex discrimination remains deeply imbedded in general employment practice in Japan." Of the businesses she surveyed, 45 percent also gave women no opportunity for promotion.[26]

The attitude of labor unions is Japan has not made the early-retirement-

Occupation Category	1960	1970	1980
Office	1.70	3.39	4.43
Skilled and manufacturing	2.40[a]	2.91	3.14
Professional and technical	0.60	1.00	1.76
Service	1.08	1.50	1.74
Sales	0.58	1.12	1.57
Laborers	--[a]	0.66	0.54
Transport and communication	0.05	0.22	0.14
Managers and officials	0.02	0.05	0.11
Farmers, lumbering, and fishing	0.24	0.10	0.10
Total	6.67	10.96	13.53

Retirement Point	Work Rule	Collective Agreement	Individual Agreement	Customary Practice
Marriage	10.9%	1.0%	2.9%	80.9%
Childbirth or pregnancy	4.6	1.0	1.8	86.2
Early age	68.1	7.4	10.5	8.3
Nepotism	3.8		1.4	87.0

***Top:* Table 69. Japan: Paid Women Workers by Occupational Category, 1960–1980 (in millions). Source: Dorothy Robins-Mowry, *The Hidden Sun, Women of Modern Japan,* Westview Press, Boulder CO, 1983, p. 171. Reprinted with permission. Notes: [a]Laborers in 1960 were included in the figure for skilled and manufacturing. *Bottom:* Table 70. Enforcement of Retirement Systems in Japan. Source: A. Cook and H. Hayashi, *Working Women in Japan,* New York State School of Industrial and Labor Relations, Cornell University, Ithaca NY, 1980, p. 26. Reprinted with permission.**

low-wages spiral of women in Japan any easier. According to Cook and Hayashi, union leaders share Japanese societal views about women at work and that women should only be transitory in the market as short term or part time workers. The fact that almost no women are visible in Japanese union leadership is an aggravating factor. Even in unions with large female membership, such as textiles, telecommunications, teaching or government service, all the top posts in the union are filled by men. There are women's divisions in the larger labor unions, but the women nominally at the head of these divisions have a hard time reconciling outside pressure by women's movements and the dictates of the union they represent.[27] Only 25 percent of female employees are unionized.[28]

Japan has a dual industrial economy. The large firms represent the upper level and provide for virtually permanent employment, at least of male workers. The medium and smaller firms are the lower level with much less secure conditions and lower wages. In addition there is a large group of companies depending heavily on part-time labor. According to researchers Alice Cook and Hiroko Hayashi in their excellent work *Working Women in Japan,* women cannot be said to be a part of the upper level, i.e., of the permanent employment system. "Women are restricted to a narrow range of occupations, all considered auxiliary and, with very few exceptions, such as teaching, low-paid. Women are promoted much more slowly than men, when they move upward in skill or scope at all. Even in government employment, the opportunities for work are not equal ... there are still nine groups of employment closed to women."[29]

Women in prestigious professions are few and far between. According to Jane Condon, "In Western eyes Japanese women's status is the lowest of all industrial society." She found that most Japanese women have grown up believing their opinions do not count. But there is the faint stirring of revolt among the younger women, particularly working women. "Young wives are less disposed to being nurses and maids at home."[30] The Ministry of Labor told Condon that great changes are to come in the next decade. Condon writes: "The momentum is building. Millions of unemployed and overeducated women are sitting at home, bowing beside the escalators, serving tea or greeting customers—just waiting for their talent to be tapped, ready to contribute to the next (Japanese) miracle."[31] It was only in the early 1980s that women first became air traffic controllers, police detectives and immigration officials. It will therefore require some sort of miracle to change the statistics of occupational segregation, which show that fewer than 10 percent of professors at universities are women, only 0.3 percent of managers, 2.6 percent of judges, and only 3.3 percent of lawyers. On the other hand almost 48 percent of the agricultural labor force, more than 50 percent of all clerical and service workers and between 50 and 90 percent of rubber and textile workers are women.[32]

Women in Politics and Government

Japan is a parliamentary democracy. The parliament (Diet) has two houses: a 511-seat House of Representatives and a 252-strong Senate. There are only a handful of women in the Japanese parliament, and proportionally even fewer women are elected to seats in the provincial, city and town councils.

Conservative party dominance and the need for consensus represent a formidable barrier to women's participation in politics. Legally, the door is open to all, but the political structure and the composition and attitudes of the parties impress upon women that politics is not considered within their accepted role.[33] As Eileen Hargadine, an Asian studies specialist, observed in *The Politics of the Second Electorate,* "...although Japanese civic culture is actively democratic and sanctions voter participation, women are not thought politically aware and therefore (not) suitable in general, for public office." In one opinion poll during the late 1970s, only 14 percent of men said they believed women's political consciousness to be high.[34]

Women face enormous difficulties in Japan to break out of their stereotype and to become active in politics. According to Susan Pharr in *Political Women in Japan,* "Japan has much in common with the undeveloped world today. This is especially true when it comes to the way in which Japanese women have gained political rights"[35] (i.e., through an outside influence, or rather, outside force—in this case the United States after the defeat of Imperial Japan during World War II). Pharr explains further that "once gained, [these ideas] have lacked roots, and the process of role redefinition necessary . . . has been a particularly onerous one. . . . The key problem for women in Japan, like that for women in so much of the world today, has been to translate the legal rights into power and to bring customs in line with what the law says."[36] In politics the results of their efforts, after South Africa and the United States, are the worst in the industrialized world. (See Table 71.)

In 1947 when the American influence was strong, a million more women than men voted, but only 39 women ended up in the House of Assembly, the Japanese House of Representatives. Thirty-three years later, women voters still outnumbered men and the voting rate among women was still 2 percent higher than that among men, yet only 9 women ended up in the Assembly.[37] The low point was the years between 1960 and 1976 when only seven women were elected to parliament. In almost every election more women voters turned out than men.[38]

For women, the most important development in decades was the election, in 1986, of a woman to head the opposition Japan Socialist Party. She was elected on September 6, 1986, to become the first woman ever to head a major political party in Japan, and took her seat in parliament with only six other women in a lower house of 512 seats. In the upper house there are now 22 women among 252 men.[39]

According to Susan Pharr, Japanese women are poised to take on men in politics. "That such roles hold attractions for Japanese women today is indicated in the results of a recent national survey in which one out of every five women questioned stated an interest in participating in civic activities—a very high number given the relatively small proportion of people in any society who becomes politically active. Socioeconomic and political factors, then, strongly support the contention that increasing numbers of women in Japan will seek out active political roles in the future." Though skeptics may doubt this, said Pharr, it should be pointed out that since the average Japanese family sees the children leave the house when the mother is about 35 years old, this means that Japanese women are left with 45 years to fill, one way or the other.[40]

The Legal World of Japanese Women

The Japanese Constitution. The so-called Showa Constitution which the Americans imposed on Japan was enacted on May 3, 1947. There are five Articles which assure fundamental rights for women. Article 14 is the central clause providing for equality before the law and prohibiting discrimination in political, economic or social relations because of race, creed, sex, social status or family origin. Article 15 guarantees women the vote. Article 24 requires that there must be mutual consent of both for marriage. Article 26 provides for equal education based on ability, and Article 44 permits women to run for elected office.

Despite the equal rights clause those rights are seldom enforced and have yet to be absorbed into the nation's consciousness. Most of the pressure for legal reform and improvement in the status of women came from outside, such as the United Nations. Sensitive to their image in the eyes of the rest of the world, Japan in 1980 signed the U.N. Convention on the Elimination of Discrimination Against Women and the Diet (parliament) ratified this in 1985, thereby giving the concept legal status in Japan.

According to Jane Condon, three areas of Japanese law had to change before the Diet could ratify the convention:

> The first related to defining Japanese nationality. Under the old law, a child born of a Japanese woman and a foreign man, even if living in Japan, retained only the father's nationality. However, the new Nationality Law, which took effect in January 1985, allows mothers for the first time to pass on their nationality to their children. The second problem area related to education. Only girls studied home economics, while boys took physical education. Although the subject is still under discussion, in the future, home economics will, most likely, be an elective for both sexes. The third problem area was the focus of the most heated debate, a bill known as the Equal Employment Opportunity Law governing the workplace, through which women will lose some protective legislation limiting overtime and night work. In turn, they gain a better (that is, equal) chance at training and promotion. However, the watered-down draft of the law which eventually passed the Diet does not punish offenders but only "encourages" employers to conform to equal opportunity guidelines.... And this is the real point. The status of women in Japan is a function not of law, but of the deeply ingrained cultural patterns. Radical change will come slowly, if at all.[41]

Marriage. Until after World War II, the idea of an individual Japanese young man marrying an individual young Japanese woman on grounds of love, personal choice or simply affection simply did not exist. Individual choice was a totally foreign concept. Women were more like property, to be acquired, and were even considered legally incompetent. Today Article 24 of the 1946 Constitution provides that marriage must be based on mutual consent. Though the girls now have a veto power, most marriages are still (probably) arranged between families. A go-between or matchmaker, the *nakodo,* is employed. The *nakodo* also ensures that the boy's family has no Korean blood, Hiroshima blood or that of the lower class *burakumin,* Japan's untouchables. Estimates of these arranged marriages vary from 25 to 60 percent of all marriages.[42] A major survey undertaken in 1982 by the massive Mitsubishi Corporation found that 40.9 percent of young women stated that "love" and "marriage" were two different things. Only 37.6 percent insisted that they would want to marry for love.[43]

Divorce. The Meiji Civil Code of 1898 gave Japanese women the right of divorce but the provisions were that (a) the husband got the children and (b) the woman received no alimony. After the divorce, she had to fend for herself. Today the tables have been turned, and 74 percent of all family court petitions for divorce are initiated by women. In 1979 more than 50 percent of women received financial settlements as part of the divorce, and mothers gained

	House of Representatives			House of Councillors				
Year	Number of Women Elected	Voting Rate, % (female)	Voting Rate, % (male)	Number of Women Elected	Number of Women in House of Councillors	Voting Rate, % (female)	Voting Rate, % (male)	Total Number of Women in Diet
1946	39	67.0	78.5					39
1947	15	61.6	74.9	11	11	54.0	68.4	26
1949	12	67.9	80.7					23
1950				5	12	66.7	78.2	24
1952	12	72.8	80.5					24
1953	9	70.4	78.4	10	19	58.9	67.8	28
1955	8	72.1	78.0					27
1956				5	15	57.7	66.9	23
1958	11	74.4	79.8					26
1959				8	13	55.2	62.6	24
1960	7	71.2	76.0					20
1962				9	17	66.5	70.1	24
1963	7	70.0	72.4					24
1965				9	17	66.1	68.0	24
1967	7	73.3	74.8					24
1968				5	13	69.0	68.9	20
1969	8	69.1	67.9					21
1971				8	13	59.3	59.1	21
1972	7	72.5	71.0					20
1974				8	18	73.6	72.7	25
1976	7	74.1	72.8					25
1977				8	16	69.3	67.7	23
1979	11	68.6	67.4		15			26
1980	9	75.4	73.7	9	17	75.4	73.7	26

custody of the children in 48 percent of the mutual-consent divorces.[44] Part of the Law of Inheritance was amended in 1980 so that the spouse's portion became one-half, formerly one-third, of the inheritance when there is a child.

The divorce rate still remains one of the lowest in the world at 20 percent or 1.5 divorces for every 1,000 marriages. (In comparison, the rate of the United States is 5.3 per thousand.[45]) According to Condon, 90 percent of divorces are through mutual agreement. The couple simply visits the local ward office and, with two witnesses required, completes a short form and signs. It is perhaps the easiest divorce procedure in the industrialized world. There are 13 reasons acceptable for divorce, of which "in-law trouble" is one. When couples cannot agree on the divorce, the case proceeds to the family court. Only if it fails in that court does a divorce end up in a regular Japanese court. Some 10 percent of divorces reach the family court and only 1 percent the regular civil court.[46] On September 2, 1987, Japan's Supreme Court also ruled that a man separated from his wife and living with his mistress (for 38 years) could file for divorce on grounds of "irreconcilable differences." The decision was hailed as a new era in divorce law, since Japanese courts previously had refused to recognize a demand for a divorce from the party at fault.

Birth Control and Abortion. Jane Condon wrote that sex education is almost totally absent from Japanese schools and the Pill is effectively banned by the Ministry of Health because of possible harmful side effects.[47] Abortion became legalized through the 1948 Eugenic Protection Law which permitted abortion, *inter alia,* for "economic reasons." A 1982 law, however, restricted the reasons for abortion to certain diseases, pregnancy as the result of rape, and endangerment of the health of the mother.

In 1983 there were more than 50,000 abortions in Japan, or about one for every three births.[48] According to the first sex survey ever conducted in Japan, two out of every three women have had at least one abortion.[49] Teenage abortions have doubled the past decade although they still form a mere 5 percent of the total.[50]

Education. Article 26 of the 1946 Constitution ordered that "all people have the right to receive an equal education, according to their ability." In 1947 the Japanese universities therefore were forced to open their doors to women. After 40 years of this open-door policy, imposed by Article 26, only about 23 percent of the four-year college students were women. Although the percentage of women of all students increased from a mere 5 percent in 1960 to 33 percent today, more than 61 percent of the girls do not enter the four-year colleges but go to the two-year insititutions which are home-oriented in the courses they offer.[51] According to Robins-Mowry the home economics major, the choice of almost 40 percent of the junior college women, is very often little more than glorified preparation for marriage and homemaking. "But most go to junior college for precisely that reason."[52]

Table 71. Japanese Women Elected to the House of Representatives and the House of Councillors, Election Years 1946–1980. Source: Dorothy Robins-Mowry: *The Hidden Sun, Women of Modern Japan,* Westview Press, Boulder CO, 1983, p. 319. Reprinted with permission.

The higher education which Japanese women have been receiving the past four decades has not brought them any better wages and income, for which occupational discrimination and the basic chauvinistic attitude of Japanese men are mostly to blame.[53] Perhaps as a result of this, only 16 percent of parents want their daughters to go to a four-year college, but 76 percent want their sons to go.[54]

Most girls end up picking home economics, teaching, education and humanities as subjects.[55] According to Jane Condon, Japan's Director of the Women and Youth Bureau of the Ministry of Labor explained that girls believed that (a) other subjects such as science, law and engineering are not useful in married life, and (b) such a four-year academic record would scare off potential suitors. Women's inferior position at higher educational levels is puzzling also because women in Japan play an enormously important role in preparing children for school and in keeping them on track after they enter school.[56]

Employment and Labor Law. Condon states that Japanese working women do have considerable protective legislation, important because it is all that women have, legally, to compensate them for their many disadvantages and the discriminatory treatment they receive on the job. These protective enactments are part of the Labor Standards Law and as such are enforced, or enforceable, by the Ministry of Labor's inspectorate, located all over Japan:

> The Labor Standards Law guarantees equal pay for equal work (Art. 4); prevents women from working during the hours from 10:00 p.m. to 5:00 a.m. (Art. 62); regulates the maximum amount of overtime allowed per day (2 hours), per week (6 hours), and per year (150 hours) (Art. 61); prohibits women from doing "dangerous work"—they may not work higher than five meters above ground nor lift specified heavy weights (Art. 63), nor may they work underground (Art. 64); they may request time off during menstruation when it interferes with their ability to work (Art. 67); they have a specified maternity leave of six weeks before and after childbirth, and the health insurance law (Art. 50, par. 2) provides for paying insured women workers 60 percent of their standard daily remuneration for six weeks before and after childbirth, if they should not work (Art. 50, par. 1). They may not be dismissed during maternity leave nor for thirty days after it (Art. 19). When a pregnant woman requires it, she may be placed on a lighter job (Art. 65). A woman may request time for nursing an infant under one year of age and receive at least thirty minutes twice a day during working hours (Art. 66).[57]

There are few company provisions for maternity leave although the Labor Standards Law makes provision for six-week pregnancy and maternity leave. But the law is not vigorously enforced. In spite of the evidence that almost 50 percent of all women work, society and employers perpetuate the myth that women are temporary employees who do not qualify for all benefits. The equal pay provision of the same law is difficult to enforce because of arguments as to what constitutes equality when comparing work and different occupations. Because labor unions are closely tied to companies they do not provide recourse for women. The Trade Union Act forbids sex-based discrimination in admission to membership but though women form some 28 percent of members, there are hardly any women in the decision-making bodies.[58]

In 1972 the Diet adopted the Working Women's Welfare Law, which aims to further the welfare and improve the status of working women by taking appropriate actions to help them reconcile their dual responsibilities of work and home or to enable them to develop and make use of their abilities. "Its adoption," said Condon, "brought Japan closer to compliance with standards on women's employment laid down in the International Labor Organization's (ILO) conventions on women's work. The law, however, was recommendatory, not mandatory."[59] Condon goes on:

> Conditions in public employment fall under a different set of laws that in some ways improve upon the provisions of the two laws noted above. Teachers in Tokyo, for example, have mandatory maternity leave eight weeks before and after childbirth with full pay, and a national law adopted in 1956 makes it mandatory that replacements be found for teachers taking maternity leave.[60]
>
> Despite all this attention to women in Japanese labor law, the code mentions sex equality only in respect to equal wages for work of equal value. The section of the law affecting conditions of work (Art. 3) speaks also of equality but limits it to creed, national origin, and social status, omitting sex. No mention is made anywhere in the law of equal opportunity in hiring, in training, in access to work or to promotion, although Article 14 of the constitution calls for equal rights of men and women before the law.[61]

According to Robins-Mowry, law and practice also diverge in Japan. She pointed out that it was not until 20 years after the date of enactment of the new Constitution and the Labor Standards Act of 1947 that the first working woman sued her employer for sex discrimination. Since that case, there have been only about 50 others concerned with unfair treatment of women, a drop of water in the ocean.[62]

The existing legislation has severe limitations for women. Despite the various protective measures, the fact remains that there is no provision for equal job opportunity. Labor disputes on this point must be raised in constitutional or civil code terms which are very general. The point is also that women's work roles are so secondary to men's in status, quality, length of service, training and opportunities that equality in these spheres has not been touched upon and the new legislation passed in 1985 is notable for its lack of enforcement. In fact the enforcement clause merely states that employers "must strive to give women equal treatment."

The Japanese government admits that working women suffer from gender discrimination. In March 1989 a spokesman for then Prime Minister Noboru Takeshita, quoting from an official report, said the number of women in the work force had increased from 12 million in 1975 to 17 million in 1988, and now form roughly 40 percent of the total work force. However, despite the 1981 Equal Opportunities Act few of these women get responsible positions in management. The report by the Prime Minister's office stated that more than 63 percent of all working women who responded to a government survey in 1987 complained of unequal treatment and discrimination. Women face discrimination in promotions, pay and working conditions.[63]

Women's Dilemma in Contemporary Japanese Society

It is an understatement, as Robins-Mowry wrote, that the situation of Japanese women in the 1970s and 1980s has not been well understood internationally and remains enigmatic to many people outside Japan.[64]

Popular Western misconceptions about Japanese women in kimonos assembling high-tech computers and laser instruments have a humorous touch to them but they do not address the question of whether Japanese women want to keep this status intact, by focusing entirely on their families, or whether they want to challenge male authority and espouse a greater individualism, either in the workplace or in politics. In reality, Japanese women have sufficient protection from existing laws to do anything. Yet, most Japanese women's lives have not been affected so much by this legal liberation as by the miracle of Japan's economic recovery after World War II. What is true is that Japanese women, facing an empty home and a long life after the children have finished school and university, have not yet decided what their future role is to be.

Women have expressed their views in political circles when they thought the moral and physical basis of the family was being undermined. They became, temporarily, political animals, like men, and yet few sought politics as a career. Japanese women, at best, are seen as very ambivalent when it comes to politics or theories of government.[65] Publicly, they would like to be known as diligent wives and housekeepers, good mothers, and this makes them appear indifferent to what is plotted and construed in the Diet. Yet they are faithful voters. The percentage of women voters is almost invariably higher than that of men. Whether women realize that they can swing an election one way or the other can be answered in the affirmative, if women are canvassed one by one. Collectively, however, publicly, this knowledge has not yet emerged as a political force.

Robins-Mowry states that women sometimes do inspire political action but that it is done through small groups, lobbyists, through neighborhood ties, rather than as a united movement. The major exception is the League of Women Voters, which often tries to mobilize women to support improvement of public and community affairs. Women, Robins-Mowry said, may even be the real prognosticators of change in Japan. "Closer to the daily life of family and community, they are the bellwethers of practical problems that emerge to require national remedy. At the local level they have pioneered procedures for coalition politics.... As guardians of their country's domestic well being, they become as well the architects of social change." Japanese politicians take heed of women's subdued voices and their talk at home because women do not represent a special-interest group and because their concerns are not politically motivated.[66]

In all of Japan there is only a small band of women who are either publicly recognized or self-proclaimed feminists, fighting for women's liberation. In her study of Japanese women, Takie Lebra found that there is no consensus in Japan itself as to where women stand. There are mutually opposing views. On the one hand, there is the view of women as deprived in status, power, and opportunity, bound by the rule of segregation and labor, submissive, feminine, and hopelessly removed from the attainment of self-fulfillment when compared with, for example, American women. On the other hand this image has been refuted as a groundless stereotype, even a myth, says Lebra. If one penetrates the surface of Japanese society, one discovers that in fact the women run the men, not the other way around. The wife enjoys dictatorial powers over household affairs with unlimited autonomy. "Rather to be pitied is the American woman who is constrained by her husband's power and interference." Women, Lebra says, are not excluded from the public domain; women choose to stay or return home.[67]

According to Lebra, there are other fundamental disagreements about the Japanese woman: on the one hand seen as the embodiment of self-denial, giving everything for her husband, the house, and the children, on the other hand she is denigrated for being so ambitious for family success that she relentlessly drives her children to study. American women can opt for a single career with impunity, even remain childless. But the stigma of female singlehood in Japan is enormous. "Over-aged" single women are seen as abnormal. The Japanese woman is extremely conscious of her role in the community and how she adjusts to the existing social structure. The structural embeddedness of sex roles—man the worker, woman the housekeeper and mother—stabilizes the sex-based hierarchy, says Lebra. Social structures as a whole dictate that women be submissive, constrained and more backstaged than men, lower in status, with less power, autonomy and role visibility. A husband who appears henpecked disturbs a sense of social order, even among the majority of women. The key to understanding the attitude of the Japanese woman who ostensibly accepts her inferior status lies in understanding how much she is bound by the norm of status asymmetry. To change this, suggests Lebra, requires a fundamental social reorganization, primarily in legislative and institutional innovations towards greater equalization.[68]

Currently, Japanese women are struggling to cope with the technological revolution, with the demand for their labor, the subsequent contraction of their roles at home and thus the denigration of their status. Millions of Japanese women are graduating from four-year colleges. Once exposed to the workplace they become discontent with the discrepancy between their educational level and the scope of occupational opportunities. A conflict is in the making. Women want to work but they also want to fulfill their role as housewives and mothers in order to fit into the social order. They want to advance in their work and do well in their careers but they also feel they must marry at an early age and have children. In the United States, women can make the choice between marriage, family, and career without violating a deeply embedded social structure. Japanese women cannot.

Kazuko Sugisaki concluded as follows:

> It is a paradox that, in Japan, working women still suffer open and hidden discrimination while their contribution makes Japan's existence as a world economic power possible. There is no simple explanation for this. It may be that the whole social system has been so rigidly based on male supremacy that it is virtually impossible to bring rapid changes, or that Japanese men have been traditionally so accustomed to treating women as their inferiors that they are not even

aware of the advantages of their superior position or the discrimination it produces. Or perhaps Japanese women themselves, having endured a low status imposed on them for generations by a society based on Confucian and Buddhist moral virtues, do not fully realize the extent of their discriminatory treatment. And regrettably there is still a tendency prevalent among middle-class women to look down upon the activists of women's liberation movements as not "ladylike." There is also a lack of interest in administrative and legislative issues that are beyond their immediate concern. All of these ingrained problems must be dealt with to bring about a true liberation of Japanese women.[69]

28. Case Study: The People's Republic of China

Communist Ideology and Women's Rights

The Chinese constitute one quarter of all humanity, and when the Communist Revolution, led by Mao Tse-tung, succeeded in 1949 to gain power, the participation of women in the new dispensation and the radical improvement of their status became a cornerstone of the new regime. Most recent research has concentrated on answering the questions (a) whether, as the Chinese government today claims, the emancipation of women and the objectives of socialism are not only compatible but the same; (b) whether the Communist Revolution has materially, legally and socially improved the status of women; (c) whether Chinese women have indeed been emancipated to the extent that equality with men in the three aforementioned areas is not just an ideological slogan but a real, measurable achievement; and (d) whether the Chinese claim of real political equality between men and women is indeed the case. The amount of research has been impressive.[1]

In claiming that there was no conflict, only mutual reinforcement between the emancipation of women and socialist development, the Chinese were echoing the standard analysis which had come to them via the Soviet Union's interpretation of the women's question begun with Lenin. This analysis held that women's emancipation depended on two things: one, their participation in production outside the home and, two, the socialization of domestic labor. Since both of these were socialist goals, women's emancipation and socialism were mutually supportive.[2] But unlike the Soviet Union, the Chinese Communist Party and the Chinese government were prepared to have the success of the Revolution measured by women's progress. Both the party and the government have held that the degree of women's liberation is an index of social progress. In 1980 China also ratified the U.N. Convention on Elimination of Discrimination Against Women.

In old China women lived at the lowest level of a suffocatingly strict patriarchal society. A woman had no right to divorce her husband, no matter how much he ill-treated her. Women, in fact, had no rights at all, except through their sons. In traditional China, Phyllis Andors pointed out, girls were freely sold as concubines or as second wives. Widows were not allowed to remarry. Betrothed girls were considered widows if their husband-to-be died before the wedding. The young widow, said Andors, could then either serve her parents-in-law, enter a Buddhist convent or commit suicide. Poorer families simply sold the widow as a concubine or slave. But if there were any children from a marriage, they were kept by the in-laws. An adulterous women could be killed by her husband without fear of punishment but not the other way around.[3] In many respects the position of women in pre-revolutionary China was much the same as women as in the hard-core Muslim countries of the world before the riches brought by runaway oil prices produced an economic upheaval and pitched them into the modern world.

Between 1899 and 1920 the denigrating social status of women and their servile subordination to men became the subject of several investigations and debates, but the real emancipation of women from their feudal status came only after the establishment of the (Communist) People's Republic of China in 1949. In fact the first law promulgated by the new revolutionary government was the Marriage Law of 1950, which not only declared the equality of women and men, but confirmed the rights and freedom of women in respect of their marriage. The new law denounced the arranged marriages and indifference to women's interests prior to 1949 as the legacy of a feudal society. For the first time Chinese women were free to divorce their husbands. Confucian Law had always regarded the patriarchal family as the foundation for social order. The law of 1950 broke with this approach and abolished the concept of supremacy of man over woman. It provided for equal rights for both sexes and the protection of the lawful interests of women and children.[4] In 1954 the first Constitution of China further reiterated that men and women were equal and that women had equal rights with men in the political, economic and social life of Socialist China.

In 1949 the new Communist government under Mao Tse-tung issued a call for women to unite with men and to participate in production and in political activities so as to improve women's political and economic status. Mao's idea was to use women as a vast pool of untapped political support to build the new socialist China. The Communists certainly made a massive attempt at the time to transform public attitudes about women on a scale women in the West can only dream of. The government staged and promoted plays, songs and study meetings. Women had their legal rights explained to them, particularly family rights within the marriage. Women were drawn into the military and the Communist Party apparatus as "comrades" of the men.[5] In fact, almost 40 years later the official Chinese definition of population policy still reads as follows: "In its commitment to raise the status of women, the government plans to use education to eradicate feudal ideas about women and to launch publicity campaigns to inform women of their legal rights."[6]

China's latest Constitution, promulgated in December 1982, contains a number of articles specifically addressed to women's rights: "Women in the People's Republic of China enjoy equal rights with men in all spheres of life, political, economic, cultural and social, including family life. The State protects the rights and interests of women, applies the principle of equal pay for equal work for men and women alike, and trains and selects cadres from among women."[7] Another article states: "Marriage, the family and the mother and child are protected by the state. Both husband and wife have the duty to practice family planning. Parents have the duty to rear and educate their minor children, and children who have come of age have the duty to support and assist their parents. Violation of the freedom of marriage is prohibited."[8]

In comparison with the first and second Constitutions of 1952 and 1978, the provisions in the 1982 Constitution are both more inclusive and more specific and reach both the domestic and public spheres of life.

Modern China, observed Elisabeth Croll, has attempted to fulfill two of the primary preconditions for improving the position of women:

> Firstly, it has broadly redefined economic, social and political structures in the interest of redistributing resources and rewards.... Secondly, it has established programmes aimed at redefining gender relations and specifically improving the position of women.... Underlying the Chinese strategy has lain the assumption that the two sets of policies are in harmony and both working towards the same goals. Policies...operate on the assumption that if they contribute to China's development and modernization, then they must also be good for women.[9]

The Fruits of the Communist Revolution

During the 1980s several prominent China specialists, sociologists, anthropologists, political scientists, economists and legalists have examined the status and role of women in contemporary China, some merely to reflect what they saw or what their research turned up. Others purposely set out to measure the declared objectives of the Chinese government against the current status of women, i.e., what, precisely, has 40 years of socialist government in China achieved for women? Certain specific situations, often common to women all over the world, are dealt with below.

Education

In 1983 women formed 70 percent of the illiterate and semi-literate population of China. According to the profile of Chinese women in *Sisterhood Is Global,* females in 1981 comprised 43.9 percent of primary school children, 39.6 of middle school and 24.4 percent of students at university. For example, at Beijing (Peking) University women formed 25 percent of the students in 1982, though it is interesting to note that 91 percent of the physics class were men.[10] Elisabeth Croll's research came up with some other figures, but not basically different, as shown in Table 72.

Both sets of figures indicate that the equality promised to women in the Constitution and which formed part of the basic Communist program has either not been realized or the policy has not been carried out. As if to underscore their own contempt for the program of equal educational opportunities, Chinese officials decided in 1982 that for women to gain entry into university they must do better in the entrance examination than men.[11] This decision is not an isolated case. It is also reflected in a decision by the Bank of China in Guandong Province that women must score 30 points more than men in applications, even for the lowly job of bank clerk.[12]

It is also suspected that the statistics which the Chinese provide on education frequently reflect the situation only in the urban areas. A report in the

Educational Institution	Percentage of Women Attending
Primary School	50
Middle School	40
Technical Schools	42
Spare-time College and Technical Schools	30
Trade Union Vocational Schools	27
Short-term Training Courses	30
College and University	30
Percentage of Women among Those Officially Classified as Illiterate	80

Table 72. Participation of Females in Education. Source: Elisabeth Croll, *Chinese Women Since Mao,* Sharpe Inc., New York, 1983, p. 46. Permission to reprint: ZED Books, London.

Chinese Bulletin of Economic Research gave the percentage of rural women receiving education in 1980 as 9.5 for junior middle school and only 3.5 for senior middle school. Though the primary school rate was given as 45 percent, the percentage of illiterate women was reported as 42 percent.[13] This is another indication that the policy of equal education for Chinese women was not so vigorously pursued in the past, otherwise the rate of illiteracy, 40 years after the Communists took over, would have been appreciably lower. Nor would the percentage of rural women receiving high school education have been so low.

Elisabeth Croll reported that in the higher educational institutions, including technical training institutes, universities and specialist colleges of various kinds, there is a shortage of facilities and that the education system has consequently become highly selective, favoring males. At each higher level of education, she pointed out, the percentage of girls decreased markedly.[14]

The education of women, even where completed, is also often disregarded. Tan Manni revealed that the hundreds of thousands of students who graduate from China's colleges every year are assigned jobs through consultation between their universities and employers, much like the placement programs of major American universities. About a quarter of this huge total are women. Yet Shanghai Fudan University found that in 1984 one-third of the employers asking for graduate student workers stipulated "men only," and some 200 employers flatly refused to take any woman graduate. It is true, said Manni, that the demand for college graduates in China is so high that it does not affect students' prospects for employment, but it does not mean that women will get the jobs they want or for which they have been trained. Partly because of this, she said, some universities now deliberately enroll more men than women, even to the extent of lowering entrance requirements for men. According to a survey by the State Science and Technology Commission's Human Resources Research Institute, quoted by Manni, some 42.7 percent of technically trained women said they believed they had no chance at all, or less chance than men, to be selected for further study. The academic degrees they hold are generally lower than those of men. All of this is finally reflected in the Academic Committee of the Chinese Academy of Sciences, where only 3.5 percent of the members are women.[15]

Esther Lee Yao's assessment is that following the Cultural Revolution of the early 1970s, formal education for women was indeed broadened since women have been trained for and obtained jobs as doctors, engineers, pilots, masons, policemen, welders, oil operators, vegetable growers and fruit pickers, all jobs previously occupied by men only.[16] However, as will be shown, the percentages are mostly so low that this is indication of change but not of equality in education.

Measured in terms of numbers at middle to advanced educational institutions, in the preponderance of women in certain areas of study, and in the number of women who are literate, equal education for men and women is more likely a propaganda slogan at this point in time than an achievement. The Revolution did bring more education to millions of women, vastly improved women's opportunities to find better employment and to improve their lives, but, as Esther Yao rightly observed, regardless of the changes in the educational model, Chinese women still have much less opportunity for education than men. Legally they have the same chances, but the statistics tell another story. When the Cultural Revolution, launched by Mao Tse-tung, *inter alia* to establish egalitarianism once and for all, finally sputtered out in 1972 and the well-known Nanking University reopened, only 27 percent of the students enrolled were women.[17] Nothing had really changed.

Political Participation

A central theme in the Communist program is that women not only enjoy total political equality with men but in order for women's emancipation to succeed, women are invited to and must play an equal role in political affairs of the country. In the 1982 Constitution there is specific provision for equal participation in the political process. "All citizens . . . who have reached the age of 18 have the right to vote and stand for election, regardless of nationality, race, sex, occupation, family background, religious belief, education, property status or length of residence. . . ."[18] As Phyllis Andors pointed out, the Communist Party in China has long claimed that women and the cause of their emancipation have, in fact, been important allies in building a successful peasant revolution and in constructing socialism.[19]

Chinese women over 18 were first granted the right to vote in the first Constitution of China in 1954. Together with men they voted to elect, and could themselves be elected, as members of the People's Congress at both local and national level. The Communist government claims that the People's Congress, China's legislative assembly and, constitutionally speaking, the supreme authority of the country, has seen impressive participation by women. Again the statistics seems to indicate otherwise.

In the six Congresses convened since 1954 women's representation varied from a high of 22.6 percent to a low of 12.3 percent. In the all-important standing committees, representation varied from a high of 25 percent to a low of 5 percent.[20]

At provincial level, in 29 autonomous provinces and regions, 26 women have been elected Vice-President or President of the Standing Committee of the Provincial People's Congress, and 10 women are now serving as Provincial Governor or Deputy Governor. However, in the State Council, the national administration for all of China, only one of the councillors is a woman. More significantly, since the real power in China, as in the Soviet Union, lies with the Communist Party, at the 12th Congress of the party in 1982 only 14 percent of the representatives were women. On the powerful Central Committee there were only 12 percent women and in the all-powerful Politburo and Party Secretariat of the Central Committee only two women made the grade.[21]

Since the Communist Party and the Chinese government have themselves made women's liberation a measurable index of the success of socialism, there is no doubt the system has been less successful than others elsewhere in the world. Of that the low representation of women in every representative institution in China, in the legislature, in government and in the party itself, is clear testimony.

There is another side to the foregoing judgment. Prior to 1949 women had no political rights whatsoever. The degree of women's political liberation, low as it is, is therefore the product of Communist objectives in China. The real question is whether they were vigorously pursuing the written objectives which they had set themselves or whether they were focusing on women's political progress through a patriarchal lens. Are we faced here with a policy which is mere tokenism?

According to Esther Yao, most Chinese held the opposite attitude towards women's political liberation than what was proclaimed by the revolutionary leadership. "As a result, competent women were often caught between the contradictory expectations of the Party and society. Married female [party] cadres where chastised by the conservative segment of society for not fulfilling the women's role at home. . . . Politically uninvolved women were not free from attack either. They were often condemned by the Party for staying at home."[22]

Margery Wolf concluded that whatever the intention of the Communist revolutionaries 40 years ago, contemporary China proves beyond a doubt that socialism and patriarchy can exist in stable harmony.[23]

It is difficult to escape the impression that women in China do not even recognize the political opportunities which currently exist, limited as they are, and that political equality, similar to that enjoyed by women in Denmark, Iceland and Sweden, is a concept which they will find hard to grasp. Ironically, women made the most progress in politics during the period 1958–1960, in the midst of the much-maligned years of the Great Leap Forward, when Chairman Mao required mass labor participation of men and women in communes, street industry and industrial management to force the pace of China's economic development. During this period women slowly developed leadership in local and regional politics, but their advance was still determined by men. Because of economic retrenchment, on the eve of the Socialist Education Campaign of 1962–1966, women not only lost ground politically but the Communist Party suddenly started to emphasize their role in reproduction and the household economy. So the young female political cadres dropped out of politics to get married, and fewer women than ever were left in active politics, even at the bottom of the totem pole.[24]

According to Xiao Lu, "The root of the problem lies in the persistence of feudal attitudes and the total control of political life by the Communist Party—which does not allow an independent women's movement to exist." The laws and the Communist Party all proclaim equality between the sexes, she said, yet feudal attitudes die hard and, given the social organization of China, these attitudes seep through every sphere of life, consciously and unconsciously affecting the making of administrative and political policy and their implementation.[25]

Women Workers and Occupational Segregation

There are few positive developments in China which can rival the emergence of women from a state of feudal degradation into the country's economic lifestream in a matter of only three decades. This has not been achieved in Africa, in the Muslim world, most of Asia or even in Latin America. That it was a forced entry, ideologically and politically motivated, as in the Soviet Union, is also true, but for most women it has brought moderate to extensive benefits.

The official policies of equal pay for equal work and of no discrimination between men and women in employment have created additional favorable conditions in economic life for women leaving the home to work.

In 1986 the total number of women employed reached nearly 47 million, or 36.6 percent of all workers. If self-employed women and women engaged in private businesses were also taken into account, women would form 43.7 percent of all workers in China. In urban areas, according to the China State Statistical Bureau, 82 percent of women of working age are now employed. Considering that prior to the Communist Revolution in 1949 women formed only 7.5 percent of all workers (about 600,000), then the 75-fold increase in women workers is an enormous achievement.[26] The result is not only that the economic status of women has improved but, together with the greater opportunities in education, and the laws pertaining to marriage and divorce, the lot of women has certainly improved considerably compared to the pre-Communist era.

Women are found in almost all trades and professions today, yet labor segregation is still so strong that, in some industries such as textiles, finance, commerce and tailoring, women are 80 percent of the workers.[27] Because the economy is centrally controlled under state socialism (to an extent Westerners would find difficult to comprehend) it needs to be emphasized that, in China, workers are allocated to industries, depending on the state's economic objectives for the time. Table 73 indicates the allocation of female labor to industry in the early 1980s.

This enforced segregation to meet centrally controlled economic objec-

Industry	Percentage of Women in Allocated Workers
Textile Industries	90
Medical Departments	80
Commerce and Industry	70
Light Industry and Handicrafts	60
Electrical and Electronics Industry	50

Occupation	Percentage women
Teachers	38.00
Scientists and technicians	33.00
Medical workers*	59.90
College lecturers and associate professors	26.00
State administrative workers	48.00
Textile workers	60.00
Agricultural workers**	40.00
Coal miners	18.00
Metal workers	14.00
Railway and construction workers	20.00
Instrument workers***	50.00

***Top:* Table 73. Allocation of Women to Industry. Source: "Equal Opportunities for Women," *China Reconstructs,* March 1982, p. 23. *Bottom:* Table 74. Women: Occupational Segregation in China. Source: China State Commission of Education; *China Reconstructs,* March 1986; Elisabeth Croll, *Chinese Women Since Mao,* Sharpe Inc., New York, 1983; *Women of China,* Chinese Embassy, United Nations. Notes: *Includes nurses, doctors and technicians. **Includes forestry workers. ***Light industry. All figures for 1980–1981.**

tives has led to the concentration of women in certain areas of employment, as shown in Table 74. But there are other also forms of occupational segregation which reflect a more universal trend and which can, more often than not, only be explained by discrimination brought on by male perceptions that a certain occupation, or the greater part of a particular trade or profession, is still for men only.

Women have become an important force for modernization in China, but they still face discrimination when it comes to promotion and the opportunity for advanced training. At university level only 32 percent of all technical personnel are women. Only 18.5 percent of engineers are women. Among the senior engineers and professors only 11.6 percent are women.[28]

According to Esther Yao, most women in China today are still segregated in sex-stereotyped jobs. Workers in child care centers and primary level teachers are predominantly women, and medicine, pediatrics, obstetrics and gynecology attract more women than other specialities. Men also dominate the top levels of all occupations. Yao states that there are several factors contributing to discriminatory hiring practices: society still holds that women should stay at home; factory managers believe that women are less efficient workers; it costs more to hire female workers because of legally enforced maternity leave (the legally required time is 56 days minimum) and the provision of child care facilities. Finally, surplus unemployed male laborers are constantly in competition with women for scarce jobs.[29] As in the United States and Europe, women's family responsibilities, particularly childbirth and childcare, are the most obvious obstacles to their increased and regular employment.

Wage Discrimination

There is also widespread wage discrimination between men and women in China, despite the stipulations of the law.

In *Women Workers in 15 Countries,* Margery Wolf said that without tracing the rise and fall of China's economy, it is fair to say that the state has managed its unemployment problem over the years at considerable cost to women. Women have not been accepted as workers who need jobs, and their benefits have never been equal to those of men. In the countryside, where 80 percent of China's people live, the slogan, "equal pay for equal work," has been heard since the Revolution, said Wolf, but in the countryside few even pretend that it has been achieved. All over rural China at the beginning of the 1980s the basic daily wage is set by a number of credits or workpoints. For men it is between 10 to 12 and for women from a low of 5.5 to a high of 8 points. According to ratios which Wolf obtained in five different communes, the points system for agricultural workers meant that women sometimes earned 44 percent of the wages paid to men for the same work and, in one commune, 70 percent. In rural factories and workshops, which required more skilled work, women's wages ranged from a low of 30 percent to a high of 79 percent of men's. Certain privileges, rights by law, which women enjoy, such as time off for menstrual periods or time off after childbirth, are simply docked against their points.[30]

In the urban areas of China, Wolf found that the wage gap existed even among the better-paid workers and was still in the vicinity of 78 percent. She also discovered that women who had middle school and higher education earned less than men who had no more than a primary school education. And the longer men worked the greater the wage differentiation. Another source of wage disparity is the unavailability to women of bonuses, overtime pay and promotions which men in the same factory enjoy. Because women have to go home to take care of the house and the children, a task men in China shirk, they cannot attend training classes that will upgrade their skills. In the urban areas women workers doing manual labor can retire with a pension of 80 percent of final wages at age 50 while others, such as clerical workers, retire at age 55—in both cases five years earlier than men. Because men generally enjoy much higher wages and retire five years later, equal income from pension is also impossible.[31]

Several other researchers have pointed to the difference in wages paid to men and women in China. Elisabeth Croll said that while remuneration for women still falls short of that of their male colleagues, at least in governmental organizations, state industrial plants and business enterprises, where men and women do the same work, women tend to receive more equal pay. In the professions wages and pensions are much higher for men. "At the present time the rates of pay received by the majority of women reflect the division of labour and their predominance in certain unskilled and service occupations."[32]

Visitors to modern China, such as Jerome Cohen, author of *Peoples China and International Law,* say that after taking in the labor scene, one is impressed by the fact that in the rural areas all of the hard work is being done by women – including fishing by net, heaving marble into carts, hoeing and digging and harvesting by hand. Cohen recalled that when Marco Polo visited China in the late thirteenth century he also observed that women did all the hard work – to which he added that when a woman was delivered of a child in the district of Dali, which he visited, the husband stayed in bed for 40 days while his friends visited him. The wife, shortly after giving birth, started doing the housework again and serving her husband food in bed.[33]

There is no suggestion that this is symptomatic of modern China, but in terms of the division of labor in the rural areas, not much seems to have changed, despite the lofty ideals promulgated in the Chinese Constitution. At best it can be said that the overwhelming preponderance of women in manual labor has somewhat decreased.

Women, Marriage and the Family

Nothing produced more misery for a woman in pre-Communist China than the fact that, after marriage, she was considered as mere property. Whereas in the pre-revolutionary days a woman had no right to divorce, that right was granted when the first Marriage Law was passed in 1950. In 1980 a new, second Marriage Law was promulgated in which freedom of marriage and divorce was redefined to ensure that if mediation between the parties failed, that "a divorce should be granted." The 1950 law used the phrase, "may be granted."

Kay Johnson observed that as the state focused more and more on economic reconstruction and cooperative transformation in the countryside, once more placing the emphasis in rural production on the family unit, rather than on collectives, it also became more concerned with maintaining family stability than with promoting women's rights. Instead of pursuing marriage reform, as it had promised women, it encouraged judges in an increasingly restrictive interpretation of the 1980 Marriage Law's divorce clause to reduce the spate of divorces, which followed the first Marriage Law in 1950 and which reached a peak in 1953. "Women found it increasingly difficult to exercise their divorce rights, and it became increasingly easy for husbands and in-laws to protect bride price investments, which even today remain widely spread in many parts of rural China."[34]

Behind the spate of divorces produced by the first Marriage Law was the Land Reform of 1950. The ownership of land as result of the Land Reform act assured women of financial independence from their husbands. That was not the intention of the party, which hoped it would encourage peasants to produce more crops and destroy the wealthy, rural land-owning gentry. When divorce became common in the early fifties the Communist Party, concerned that the family as an institution was being threatened, began to moderate their stand.[35]

The family and women's relationship to it has remained one of the most traditional features of the predominantly rural Chinese society, said Johnson. Studies have revealed a substantial gap between the Chinese government's national goals in terms of marriage and local rural practice. "With respect to 'buying and selling' marriages, bride price practises, the realization of women's property, child custody and divorce rights, little if any change has occurred in many rural areas."[36]

The new economic policies for rural China are referred to as the family responsibility system or the household production system. Under the new system every head of household, the man, becomes head of his own production team. As Margery Wolf found: "In effect the state has handed back to men in what amounts to a decollectivization of Chinese agriculture."[37] There is a greater emphasis on a form of free enterprise in the urban areas, and the new policy is not likely to have much effect on women's marriage and the family in the cities—but, again, 80 percent of China's population live in the rural areas. China is an agricultural country and 40 percent of the workers in agriculture are women. Insofar as women in the rural areas are concerned, the Chinese government has effectively backed away from its own political ideology, and from the spirit of the Constitution.

Another painful contradiction between the new economic policies and the well-being of women, said Wolf, derives from the conflict between those policies and the intensification of the birth limitation program. "Men are again likely to become structural as well as ideological patriarchs. A man with a married son now forms a viable production team . . . but a woman who produces only female children for her husband's production team brings disaster to the family."[38] In *Chinese Women Since Mao,* Elisabeth Croll confirmed this observation, saying that there has been a new wave of preference for parents to have only sons. In a survey of peasant households of 1982 a mere 2.2 percent wanted to have a daughter as an only child. "The desire for boys is so great in the single-child family that it has led to an unforeseen re-appearance of female infanticide and violence against women who bear daughters."[39]

In 1982 penalties for having more than one child included 15 percent tax of an entire family's income until the child is aged seven. This was one of the reasons for the upsurge in female infanticide. Ironically, the government, which is the cause of this situation, also forcibly condemns the crimes. According to the *People's Daily* newspaper, "the phenomenon of butchering, drowning and leaving to die female infants and maltreating women who gave birth to these infants is a grave social problem."[40]

Wolf cited reports by the Anhui Provincial Women's Federation, which investigated reports of female infanticide and found that in the Suixi and Huaiyuan counties there were 16.4 percent more boys born than girls. A normal birth ratio, she observed, would show 6 percent more boys than girls. That left a startling 10 percent of girls "missing." In some communes the discrepancy was even more frightening, the highest being a 27 percent predominance of male births over female births.[41] At that rate for all of rural China a sociological disaster could be lurking, just around the corner, since statistical projections dictate that in two decades a substantial percentage of males would simply not be able to find any women to marry.

Because of national economic considerations, China is now obviously more concerned with rural family planning and population control than in women's rights per se. As Johnson stated: "Women have been pressed since the 1970's to drastically reduce their fertility rate, in many cases through late abortion, while remaining trapped in unreformed family structures in which their status, personal influence and security, indeed their very membership in their husband's family and the village, depend on traditional child bearing functions. . . ."[42] Obviously this produces a clash between unreformed family structures and government enforced demands for one or at most two children per family.

The shift in controls and operation of production to the household as the basic unit of production in rural China can only have the result that women's labor will increasingly be confined to productive activities within the household. In this way it will reverse the previous advantages of collectivism, such as individual remuneration of women and reduction in the controls of the man as head of the household. This will encourage the re-emergence of the patriarchal Confucian-type family, which is exactly what the Revolution in China had been fighting to eradicate since 1949. Theoretically married women in rural China have come full circle. As Kay Johnson observed: "Today the family . . . remains one of the most traditional features of a predominantly rural Chinese society. The outcome of . . . upheaval and revolution . . . has done more to restore the traditional role and structure of the family than to fundamentally reform it." As proof she also points to the perpetuation of semi-arranged marriages, unequal family roles and burdens for women, male supremacist attitudes, the preference for sons and the differential treatment meted out to daughters.[43]

Ideology and Reality

In its reports to the United Nations, the Chinese government still asserts that it is committed to raising the status of women and that the government is dedicated to stamping out feudal ideas. It claims that it has set up free legal advisory centers to inform women of their legal rights under the Constitution and under the Marriage Law of 1980. It states that the bride price has been made illegal, concubinage and polygamy prohibited and the minimum age for marriage for women raised to 20 and for men to 22.[44] But the gap between policy and reality is too wide to ignore. The much-touted legal centers, for example, are almost all located in the major cities and not in the rural areas.

Legal experts, for example Cohen, point out that taking legal action in China in order to redress discrimination is not easy, simply because case law is still largely non-existent. It was not until late 1978, said Cohen, that China started to put together a body of legislation covering the whole range of the law, from civil liberties to inheritance. Up until 1981, really good Chinese lawyers were extremely difficult to find. China has gone from virtually no legal education in the 1960s to 45 law schools with 15,000 students in 1986. But for a country with a population in excess of a billion people that is a drop in the ocean.[45] Based on figures provided by the American Bar Association and the Chinese delegation to the United Nations, in 1988 the United States had one qualified lawyer for every 260 people. In China it was one for every 120,000 people, and that includes the current crop of law students at Chinese universities and law schools.

In *The Unfinished Liberation of Chinese Women,* Phyllis Andors concluded that while the status of women, compared to the pre-Communist period, has changed for the better, even dramatically so, economic development and social change according to the Communist ideology have not brought the promised equality to women. In fact, Andors states, women's lot was probably more improved during Mao's Cultural Revolution, since they were at least drawn into the mainstream of the economy. "In paying attention only to ideological issues, the Chinese did not analyze the important structural impediments with which women still had to cope . . . nor was there any social analysis of the increasing stratification of the female labour force and the conflict between class interests and sex interests."[46]

Even if well meant, and in the context of Communist history in the Soviet Union and China such intentions can only be cast in doubt, the Chinese objectives for women after 1949 were repeatedly derailed by political, cultural and economic forces and priorities. The fact is that the anti-feudal Revolution, from which women gained so much, was never completed. It was overtaken by economic priorities and the need to modernize the bureaucracy of China, not to mention the struggle of the Communist party to maintain its grip in rural China and the constant battles for control in the upper echelon. There is no guarantee that future redefinition of Communist objectives will not occur.

Family reform, which Mao Tse-tung rightly described as a life and death matter for females, is still incomplete, 40 years after it began. "In China," Margery Wolf concluded, "a woman's life is still determined by her relationship to a man, be he father or husband, not by her own efforts or failures. The revolution promised women something more, but that promise has not been fulfilled."[47]

Life for the average woman in China has certainly been raised to standards beyond the hope of the previous generation, said Wolf. But what should be of great concern is the frequency with which successive Chinese governments or factions have stepped aside from the goal of equality which they themselves claimed was part and parcel of the "success" of the Revolution. Gender equality, she said, has never been repudiated, but it has often been postponed. Under the new policies, the so-called Four Modernizations, women are being told to step aside again in the interest of China. They are being encouraged to give up their jobs in favor of their children. She can thus only concur with Andors that in political-ideological terms, the resolution of the women question in China is to be dependent upon the future success of economic modernization.[48]

Will the new Communist leadership oversee a successful modernization? It is extremely doubtful. Economic modernization in the Soviet Union under a system of state socialism has failed. The chances of success in China because of the Chinese recipe are equally dismal. Every study of socialism versus capitalism worth mentioning has shown time and again that socialism, state socialism, has failed in the undeveloped regions of the world to achieve momentum towards sustained, meaningful economic growth and a resultant rise in living standards and individual freedoms. It failed in socialist Tanzania, Zambia, Ghana, North Korea, Poland, Rumania and a host of other states while it succeeded in the free market economies of South Korea, Taiwan, Singapore, Hong Kong and other countries.

Women hold up half the sky, says an old Chinese proverb, but a recent United Nations-funded workshop on how to improve statistics on women in China (held in Beijing, June 1989) revealed that the development of 500 million Chinese women is not nearly adequately reflected in official statistics. Though a vast amount of data is collected regularly, in many areas it is not disaggregated by gender.[49] To a certain extent the bamboo curtain obscuring the true status of women in China remains only half raised.

Part Ten: Conclusions, Recommendations, Guide to Data, and Research Proposals

29. Summary and Conclusions

The consensus of almost all qualified observers is that women, worldwide, have made their greatest gains the past 20 years in the purely legislative field. It is true this was accompanied by a vast increase in the number of women in employment and education, but the social, economic and political status of women, compared to that of men, is still one of subordination. And in the workplace wage discrimination and occupational segregation, often the result of government intervention, is still widespread.

There are islands in the women's world where individual countries have marked up progress towards equality over a broader spectrum. In certain individual countries (Norway and Sweden, for example), women have made remarkable progress under laws designed specifically to eliminate discrimination on grounds of gender and to give women an equal chance in the field of politics, education, and employment. Not one country in the African, Asian, Latin American or the Communist world can be included in this group, which is mostly European, North American, or Nordic.

On paper, the Communist world has the most comprehensive set of laws to ensure women's equality, but it is an equality only on paper and in terms of ideology. Of this the Soviet Union is a worse culprit than China. In the Third World the gap between what appears on paper and what is happening in practice has increased rather than decreased. United Nations member states which helped launch the Decade for Women (with considerable fanfare) have openly expressed their disappointment with this development, or, rather, lack of development. "All the results point to a highly unsatisfactory situation and a deteriorating trend in the position of women in developing countries," the representative of India at the United Nations pointed out in a letter to the Secretary General of March 30, 1983. He pointed out that this deterioration took place despite the U.N. Conference on the Role of Women in the Developing States, held at Bagdad in May 1979, which specifically called for progress in women's status to become part of the national strategies of developing states. He also referred to the Seventh Conference of Heads of States of Non-aligned Countries, held at New Delhi in 1983, which gave further support to this goal. The problem is that India itself is one of the worst examples of equality that exists only on paper.

In a United Nations Report, *The Decade for Women in Latin America and the Caribbean* (Santiago, Chile, 1988), the *rapporteur* said that there is no doubt that the *de juro* and *de facto* treatment of women in this area of the world are also two different matters. "Experience has shown that the laws are inadequate except as a means of expressing an ideal." Significant progress has been made in expanding the opportunities for the young to study in middle and higher education, he said, and in the participation of women in new fields of activities; however, in spite of the ostensible democratic dispensation, the role of women in the leadership of political parties, in parliament and in trade unions in these countries is still severely limited.

In Africa south of the Sahara, inequitable values, political hypocrisy, gaps between policy and practice, and discriminatory practice in social, economic and political life, openly favoring males, continue to harm women and the national development of their own states. As Lance Morrow wrote in *The Cross Cultural Study of Women,* these problems are being perpetuated by discriminatory social structures and power relationships such as the granting of land titles only to males, limited educational and economic opportunities for women and male domination of decision making. "If this trend is not reversed soon, these policies will undermine the future of both men and women for generations to come." Considering that women form half of the full-time labor force in Africa, productivity cannot be increased by more restrictions which institutionalize male dominance and female dependence in all areas of life. "Once embedded in the family, educational, employment and power structures of the . . . social order," Morrow concluded, "the modernised pattern of sexual discrimination may become as resistant to change in Africa as it has been in Western countries that have already been struggling painfully through the industrial and bureaucratic transformation of society."[1]

Women all over the world are hopelessly under-represented in the policy-making and decision-making levels of society, whether this be in the Communist East Bloc, in the West (except for the Nordic states), Africa, Asia or Latin America. Yet women almost always form not only the majority of the population but, frequently, the majority of the voters. Just as frequently a higher percentage of women than of men vote in elections for the legislature, for example in Japan, West Germany and South Africa.

There are many role models among the women of Europe, women who sit in the cabinet or in the European Parliament in Strasbourg. But for the majority of women who are interested in seeing a broad-based change there is not much for their comfort. As Joelle Juillard wrote in "Policy Impacts and Women's Role in France" *(Women in the World),* the increase of women deputies in the French National Assembly from five in 1975 to 28 in 1985 is really not that impressive when one considers that there are 491 deputies. And occupational segregation is still so massive that of 300 officially listed occupations in France, women are found overwhelmingly in less than 10 percent. The percentage in higher-status positions is only about 5 percent, all of this despite the law on sexual equality in employment passed by the French Assembly in 1983.

The first stirrings of a feminist revolt against women's exclusion from the decision-making process was seen in Iceland in 1987. In national elections some 10 percent of the voters cast their ballots for the Women's Alliance, which went on to win six of the 63 seats in parliament. Since the election gave no party or coalition a governing majority, these six women held the pivotal role in the formation of any new government. The signal should be clear to women (and to men) all over the world. If women are not taken up in the decision-making process in greater numbers, a well-organized women's political movement could create enormous problems for the overwhelmingly male-dominated parties.

It is both fitting and historic that women should have achieved this victory in the Icelandic *Althing* because it is the oldest parliament in the world, dating from the Vikings in the year 930. In all the years there had been only a dozen women ever elected to parliament. Now the Women's Alliance is going to demand, and obtain, parliamentary action for better wages, longer maternity leave, better child care, all the familiar demands women have been making in other countries without getting anywhere. And the country has a woman as President for the second time in a row.

Joni Lovenduski has provided pointed and accurate conclusions about women's status in politics. Under-representation in policy and decision-making bodies is of vital concern to women, she wrote, because most areas of women's lives are affected by public policy. Marriage laws, control of fertility, rights and duties as mothers, property rights (in Africa and Asia), the control of wealth and income, employment practices, salaries, pension schemes and medical benefits—all of these are the subjects of legislation, regulation and other forms of state control. Governments and political parties may appear to be interested in women's rights, she said, but no country or party has come close to treating women as autonomous individuals and only a handful have marriage laws which treat the couple as equal partners. Changing the structure of male-dominated governments and administrations is extremely difficult because gender discrimination is one of the foundation stones of that structure. As Lovenduski observed: "Those who wish to reform the status of women via the political system face a pre-structured policy process in which gaining agenda status for (women's) issues is only the first of many difficult steps."[2]

Thus the gap between what the law provides for and what really happens in the workplace is present in every country in the world to some degree. It is at its worst in Africa, followed by Asia, Latin America, the United States, Western Europe and the Communist states, whose major crime is less in terms of occupational segregation and wage discrimination than in the almost total exclusion of women from the decision-making process.

There are some countries which have excelled in cynical deception on the women's question. India is a prime example. For a country which pretends to be the spokesman for the Third World in terms of human rights, it succeeded in posting one of the lowest rates of literacy for women, and even where women were qualified for higher education only some 20 percent (1985) were admitted to higher education, the lowest rate in the world. India is a good example of a country with an abysmal gap between policy and practice. A fine Constitution, on paper, but one which means little to women, even to those in the legal profession.

There is hardly room for complacency in the West. Despite the plethora of laws which the federal government of Australia has passed to fight discrimination against women, the gap between policy and practice down under is still enormous. In fact, one of the most recent studies shows that Australia has one of the highest degrees of sex segregation in the workforce of any of the industrially developed countries. The predominantly female occupations are characterized by poor conditions and low pay; furthermore, such conditions cannot easily be challenged by women, who face great problems with the procedures involved in any challenge in court.

Almost every prominent scholar has also come to the conclusion that the mere presence of laws does not help the progress of women towards equality; only vigorous enforcement and publicity helps. The laws cannot be taken as guarantees of implementation, said Lovenduski, because laws, like policies, must be viewed in the context of the social, political and economic environment. In China and Russia, well-written laws are all subordinate to the economic objectives of the state. In Europe, the new equality laws were largely focused upon the labor market but have statute law as their major source. But these laws, she observed, were not set up to promote the interest of an already entirely disadvantaged group, such as women. It also depends whether the law requires the burden of application to be placed on the individual who has been wronged or on the state. Proving discrimination is difficult, and the placement of the burden of proof on the complainant has been found to be an important constraint in almost all European states.[3]

Where powerful economic organizations are involved, their opposition to government regulatory "intervention" in their free enterprise operation has also turned out to be an important impediment to the effective application of anti-discriminatory legislation. The conclusion, in Lovenduski's words, "is that equality legislation is important to the achievement of women's rights in employment but there seems to be little chance that laws alone will solve the problem. There are rather an essential pre-condition to which must be added political will and political organization. Real equality of opportunity will depend on women's activities across the political spectrum and this is difficult because women have only token representation in most political institutions."

Britain is a prime example of a state which has passed a significant body of legislation focusing on the removal of various impediments to women's employment but where institutions and structures have altered little—in fact, the least in all of Europe—to accommodate women's demands. This failure, said Lovenduski, also meant that the laws had the least effect. Britain's women are among the lowest paid in Europe and as a percentage of men's income their wages stood at only 66 percent in 1982, as against the 81 percent which Sweden had already reached in 1980. Italy had reached 86 percent in 1982 and France 78 percent.

The lack of impact of British legislation has been a great disappointment. The Equal Opportunities Commission adopted a policy of persuasion rather than vigorous law enforcement, said Lovenduski, reflecting the traditional British attitude in matters of dispute. The trade unions sat on their hands because they were dominated by men.

Sex equality was given a low priority by the British executive, even though headed by a woman Prime Minister. From 1979 the British E.O.C. had to look to E.E.C. law for sources of change rather than to the British executive. When the Equal Pay Act was amended in 1983 to include work of equal value, this was the result of a finding of the European Court of Justice that the British legislation did not meet the requirements of the European Community law.[4]

Women in Britain have, of course, gained from the Sex Discrimination and Equal Pay acts, said Lovenduski, but the gain could have been much wider, affecting infinitely more women, if the policy makers had been more willing to take an interest in the subject and if both government and the structure of economic society had made regular comprehensive overviews of the disadvantaged status of women. Thus Britain, in Lovenduski's opinion, passed the necessary laws only to have their application mired in lack of enforcement because the political and economic structures would not adjust to the spirit of the law, killing it by lack of interest and inactivity.

Because structures in the United States have also shown almost no change the past two decades, the wage gap between the average male and female worker showed only a small decrease despite the important laws passed during the 1970s to eliminate occupational and wage discrimination, and despite the fact that (currently) the average woman worker is even better educated than the average male worker.

Positive developments in the United States have often been offset by negative ones, negative in the sense of a lack of change. A new trend, which could become one of the most significant economic developments in decades, is the upsurge in women-owned businesses. It has become an important factor in the economy of the country. Revenues from women-owned companies now top $100 billion, and their total tax contribution exceeds $50 billion. Of the 13 million sole proprietorships in the United States in 1988, at least 3.7 million are owned by women, nearly double what they owned in 1978. This development took place despite the fact (confirmed by the House Small Business Committee in 1987) that women business owners face considerable difficulties in gaining access to commercial credit and bidding on government contracts (see *Time,* July 4, 1988, pp. 54–57).

On the other hand, there has been a stagnation in the academic world. Though there have been bright spots and some impressive gains, as indicated in Angela Simeon's work *Academic Women* (1988), universities still implement women's subordination through their institutional policy, their academic disciplines and their "ideological aerobics." In *The Dissenting Feminist Academy* (American University Studies, New York, 1987), Gisele Thibault explores the barriers which higher education erects to women in general and to feminism specifically. It is an indication of how much still needs to change at university level, politically, economically, and socially, she observed, before feminist scholarship becomes accepted and not just tolerated on a small scale.

Some General Conclusions on Europe

In the first place, pay differentials between male and female workers have been reduced from roughly one-third to roughly one-quarter; new laws have been passed tightening the rules against discrimination; and assistance to women workers with children has continued to increase. But the reduction in the wage gap cannot be linked to a reduction in occupational segregation.

Education for women and technical training have improved both in quantity and quality. The so-called prime-age male is no longer the major demographic group in the labor force in the majority of countries, a statistical fact also reflected in the United States. Women no longer can be viewed as a tenuous attachment to the labor force. The conception that most employed women work part time no longer holds true for the majority of the European countries. There is an increased labor-force participation by women during their childbearing years and by women with young children. Finally, there has been greater support for divorced women, pregnant women and working mothers with small children.

Support policies for divorced women with children are not limited to Scandinavia but can be found in West Germany, Italy, Britain and France as well. Many European countries, e.g. West Germany and Sweden, have systems which guarantee custodial parents a minimum child support payment. In Italy a pregnant women is entitled to five months' leave followed by a further six months at 30 percent of her wages. What is important is that her job is held for her for both time periods. All of the E.C. countries have benefit packages for pregnant women. That of Italy is generous. That of Sweden is the best, with paid parental leave of nine months at the birth of a child.

The general trend in Europe is for the various states to improve on child support systems, particularly so for working women, though the central governments are trying to get out of the childcare business by devolving responsibility to local authorities. France has been providing outstanding care through her free public nursery schools and day nurseries for working mothers. Some 90 percent of three- to five-year-olds attend state-funded childcare facilities. Though only a recent development in Italy, by 1987 nearly 90 percent of three- to six-year-olds were attending public-funded nursery schools. France is spending nearly 4 percent of its gross national product on subsidies for preschool children, not only for the sake of the working mother but also as an investment in the future.

All of what women have achieved in Europe through the various women's movements differs in concept substantially from the approach to women's equality in the United States. The departure point is the recognition, in Europe, that almost all working women will have children and without public support policies women cannot cope with both motherhood and a career. In Britain the women's movement worked quietly and effectively within the bastions of established male power. The same approach was used by Swedish women and by the Italians, who worked within the trade unions, the political parties and the powerful Catholic Church.

In several European states—Greece, Portugal, Spain—the progress towards equal treatment between men and women has been much slower than in the northern European states. Spain, for example, is only on the threshold of women's rights and until recently had no real conception of the extent of discrimination against women. The first extensive study of job discrimination and sexual harassment of women in Spain was completed only in mid-1987. The report, by the women's department of the General Workers Union, Spain's largest labor organization, said 84 percent of the women surveyed had experienced some form of sexual harassment. The researchers found discrimination in salaries and promotions, particularly in manual labor and blue collar jobs. Job segregation in the labor force, both public and private, is still rife. The country's security agency, the Civil Guard, in 1987 employed 63,000 men and only one woman in a public relations post. The *Guardia Civil,* in fact, reflects the male-dominated, Roman Catholic–inspired conservatism that has held Spain in its grip for several decades now. It was only after the death of General Francisco Franco in 1975, and the introduction of a democratic Constitution shortly afterwards, that Spain slowly, and painfully, began to assess women's subordination. Under Franco, women were not allowed to start businesses, open bank accounts, have passports without their husbands' written permission or retain custody of their children in divorce. Only women were punished for adultery. Women were barred from being judges or prosecutors.

Since Franco's death the Spanish government has legalized abortion (in certain cases) and the purchase of contraceptives, and has changed the laws on divorce and adultery. There are now 24 women parliamentary deputies and 172 women mayors. Of course, Spain still has far to go. As the Madrid newspaper *El País* wrote in an editorial on July 30, 1987: "Beneath the traditionally Spanish macho mask lies a system of segregation that allows (only) men to make the decisions."

The East Bloc and the Soviet Union

According to all of the leading experts—Buckley, Lapidus, Hough, Heitlinger, Holt, Wolchik, Sachs, Lovenduski, McCauley, Chapman, Moses, Hansonn, Willis, and others—the gap between ideology, policy, and reality has not been bridged.

Disparities between men and women in salary and in grade classifications persist despite the fact that, in the Soviet Union for example, women equal or surpass men in total completed years of general secondary and higher education. Women continue to be manipulated for political and economic reasons, and entry into technical and vocational schools is still highly restricted. Though all citizens in the Communist states are constitutionally as equal as they can be made on paper, women in unskilled labor far outnumber men, while there are twice as many men in skilled labor as women.

As in Western economies, women in the Soviet Union are notably absent in the seats of political power or in senior positions of management. In the spirit of *glasnost* encouraged by Mikhail Gorbachev, Zoia Pukhova, head of the Soviet Union's Women's Committee, in 1987 drew public attention to the foregoing in an article in the Communist Party journal *Kommunist.* "Some spheres of government activity turn out to be virtually barred to women...," she wrote. Though her figures varied from those of Western observers (see Chapter 18), she said that women make up 50.8 percent of the total workforce but only 12 percent of the managerial staff. She said that 40 percent of the people in the academic and scientific fields were women; yet women make up only 2 percent of the Academy of Sciences. Gorbachev himself said at an international conference on women in Moscow in 1987 that everything with women is not in order.

In a mirror-like reflection of the United States, women in the Soviet Union still make up 95 percent of all secretaries, 94 percent of cashiers, 99 percent of hospital staff and almost 80 percent of shop attendants. This occupational segregation is made worse by the fact that the Soviet Union and other Communist countries in the East Bloc persist in telling the world that the women's problem does not exist in socialist societies and that women, by law, enjoy the same opportunities as men. In fact women in the East Bloc are overwhelmingly channelled by undeclared but *de facto* state policy into the least skilled, lowest paying, most personally and physically demanding and least prestigious positions. Even the much-lauded women doctors in the Soviet Union (almost 70 percent of all medical doctors) suffer the indignity of receiving a salary which represents only 66 percent of the take-home pay packet of the average male welder in industry.[5]

Women in the East Bloc are seen by the Communist Party bosses, not as autonomous individuals, but as a collective labor pool, a utility. True, the commitment on paper to an egalitarian society is impressive, but it is only on paper. True, there are impressive state subsidies for pre-school facilities, housing and child support. But women must not only work and raise the children, they must also keep house and shop, all as part of a double burden which is shared less by men in the East Bloc than in any other society. The Communist egalitarian state and social equality are as much a myth for women as is the liberation of women in the United States, only the United States government does not formally declare the liberation of women to be a fact. The Communist Party in the East Bloc and the various Politburos have the only say in how many rights women may enjoy in practice, and women are almost totally excluded from these decision-making bodies.

The Muslim World

By Western understanding of the principle of equality, there will and can be no equality for women in the Muslim world while Islamic law, based on the *Qur'an,* determines the fabric of society.

When Islamic laws were largely ignored in Iran during the last decade of the Shah, women were making enormous strides in business and education while their social mobility was no less and no more restricted than that of men, at least in the major urban areas, as the author personally observed during visits to Iran in 1974 and 1976. At major social functions at leading hotels the women, invariably, dressed in fashionable Western styles.

Not only has Islamic law changed all this, but it has effectively closed the door to any organization (of men and women) which seeks to work for women's equality with men, unless this takes place within the strictures of the law. In a Catch-22 situation, these strictures guarantee that no change will take place.

The *Qur'an,* the word of God as revealed to the Prophet Mohammed, is the most authoritative injunction in Islamic law. The *hadiths* or sayings attributed to Mohammed are of varying degrees of authority. Religious scholars classify these from "certain" to "false." Whole schools of legal and theological interpretation turn on whether a *hadith* is considered true or false. The *Qur'an* and the *hadiths* form the *Shari'a* or Muslim law. Margot Duley, commenting on this in *The Cross Cultural Study of Women,* concluded: "Regardless of the original thrust of Islamic law regarding women's status, the indisputable fact remains that inequalities are now embodied in legal codes."[6]

Other scholars such as Rauf and Fischer have indicated that the inequality of women was in fact Mohammed's intent.[7] A key verse from the *Qur'an* is the following: "Men are in charge of women, because Allah hath made the one of them to excel the other and because they spend of their property for the support of women."[8] Translated into Western idiom, this reads that man is the master because God made him a better human being than woman and because he spends money on her well-being.

In the early centuries of Islam, women were important scholars and attained considerable eminence.[9] But despite those early achievements a concept of unequal and separate status has rigidified over time and is currently strongly supported by the so-called fundamentalists. Nadia Youssef, an Egyptian sociologist, observed: "By the standards of the twentieth century, the religious sanctioning of polygamy and concubinage, divorce at will by the husband, guardianship of children to the father, unequal female inheritance, unequal weight to the legal testimony of women, are hardly consonant with a woman's equitable position in the modern world."[10]

Several states which do not classify as Muslim states but which have large Muslim communities are faced with the conflict between the laws of man, as promulgated by their elected representatives in parliament, and the Islamic laws, to which Muslims refer as the law of God. A classic case is India, where there are some 80 million Muslims. In this sovereign state with parliamentary government, are Muslims Indians first or Muslims first? Are Muslims to be governed, as Indians, by the secular laws of modern India, or as Muslims by the canonical laws of their ancient religion based on Allah's commandments and on words and deeds of Muhammad—of which Muslim personal law was a part? A Muslim woman, married for nearly 50 years to her Indian (Muslim) husband and who had borne him half a dozen children, can be thrown out of her house on a whim of the husband. The husband, according to Muslim law, could then divorce her simply by repeating three times, "I divorce you," and, since she is then no longer his wife, the courts of India have no jurisdiction in the matter. All that she is entitled to, in terms of Muslim law, is a maintenance allowance for three months.[11]

In February 1986 the Indian government introduced the Muslim Women's (Protection of Rights on Divorce) Bill, which placed the responsibility for supporting indigent divorced women not on their husbands but on their parents and other relatives and on *wakfs,* or Muslim charitable trusts, thereby guaranteeing continuation of the dispute. The bill became law in May 1986.[12]

The Third World

The Washington-based Population Crisis Committee rightly found in its *Population Briefing Paper No. 20* of 1988 that women in the Third World are largely poor, powerless and pregnant. Most of the women in the poor countries are not merely poor, the Committee found, but live on the edge of subsistence. They are economically dependent and vulnerable, politically and legally powerless. They are caught in a life cycle that begins with early marriage and too often ends with death in childbirth. They work longer hours and sometimes work harder than men, but their work is typically unpaid and undervalued. They are concentrated in the lowest-paid occupations, grossly under-represented in institutions of government. They bear nearly total responsibility for child care and the household, regardless of their contribution to family income. They are the illiterates of the world and bear three or more times as many children as women in Western society; yet, with the exception of Taiwan, Hong Kong, and Singapore, which now rank with the more developed countries, they have almost no access to birth control.

In *Population Briefing Paper No. 19* of 1987, the Population Crisis Committee pointed to the fact that in 80 of the 95 Third World countries studied, adequate services for birth control are not available. Data from its survey also indicated that almost 50 percent of women in the Third World did not want any more children. Altogether some 250 million women in developing countries do not have access to birth control or lack the education to use it.

Governments of the Third World have made almost no effort on their own to study the question of the value of women's labor. They have had to be prodded in this direction by the United Nations, the World Bank, and other international agencies. In most Third World countries there are constitutional provisions for women's equality and for equal opportunities which, on paper, are on par with those of the Nordic states. The same Third World countries have constitutional and statutory protection for women against unfair discrimination in terms of work and education which are equally impressive. But in practice this all represents a cynical political exercise by governments who are more interested in the political face which they present to the world (on paper) than in carrying out their legal obligations. Many African and Asian countries proclaim equality for women in law, but their ideologies define female labor as the property of men. Whatever women earn is claimed, or simply taken, by men (more specifically in Malaysia, Sudan, Iran, Bangladesh, Ghana, Tanzania, Indonesia, Brazil, Morocco, and India) in what researchers (*Women, Work and Ideology in the Third World,* edited by Haleh Afshar) called the process of "proletarization of women."

Thus the one overwhelming conclusion reached about countries in the Third World is that vast gaps exist between general policy and practice as well as between constitutional and statutory provisions in respect to women's rights and what really happens at school, at home, in the workplace, in politics and in the social and economic milieu. In Chapter 32 of this book the proposal is made that a study be undertaken to ascertain the extent of the gap. The chapter contains numerous extracts from the constitutions and laws of scores of Third

World countries where, on paper, equality between men and women—political, social and economic—is equal to that of the most advanced Western democracies, equal to that of all the Nordic countries. Yet every study made of women's rights in Africa, of women's opportunities, of equal access and equal representation, of wages and occupational segregation, of family and marital rights, has revealed that the laudable provisions of the constitutions and of existing statutes are grotesque in their inapplication.

The equally overwhelming impression is also that when the United Nations voted on the various conventions dealing with women's rights, the male-dominated Third World governments simply parroted the declarations and embodied these in legislation, either by amending the constitution or by passing legislation to take care of the matter—without the slightest concern as to whether the laws could be implemented in the near future or what would happen if women were to apply *en masse* to the courts for their application. Once passed, the provisions became dead-letter laws.

In Africa the situation was aggravated by the fact that military governments invariably suspended the Constitution, on occasions several times in one decade, e.g. Nigeria, or a state of emergency was allowed to remain in force indefinitely, thereby nullifying the legal protection enjoyed by men and women in terms of the Constitution. In Zambia the state of emergency has now lasted more than 20 years, although that has not deterred the Zambian government, notably its President (Kenneth Kuanda), from constantly crying about the human rights of men and women in other parts of Africa.

Because the laws were ignored, scoffed at, suspended or simply not applied, women's progress in Africa, and most other countries of the Third World during the past two decades, was largely nonexistent.

When the United Nations staged its 1985 international conference in Nairobi to mark the end of the women's decade, the real focus was not women in the world, but women in the Third World, mostly Africa, Asia and Latin America. The bulk of the publications which the United Nations or its various agencies produced just prior to and after the Nairobi conference concentrated on Third World countries. The principal subjects were women's poverty; women's lack of education; women's failure to make headway on the issue of property ownership; wage discrimination; occupational segregation; the absence of women from the national legislature; the need for birth control; the dangers of a continuation of the population explosion in Africa; sexual mutilation of women; women's lack of technical training; lack of assistance in food production; the high rates of mortality in childbirth; the organization of women's movements; and related items.

When reference was made to the fact that women perform two-thirds of the world's labor, but receive only 5 percent of the income and own less than 1 percent of the assets, it was women in the Third World, in most of North, East, West and Central Africa, in Bangladesh, Pakistan, and India, in Syria and Iraq, in Colombia, Ecuador and various other Latin American states, that the conference had in mind, not women in Western Europe, North America or in the Communist East Bloc.

There are individual countries in the Third World where women, in specific areas, have made some notable progress, either in the increased number who have become literate, the increase of women in the labor force, or the inroads in some traditional male areas of employment. But the overwhelming impression is that women in the Third World are poor, often hungry, have too many children, are not trained for employment and lack formal education and live in an utterly male-dominated society. A mockery of the concept of equality contained in the fine-sounding constitutions of so many states. Women will probably be no better off by the year 2000 than they were in 1950 unless governments and entire male societies radically change their outlook. The chances for this happening by the year 2000 are virtually nil.

In Africa successive black governments are still seeking the political kingdom first. The fundamental changes in African and Asian societies which are required to really liberate women are so massive, and will occur with such agonizing slowness, that it may be well halfway into the twenty-first century before women will receive sufficient representation in policy-making and decision-making bodies to enable them to produce the equal opportunities, education and effective legal equality which are a pre-requisite for women's equality. Only then (unless men are prodded into a rapid pace of change by an unspeakable disaster of mass starvation, brought about by unwise agro-economics in food production and unrestrained population growth) will women be able to decide to have only two instead of the seven or eight children for whom they must now eke out a precarious existence.

Latin America has by far the best chance of a significant change in attitudes among governing elites and male society from which women could benefit. Those with the fewest chances are women in Africa where tribal and traditional laws are officially permitted to survive. Those with no chance at all are women in the Arab and Muslim societies of Asia Minor and Major, the Middle East and North Africa, where the laws of Islam with their ingrained second-class status for women are impossible to cross and where the religious text of Hindu teachings encourages the murder of widows.

The United States

For the United States, the greatest strides made during the past decade were in the number of women who had entered the professional market and women who have set up their own business. Progress was also made in the courts towards further elimination of discriminatory measures against women. Supreme Court decisions which reaffirmed a woman's right to abortion and defined sexual harassment as a form of sexual discrimination, plus preferential treatment for women in hiring and promoting when there is an imbalance in the marketplace, are among the most important legal developments at the national level.

The biggest disappointments were the failure to significantly close the wage gap between men and women and the continuance of widespread occupational segregation.

At the state level, the progress made towards equal payment for work of comparable worth was equally important, but the issue still has to be settled at the national level. At the same time, sex (and race) remain the key factors in setting wages while the stereotyping of women, resulting in hurtful discrimination, remains a fundamental problem for United States society.

Women's greatest problem remains reconciling the demands of childbirth and childrearing with those of earning a living.

Some fundamental differences have developed among the various women's movements as to future efforts on behalf of women. This springs partly from the negative consequences of some actions which women had strongly advocated in the past, for example, the concept of a no-fault divorce. In her book *The Divorce Revolution,* Leonora Weitzman of Stanford University said that no-fault divorce was "an economic disaster" for women in every state. She said that the trauma had been reduced but not the economic consequences, pointing to the fact that women and children experienced a 73 percent decline in their standards of living in 2,500 court cases which she examined in Los Angeles and San Francisco. At the same time, the husbands experienced a 42 percent average increase in their standards of living.[13]

Betty Friedan, author of the 1953 classic *The Feminine Mystique* and leading feminist, said in 1986 at the annual meeting of the American Society of Sociologists that the changes in the divorce laws have backfired: "There is a false illusion of equality in current divorce proceedings." She now states, "There can't be real equality without recognizing differences."[14]

The feminist dream of laws requiring equal division of property after divorce also ended in disaster because in two out of three cases the woman who ended up with the house had to sell the property at a time when her children most needed stability. Dr. Weitzman said that 85 percent of divorced women in the United States do not receive a cent in alimony, although judges put the figure at 40 percent, which is bad enough. She said that under old laws alimony was an open-ended commitment but that the average today was about 25 months.[15] Yet, "alimony is a woman's due, her entitlement and part of her compensation for contributions to her husband's and children's welfare."

Permanent alimony awards are now making a comeback to the benefit of women. "We are just beginning to see the tide turning back in terms of common sense," said Judith Younger, former Dean of the Syracuse School of Law in New York. This was confirmed by Doris Freed, a New York lawyer who writes a yearly treatise, "Family Law in the 50 States." Both New York State and Minnesota have had to amend the divorce laws passed in the 1970s at the behest of the women's rights movement. Ms. Freed said that the laws passed to help women, in the end, contributed to the "feminization" of poverty. Florida's Supreme Court, in a 1985 decision, reprimanded a lower court for stating that permanent alimony should be awarded only "as a last resort."[16]

The women's movement also came under attack for not getting its fundamental objectives right. Dr. Sylvia Hewlett's book on the myth of women's liberation in the United States openly blames the movement for concentrating on workplace progress at the expense of motherhood. She found that the consequences of their action had done nothing to alleviate the double burden of women: being both mother and worker. She said that today almost 80 percent of poor people in America are women and children. Dr. Hewlett, a United

Nations economist and dedicated feminist, also said that her main criticism of the women's movement is that it sought equality with men, ignoring the special predicament that women with children face in society. Dr. Hewlett's view is that there should be special protection for women, whereas the women's movement was still set in its belief that only equality with men will work.[17]

The United States Supreme Court's decision that women were entitled to preferential treatment was hailed across the board by almost all women's movements, in a way confirming Dr. Hewlett's conclusions as correct.

There is consensus now that the women's movement in the United States is somewhat in disarray and despair because feminism has turned against itself after viewing the consequences of women's progress the past decade. Germaine Greer's 1984 book *Sex and Destiny* has made the essential point that women have been harmed, rather than helped, by the sexual revolution and are now worse off.

It is true that American women have made remarkable progress in the professional fields and are scaling higher rungs on the political ladder, yet most leading figures who were hailed for their wisdom and public statements by the feminist movement in the 1970s now use words such as "despair," "decay," "demoralization," and "paralysis" in talking of the movement.

In an article in *Policy Review* in 1986, Managing Editor Dinesh d'Souza quotes Jean Elshtain, a feminist professor at the University of Massachusetts, as saying that the women's movement is now perceived by younger women as harboring contempt for the female body, for pregnancy, childbirth and child rearing. Making divorce easier has resulted in the number of cases rising from 479,000 in 1965 to over a million in 1985. Divorced women, because of their lower job training, ended up working harder, earning less and becoming poorer. "But the feminization of poverty in this country has come about precisely as sexual discrimination has decreased—thanks to social and legal prohibition," d'Souza wrote.

All the feminist literature of the 1970s inveighed against the traditional marriage and against having children within marriage. The result was increased federal and state aid to female-headed households and unwed mothers, a program which, judging by the statistical results, failed. The number of female-headed black households has more than doubled since 1965. D'Souza also pointed out that feminism ends up at odds with itself when women who do not espouse the feminist agenda rise to the top of their profession, people such as former Ambassador Jeanne Kirkpatrick, former United States Secretary of Transportation Elizabeth Dole, Supreme Court Justice Sandra Day O'Connor, Senators Paula Hawkins and Nancy Kassebaum, and others.[18]

The founder of Conservative Women for America (C.W.A.), Beverly LaHaye, openly criticized N.O.W. and the feminist movement in general for going too far, making too many strident demands and ignoring family values. The C.W.A. now claims to have 565,000 members, considerably more than N.O.W. or any other feminist organization.[19]

An article in *The New York Times* in 1986 also stated that the National Organization of Women was being criticized by some observers for being too intent on public issues, such as abortion and job and pay equity, and failing to tackle in any comprehensive way the kinds of problems with which women are confronted daily, such as supporting children alone, insufficient incomes, having children without jeopardizing their careers, etc. The *Times* quoted Ruth Mandel, Director for the Center for Women and Politics at Rutgers University (New Jersey) as saying that the biggest challenge facing N.O.W. is the need to identify the American woman, discover her greatest needs and turn those needs into an activist agenda.[20]

Public and private disillusionment with the objectives and tactics of N.O.W. has become more noticeable. In 1977 the first National Women's Conference, organized by N.O.W. supporters in Houston, had $5 million in federal funds, had the backing of the President's wife (Rosalynn Carter) and was attended by more than 2,000 delegates, cheered on by some 15,000 spectators under the watchful gaze of 1,500 members of the media. A decade later, in November 1987, only 900 feminists gathered in a Washington hotel to analyze the results of developments since the Houston conference. There were only about a thousand supporters; a total of 23 corporations managed to scrape together a bare $20,000 for the conference, forcing N.O.W. and the delegates to use their own money and to run the meeting without any paid staff. Instead of 1,500 newspaper, radio and television reporters, this time about 50 showed up. Worse, of the 900 delegates only a handful were young people.

There are still members of N.O.W. who have not seen the writing on the wall and whose approach to the problems women face can serve only to mislead and, eventually, to disillusion on the national level. Robin Morgan, writing the foreword to *Women and Russia,* said that Soviet women and United States women share the same basic situation of powerlessness. "Our pain differs more in detail than in kind, and our respective governments, while claiming major ideological distinction from one another, share the same patriarchal indifference to and suppression of their female citizens."[21] This, of course, is manifestly untrue and a false comparison. The government of the Soviet Union is the Communist Party, and the only party permitted. There are no free elections. It is not a multi-party system and not a democracy. Comparing the United States government with the Supreme Soviet and the Kremlin is comparing apples with oranges.

It is true that a male-dominated *society* in the United States, because of mistaken perceptions of women's role, has prevented the women's movement from achieving more success, but to state that the United States government "suppresses its female citizens" is factually wrong and legally absurd. The United States government executes and administers the laws of a freely elected Congress. In the Soviet Union, the Communist Party not only makes the laws but implements them as well. Unlike the United States, the Soviet economy is also centrally managed. Women are suppressed in the Soviet Union, for economic reasons, suppressed by a political party. But in the United States the "government" is both Congress and the administration as well as the judiciary.

Robin Morgan also stated that it is vital that women speak and listen to each other and join forces. But then she added: "There is no solution to humanity's agony as long as a minority (men) holds and abuses power. Feminism is the politics of the 21st century, or there simply will be no 21st century on earth."

Even allowing for rhetorical extravagance, this is a politically immature assessment. Not all male governments in the world held and abused power. Did Ms. Ghandi (India), Ms. Bandaranaike (Sri Lanka), Ms. Golda Meir (Israel), Ms. Peron (Argentina), and various other women leaders never abuse their power?

It is ironic that seven years after Robin Morgan wrote these words, two men, Mikhail Gorbachev of the Soviet Union and Ronald Reagan of the United States, have pulled the world closer to global peace in the 21st century than any other two leaders since the end of World War II. And it was the United States system of free enterprise, a system not forced on women by its government, as Morgan alleged, which won out over the imposed socialism of the Communist Party.

The sort of radical, revolutionary political feminism espoused by Morgan and others is inadequate to achieve women's goals nationally or internationally and is even destructive. As Lynne Segal wrote in her book *Is the Future Female,* this can only lead to a feminism which is biologically determinist and ahistorical and therefore unable to deal with change.[22]

Despite the fact that the feminist revolution has now been rolling in the United States for 20 years, women are only marginally better off in most areas than a decade or two ago. In her provocative book *The Equality Trap* Mary Ann Mason points out that women bank executives, surgeons, and corporate lawyers shine in magazine and television programs but the vast majority of women are still in low-paying jobs. Women work more hours per week in the house and outside than ever before, and a paying job has become a necessity for women. The blame, she said, must be shared, at least partially, by the women's movement which moved away from the objective of *women's* rights to that of *equal* rights. This has worsened the situation for the vast bulk of American women, who are working women.[23]

Equality, Mason observed, has ruined the lives of women who divorced. It has weakened the bond between men and women. It has prevented women from realizing that the real revolution in the United States was an economic one. In fact, the members of the new generation of women are the first to experience a *lower* standard of living than their parents. They pay twice as much (44 percent) of their paycheck for the mortgage payment than people in the 1970s. They spend 30 percent less on clothing, give 38 percent less to charity, and have 75 percent less savings than their parents. The women's movement (N.O.W. in particular) provided the ideological base for the economy's new need for women workers, said Mason. Women are now equally responsible for supporting the family. But this concept of equality was a trap because equal rights does not challenge the structure of the economy or the role of the government. Women were to be as free and equal as men in every respect and 70 percent of men who never married ended up looking on marriage as "restrictive." Equality for women abetted the male flight from the economic and emotional responsibilities of family. Equality makes no sense when the mother, for obvious reasons, deserves first priority in parental leave, said Mason, but because of the emphasis on equality, men are now challenging this assumption.[24]

Feminists in America believe that women should be treated as individuals and not as individuals who are also members of a sex, and that free and open competition with men in the marketplace must be the goal. This, however, is bad for women with children, and the majority of working women have children. The rigid ideology of equality, Mason argues, should be abandoned for a return to flexible women's rights. The women's movement needs to draw up a new women's rights agenda that will benefit all women, particularly working women with children.[25]

The overall impression is that the crux of the debate on the future of the women's movement in the United States is now back where it was one or two decades ago: strongly pro-family women versus women who sometimes speak of child rearing as a major obstacle to achieving feminist goals. Historian Rosalind Rosenberg, author of *Beyond Separate Spheres: Intellectual Roots of Modern Feminism*, states that "if women as a group are allowed special benefits, you open up the group to charges that it is inferior. But if we deny all differences, as the women's movement has so often done, you deflect attention from the disadvantages women labor under." Either way, she says, women can lose.[26]

What do women really want in terms of career and a family? During 1986, there were several important and comprehensive surveys on women, almost all of which indicated that women overwhelmingly valued financial security and their families. Surveys by Procter and Gamble, *Redbook* magazine and Ethan Allan, Inc., show women highly value their careers. Also, more than 60,000 women responded to a survey conducted by *Woman's Day* in 1986, in which the overwhelming majority indicated that they want to hold jobs and must hold jobs to make ends meet.[27] On the other hand, a 1985 nationwide Gallup Poll has also revealed that 72 percent of women find the traditional role of wife and mother "ideal."

A re-evaluation of women's position in the United States seems overdue. In almost every respect, except in terms of the law and in terms of court rulings, there has been a sense of disillusionment.

In their book *Success and Betrayal,* authors Sarah Hardesty and Nehama Jacobs looked at the crisis of women in corporate America and pointed out that a substantial percentage of women in middle-management corporate positions feel disillusioned both with the nature of rewards they have received to date and their limited (future) career-advancement opportunities.[28] Women, they said, still hold only 4 percent of the 12,000 directorships in America's top companies. Of 6,500 public companies, only 15 are headed by women.

According to Sylvia Hewlett, the problems of contemporary American women are not necessarily the result of some massive or inevitable conflict between work and family life. Rather, they result from the fact that the United States does less than any other advanced country to make life easier for working mothers. There is less maternity leave, less subsidized child care and less job flexibility. The crux of the problem, she states, is "that there have been no cultural or institutional changes in the way children are supposed to be raised." For this reason, she argues, the European women's movement did the right thing by pressing, not only for equal rights, but for social benefits to ease the family responsibilities of working women.[29]

Hewlett believes American women are locked in a no-win situation. They have lost the guarantees and protection of the past, since marriage has broken down, and yet they have failed to improve their earning power in the labor market, since the wage gap remains almost as wide as ever. In Hewlett's opinion, American women are in bad shape, while the future does not hold out many prospects as divorce increases. She cites demographers who predict that two out of every three new marriages will end in divorce.[30]

Hewlett also believes that a decade of militant feminism has not succeeded in upgrading the economic conditions of women's lives. The reason for this is that American feminists have emphasized formal equality and encouraged women to enter the world of work on male terms. "The last thing most American feminists would admit is that working mothers might just need special concessions. . . ." She cites the example of the Scandinavians, who believe that women do need special benefits and services in order to be able to compete on an equal footing with men. Hewlett, with justification, is very critical of the militant feminists of the United States whose agitation has not brought help to women to deal with the concrete realities of life, i.e., reconciling motherhood with a job, whereas in Europe they have succeeded in doing just that. They may have fewer women executives in Europe than in the United States, says Hewlett, but the wage gap is closing and there is generous maternity leave and all other kinds of assistance to working mothers which the United States does not have. Equal rights and sexual freedom, she said, are what the women's movement in the United States fought for, whereas in Europe the fight was balanced between legal rights and the need to institute family support systems. In the United States the critical problems of having children and being a mother while trying to hold down a job have been downplayed by the women's movement, sidetracked, even ignored, said Hewlett, citing one of the leaders in the Italian movement, Daniela Colombo: ". . . the feminist movement (in the United States) has been more interested in abortion and sexuality than in work and family issues."[31]

Such criticism by Hewlett and others on the objectives of the women's movement in the United States is indeed not unfounded. Beyond the arguments which they have presented there is the undeniable fact that the actual programs of such organizations as W.E.A.L. and N.O.W. gave top priority to legal issues such as the Equal Rights Amendment and to other high-publicity questions such as abortion. The so-called National Plan of Action produced after the International Women's Year Conference in Houston barely touched upon the question of women and their children. Friedman in her book *The Second Stage* admits that as late as 1979 her appeal for the movement to come to grips with the practical problems of the family fell on deaf ears. Germaine Greer in *Sex and Destiny* (1984) accused modern society, and by implication N.O.W., of being profoundly hostile to children.

The consequence of all this was that the women's movement split into two opposing sides—the pro–E.R.A. group and the stop–E.R.A. group—one still emphasizing the legal, so-called male-clone approach, the other appealing to measures to strengthen the family and to assist working women with their dual burdens of being worker and mother.

Ethel Klein believes that discrimination against women in the United States today is not due simply to individual prejudice, or to errant employers who prefer to pay men more than women for the same work. "It is largely rooted in a sex segregated labour market that confines women to a limited number of low-paying jobs." She points out that nearly 80 percent of women are employed in clerical, sales, service and factory or plant jobs that pay on the average less than $10,000 per year. She admits that women have made some inroads into the traditional male areas; "yet for every woman who moved into a traditionally male dominated job, thousands of women have remained in low paying occupations...," citing clerical workers (80 percent), non-college teachers (71 percent), librarians (81 percent), health technicians (70 percent) and nurses (97 percent).[32]

According to Klein, an end to wage differences between men and women and occupational segregation is only part of the process that will integrate women into the marketplace. What is also required is that both husband and wife share in women's responsibilities for home and child care, and that women's values and perspectives be incorporated in the organization of labor. Without a major restructuring in the relationship between work and family, women's burden will not be lightened. "The demands of family work and paid work are currently in competition with one another. Once women's role in the labour force is accepted, society is forced to address the question of child care." In this regard, she states that surveys show the general public to be strongly in favor of more day care centers.

The concept of sex equality need not presume that the development of a place for women in the marketplace is more important than women's places in their private families, Klein argued. Although women have to be paid for their work in order to survive, women's contribution as employed workers is not more valuable than their traditional home and child care responsibilities. Klein calculates that a full-time homemaker is worth a minimum of $20,000 per year, a figure considered conservative by other analysts. Receiving wages for housework is one way for women to gain economic independence.[33]

Increasingly, the contribution of homemakers to the national economy is seen as something which can no longer be ignored, and the nature and value of the productive services provided by the housewife is worth investigation. As economist Barbara Bergmann points out, "even in its dwindled state, the housewife occupation remains the largest single occupation in the USA." In January 1986 almost 30 million women were housekeepers or homemakers.[34]

The vexing questions of abortion and child care, more than anything else, are shaping up as the two major issues of the early 1990s. Other issues which are still current are election of more women to political office; pay equity, rape, and domestic violence; and the feminization of poverty.

The pros and cons of abortion have been bandied about in the press and on television, sorted out and analyzed in numerous studies and books, and during 1988 and 1989 even debated on the street during, sometimes, violent public confrontations. The crucial fact is that every year there are three million unintended pregnancies in the United States and, according to the Alan Guttmacher Institute, the United States now has the highest rate of teen pregnancy in the industrialized world. How is that to be overcome?

The very principle of abortion is obscured by the argument as to when a human life really begins. Those opposed to abortion, on religious, medical, and other grounds, say that life begins at conception. On the other hand, doctors say that, if death can be certified only when the heart stops beating and the brain no longer responds to any stimuli, that life should be counted from the moment the heart begins to beat and the brain begins to react. The debate has not been settled.

The Alan Guttmacher Institute shows most women get abortions because they cannot afford a child or they fear a child would interfere with their work, school, or family responsibilities. The study, published in *Family Planning Perspectives* and released on May 9, 1988, is the first in the United States to take a close look at the reasons why women have abortions.

Planned Parenthood has set out the pro-choice case in full-page newspaper advertisements in which the following points are made. (a) Laws against abortion kill women. In the two decades before abortion was legal in the United States it was estimated that nearly a million women sought abortions. Thousands died. Those who did not die were stamped as criminals. (b) Legal abortion protects women's health because for thousands childbirth will result in serious complications. (c) It is unfair and illogical to confer upon an egg which has just been fertilized by man's sperm, rights equal to or superior to those of a woman's. (d) An accident with a birth control method, or a moment of forgetfulness, or rape, can cause a pregnancy and end a woman's economic and personal freedom. (e) Anti-abortion laws discriminate against low-income women, who are driven to dangerous, self-induced, or back-alley abortions, while the wealthy can obtain a safe abortion. (f) Compulsory pregnancy laws are incompatible with a free society. There can be no greater violation of privacy than compelling a woman to carry an unwanted pregnancy to term. (g) If abortion is outlawed, again, more children will bear children for which they cannot care. It is a fact of life than 40 percent of 14-year-old girls will become pregnant before they are 20. The most tragic cases in society are those of unwanted children. (h) An unintended pregnancy can push people below the line of economic survival. It is estimated that in 1988 it costs $100,000 to raise a middle-class child to adulthood. This does not include college education after high school.

Opponents of abortion claim that they are acting in defense of life, that they are trying to save children and that abortion is murder. They believe that abortion permits so much freedom that it destroys every vestige of responsibility on the part of married or unmarried couples. The anti-abortion school has not yet taken a public stand on the estimated four million fertilized embryos (and therefore a human being according to their position) which are *spontaneously* aborted in the United States every year. Are these to be classified, not as murder, because there was no intent on the mother's part, but manslaughter? But the basis of their objection is that abortion is immoral and a pregnancy should be terminated only in extreme circumstances, such as rape and incest, or to save the mother's life. It should never be used for gender selection or birth control.

In 1973, the year in which the Supreme Court handed down its ruling in *Roe* vs. *Wade,* nearly 745,000 abortions were performed in the United States. The number gradually increased and, since the '80s, has averaged more then 1.6 million per year. Figures from the Alan Guttmacher Institute Survey of 1987 indicates that the majority of abortions performed in the United States are obtained by young (62 percent) white (70 percent) women of Christian religion (73.4 percent), unmarried (81 percent), while the highest rate of abortion of any age group is among women aged 18–19 years. These figures would seem to support the anti-abortion argument that the overwhelming majority of women, particularly young, unmarried white women, are using abortion primarily as a method of birth control. All of the moral, sociological and legal implications were not addressed by the U.S. Supreme Court in its deliberation in 1989 of the case of *Webster* vs. *Reproductive Health Services.* But in a clear setback for the pro-abortion element the court did rule, in effect, that states have the right to make laws which will prevent abortion on demand being financed by taxpayers' money, thus setting the stage for a local, instead of a national debate on the issue.

As if not already one of the most vexing problems of the century, the abortion debate was complicated even more by the question of whether or not a father has a right to be informed about an abortion and to take steps to prevent it. The United States Supreme Court has already ruled that abortion is solely the woman's choice. As New York University law professor Sylvia Law once observed, "There is no way that one can treat a man and a woman evenhandedly when the biological reality is that woman has to bear the child." But courts may require the wisdom of Solomon, in a legal sense, since men are not challenging a woman's right to have an abortion but are seeking ways in which her right to an abortion can be restricted. The argument is that the Supreme Court has never found that women have an absolute right to abortion. The court, in fact, has recognized that there are several factors which can offset that right, e.g., the age of the fetus and, for minors, parental or court consent. The new debate will be whether the judges should balance the fundamental rights of both father and mother. In this respect the question still to be settled is whether abortion is a purely legal issue or a women's rights issue.

The debate over day care for children of working mothers asks whether the United States government, state government, or private enterprise should pay to help take care of the children of mothers who simply must work to keep things together. The statistics are almost self-explanatory. Some 66 percent of mothers in the age group 18–44 work, including 51 percent with children less than a year old. Susan Brooks of the United States Department of Health Services in Atlanta states that, according to the 1986 census data, there are 8.8 million mothers rearing children whose fathers are absent from home. Columnist Ellen Goodman of *The Boston Globe* cites figures that there are 10.5 million children under six being cared for by people other than their parents and that by 1995 two-thirds of all preschool children and four out of five of all school children will have both parents in the work force. "We have drifted into a national childcare crisis," she said.

The fundamental question being posed is where family responsibilities end and government responsibilities for easing this crisis begin. Some proposals, for example that the government should convert today's patchwork system into a subsidized network, run by strict standards, carry costs estimated at $62 billion for child care for those under six.

Day care for children traditionally has been regulated by individual states, but in 1989 Congress began the first serious debate whether to enact minimum federal standards. More than two dozen child care bills are pending in Congress, some of them the carry-over of previous years when the principle of federal encroachment erupted into a major controversy, delaying passage of several bills.

Congress has recognized the problem of non-payment of court-ordered child support with the passage of the Family Support Act of 1988. But that is not what the pro–child care lobby is aiming at. Their argument is that women must work; the economy needs their input; the majority of working women have children that must be taken care of and, sooner, rather than later, the majority of the labor force in the United States will be women. More and more they are pointing to what the countries of the European Community are doing. The 1988 report of the European Commission, *Child Care and Equality of Opportunities,* shows that, with the exception of Portugal, all 12 countries provide state-funded childcare facilities to children aged three to five, ranging from 45 percent of all children in this age bracket in Britain to 90 percent in France and Belgium.

In the United States in 1986 there were only enough child care facilities (day care centers or licensed day care homes) for 2.1 million children. But in the same year there were already more than 10 million children under the age of six with two working parents or a single parent to support the family. A survey of more than 10,000 United States corporations in 1987 showed that 61 percent had specific policies, such as flexitime, parental leave, job sharing and work-at-home programs, to help make child care easier, while 11 percent offered day care. (There are 44,000 United States companies with 100 or more workers.) At the bottom of the scale in Europe, Portugal provides state-funded day care centers for 20 percent of all children aged three to five and for 50 percent aged three and younger. Very few of the American companies have the sort of package for working fathers and mothers which IBM introduced in 1988. Apart from flexitime, all of the IBM female employees with children may now take as many as three years of leave, without pay, to take care of their young. Health and retirement benefits will continue while workers are on leave, and IBM guarantees them a job when they return from leave.

The wide-ranging debate on child care assistance for working mothers gained momentum during the 1988 Presidential election and has generated considerable publicity and argument. The consensus is that the principle of child care has been accepted. All that remains to be settled is who is going to pay for the service.[35]

30. Recommendations

There is no shortage of recommendations for governments, women's organizations and individuals as to what could be done to eliminate discrimination against women and to improve their status in society. At the same time, there are many disagreements, even amongst qualified observers, as to the most important objectives and which of the problems require the most urgent attention. There are also major differences of opinion concerning the methods and tactics to be employed to achieve the principal objectives.

The question of reducing the inequality between women's and men's earnings is the one subject all are agreed upon. Women also deserve greater political representation. Almost everyone also agrees that tightening up the wage laws is a good beginning but that legislation by itself cannot eliminate the fundamental inequality of women's social role that compels her to carry the burden of domestic work alone. But in the final analysis the need to change men's perceptions of the problem and alleviation of the dual burden of motherhood and employment is at the heart of the problem.

A study of women's rights reveals that the perceptions of women in society, which end up hurting women, are often the product of the most virtuous of intentions.

During the early years of Christianity, women enjoyed a position of relative equality in the church, but soon many doors were closed to them. The cult of Mary, the symbolic elevation of motherhood, in fact established a subordinate position for women. The cult of the Virgin Mary may function as a source of strength for women in Latin America, but it does not challenge the social order of male dominance inside and outside the cathedrals. In *The Cross Cultural Study of Women* it is pointed out that a similar decline in importance and status of women over time has been documented for Hinduism, Islam and Buddhism. In Hinduism women may be venerated but their role is circumscribed.[1]

Margot Duley and Mary Edwards observed that on a global scale there are over 200 recommendations which can be made for improving the status of women and eliminating discrimination. The most important include: full and equal employment opportunities; development of accessible family planning; facilities to lighten women's work; introduction of appropriate technology to do this; target dates for the elimination of male/female differentials in literacy rates; equal access to technological innovations for women in agriculture; involvement of rural women in agricultural policy making; equal rights of land ownership; special attention to women's health needs; redefinition of concepts of work to include women's unpaid labor in the G.N.P.; removal of sex bias from educational curricula; and promotion for education for women at home. The cumulative effect of these programs, they wrote, would be immense.

Interestingly enough, this set of recommendations does not address the problem of women and the law. In the evaluations and recommendations made in *The Decade for Women in Latin America and the Caribbean* (United Nations: Santiago, Chile, 1988), the *rapporteur* stated: "A curious fact which invites speculation is that laws have been an important instrument of change, or at least reflect the existence of certain levels of awareness and sensitivity to the problem of women's rights, but that if women do not assume responsibility for the application of those laws, they will remain inoperative, at least insofar as the majority of women is concerned." The *rapporteur* said that it was agreed that legislative measures cannot by themselves modify the situation of discrimination against women, but they can facilitate the conditions for eliminating it.

Based on the information in this book, it requires little imagination to see that the one area in the world which would benefit most in the short and long term from the application of such programs would be Africa, provided the male hierarchy is prepared to surrender most if not all of its exclusive privileges. In Africa, Asia and to a lesser extent Latin America, that does not appear likely to happen in this century.

In *Empowerment and the Law* there is an excellent matrix which summarizes the major strategies available to organized women's movements according to focus, goals, objectives and activities. While an oversimplification (which fails to convey the interaction of the components), it is nevertheless an excellent starting point for almost any nationally organized women's movement. The starting point, said author Margaret Schuler, is acceptance of the premise that ignorance and powerlessness are rooted in social structures that determine the unequal exercise of power in society. The remedy is a social transformation, not only of laws, but also of attitudes, which, in turn, requires education, not only of and for the victims, but of society as to the unequal status of its own voters and taxpayers—who happen to be female.[2]

Political and government specialists Joni Lovenduski and Jill Hills, both British, wrote that "in order to change an unfavorable economic, social and domestic condition women must seek not only to enter the political arena in greater numbers, but must also expand it to include private issues on the public agenda. Women currently in positions of political leadership bear major responsibility for initiating this dual strategy." Unfortunately, Lovenduski and Hills points out,

> There is evidence that many women directly owe their positions to other women, and are therefore not required to distinguish the special needs of their women constituents. This suggests that women have never exercised the vote to its full extent, have never turned the apparent disadvantage of being a second electorate into a political weapon. Women's massive voting strength thoughtfully used, or withheld, could activate even apparently moribund political leaders ... only when women begin to vote and mobilise as women over the whole range of political issues will political leaders ... perceive and act upon obligations to women electors. Then and only then will an effective re-ordering of public priorities ... take place.[3]

The recommendations made in this chapter are neither global nor aimed at any specific region or country, except for the United States and the Republic of South Africa, which are two special cases. Of all the world's industrially developed or rich countries, they have the worst record in wage discrimination and occupational segregation and both lack national policies, and legislation, aimed at providing for working women during and after childbirth and for working women with small children at home. But the recommendations, even in the case of South Africa and the United States, should not be seen as totally comprehensive.

The first part of this chapter will deal with certain general recommendations, based on the decisions taken during the World Conference of Women in Nairobi in 1985, followed by some regional suggestions and then the two special cases of South Africa and the United States. Finally, affirmative action and comparable worth will be analyzed as recommended lines of action.

General Recommendations

The report on the non-governmental meeting (N.G.O.) for women in Nairobi, which coincided with the United Nations–sponsored world conference to assess the achievements of the Decade for Women, is an excellent example of what women ought to and ought *not* to do in their struggle to further the cause of sexual equality in government, before the courts, in industry, trade, education, politics, agriculture and the service sector.

The idea of the N.G.O. meeting was to find the most effective collaborative means of achieving meaningful and lasting change in the position of women. The nine subjects dealt with—development, equality, education, health, employment, refugees, etc.—were all appropriate for the occasion.[4]

Studying the various recommendations and findings it is evident that women have indeed achieved a new level of sophistication in their analysis of the problems which their sex still faces all over the world. At the same time, some of the conclusions were either premature or far off the mark, and some of the recommendations were so ambitious or overlapping (with what has already been done) that they almost lost sight of the original objective, which was to improve the existing status of women.

That women saw themselves as forces of change, not just for women, but for all of society, is an admirable spirit but the idea that men and women should be considered as "separate forces in the quest for world peace," to quote one recommendation, is distressing. One cannot, should not, strive for an equal say as a separate force when the entire objective has always been to have an equal say within the same force. World peace is something which men and women should tackle together, not as separate forces.

It is even more distressing to read the following in the N.G.O. report: "Participants expressed little hope for the ability or willingness of present governments to help realise women's alternative visions. . . ." This is surely not a charge which can be leveled at the Nordic governments, or at those governments in West Germany, France, Canada, Italy, Australia and elsewhere which have at least enacted far-reaching legislation during the period 1975–1985 to meet the legitimate demands of women. Sometimes governments in the West have even gone beyond what the law or international conventions require. For example, France, which has had an Equal Rights Amendment Act for many years, has been making an extraordinary effort to overcome sex stereotyping of jobs by offering "bridging" courses and requiring employers to train women for technological and computer jobs.

When the law is in place to ensure equality then the energies of women should be directed towards its rigorous enforcement and implementation, but in cooperation with men.

Energies should also be directed towards men in general, the male-dominated society, to effect a change in attitude. Anthony Strachan wrote in *The New York Times* that many men actually feel threatened by the changing roles of the women in their lives.[5] Some women recognize this. At an international conference on women held in Washington DC in 1986, one of the main conclusions was that traditional beliefs pose one of the greatest challenges to progress for women throughout the world and the perceptions of men in general represent one of the biggest hurdles to overcome.[6]

In respect of the foregoing it is surprising that women have not sufficiently taken the initiative in promoting social and economic changes through the mass media. It is true that women are under-represented in the media, and there is often a tendency within the media to establish a stereotype of women or even distorted images of them.[7] It is true that coverage by the media of women as participants in economic activity has been inadequate. Women are rarely connected with issues of global importance, except if a woman happens to be head of government, like Margaret Thatcher of Great Britain. Women are not connected in the media with issues such as unemployment, inflation, budget deficits, pollution or scientific and technological development, except as part of the family. Experts believe women should recognize the previously unexplored potential of the media in their quest for equality and integration in the development of the country.[8]

There are perhaps a dozen targets for the women's movement which almost select themselves. Education is one. There is striking evidence that a woman's level of education is one of the most significant factors in the health of her children. In countries where infant mortality levels are at their highest, the male/female ratio of literate adults is 42 to 19. Where the mortality rate is lowest it is 96 to 94.[9]

As to family planning, it has been repeatedly shown that the higher the level of a woman's education, the fewer children she is likely to have. In Western Europe, where some 98 percent of women enjoy literacy, the average number of children per woman is 1.6. In East Africa, where the literacy rate of women is only 14 percent, the average number of children per woman is 6.8.[10]

Eliminating all vestiges of discrimination on the statute books is another target. So is greater participation in the legislative process and in government. So are equality in the workplace, equal pay for equal work, and equal opportunities in employment—to name but a few. These objectives need to be tackled on a priority basis. Concentration of energies, womanpower, money and other resources are called for to obtain such change that women all over the world would gain courage by recognizing that dramatic progress is possible and visible.

When the N.G.O. workshops recommended that there should be links between influential women or groups of women and the forces working for "national liberation," substance and reality flew out of the window. "National liberation" can mean a Communist insurgency against a democratically elected government, such as in the Philippines, or against a Communist government imposed on the people, such as in Afghanistan, or the struggle of blacks in South Africa to obtain voting rights in the national legislature. The women's movement has enough hay on its fork without attempting to deal with issues mired worldwide in political quicksand.

Recommending that women form their own labor unions, as women, is exactly the sort of development which women have been *opposing* the past 20 years. It also suggests that existing labor unions have not been sympathetic to the women's movement, or refused women membership, which may be true in many cases but is also untrue in as many others. The objective should rather be to improve the unions' strength with greater membership by both women and men, with more women on the executive, pulling in the same harness.

The tendency to adopt recommendations which have a splinter effect on women's movements was seen in several areas and workshops in Nairobi. A "black caucus" met every day to plan its own strategy but the entire meeting was about discrimination against women, period, and not about racial discrimination. Would it have been sensible and suitable for the white women, who were a distinct minority at the meeting, to organize themselves into a white caucus? It requires little imagination to see that such a step would have been attacked by the black caucus as "racist," probably on the grounds that white women are not an "oppressed" group.

The following resolution, in abbreviated form, is a further example of the inpracticality of the buckshot approach which cannot serve the interests of women: "The threat to peace resulting from . . . wars, armed conflict . . . violation of human rights, terrorism . . . [these things] are major obstacles . . . specifically to the advancement of women."[11] The fact is that war, aggression, terrorism, violation of human rights, etc., are just as abhorrent to the vast majority of males and just as much an obstacle to the advancement of individual men as to that of women.

The foregoing approach created the impression that a large segment of the international women's movement would prefer a separate United Nations, where all the delegates would be women, when realistically they should be working for far greater participation in the governments of their own countries and thus for greater, if not equal, representation at the United Nations and other world organizations.

On the other hand, consider the following resolution, also somewhat abbreviated, taken at the same meeting: "Education is the basis for the full promotion and improvement of the status of women . . . governments should strengthen the participation of women at all levels of national education policy and in formulating and implementing plans, programmes and projects. Special measures should be adopted to revise and adapt women's education to the realities of the developing world."[12] This proposal makes admirable sense because it implies a coordinated effort by governments in which men and women should play as nearly as possible an equal role.

There are other examples of practical and sensible recommendations produced by the non-governmental meeting in Nairobi. Take the following, which is based largely on the fact that in several Third World countries, certainly in most of Africa, women are the principal producers of food: Emphasize sustainable organic farming that does not destroy the land; involve women in feasibility studies of dams; strengthen existing networks of agricultural assistance; train rural women in planning, implementing and evaluating agricultural programs; identify technology suitable to women's needs and teach women those skills; help women establish their own agricultural union if it proves to be impossible for women to gain decision-making positions in mixed-membership unions.[13]

Analyzing the specific actions undertaken by women's movements in various fields and in various parts of the world, one is struck by the same gap between practical, worthwhile projects, with a good chance of success in the short term, and those which, currently, make no sense, given the priorities which women have set for themselves.

Let us look at some of the negative actions first.

(i) An international organization was set up in Rio de Janiero, Brazil, to gather and assess development strategies and themes of the women's movement. There is nothing wrong with this. It is, in fact, necessary. Yet the first study published dealt with the impact of global economic and political crises on women. But these crises have an impact on men as well, on all of society. Time, money and energy would have been better spent to study how governments have set about, in each country, to legislate for and execute the provisions of the various international conventions on discrimination against women, particularly those which have already been ratified.

(ii) The Women's Society for International Development, with its secretariat in Rome, has spent time studying and discussing the social impact of the international debt crisis, which, again, is a matter of enormous concern to entire communities and governments all over the world, not just to women. Hardly a day passes without the crisis being subject to scrutiny of the world media.

(iii) The Nordic Alternative Campaign in Denmark has published an 80-page book dealing with the dangers of war and ecological problems. Surely the suggestion cannot be made that not enough responsible men are aware of the dangers of war or of the world's ecological problems? There are men, many men, who have devoted their lives to these problems. In the Netherlands they have a saying: *"Eendracht Maakt Macht."* In Britain they say: "Strength in Unity." It's a universal truth that some problems are too big for one segment of the population. Women should not establish organizations to deal with problems where similar organizations already exist; instead, they should attempt to gain membership and get on the board of directors.

(iv) An International Union for the Conservation of Nature was formed, with its head office in Nairobi, Kenya. Again, individual men, or men as a group, are as much concerned with nature conservation as women. Otherwise a case could be made out that there should be an Audubon Society for men and one for women. Or an Academy of Science for men and one for women. There would be a problem if not enough women are members of those societies or are not adequately represented in the decision-making bodies.

(v) A meeting was held in January 1986 between representatives of the Soviet Women's Committee and the Women and Foundations Organization from the United States to discuss women's joint actions for peace. Such a meeting is futile. It has been proved empirically, a thousand times, that individuals and citizens' groups domiciled in the U.S.S.R. cannot and will not act in the international sphere except at the behest, and with the authority and connivance, of the Soviet government. It is equally true that in the United States private foundations and organizations are exactly what they claim to be, private and independent, funded privately and not beholden to the state or any political party. They will and do act in ways which the administration of the day disapproves of or approves of, depending on the merits of their cause. The fact is that the private American group, in this case, was dealing with the Soviet government.

(vi) Much the same can be said about the so-called "Action Alert" network started by several women's movements in Europe, coordinated from Copenhagen by the Women and Development Committee of the Association for International Development, to create awareness about what is being done or needs to be done to stop apartheid. Given the actions of the United Nations in this field, and of various governments, through trade and financial embargoes, diplomatic isolation, sanctions legislation, etc., this seems a sheer waste of time.

In contrast, the women's movement was also responsible for some important new actions which can be highly recommended. Take the following:

(i) A network of women in the field of political science was formed to integrate findings into their academic research and teaching.[14]

(ii) A video explaining women's legal rights has been made and shown to labor unions in Brazil. A publications exchange among 200 to 300 women's research centers has been set up as well as a women's political participation network.[15]

(iii) The Vatican was criticized for sending only male representatives to the Nairobi conference and for not ratifying the United Nations Convention for the Elimination of Discrimination Against Women. The N.G.O. recommended that a committee of Third World women be established to voice concern and mobilize public opinion against the violation of civil, legal and human rights of women in the Third World; to work towards the establishment of an International Commission on women's rights; to conduct regional conferences on legal rights and legal remedies for women and to launch a campaign to inform women of their legal rights.[16]

(iv) A meeting was held in Germany in 1986 to discuss the role of agricultural organizations in enhancing the status of women farmers.[17]

(v) *L'Union Europeene Feminine* adopted a program of work called *Les*

Femmes et l'Horizon 2000 which will treat problems of health, migration, agriculture and food as well as monitor and discuss the economic and social rights of women. Representatives from all the European countries met in Stockholm in 1986 and in Vienna in 1987 to continue the work.

All five of the foregoing actions make good sense, given the objectives which women have set themselves and given the boundaries of practicality.

What else can be recommended in which not only women but everyone could and should play a part, particularly the male-dominated legislatures?

To correct basic pay inequality, further progress will have to be made through statutory minimum wages for all wage earners; broader access for women to all occupations and to higher-paying jobs in the civil service and in the private sector, and wider acceptance of equal pay for jobs of comparable worth. Admittedly, equal pay for comparable worth is a vexing question, difficult to formulate in rules and regulations because of the difficulty in judging whether, for example, the job of a nurse (considering the hours worked, responsibilities and training) is equal in value to that of a dental technician. Many countries, provinces, states and city councils are therefore loath to tackle the subject of comparable worth at all. Perhaps a start could be made with some common categories, including that of housepainter and nurse, if not in the private sector, where the laws of supply and demand create additional problems, then in the civil service. After all, as Nina Rothschild said in the United States, if a nurse makes a mistake she could kill you. If a housepainter makes a mistake he merely annoys you, and he has to correct the mistake at no further cost to you. Why then should a painter be paid more than a nurse?

Most governments should not find it too difficult to make a tangible effort to try to combat the stereotypes with which women are confronted from day one in school and in the education process itself. In fact, most school curricula virtually impose these stereotypes on girls from an early age. This could be changed in textbooks and through the curricula itself and in most states of the world it would not even require legislation. It is a question of pedagogy, something which can be done for government-funded schools by administrative fiat, by proclamation, by regulation or by putting pressure on the school board.

A study of textbooks in the United States has shown that 75 percent of illustrations showed activities of men and boys only, particularly if machinery appeared in the illustration. In Latin America, a United Nations commission found that books at the primary level, where attitudes are most easily and permanently formed, continue to be highly discriminatory in the images that they convey, reflecting cultural emphasis on male domination and women in passive roles as housewives. A study prepared for the European parliament reports little change over the years in European school textbooks as well, in which stereotypes are also embodied. Given curriculum choices, girls generally tend to select subjects which conform to their cultural image and not to their own potential or ability. As one expert observer, Ruth Sivard, noted: "Textbook stereotypes, in other words, become self-fulfilling prophecies."[18]

Since the most pervasive discrimination against women is often that which assigns to men and women different rights in employment and retirement, the obvious target for legislators should be to amend those statutes so as to place men and women on an equal footing. To give teeth to such amendments, or new legislation, a woman who suffered damage as the result of unjustified discrimination on the grounds of sex should be able to apply, under statute, to an appropriate court for a declaration as to her rights, an injunction, specific performance or damages or both. It is axiomatic that "unjustifiable discrimination" should be defined by statute and that jurisdiction should be conferred, also by statute upon the appropriate court, perhaps a special court, to enable it to make declarations, grant injunctions, give instructions for specific performance and award damages.

For Western countries, where the freedom of the press and academic institutions provide a platform for reasonable targets set by women, women's organizations would be well advised to establish a short list insofar as legislative action is concerned. Any new legislation advancing women's rights should be distributed as widely as possible by women's organizations, by women in the legal profession and with the help of the media. They should aim to make the study of women's basic rights a central part of all high school curricula. They should also create a national body to monitor the implementation of laws requiring equality for women. To give some teeth to this body they should create an affiliated organization of legal scholars and women jurists, lawyers and advocates, who are willing to support the case of any woman who wishes to bring an action which can prove legal discrimination. The purpose is to create case law, on which so many Western law courts base their decisions.[19]

In this respect an immediate target should be the preparation and publication of a study of women and the law in each country, a work which needs to be updated every two to three years. An excellent example of the type of study required is *Women and the Law,* written by T.N. Srivastana, concerning women and the law in India. The book deals with women and the Constitution, women and criminal law, the family laws on marriage, marital relief and divorce, maintenance and custody of children, inheritance and succession as well as adoption, women and industrial law and women and social welfare. It answers such questions as: What are the legal rights of a woman in India? What legal steps can she take to protect herself against exploitation and injustice? How can she assert her legal rights?[20]

Since enactment of the law is not enough, women should be made aware of the laws which protect them. If they believe they have been discriminated against, then they need also to know how to set about eliminating the discrimination and to seek compensation for any losses which they may have suffered.

Getting women to use the law to enforce existing anti-discriminatory legislation and constitutional rights is becoming extremely important. It is as applicable to the United States as it is to Kenya, South Africa, India, Britain, or Brazil, anywhere where there is free or reasonably free judiciary. Mary Robinson, a Senator in the Irish parliament, posed the questions: Who has been making the law? Who has been interpreting the law? Who has been administering the law? Who has been enforcing the law? Who has been providing legal services? The answer, she said, is the same in each case: "Either exclusively or predominantly men." Addressing the plenary session on Women in Ireland at the Third International Interdisciplinary Congress on Women in Dublin in July 1987, she observed that law can be an important instrument of social change. "But given that the numerical situation is unlikely to change in the short term, in that men will probably be dominant in the power structures for the foreseeable future, can an effective strategy be devised to redress this imbalance?" The answer is "Yes," but the approach must be strategic and effective. The following factors, she said, are relevant to the formation of such a strategy:

- It is vital that a sufficient number of women recognize that the domination by men in the power structures of society *does* matter.
- They must recognize that it is an imbalance which affects the ethos and priorities of that society, and that it must be altered in a concerted manner.
- Knowledge is power. Unless women's groups and women more generally have access to knowledge of the laws and institutions which affect them, they cannot seek to exert effective influence.
- Because women are outnumbered in the various power structures, it is all the more important that they develop skills of effective lobbying in order to influence priorities and bring about change.
- Consideration should be given in appropriate circumstances to the use of the test case to accelerate legal change. Women's organizations could consider establishing a legal fund to help support test cases in appropriate areas.
- Women activists in the trade union movement should examine their ambivalence towards lawyers and the courts. However understandable their reservations in that regard, equality law cannot be fully effective until there is a healthy jurisprudence developed both in the Labor Court and on appeal on a point of law to the High Court.
- In recent years there has been a welcome development of women's studies in third level colleges and extra-curricular courses throughout Ireland. An important component in such courses should be a basic grounding in law.
- Women judges and lawyers could be more active in challenging any traditions of their profession which are blatantly sexist.

Selecting targets for legal action is extremely important, and women should avoid picking targets which clearly are not in the public eye, of which few people are aware, and where the end result would be only (a) another statement made or (b) something a few, highly selective, upwardly mobile superachievers would benefit from. One such area is private clubs. A private club's membership should not be the business of the government or be attacked in court unless it is a place where business is generally transacted or if membership clearly would improve the status, career opportunities, income, legal or educational standing of an individual woman. The idea of men- or women-only clubs may be archaic and even ridiculous in this age, but it is not necessarily a barrier to women's progress. There are clubs where it is even the unwritten law that business matters are not to be dragged into the pool room or the restaurant. Attacking such clubs or organizations in the United States appears to many sympathetic supporters of the women's movement as an attack on the constitutional freedom of association. There is privacy, even a right of privacy, inherent in a club whose objectives, insofar as women are concerned, are neither pernicious nor malicious.

Getting the government and the courts involved in every action of men or women which smacks of some sort of association invites what Robert Nisbet describes in his book *The Present Age: Progress and Anarchy in Modern America* (Harper & Row, 1988) as "a new absolutism," almost totalitarian in its approach and earmarked by "legal and administrative tyranny." Targeting clubs and organizations not involved in public activities or causes and where private choices are exercised can be only counterproductive, time-consuming, expensive, and energy-sapping. There are many other, worthwhile, dragons to slay.

The most difficult situations for women are those in countries where religion very often dominates the institutions of state, such as in the Muslim countries and in Israel. Recommending an action which would have to face up to deeply held religious convictions is often impossible. Take the case of Israel. Rabbinical courts have exclusive jurisdiction over marriage and divorce of Jews and will not dissolve a marriage unless both partners agree. There is a Catch-22 for women. Under the law administered by the Rabbinical court, a still-married man has more freedom than a woman unable to obtain divorce. There is inequality codified in the Jewish law pertaining to married women. Children of a married man's illegitimate union with a so-called common-law wife are legitimate so long as she is Jewish and not married to another man. But children of a married woman's illicit union are considered bastards and unmarriageable in Israel. A married woman who lives with another man can face losing custody of her children, and Jewish law forbids the "adulteress" to return to her husband or to marry her lover, even if she later obtains a divorce. Where both spouses are Jewish, there is no recourse to the civil courts. Finding a solution to this inequality would mean a change in basic Jewish religious law, which is almost impossible.[21]

Science and Technology

Because of the extreme importance attached to scientific and technological development in the 1990s, a special effort should be made to draw more women into science and technology. A special panel of scientists at a conference cosponsored by the American Association for the Advancement of Science and the United Nations Advisory Committee for Science and Technology, held at Mount Holyoke College, Massachusetts, in September 1983, considered various proposals. The following are some of the specific recommendations made and addressed to national and local governments—as well as to the United Nations.

> 30. Governments should appoint or nominate (where appropriate) women to participate in international, regional and national bodies that deal with science and technology for development.
>
> 32. We urge national Governments, particularly those of developing countries, to build indigenous research and development capabilities by adopting on a priority

basis a policy of total human resource development that would give women full representation.

38. We urge Governments to invest a high percentage of the national budget in science and technology training for women. Scholarships and other forms of financial support should be provided to enable women with demonstrated ability to pursue advanced study in the fields of science and technology.

41. Governments and educational institutions should adopt policies to ensure equivalent access to education, employment and advancement in science and technology by men and women.

42. We recommend development of innovative curriculum and admission policies that would facilitate a breakdown of gender stereotyping in schools and training institutions. A review and revision of such curricula should be undertaken to ensure that young women have equal access to and gain training in science and technology-related fields, with a practical application to employment opportunities once training is completed.

47. National Governments should ensure that women scientists and engineers are provided with equal access to all installations (for example, libraries, instrumentation facilities, oceanographic vessels) and placements, social and technological, to enable them to study and participate in science and technology to the fullest extent possible. This is particularly critical in situations where boys and girls receive a separate education that is not always equal.

50. Governments should ensure that employers in science and technology utilize the talents of women in these fields throughout their organizational structure—fairly, proportionately and based on capabilities. Neither family responsibilities nor marital status should be used as a deterrent or excuse to prevent employment or to restrict upward mobility in employment by women in science and technology.

60. Increased contact should be encouraged between women scientists and women's organizations to promote better understanding of the issues, concerns and constraints of both groups, to assist the "demystification" of science and technology to women's groups, and to lay the groundwork for effective future collaboration.

63. Recipient countries should require national and international institutions and organizations involved in the transfer of technology to provide information on the potential negative effects, as well as the positive effects, of new technologies, including their potential impact on women and women's activities.

64. We urge national Governments to set up science and technology advisory committees to monitor the import and impact of exogenous technology. Women should be given full representation on these committees with a view to monitoring the effects of new science and technology on the quality of life.

72. Noting that sex bias in the introduction of new technologies has frequently become institutionalized, excluding women from the benefits of new technologies, measures—including administrative, legislative and educational—should be taken to ensure that women have access to information, knowledge, training and retraining and employment associated with these technologies.

79. Governments should be urged to nominate women as well as men to the Advisory Committee and the Intergovernmental Committee on Science and Technology for Development. Given that there exists a large pool of eminent women in science and technology available to serve in advisory capacities, we recommend that in addition to geographical distribution there be gender representation on every committee related to science and technology. This representation should increase over time to reflect the representation of women in the world populations.

The Communist World

Any recommendation made in respect of women in any of the Communist countries dealt with in this book is of purely academic interest as long as every important decision affecting the status of women, their subordination, and discrimination against them on grounds of gender, is firmly in the hands of a Communist Party elite consisting of from 88 percent to 100 percent men.

The fact that there is no free debate and public discourse permissible on any contentious subject in the Communist world, including women's rights, adds to the impossibility of making any meaningful recommendation. The reality is that a recommendation on any subject in the Communist system has no hope of being accepted unless it serves the political objectives and ideology of the party, in particular, those who control the party.

Women's organizations in the Soviet Union and China are not free. They are staffed by individuals who are quite capable of independent judgment and objective analysis of women's rights, but they must toe the party line. The same applies to the sociologists and political scientists at the various state universities. In addition, in both the Soviet Union and China, women are considered by the hard core of the ruling elite simply as a national utility, either to swell the population, such as in Rumania, to provide for labor shortages, such as in the Soviet Union, or, as in the case of China, simply a cog in an ideological restructuring of society.

Many other observers have made recommendations to try to fit in with the existing realities in the Communist states, but all have hedged these with reference to the all-powerful role of the Communist Party.

One of the most concise pictures of the problems and needs of women in China is drawn by Xiao Lu in *Sisterhood Is Global.* Her conclusion is that all of the problems, including feudal attitudes, can be met if the government is prepared to do so. What is needed to overcome these and other problems for women, she adds, is greater gender equality and more egalitarian family structures, plus a vigorous promotion of free-choice marriage—in other words, the real application of stated Communist policy and respect for the existing laws. The problem, she points out, lies in the persistence of feudal attitudes and the total control of political life by the Chinese Communist Party, which does not even allow an independent women's movement to exist. All existing women's organizations, such as the All China Federation of Women, in reality are nothing but extensions of the C.C.P.[22]

Phyllis Andors indicated in her study of the liberation of Chinese women that, when the era of Mao ended and that of Hua Guofeng-Deng Xiaoping began, the question of women's role in China came in for re-examination. In the 1970s women's interests were clearly defined as class interests. Sexual oppression was acknowledged. Now the Party stressed only the generic interests of women and neglected the question of class. Family planning and women's roles at home became the main theme. The goal was set to reduce population growth to less than 1 percent a year by the early '80s. The new regime was intent on economic growth and cutting down on the expenses incurred in providing for women and children; thus, in purely political-ideological terms, the resolution of the women's question in China is to be dependent on the future success of economic modernization. The politics of women's liberation are thus diffused, and women must be content to identify with home and family and only certain kinds of employment.[23]

Africa

Perhaps the four most important recommendations which can be made in respect of most African countries are (a) to impartially enforce their own Constitution and laws, (b) to cease their glorifying annual billion-dollar military buildup and concentrate on expanding education to include women, (c) to develop regular water supplies and increase the production of basic foodstuffs, and (d) to become serious about fighting the population explosion.

Ethiopia is a prime example of a country which puts egoistic trappings before the feeding of its own population. During the height of the 1986 famine, it accepted some $75 million from the United Nations to build a conference facility for its political elite. Kenya, Nigeria, Tanzania, Zambia, Zaire and Ghana are examples of countries whose women would be infinitely better off if the laws passed to protect them and to eliminate discrimination were taken seriously by the people who wrote the laws, i.e., the government. (See the constitutional provisions for equality extracted in Chapter 32.) In many states the constitution has been suspended because of a state of emergency or military rule—for example Nigeria, Liberia, Zambia—so that the first recommendation becomes a moot point.

To indicate how important it is for African states to launch a massive and continuous family planning campaign, consider the following calculations made by the World Bank after their recent thorough and in-depth analysis of population programs in Africa. If all African women who want no more children were actually to have no more, roughly one-sixth of all maternal deaths could be avoided. If no woman had a child after the age of 40, as much as another 33 percent of maternal deaths could be avoided. The same dramatic results would be achieved in infant mortality rates.[24]

Improving women's education and raising their status by law and regulation, for example in marriage and property rights, will help free them from the traditional roles that encourage high fertility and thus deny society the benefits of their potential contribution. But in this respect more than talk is required. "The commitment of government leaders to the development of population policy must extend beyond lip service and be translated into effective action," the World Bank wrote.[25] In all of Africa in 1985 (South Africa excluded) only Zimbabwe provided substantial access to family planning for those outside the urban areas. Botswana and Kenya have programs in the pipeline, but actual access is still very limited. Others—Ghana, Liberia, Malawi, Rwanda and Tanzania—can only claim limited progress.

That there is a direct relation between women's education and declining fertility has proved to be true not only in Africa but also in all other societies, even among the Arab states. In her article, "Women's Education and Fertility," based on field research and questionnaires, Ann Al-Kadhi wrote that women with no education in the Middle East had the largest families, while increased levels of education corresponded directly with a decrease in family size.[26]

In traditional African society, outside the cities, women still do most of the farming, gather the fuel wood and draw the water. In fact, as the International Labor Organization pointed out, women are the major producers of food in Africa yet most of them work under extremely harsh conditions with poor tools and low levels of input in terms of new knowledge of production techniques, seeds, fertilizers, irrigation, etc.[27] Women, in fact, and not men, are the real farmers in Africa south of the Sahara, South Africa excluded. In four countries—Ghana, Senegal, Togo and Upper Volta—women form between 42 and 46 percent of the agricultural workers. In seven countries—Zambia, Mali, Ivory Coast, Malawi, Mali and Zaire—about half the agricultural labor force are also women. In Botswana, Tanzania, Cameroon and Sierra Leone—the percentage is above 50 percent. In all other African states, the percentage varies from 31 to 39 percent. The only exceptions are the Muslim states such as Mauritania, Benin and Niger.[28]

The World Bank, recognizing the foregoing pattern, set out to make a number of specific proposals, recommendations, in respect of women:

> Enhancing the status of women economically and politically, and thereby expanding their range of opportunities, is of critical importance in strengthening the demand for smaller families. In Africa, the prevailing young age of marriage for women, the frequency of polygamy, an unequal work burden between the sexes, and the low educational levels of women all combine to perpetuate the low status of women. . . .
>
> Legislative changes can be useful in promoting smaller families. First, they can affirm that basic human rights include the right of each couple to determine the spacing and number of their children, and can recognize that the practical exercise of this right requires access to family planning services and information. (The U.N. World Population Plan of Action of 1974, which was reaffirmed in 1984, expressed these principles and is supported by almost all governments.)
>
> Legislative change cannot in itself bring major changes in women's status in the short run. But in the long run it can help to broaden views of what is socially acceptable and encourage changes in attitude that will eventually contribute to changes in behavior. For example, legislation to raise the minimum legal age of marriage can encourage young women to delay marriage if they so wish, and it symbolizes the government's commitment to improving the status of women.
>
> Legislative change can be supplemented by specific efforts to reorient government programs to better serve women. This is especially the case in agriculture. Measures can be designed to increase women's access not only to land but also to new production technology for food crops, basic skills training, credit, and cooperatives. This reorientation will not be easy to bring about in the face of present attitudes and given the political weakness of women. Women will need to be trained as extension workers, teachers, and health auxiliaries and to become professionals, technicians, civil servants, and party officials. . . .
>
> Strengthening women's organizations, by expanding women's opportunities and providing outlets for women to assert control over their environment, can also help raise women's status. In several African countries women are establishing self-help organizations that build on communal traditions of cooperation. Such organizations can be more effective than individuals in obtaining credit, technical assistance, and help from government and other bodies. Women involved in such organizations often come to prefer smaller families and demand family planning. Nearly 22

> percent of the women belonging to Kenya's national women's organization, *Maendeleo ya Wanawake,* use contraception, compared with only 8 percent nationwide.... Experience has been similar in such diverse settings as Bangladesh, Indonesia, and Mexico.[29]

The Case of South Africa

Among countries which present difficulties of a truly vexing nature is South Africa because of its Western and non-Western sector. In addition, black women's progress is tied not only to political and ideological problems but also to native custom and tradition in the politically autonomous black homelands. For black women the bottom line is that as long as the central government pursues a policy of discrimination against blacks (which is constitutionally entrenched) their struggle for equal treatment will remain infinitely more difficult than that of white women.

In 1986 the governing National Party government, led by President Pieter Botha, committed itself in writing to political power-sharing between black and white on the basis of a just and democratic dispensation and in structures of government which are to be agreed upon by a constitutional *Indaba,* or major conference, between black and white leaders. Between 1980 and 1988 numerous laws and other pieces of legislation discriminating against people on grounds of pigmentation have been scrapped in preparation for the post-apartheid society (see Chapter 9 of this book), leaving only three key laws to be dealt with before legal equality between black and white can be achieved: (a) The Population Registration Act, which determines, *inter alia,* who may vote for the central government and to which school one can go; (b) the Land Act, which determines the areas which are exclusively for black or white ownership; and (c) the Group Areas Act, which determines which race may live where in the rural and urban towns and cities. Logic and numbers seem to dictate that in a power-sharing structure, based on democracy and justice, the central government would finally be constituted of a black majority. In that case, these last, major, vestiges of racial segregation will fall away and positively affect the opportunities for all black people, including black women. The search for consensus on the final constitutional structure is now on, and whether the current government is sincere and capable of crossing the Rubicon and implementing real power sharing remains to be seen.[30]

Generally speaking, South African written law with regard to women is comparable to that of most Western democracies. What is missing is an overall act to end discrimination against women, based on the terms of the United Nations Convention of 1982. Such an act would be impossible under existing political dispensation in South Africa since an act banning all forms of discrimination against women would mean banning discrimination against black women as well.

For white women in South Africa, the major discrimination is in the labor market, both in the private and civil sector. The same problems of attitude, sexual stereotypes, men's perception of women's role, women's perception of their own roles and an educational program tailor-made to perpetuate sexual stereotypes, are the targets for which women should aim. In this respect they could put considerably more pressure on the media, who know only too well that women also buy and read newspapers, that women are extremely important to their major advertisers and that women form a larger block of voters than men. But the starting point in South Africa should and could only be the home itself, followed by primary and secondary school.

Stereotypes are cast at home but are given shape and refined at school. By the time the girls leave high school they are already in a disadvantaged position. If the parents could bring sufficient pressure to bear, and the educational authorities were to embark on a clearly defined path to break down the stereotyping of girls, it would do more for women in their quest for equal treatment than anything else in sight.

Women's movements in South Africa, rather than attacking legislation, should gear their activities to educating the public, said Dr. Johan van der Vyver, Professor of Law at the University of Witwatersrand. "While the situation in South Africa reveals some discrimination against women, particularly in the labour market, this is not founded on law." He said that the blame for existing discrimination is to be found in public bias, prejudice, and not legal sanction. Professor van der Vyver pointed out that more and more gender-based discrimination has been removed from South African legislation the past few years. He categorized discrimination into those laws that afford differential treatment to women because they are female, and those which differentiate because they are female and married.[31]

Finally, the South African legislature itself could play a major role in eliminating remaining discrimination against women, either by enacting further laws in terms of equal wages in the private sector, or by launching a decade for women in South Africa. The state could easily utilize the state-owned and -controlled television and radio for the necessary publicity and, in government schools, explain that there is nothing in the world which prevents girls from becoming engineers, pilots, architects, managers, and, yes, heads of government agencies and cabinet ministers. If, in addition, the teachers' training colleges in South Africa, all state-owned, were to include a compulsory two-year course on women's rights and the status of women, down the road a new generation of teachers would be in a strong position to destroy the stereotyping of South African women. In the case of whites, that stereotyping is certainly at the heart of the problem—stereotyping and male ignorance and prejudice as to what women can achieve and have achieved in the world when given equal opportunities.

A specific law which South Africa should enact to promote equality for women would be a law requiring equal payment for work of equal worth in all parastatal organizations, provincial and municipal bodies, the civil service, including the police and army, universities and public educational institutions, including public industries and utilities such as the S.A.B.C., Iscor, Sats, Escom and others. Since unmarried and independent women pay tax on the same scale as men there is no reason why their taxes should be applied dissimilarly in compensating them for work of equal value.

Such a law or state regulation on equal pay for work of comparable worth, backed by a general law to enforce equal pay for women doing equal work in the marketplace (to which both the private and public sector would have to answer), plus an imaginative educational program to destroy the current perceptions of women (stereotyping), will do more to create a just and equal situation for women, with equal opportunities, than any other program.

Down the line the country will have to deal, like most other states, with the lack of compulsory maternity leave, deletion of early retirement of women, provision of equal pensions, greater technical and vocational training for women and the removal of the remaining restraints (such as their gross under-representation in the legislature, judiciary, civil service, and the cabinet) which place women on an unequal footing in competition with men.

Both the United States and South Africa need to adopt a national policy that supports women in their domestic roles and as working mothers so that they can do better in the labor market. As Sylvia Hewlett pointed out, this will enable many women to take fewer years off from employment to wait until their children are grown enough to attend school and thus to pay a smaller penalty in terms of lower wages when they return to work. This is the only policy that will bring about a real narrowing of the wage gap. In the United States a five-year break in employment lowers average earnings by 19 percent.[32]

Ignoring women's double burden is also a *guarantee* that they will remain second-class citizens in the marketplace, whether they live and work in Cape Town and Johannesburg or in Los Angeles and New York. In the process not only women but also society suffers. Since many women (the vast majority in fact) must work, children whom they may neglect later grow up to be problem-ridden, unproductive adults on which the state then proceeds to spend billions either in unemployment insurance, welfare, imprisonment or drug treatment. In 1985 there were more than 17,000 divorces among white women in South Africa, affecting more than 20,000 children. This is why everyone welcomed the law proposed in May 1987 to provide for the appointment of a family advocate to look after the interests of children in divorce proceedings.

In order to provide women, and their children, with an equal chance in life, they not only require special assistance but also *different* treatment. Only the angry liberal wing of women's organizations still believes, erroneously, in even more rigid legal equality, whereas in reality *de facto* equal opportunity is of much greater worth to both women and society. But equal opportunity can never be provided unless women who bear children receive special consideration—not the token kind found in most parts of South African and American society but real, tangible, meaningful consideration. It is not necessary to belabor this point. Had men been able to bear children, there would have been no argument to begin with. Alternatively, if a woman wishes to be an equal, and she has a right to equality as a human being, as a citizen of the country and as a taxpayer, she needs (a) to be unmarried and (b) to remain childless. If it were put to young men entering business that they can succeed only if they never married and had no children, there would be no business structure. In a 1982 survey, the prestigious *Wall Street Journal* found that only 48 percent of women executives in the United States were married and 61 percent of those married had no children. In comparison, 96 percent of male executives were married and 89 percent had children. Similar results were uncovered in 1985 by Basia Hellwig in a special survey for *Working Women.*[33] The chances are good that the same statistics will come up in South Africa.

Government and society in both the United States and South Africa will have to radically re-evaluate their attitudes towards pre-school children and young children at school with working mothers. What is needed is a statutory maternity policy that guarantees certain rights and benefits to working women before and after childbirth. The United States does have a Pregnancy Disability Amendment Act, but it is riddled with shortcomings, for example, its provisions on compulsory disability insurance. Private companies, both in South Africa and the United States, have excellent programs, but fewer than 25 percent of women in both countries work for the behemoths who can afford maternity benefits equal to those provided by law in countries such as France and Italy.

In law and in practice the East German Communist dictatorship has provided the best legal and practical benefits to working women with children.[34] The example set by a Communist state should be no reason for any country in the free world to back off from such a system. Some of the most prominent, in fact, most of the prominent members of the free world have long had similar systems which did not harm their capitalist structures in any way. Italy, Germany and the Netherlands have all made great strides towards providing publicly funded child care and they all remain staunch members of N.A.T.O.

France spends 4 percent of its gross national product on subsidies to preschool children.

The French logic is impeccable. They do not wish to pour even more money than this down the drain at primary and secondary school levels because pre-schoolers were grossly neglected. Every sociologist worth his or her name will be able to show what an enormous percentage of juvenile delinquency (ending up with costly imprisonment and loss of productive manpower) begins with poverty and neglect of small children.

The crux is that women cannot be provided with equal opportunities or ever hope to achieve economic equality with men, without family support structures such as maternity leave of at least six months, a guaranteed return to employment, child allowance and public day care for their children. In South Africa young men going off to army camp, without small children, are better taken care of in terms of protected employment and salaries than working women with children.

Thus, in the case of South Africa, there needs to be (a) an Equal Pay for Equal Work Act, applicable to the public and private sectors, (b) an Equal Opportunities Act, (c) a Maternity Leave Act, and (d) a National Child Care Act.

The expenses will be enormous but the benefits will be even higher in terms of more productive human resources.

If these proposals are too demanding then at least some aspects of the French system need to be adopted and enacted in legislation of (a) the appointment of a woman, preferably a senior advocate, as a Deputy Minister responsible for women's rights, (b) equal payment for equal work in all state, provincial, educational, municipal and parastatal organizations, (c) a legal requirement for all employers to produce annual reports on the comparative incomes of men and women on their payrolls, (d) the appointment of an Equal Employment Opportunity Commission responsible to parliament and not to the state, and (e) compulsory maternity leave for both the private and public sectors.

In France the Ministry of Women's Rights developed policies to encourage women's entry into the professional world and their access to professional and technical training; coordinated reports and studies on women's rights; coordinated positive discriminatory policies permitting temporary action favoring women to enable them to catch up with men (similar to temporary affirmative action); established programs of special training for women and coordinated research on legislation affecting women.[35]

The United States

"Affirmative Action" and "Comparable Worth" are two concepts as well as methods by which women in the United States could (a) catch up financially with men, (b) narrow and eliminate the wage gap, (c) overcome occupational segregation, and (d) achieve equal preferential treatment in hiring and promotion to overcome a manifest imbalance in the marketplace.

Both concepts are approaches to the problem of discrimination against women peculiar to the situation in the United States and will therefore be considered in American terms and as seen through the eyes of American experts. Before doing so, and in addition to the suggestions and recommendations already made in the previous section dealing with both South Africa and the United States, there are a number of points about women in the United States that need restating.

Since reconciling the demands of childbirth and childrearing with those of earning a living is clearly the most urgent problem facing modern American women, it follows logically that (a) the women's movement should address itself to this issue and (b) that at federal and state levels, administrators, budget directors and the policymakers should take a close look at how the governments in Europe have packaged family and child support to ease the dual burden carried by working women with children. In the 1987 Afterword to her book *A Lesser Life,* Sylvia Hewlett said that such a policy should receive priority because ". . . we tended to forget that 90 percent of women chose to have children, and that women will remain seriously handicapped in the workplace unless we establish a new system of family supports."[36]

Hewlett's views on this subject are also shared by economist Barbara Bergmann who states that child care assistance, support payments and flexible work schedules would help women stay in the mainstream even if they lack a man's support.[37]

Thus far, efforts to eliminate discrimination in the job market have been seriously limited because they have failed to deal with women's double burden. Hewlett quite rightly states that "unless women get some relief from their domestic responsibilities, they will continue to fare badly in the labor force."

It is the interruption to women's careers brought on by childbirth and the rearing of the young that ruins their careers in mid-life and depresses their earnings. High quality subsidized childcare such as is provided in France would enable many women to take fewer years out of the labor force and thus pay a smaller penalty in terms of lower wages when they re-enter the market. As Hewlett points out, a five-year break in employment lowers average earnings for women in the United States by 19 percent.

The vast majority of women desperately need to keep on working to support themselves and their families; there is therefore no substitute for a statutory maternity policy that guarantees essential rights and benefits to working women when they give birth. Thus, Hewlett wrote, working women need more than just equal treatment or equality in terms of the law. Men, after all, do not bear children. And it makes sense, economic sense, she said, for the federal government to invest financially in the health and well-being of small children. France has managed to build a consensus around family policy. It is supported by Communists, Socialists and Conservatives. The French regard motherhood as a social function similar to military service for men, something that has to be financially supported by the whole community.[38] Interestingly enough, Ethel Klein has observed that 66 percent of the United States public already supports federal assistance for child care centers.[39]

It must be recommended to women that they join labor unions and press vigorously for a greater say in the executive, more in keeping with their membership. The reason for this is very simple. Unionized workers in the United States earn, on the average, 30 percent more than non-unionized members. Ask any male worker whether he would join a union if he knew that, on the average, this would mean a rise in his salary from $20,000 to nearly $30,000 or from $40,000 to nearly $52,000 or from $70,000 to $100,000 and many will be trampled in the rush to vote "yes." It is therefore incomprehensible that only 14 percent of working women in the United States belong to any labor union, prompting many men to point out that women often have only themselves to blame for their low incomes.

Sylvia Hewlett was one to point out that over the past decade organized labor (the unions) has suffered massive losses in membership in the industrial sector. It thus seems obvious that unions should look at the flood of women entering the market for new life blood, as some unions did with enormous success, not only to themselves, but also to their members. The best example is the American Federation of State, County and Municipal Employers (A.F.S.C.M.E.), whose success in the courts in terms of child care leave and comparable worth has put millions into the pockets of their female members. A.F.S.C.M.E. has been successful in negotiating pay equity raises for its members in eight different states. For an individual it is enormously expensive to fight occupational discrimination. Unions are a natural vehicle. For unions, Hewlett suggests, it means stepping away from their historical identification with male workers. The figures are staring them in the face. During the period 1980–1984 some 800,000 jobs were lost in the industrial sector whereas the employment in the services sector grew by five million, of whom 60 percent were women. The success of women in breaking down occupational segregation and narrowing the wage gap so dramatically in Sweden would have been impossible without the unions, said Hewlett, and also impossible for the unions without a massive female membership. It was the same in Britain, where female membership rose by 50 percent between 1971 and 1981 so that 40 percent of women workers are now organized in unions. American men and women should look at these figures, she said, and realize that in 1984, for the first time, white males did not represent a majority of the available labor force.[40]

Women, too, suffered because of the labor unions' seeming reluctance to benefit from the upsurge of their numbers in the marketplace. But even such reluctance should not be reason for a sackcloth-and-ash attitude on the part of women. If male-led unions fail to grasp the importance of what is happening, women can do something themselves. In order to begin to realize their potential for economic power, women perhaps need to be organized both as an oppressed gender and as workers. This is not a novel thesis and has been developed in depth by many others, including Diane Balser in her provocative work *Sisterhood and Solidarity: Feminism and Labor in Modern Times* (South End Press, Boston, 1987) in which she employs case studies to illustrate previous attempts at organization. Balser's book challenges national women's organizations, particularly feminists, to consider that electing women to local and national political office in the United States cannot be the primary strength for empowering women, because political power is rooted in economic power. Women, she said, should stop complaining and get organized. In her opinion, unionization of women should be a major objective of feminist women.

Affirmative Action and Comparable Worth

Affirmative action has been blessed by the United States Supreme Court in its landmark decision of 1987: women may be hired and promoted, in preference to men, in order to redress a manifest imbalance in the marketplace.

In Chapters 5 and 16, some of the pros and cons of affirmative action have already been set out and in this section the emphasis will be on comparable worth as a recommended action to achieve equality for women.

It is interesting to note that labor unions in the United States, reversing themselves, are now fighting to maintain seniority rights over affirmative action, arguing that seniority is the worker's only protection against unfair firing. During the 1980 and 1984 presidential campaigns, the unions were counted among the most vociferous supporters of affirmative action because the policy was not favored by the (winning) Republican candidate, President Ronald Reagan. All the arguments which the unions employed at the time have now either escaped them or are returning to haunt them.

One other pattern which is emerging is that not only the unions but also the general public has become concerned about what they see as reverse discrimination against white males. In her book *Gender Politics,* Ethel Klein observed, rightly, that even supporters of affirmative action are worried that the public will perceive all minority (i.e., black) and female hirings as "inferior." In the process "the fundamental question of women's economic survival is becoming blurred or ignored in the midst of all this controversy."[41] But right now affirmative action is still seen as sound policy, not only in the United States but elsewhere. The International Labor Organization stated: "To redress the historical inequalities between men and women, preferential policies and policies of positive discrimination in favour of women are called for."[42]

A note of caution has also been sounded not to expect too much too soon from affirmative action. According to Margaret Thornton, affirmative action measures are unable to deal with the manifestations of structural discrimination. Examining wage-setting in Australia, she points out that the principle of equal pay for equal work has been accepted and passed into law. But it has had no practical effect, or very little effect, on the female occupations in the male-dominated arbitration arena. All that the laws have demonstrated is their limited capacity in affecting change where the ideology of patriarchy operates in its many ways.[43]

In her excellently written book *The Economic Emergence of Women,* economist Barbara Bergmann provided sound arguments for why affirmative action is not only the just but also the right way to fight discrimination against women. She wrote that discrimination against women in the job market has two major aspects—exclusion and low pay—and the two aspects are connected. "Women's exclusion from some jobs pushes them into a labor market separate from that of men, a fenced-off market in which supply and demand decree low rates of pay. If more rapid progress is to be made, both aspects of discrimination need to be attacked. The main attack on exclusion is through affirmative action. Under affirmative action, employers draw up and implement plans to recruit women and minority men into jobs in which their presence has been low. The main attack on low wages is through the pay equity campaign. Its goal is to get employers to raise the pay in jobs where women predominate and so to close the wage gap between women and men by direct action."[44]

Bergmann argues that it is a good thing that affirmative action be enforced by a government agency such as the Equal Opportunities Employment Commission, even though she criticizes the E.E.O.C. for not being active enough.

> Affirmative action enforced by a government agency offers a way to break the vicious circle—the firm's management is forced to institute selection procedures that get around individual managers' and workers' prejudices. Since the employer's hand is forced, the male workers can be told that the firm has no alternative but to integrate. The power of low-level employees to veto candidates on the basis of race or sex is reduced. The hostility generated by the integration is displaced from the employer to the government. The welcome that affirmative action has received from some employers probably derives from this source. The imposition of numerical goals and timetables is the only way that has been found to hold firms accountable.[45]

To the foregoing Bergmann added:

> If discrimination still is rife, then a rigorously administered affirmative action program should result in the hiring and promoting of competent female and minority candidates who would have been excluded. In this case, affirmative action promotes

> the hiring of the more competent and prevents the hiring of the less competent. The strong evidence we have that points to current widespread discrimination ... supports the view that meritocratic hiring procedures are on balance promoted by affirmative action rather than thwarted by it.[46]

Bergmann admits that affirmative action will cause some innocent white men to be treated unfairly, which is regrettable; however, the absence of affirmative action also causes injustices. "In reality we are always choosing among imperfect alternatives, and the verdict we bring in on affirmative action should not be based on the false idea that the alternative to affirmative action is a perfectly fair system in which everyone is dealt with according to merit. On the contrary, we must compare the benefits and injustices under each imperfect alternative and make a choice."[47]

If affirmative action is inefficiently applied and the wrong people are hired, Bergmann concluded, the people unjustly excluded will most likely be the competent women who should have been hired in the first place. Affirmative action goals are temporary expedients meant to remedy a highly discriminatory situation that otherwise could not be dismantled. The situation that most justifies affirmative action, she said, is where the discriminators have excluded women completely, having set their quota at zero.[48]

Comparable worth is a totally different kettle of fish compared to both affirmative action and equal pay for equal work.

To understand comparable worth, one can compare the work of kindergarten teachers in New York City with that of zoo keepers. The teachers are required to be university graduates and their parents may have spent some $36,000 to $40,000 to have them graduate, based on out-of-state tuition fees and accommodation expenses. On the other hand, to become a zoo keeper requires no education beyond, perhaps, reading and writing. Yet, the starting salary for the teachers, overwhelmingly women, is $14,500 while the keepers of the animals, overwhelmingly men, start at almost $20,000.[49]

The foregoing example is, of course, only one end of the spectrum. It is a case which, for obvious reasons, cries out to be corrected. On the other end of the spectrum, you find a male precision tool maker in a missile plant, or in a factory which produces passenger aircraft, and a woman laboratory technician producing instruments for surgeons or dentists. How does one even begin to compare the worth of each occupation for the purposes of adjusting salaries? Is the law of demand and supply in the last case not the overriding factor?

Gilda Berger states that those who consider the cost of comparable worth too high should consider that it may cost more to continue what is unfair, and probably illegal, than to correct the inequities. In the case of the Minnesota State University System, the legislature discovered that the amount of money needed to defend the unfair salaries of women on the teaching staff of the university would exceed the sum required to effect comparable salaries. So it wisely, and simply, passed a law to take care of the salaries.[50]

Ethel Klein's view is that comparable worth is not such a simple solution to sex discrimination. It is likely to cost employers billions and the business community maintains that raising salaries to comparable levels would be inflationary and, furthermore, that supply and demand, not the government through some law, should determine the wage levels.[51]

Comparable worth is seen by many women's organizations, such as N.O.W., as the number one shortcut to achieving equality in the marketplace. They may be right. Four recently published studies examined the question.

In *New Directions for Research,* Heidi Hartmann (editor) concluded that comparable worth claims and strategies for adjusting wages based on such claims need to be understood as part of the larger process of wage adjustment.[52] Obviously, Hartmann did not see comparable worth as the beginning and end to wage discrimination. This book is the result of a seminar by recognized experts on comparable worth organized by the National Research Council of the Committee on Women's Employment and Related Social Issues and was sponsored by the Ford Foundation. It is an excellent guide to the aspects of comparable worth which require research and the types of questions to be pursued.

In *Comparable Worth and Wage Discrimination* (currently the most comprehensive book on the subject), editor Helen Remick quotes the former director of the Equal Employment Opportunity Commission as saying that comparable worth is pregnant with the possibility of disrupting the entire economic system of the United States. Remick states that recent research has shown that wage discrimination is only partly explained by worker or job characteristics; the remaining differences, about half of the total, is associated with the sex of the people doing the work. "In fact, the sex of the workers performing a job is the best single predicator of the compensation for that job, surpassing in importance education, experience or unionization."[53]

Efforts to improve women's earnings by integrating women into men's jobs have met with many obstacles. This has been resisted by men. Comparable worth, Remick says, addresses the sex difference in compensation that cannot otherwise be explained and says that wages should be based upon the worth of the work and not upon the sex of the person. But comparable worth is a complex matter and, as a policy, is only in a formative stage. To understand comparable worth, one should accept the analysis of job evaluation, an intricate and technical process in which the job is finally allocated a certain number of points. "As long as job evaluation in its many forms remains the central tool for measuring salary inequities, it holds the key to demonstrating and correcting this major form of discrimination...."[54]

According to Remick, comparable worth and its implementation may not be as difficult or disrupting as some critics fear, pointing to developments in Canada where a law mandating comparable worth has already been on the statute book for a decade. Still, while job evaluation is now widely acknowledged there is no consensus yet on how to measure and correct the accompanying wage disparity.[55] The Canadian Human Rights Act of 1977 which provided for equal pay for work of equal value[56] is being carefully monitored in the United States. Unfortunately it applies only in matters of employment in the workforce that falls under the federal government, which, by 1985, was about 11 percent of the total labor force. Other workers are under provincial jurisdiction and only Quebec has enacted a similar law.

In *Comparable Worth and Wage Discrimination,* Rita Cadieux points out that though it is receiving tremendous support from women's organizations and labor unions, there is a world of difference between adopting sound legislation and putting it into effect. The Canadian Human Rights Commission was to set up the mechanism for implementing the law, and Cadieux was a member of that Commission. After consulting with a cross-section of Canadian employers and employees, experts, labor unions and women's organizations, guidelines for the implementation were approved by the Commission and issued in the *Canada Gazette* in September 1978 as Appendix II. The criteria for determining the value of the work were skill, effort, responsibility and conditions of work. Between March 1978 and November 1983, the Commission received only 60 complaints from federal employees. But while a few settlements have had some impact, "the legislation has eliminated only a small fraction of existing discrimination in pay between men and women in the rest of the workforce," said Cadieux. The problem was that enforcement could take place only through a process of complaints and few employers have volunteered to review their job evaluation and compensation systems to comply with the spirit of the act.[57]

In December 1981 the Canadian Commission approved amendments to its Equal Wages Guidelines to cover labor shortages and changes in work that cause a decrease in the value of the work. In her conclusion, Cadieux states: "I believe that the concept of equal pay for work of equal value will, in time, be included in all Canadian human rights legislation. Widespread application of the concept will not create chaos in the country's pay system, as the pessimists say. It will, however, help ensure that women receive compensation . . . that reflects the fact that they have had fewer employment options than men."[58]

A different point of view is taken by two legal experts, Robert Williams and Lorence Kessler, in a monograph prepared for and published by the National Foundation for the Study of Equal Employment in Washington.[59] According to them, comparable worth's theoretical simplicity has an emotional appeal, but that alone cannot guarantee comparable worth in practice. They question the value of job evaluation systems because these are not objective or scientific methodologies, are intended to operate in dynamic fashion, and are not designed to function totally without respect to the influences of the market or the economy. If there is no objective method of measuring worth, they say, the practicality of the comparable worth theory remains seriously flawed.

Williams and Kessler believe many of the reasons for pay differentials can be dealt with under existing laws. They question the statistics which are presented to describe the need for comparable worth. It is noted that a system that fails to recognize legitimate market-based differences in pay rates for different jobs would require the establishment of new mechanisms for evaluating job worth. They claim these mechanisms have not been defined by anyone. According to them, all experts question whether a court, a legislature or a regulatory agency can use current job evaluation techniques to improve and enforce pay equity. They suggest that job evaluation is at best a systematic way of making subjective value judgments useful to managers and administrators. In a free market system, it has traditionally been the value of the job to the purchaser of the services performed, i.e., its value to the employer, that has governed rates of pay.[60]

To support their view of comparable worth's down-side, Williams and Kessler refer to the 1981 study *Women, Work and Wages* by the National Academy of Sciences, which observed that because comparable worth involves intervention in the operation of free market forces, it has the potential of creating unintended, counterproductive consequences. Of particular concern to the experts who completed this study is that comparable worth could lead to considerable unemployment or dislocation of workers in the very group it is intended to benefit. They said that comparable worth had been tried by the Australian government with adverse effects. (The Canadian effort was not mentioned.) As to the argument that discriminatory pay practices cannot be justified on the grounds that they save employers money, experts caution that some estimate of the cost must first be made. As part of a cost-benefit analysis of comparable worth, the Williams and Kessler work contains a chapter which looks at a workable alternative, asking: "Would a strong policy to assure women equal access to higher paying jobs, combined with effective enforcement of existing equal pay laws, have the potential for narrowing the wage gap without the negative consequences attached to the comparable worth theory?"[61]

The views of Williams and Kessler also reflect the views of the senior judiciary in the United States. In 1985 a three-judge panel of the Ninth United States Circuit Court of Appeals ruled in Sacramento, California, against female workers in the state of Washington who sought equality in pay with men holding comparable jobs. The court said the disparity in pay, without proof of a discriminatory motive, first of all did not violate a federal law banning on-the-job sex bias. "It is evident," the court found, "that Congress, after explicit consideration, rejected proposals that would have prohibited lower wages for comparable work as contrasted with equal work." The court ruled that the state could not be held responsible for "an inequality which it did not create.... Neither law nor logic deems the free market a suspect enterprise."[62]

Considering all the views above, and those of others, one is inclined to believe that the implementation of comparable worth and the methods of job evaluation (to ascertain which jobs are of the same worth) still require an enormous amount of research but that a call to use existing laws and agencies, which have made no dent in pay disparities over the past decade, is bound to fail, also on the principle of practicality. Furthermore, there are obvious cases in the public service sector (of federal and state governments) where comparable worth action is almost axiomatic, as in the case of the school teachers and the zoo keepers. The worst scenario would be that the teachers would be paid the same salary as the zoo keepers. If, in the end, they receive more, the zoo keepers still would not have had their income reduced. Provided the adjustment under comparable worth is upward, for the aggrieved party, and not downward for the other party, the absence of a scientifically perfect job evaluation system may represent a flaw but certainly not a serious one and far from fatal.

31. Data: Guide to Information Sources

Sources of information are presented in the following order:

1. An overview of the availability of source material and gaps in our information about women's progress towards equality.
2. Studies, reports, and surveys which are concerned with several countries at a time, in different continents, or which present information on women in an international context.
3. Sources on women in Europe.
4. The Communist East Bloc.
5. Asia.
6. Africa.
7. Latin America.
8. The Arab-Muslim World.
9. The United States.
10. Law and scientific journals and newspapers which have been consulted in preparation of the manuscript for this book and which, regularly, contain articles about women's status and women's rights.

1. Overview. There is a wealth of recently published material (1975–1987) on the progress, or lack of progress, made during the United Nations Decade for Women and which started off with the world conference in Mexico in 1975. Several books have been published by major research institutes, detailing the status of women in 1975 and comparing their situation with the circumstances of 1985 and by individual economists, sociologists, and political scientists. There have been numerous articles on women's rights published in the press and, by more qualified observers, in scientific journals.

Many surveys and investigations have been completed by individual governments and by states, within federations and unions, by law commissions and by women's organizations.

International organizations, and the United Nations itself, have also produced a significant volume of material dealing either with discrimination against women, the status of women in several different fields such as health, education, economic development or with the progress made by member states in the elimination of discrimination during the past decade. The weakness of official reports is the fact that the United Nations has no option but to accept at face value the records filed by member states. Perhaps only a third of those reports are reasonably accurate and objective.

To the novice researcher in the United States or Europe, there is an *embarras de richesse* and material on women's rights now abounds. But of comparative analyses, particularly in the strictly legal field or in the field of Constitutional law, there are few really good studies. The literature on women's rights is also mostly one-dimensional. There are few overall studies covering statutes or covering cases, and there are no comparative analyses of voting rights or restrictive inheritance practices around the world, with the exception of population studies which cover the world's family planning and abortion laws.

There is a lack of documented information on the interrelationship between women's education and the law. There are several other fields which are almost blank. Have the international community, nations, and governments dwelled on racial discrimination to the detriment of other forms of discrimination, such as religious discrimination and discrimination against women on grounds of gender?

There is an enormous lack of research material on how the various laws passed to end discrimination against women, or to protect women, have fared in practice. There is an equal lack of documented material to prove that the various laws passed in so many countries have had any notable effect on women's status, one way or the other. Have the laws been advertised, implemented, and applied? Is there a correlation, as there surely must be, between discrimination against women and lack of knowledge of what the law provides? There are African and Asian states where the vast majority of women have never even heard of the provisions in the country's Constitution, or of statutory laws passed to help them. How much is being spent in schools, in colleges, and in the marketplace to teach women what the law provides or prohibits? How many major corporations, employing thousands of women, have documented material to show that they have fully alerted their women workers to their rights? How many government schools in the world contain a section concerning gender discrimination in their regular curriculum?

These are vast gaps in our knowledge of the women's question, not only in respect of individual states, but even more in comparative analysis between countries or on a regional basis. Generally speaking, the most important information we lack is whether or not countries are paying mere lip service to the international conventions which they have ratified and the laws which their parliaments have passed, prohibiting discrimination against women. Second to that is the lack of reliable and reasonably current statistics on women's education, occupational segregation, wage differentials, and related matters. Currently, most African and Asian statistics are 10 to 15 years old. The net result is that governments adopt resolutions and pass laws affecting women, but no verification is possible until a decade later, by which time a new government is in power which can then proceed to blame its predecessor for not carrying out its own policy.

Perhaps in recognition of the fact that too many governments are paying lip service to the elimination of discrimination against women, one of the recommendations contained in *The Decade for Women in Latin America and the Caribbean* (United Nations, Santiago, Chile, 1988) reads as follows:

> To conduct research on the legal status of women in each of the national bodies of legislation of the countries of the region, for the purpose of elaborating up-to-date diagnostic analyses and a general study in comparative law. In both cases an effort should be made to delve into the rights proclaimed, the omitted or poorly developed aspects, the level of equality attained in the different fields of law (labour, penal, agrarian, etc.) and the differences between the *de facto* and *de jure* situations. On the basis of these studies and of the existing diagnosis of international legislation and related resolutions referring to women, there should be an evaluation of the level at which international legislation and the resolutions and mandates of the United Nations are reflected in the national bodies of legislation of the countries of the region, measured in terms of ratifications, accessions, degree of orientation of actions and level of actual implementation.

There is still a lack of reliable source material which proves how women are legally discriminated against—using discrimination in its Western context and for comparative purposes.

One of the best books on the rights of women was written by Susan Ross of the Civil Rights Division of the United States Department of Justice and by Ann Barcher, an attorney in New York, but the book, *The Rights of Women,* deals exclusively with women's rights in the United States under existing United States laws. If a similar book existed on the rights of women in Pakistan then we could begin with a comparative analysis, something similar to that prepared by Margaret Rogers for the Commonwealth Secretariat in London, entitled *A Decade of Women and the Law.* (This work, published in 1985, is discussed elsewhere in this chapter.) While not entirely of the same nature *Empowerment and the Law,* edited by Margaret Schuler and published in 1986, is also the sort of book of which one would like to see more (also discussed farther on in this chapter). Another good work is *African Women and the Law,* published by Boston University in 1982.

There are several books on the market listing the resources available to individuals, schools, and colleges for the study of discrimination against women and other feminist subjects. No one should undertake any research without first consulting at least one of these guides. For example, the Feminist Press, City University, New York, has a book, *Feminist Resources for Schools and Colleges,* which contains annotated entries for 445 print and audiovisual materials—books, articles, periodicals, films, records, cassettes, and slides. Resources for Feminist Research, Toronto, Canada, publishes *International Guide to Women's Periodicals and Research.* Libraries Unlimited in Littleton, Colorado, has published Esther Stineman and Catherine Loeb's *Women Studies: A Recommended Core Bibliography.* In 1980, Gale Press, in Detroit, published *Women in America: A Guide to Information Sources,* edited by Virginia Terris and containing nearly 2,500 entries arranged in 10 categories ranging from history, image, and status to health and sexuality. In the United States facilities exist to obtain microfilm or complete copies, in soft or hard cover, of almost every Master's thesis or Doctoral dissertation completed in the past two decades on all subjects, including those pertaining to discrimination against women, women's status, and women's rights. Companies providing these services, for example, University Microfilm International in Ann Arbor, Michigan, will even do computer searches for key subjects to screen out unrequired data.

A prime secondary source of information is the United States Library of Congress where, in the main catalog, under the subject "Women," there are six printed pages, three columns each, covering 420 subjects on women from Women and Buddhism to Women's Studies. In between, there is every conceivable subject. On women's rights alone, there are sexual discrimination, legal statutes, suffrage, emancipation, women's liberation, feminism, services for women, women's studies, female studies and feminist studies.

Most of the world's major newspapers are now also so carefully indexed and readily available in major public libraries around the world that they can also be considered a major secondary source of information on women, particularly in regard to government policies, statements, events and actualities, political and ideological debates and various conferences. *The New York Times* reveals 379 subjects on women covered by reporters, contributors, editorialists and guest analysts.

Another source of information is the various women's study groups and the monthly and annual publications produced by women's study departments at various Western universities. Many new researchers have been noted and new fields are being covered. There is now also a National Women's Studies Association. In addition, there are studies, summaries, and surveys by various other organizations.

The International Women's Rights Action Watch (I.W.R.A.W.) was formed to monitor, analyze and encourage law and policy reform in accordance with the principles of the United Nations convention on the elimination of all forms of discrimination against women. I.W.R.A.W. grew out of a series of workshops on the convention held at the nongovernmental organization forum in Nairobi in 1985 during the world conference which ended the United Nation's Decade of Women. I.W.R.A.W. now serves as an international, nongovernmental clearinghouse for research and as an information center on law and policy reform aimed at improving the status of women. I.W.R.A.W. is operated jointly by the Hubert H. Humphrey Institute on Public Affairs (Women, Public Policy and Development Project) at the University of Minnesota and by the Development Law and Policy Project in the Center for Population and Family Health at Columbia University in New York. I.W.R.A.W. is a major source of data on the status of women.

The Litlaw Foundation, Los Angeles, deals with (1) labor provisions in constitutions of Europe; (2) labor provisions in Asian constitutions; and (3) labor law in Latin American constitutions. Publications are edited by David Ziskind.

The National Organization of Women's Legal Defense and Education Fund produces the *State by State Guide to Women's Legal Rights for the USA*. The book annually reviews laws on marriage, divorce, domestic violence, inheritance rights, reproductive rights, unmarried couples, equal pay, fair employment, credit, housing, insurance and public accommodation for each of the 50 states and gives the state code citation for each law.

The National Foundation for the Study of Equal Employment Policy is a tax-exempt educational organization formed in 1983 to engage in research on the development of policy and law designed to eliminate all aspects of employment discrimination, whether based on race, color, religion, sex, national origin, age, handicap, veteran status, or other classification. Its purpose is to supply objective explanations of the background, controlling factors, applicable law, and practical considerations involved in dealing with these issues. Included are analyses of the impact on workers, employers and the general public of existing laws and enforcement policies, government regulations, and private and public sector voluntary programs and assessments of their effectiveness. Both the practical and legal problems involved are considered and, where necessary, empirical data are developed. In 1984 the foundation published *A Closer Look at Comparable Worth.*

Rush Publications, Rush, New York, produces *Women's Studies Abstracts,* a quarterly journal summarizing new publications and newspaper and magazine articles on women's subjects which comes with an annual index. This publication is excellent for checking what is new in the field of women's studies, and also covers newspaper reports and other countries.

Research at government levels has shown a corresponding rise; however, exceptional care must be taken not to accept at face value the reports which governments submit to the United Nations, unless the statistics and information correspond with what has been uncovered by private researchers. This is particularly true of the reports submitted by certain African, Muslim and Asian states and, without exception, by every Communist state.

An example of the foregoing are the reports submitted to the United Nation's Committee on the Elimination of Discrimination Against Women. According to the report submitted by the representative of Mongolia, this Soviet republic is the closest thing to heaven on earth for women. Since the revolution of 1921, the report pointed out, so much has been achieved that full equality between men and women in all aspects of life is no longer an objective, or policy, but has become a fact. Mongolian women formed (officially) just one-half of those working in economic and cultural activities. In the days of the Tsar, illiteracy among women stood at 98 percent (according to the Mongolian delegate) but it has now been totally eliminated. Female students made up almost 56 percent of the student population. There was no unemployment and equal pay for equal work was "guaranteed." The delegate did not state merely that it was the law, but that it was *guaranteed* by the state. Women had total equality in marriage. Where work was prohibited for women it was purely in their own interests.

When the Mongolian report was discussed, a Western delegate noted that in the legal annexes there appears to be an overprotection of women in their maternal role while the terminology used in the report itself made women either "invisible" or "simple numerical averages." The report had no information about prostitution, participation in public life or health. The omission was understandable since the upper echelon of Mongolian politics was a desert as far as women were concerned. Another Western expert remarked that the divorce laws in Mongolia constricted rather than freed women since marriage could be dissolved only by mutual consent.

The report by Czechoslovakia was not much different but at least it had more flair in its extravagant and propagandistic claims. There was a long historical tradition for women's rights in Czechoslovakia, the report stated, dating back to the 15th century. (This historical claim was a fact which, somehow, had escaped most reputable Western historians.) The report stated that most women enjoyed full equality in every respect, in employment, wages and pensions. They, the women, formed 51.4 percent of the population and 80.9 percent were engaged in "social" work. (No definition of social work was provided.) One of the Western experts observed that, in fact, the social roles of the two sexes were still different, as well as the sexual division of labor. Another observed that, despite all the equality which they allegedly enjoyed, women were not entering technical and vocational training institutions at the same pace as men. On the question of prostitution, the Czechoslovakian delegate surprised sociologists all over the world when he observed that the Penal Code contained no provision outlawing prostitution for the simple reason that when the code was passed in 1961 the problem of prostitution did not exist. The Communist delegate stated blandly that it was only with the development of tourism (from the West) that prostitution surfaced in Czechoslovakia.

The obvious lack of candor and verifiable facts in the reports by Communist state delegates runs like a refrain through all the reports, and the explanations provided by their representatives easily stretch credulity. The Vietnamese also claimed total equality for women but although 13 out of 23 million voters were women their representation by elected representatives was extremely low. Women were also prohibited from working in several major professions and there was a difference in the retirement age between men and women.

It was not only reports such as the foregoing which have to be scrutinized and verified in almost every respect, if verification is at all possible, but the entire Data Bank on women which has been established in the United Nation's Centre for Social and Humanitarian Affairs. All of the data in the bank originate from member states. The present data cover such areas as education, demography, health, labor force and other issues. In any case, it is extraordinarily difficult for independent researchers to gain access to the data bank. The author was told that it was for use only by United Nations delegates and their staffs, to United Nations secretariat employees, or to staff members from other United Nations organizations.

2. International. *Women in the World, an International Atlas,* by Joni Seager and Ann Olson, Simon and Schuster, New York, 1986, is the best overview currently available. In 40 color maps, this atlas of 126 pages presents a full and detailed picture of the status of women worldwide. Statistics translated into visual graphics become more accessible, understandable and appealing. Each map spread focuses on a central topic, with one or two subtopics. A short text introduces and interrelates the graphics. At the end, notes for each map provide comments, background information and bibliography. Data are arranged along broad lines: marriage, motherhood, women in the labor force, resources, welfare, authority, women in politics, change and statistical politics, going into specific subthemes such as young brides, women in the media, education and illiteracy, life expectancy, military service, rape and channels of change. As the introduction to this vital reference work says, mapping the world of women reveals patterns usually obscured in statistical tables or in narratives: the similarities and differences, the continuities and contrasts.

The best general *introduction* to the study of women and women's rights is Ruth Sivard's *Women: A World Survey,* published by World Priorities, Washington, D.C., 1985, and funded by the Carnegie Corporation, the Ford Foundation and the Rockefeller Foundation. Using maps, diagrams, charts and statistical tables, Ms. Sivard has set out the status of women in terms of population growth, economic development, social change, labor, unemployment, the wage gap, job segregation, poverty, educational enrollment, literacy, curricula of school courses, teaching staffs, fields of specialization, women's health, life expectancy, factors affecting health, health care, government and laws in respect of women's suffrage, women's legal rights and women in government.

Second on the list is *Women in Economic Activity: A Global Statistical Survey: 1950–2000,* a joint publication of the International Labor Organization in Geneva and the United Nations Research and Training Institute for the Advancement of Women in New York. Published in 1986, the work profiles working women (women in economic activity) in Africa, Asia, Latin America and the Caribbean, the European Market Economy countries (mostly Western Europe), North America, Oceania, and Eastern Europe (all the Communist Bloc countries) with selected bibliographical references and statistical appendices, including one of men's and women's wages.

The third choice should be the *World Survey on the Role of Women in Development,* prepared by the United Nation's Department of International Economic and Social Affairs and published in 1986. The 238-page report gives an overview of the role of women in development, specifically economic development, the role of women in agriculture, the role of women in industrial development, in money and finance, in science and technology, in trade, and in the development, use and conservation of energy resources. It ends with a section dealing with the concept of self-reliance and the integration of women in development. A mass of statistical information is presented by way of tables. The weakness of the survey is its enormous reliance on government sources when at least those of many Third World and Communist states are known and have been proved to be suspect. Altogether, 124 countries are covered (32 developed and 92 developing) and statistics are for three benchmark years: 1960–1970–1980.

Lynne Iglitzin and Ruth Ross (editors): *Women in the World 1975–1985,* 2nd ed., ABC-Clio Inc., Santa Barbara, California, 1986. This is one of the most important source books for the study of women in the world. Considerable light is thrown on the women's movement. Is the movement in fact moving, or mired? If it is moving, how rapidly and in what direction? If mired, by whom and/or what, and what are the current options for correction? Are the advances that finally receive official sanction more honored in the breach than in the observance? And what kinds of meaningful cross-cultural comparisons in the status of women can be made? The 1976 edition of *Women in the World* assessed centuries of women's history. In this new edition, the authors focus on the 10-year period following the 1976 publication—1975–1985; hence its subtitle, *The Women's Decade.* Here, writers of both sexes provide facts, statistics, graphs, and personal observations, candidly revealing their findings and evaluations to the researcher, scholar, student, and the general public.

Margaret Rogers: *A Decade of Women and the Law,* Commonwealth Secretariat, London, 1985. This is a comprehensive study of 25 Commonwealth countries and was published in 1985 through a grant from the Hubert Humphrey Institute of Public Affairs at the University of Minnesota but published by Commonwealth Secretariat Publications, Marlborough House, London, 1985. The survey is based on materials contained in 45 issues of the Commonwealth Law Bulletin of the period 1974–1985. It is an excellent publication to analyze how laws were changed, scrapped, rewritten and otherwise employed during the same 10-year period in the quest for equal treatment for women. Numerous court cases are summarized in the report dealing with constitutional law, practice and procedures in court, criminal law, the law of evidence, family law, industrial relations, health, education and social welfare, administrative law, bankruptcy and other subjects in the 35 Commonwealth countries.

Debbie Taylor (editor): *Women: A World Report,* Oxford University Press, London, 1985. This book was written to coincide with the end of the "Decade for Women." It consists of three parts. Part I by Debbie Taylor is an excellent analysis of the status of women, worldwide, dealing with the family, women's role in agriculture and industry, women and health, sex, education and politics. The second part is a series of personal reports by women about women and can safely be skipped. Part III, entitled "The Facts," is an excellent statistical survey.

Joni Lovenduski and Jill Hills (editors): *The Politics of the Second Electorate,* Routledge & Kegan Paul, London, 1981. This is an analysis of the political role played by women in Australia, Canada, the United States, Japan, the Soviet Union, Eastern Europe, Sweden, France, Spain, West Germany, Italy and Finland. All in all, the 14 contributors map out the political behavior of women in 20 countries, such as voting, their presence in public office, among political elites and in politics outside the formal structure of government. This is an excellent cross-national coverage looking at the forces of history, current trends and future possibilities.

Robin Morgan (editor): *Sisterhood Is Global,* Anchor Books, Garden City, New York, 1984. This massive work covers almost every country in the world, analyzing, country by country, the status of women, their numbers, divorce rate, fertility rate, educational status, the various laws which affect them, their position in the governing elites, wage discrimination, occupational segregation and other subjects. The material is very concisely presented and condensed into a few pages per country, followed by one article written by a prominent expert on the role and fate of women in the country under review. Some of the articles are a little strident in their feminism; others are models of research and restrained comment. The book is the closest thing in existence to an encyclopedia on the status of women.

Margaret Schuler (editor): *Empowerment and the Law,* O.E.F. International, Washington, DC, 1986. This is one of the most important books on women's rights to be published in the past two decades because of its understanding of the power of the law. The book is written in four parts. Part I is an approach to women, law and development. Part II deals with patriarchal, class and ethnic biases in the law. Part III deals with using the law or challenging the law, while Part IV is basically a report on the Nairobi meeting of the Third World Forum on Women, Law and Development. Sixty women contributed chapters to this book about Third World women and the law. It is about how society creates and reinforces female oppression, and about women's efforts to confront that oppression. This book is about the empowerment of women who suffer the double burden of being poor and being female. It is also about women deepening their understanding of the legal, cultural, political, and economic underpinnings of their subordination. It is about women gaining the skills needed to utilize the "system" (where necessary), in order to assert rights, redress injustices, and access economic and political resources. The 55 case studies contained in this volume document the problems confronting women in 32 countries of Asia, Africa, and Latin America. The papers also document the strategies and programs women are using as they struggle to take their place as participants, contributors, and beneficiaries of development.

Margot Duley and Mary Edwards (editors): *The Cross Cultural Study of Women,* The Feminist Press, New York, 1986. An excellent introduction to the study of women's rights. The book contains two parts, one dealing with theoretical perspectives and the other with area studies. In the latter, the status of women is analyzed in India, China, Oceania, sub-Saharan Africa, Latin America and the Islamic Middle East and North Africa. This book is highly recommended to those who wish to teach women's studies at the university level.

Women of the World, United States Department of Commerce, Bureau of the Census, Washington, D.C., 1984 and 1985. A series of four works, WID1-4, prepared under a resources support service agreement with the Office of Women in Development, Bureau for Program and Policy Co-ordination, United States Agency for International Development. The four works include Asia and the Pacific, Africa, Latin America and the Middle East. Contains substantial statistical data, tables, and diagrams, plus a good bibliography. An excellent introduction to women of the various regions.

Women, Work and Ideology in the Third World, Haleh Afshar, editor, Tavistock Publications, New York, 1985. A wide-ranging analysis of female labor in Malaysia, Sudan, Iran, Bangladesh, Ghana, Tanzania, Indonesia, Brazil, Morocco, and India.

Women Workers in Fifteen Countries, Jennie Farley, editor, ILR Press, Cornell University, New York, 1985. A thorough examination of the extraordinary influx of women into the work force in 15 major countries, written by authors each representing one of the 15 countries. Though basically an examination of the conditions under which women work in different economic systems, it covers such topics as subordination at home and at work; job segregation; childcare facilities; gender-limited opportunities; inadequate representation of women in labor unions; and pay inequities. Government and business policies in each country is examined as well as the effects of protective and antidiscriminatory legislation. Most of the contributors are professors of sociology and economics at various universities, including such well known writers as Barbara Bergmann, Bianca Beccalli, Gail Lapidus, Margery Wolf, Hiroko Hayashi, Ylva Ericsson, Marion Janjic, Olivera Buric, Emma MacLennan, and others. The countries include, among others, the Soviet Union, China, Yugoslavia, Japan, Israel, Great Britain, France, Italy, West Germany, Sweden, and Switzerland and is an indispensable work for understanding women's subordinate status in disparate regions of the world.

I.N.S.T.R.A.W.: *Women in the World Economy,* Oxford University Press, New York, 1986. Edited by Susan Joekes, this book is a synthesis of eight previous monographs that analyzed women and industrial development, agriculture, trade, money, and finance, technological innovations and other issues. Several internationally renowned research institutions and United Nations organizations such as U.N.C.T.A.D. contributed data.

Sheile Lewenhak: *The Revaluation of Women's Work,* Croom Helm Publishers, Sydney, 1988. The intention of this book is to challenge narrow concepts of work, value and women's worth in industrial and nonindustrial countries alike. The thrust of the book is that the general undervaluing of women's work, that has paralleled the development of the international market economy, distorts the estimates of the national product of countries. International institutes should help to redefine the value of women's work.

Population Crisis Committee: *A World Assessment of Access to Birth Control, Population Briefing Paper No. 19,* Washington, D.C., 1987. A study of birth control in 95 countries. The eight-page document contains diagrams and tables and is accompanied by a wall map in full color. The assessment covers access to birth control education and methods of control in the developed countries, the undeveloped countries, and regional comparisons and measures of the impact of birth control. The most up-to-date study of its kind.

Population Crisis Committee: *Country Rankings of the Status of Women, Population Briefing Paper, No. 20,* Washington, D.C., 1988. An excellent 10-page overview of the status of women in 99 countries of the world, representing 2.3 billion women, or 92 percent of the female population of the world. The paper is illustrated with diagrams and is accompanied by a large wall map. The areas covered are female, infant, and child mortality; female mortality in childbearing years; the gender gap and male and female life expectancy; early marriage and childbearing; number of children and use of contraceptives; single women and women without husbands; girls in school; women as teachers; university enrollment; the gap in literacy between men and women; women in paid employment; self-employed women; professional women; women's share of the paid labor force; political and legal equality; economic equality and equality in marriage and the family. Countries are graded by a points system in respect to the following major divisions: social equality, health, marriage, education, and employment.

Sex Inequalities in Urban Employment in the Third World, edited by Richard Anker and Catherine Hein, is a study prepared for the International Labour Office and published in Geneva in 1986. This collection of country studies examines women's employment in the modern nonagricultural sector, the fastest growing sector of the economy as development proceeds. The introductory chapter describes the main explanations for the disadvantaged position of women workers (neo-classical, labor market segmentation and gender or feminist theories). Other determinants examined are the organization of work in the modern sector along the lines set in the industrialized countries; management attitudes and practices; education; cultural restrictions as women, and the household division of labor. The country case studies (Cyprus, Ghana, India, Mauritius, Nigeria, Sri Lanka and Peru) investigate the limits to women's employment in the modern sector. Blending macro and micro-level data, the case studies raise issues such as inequality in earnings between male and female workers; differences in recruitment, hiring, firing and promotion practices for men and women; the effect of family responsibilities on career development and worker productivity. Women's position in the labor market is a major determinant of their overall status in society; thus, the studies go beyond employment statistics to seek the reasons behind gender-based occupational segregation and inequalities. Despite the diversity of cultural and institutional contexts analyzed, the studies show remarkable similarities in the discrimination women face in the labor market, tracing it to the sexual division of labor within the household in Third World countries.

Women's Movements in the World 1988 is a new edition to Keesings Reference Publications and describes more than 800 women's movements in substantial detail. Published by the Longman Group, High Harlow, Essex, England.

The following United Nations publications are of importance.

United Nations: *World Population Policies,* New York, 1987. Member states of the United Nations report on population policies, including the status of women. Contains a wealth of official data provided by the various governments.

World Health Organization: *Women, Health and Development,* Geneva, 1985; International Labour Office: *Resources, Power and Women,* Geneva, 1985; International Labour Office: *Sex Inequalities in Urban Employment,* Geneva, 1986 and by the United Nations International Research and Training Institute for the Advancement of Women: *The Changing Role of Women in International Economic Relations.* Study prepared by Brigitte Stern at the request of I.N.S.T.R.A.W., pp. 56, Santo Domingo, 1985. Research Study No. 1-A; *Impact of Monetary and Financial Policies upon Women.* Study prepared by Sushila Gidwani at the request of I.N.S.T.R.A.W, pp. 52, Santo Domingo, 1985. Research Study No. 1-F; *Industrialization, Trade and Female Employment in Developing Countries: Experiences of the 1970s and After.* Study prepared by Susan P. Joekes at the request of I.N.S.T.R.A.W., pp. 65, Santo Domingo, 1986. Research Study No. 1-J; *Women in Economic Activity: A Global Statistical Survey (1950–2000)* I.L.O./I.N.S.T.R.A.W., pp. 170, Santo Domingo, 1985. Statistical Publication No. 1.

U.N.E.S.C.O.: *Institutions Engaged in Research on Women: Asia-Pacific,* Bangkok, 1987. This directory, produced by Unesco's Regional Unit for Social and Human Sciences, contains information on institutions wholly or partly engaged in research and teaching of women's studies in the Asia and Pacific region, both governmental and nongovernmental.

3. Europe. The most recent documentation to consult about women's status in Europe in general, as well as in respect of employment, education, legal rights, women in the family, divorce and separation, legal rights, women in the family, divorce and separation, child care, occupation and wage discrimination, women's actions and women in politics, is undoubtedly that produced by the Directorate-General of Information of the Commission of the European Communities in Brussels. The Women's Information Service publishes the bi-monthly *Women of Europe,* in English and eight other languages. Apart from being an excellent source of developments in individual countries, *Women of Europe* also contains feature articles on special subjects and provides details about debates and resolutions adopted by the European parliament, and of directives issued by the Council of Ministers of the E.E.C.

Based in Brussels, the Women's Information Service from time to time also publishes thoroughly researched supplements such as *Women in Spain, Women in Portugal, Women in Agriculture, Women in Statistics, Women and Voting, Women at Work, Women in Paid Employment, Community Law and Women, Women and Music, Attitudes of Men and Women in Europe, Women and Television* and action programs to create equal opportunities. Those mentioned have all been published between 1984–1988.

The best general overview is the supplement *Women of Europe* (No. 27 of June 1988) which give details of women's progress during 1978–1988 in the 12 European countries which make up the community. This 60-page supplement should be read in conjunction with *Community Law and Women* (Supplement No. 25 of 1986) which sets out what conventions and directives the various European Community institutions have passed in respect of women. The 158 page study also provides details on how the various countries have set about the implementation of the laws and directives, the community's various action programs and the role of the European Court of Justice, complete with relevant case studies and judgments of the court.

Details of women's studies in Europe, complete with the names and addresses of research institutes, centers, councils, the names of faculties and universities and of various publications are contained in supplement No. 18 of 1984 entitled *Women's Studies.*

The European Commissions Automated Central Documentation Department in Brussels has devoted an entire issue of its 1988 Bibliographies Review to women's affairs. It contains more than 200 pages of orderly bibliographical references on European Community legislation, publications edited by the European Commission, and articles and documents on women's affairs published in the 12 different member states of the E.C.

Two works which are extremely useful for getting started on research in Europe, both Eastern and Western Europe, are *The Politics of the Second*

Electorate, edited by Joni Lovenduski and Jill Hills and that of Gisbert Flanz. (Below.)

While *The Politics of the Second Electorate* is really a study of the political role of women, in which the authors mapped out the political behavior of women in 20 industrially developed countries, mostly Western Europe, each essay contains a mass of detail on women's status in general in terms of work, wages, education, socio-economic environment and historical background.

Gisbert Flanz: *Comparative Women's Rights and Political Participation in Europe,* Transitional Publishers, Dobbs Ferry, New York, 1983. Contains valuable information on women in Europe and also provides the reader with the opportunity to compare trends in individual countries.

Another important source of information on Europe is a special report, *The Economic Role of Women in the ECE Region,* published by the United Nations for the Economic Commission for Europe. The 94-page report covers developments during the period 1975 to 1985 and has an extremely comprehensive list of tables, totaling 72 with seven diagrams. It was the most detailed and up-to-date study of its kind in existence available in 1987.

The best country-by-country survey of the changing political and economic history of women in Europe is Joni Lovenduski's *Women and European Politics,* published by the University of Massachusetts Press in 1986. This thoroughly researched work is a truly comprehensive survey of the changing position of European women and is an outstanding contribution not only to women's studies but also to comparative politics.

Two other books which are important are concerned with the Nordic countries and Britain.

The Unfinished Democracy—Women in Nordic Politics, Elina Haavio-Mannila, editor, Pergammon Press, Oxford, 1985, is probably the best comparative study of women's participation in politics and government in the five Nordic countries. The book, written by various contributors, examines the functions of women's organizations, women's participation in politics, both at the parliamentary and the local level, representation in business, and the policy of public equality.

Lynne Segal: *Is the Future Female?,* Virago Press, London, 1987, is a thorough and well-researched analysis of the importance and centrality of socialist feminism in the construction of the future. The book is a critical history of the present wave of feminism but primarily reflects the author's experience with the Women's Liberation Movement in England. Segal describes the demise of socialist feminism, which she sees as a reflection of the fragmentation of the women's movement generally. The decline of the movement is laid at the door of the radical, revolutionary feminists whom she accuses of having become addicted to an ideology close to biological determinism.

4. The Communist East Bloc. The most difficult area on which to obtain reliable resource material is the East Bloc Communist countries, including the Soviet Union. The Communist countries have not been reluctant to deposit reports on the status of women with the United Nations agencies, such as the I.L.O., but because it is so difficult for Westerners to verify the statistics, most of the material remains suspect.

There is also a lack of up-to-date works on women in the Soviet Union. Gail Lapidus has produced some excellent works on the Soviet Union of which her book *Women in Soviet Society,* published by the University of California Press in 1978, is the best general introduction to the study of women in the Soviet Union. A more recent work and also an excellent source is that of A. McCauley: *Women's Work and Wages in the Soviet Union,* published by George Allen & Unwin, London, in 1981. He mentions that in a catalogue of doctoral dissertations in the United States on feminism and women's studies only 2 out of 680 were concerned with the position of women in the Soviet Union and Eastern Europe. McCauley's work is a rigorous analysis of the economic role of women in the Soviet Union and evaluates those social and economic policies pursued by the Soviet government to reduce if not eliminate sexual inequalities in the labor market. He also provides the first detailed analysis of the nature and extent of occupational segregation. The second half of the book explores the factors that contribute to the maintenance of this state of affairs—differential socialization and education, protective legislation and the difficulties faced by women in combining their domestic roles with paid employment. McCauley presents a wealth of up-to-date empirical material on all of these topics, examines the way in which policy has evolved over the past 40 years or so, and explores the reasons why the Soviet Union has so far failed to achieve its stated policy goal of eliminating sexual inequality entirely. McCauley deals not only with the urban labor force, but also examines the position of women in agriculture and analyzes occupational structures for the Soviet Union as a whole and on a regional basis. In addition, he provides the first truly comprehensive account of the development of protective legislation and social security provisions for women from the revolution to the present day.

Women in Soviet Society is an enormous contribution to the field of Soviet studies and on women and society. It is meticulously researched and a trenchant analysis of the impact of Soviet economic development on the status of women since the Communists took over. It is probably the most valuable work of the past three decades on women in the Soviet Union.

Another recent and important book is David Willis: *Klass,* St. Martin's Press, New York, 1985. Willis was the bureau chief of the *Christian Science Monitor* in Moscow for more than four years and this book is an excellent presentation of his observations over the years, including a section on women with some very revealing information. The Soviet Union, according to Willis, is really a very class-conscious nation, despite the egalitarian ideology of the Communist Party, and the majority of women, compared to men, remain the statusless sex.

Soviet Sisterhood, Barbara Holland, editor, Indiana University Press, 1985, is a wide-ranging analysis of the status of women in the Soviet Union, written by eight leading experts. Official Soviet interpretation of the women's question is analyzed as are Soviet views of sex differences, Soviet women's magazines, women workers and the demographic crisis, maternity care, Soviet rural women, Soviet politics and women, and Soviet feminists. It is an indispensable work for anyone trying to establish the state of women's affairs in the Soviet Union. Genia Browning and Mary Buckley, respectively, are responsible for excellent contributions on the real scope of the women's question and women's lack of real participation in Soviet politics.

Women and Russia, Tantyana Mamonova, editor, Beacon Press, Boston, 1984, is a timely work in which Russian women speak for themselves. The contents are comprised of an expose of the patriarchal structure in the family, in marriage, in society, and in the higher echelons of Soviet politics.

As far as other books on Eastern Europe are concerned, Sharon Wolchik's dissertation *Politics, Ideology and Equality: The Status of Women in Eastern Europe,* University of Michigan, 1978, is a first class work, as is Barbara Jancar's *Women Under Communism,* Johns Hopkins Press, Baltimore, 1978. Another good work is that of Alena Heitlinger, *Women and State Socialism: Sex Inequality in the Soviet Union and Czechoslovakia,* McGill-Queens University Press, Montreal, Canada, 1979. Other sources are the yearbooks on international Communist affairs produced by the Hoover Institute of the University of Stanford.

The journal *Comparative Politics* contains very useful articles and the U.S. State Department also publishes area handbooks on various Communist countries. Radio Free Europe produces various situation reports worth examining. Finally, from time to time, the *Slavic Review* has published first class essays on Eastern European women—for example, Sharon Wolchik's piece "The Status of Women in a Socialist Order: The Case of Czechoslovakia," Vol. 38, No. 4, pages 583–602.

Sources on women in the Soviet Union, apart from those already mentioned above (Lapidus, Wolchik, McCauley and others) include *Women in Russia,* edited by Atkinson, Dallin and Lapidus and published by Harvester Press, Hassocks, England, in 1978. This contains a whole number of excellently written chapters on various aspects of women's status in the Soviet Union. Other sources to watch are various articles in *Comparative Politics* and also S. White's book *Political Culture and Soviet Politics,* published by MacMillans in England in 1979.

5. Asia. An important reference work on women's studies in Asia, notably India, Pakistan, Bangladesh, Nepal and Sri Lanka is *South Asian Women at Home and Abroad: A Guide to Resources,* edited by Jyotsna Vaid, Barbara D. Miller and Janice Hyde and published in 1984 by the University of Michigan at Ann Arbor under the auspices of the Committee on Women in Asian Studies of the Association for Asian Studies. Not only does this volume contain a bibliography of recent books, articles and working papers on women but also a list of films, periodicals and organizations.

United Nations: *Women's Economic Participation in Asia and the Pacific,* Economic Commission for Asia and the Pacific, Bangkok, 1987. The volume contains 11 studies of the role of women in the economies of Bangladesh, China, India, Indonesia, Pakistan, Malaysia, the Philippines and Thailand, Hong Kong, Korea and Singapore, and Japan and New Zealand. All the studies focus on two measures of women's economic status: their role of participation in the modern sector of the economy and their earnings as compared to those of men. It is an indispensable work if one is to understand to what extent women's work is of a lower status than men's and why women are clustered in low-paying jobs and have lower levels of education.

Also of interest for those studying the status of women in Asia is the newsletter of the Asian Women's Research and Action Network (A.W.R.A.N.) at the Kahayug Foundation, Davao City, Philippines. The University of Philippines Law Center and the Asia Foundation has also published several papers and books, notably *Women and the Law,* 1983, edited by Flerida Romero. In Bangladesh the Institute of Law and International Affairs in Dacca published *Women and Development: Perspectives from South and Southeast Asia* in 1979, edited by Rounaq Jahan and Hanna Papanek.

An indispensable source for research on women in Asia is *Women of South Asia: A Guide to Resources* by Carol Sakala, Kraus International Publications, New York, 1980, an annotated bibliography which contains nearly 5,000 entries. Equally indispensable is the reference work *South Asian Women at Home and Abroad: A Guide to Resources.* Prepared by Jyotsna Vaid and Barbara Miller and published by the Association of Asian Students in London, 1984, the work includes demographic, educational, employment, fertility and legal data as well as a bibliography of recent publications, a directory of periodicals and newspaper articles on women's issues in South Asia, a directory of South Asian women's groups at home and abroad, a research directory and a listing of relevant documentary and feature films.

One of the best overall study guides and reviews of historical and current issues on women's rights in India is contained in *The Cross Cultural Study of Women.* Written by Margot Duley (who edited the book together with Mary Edwards), pages 127 to 236 are a veritable gold mine of information.

An indispensable point of contact on research is the *Women's International Network News,* Grant Street, Lexington, Massachusetts. *WIN News* abstracts news reports and government documents worldwide. Another is *Women's Studies International Forum.* In addition, *The International Journal of the Sociology of Law* also publishes articles of importance such as the one on legal reform in Democratic *(sic)* Yemen in Vol. 13, No. 2, May 1985, pages 147–172.

Because the Chinese constitute one quarter of humankind, the study of women's status and discrimination against women in China is a formidable objective. An extremely helpful bibliographical tool was recently published by Greenwood Press (1984) in Westport, Connecticut. Written by Kasren T. Wei, the book *Women in China: A Selected and Annotated Bibliography,* contains 1,100 annotated entries arranged under 14 topic headings: bibliographies, biography, autobiography and memoirs; economics and employment; education; family planning; fertility and health; female roles, social customs and status; feminism and the women's movement; general works and history; legal status and laws; literature and the arts; marriage and the family; philosophy and religion; politics and government and special features of journals.

An excellent book which examines the policies and changes affecting rural women under Communist leadership is Kay Johnson's *Women, the Family and Peasant Revolution in China,* University of Chicago Press, 1983. Johnson focuses on reform of marriage and the family; kinship practices; women's place in society in rural society and the dogma of socialism. The book contains excellent historical material and has both anthropological, sociological, and political value. Johnson's key finding is that though the Chinese Communist Party has always favored women's rights and family reform as part of the revolution to destroy a feudal past, it has rarely pushed for such reforms; furthermore, its centrally planned economic objectives for economic and military purposes have often reinforced the traditional role of women.

Ester Yao: *Chinese Women, Past and Present,* Ide House, Mesquite, Texas, 1983. Dr. Yao is an expert on China, and this work, supported by original documents newly translated, is a major study of the history of China, focusing on women. The chapters cover every major period in Chinese history, from women before 208 B.C. to the new China after Mao Tse-tung. The analysis covers Chinese women in individual and collective setting. Their education, arts, business, work, industry, marriage, and political life. The book also contains a comparative analysis of women on mainland China and Chinese women in Taiwan. In the section about the contemporary period, there are chapters on political change and the legal status on women; on education, industrialization, and the female labor force; on women's role in society; and on the family role of women and the comparison with women in Taiwan. It is an excellent work, well researched and indispensable in the study of women under Communism in China.

Elisabeth Croll: *Chinese Women Since Mao,* Sharpe Inc., New York, 1983. The book is an excellently researched, wide-ranging work on women in China, covering their social status, marriage, family planning, sexual division in the labor force, wage segregation, education, and political participation. The various chapters cover the first 30 years of Communist government; the new era after Mao; peasant women; urban working women; domestic labor and child care; marriage and divorce; the one-child family; images of women; the politics of the women's movement in China; and, finally, women and socialist modernization. Elisabeth Croll is an expert on China and her reflections on the implications of women's involvement in new political developments in China reveal her solid grasp of current politics.

Margery Wolf: *Revolution Postponed, Women in Contemporary China,* Stanford University Press, California, 1985, has made a close examination of women's status in the political, social, educational, and economic field in China. Based on field research and wide-ranging interviews with Chinese women, the book specifically addresses the gap between government promises and ideology and women's real status, as well as the consequences of the new economic policy of the 1980s. To date, Wolf concludes, nothing approximating equality has been achieved in working conditions, in pay, in educational opportunities, and in upper-level politics.

For another excellent overview of the status of women in China also see Duley and Edwards: *The Cross Cultural Study of Women,* pages 237–270 and Phyllis Andors: *The Unfinished Liberation of Chinese Women, 1949–1980,* Indiana University Press, Bloomington, Indiana, 1983. A careful and well-researched study of the changing status of women, first during the early years of Mao Tse-tung, during the cultural revolution, and finally in the post Mao Tse-tung era.

Japanese women are put under the microscope in Takie S. Lebra's *Japanese Women,* University of Hawaii Press, 1984. An excellent in-depth view, based on field study and observation over a five-year period, as well as on wide-ranging interviews with Japanese women. The book reveals the persistence of opposition to women's liberation. Lebra carefully analyzes the mutually opposing views in Japan and in the West about women's true place in society.

Dorothy Robins-Mowry: *The Hidden Sun, Women of Modern Japan,* Westview Press, Boulder, Colorado, 1983, has written an excellent book analyzing perceptions of equality between men and women in Japanese society; social patterns, such as life styles and leisure patterns; women in economics and women as consumers; the political process and women's role in local and national representative politics; and Japanese women's attitudes towards the rest of the world. Her book is an essential source for understanding women's position in modern Japan.

Jane Condon: *Japanese Women in the 80's,* Dodd Mead & Co., New York, 1985. Currently the best and most up-to-date book on the status of women in Japan. Covers all aspects relative to women's status in the home, education, training, vocation, occupational segregation, wage discrimination, roles in politics and administration, laws pertaining to women, divorce and customs. Well researched and documented.

Susan Pharr: *Political Women in Japan,* University of California Press, 1981. This book describes the enormous difficulties women face in Japan to break out of their stereotype and to become more active in politics.

Alice Cook and Hiroko Hayashi: *Working Women in Japan,* Cornell University Press, New York, 1980. Although this book is only 125 pages, it is an excellent analysis of the status, disadvantages and future of working women in Japan.

6. Africa. In studying the women of Africa (south of the Sahara) there are three important journals to consult: *African Studies Review, The Journal of Southern African Studies* and *The Journal of Modern African Studies.* In *The Journal of Southern African Studies* of October 1983 there is a special issue dealing with African women. Deborah Gaitskell's introduction is particularly interesting. The issue reviews major themes in previous studies and introduces six new themes, namely: female immigrants from Britain, subordination of Tswana women, women and the pass laws in South Africa (the pass laws were effectively abolished in 1987), negative effects of agricultural changes, matrilineal supports for women and major issues in recent research.

Almost every major industrial country has at least one important journal dealing with developments in Africa. The *Canadian Journal of African Studies* is a good example.

There are also some outstanding law journals which often contain information and discussion of laws affecting women. The best to come out of Africa is undoubtedly *The Comparative and International Law Journal on Southern Africa,* published quarterly by the Institute of Foreign and Comparative Law of the University of South Africa in Pretoria. Others include Christopher Adei: *African Law South of the Sahara,* International Institute for Advanced Studies, Missouri, 1981, and J.F. O'Barr: *Perspectives on Power: Women in Africa, Asia and Latin America,* Duke University Center for International Studies, Durham, North Carolina, 1982.

Overall, the best plan to keep up-to-date on studies of African women being published or reviewed in various journals is to consult such aids as the *Social Sciences Citation Index* and to subscribe to *Signs: Journal of Women in Culture and Science,* published by the University of Chicago Press. For example in *Signs,* Vol. 8, No. 1 (Autumn 1982) there was an article by Margaret Strobel, "African Women," which is an excellent update (at that time) on current issues and published literature on a wide variety of subjects concerning women, including marriage and legal relationships, female political roles and activity and women's positions in ritual, religion and secular ideology.

Given the extremely important problem of the population explosion in Africa, the World Bank's policy study *Population Growth and Policies in Sub-Saharan Africa* (1985) is a must for anyone investigating the current and future status of women in Africa. The 102-page report contains numerous diagrams, tables and graphs and has an excellent bibliography.

Many American, Canadian and British universities have African studies programs. It is impossible to select only one because there are so many good schools today. Other universities include African studies in their international research programs, for example, Duke University Center for International Studies puts out occasional papers dealing with women in Africa. Paper Number 13 of 1982 is a good example as it contains Karen Sack's excellent article, "An Overview of Women and Power in Africa," in *Perspectives on Power: Women in Africa, Asia and Latin America,* edited by Jean F. O'Barr. Boston University's African Studies Center has published various valuable papers, for example, *African Women and the Law: Historical Perspectives,* edited by Margaret Hay and Marcia Wright, Boston University, 1982, No. 7.

Probably the most comprehensive study on modern African women is *African Women South of the Sahara,* edited by Margaret Hay and Sharon Stichter and published in 1984 by Longmans in New York. The book deals with women's changing roles in Africa; changes in rural and economic life; family relationships; religion and ideology, literature, the arts, politics, so-called national liberation movements; and women and economic development. The book covers all of Southern Africa including the Republic of South Africa.

Among several other books worth looking at is *Female and Male in West Africa,* edited by Christine Oppong and published by Allen and Unwin, London, 1983. The work contains three valuable statistical chapters comparing female and male life cycles, work experiences and migration. There are 22 case studies including one on female disadvantages in access to opportunities and resources. Another book is *African History and Culture,* published by Longmans in London, 1982, and edited by Richard Olaniyan.

Particularly useful is *Women of the World: Sub Saharan Africa,* written by Jeanne Newman for the Bureau of Census, United States Department of Commerce in 1984. The study presents demographic and economic data, details about literacy, education, economic activity, marital status, fertility and mortality, and includes an excellent bibliography and discussions on the value of census data available regarding women. Also of importance is *Comparative Perspectives of Third World Women; The Impact of Race, Sex and Class,* Praeger Publishers, New York, 1980, edited by Beverly Lindsy.

In view of the enormous importance of education in Africa it is worth looking at Lois Adams' chapter in the Lindsy book (pages 55–77) entitled "Women in Zaire: Disparate Status and Roles." Another good book on women's education in Africa is *Women's Education in the Third World* published by the State University of New York, Albany, 1982, and edited by Gail Kelly and Carolyn Elliot. Although somewhat dated, Barbara Roger's book *The Domestication of Women: Discrimination in Developing Societies,* published by St. Martin's Press, New York, in 1979, is still worth looking at. Finally, *Women in Developing Countries: A Policy Focus* edited by Kathleen Staudt and Jane Jacquette, published by Haworth Press in New York, 1983, contains important sections on the gap between policy and practice. "Efforts Towards Women's Development in Tanzania: Gender Rhetoric versus Gender Realities," by Susan Rogers is a good example.

Other works which need to be consulted are listed in the notes for Chapter 6 at the end of this book.

7. Latin America. In the absence of studies (in English) by private organizations and individuals on the status of women in Latin America, the two most important sources are both government or official. The United Nations' *The Decade for Women in Latin America and the Caribbean,* published in Santiago, Chile, in 1988 is certainly indispensable although the statistics contained therein are not much more recent than those for Africa or other Third World countries in Asia. In 1984, the Agency for International Development of the United States Department of Commerce published its study of *Women in the World: Latin America.* This is an excellent overview containing statistics and easy to read diagrams and tables.

June Nash and Helen Safa, editors: *Women and Change in Latin America,* Bergin Publishers, New York, 1988, has provided a detailed presentation of women's powerlessness in Latin America and the oppression which they suffer. All of the major issues facing feminist research is well covered by several contributors and the book is an excellent gauge of women's adaptation to economic, political, and social transformations in various Latin American countries.

For Latin American studies it also should be noted that several works mentioned under the section dealing with women's studies in general, and Africa and Asia, are also relevant for Latin America—for example, *Comparative Perspectives of Third World Women; Perspective on Power: Women in Asia, Africa and Latin America; Women in Developing Countries: A Policy Focus; Women's Education in the Third World,* and *Women in Developing Countries.* All have been discussed in this chapter.

As in the case of African and Asian studies there are several well established research centers and journals such as *The Journal of Inter American Studies and World Affairs; Hispanic American Historical Review; The Journal of Social History; Report on the Americas; Latin American Perspectives; Latin American Research Review; Comparative Studies in Society and History;* and *The International Journal of Women's Studies.*

One work of particular importance and one which is a very useful introduction to the area is *Sex and Class in Latin America,* edited by June Nash and Helen Safa and published in 1980 by J.F. Bergin in Brooklyn, New York; also *Women in Latin America: An Anthology from Latin American Perspectives,* published by the journal *Latin American Perspectives,* Riverside, California, in 1979.

For those who can read Spanish, there is a 408-page work published in Montevideo by the U.N.'s Economic Commission for Latin America and the Caribbean in 1985 containing the papers read at the 1984 conference in Santiago, Chile, entitled: *Thinking about Young Women.* The work is a valuable tool to understand the situation of young women in Latin America and the struggles which they face. Also consult the books and studies listed in the notes for Chapter 19 at the end of this book.

8. The Arab-Muslim World. There is considerable literature available in English on the status of women in the Islamic region and on Islamic women's formal rights and relationships. In Ayad Al-Quzzaz's annotated bibliography: *Women in the Middle East and North Africa,* published by the University of Texas Press in 1978, there are over 200 English language titles, indexed by country and topic. In Michelle Raccagni's bibliography, *The Modern Arab Woman,* published by Scarecrow Press, New Jersey, in 1978, there are over 3,000 entries including books, articles, and dissertations in Western languages, mostly French and English, as well as Arabic. The United States Agency for International Development also published a bibliography on women in the Near East in 1977, prepared by Roxann Van Dusen and, in 1984, an excellent overview of women in the Middle East as part of its series *Women in the World.*

As a general background source on women in the Arab world, *Women and World Development: An Annotated Bibliography* published by the Overseas Development Council in Washington in 1976 and edited by May Ahdab-Yehia and Mary Rihani is particularly valuable. The literature on particular measures of women and development (education, work, political participation, health and fertility) can easily be traced in these bibliographies. In addition the best, most useful general overview is provided by *Women in the Muslim World,* Harvard University Press, 1978, and edited by Lois Beck and Nikki Keddie. This work contains 33 original essays on women in the Muslim world. Another important work dealing with an equally important region is that by Elizabeth Sanasarian: *The Women's Rights Movement in Iran: Mutiny, Appeasement and Repression from 1900 to Khomeini,* Praeger Publishers, New York, 1982.

There are scores of publications by various institutes and universities and other learned societies on women in the Arab-Muslim world. One which has been doing some interesting work is The Institute for Women's Studies in the Arab World at Beirut University College. The Institute publishes *Al-Raida,* a journal about women in Arab societies, and various papers and books, for example, Nasr J. Abu and N. Khoury (eds.) *Women, Employment and Development in the Arab World,* Mouton Publishers, Berlin, 1985. Another very useful source is *The International Journal of Middle East Studies.*

To understand the spirit of Islam and the role played by the prophet Mohammed in establishing that spirit, one could turn to Reuben Levy's work *The Social Structure of Islam,* published by Cambridge University Press in England in 1965, and Muhammad Abdul-Rauf's study *The Islamic View of Women and the Family,* Speler Publications, New York, 1977. For information on Islamic legal reform there is John Esposito's *Women in Muslim Family Law,* published by Syracuse University Press, New York, 1982. An excellent study on the suffering brought to women by the Arab Muslim practice of female circumcision is Kathleen Barry's *Female Sexual Slavery,* Prentice Hall, Englewood Cliffs, New Jersey, 1979, and Lillian Sanderson's book: *Against the Mutilation of Women,* Ithaca Press, London, 1981. Most other works are listed in the notes for Chapter 21 at the end of this book.

9. The United States. It would be an impossible task, within the confines of this chapter, to discuss even a reasonable number of the many works published in the United States from 1979 to 1989 on the women's question. The works which are mentioned below are included primarily because they are the latest published. The work of such prominent scholars as Lenore Weitzman *(The Divorce Revolution),* Barbara Bergmann's *The Economic Emergence of Women,* and Sylvia Hewlett's *A Lesser Life,* to name only three important and valuable studies, were all discussed in great detail in the chapter concerning the United States. Others were mentioned in the overview section of this chapter. The reader is also referred to the studies listed in the notes for Chapter 16 at the end of this book.

The American Woman 1988–1989, edited by Sara Rix for the Women's Research and Education Institute, W.W. Norton & Co., New York, 1988. The second annual report on the status of women in the United States, prepared by the research arm of the bi-partisan Congressional Caucus for Women's Issues, this work is one of the most authoritative sources on the social, political, and economic characteristics of United States women. The book contains numerous tables and diagrams, and it examines such topics as women in the economy, women in the political process, women and the family, black women, women in nursing, the arts, military, media, sports, and science. Statistics focus on education, income, health, fertility, age, distribution, employment, marital status, and other subjects. It is undoubtedly the first book to read to obtain an overall view of women's status in the United States.

Women's Changing Role, Information Aids Inc., Wylie, Texas, 1988. Though only 98 pages, this information series issue is packed with up-to-date information about women in the United States, and includes extremely useful tables and diagrams. It covers women in the labor force, occupational segregation, money, poverty and the wage gap between men and women, women and education, office holding, voting and politics, women and their children, child care, and displaced women and single parents. Though concisely written but far from as extensive, it is at least as authoritative, as *The American Woman 1988–1989* insofar as its sources are concerned.

Leslie Goldstein: *The Constitutional Rights of Women,* University of Wisconsin Press, 1988. Goldstein examines ways in which the United States Supreme Court initiates and responds to social change, in this case the rights of women. The book covers all major Supreme Court decisions, on a case-by-case basis, that affected gender equality and reproductive rights. The case studies include excerpts from dissents and concurrences as well as majority opinions. The book also contains an introduction to the judicial process and a careful historical treatment of women's constitutional rights. Five major areas are covered: the historical aspects; the equal protection clause and gender discrimination from 1868–1975; gender and the court's more rigid scrutiny of fathers' rights, marriage, women in the military, and rape; women, procreation and the right of privacy; and, lastly, Congressional enforcement of equal protection. Altogether, 37 individual issues are covered from sterilization and abortion to pensions, education, and affirmative action.

N.O.W. Legal Defense and Education Fund: *The State-by-State Guide to Women's Legal Rights,* Renee Cherow-O'Leary, editor, New York, 1987. Part one of the book gives an overview of women's legal rights, including the legal process; home and the family; education; employment and women in the community, i.e., women and the criminal justice system; rape; women in the military; economic equality; housing; and women and political action. Part two is a state-by-state guide. There is an annexure on divorce and on child custody.

Mary Ann Mason: *The Equality Trap,* Simon & Schuster, New York, 1988. A well-reasoned, carefully researched, and comprehensive analysis of why the feminist drive for total legal equality with men in the United States has actually made things worse for women, this original analysis draws on both legal and social history and contains details about the status of women in respect to marriage and divorce, employment, wage discrimination, occupational segregation, the disintegration of the family, women's dual burden as mothers and workers, child care, public and government attitudes, and the ideology, objectives, victories, and mistakes made by the feminist movement.

Lynne Segal: *Is the Future Female?,* Peter Bedrick Books, New York, 1987. Segal challenges many current feminist orthodoxies on a wide range of issues from war and peace to sexuality and pornography. She is opposed to the exponents of "apocalyptic feminism," which says that men hold power through greed and violence and that only women, because of their essentially greater humanity, can save the world from social, ecological, and nuclear disaster. Instead, she argues that women must build on the changes which have occurred and improved women's lives and, combining autonomy with alliances, try to alter power relations and forge a new future for women and men.

Gisele Thibault: *The Dissenting Feminist Academy,* American University Studies, New York, 1987. The book deals exhaustively with universities and their response to an interaction with feminism. It contains a detailed description of how the universities have erected barriers to both feminist philosophy and to women. Thibault examines how the university, politically, economically, and socially, implements women's subordination through its institutional polity and its academic disciplines. The book is basically a historical analysis of the profound contradictory relationship of feminist scholarship to the university in the United States.

Angela Simeone: *Academic Women, Working Towards Equality,* New York, 1987. This book explores women's current status and gains over the past 20 years and the impact of institutional sexism on women's careers. Simeone indicates how much remains to be done to bring about women's equality with men, despite affirmative action laws and, what she terms, the presumed progressiveness of U.S. colleges and universities. It is an update of women's progress, and lack of it, in higher education in the United States up to the mid-1980s.

Gilda Berger: *Women, Work and Wages,* Franklin Watts Publishers, New York, 1986. Berger's work is an excellent introduction to the status of working women in the United States including a discussion of key legislation.

Barbara Bergmann's *The Economic Emergence of Women,* Basic Books Inc., New York, 1986, is probably the best and the first complete assessment of women's massive entry into the workplace, the economic revolution which Bergmann describes as "the break-up of the ancient sex-role caste system." The book deals with the economic impetus behind the revolution, the social factors, sex segregation in the marketplace, women's wages, affirmative action, poverty and single parents, the economics and politics of family care and several other important subjects.

Sylvia Hewlett: *A Lesser Life: The Myth of Women's Liberation in America,* Warner Books, New York, 1986. Hewlett's *A Lesser Life,* severely criticized by the women's movement led by the National Organization of Women and other more militant feminists, is widely hailed and applauded as the best analysis of the true status of women in the United States in the aftermath of the "Decade of Women." The book deals, *inter alia,* with the economic fall-out of the divorce arrangements which the women's movement had fought for, with the wage gap, the neglect of American children, the advantage of social benefits to working mothers with small children as opposed to equal (legal) rights only, women's liberation and the betrayal of motherhood, the male rebellion, contemporary women, the unions and the American administration's approach to the problems of women's double burden as mother and as worker.

10. Law and Scientific Journals and Newspapers and News Magazines. See the *Bibliography* for government journals, reports, yearbooks and newspapers.

32. Research Proposals

Research on the status of women by the public sector is currently at much higher levels than 10 years ago, particularly in the economic sphere, perhaps because governments have finally realized that it is to their own advantage to have as much information as possible readily available. As the International Labor Organization has pointed out:

> Lack of knowledge with respect to women's actual, as well as potential, participation in the labour force will always have a detrimental effect, not only on women themselves, but on national development processes in general. Awareness of the real extent which women's activity has reached, of the importance of women's income for family welfare and of the contribution of women for family development is essential to the formulation of adequate policy measures and the adjustment of strategies in such a way as to benefit both women and men in the area of employment and, in turn, to enhance the development process as a whole. (I.L.O. and U.N. Research and Training Institute for the Advancement of Women: *Women in Economic Activity 1950–2000,* Geneva, 1985, p. 5.)

In future research the perspective should be that women have legitimate aspirations which have not yet been met.

There is an absence of unanimity as to what the real aspirations of women are. Questions to be answered deal with practicalities, for example: Are there enough jobs to go around? Are there sufficient resources to give women what they seek? Does women's equality require a sacrifice for men? What has been the result of legislation aimed at helping women in cities, states and countries?

Any research which has law as its fulcrum should first examine the role of the legal process, what the constitution provides, the general nature of legislation and court decisions, limitations on the legal process and, finally, administrative enforcement policies. This should then be followed by an examination of what the law has and has not done in respect of biological problems, cultural obstacles, educational obstacles, poverty, wage differentials, unequal pensions, marital rights and religious obstacles as with Islam and Catholicism.

Research which examines *the demand for equality* should cover participation in decision making with men, voting, representation, political party representation, civil service, political leadership positions, and women in corporations. In the job market one should look at work opportunities, equal pay and wage gaps, unfair dismissal, public and private pensions, sexual harassment, police and military and private executive opportunities and, finally, property and business, title to property, contract rights and credit and inheritance.

The subject of *conflict with men* can be dealt with under two main headings: marriage, and separation and divorce. Under marriage the following need to be included: marital choice, marital property, control over children, shared responsibilities, domestic violence (wife abuse) and family planning. Under the second subject, there is the availability of alimony and child support.

What is also required is research on *women as women*. There are five main points to be dealt with: (i) dignity as individuals, including slavery, prostitution and forced marriage; (ii) health, special health care, protective legislation, maternity leave and sexual mutilation; (iii) reproductive choices, family planning and abortion; (iv) helpless women, elderly, handicapped and the poor; and (v) the mother role—control over children, day care, adoptions.

One overall study could be *the inter-relationship between education and the law* and what educated women can accomplish not only in law but also in extra-legal efforts. Concerning education there needs to be research on access to education, equal treatment, training for professions and technical education. Perhaps there should be a quest for minimum standards of education for all women. For more than 30 years there have been minimum standards agreed to by the United Nations and by member states for the treatment of criminals. Many states have made a real effort to comply with those standards. Why should it be any more difficult to set minimum rules for the treatment of innocent, law abiding, tax-paying and voting women? (U.N.: *First United Nations Congress on the Prevention of Crime and the Treatment of Offenders,* A/Conf./6/1, New York, 1956.)

The following is a proposed outline for major research at doctoral levels, for either individual or group effort, based on those subjects which most affect women in their daily lives. Perhaps a working title should be *Fundamental Concerns of Women.*

I. Status and Political Rights

- A. Women's Standing under Law with Respect to:
  - 1. Voting
  - 2. Right to Hold Public Office
  - 3. Nationality and Citizenship (Including Treatment of Foreign Nationals)

II. Property Ownership

- A. Right to Hold Title
- B. Right to Contract Credit, Insurance, etc.
- C. Inheritance and Succession
- D. Tax Discrimination

III. Labor

- A. Employment and Promotion Opportunities
- B. Military and Alternative Service
- C. Maternity, Day Care
- D. Insurance, Pensions
- E. Protective Practices

IV. Education

- A. Availability

B. Discrimination in Access
C. Discrimination with Regard to:
1. Curricula
2. Texts
3. Education Practices
D. Teaching Roles

V. Crime

A. Definition of and Treatment Afforded to Female Offenders
B. Statutory and Societal Regulation of Sexual Behavior:
1. Prostitution
2. Rape
3. Lesbianism

VI. Slavery

(A Tentative Cross-Reference Topic)

VII. The Family

A. Special Status Afforded to the Family under Promotional and Protective Policies
B. State Intrusion: Family Bonuses and Allowances
C. Marriage:
1. Laws and Customs
2. Religious and Cultural Rules Concerning Marriage
3. Sex Relations
4. Financial Relations
D. Divorce
E. Maintenance
F. Unilateral Divorce
G. Child Custody
H. Widows' Status, Benefits, etc.
I. Family Planning
J. Control over One's Own Body
K. Methods and Social/Religious Controls:
1. Abortion
2. Contraception
L. Women and Children:
1. Special Status and Protective Policies
2. Parental Rights
3. Mothers' Rights
4. Guardianship
5. Adoption
6. Unmarried Mother
a. The Child Born out of Wedlock

VIII. Women and Religion

A. The Relationship Between Religions and Sex Discrimination

In the Introduction to this book, five theses were mentioned, ideal for research at the doctoral level. From the point of view of research these require further illustration and substantiation.

Thesis One: Attitudes of men in general determine the pace and extent of women's advance in society, and not so much constitutional or other legal provisions.

The position of management comes to mind. Between 1965 and 1983, the number of women in executive positions in private industry in the United States doubled. The main reason was that at the same time male views about women as executives were also changing. The *Harvard Business Review* published a survey on male attitudes which revealed that in 1965 only about 9 percent of the men held a favorable attitude. By 1985 this had grown to 33 percent. The law had nothing to do with this change in attitude. The Equal Rights Amendment failed in the United States after a massive effort but France adopted an E.R.A. 20 years ago, mainly because surveys revealed that the majority of French men did not have the same hang-ups as American men. In the '70s French men voted overwhelmingly that they had no objection to women having a better job or holding more important positions than they did, and almost 70 percent voted that they would accept a woman for a boss. France today has a higher percentage of lawyers and engineers who are women than the United States. There were other reasons why the E.R.A. failed in the United States, but the attitude of men was extremely important.

Thesis Two: Women are hampered in their quest for equality by cultural, religious and social traditions in the Western world, far more than by legal impediments.

One has only to look at women's place in the world of music. Because women have been so discriminated against in the world of music, as composers, conductors and performers, they have been forced to arrange international conferences to publicize their plight. The Fourth International Congress of Women in Music was held in Atlanta, Georgia, in March 1986. The previous congresses were held in New York, Los Angeles and Mexico City. At the Atlanta congress, the music of 90 women composers was looked at. The Spanish composer Maria Luisa Ozaita explained to the press that "legal egalitarianism is one thing while the reality of getting one's music before the public is another." The New York Philharmonic only hired its first full-time woman member in 1966. The Berlin Philharmonic still has an all-male policy. No woman has ever served (so far) as music director of a major symphony orchestra. Women composers have fared no better. Authoritative studies show that the reason for this problem can possibly be found in religious attitudes. The major institution shaping the initial 1,500 years of Western music was the church. And the only place in the church where a woman could sing was as a nun in a convent. Pope Sixtus V even banned the appearance of women in opera. Today the problem is still to a large extent that of church and society and the reluctance of male-dominated institutions in the music world to accommodate women composers. The most gifted woman composer in Germany will die unnoticed unless her work can be performed by a great orchestra—such as the Berlin Philharmonic.

Thesis Three: Discrimination against women on grounds of gender, in respect of wages, class of employment, birth control, family size, property ownership, marital rights, freedom of speech and freedom of movement and association, is worse in most African and Muslim states than discrimination against blacks on grounds of race in countries with a multi-racial population structure, such as South Africa.

In this case, one need only look at the Muslim world, where the evidence of one man in court automatically cancels out the evidence of two women. Pakistan's national women's field hockey team may never compete at the Olympic Games, but the men do. In the Islamic law of succession a woman's portion is equal to only half of a man's. The right of banishment of a woman from her home is entirely the man's prerogative. No alimony is due to a woman in case she is unjustly arrested or raped or suffers any condition "which renders her useless as a wife." In Saudi Arabia a woman may not drive a car and may not work openly. Nowhere in the Republic of South Africa, generally accused of being the most racist society in the world, are blacks, both men and women, discriminated against to the same extent, in fact not even nearly to the same extent, on the basis of race.

Thesis Four: Laws passed to protect the position of women have not always had the desired effect, in fact, in certain areas have worked to women's detriment.

A good illustration is the no-fault divorce law in the United States, which has turned out to be an economic disaster for divorced women. The trauma and acrimony have been reduced by the law, true, but, for example, in San Francisco, women and children have experienced a 73 percent *decline* in their standard of living in the first year after divorce, while divorced men experienced a 42 percent *increase* during the same period. A 1979 state law in California, requiring equal division of property, was hailed as a feminist dream come true. In practice, however, it has hurt women because now one out of every three homes involved is sold, disrupting the family when stability is most required.

Thesis Five: Constitutional and statutory provisions for the rights of women and laws promulgated to implement ratification of the United Nations convention to eliminate all discrimination against persons on grounds of gender are no guarantee that the laws are applied or the objectives vigorously pursued; in fact, behind the facade of these laws, discrimination against women not only persists but, in some countries, has increased.

This book has proved this to be true. One need only compare the status of women in Third World countries in Asia, Africa, the East Bloc and Latin America with the constitutional provisions extracted further on in this chapter, in respect of employment rights, to grasp the gulf between paper equality and equality in the workplace.

What appears to be most needed in the short term is a solid body of source material on constitutional provisions and statutes, both national and state, similar to the work which N.O.W. has produced for the United States, but including each country of the world. Perhaps a computer data base could be produced, updated annually, and used as an authoritative source for the purposes of comparative analysis. Perhaps this task would be more a work of massive compilation than of genuine research, but such a compilation, carefully prepared and regularly updated, would be the best tool for judging whether countries are simply paying lip service to their constitutions. A first companion work would then be an analysis on a country basis, and then by region (for example the E.C.E.) or by religion (for example the Muslim states) to see whether the existing legislation to protect women and to promote their status is being complied with. In short, the most important research which could possibly be tackled is an assessment of the gap between policy and practice.

Are governments applying their own laws, or are the laws merely window dressing? What is the status of case law? Are women being made aware of their rights and how the abuse of those rights can be brought to court? Is the state vigorously prosecuting those companies or organizations which discriminate against women in violation of the statutes or the constitution of the country? Are governments hearing of violations but not reacting? Information of this nature, produced on a regular basis, will place a weapon in the hands of women in those countries, notably in Africa, Latin America and Asia, whose rhetoric at the U.N. and subscription to every U.N. convention against discrimination is overwhelmingly more impressive than their track records in the field. Without the data base referred to above, this assistance cannot be provided to women.

The remainder of this chapter is taken up by two research proposals, already fully researched in terms of basic data: **Employment Rights** and **Voting Rights for Women** in Africa, the Middle East, the Far East, Indochina, and Southeast Asia, the South Pacific, the Caribbean and North America.

A total of 64 countries is included.

The right to vote and the right to be employed are the two most fundamental rights for women because all other rights arise from these freedoms. The right to a democratic government and all the protection which that implies is implicit in the right to vote. The right to fair wages, a nondiscriminatory workplace, maternity and pension rights and other benefits are implicit in employment rights. In short, those two rights are the answer to the average woman's demands: "I want a voice in the making of the laws of this country and in the government and I want to be able to work, as men do, to earn a decent wage."

Each outline is accompanied by complete footnotes on the source for each subject for each country and for each law or executive provision. The material for employment rights is subdivided to cover employment opportunity, equal pay, protective provisions and maternity benefits. In the case of voting rights there is, of course, no subdivision possible.

Those who are interested in various regions of the world will have the basic references, the most time-consuming part of the research, already documented.

In the interests of promoting research, copyright to these two themes, as they appear in this book, is hereby waived.

Employment Rights

Equality of employment cannot be achieved by a blanket constitutional provision mandating sexual equality.

Securing women's rights in the labor field must begin with constitutional/legislative provisions outlawing discrimination in obtaining employment. This involves special protections for married and pregnant women and in many societies also requires freedom from the control of husbands who might otherwise legally forbid their wives to work outside of the home.

Secondly, women need the guarantee of equal pay for equal work. And a considerable number of women activists are increasingly demanding equal pay for jobs of "comparable worth."

Conflict exists on whether the adoption of "protective" legal provisions advances or denies employment equality for women. Are the laws regulating the jobs in which women may be employed (underground mining, for example), the laws prohibiting work during specified hours, etc., a type of affirmative action? Do they give women increased access to preferred employment? Or do they simply restrict the scope of the labor available to women?

Finally, women's rights in the marketplace necessitate legal protection for working mothers: "maternity benefits" of varying types. Pregnant women need legal protection from discharge; they need guarantees of reemployment after their babies are born. They need facilities and time off for nursing and child care, including nurseries or even pre-school care.

The following pages outline the major constitutional and legislative protections afforded women throughout the world. (It should be borne in mind that the constitutions of some two dozen and more African states are currently suspended because of a military take-over or a state of emergency, e.g., Nigeria, Ethiopia, Tanzania, Zambia, Liberia and Ghana.)

Employment Rights for Women in Africa

Employment Opportunity. Most countries have some constitutional provision relating to the right to work, freedom to choose one's occupation, etc.: Algeria,[1] Angola,[2] Benin,[3] Burundi,[4] Cameroon,[5] Central African Republic,[6] Congo,[7] Egypt,[8] Eq. Guinea,[9] Ethiopia,[10] Ghana,[11] Guinea,[12] Guinea-Bissau,[13] Madagascar,[14] Mali,[15] Morocco,[16] Mozambique,[17] Nigeria,[18] Rwanda,[19] Senegal,[20] Somali Dem. Rep.,[21] Sudan,[22] Tanzania,[23] Togo,[24] Upper Volta,[25] Zaire.[26]

Of these, only a handful specifically include women, or prohibit employment opportunity discrimination on account of sex: Central African Rep., Mozambique, Sudan, Zaire. Egypt's constitutional provision qualifies somewhat women's employment equality.[27]

Ethiopia also has legislation pertaining to employment rights, but it does not specifically have to do with women.[28]

Equal Pay. A minority of countries have some kind of constitutional provision having to do with fair remuneration: Algeria,[29] Angola,[30] Congo,[31] Eq. Guinea,[32] Ethiopia,[33] Ghana,[34] Libya,[35] Madagascar,[36] Nigeria,[37] Rwanda,[38] Somali Dem. Rep.,[39] Sudan.[40]

Only about half of these, however, make mention of sex as a prohibited basis of discrimination, or of the right of women to equal salaries: Congo, Ethiopia, Ghana, Nigeria, Sudan.

Protective Provisions. No country has a constitutional provision which specifically limits the type of work, working conditions or hours for women. The Constitution of Sudan, however, does state that "no person shall, on grounds of need, be forced to perform work not suitable to his age, sex, or health."[41]

Nigeria's Constitution guarantees the protection of workers' health, safety and welfare, without restricting women's employment opportunities for this reason.[42] However, Nigeria does have other provisions which prohibit women from engaging in night work and allow other restrictive regulations.[43]

Ethiopia and Kenya also have protective legislation. Kenya, like Nigeria, prohibits women, with some exceptions, from working during certain hours.[44]

Ethiopia, however, generally treats men and women more equally, and its protective provisions are framed in more general terms.[45]

Maternity Benefits. A few constitutions have general provisions which aim at helping working mothers: Angola,[46] Benin,[47] Egypt,[48] Gabon,[49] Ghana,[50] Libya,[51] Madagascar,[52] Somali Dem. Rep.,[53] Sudan.[54]

Benin specifically guarantees the right to maternity leave, and Somali Dem. Rep. declares that the state shall provide child care homes.

Some countries also have legislation which provides aid to working mothers in the form of maternity leave: Ethiopia,[55] Ghana,[56] Kenya,[57] Togo.[58] (Togo also provides for rest periods for working mothers.)

A good number of countries have no constitutional provisions concerning women's economic opportunities: Botswana, Chad, Djibouti, Gambia, Ivory Coast, Kenya, Kribati, Lesotho, Liberia, Malawi, Mauritania, Nigeria, Sierra Leone, South Africa, Swaziland, Tonga, Tunisia, Uganda, Zambia, Zimbabwe.

Employment Rights for Women in the Middle East/Arabian Gulf

Employment Opportunities. Most countries have some constitutional provision relating to the right to work, freedom to choose one's occupation, etc.: Bahrain,[1] Egypt,[2] Iran,[3] Iraq,[4] Jordan,[5] Kuwait,[6] Lebanon,[7] Qatar,[8] Syria[9] Turkey,[10] UAE,[11] Dem. Rep. of Yemen,[12] Yemen Arab Rep.[13]

Iran[14] and Israel[15] have legislation relating to employment opportunity rights.

Of these countries, more than half specifically mention sex in relation to employment: Egypt, Iran, Israel, Syria, Turkey, Dem. Rep. Yemen.

The constitutional provisions of Iran[16] and Turkey[17] are somewhat restrictive of women's employment rights, however.

Equal pay. Only five countries have any kind of constitutional protection of fair remuneration: Bahrain,[18] Jordan,[19] Kuwait,[20] Syria,[21] Turkey.[22]

The applicable provisions, however, do not specifically call for equal pay for men and women.

Iran[23] and Israel[24] both have legislative provisions which recognize the principle of equal pay for men and women for the same work.

Lebanon[25] has a legislative provision which specifies that laws governing minimum wages apply to women only if the work involved is the same type of work as performed by men.

Protective Provisions. The constitutions of Jordan[26] and Turkey[27] contain general provisions that call for special conditions for women workers.

Iran,[28] Israel[29] and Lebanon[30] forbid or restrict the employment of women in certain types of labor, or during certain hours, by means of legislative enactments.

Maternity Benefits. The Constitution of Egypt[31] guarantees maternal and child care in general, while the Constitution of the Dem. Rep. Yemen[32] guarantees paid maternity leave and child care for working mothers.

Maternity leave, nursing time and child care are also given to working women through legislation in Iran,[33] Israel[34] and Lebanon.[34]

Oman[35] and Saudi Arabia[36] have no constitutional provisions.

Employment Rights for Women in the Far East

Employment Opportunity. People's Rep. of China,[1] Japan,[2] Korean People's Dem. Rep.,[3] Rep. of Korea,[4] Mongolian People's Rep.,[5] and Taiwan[6] all have constitutional provisions relating to employment opportunity. However, only People's Rep. of China, Korean People's Dem. Rep. and Mongolian People's Rep. guarantee the equality of women's and men's economic rights.

Equal Pay. Almost all of the countries have either a constitutional or a legislative provision for fair remuneration: People's Rep. of China,[7] Japan,[8] Rep. of Korea,[9] Mongolian People's Rep.[10]

However, the right of equal pay between men and women is specifically protected only by the Constitution of the People's Rep. of China and by the Labor Standards Law of the Rep. of Korea.

Protective Provisions. The only constitutional protective provisions are general, non-restrictive provisions found in the constitutions of the Rep. of Korea[11] and Taiwan.[12]

Maternity Benefits. The constitutions of Korean People's Dem. Rep.[13] and Mongolian People's Rep.,[14] as well as legislation and other provisions in the People's Rep. of China,[15] and Japan,[16] guarantee maternity leave, nursing time, and child care for the working mother.

Employment Rights for Women in Indochina/Southeast Asia

Employment Opportunity. The constitutions of Indonesia,[1] Dem. Kampuchea,[2] Philippines,[3] Thailand,[4] and Soc. Rep. of Vietnam[5] all make some provision for the right or duty of citizens to work.

Only the Philippines'[6] Constitution and Indonesian[7] legislation make mention of equal treatment of the sexes in employment.

Equal Pay. Only the Soc. Rep. of Vietnam[8] has a constitutional guarantee of equal pay for equal work between men and women.

Indonesia[9] and the Philippines[10] have legislative guarantees of equal pay between the sexes.

Protective Provisions. A general protective provision is found in the Constitution of the Soc. Rep. of Vietnam[11] only, although there were more specific restrictive decrees from the Dem. Rep. of Vietnam.[12]

Indonesia[13] and the Philippines[14] both have laws which restrict women's working hours and types of occupation.

Maternity Benefits. The Soc. Rep. of Vietnam, through its Constitution[15] (and by earlier decrees),[16] and Indonesia[17] and the Philippines[18] (through legislation) provide such benefits to the working mother as maternity leave, nursing time, and child care. Singapore also has some maternity leave entitlements for unwed, as well as married, women.[19]

The Laos People's Dem. Rep., Malaysia, and Singapore have no applicable constitutional provisions.

Employment Rights for Women in the South Pacific

Employment Opportunity. Two constitutions specify the right or duty to work in general: Papua New Guinea,[1] Vanutu.[2]

New Zealand prohibits discrimination by any employer on account of sex, marital status or religious belief.[3]

Australia has no applicable constitutional provision, but certain legislative enactments in some states discriminate against women in employment. Generally, however, there are no legal restrictions on recruitment and promotional policies and practices, retirement, income tax, etc.[4]

Equal Pay. In Australia, equal pay provisions have been established by decisions of the Conciliation and Arbitration Commission in the Equal Pay Cases of 1969 and 1972, and by state equal pay legislation prior to 1969. The principle of equal pay for equal work has also been implemented in the public services.[5] However, in the 1972 joint National Wage and Equal Pay Cases, the Commission refused to extend the minimum wage provisions to females.[6]

The Constitution of New Zealand forbids an employer to offer different terms of employment to persons similarly qualified and employed in the same or similar circumstances, by reason of sex.[7] Equal pay rate is also referred to in the Committee Report on Equal Pay Implementation.[8]

Protective Provisions. In Australia, limitations on the employment of women exist by means of legislation in each state and in the Commonwealth.[9]

Maternity Benefits. The Human Rights Commission Act of New Zealand states that preferential treatment granted by reason of a woman's pregnancy or childbirth does not constitute a breach of the prohibition against sexual discrimination in employment.[10]

Australia provides maternity benefits through various legislative provisions enabled by the Commonwealth Constitution, including Maternity Allowance, Child Endowment, and Maternity Leave for public sector employees.[11]

A good number of South Pacific constitutions have no provisions pertaining to economic or employment rights: Fiji, Kiribati, Nauru, Solomon Islands, Tuvalu, Western Samoa.

Employment Rights for Women in the Caribbean

Employment Opportunity. The Constitution of the Dominican Republic[1] states that every individual has the obligation to work.

The Constitution of Haiti[2] prohibits discrimination in general in the appointment of government services personnel.

The Constitution of Dominica[3] prohibits any employment provision requiring standards or qualifications specifically relating to sex.

Cuba[4] constitutionally guarantees a job to every woman as well as man; Guyana[5] also constitutionally protects women's right to work.

Trinidad and Tobago[6] guarantee to every person the right to work, and also require that all persons respect the rights and freedoms of others without regard to race, sex or creed.

Equal Pay. Haiti's[7] Constitution prohibits discrimination in the terms of employment of government services personnel and guarantees a fair wage.

Cuba[8] has a general constitutional provision guaranteeing equal pay.

Guyana[9] specifically guarantees women's right to equal pay.

Protective Provisions. Jamaica has legislation which restricts the employment of women in night work. Also, the Minister of Labor is empowered to make regulations restricting or prohibiting altogether the employment of women under certain circumstances.[10]

Cuba[11] and Guyana[12] have general constitutional provisions which may tend to restrict women's employment opportunities.

Maternity Benefits. Barbados provides day-care facilities for working mothers and government programs to improve the quality of staff operating centers.[13]

Cuba[14] and Guyana[15] have constitutional provisions concerning help for working mothers.

Most Caribbean constitutions have no provisions relating to employment rights: Antigua, Bahamas, Barbados, Belize, Grenada, St. Lucia, St. Vincent, Suriname.

Employment Rights of Women in North America

Employment Opportunity. The United States has no constitutional protection of employment rights. However, federal legislation prohibits employment discrimination on the basis of sex.[1] Furthermore, at least 34 states have some kind of fair employment practices law forbidding employment discrimination on account of sex.[2]

Equal Pay. The United States also has federal legislation prohibiting wage discrimination based on sex in public and private employment.[3] As of 1975, 38 states also had equal pay laws.[4]

Canada, too, has passed equal wages legislation.[5]

Protective Provisions. Seventeen states barred certain occupations to women as of 1975. Most of these were jobs in mining or jobs having to do with the sale of alcoholic beverages. Some states had more general provisions prohibiting women from "unhealthful," "immoral," "dangerous," or "unsuitable" employment.[6] Also, at that time 30 states had laws establishing maximum working hours for women.[7]

Voting Rights

While few countries, notably Liechtenstein and Switzerland (in part), until recently still denied women the right to vote, such right is not necessarily specified in countries when there is equality at the ballot box.

Some constitutions do so provide, specifically granting voting rights to women or stating that women have the same voting rights as men or stating that there is no voting discrimination based on sex. This is most common in the Far East and the South Pacific. In other constitutions there is merely a general provision on voting without any reference to sex and this has been understood as granting equal electoral rights.

Voting equality has also been protected by general provisions on sexual equality or merely statements that all persons are equal. This is typical of the nations of Africa and the Middle East.

Voting Rights for Women in Africa

Several countries have a single constitutional provision that gives the right to vote to women as well as men: Guinea,[1] Ivory Coast,[2] Liberia,[3] Mali,[4] Mauritania,[5] Morocco,[6] Niger,[7] Senegal,[8] Togo,[9] Upper Volta.[10]

Many countries have more than one constitutional provision, relating to equality of the sexes and voting rights, which combined, give women the right to vote: Algeria,[11] Angola,[12] Benin,[13] Botswana,[14] Central African Rep.,[15] Congo,[16] Djibouti,[17] Egypt,[18] Eq. Guinea,[19] Ethiopia,[20] Gambia,[21] Ghana,[22] Guinea-Bissau,[23] Kenya,[24] Dem. Rep. of Madagascar,[25] Mozambique,[26] Nigeria,[27] Rwanda,[28] Sierra Leone,[29] Somali Dem. Rep.,[30] Sudan,[31] Tanzania,[32] Zaire,[33] Zambia,[34] Zimbabwe.[35]

The Constitution of Burundi[36] calls for the equality of the sexes but does not specify the right to vote.

The constitutions of Malawi[37] and Tunisia[38] have provisions concerning the equality of all citizens and voting rights, but do not specify equality of the sexes.

Some countries have no applicable constitutional provisions: Chad, Gabon, Lesotho, Libya, South Africa, Swaziland, Tonga, Uganda.

Voting Rights for Women in the Middle East/Arabian Gulf

A few countries grant to women the right to vote on equal terms with men by means of various constitutional, legislative and declaratory provisions: Egypt,[1] Iran,[2] Israel,[3] Lebanon,[4] Turkey,[5] People's Dem. Rep. of Yemen.[6]

In a few other countries, equality of the sexes is specified in the constitution, without explicit mention of the right to vote: Iraq,[7] Qatar,[8] Yemen Arab Republic.[9]

The constitutions of Jordan,[10] Syria,[11] and the United Arab Emirates,[12] call for equality of all persons or citizens, but without mention of sex as a prohibited ground for discrimination.

Other countries have no applicable constitutional provisions: Bahrain, Kuwait, Oman, Saudi Arabia.

Voting Rights for Women in the Far East

Only the Korean People's Dem. Rep.[1] has a single constitutional provision that gives the right to vote to all citizens, regardless of sex.

Most other countries give women the right to vote by a combination of constitutional provisions: People's Rep. of China,[2] Japan,[3] Mongolian People's Rep.,[4] Rep. of Korea,[5] Taiwan.[6]

The People's Rep. of China also has an Electoral Law that states that "women shall have the right to elect and to be elected on equal terms with men."[7]

Voting Rights for Women in Indochina/Southeast Asia

Only one country's constitution protects the right to vote, regardless of sex: Socialist Rep. of Vietnam.[1]

The constitutions of Indonesia,[2] Malaysia,[3] Singapore,[4] and Thailand[5] assure the equality of all persons, but not specifically between the sexes. Of these, Malaysia[6] has a constitutional guarantee of the right to vote. Indonesia guarantees that women share equally with men the right to vote by means of law.[7]

The Constitution of the Philippines[8] has a voting provision, but the right of suffrage is specifically granted to women by law.[9]

The Constitution of Dem. Kampuchea[10] states that men and women are equal, but has no voting provisions.

The Lao People's Dem. Rep.[11] has no applicable constitutional provisions.

Voting Rights for Women in the South Pacific

Most constitutions of the South Pacific guarantee fundamental, individual rights and freedom regardless of sex and also provide for voting qualifications: Fiji,[1] Kiribati,[2] Nauru,[3] Papua New Guinea,[4] Solomon Islands,[5] Tuvalu,[6] Vanuatu,[7] Western Samoa.[8]

Australia and New Zealand have no applicable voting rights provisions in their constitutions. Australia does have a general qualification of electors provision,[9] and New Zealand has extended to women the right to vote on the same basis as men by means of legislation.[10]

Voting Rights for Women in the Caribbean

Most Caribbean constitutions, in addition to providing for voting, guarantee the fundamental rights of individuals regardless of sex, and/or prohibit discrimination on the basis of sex: Antigua,[1] Bahamas,[2] Barbados,[3] Belize,[4] Dominica,[5] Grenada,[6] Guyana,[7] Jamaica,[8] St. Lucia,[9] St. Vincent,[10] Trinidad and Tobago.[11]

Women in Jamaica also have the right to vote protected by law.[12]

In a few other countries, women's voting rights are protected by the application of more than one constitutional provision: Dominican Rep.,[13] Haiti,[14] Suriname.[15]

The Constitution of Cuba contains one provision that gives the right to vote to women as well as men.[16]

Voting Rights for Women in North America

Canada guarantees everyone the right to vote by means of the Constitution Act.[1]

The Constitution of the United States specifically provides that the right of citizens to vote shall not be denied or abridged on account of sex.[2]

Notes

Chapter 2. The Status of Women: A Global View

1. Margaret Alic, *Hypatia's Heritage: A History of Women in Science,* Beacon Press, Boston, 1986. For Hypatia, see pp. 41–47. See also Caroline Herzenberg, "Women in Science During Antiquity and the Middle-Ages," *Journal of College Science Teaching,* November 1987, pp. 124–127, and Else Hoyrup, *Women of Science, Technology and Medicine* (Bibliography), Roskilde University, Denmark, 1987.

2. See Carl Sagan, *Cosmos,* Ballantine Books, New York, 1980, pp. 278–279.

3. *American Health,* June 1986, p. 10.

4. *National Geographic,* Vol. 168, No. 3, 1986, p. 313.

5. "Most Gains for Women's Rights Were Achieved in the Last 25 Years," *The St. Louis Post-Dispatch,* December 13, 1987.

6. "Sex Discrimination, Theory and Research," in *Case Studies on Human Rights,* W. Veenhoven (ed.), Nijhof, The Hague, 1975, Vol. V, p. 140.

7. *Voice of Women,* Sri Lanka, Colombo, No. 7, 1985, contains an article on this subject.

8. See J.D. van der Vyver, *Die Beskerming van Menseregte in Suid-Afrika,* Juta, Cape Town, 1975. For a review in English see *South African Yearbook of International Law,* UNISA, Pretoria, 1975, Vol. 1, p. 230.

9. Southern African Editorial Services, *Fact Sheet,* Sandton, July 1987; *South African Digest,* Pretoria, January 30, 1987, pp. 1–2, and November 27, 1987, in "Viewpoint," p. 2, lists the various laws repealed.

10. *Women: A World Survey,* World Priority, Washington DC, 1985, p. 5.

11. *Ibid.,* p. 6.

12. Joni Seager and Ann Olson, *Atlas: Women in the World,* Simon & Schuster, New York, 1986, p. 7.

13. *Population Briefing Paper,* No. 20, June 1988, p. 3.

14. United Nations, *World Survey of the Role of Women in Development,* New York, 1985, p. 34.

15. *The American Woman 1988–1989: A Status Report,* Sara Rix (ed.), W.W. Norton, New York, 1988, p. 90.

16. Population Crisis Committee, *Population Briefing Paper,* Washington DC, No. 20, June 1988, p. 9.

17. John Paul's Apostolic Letter "On the Dignity and Vocation of Women," *The Atlanta Journal and Constitution,* October 1988, p. 18. Cf. *Newsweek,* April 18, 1988, p. 85.

18. *The Atlanta Journal and Constitution,* July 6, 1986, p. 15.

19. *The Atlanta Constitution,* June 22, 1988, p. D3; August 2, 1988, p. A3; September 25, 1988, p. A6; *International Herald Tribune,* Paris, August 1, 1988, p. 2.

20. United States Department of Commerce, *Women of the World,* Washington DC, May 1984, pp. 63, 76.

21. *The Female World from a Global Perspective,* Indiana University Press, Bloomington, 1987, pp. 172–173.

22. Shirley Joseph, "Statement on the Copenhagen Conference," *Lilith,* No. 8,

1981, p. 34. Cf. Jessie Bernard, *The Female World from a Global Perspective,* pp. 176–178.

23. *The New York Times,* July 24, 1985.

24. See Chapters 5 and 8.

25. "Women Are the Poor," *Development Forum,* United Nations, New York, 1985, p. 7.

26. United Nations Secretariat: *U.N. Decade for Women,* conference issue, July 1985, p. 2.

27. Report by Harden and Battiata, July 18, 1985.

28. Simon & Schuster, New York, 1988, pp. 376–377.

29. *Population Briefing Paper,* No. 20, June 1988.

30. See Chapters 16 and 29.

31. Betty Vetter, "Women's Progress," *Mosaic,* National Science Foundation, Vol. 18, No. 1, 1987, pp. 2–5.

32. See A. Bernstein, "So You Think You Have Come a Long Way?" *Business Week,* February 29, 1988, pp. 48–49.

33. Sara Rix (ed.), Norton, New York, 1988, pp. 91–93.

34. September 1987, pp. 92–95.

35. Oxford University Press, 1985, Preface.

36. *Women's Work, Men's Work: Sex Segregation on the Job,* National Academy Press, Washington DC, 1986, p. 130.

37. United Nations, *Review and Appraisal,* Part I, A/CONF/116/5.

38. See Gerda Lerner, *The Creation of Patriarchy,* Oxford University Press, 1986; and *Women in World Religions,* Arvind Sharma (ed.), New York State University Press, 1987.

39. See "The Gap Between Policy and Practice," Chapter 5.

40. Jessie Bernard, *The Female World from a Global Perspective,* p. 149.

41. National Science Foundation, *Mosaic,* Vol. 18, No. 1, p. 2.

42. Genia Browning, "Soviet Politics—Where Are the Women?" in *Soviet Sisterhood,* Barbara Holland (ed.), Indiana University Press, 1985, pp. 207–211.

43. *The Female World from a Global Perspective,* p. 184.

44. *The American Woman 1988–1989,* p. 90, table 2.1.

45. *The Politics of the Second Electorate,* Joni Lovenduski and Jill Hills, eds., Routledge & Kegan Paul, London, 1981.

46. "Women and Men of Europe in 1983," Supplement No. 16 to *Women of Europe,* Commission of the E.E.C., Brussels, 1984.

47. See Sheile Lewenhak: *The Revaluation of Women's Work,* Croom Helm, Sydney, 1988.

48. Warner Books, New York, 1986, p. 89.

49. *Journal of Economic Issues,* Vol. 22, No. 3, September 1988, p. 792.

50. M. Buvenic and N. Youssef, "Women Headed Households," paper of the United States Agency for International Development, Washington DC, 1978.

51. *Women of the World: Sub-Saharan Africa,* United States Bureau of Census and the United States Office of Women in Development, Washington DC, 1984, p. 119.

52. See *Women in the World Economy,* Oxford University Press, New York, 1987, last chapter.

53. K. Newland, *Women, Men and the Division of Labor,* Worldwatch Institute, Washington DC, Worldwatch Paper No. 37, May 1980.

54. See Chapters 10, 19 and 25.

55. *Women's Changing Role,* Carol Foster et al. (eds.), Information Aids, Wylie TX, 1988, p. 10.

56. *Women: A World Report,* p. 27.

57. United Nations, *World Survey: Women in Agriculture,* A/CONF/116/4, 1985.

58. United Nations Economic Commission for Africa, E/ECA/REIWD/OAU/4, 1984.
59. United Nations, Information Pack, World Assembly on Aging, Vienna, 1982.
60. Gisela Wild, *Comparative Law Yearbook,* 1985, Vol. 8, p. 9.
61. *Indian Bar Council Review,* Vol. X (4), 1983, p. 553.
62. *Women: A World Survey,* p. 6.
63. See Gail Lapidus, *Women in Soviet Society,* University of California Press, 1978.
64. *Women, Work and Ideology in the Third World,* Haleh Afshar (ed.), Tavistock Publications, New York, 1985, Introduction.
65. J.P. Scanlan, "The Feminization of Poverty," *Current Magazine,* Washington DC, 302: 15–16, May 1988.
66. *The American Woman 1988–1989,* p. 139.
67. United States Bureau of Census, *Poverty in the United States,* Washington DC, 1987.
68. *Male, Female Differences in Work Experience and Earnings,* Washington DC, 1987.
69. *The American Woman 1988–1989,* p. 30.
70. *The Atlanta Journal and Constitution,* June 27, 1988, p. A5.
71. *Ibid.,* November 27, 1988, p. A2.
72. *Ibid.,* November 6, 1988, p. A1.
73. *The Invisible Bar: The Woman Lawyer in America 1638 to the Present,* Beacon Press, Boston, 1986, pp. 218, 250. Cf. J. Abramson: "For Women Lawyers an Uphill Struggle," *New York Times Magazine,* June 1988, pp. 36–37.
74. *Newsweek,* April 28, 1989, p. 71, and the *Atlanta Constitution,* April 14, 1989, p. 2D.
75. Joni Seager and Ann Olson, *Atlas: Women in the World.*
76. *Haagsche Courant.* The Hague, March 22, 1982, *HC Achtergrond.*

Chapter 3. The Environment of Discrimination

1. Dorothy Robins-Mowry, *The Hidden Sun: Women of Modern Japan,* Westview Press, Boulder CO, 1983, Appendix B, p. 319.
2. Joelle Juillard, "Policy Impacts and Women's Role in France," in *Women in the World,* Lynn Iglitzin and Ruth Ross (eds.), 2nd edition, ABC–CLIO, Santa Barbara CA, 1986, p. 16.
3. Yenlin Ku, "The Changing Status of Women in Taiwan," in *Women's Studies International Forum,* Vol. 11, No. 3, p. 179.
4. *Women's Studies International Forum,* Vol. 11, No. 5, p. 459.
5. *Unfinished Democracy: Women in Nordic Politics,* Elina Haavio-Manilla (ed.), Pergamon, Oxford, England, 1985.
6. "Elusive Equality: The Limits of Public Policy," in *Women in the World,* p. 7.
7. *The Politics of the Second Electorate,* Routledge & Kegan Paul, London, 1981, p. 325.
8. *Women: A World Report,* Debbie Taylor (ed.), Oxford University Press, New York, 1985, p. 82.
9. United Nations, *World Population Policies,* New York, 1987, Vol. 1, p. 85.
10. I.L. Markowitz, *Studies in Power and Class in Africa,* Oxford University Press, New York, 1987.
11. "Women, the Family and Social Change in Latin America," *World Affairs,* Washington DC, Vol. 150, No. 2, Fall 1987, pp. 117–120.
12. *Women's Studies International Forum,* Vol. 11, No. 4, 1988, p. 352.
13. *Atlas: Women in the World,* Simon & Schuster, New York, 1986, p. 8.
14. Joni Lovenduski, *Women and European Politics,* University of Massachusetts Press, Amherst, 1986, Chapter 6.

15. Published respectively by: Routledge & Kegan Paul, London, 1981, and the University of Massachusetts Press, Amherst, 1986.

16. International Labour Organization, *Women at Work,* Geneva, 1988, Vol. 1, p. 29.

17. *Ibid.,* p. 45.

18. *Ibid.,* p. 29.

19. *Ibid.,* Vol. 2, p. 6.

20. Wan Shanping, in *Women's Studies International Forum,* Vol. 11, No. 5, 1988, p. 455.

21. United States Department of Labor, Bureau of Labor Statistics.

22. United Nations, *World Survey of the Role of Women in Development,* New York, E.86.IV.3, 1986.

23. *The American Woman 1988–1989: A Status Report,* Sara Rix (ed.), W.W. Norton, New York, 1988.

24. International Labour Organization, *Recruitment, Training and Career Development in the Public Service,* Geneva, Report 11, Joint Committee on the Public Service, 1983.

25. United Nations, *World Survey of the Role of Women in Development,* 1983, p. 20.

26. International Labour Organization, *Women at Work,* 1987, Vol. 2, p. 25.

27. See Susan Joekes, *Women in the World Economy,* Oxford University Press, New York, 1984.

28. See "Occupation and Industrial Distribution in the ECE Region," Part 1, Seminar on the Economic Role of Women in the ECE Region, Vienna, ECE/SEM/6/R.4, 1984; and United Nations, *World Survey of Role of Women in Development,* 1986, p. 25, Table 3.

29. Equal Opportunities Commission, London, 1980.

30. International Labour Organization, *Rural Labour Markets and Employment Policies,* Geneva, ACRD X/1983/111, pp. 19–20.

31. United States Bureau of Labor Statistics, *Employment and Earnings,* January 1987, Table 22.

32. See Organization for Economic and Cooperative Development, *Employment Trends,* October 16, 1986, p. 21.

33. United States Department of Education, *Digest of Educational Statistics,* 1987, Table 164.

34. See *The Pretoria News,* October 16, 1986, p. 21.

35. Eisold, E., "Young Women Workers in Export Industries," WEP Working Paper, International Labour Organization, Geneva, 1984; Robert A., "The Effects of the International Division of Labour on Female Workers in the Textile and Clothing Industries," in *Development and Change,* Vol. 14, No. 1, January 1983; and see also United Nations, *Export Processing Zones,* 1983.

36. United Nations, *World Economic Survey 1988: Current Trends and Policies in the World Economy,* New York, 1988, p. 154.

37. Sivard, Ruth, *Women: A World Survey,* World Priority, Washington DC, 1986, pp. 11–17.

38. *Ibid.,* pp. 18–20.

39. *Women: A World Report,* p. 75.

40. *Population Briefing Paper,* No. 20, June 1988, p. 6.

41. U.N.E.S.C.O.: *Yearbook,* 1982, pp. V-24 and V-25; and Moussa, Favag, *Les Femmes Inventeurs Existent,* Geneva, 1986.

42. "Women in Science During Antiquity and the Middle Ages," *Journal of College Science Teaching,* Nov. 1987, pp. 124–127.

43. *Hypatia's Heritage: A History of Women in Science,* Beacon, Boston, 1986.

44. United Nations, *World Survey on the Role of Women in Development,* p. 142.

45. Boulding, Elise, "Integration into What?" in *Women and Technological Change in Developing Countries,* Rosslyn Dauber and Melinda Cain (eds.), Westview Press, Boulder CO, 1981, pp. 16–17. Cf. Pamela D'Onofrio-Flores, "Technology, Development and the Division of Labour by Sex," in *Scientific-Technological Change and the Role of Women in Development,* P. D'Onofrio-Flores and Sheila Pfafflin (eds.), Westview, Boulder CO, 1982.

46. Horowitz, Bruce, "Energy Future Has a Role for Women Too," *Industry Week,* September 21, 1981.

47. "Women in Science and Engineering," *Mosaic,* National Science Foundation, Vol. 18, No. 1, pp. 2–7.

48. World Health Organization, *Women, Health and Development,* Geneva, 1985, p. 10.

49. Pezzullo, Caroline, *For the Record,* Forum 1985, International Women's Tribune Center, New York, 1985, p. 31.

50. *Ibid.,* p. 17.

51. *Ibid.,* p. 9.

52. *The American Woman 1988–1989,* pp. 91–94.

53. Department of Foreign Affairs and Information, *Official Yearbook,* Pretoria, 1986.

54. "An Experiment in Women Power," *Time,* October 6, 1986.

55. *Sex Inequalities in Urban Employment in the Third World,* Richard Anker and Catherine Hein (eds.), International Labour Organization, Geneva, 1986.

56. World Health Organization, *Women, Health and Development,* Geneva, 1985, p. 4.

57. See Chapter 28.

58. Indiana University Press, Bloomington, Indiana, 1983, p. 173.

59. *Ibid.,* p. 77.

60. Population Crisis Committee, *Access to Birth Control: A World Assessment,* Population Briefing Paper No. 19, Washington DC, October 1987.

61. *Ibid.*

62. *Ibid.*

63. World Health Organization, *Women Health and Development,* Table 1, p. 6.

64. *Ibid.,* p. 22.

Chapter 4. The International World

1. *The Female World from a Global Perspective,* Indiana University Press, 1987, p. 169.

2. *Ibid.,* p. 170.

3. The International Labour Organization, Geneva, publishes an annual report on the status of ratification of the various conventions. See also the I.L.O. publication *Women at Work,* 1987, Vol. 2.

4. Conventions 13, 81, 87, 97, 102, 110, 111, 117, 122, 127, 128, 136, and 140.

5. Convention dates are those when the convention came into force and not when it was adopted by the General Assembly of the United Nations. Sometimes as many as three years may pass before a convention comes into force. For dates of ratification see I.L.O., *Women at Work,* 1987, Vol. 2, pp. 34–40.

6. *Women: A World Survey,* World Priority, Washington DC, 1985, p. 31.

7. *Women at Work,* Vol. 2, pp. 34–40.

8. A/CONF/116/28/Rev.1, para. 97, p. 231.

9. General Assembly Resolution 22111 (XXI).

10. Source: United Nations Secretariat, New York.

11. Robin Morgan (ed.), Doubleday, New York, 1984, p. 690.

12. Paragraph 315, p. 77, A/CONF/116/28/Rev.1. See also INSTRAW *News,* Santo Domingo, No. 8, 1987, p. 24.

13. *Women and European Politics,* University of Massachusetts Press, Amherst, 1986, p. 238.

14. The history of this period is recounted in a U.N. document, *The United Nations and Status of Women,* 64-04650-20M (May 1964), p. 305.

15. Charter, Article 1, para. 3. See also Articles 13(1)(6)55(c), 56, 62(2) and 76(c).

16. Its reports are issued regularly with the indicator E/CN.6/. A good discussion of the work of this group is presented by Margaret E. Galey, "Promoting Non-discrimination Against Women! The UN Commission on the Status of Women," *International Studies Quarterly,* Vol. 23, June 1979, pp. 273–302.

17. Universal Declaration of Human Rights, Article 16.

18. *Ibid.,* Article 213.

19. *Ibid.,* Article 25.

20. Commission of the European Communities, *Community Law and Women,* Supplement 25 of *Women of Europe,* Women's Information Service, Brussels, 1986, pp. 6–8, 35–38, 74–83 and 84–87.

21. *Sample Survey of Work Forces,* Eurostat, Statistical Office of the E.C., Brussels, 1983, p. 88.

22. *Europe,* July/August 1984, pp. 26–28.

23. *Women and European Politics,* p. 285.

24. Resolution 640 (VII).

25. Article 4.

26. Article 25(a) and (c).

27. 27th Ordinary Session Recommendation 606 (1975) on the political rights and position of women.

28. Article 16.

29. *Ibid.*

30. Article 2.

31. Article 3.

32. Article 2.

33. Article 16.

34. Article 23.

35. Article 6.

36. *Ibid.*

37. Case of Abdilaziz, Cabales and Balkandali, Nos. 9214/80, 9473/and 1474/81.

38. See N. Burrows, "Promotion of Women's Rights by the European Economic Community," *Common Market Law Review,* Vol. 17, 1980, pp. 191–209.

39. A/CONF/116/28/Rev.1, para. 68, p. 21.

40. Article 6(a).

41. International Labor Office, *List of Ratifications of Conventions,* International Labor Office, Geneva, 1982.

42. Convention Concerning Night Work of Women Employed in Industry, International Labor Office, 1982.

43. Article 3.

44. Article 8.

45. Article 15.

46. Convention No. 100, June 1951.

47. Convention No. 102, June 1952.

48. Article 2.

49. Article 7.

50. Article 7(i).

51. Part I, European Treaty Series, No. 35, 1978.

52. Council Directive 75/117/EEC, Article 2.

53. See E.M. Biddison, "Recent Developments: Sex Discrimination—UK Law Fails to Satisfy EEC Equal Pay Directive," *Texas International Law Review,* Vol. 18, 1983, pp. 380-388.

54. See J.M. Steiner, "Sex Discrimination Under UK and EEC Law," *International and Comparative Law Review,* Vol. 32, 1983, pp. 399-423; and S. Weisman, "Sex Discrimination: Some Recent Decisions of the European Court of Justice," *Columbia Journal of Transnational Law,* Vol. 21, 1983, pp. 621-640.

55. Resolution 2263 (XXII).

56. Article 11.

57. Alan Whittaker, "Slavery, Myths and Reality," *The International Yearbook 1987,* Skinner Directories, Windsor Court, England, 1988.

58. Article 4, Universal Declaration of Human Rights, 1948, reads: "No one shall be held in slavery or servitude; slavery and the slave trade shall be prohibited in all their forms."

59. *India Today,* January 31, 1988, p. 68.

60. See Eschel Rhoodie, *Power and the Presidency,* Strydom Publishers, Johannesburg, 1989.

61. Kurt Glaser and Stefan Possony, *Victims of Politics—The State of Human Rights,* Columbia University Press, N.Y., 1979, pp. 285-286, 371-372.

62. *Insight Magazine,* New York, March 6, 1989, p. 39.

Chapter 5. Constitutional and Statutory Provisions

1. Eschel Rhoodie, *Discrimination in the Constitutions of the World,* Brentwood, Columbus GA, 1984, pp. 1-2.

2. Henk Van Marseveen and Ger Van der Tang, *Written Constitutions,* Oceana Publications, New York, 1978, pp. 273-280.

3. "Women's Equality in the World's Constitutions," *Populi,* Vol. 12, No. 2, 1985.

4. *The State of the World's Women,* New Internationalist Publications, Oxford, 1985, p. 17.

5. "Women's Equality in the World's Constitutions."

6. Civil Code: Article 1002.

7. *Ibid.,* Article 1059.

8. *Ibid.,* Article 1018.

9. Article 134.

10. See The Asian Women's Research and Action Network, *A 14 Country Alternative Asian Report on the Impact of the UN Decade for Women,* Davoa, Philippines, 1985.

11. "Women's Equality in the World's Constitutions."

12. Codified in the International Covenant on Civil and Political Rights and the International Covenant on Economic, Cultural and Social Rights.

13. "Women's Equality in the World's Constitutions."

14. *The State of the World's Women,* p. 9.

15. Albania, Article 41 para. 2; Poland, Article 78(2)(1); Switzerland, Article 4(2).

16. See David Ziskind, *Labor Provisions in Asian Constitutions,* Litlaw Foundation, Los Angeles, 1984; Ziskind, David, "Labor Law in Latin American Constitutions," *Comparative Labor Law,* University of California, Vol. 6 No. 1, Winter 1984; and Ziskind, David, *Labor Provisions in Constitutions of Europe,* Litlaw Foundation, Los Angeles, 1985.

17. *Labor Provisions in Constitutions of Europe,* pp. 57-58.

18. *Labor Provisions in Asian Constitutions,* pp. 28-29.

19. *Ibid.,* p. 61.

20. *Labor Provisions in Constitutions of Europe,* p. 17.

21. *Ibid.,* p. 21.

22. *Ibid.,* p. 55.
23. "Labor Law in Latin American Constitutions," p. 11.
24. *Ibid.,* p. 12.
25. *Ibid.,* p. 12.
26. "Women's Equality in the World's Constitutions."
27. "The Status of Women in Mexico," in *Women in the World,* Lynn Iglitzin and Ruth Ross (eds.), 2nd edition, ABC-CLIO, Santa Barbara CA, 1986, p. 317.
28. Margaret Schuler, *Empowerment and the Law,* OEF International, Washington DC, 1986, p. 67.
29. *Ibid.,* p. 76.
30. United Nations, *The Decade for Women in Latin America and the Caribbean,* Santiago, Chile, 1988, p. 130.
31. *Ibid.,* p. 178.
32. See de Villiers, et al., *African Problems and Challenges,* Valiant Publishers, Johannesburg, 1976, p. 67.
33. Schuler, p. 250.
34. Announced by A.Z.A.P., Kinshasha, Zaire, November 24, 1988.
35. *A Decade of Women and the Law,* Margaret Rogers (ed.), Commonwealth Secretariat, Legal Division, London, 1985, p. 335; and *Commonwealth Law Bulletin,* January 1978, p. 182.
36. United Nations, *Human Rights: International Instruments,* New York, ST/HR/4/Rev. 4, July 1, 1982.
37. *The State of the World's Women,* p. 17.
38. *The Cross Cultural Study of Women,* Feminist Press, City University of New York, 1986, p. 74.
39. G.R. Tamarin, "Israeli Society: Authoritarian Traditionalism vs. Pluralist Democracy," in *Case Studies on Human Rights,* Willem Veenhoven (ed.), Vol. 11, p. 119, Martinus Nijhof, The Hague, 1975. Cf. Svi Berinson: "Freedom of Religion and Conscience in the State of Israel," *Israel Yearbook of Human Rights,* 1973; and Pnina Lahav: "The Status of Women in Israel: Myth and Reality," *American Journal of Comparative Law,* Vol. 22, No. 107, 1974.
40. See G.R. Tamarin, *The Israeli Dilemma,* Rotterdam University Press, 1973, pp. 33–34.
41. See Lesley Hazleton, *Israeli Women: The Reality Behind the Myths,* Simon & Schuster, New York, 1987.
42. In Schuler, pp. 174–177.
43. *Ibid.*
44. Pakistan Survey, *The Economist,* London, January 17, 1987, p. 11.
45. Schuler, p. 3.
46. *Ibid.,* pp. 3–4. Cf. Diane Polan, "Towards a Theory of Law and Patriarchy," in *The Politics of Law: A Progressive Critique,* Pantheon Books, New York, 1982.
47. Pp. 175–176.
48. "The Equality Principle and the Section Division of Labour," *Women's Studies International Forum,* Vol. 9, No. 1, 1986, pp. 13–18.
49. *A Decade of Women and the Law,* pp. 175–176; *Commonwealth Law Bulletin,* July 1978, pp. 598–599; and *Commonwealth Law Bulletin,* October 1984, pp. 1958–1959.
50. *Commonwealth Law Bulletin,* January 1984, pp. 368–369.
51. See Rose Pearson and Albie Sachs, "Barristers and Gentlemen: A Critical Look at Sexism in the Legal Profession," *Modern Law Review,* Vol. 43, 1980, p. 400; and D. Podmore and A. Spencer, "The Law as a Sex-Typed Profession," 9 *Journal of Law and Society,* Vol. 9, 1982, p. 21.
52. Kumari Jayawardene, "A Note on Violence Against Women," *Voice of Women,* Colombo, Sri Lanka, Vol. 2, No. 7, 1985; "The Sad Plight of Iranian Women," *Bulletin,* Center for Women's Development Study, New Delhi, India, Vol. 2, No. 2,

1984; and cf. M.J. Hay and E.G. Bay, *Women in Africa: Studies in Social and Economic Change,* Stanford University Press, 1976, and, by the same authors, *African Women South of the Sahara,* Longman, New York, 1984.

53. "Islamic Law in Pakistan Punishes Rape Victims," *Voice of Women,* Colombo, Sri Lanka, No. 7, 1985, p. 38.

54. This entails the removal of the external genitalia while the outer vaginal lips are sewn shut, leaving just a tiny opening for urine and menstrual blood to pass. The operation is known as "Phaoronic circumcision."

55. *Women: A World Report,* Debbie Taylor (ed.), Oxford University Press, New York, 1985, p. 57.

56. *For the Record,* Caroline Pezzullo (ed.), International Women's Tribune Center, New York, 1985, p. 35.

57. *The State of the World's Women,* p. 17.

58. *Women: A World Survey,* World Priority Publications, Washington DC, 1985, pp. 31–33.

59. *Ibid.,* p. 31.

60. *Ibid.,* p. 32.

61. *Ibid.,* pp. 32–33.

62. See International Labour Organization, *Resources, Power and Women,* 1985, pp. 44–45.

63. Food and Agricultural Organization, *The Legal Status of Rural Women,* Rome, 1979; A.P. Okeyo, "The Joluo Equation," *Ceres,* Vol. 13, No. 3, 1983, pp. 37–42; and cf. *Female Power, Autonomy and Demographic Change in the Third World,* Richard Anker (ed.), Croom Helm, London, 1982, pp. 117–132.

64. *Time,* July 7, 1986, p. 40.

65. "Women and the Law in Ireland," *Women's Studies International Forum,* Vol. 2, No. 4, 1988, pp. 351–353.

66. 1937 Constitution, Article 41.3.2.

67. Patricia Prendiville, "Divorce in Ireland," in *Women's Studies International Forum,* Vol. 2, No. 4, 1988, p. 355.

68. University of Wisconsin Press, 1988.

69. *The Atlanta Journal and Constitution,* November 10, 1988, p. A9.

70. Reproduced in *The Atlanta Constitution,* October 1, 1988, p. A2.

71. *Time,* April 17, 1989, pp. 51–52.

Chapter 6. General Survey

1. K. Glaser and S. Possony, *Victims of Politics,* Columbia University Press, New York, 1979, p. 270.

2. Peggy Sanday, "Towards a Theory on the Status of Women," *American Anthropologist,* Vol. 76, 1976, p. 1696.

3. "Tradition Binds African Women to Circumcision Rite," *The Washington Post,* foreign news service, reprinted in *The Minneapolis Star and Tribune,* July 21, 1985, p. B1.

4. *Official Yearbook,* Department of Information, 1977, pp. 305–306. Cf. Marielouise Jannsen-Jurreit, *Sexism,* McGraw-Hill, New York, 1982, pp. 224–225; and M.J. Mbilinyi, "The State of Women in Tanzania," *Canadian Journal of African Studies,* 6/371, 1972.

5. *The Star,* Johannesburg, airmail edition, 22 June 1988.

6. *Ibid.,* November 23, World View, p. 7.

7. *Ibid.*

8. *The Houston Post,* November 17, 1988, p. A20.

9. International Labour Organization, *Rural Development and Women in Africa,* Geneva, 1984, pp. 53–54.

10. *Ibid.*, pp. 55–57.
11. *Ibid.*, p. 58.
12. *Women in Economic Activity,* Geneva, p. 41; International Labour Organization, *1982 Year Book of Labour Statistics,* Geneva, 1983, Table 1.
13. International Bank for Reconstruction and Development, *Population Growth and Policies in Sub-Saharan Africa,* Washington DC, August 1986.
14. *Ibid.*, p. 4.
15. United Nations, *World Population Trends and Politics,* Population Studies 103, 1988, p. 6.
16. *Why Africa Is Poor,* Citizens for Foreign Aid Reform, Toronto, Canada, 1987, p. 6.
17. *Ibid.*, pp. 8–13.
18. Worldwatch Institute, *Reversing Africa's Decline,* Washington DC, Worldwatch Paper No. 65, 1985; L. Timberlake, *Africa in Crisis,* International Institute for Environment and Development, Washington DC, 1985; and E.C. Wol, *Beyond the Green Revolution,* Worldwatch Institute, Washington DC, Worldwatch Paper No. 73, 1986.
19. *Population Growth and Policies in Sub-Saharan Africa,* p. 4.
20. United States Department of Commerce, *Women of the World,* Washington DC, May 1984, p. 2.
21. *Ibid.*, p. 53.
22. *Ibid.*, p. 54, quoting figures provided by the Central Bureau for Statistics, Nairobi, Kenya, for 1978.
23. *Ibid.*, p. 56.
24. *Ibid.*
25. *The Cross Cultural Study of Women,* Margot Duley and Mary Edwards (eds.), Feminist Press, City University of New York, 1986, p. 346. See "Women's Role in Economic Development," chapters 7 and 12, dealing with the educated black women and the design of female education.
26. Beverly Lindsy, "Issues Confronting Professional African Women," in *Comparative Perspectives of Third World Women,* Beverly Lindsy (ed.), Praeger Publishers, New York, 1980, pp. 78–95.
27. See Barbara Rogers, *The Domestication of Women: Discrimination in Developing Societies,* St. Martin's Press, New York, 1979.
28. *The Cross Cultural Study of Women,* p. 352.
29. *For the Record,* Caroline Pezzullo (ed.), International Women's Tribune Center, New York, 1985.
30. International Labour Organization, *Resources, Power and Women,* Geneva, 1985, p. 37.
31. International Labour Organization, *Women in Economic Activity,* Geneva, pp. 24–25; and cf. *Agrarian Policies and Rural Poverty in Africa,* D. Ghai and S. Radwan (eds.), International Labour Organization, Geneva, 1983, pp. 12–15.
32. International Labour Organization, *Women in Economic Activity,* p. 25.
33. International Labour Organization, Report II, Sixth African Regional Conference, Tunis, 1983, p. 93.
34. K. Akadiri, *The Modern Employment Market in Selected African Countries,* International Labour Organization, Geneva, 1984.
35. Population Crisis Committee, *Population Briefing Paper No. 20,* Washington DC, June 1988, pp. 6–7.
36. "Women in Zaire: Disparate Status and Roles," in *Comparative Perspectives of Third World Women,* pp. 55–77.
37. *The Cross Cultural Study of Women,* p. 352.
38. Veronique Dagadzi, "Law and the Status of Women in Togo," *Columbia Human Rights Law Review,* Vol. 8, No. 1, 1976, p. 295.

39. *The Female World from a Global Perspective,* Indiana University Press, Bloomington, 1987, pp. 88-95.

40. *The Cross Cultural Study of Women,* pp. 367-368.

41. Susan Roberts, "Efforts to Women's Development in Tanzania: Gender Rhetoric versus Gender Realities," in *Women in Developing Countries,* Kathleen Staudt and Jane Jacquette (eds.), Haworth Press, New York, 1983, pp. 23-41.

42. Audrey Wipper, "The Politics of Sex," *African Studies Review,* Vol. 14, No. 3, 1971, pp. 463-482.

43. Lance Morrow, in *The Cross Cultural Study of Women,* p. 369.

44. "Law, Education and Social Change: Implications for Hausa Muslim Women in Nigeria," in *Women in the World,* Lynn Iglitzin and Ruth Ross (eds.), 2nd edition, ABC-CLIO, Santa Barbara CA, 1986, p. 188.

45. *Ibid.,* p. 189.

46. *Muslim Peoples,* Richard V. Weekes (ed.), Greenwood Press, Westport CT, 1984, contains an excellent presentation of Muslim Law.

47. *Women in the World,* p. 183.

48. *Ibid.,* pp. 196-199.

Chapter 7. Case Study: Nigeria

1. The High Court Laws of the Eastern Region and the Western Region and the High Court of Lagos Act each provide for the application, as a first choice, of customary law where the parties are all Nigerians or where the justice of the case so requires, even if one or more parties are not Nigerians, provided that the customary law in question is not repugnant to natural justice, equity and good conscience, nor incompatible with the provisions of a written law, and provided further that the parties themselves had not previously agreed—either expressly or by necessary implication—that the transaction should be governed by some law other than customary law. S.N. Chinwuba Obi, *Modern Family Law in Southern Nigeria,* Sweet & Maxwell, London, 1966, p. 6.

2. Nancy J. Hafkin and Edna G. Bay (eds.), *Women in Africa: Studies in Social and Economic Change,* Stanford University Press, Stanford CA, 1975, p. 45.

3. Christopher Y.O. Adei, *African Law South of the Sahara,* International Institute for Advanced Studies, Missouri, 1981, p. 37.

4. Hafkin and Bay, p. 46.

5. *Ibid.,* pp. 47-48.

6. *Ibid.,* pp. 49-50.

7. *Ibid.,* p. 51.

8. *Ibid.,* p. 55.

9. *Ibid.,* pp. 55-56.

10. A more accurate term to be used is "polyandry" since there may be situations where there is one husband with many wives, but no situation of one wife with multiple husbands.

11. Adei, p. 21.

12. Obi, pp. 103-104.

13. The age of Marriage Law, 1956, of the Eastern Region, provides in Section 3(1) that "A . . . promise or offer of marriage between, or in respect of persons either of whom is under the age of sixteen shall be void." Obi, pp. 106-109.

14. Adei, p. 40.

15. Obi, p. 114.

16. *Ibid.,* p. 129.

17. *Ibid.,* p. 141.

18. *Ibid.,* p. 204.

19. *Ibid.,* p. 55.

20. *Ibid.,* p. 203.

21. *Ibid.,* p. 41.
22. *Ibid.,* p. 245.
23. *Ibid.,* pp. 245–246.
24. *Ibid.,* p. 247.
25. *Ibid.,* p. 215.
26. However, a husband remains under the duty to maintain if he deserts his wife. *Ibid.,* p. 248.
27. *Ibid.,* pp. 227–229.
28. *Ibid.,* pp. 263–264.
29. *Ibid.,* p. 42.
30. See generally *Ibid.,* pp. 248–252.
31. See *Ibid.,* pp. 252–254.
32. *Ibid.,* p. 256.
33. *Ibid.,* p. 254.
34. *Ibid.,* p. 257.
35. *Ibid.,* p. 257.
36. *Ibid.,* p. 257.
37. For further information, see footnote 54 in *Ibid.,* p. 258.
38. *Ibid.,* p. 258.
39. *Ibid.,* pp. 255–256.
40. *Ibid.,* p. 56.
41. *Ibid.,* p. 280.
42. *Ibid.,* p. 281.
43. See generally *Ibid.,* pp. 280–284.
44. "UN Honors Farm Women of Africa," *The New York Times,* May 16, 1986, p. 7.
45. Adei, p. 37.
46. *Ibid.,* p. 37.
47. See also the section on Personal Autonomy, this chapter. Nigerians living in villages know of the pressures young women in urban areas face to form relationships with men in order to ensure financial stability, and many parents fear sending their daughters to such a fate. See generally "Victimization of Babies in Nigerian Urban Centers," Nwokocha K.U. Nkpa, in *Victimology: An International Journal,* Emilio Viano (ed.), Vol. 5, 1980, pp. 251–262.
48. Hafkin and Bay, pp. 56–57.
49. *Ibid.,* pp. 57–58.
50. Jadesola O. Akande, *Introduction to the Nigerian Constitution (of 1979),* Sweet & Maxwell, London, 1982, Commentary on Article 39, section 1.
51. Hafkin and Bay, p. 46.
52. Rebecca J. Cook and Bernard M. Dickens, "Abortion Laws in African Commonwealth Countries," in *Journal of African Law,* A.N. Allott, H.F. Morris, and S.A. Roberts (eds.), Autumn 1981, Vol. 25, No. 2, p. 61.
53. *Ibid.,* p. 61.
54. *Ibid.,* p. 61.
55. Nkpa, p. 253.
56. *Ibid.,* p. 252.
57. *Ibid.,* pp. 255–256.
58. Obi, p. 105.
59. *Ibid.,* pp. 103–106.
60. Akande, Commentary on Article 39, section 1.
61. Obi, p. 119.
62. *Ibid.,* p. 381.
63. *Ibid.,* p. 382.

Chapter 8. Cast Study: Kenya

1. Rose, Maina, V.W. Muchai, and S.B.O. Gutto, "Law and the Status of Women in Kenya" in *Columbia Human Rights Law Review,* Vol. 8, No. 1, Spring-Summer 1976, p. 186.

2. U.U. Uche, *Law and Population Growth in Kenya,* background paper for workshop on the Teaching of Population Dynamics in Law Schools, University of Nairobi, 1974, p. 2.

3. Note: Section 13 of the African Christian Marriage and Divorce Act (Laws of Kenya, Chapter 151) removes compelled wife inheritance from polygamous marriages. One section provides that any African woman married in accordance with that Act, the Marriage Act, or under the repealed Native Christian Marriage Act, shall not be bound to cohabit with the brother or any other relative of her deceased husband or any other person, but shall have the same right to support for herself and her children of such marriage from such brother or other relative as she would have had if she had not been married under any of those provisions. (Uche, p. 22.)

4. *Ibid.,* p. 2.

5. *Ibid.*

6. A 1971 survey for the Family Planning Association of Kenya revealed that the majority of Kenyans still feel that it is right to have more than one wife. Even a good proportion of the educated elite seemed to share the view. *(Ibid.)*

7. Maina *et al.,* p. 189.

8. *Ibid.,* p. 189.

9. Wilson *v.* Glossop, 20 Q.B.D. 354, 357 (1888); Weingerteen *v.* Engle, 1 All. E.R. 425 (1947).

10. Note, however, that most husbands, lovers, wives and mistresses do not know of this legal right, and thus women do not exploit such a right (Maina, p. 188.)

11. *Ibid.,* p. 190.

12. Matrimonial Causes Act, Section 3.

13. Maina, p. 192.

14. *Ibid.*

15. Maina, p. 193.

16. *Ibid.*

17. *Ibid.*

18. Subordinate Courts (Separation and Maintenance) Act, Laws of Kenya, Chapter 153.

19. Maina, p. 192.

20. Laws of Kenya, Chapter 144.

21. Maina, pp. 193–194.

22. Kenya constitution §82(3) (1969).

23. Maina, pp. 186–187.

24. *Ibid.,* p. 194.

25. *Ibid.,* pp. 186–187.

26. *Ibid.,* pp. 192–193.

27. Law of Succession Act §5(2) (1972).

28. *Ibid.*

29. Maina, p. 195.

30. *Ibid.*

31. *Ibid.*

32. Uche, pp. 203.

33. Law of Succession Act (1972) clause 29.

34. See Margaret Schuler, *Empowerment and the Law,* OEF International, Washington DC, 1986, p. 3.

35. Maina, generally pp. 185–206.

36. Employment Act, no. 2/1976.
37. Maina, p. 185.
38. For another example beyond that discussed below, see pp. 51–56 in Audrey Wipper, "Riot and Rebellion Among African Women: Three Examples of Women's Political Clout," in Jean F. O'Barr, *Perspectives on Power: Women in Africa, Asia and Latin America,* Durham NC, Duke University Center for International Studies (1982), pp. 50–72.
39. The social hierarchy of the East African or Swahili coast has evolved over hundreds of years of migration and interaction by various peoples. The upper class included wealthy slave-owning families which grew out of intermarriage between long-time coastal residents—the Twelve Tribes of Mombasa—and immigrants from the Hadramaut and Oman in Arabia; the middle layers included some slave-owners among the traders, sailors, artisans, and laborers who were drawn from the poorer ranks of Twelve Tribes and Arab society as well as some freed slaves who rose to this level; the lower classes were comprised of slaves from the hinterland Mijikenda peoples and from central and east Africa. (Margaret Strobel, "From *Lelemama* to Lobbying: Women's Associations in Mombasa, Kenya," in *Women in Africa: Studies in Social and Economic Change,* Nancy J. Hafkin and Edna G. Bay (eds.), Stanford CA, Stanford University Press, 1976, pp. 183–211.
40. *Ibid.,* p. 183.
41. *Ibid.,* p. 184.
42. The heyday of *lelemama* groups was from 1920–1945, although the associations exist today on a reduced scale. For a more complete history and description of various groups, see generally Strobel, pp. 183–211.
43. *Ibid.,* p. 187.
44. *Ibid.,* p. 188.
45. *Ibid.,* pp. 188–189.
46. *Ibid.,* p. 192.
47. *Ibid.*
48. *Ibid.,* pp. 192–193.
49. The dance associations did not die a natural death. Instead, the effective demise of *lelemama* occurred when the competitions got out of hand and hostilities became overt in the "Battle of Kuze Road," after which the government banned *lelemama* for a time and disallowed dance permits for weddings or religious celebration. Hostilities cooled, but without competition interest died out and the dance associations lost their strength. In retrospect, many women now see the *ngoma* (the dances) as a waste of money. (Strobel, pp. 195–197.)
50. *Ibid.,* p. 200.
51. *Ibid.,* pp. 198–199.
52. *Ibid.,* pp. 205–206.
53. *Ibid.,* pp. 207–208.
54. *Ibid.,* pp. 208–211.
55. Maina, p. 195.
56. Uche, p. 2.
57. *Ibid.,* p. 4.
58. *Ibid.,* p. 2.
59. *Ibid.,* p. 1.
60. *Women's International Network News,* Vol. 12, Autumn 1986, p. 37.
61. Uche, p. 9.
62. *Women's International Network News,* p. 37.
63. Uche, p. 15.
64. *Ibid.,* p. 17.
65. *Ibid.*
66. Kathleen Barry, *Female Sexual Slavery,* Englewood Cliffs NJ, Prentice Hall, 1969, p. 161.

67. J.G. Kigondu, and M. Odera, "The Dangers of Female Circumcision/Genital Mutilation," *Women's International Network News,* Vol. 12, Autumn 1986, p. 24.

68. Kigondu and Odera, p. 24.

69. Barry, p. 161.

Chapter 9. Case Study: South Africa

1. See David Harrison, *The White Tribe of Africa,* Macmillan and the British Broadcasting Corporation, London, 1981; John Fisher, *The Afrikaners,* Cassell, London, 1969; and Robert Lacour-Gayet, *A History of South Africa,* Cassell, London, 1977.

2. NedBank, *South Africa: An Appraisal,* Johannesburg, 1977.

3. Leslie Dellatolla, "Women in the Economy," *Southern Africa Today,* Johannesburg, March 1988, pp. 1–8; "Changing Rights of Black Women," *Metropolitan Digest,* Johannesburg, January 15, 1988, p. 5; "Law Changes to Benefit Black Married Women," *Business Day,* Johannesburg, February 22, 1988; and "Black Women Increase Business Presence," *Business Day,* Johannesburg, November 14, 1986, p. 7.

4. Sinnah Kunene, "Discrimination in a Man's World," *City Press,* Johannesburg, April 8, 1988; and Daphne Nene, "A Survey of African Women Petty Traders," *Rural Development and Women in Africa,* International Labour Organization, Geneva, 1984, pp. 147–153.

5. Johannesburg, May 1987.

6. See "Study Shows Change in SA Women's Role," summary of Barbara Ross's speech "Tomorrow's Women," in *The Pretoria News,* August 19, 1986.

7. *The Work Situation of South African Women,* Ros Hirschowitz and Gerrie Cilliers (eds.), Human Sciences Research Council, Pretoria, 1987, p. 89.

8. "Tukkies Skaf Die Beperking Op Vrouestudente Af," *Beeld,* Johannesburg, June 15, 1984.

9. East London, May 5, 1987, text in hand.

10. *Beeld,* Johannesburg, September 12, 1984, p. 4.

11. *The Star,* Johannesburg, September 11, 1984, p. 5.

12. *The Work Situation of South African Women,* pp. 126–128.

13. *The Atlanta Constitution,* editorial, May 30, 1987.

14. South African Press Association, Johannesburg, March 19, 1986.

15. See Chapters 29 and 30 for conclusions and recommendations concerning comparable worth.

16. *The Citizen,* Johannesburg, July 28, 1987.

17. Address to the Gold Awards Ceremony of the South African Federation of Business and Professional Women, Johannesburg, October 1988.

18. Marika Sboros, "Some Women Are Not So Equal," *The Star,* Johannesburg, airmail edition, October 26, 1988, p. 12.

19. *The Work Situation of South African Women,* p. 138.

20. In May 1988 the government announced the appointment of Cecile Schmidt as South African Ambassador to Austria and Annette de Kock Joubert as Consul General in Glasgow, Scotland, the first women envoys ever. See *The Star,* Johannesburg, airmail edition, May 11, 1988, p. 8.

21. The Transkei is legally an independent state, at least in terms of South African constitutional provisions and in its right to enact its own laws, raise taxes, enter into agreements with foreign states, etc., and thus Ms. Sicgau's position is not discussed as part of the pattern of discrimination in the Republic of South Africa itself.

22. *The Work Situation of South African Women,* p. 5.

23. *Ibid.,* pp. 21–3, 10, 12.

24. *Ibid.,* p. 146.
25. Address by Prof. Danie Joubert, President of the University of Pretoria, *Beeld,* Johannesburg, May 23, 1984, p. 18.
26. *The Sunday Star,* Johannesburg, November 2, 1986, Financial Section, p. 7.
27. "Vroue Bly Steeds Mans Se Slawe," in *Rooi Rose,* January 7, 1987, pp. 28–30, 75.
28. *Ibid.*
29. *Ibid.*
30. *Ibid.*
31. Report on file dated December 1, 1986.
32. Christine M. Darden, 1987.
33. Department of Foreign Affairs, *Official Yearbook,* 1985, pp. 483–487.
34. *The Work Situation of South African Women,* pp. 84–85.
35. *Die Vaderland,* Johannesburg, September 9, 1984, p. 8.
36. *South African Digest,* June 27, 1986, p. 575.
37. *South African Digest,* November 21, 1986, p. 1074.
38. "Talle Rolle Bring Ook Konflik," *Die Vaderland,* Pretoria, May 13, 1987.
39. "How Women Can Achieve True Liberation," *The Star,* Johannesburg, May 10, 1986.
40. In 1988 there were also four women serving on the President's Council, a nominated advisory body; three women in the (elected) Colored House of Representatives; and one woman in the (elected) Indian House of Delegates. See "Politiek: SA Vrou Is Ver Agter," *Die Vaderland,* Johannesburg, March 9, 1988.
41. "The Four Women in Parliament," *The Star,* Johannesburg, May 11, 1987.
42. *The Star,* Johannesburg, March 23, 1987.
43. "Women Must Bargain for a Much Better Deal," *The Pretoria News,* April 30, 1987.
44. *Focus,* Part 5, No. 2, October 1986.
45. *The Star,* Johannesburg, September 9, 1984, p. 5.
46. "Doen Iets Aan Seksime In Handboeke," *Beeld,* Johannesburg, March 19, 1988, p. 6.
47. *The Work Situation of South African Women,* p. 75. See also D.K. De Meis and E. Hock, "The Balance of Employment and Motherhood," *Developmental Psychology,* Vol. 22, No. 5, pp. 627–632.
48. See E. Prinsloo, *Ek, My Kind of My Werk,* HAUM Publishers, Pretoria, 1987.
49. *The Work Situation of South African Women,* pp. 70–72, 81.
50. Wiehahn Report, paragraph 5.15.19.
51. See Wiehahn Commission report, Part 5, Chapter 5, "Women in Employment."
52. "Emancipation and Depression," *The Star,* Johannesburg, February 10, 1987, p. 13.
53. *The Star,* Johannesburg, July 8, 1986, p. 13.
54. "Women at Work: A Review of Staff Pension Schemes in the South African Labour Market," *IR Journal,* Pretoria, 2nd Quarter, 1986, pp. 22–31.
55. *The Citizen,* Johannesburg, June 6, 1984, p. 10.
56. *Die Vaderland,* Johannesburg, May 10, 1983.
57. *The Star,* Johannesburg, and *The Pretoria News,* May 10, 1983.
58. Women's Legal Status Committee, "Memorandum to the Commission of Inquiry into Labour Legislation," Johannesburg, September 1978. For an interesting comparison see Y.E. Polson, "Rights of Working Women," *Virginia International Law Review,* 15/729, 1974.
59. *Women: The Quiet Revolution,* Johannesburg, April 1985.
60. See Peter Stephan, "Oor Vroue en Belasting," *Fokus,* Part 5, No. 1, July 1986, p. 3.

61. "Women and the Law: Aspects of Discrimination."

62. January 28, 1987, signed by Margaret Lessing, Director of the Women's Bureau. See *The Pretoria News,* September 9, 1986, p. 6.

63. Debra Cleveland, "Women of the Cloth," *The Sunday Times,* Johannesburg, April 27, 1986, Life Style Section, p. 1.

64. *The Star,* Johannesburg, airmail edition, June 20, 1988.

65. Department of Foreign Affairs and Information, *Official Yearbook,* Pretoria, 1985, p. 799.

66. *Ibid.,* p. 916.

67. Department of Foreign Affairs, *South African Digest,* Pretoria, May 8, 1987, p. 15.

68. See *Factory and Family: The Divided Lives of South African Women,* Fatima Meer (ed.), Institute of Black Research, Durban, 1985; and Daphne Nene in *Rural Development and Women in Africa,* International Labour Organization, Geneva, 1985, pp. 147–153.

69. *The Star,* Johannesburg, March 17, 1986, p. 10; cf. Marina Maponya, "Problems and Challenges from a Black Woman's Point of View," in *South Africa: The Road Ahead,* G.F. Jacobs (ed.), Jonathan Ball Publishers, Johannesburg, 1986, pp. 206–208.

70. Helen Wishart, "Law Changes to Benefit Black Married Women," *Business Day,* Johannesburg, February 22, 1988. Cf. "Marital Status of Blacks Boosted," *The Star,* December 14, 1988, airmail edition, p. 11.

71. "Women's Role in Building Bridges and Seeking Solutions," in *South Africa: The Road Ahead,* p. 213.

72. "Changing Rights of Black Women," *Metropolitan Digest,* Johannesburg, January 15, 1988, p. 5; "Women Do Have Some Rights," *The Pretoria News,* February 2, 1987.

73. *South African Digest,* Pretoria, November 21, 1986, pp. 1074–1075. Cf. "Black Women Are Quietly Overcoming Prejudice," *The Citizen,* Johannesburg, November 13, 1986.

74. *South African Digest,* April 3, 1987, p. 15.

75. "Vrou Kry 'n Kans Om Te Leer," *Beeld,* Johannesburg, January 7, 1987.

76. *The Cape Times,* Cape Town, December 3, 1985, p. 2.

77. Sinnah Kunene, "Discrimination in a Man's World," *City Press,* Johannesburg, April 8, 1984; and "NdeBele Women Flex Their Muscle," *The Star,* Johannesburg, airmail edition, December 21, 1988.

78. "Black Advancement Race Is On," *The Star,* Johannesburg, airmail edition, December 21, 1988.

79. In *Fair Lady,* March 18, 1987, p. 123.

80. See "Restraints on Black Women Cast Aside," *The Star,* Johannesburg, May 19, 1986, p. 7.

81. *South African Digest,* Pretoria, November 23, 1984, p. 22.

82. *Southern Africa Today,* Johannesburg, March 1988, pp. 1–7.

83. Repeal of the Black (Urban Areas) Consolidation Act of 1945; Repeal of the Black Labor Act 67 of 1964, published in *The Government Gazette,* Pretoria, July 1, 1986; and Restoration of South Africa Citizenship Act 73 of 1986. See *South African Digest,* Pretoria, January 30, 1987, p. 2, and November 27, 1987, p. 2.

84. See D.M. Mabiletsa, "Black Women's Progress Despite Problems," speech delivered to the Catholic Women's League, February 6, 1985.

85. In terms of the 1983 Constitution, Indian and colored women may vote on an equal basis with men for representatives in the Indian and Colored chambers of the central Parliament. In 1976 Alathea Jansen, a colored woman, was appointed Chairman of the (elected) Colored Persons Representative Council.

86. "SADF Treats All Members Alike," *The Pretoria News,* May 16, 1986.

87. *The Herald,* Port Elizabeth, May 7, 1985, p. 8.
88. *The Star,* Johannesburg, September 11, 1984, p. 5.
89. "Women's Lib Means Political Liberation," *The Star,* Johannesburg, August 4, 1986, p. 12.
90. *The Star,* Johannesburg, August 4, 1986, p. 12, and September 11, p. 5.
91. "Role Expectation of Women and Their Husbands," in *The Work Situation of South African Women,* pp. 89–112.
92. *The Politics of the Second Electorate,* Joni Lovenduski and Jill Hills (eds.), Routledge and Kegan Paul, London, 1981, p. 328.
93. "Studeer Hulle Vergeefs," *Beeld,* Johannesburg, April 28, 1987.
94. *The Work Situation of South African Women,* pp. 130–131.
95. University of the Orange Free State Research Institute for Educational Planning, *Education and Manpower Development Study,* Bloemfontein, 1988.
96. Eleanor Preston-Whyte and Jennifer Louw, "The End of Childhood," in *Growing Up in a Divided Society,* Eleanor Preston-Whyte and Jennifer Louw (eds.), Ravan Press, Johannesburg, 1986, pp. 361-362.
97. Unpublished article about the future of education in South Africa, HAUM Publishers, Pretoria, 1987.
98. See *Focus,* Part 5, No. 3, January 1987, p. 2.
99. *Ibid.,* p. 6. Cf. S. van der Walt, *Die Vrou in Die Werksituasie in die RSA: 'n Verwysingsraamwerk,* Human Sciences Research Council, Pretoria, 1986.
100. *The Star,* Johannesburg, June 24, 1987, p. 8.

Chapter 10. General Survey

1. Commission of the European Communities, *Equal Opportunities 2nd Action Programme 1986–1990,* Women's Information Service, Supplement No. 23 to *Women of Europe,* Women's Information Service, Brussels, 1985, Preface, and *Men and Women of Europe in 1987,* Supplement No. 26 to *Women of Europe,* Women's Information Service, Brussels, December 1987.
2. Britain, Home Office, *New Earnings Survey,* part A, Table 15, April 1979.
3. Britain's Equal Opportunities Commission, quoted in *The International Herald Tribune,* Paris, July 18, 1986.
4. *Time,* July 7, 1986, p. 40.
5. *Europe,* July/August 1984, pp. 26–28.
6. International Labour Organization, *Women in Economic Activity,* pp. 89–99.
7. International Labour Organization, *The Economic Role of Women in the ECE Region,* Geneva, 1985, p. 11.
8. *Ibid.*
9. H.M. Hernes, "Women and the Welfare State," in *Patriarchy in a Welfare Society,* H. Holter (ed.), Oslo University Press, 1984.
10. International Labour Organization, *The Economic Role of Women in the ECE Region,* p. 57.
11. International Labour Organization, *The Economic Role of Women in the ECE Region,* E.80.II.E.6, Table III, 13.
12. *Ibid.,* pp. 61–62.
13. Article III of the 1948 Constitution.
14. *The Sunday Telegraph,* London, May 22, 1988, International, p. 9.
15. See Lucia Birnbaum, *Feminism in Italy,* Wesleyan University Press, 1987.
16. Bianca Becalli, in *Women Workers in Fifteen Countries,* Jennie Farley (ed.), ILR Press, Ithaca NY, 1985, p. 154.
17. Bianca Becalli and Rita Invernizzi, "Women in Non-Traditional Jobs, the

Italian Case," paper presented at the Conference on the Empowerment of Women, Groningen, Sweden, 1984.

18. Shari Steiner, *The Female Factor: Women in West Europe,* Intercultural Press, Chicago, 1977, p. 126.

19. *The Atlanta Constitution,* January 21, 1988, p. A2.

20. *The Wall Street Journal,* New York, September 23, 1985, p. 34; and *Time,* October 7, 1985, p. 47.

21. See *Time,* American edition, April 11, 1985, p. 53.

22. *The Atlanta Constitution,* May 8, 1987, p. 23.

23. *The Atlanta Constitution,* June 27, 1988, p. A5.

24. A.M.C. Makkee, in *Comparative Law Yearbook,* Vol. 8, p. 23.

25. See Pessers, "Kroniek Femminisme en Recht," *Nederlands Juristenblad,* 1984.

26. Makkee in *Comparative Law Yearbook,* Vol. 8, p. 28.

27. University of Massachusetts Press, Amherst, 1986, p. 223.

28. Shari Steiner, p. 296.

29. *Ibid.,* p. 300. Cf. Anna P. Schreiber, "The Status of Women in the United States and Scandinavian Countries" in Richard Claude (ed.), *Comparative Human Rights,* Johns Hopkins University Press, Baltimore, 1976; and Helene Thalman-Antenen, "Equal Pay: The Position in Switzerland," *International Law Review,* 104/275, 19712.

30. *Women and European Politics,* p. 234.

31. "Switzerland," in *Women Workers in Fifteen Countries,* pp. 147–153.

32. "Gender and Race Differences in Criminal Justice Processing," *Women's Studies International Forum,* Vol. 9, No. 1, 1986, pp. 89–99.

33. Vol. 9, No. 1, 1986, pp. 19–24.

34. See Georgina Ferry, "Was WISE Worthwhile," in *New Scientist,* January 3, 1985, pp. 28–31.

35. "Great Britain," in *Women Workers in Fifteen Countries,* p. 110.

36. "Italy," in *Women Workers in Fifteen Countries,* pp. 155–156.

37. "Federal Republic of Germany," in *Women Workers in Fifteen Countries,* p. 135.

38. Commission of the European Communities, *Child Care and Equality of Opportunities,* Strasbourg, 1988.

39. August 22, 1988, p. 36.

40. See Sylvia Hewlett, *A Lesser Life,* Warner Books, 1986, Chapters Four and Five.

41. *Ibid.,* p. 68.

42. 1975 Employment Protection Act as amended by the Employment Protection (Consolidation) Act of 1978 and the Employment Act of 1980.

43. Commission of the European Communities, *Men and Women of Europe in 1987,* Supplement No. 26 to *Women of Europe,* Women's Information Service, Brussels, December 1987, pp. 32–33, 35 and 54–55.

44. *Women of Europe,* May-July 1986.

45. Commission of the European Communities, *Women and Television in Europe,* Supplement No. 28 to *Women of Europe,* Women's Information Service, Brussels, September 1988, pp. 18, 20 and 24.

46. *Women of Europe,* September/October 1988, p. 28.

47. *Women of Europe,* November 87/January 88, pp. 3–4.

48. *Women of Europe,* September/October 1988, p. 13.

Chapter 11. Case Study: The United Kingdom

1. 1970, ch. 41.
2. 1975, ch. 65.
3. Steiner, "Sex Discrimination under UK and EEC Law: Two Plus Four Equals One," *International and Comparative Law Review,* Vol. 32, 1983, p. 399.
4. (1979) 1 ALL ER 456, 463.
5. (1979) 1 ALL ER 456, 463.
6. Steiner, p. 403.
7. (1981) IRLR 388 (EAT).
8. Steiner, p. 403.
9. New Zealand and Israel are the only other nations which do not have or are not committed to one-document constitutions.
10. 7 & 8 Geo. V, c. 64 (1918).
11. For a comprehensive study of women's rights at the polls in the United Kingdom, see Constance Rover, *Women's Suffrage and Party Politics in Britain, 1866–1914,* Routledge & Kegan Paul, London, 1967.
12. Prior to being given the vote in national elections, women of America held the franchise in 20 states.
13. 1967, ch. 56.
14. 1976, ch. 50.
15. 1969, ch. 55.
16. 1973, ch. 18.
17. *Sexism and the Law: A Study of Male Beliefs and Legal Bias in Britain and the United States.* Free Press, New York, 1979, p. 143.
18. *Ibid.,* 142.
19. 1970, ch. 45.
20. 1973, ch. 18.
21. Michael L. Rakusen and D. Peter Hunt, *Distribution of Matrimonial Assets on Divorce,* Butterworths, London, 1982.
22. (1973) 1 ALL ER 829, CA.
23. Id. at 836.
24. 1882, ch. 75.
25. Albie Sachs and John Huff Wilson, *Sexism and the Law.*
26. (1973) 1 ALL ER 829, CA.
27. *Ibid.*
28. *Britain 1985,* Her Majesty's Stationery Office, London, 1985, p. 20.
29. *Ibid.*
30. 1975, ch. 73. Prior to this Act, it had been possible since 1938 for destitute surviving spouses to apply to the courts for maintenance monies from the estates of their deceased husbands.
31. 1970, ch. 41.
32. 1975, ch. 65.
33. Erica Szysczak, "Pay Inequalities and Equal Value Claims," *Modern Law Review,* Vol. 48, 1985, p. 129.
34. See E.E.C. Council Directives 75/117, 76/207 and 79/7.
35. Vivien Shrubsall, "Sex Discrimination: Retirement and Pensions," *Modern Law Review,* Vol. 48, 1985, p. 373.
36. By contrast, the Commission for Racial Equality has a larger budget for a smaller number of applicants.
37. Cosmo Graham and Norman Lewis, *The Role of ACAS Conciliation in Equal Pay and Sex Discrimination Cases,* Equal Opportunities Commission, London, 1985.
38. 1878, ch. 19. One could even go back to 1828, when wife abuse could be prosecuted under the criminal law, and to the Offenses Against the Person Act, 1861. But

it was not until the 1878 Act that a direct remedy was available—magistrates were now authorized to grant separation and maintenance orders to wives who had been assaulted by their husbands where such assaults had resulted in convictions.

39. 1976, ch. 50. This Act provides protections in the county courts.

40. 1978, ch. 22. Amends 1976 Act in part.

41. Kathryn McCann, "Battered Women and the Law: The Limits of the Legislation," Chapter 4 in *Women-in-Law: Explorations in Law, Family and Sexuality,* Julia Brophy and Carol Smart (eds.), Routledge & Kegan Paul, London, 1985, p. 71.

42. *Ibid.*

43. *Ibid.,* p. 94.

44. *Ibid.,* p. 71.

45. See L. Chester and S. Boston, "Secret Memo Aims to Stop Equal Pay for Women," *The Sunday Times,* London, February 11, 1973.

46. Shari Steiner, *The Female Factor: Women in West Europe,* Intercultural Press, Chicago, 1977, p. 182.

47. See Judith Blake, "The Changing Status of Women in Developed Countries," *Scientific American,* Vol. 231, 1974, pp. 127–147.

48. *The Politics of the Second Electorate,* Joni Lovenduski and Jill Hills (eds.), Routledge & Kegan Paul, London, 1981, p. 8.

49. *Ibid.,* p. 11.

50. *Employment Gazette,* London, March 1980, p. 280.

51. *The Daily Telegraph,* London, April 3, 1986, p. 6.

52. *The Daily Telegraph,* London, April 2, 1986, p. 1.

53. Pp. 13–14.

Chapter 12. Case Study: France

1. G. Eisenhardt, *Deutsche Rechtsgeschichte,* Beck Verlag, West Germany, 1984, p. 185.

2. *Citoyennes à part entière,* No. 43, June 1985.

3. *Historical Development and Descriptive Analysis of National Machinery Set Up in Member States of the Council of Europe to Promote Equality Between Women and Men,* Council of Europe, Strasbourg, 1982, pp. 16–19, 47–49; *National Institutional and Non-institutional Machinery Established in the Council of Europe Member States to Promote Equality Between Women and Men,* Council of Europe, Strasbourg, 1985, pp. 22–28, 72–73.

4. *Frauen Europas,* Kommission der Europaischen Gemeinschaft, Brussels, No. 45, March-May 1986, p. 21.

5. John Ardagh, *France in the 1980s,* Penguin Books, New York, p. 349.

6. *Frauen Europas,* p. 21.

7. *European Ministerial Conference on Equality Between Women and Men,* Strasbourg, March 4, 1986, p. 3; and "Policy and Strategies to Achieve Equality in Decision-Making," report submitted by the French delegation, in *European Ministerial Conference,* p. 4.

8. *Positive Action for the Benefit of Women,* Andrée Michel (ed.), Council of Europe, Strasbourg, 1986, p. 9.

9. *Ibid.,* Vol. 3, p. 4.

10. Ardagh, p. 349.

11. *Equality Between Women and Men,* Proceedings of the seminar, "Contribution of the Media to the Promotion of Equality Between Women and Men," Council of Europe, Strasbourg, June 21–23, 1985, pp. 178–183.

12. Ardagh, pp. 14–15.

13. *Ibid.,* p. 347.

14. *Guide des droits des femmes,* Centre National d'Information sur les Droits des Femmes, 1986, pp. 66–69.

15. *Ibid.,* pp. 72–79.

16. *Report on the Situation of Women in Europe,* European Parliament, 1984, Doc. 1-1229/83/C, p. 415.

17. *Guide des droits des femmes,* p. 93.

18. *Ibid.,* p. 95.

19. *Ibid.,* pp. 78–85.

20. *Le concubinage: vos droits,* Centre National d'Information sur les Droits des Femmes, 1986.

21. *Citoyennes à part entière,* No. 50, February 1986, pp. 12–13.

22. *Guide des droits des femmes,* pp. 105–107.

23. *Egalité(e), 1981 les droits des femmes vers l'an 1000,* Ministère des Droits de la Femme.

24. *Citoyennes à part entière,* No. 49, January 1986, p. 4.

25. *Positive Action for the Benefit of Women,* Vol. 3, p. 16.

26. *Ibid.,* Vol. 1, pp. 11, 31.

27. *Ibid.,* p. 17.

28. EG (86) 1, p. 20.

29. EG (86) 1, pp. 31, 41.

30. MEG (86) 3, p. 13.

31. *Frauen Europas,* No. 42, Sept.-Nov. 1985.

32. *Positive Action for the Benefit of Women,* Vol. 1, p. 18; *Frauen Europas,* No. 38, Nov. 1984–Jan. 1985, p. 21.

33. *Guide des droits des femmes,* p. 38.

34. *Ibid.,* p. 39.

35. *Ibid.,* pp. 175–185.

36. *Ibid.,* pp. 360, 361.

37. *Ibid.,* pp. 363, 365.

38. *Ibid.,* pp. 124–131.

39. EG (86) 1, p. 15.

40. MEG (86) 3, p. 9.

41. EG (86) 1, p. 15.

42. Shari Steiner, *The Female Factor: Women in West Europe,* Intercultural Press, Chicago, 1977, p. 182.

43. *Ibid.,* p. 134.

44. *Le Nouvelle Observateur,* Paris, January 28, 1983.

45. Data by United States Department of Commerce and Labor, Equal Employment Commission, and graphically set out in *U.S. News and World Report,* November 29, 1982, p. 55.

46. *The Politics of the Second Electorate,* Joni Lovenduski and Jill Hills (eds.), Routledge & Kegan Paul, London, 1981, pp. 113–114.

47. *Ibid.,* pp. 119–120.

48. *Women Workers in Fifteen Countries,* Jennie Farley (ed.), ILR Press, Ithaca NY, 1985, p. 113.

Chapter 13. Case Study: West Germany

1. Ines Reich-Hilweg, *Männer und Frauen sind gleichberechtigt,* Article 3 Abs.2 GG, Europaische Verlagsanstalt, 1979, pp. 44–45.

2. Faschismusforschung Frauengruppe, *Mutterkreuz und Arbeitsbuch, Zur Geschichte der Frauen in der Weimarer Republik und im Nationalsozialismus,* Fischer Taschenbuch Verlag, pp. 7–13, 50, 54.

3. For a very cohesive discussion on Article 3 see Reich-Hilweg.

4. Reich-Hilweg, p. 31.

5. Constitutional Court decision, BVerfGE ("Bundesverfassungsgerichtsentscheidung") 10, 59ff.

6. Reich-Hilweg, p. 139.

7. *Frauen in der Bundesrepublik Deutschland,* Bundesminister für Jugend, Familie und Gesundheit, Summer 1984, p. 43.

8. *Equality Between Women and Men,* Proceedings of the seminar, "Contribution of the Media to the Promotion of Equality Between Women and Men," Council of Europe, Strasbourg, June 21–23, 1983, pp. 97–117.

9. For general reading on the family see a) *Grundgesetz Alternativ-Kommentar,* Luchterhand, 1984, Band 1 Article 3 und 6 GG; b) Gerrit Langenfeld, *Der Ehevertrag,* 1985; and c) Siegfried de Witt and Johann-Friedrich Huffman, *Nicht-eheliche Lebensgemeinschaft,* NJW-Schriftenreihe 2., 1986.

10. BVerfGE 6/55,72.

11. Continuous jurisdiction of the Constitutional Court.

12. BVerfGE 6/55;53/224, 257.

13. Langenfeld, p. 34ff.

14. *Ibid.,* p. 142.

15. *Frauen in der Bundesrepublik Deutschland,* pp. 21–26.

16. *Daten zur Frauenarbeitslosigkeit und Frauenerwerbstatigkeit,* Bundesminister für Arbeit und Soziales, Bonn, April 16, 1986.

17. *National Institutional and Non-institutional Machinery Established in the Council of Europe Member States to Promote Equality Between Women and Men,* Council of Europe, Strasbourg, 1985, pp. 29, 30, 74.

18. Heide Pfarr, "Quotierung und Rechtswissenschaft," in H. Daubler-Gmelin, H. Pfarr, M. Weg, "Mehr als nur gleicher Lohn," *Hanbuch zur beruflichen Forderung von Frauen,* VSA Verlag, 1985, pp. 86–87.

19. *Neue Juristische Wochenzeitschrift,* NJW, 1984, p. 202.

20. Pfarr, p. 88.

21. For the discussion see Pfarr, pp. 86–87, and *Frauenforderplane,* Wissenchaftlich Abteilung des Bundestages, Bonn, February 1986.

22. Die Gruenen, *Vorlaufiger Entwurf eines Anti-Diskriminierungs gesetzes,* January 1986.

23. *Frauen in der Bundesrepublik Deutschland,* p. 51.

24. Gisela Wild, in *Comparative Law Yearbook,* Vol. 8, 1985, p. 9.

25. *Ibid.,* p. 12.

26. Article 109, paragraph 2.

27. Wild, p. 14.

28. *The Politics of the Second Electorate,* Joni Lovenduski and Jill Hills (eds.), Routledge & Kegan Paul, London, 1981, p. 155.

29. *Ibid.,* p. 177.

30. Shari Steiner, *The Female Factor: Women in West Europe,* Intercultural Press, Chicago, 1977, pp. 213–214; and see also Herta Kuhrig, *Equal Rights for Women in the German Democratic Republic,* publication of the G.D.R. Committee for Human Rights, 1973.

31. See *Abortion Law and Public Policy,* Dennis Campbell (ed.), Martinus Nijhof, The Hague, 1984.

32. "Federal Republic of Germany," in *Women Workers in Fifteen Countries,* Jennie Farley (ed.), ILR Press, Ithaca NY, 1985, p. 154.

Chapter 14. Case Study: Switzerland

1. Arthur Haefliger, *Alle Schweizer sind vor dem Gesetze gleich,* Zur Tragweite des Article 4 der Bundesverfassung, Bern, 1985, p. 19.

2. *Ibid.*, p. 30.

3. Martine Chaponniere-Grandjean, *Geschichte einer Initiative, gleiche Rechte für Mann und Frau,* 1983 – summary of the events leading to women's vote and equality.

4. Haefliger, pp. 78, 179.

5. *Ibid.*, p. 42; and Lili Nabholz-Haidegger, "Die rechtliche Situation der Frau in der Schweiz," in *Frau Realitat und Utopie,* Christa Koppel, Ruth Sommerauer, 1984.

6. See *La Situation de la femme en Suisse,* Elisabeth Veya, 1983.

7. *Frauenfragen,* Eidgenossischen Kommission für Frauenfragen, Bern, No. 1, March 1986, p. 97.

8. "The Situation of Women in the Political Process in Europe, Part II," *Women in the Political World in Europe,* Council of Europe, Strasbourg, 1984, pp. 16, 17.

9. *Ibid.*, pp. 93, 107.

10. *Fakten zur Emanzipation von Frau und Mann,* "Ausgelaugt bis Zartlichkeit," Eidgenossischen Kommission für Frauenfragen, Bern/Zurich, 1983, see head-word "Parliament."

11. *Ibid.*, see head-word "Stimmbeteiligung."

12. Haefliger, p. 33.

13. *International Herald Tribune,* August 7, 1986.

14. *Fakten zur Emanzipation von Frau und Mann,* see head-word "Politik, Bundesverwaltung."

15. *Ibid.*, see head-word "Politik, offentliches Leben."

16. *Ibid.*, see head-word "gesamtverteidigung"; also *Frauenfragen,* April 1985, p. 47.

17. *Fakten zur Emanzipation von Frau und Mann,* see head-word "Partnerschaft."

18. *Frauenfragen,* April 1985, p. 48.

19. *Rapport,* note 6, p. 19.

20. *Rapport,* note 6, pp. 19, 20.

21. *Fakten zur Emanzipation von Frau und Mann,* see head-word "Familienrecht."

22. *Rapport,* p. 32.

23. *Fakten zur Emanzipation von Frau und Mann,* see head-word "Steuerrecht"; *Rapport,* pp. 43–47.

24. *Frauenfragen,* January 1986, p. 9.

25. *Fakten zur Emanzipation von Frau und Mann,* see head-word "AHV Alter-s-und Hinterlassenenversicherung."

26. *Ibid.*, see head-word "Familienrecht"; and *Frauenfragen,* January 1985, p. 27ff.

27. *Fakten zur Emanzipation von Frau und Mann,* see head-word "Arbeitslosigkeit"; and *Statistisches Jahrbuch der Schweiz,* 1985.

28. Haefliger, pp. 83, 84.

29. *Ibid.*, p. 84, BGE (Bundesgerichtshofentscheidung) 108Ia 22.

30. *Frauenfragen,* January 1986, p. 97.

31. *Fakten zur Emanzipation von Frau und Mann,* see head-word "Gesamtarbeitsvertrage, Lohn."

32. Claudia Kaufmann, "Kompensatorische Massnahmen zur Gleichstellung von Frau and Mann," *Frauenfragen,* February 1985.

33. *Frauenfragen,* February 1985, "Berichte," pp. 16, 25, 40, 49.

34. *Positive Action for the Benefit of Women,* Council of Europe, Strasbourg 1986, Vol. 1, pp. 22, 3, 39.

35. *International Herald Tribune,* June 4, 1986, p. 14.

36. *Fakten zur Emanzipation von Frau und Mann,* see head-word "Paritatslohn, Primarsektor."

37. *Rapport,* p. 84.

38. *Ibid.*, pp. 52–55.

39. Nabholz-Haidegger.

40. *Fakten zur Emanzipation von Frau und Mann,* see head-word "Mutterschaftschutz."
41. *Ibid.;* also "Frauenhauser," *Badische Zeitung,* August 5, 1986.
42. Gunter Stratenwerth, "Revision des Sexualstrafrecht," *Frauenfragen,* January 1986, pp. 54–58.
43. *Frauenfragen,* January 1986, p. 97.
44. *Historical Development and Descriptive Analysis of National Machinery Set Up in Member States of the Council of Europe to Promote the Equality Between Women and Men,* Council of Europe, Strasbourg, 1982, pp. 42, 63.
45. "Egalité des droits entre hommes et femmes," *Rapport sur le programme legislatif,* February 26, 1986 (86.008).

Chapter 15. Canada

1. Peter W. Hogg, *Constitutional Law of Canada,* 2nd ed., Carswell Co., Toronto, 1985, p. 723.
2. *Sisterhood Is Global,* Robin Morgan (ed.), Anchor Press/Doubleday, Garden City NY, 1984, p. 100.
3. Hogg, p. 723.
4. *Sisterhood Is Global,* p. 100.
5. Penney Kome, *Women of Influence,* Doubleday Canada, Toronto, 1985, p. 31.
6. Mary Eberts, "Women and Constitutional Renewal," in *Women and the Constitution in Canada,* Audrey Doerr and Micheline Carrier (eds.), Canadian Advisory Council on the Status of Women, Ottawa, 1981, pp. 7–8; *Edwards v. A.-G. Can.* (1930) A.C. 124.
7. Hogg, p. 726.
8. *Ibid.,* p. 726.
9. Eberts, p. 8.
10. Janet Kask, "Women and the Law," in *Mother Was Not a Person,* Margret Andersen (ed.), Content Publishing and Black Rose Books, Montreal, 1972, p. 47.
11. Kask, p. 47.
12. *Ibid.,* p. 48.
13. Hogg, p. 453.
14. *Ibid.,* p. 475.
15. Claire L'Heureux-Dube, "The Quebec Experience: Codification of Family Law and a Proposal for the Creation of a Family Court System," *Louisiana Law Review,* Vol. 44, 1984, p. 1592.
16. L'Heureux-Dube, pp. 1593–94.
17. Josephine F. Milburn, *Women as Citizens,* Sage Publications, London, 1976, p. 14.
18. Milburn, p. 15.
19. L'Heureux-Dube, p. 1593.
20. *Ibid.,* p. 1594.
21. Kask, p. 50.
22. L'Heureux-Dube, p. 1595.
23. *Ibid.,* p. 1595.
24. *Ibid.,* p. 1604.
25. *Ibid.,* p. 1604.
26. *Ibid.,* p. 1605.
27. Kask, p. 48.
28. *Ibid.,* p. 48.
29. *Ibid.,* p. 48.
30. L'Heureux-Dube, p. 1596.
31. *Ibid.,* p. 1597.

32. See *Women and the Constitution in Canada,* Audrey Doerr and Micheline Carrier (eds.), Canadian Advisory Council on the Status of Women, Ottawa, 1981; and Labreche, "Women's Pressure Groups – What's Their Role in the Eighties," *Chatelaine,* July 1982.
33. *The Atlanta Journal and Constitution,* January 29, 1988, p. A3.
34. (1983) 4 D.L.R. (4th) 112 (Sask. Q.B.).
35. Hogg, p. 744.
36. Morgan, p. 101.
37. *Ibid.,* p. 101.
38. Kask, p. 154.
39. Sherri Aikenhead, "Abortion on the Docket," *Maclean's,* October 20, 1986, p. 56.
40. *Ibid.,* p. 56.
41. *Ibid.,* p. 56.
42. Hogg, p. 533.
43. Eberts, p. 15.
44. Hogg, p. 535.
45. *Ibid.,* pp. 536, 534.
46. *Ibid.,* p. 635.
47. *Ibid.,* p. 534.
48. Morgan, p. 102.
49. *Ibid.,* p. 102.
50. *Ibid.,* p. 102.
51. *Ibid.,* p. 101.
52. L'Heureux-Dube, pp. 1598–99.
53. Hogg, p. 552.
54. *Ibid.,* p. 552–53.
55. Beverly Baines, "Women, Human Rights and the Constitution," in *Women and the Constitution in Canada,* Audrey Doerr and Micheline Carrier (eds.), Canadian Advisory Council on the Status of Women, Ottawa, 1981, p. 47.
56. (1974) S.C.R. 1249.
57. Baines, p. 48.
58. "Statement by Native Women's Association of Canada on Native Women's Rights," in *Women and the Constitution in Canada,* Audrey Doerr and Micheline Carrier (eds.), Canadian Advisory Council on the Status of Women, Ottawa, 1981, p. 66.
59. Hogg, p. 552.
60. *Ibid.,* p. 536.
61. Morgan, p. 101.
62. Kask, p. 51.
63. Hogg, p. 537.
64. Eberts, p. 18.
65. *Ibid.,* p. 18.
66. Hogg, p. 798.
67. (1978) 23 N.R. 527 (S.C.C.).
68. Eberts, p. 11.
69. *Ibid.,* p. 11.
70. Hogg, p. 791.
71. *Ibid.,* p. 798.
72. *Ibid.,* p. 798.
73. *Ibid.,* p. 801.
74. *Ibid.,* p. 632.
75. Greta Hofmann Nemiroff, "Canada, the Empowerment of Women," in *Sisterhood Is Global,* Robin Morgan (ed.), Anchor Press/Doubleday, Garden City NY, 1984, p. 105.

76. Sherri Aikenhead, Doug Smith, and Jennifer Henderson, "Women's Battle to Close the Wage Gap," *Maclean's,* October 27, 1986, p. 58.
77. *Ibid.,* p. 58.
78. *Ibid.,* p. 58.
79. *Ibid.,* p. 58.
80. Morgan, p. 101.
81. *Ibid.,* p. 101.
82. John Barber, *et al.,* "Parents, Jobs and Children," *Maclean's,* November 10, 1986, p. 46.
83. *Ibid.,* p. 46.
84. *Comparative Law Yearbook,* Vol. 8, 1985, p. 3.
85. *Ibid.,* p. 4.
86. *Report of the Royal Commission on the Status of Women,* Government of Canada, 1970, p. 262.
87. Cited by Sylvai Bashevkin, *Comparative Law Yearbook,* Vol. 8, p. 6.

Chapter 16. Case Study: The USA

1. United States Bureau of the Census, *Estimates of the Population of the United States by Age, Sex and Race,* Washington DC, 1987; National Center for Health Statistics, *1986 Annual Summary of Births, Marriages, Divorces and Deaths,* Washington DC, 1987.
2. G. Miller in *New York State Journal of Medicine,* February 1986.
3. *Women's Changing Role,* Information Aids, Wylie TX, 1988, pp. 2–4.
4. John F. Stinson, "Moonlighting by Women," in *Monthly Labor Review,* United States Bureau of Labor Statistics, Washington DC, November 1986. Cf. Maureen Downey, "America's New Work Force," *The Atlanta Journal and Constitution,* February 1, 1988, p. C1.
5. *Wall Street Journal,* September 16, 1985, p. 5, col. 1.
6. *The American Woman 1988–1989: A Status Report,* Sara Rix (ed.), W.W. Norton, New York, 1988, Table 3.2, p. 130.
7. United States Bureau of the Census, *Fertility of American Women 1984,* Washington DC 1985.
8. United States Bureau of Labor Statistics, Washington DC, October 26, 1987.
9. Ellen Goodman in *The Atlanta Constitution,* March 22, 1988, p. A23.
10. *The Atlanta Constitution,* January 10, 1988, p. A5, and June 15, 1988, p. A1.
11. *U.S. News and World Report,* September 19, 1988, p. 43.
12. United States Travel Data Service statistics, Washington DC, 1985.
13. I.A.P.A., *First Class,* November/December 1985, p. 26.
14. United States Department of Labor, Bureau of Labor Statistics.
15. *The American Woman 1988–1989,* Table 13, p. 371.
16. *The New York Times,* February 6, 1937, p. D-2.
17. *INC. Magazine,* January 1987, p. 11.
18. July 1986, pp. 45–46.
19. "Women and the New Enterprise Ethic," April 1988, pp. 87–88.
20. *Time,* July 4, 1988, p. 54.
21. Anne B. Fisher, "Credit Where Credit Is Due," in *Savvy Woman,* Palm Coast, Florida, November 1988, pp. 32–33.
22. *The Economic Emergence of Women,* Basic Books, New York, 1986, p. 27.
23. *Ibid.,* p. 48.
24. *Ibid.,* p. 53.
25. *The Divorce Revolution,* Free Press, New York, 1985, p. 400.
26. *A Lesser Life: The Myth of Women's Liberation in the U.S.A.,* Warner Books, New York, 1986, pp. 60–62, 66–67.

27. *The Equality Trap,* Simon & Schuster, New York, 1988, p. 22.

28. Barbara Bergmann, *The Economic Emergence of Women,* pp. 50–51.

29. *Economic Report of the President to Congress,* United States Government Printing Office, Washington DC, 1987, p. 216.

30. *Ibid.,* p. 209.

31. *Ibid.,* p. 211.

32. *A Lesser Life,* p. 13.

33. *Ibid.,* pp. 30, 71.

34. *Economic Report of the President,* p. 210.

35. *Ibid.,* p. 213.

36. "State Farm to Pay Millions to Settle Sex Bias Law Suit," *The Atlanta Constitution,* January 17, 1988, p. A1.

37. *Insight,* August 29, 1988, p. 25; and *Time,* October 17, 1988, p. 33.

38. *The Atlanta Constitution,* November 6, 1988, p. A1.

39. Beth Schneiderman, "Professors' Salaries in Women's Studies Programs," *Chronicle of Higher Education,* Vol. 33, No. 17, March 11, 1987.

40. Gilda Berger, *Women, Work and Wages,* Franklin Watts, New York, 1986, pp. 6–9, 26.

41. A. Gates and K. Shelley, *Fringe Benefits,* Donald I. Fine, New York, 1986.

42. *The Economic Emergence of Women,* pp. 92–93.

43. United States Department of Commerce, Bureau of the Census, Washington DC, 1987.

44. United States Press Institute, Washington DC.

45. United States Department of Labor Statistics, Washington DC.

46. United States Department of Commerce, Bureau of the Census, Washington DC, 1987.

47. American Association of University Professors, May 1986.

48. *The Politics of the Second Electorate,* Joni Lovenduski and Jill Hills, eds., Routledge and Kegan Paul, Ltd., London, 1981, p. 48.

49. L. Checco and A. Alexander, "Congress Still Biased," *The Atlanta Journal and Constitution,* August 21, 1983, p. A6.

50. National Information Bank on Women in Public Office, Center for the American Woman in Politics, Rutgers University, New Jersey, 1988.

51. *The American Woman 1988–1989,* Tables 2.1 and 2.2, pp. 89–91.

52. N. Agarwal, "Male-Female Pay Inequality and Public Policy in Canada and the USA," *Relations Industrielle,* University Laval, No. 4, 1982.

53. C.N. Halaby, "Sex Inequality in the Workplace," *Social Science Research,* March 1979.

54. D. Treiman and H. Hartmann, *Women, Work and Wages: Equal Pay for Jobs of Equal Value,* National Academy Press, Washington DC, 1981; M. Ferber and J. Spaeth, "Work Characteristics and the Male-Female Earnings Gap," *The American Economic Review,* Vol. 74, No. 2, May 1984; M. Gold, *A Dialogue on Comparable Worth,* ILR Press, Ithaca NY, 1983. Cf. C. Saunders and D. Marsden, *Pay Inequalities in the European Community,* Butterworth, London, 1981.

55. *Economic Report of the President.*

56. Barbara Reskin and Heidi Hartman, eds., National Academy Press, Washington DC, 1986.

57. C. Craig, E. Garnsey and J. Rubery, "Women's Pay in Informal Payment Systems," *Employment Gazette,* United Kingdom Department of Employment, London, April 1983.

58. International Labour Organization, *The Economic Role of Women in the ECE Region,* Geneva, 1985, Table IV.11, p. 59.

59. *Johnson v. Santa Clara County Transportation Agency,* March 25, 1987.

60. *The Atlanta Journal and Constitution,* March 27, 1987, p. 3.

61. *The Atlanta Constitution,* March 26, 1987, p. 8.

62. Maureen Downey, "Georgia Feminists Hail Supreme Court Ruling," *The Atlanta Constitution,* June 20, 1986.

63. *The Atlanta Constitution,* June 4, 1987, p. A13.

64. United States District Court, Washington DC, Judge John Lewis, *Palmer v. Schultz,* July 2, 1987.

65. United States Court of Appeals, Washington DC, *Ann Hopkins v. Price Waterhouse,* August 4, 1987.

66. See Nathan Glazer, *Affirmative Discrimination,* Basic Books, New York, 1975, pp. 196–221.

67. International Labour Organization, *The Economic Role of Women.*

68. W.T. Bielby and J.N. Baron, *Women's Place Is with Other Women: Sex Segregation in the Workplace,* University of California, 1983, study sponsored by the National Academy of Sciences.

69. International Labour Organization, p. 67.

70. National Association of Working Women, *The Profile of Working Women,* Washington DC, April 1987.

71. *Time,* July 12, 1982, p. 23.

72. *The Economic Emergence of Women,* pp. 81, 82–83.

73. *Economic Report of the President,* p. 221; and *The Atlanta Constitution,* September 4, 1986, pp. 1, 10.

74. Berger, *Women, Work and Wages,* pp. 68–69.

75. *A Lesser Life,* p. 85.

76. *Ibid.,* p. 84.

77. United States Bureau of the Census, Current Population Reports, *Money Income of Households, Family and Persons in the United States, 1984,* Washington DC, 1987; *Male-Female Differences in Work Experience, Occupations and Earnings,* Washington DC, 1987; and *Economic Report of the President.*

78. *Male-Female Differences in Work Experience, Occupations and Earnings.*

79. *The American Woman 1988–1989.*

80. *The Atlanta Constitution,* January 2, 1988, p. A5.

81. "Professors' Salaries," *Chronicle of Higher Education,* Vol. 33, No. 17, March 11, 1987.

82. *The Atlanta Journal and Constitution,* September 4, 1988, p. A18.

83. *The Atlanta Constitution,* October 19, 1984, p. A1.

84. Claudia Wayne, Executive Director, National Committee on Pay Equity, Washington DC, 1986.

85. "Comparable Worth Is Putting More in Women's Pockets," *The Atlanta Constitution,* August 28, 1986, p. 16.

86. Georgia Professional Standards Commission of the State Board of Education, Atlanta, November 1986.

87. K. Glaser and S. Possony, *Victims of Politics—The State of Human Rights,* Columbia University Press, New York, 1979, p. 333.

88. See National Organization of Women, *State by State Guide to Women's Legal Rights,* McGraw-Hill, New York, 1987.

89. *Ibid.*

90. National Association of Working Women, *Profile of Working Women.*

91. *Catalyst,* New York, 1987.

92. Leslie Goldstein, *The Constitutional Rights of Women,* University of Wisconsin Press, 1988, p. 49.

93. See *INC. Magazine,* June 1986, p. 19.

94. See *The Economist,* London, January 24, 1987, p. 27.

95. Berger, *Women, Work and Wages,* p. 20.

96. See *Women and the Equal Rights Amendment,* Catherine Simpson, ed., R.R. Bowker, New York, 1972.

97. McGraw-Hill, New York, 1987, and Univ. of Wisconsin Press, 1988.

98. *The Atlanta Journal and Constitution,* January 19, 1986, Section 4-M, p. 2.

99. See *The Wall Street Journal,* November 13, 1985, p. 10, col. 1.

100. *U.S. News and World Report,* July 4, 1988, p. 11.

101. Simon & Schuster, New York, 1988, p. 377.

102. "Army Opens More Jobs to Women," *The Houston Chronicle,* November 15, 1988, p. A3.

103. *The Atlanta Constitution,* July 14, 1988, p. A2.

104. *Insight,* October 31, 1988, p. 26.

105. *The Atlanta Constitution,* February 3, 1988, p. A3; and *Insight,* June 27, 1988, p. 18.

106. *The Rights of Women,* Bantam Books, New York, rev. ed., 1983, pp. 1–4. Cf. Brown, Freedman, Katz and Price, *Women's Rights and the Law,* Frederic Praeger, New York, 1977, which contains a comprehensive survey of sex discriminatory state laws; and J.M. Picker, "Laws and the Status of Women in the United States," *Human Rights Law Review,* Vol. 8, p. 1139, 1977.

107. *The Atlanta Constitution,* February 25, 1987.

108. *The Atlanta Constitution,* March 26, 1987, pp. 1 and 8.

109. *Time,* April 6, 1987, p. 19.

110. *Ibid.,* p. 20.

111. *The Atlanta Constitution,* March 27, 1987, p. 3.

112. *The Atlanta Constitution,* May 4, 1987, p. 1.

113. *Comparable Worth and Wage Discrimination,* Helen Remick, ed., Temple University Press, Philadelphia, 1984, preface, p. ix.

114. *The Economic Emergence of Women,* p. 5.

115. Pp. 13–15.

116. *A Lesser Life,* pp. 14–15, 96–97.

117. *Ibid.,* pp. 46–47, 74–76.

118. *Ibid.,* pp. 142–143, 177, 402.

119. Simon & Schuster, New York, 1988, pp. 22–25, 30–31, and 44.

120. *The Equality Trap,* p. 45.

121. See Hewlett, *A Lesser Life,* p. 80.

122. *The Atlanta Constitution,* May 30, 1986, p. 25.

123. Government of the State of Georgia, 1986.

124. Harvard University Press, Cambridge MA, 1984, Table 2.1 and pp. 42–43.

125. Klein, *Gender Politics,* p. 166.

126. *Time,* June 29, 1988, p. 4.

127. *Insight,* September 26, 1988, p. 18.

128. Ronni Sandorf, "Sexual Harassment in Fortune 500," *Working Woman,* December 1988, pp. 69–79.

129. *Women's Work, Men's Work: Sex Segregation on the Job,* Barbara Reskin and Heidi Hartman, eds., National Academy Press, Washington DC, 1986, p. 130.

130. *The Invisible Bar,* Beacon Press, Boston, 1986, pp. 218, 250.

131. *The Atlanta Constitution,* August 10, 1988, p. A12.

132. *Women's Changing Role,* Information Aids, Wylie TX, 1988, p. 29.

133. "Women's Issues in 1988," *Creative Loafing,* Atlanta, Vol. 16, No. 36, February 6, 1988, p. A5.

Chapter 17. General Survey

1. Jessie Bernard, *The Female World from a Global Perspective,* Indiana University Press, Bloomington, 1987, p. 172.

2. *Women Under Communism,* Johns Hopkins University Press, Baltimore, 1978.

3. *Ibid.,* p. 207.

4. General Assembly, Official Records, 41st Session, Supplement 45 A/41/45, New York, 1986, pp. 10–15.

5. *Ibid.,* pp. 23–25.

6. See Gail Lapidus, *Women in Soviet Society,* University of California Press, 1978; *Soviet Sisterhood,* Barbara Holland, ed., Indiana University Press, Bloomington, 1985; *Women and Russia,* Tatyana Mamonova, ed., Beacon Press, Boston, 1984; Barbara Jancar, *Women Under Communism,* Johns Hopkins University Press, Baltimore, 1978; Alena Heitlinger, *Women and State Socialism: Sex Inequality in the Soviet Union and Czechoslovakia,* McGill-Queens University Press, Montreal, 1979.

7. It should be noted that these statistics obtained at the United Nations are from official communist state sources, in particular the census figures for 1975–1981.

8. International Labour Organization, *Women in Economic Activity,* Geneva, 1985, pp. 141–143.

9. "The Non-Existence of Women's Emancipation," pp. 290–292.

10. Chapter 9.

11. "Let's Pull Down the Bastilles Before They Are Built," in *Sisterhood Is Global,* Robin Morgan, ed., Doubleday, New York, 1984, p. 561.

12. *Sisterhood Is Global,* p. 576.

13. Labor Code, Articles 46, 152–158.

14. Lynn Iglitzin and Ruth Ross, eds., 2nd edition, ABC–CLIO, Santa Barbara CA, 1986, p. 426.

15. Official *Gazette,* Yugoslavia, No. 18, 1978.

16. See Chapter 31, this book, for a discussion of the report.

17. "Neofeminism and Its Six Mortal Sins," p. 735.

18. *Ibid.,* pp. 736–737.

19. *Women in the World,* Lynn Iglitzin and Ruth Ross, eds., p. 426.

20. *Women Workers in Fifteen Countries,* Jennie Farley, ed., I.L.R. Press, Ithaca NY, 1985, pp. 49–51.

21. *Women in the World,* p. 428.

22. P. 55.

23. *Women and European Politics,* University of Massachusetts Press, Amherst, 1986, p. 130.

24. *Ibid.,* p. 157.

25. *Ibid.,* p. 199.

26. *Ibid.,* p. 288.

27. *Ibid.,* pp. 286–287.

28. *Ibid.,* pp. 287–288.

29. In *The Politics of the Second Electorate,* Joni Lovenduski and Jill Hills, eds., Routledge & Kegan Paul, London, 1981, pp. 253–254.

30. *Ibid.,* p. 255.

31. R.D. Putnam, *The Comparative Study of Political Elites,* Prentice Hall, Englewood Cliffs NJ, 1978, p. 33.

32. *The Politics of the Second Electorate,* p. 259.

33. P. 271.

Chapter 18. Case Study: The Soviet Union

1. D. Willis, *Klass,* St. Martin's Press, New York, 1985, p. 179.

2. "The Soviet Union," in *Women Workers in Fifteen Countries,* Jennie Farley, ed., I.L.R. Press, Ithaca NY, 1985, pp. 14–15.

3. *Sisterhood Is Global,* Ruth Morgan, ed., Doubleday, New York, 1984, p. 682.

4. *Ibid.*
5. Gail Lapidus, *Women in Soviet Society,* University of California Press, 1978, pp. 304–306.
6. *The Politics of the Second Electorate,* Joni Lovenduski and Jill Hills, eds., Routledge & Kegan Paul, London, 1981, p. 282.
7. See Joanna Hubbs, *Mother Russia,* Indiana University Press, Bloomington, 1988.
8. *The Atlanta Constitution,* October 1, 1988, p. A14.
9. Census of 1979.
10. *Time,* June 6, 1988, p. 29.
11. "Soviet Politics" in *Soviet Sisterhood,* Barbara Holland, ed., Indiana University Press, Bloomington, 1985, p. 207.
12. *Ibid.,* pp. 209–210.
13. *The Politics of the Second Electorate,* p. 278.
14. Pp. 213–217.
15. J. Hough, *The Soviet Union and Social Science Theory,* Princeton University Press, Princeton NJ, 1977, p. 356.
16. George Allen & Unwin, London, 1981, p. 1.
17. *Women of the World,* WID1-4, United States Agency for International Development, United States Department of Commerce, Washington DC, 1984 and 1985.
18. J.A. Chapman, "Equal Pay for Equal Work," in *Women in Russia,* Atkinson, Dallin and Lapidus, eds., Harvester Press, Hassocks, England, 1978, p. 225; and Lapidus, *Women in Soviet Society,* p. 191.
19. *Women's Work and Wages in the Soviet Union,* p. 20.
20. *Ibid.,* pp. 206–207.
21. June 6, 1988, p. 30.
22. *Vestnik statistiki,* Census Ministry, Moscow, 1984, No. 1, p. 65.
23. *Time,* June 6, 1988, p. 29.
24. "The Soviet Women," in *Women Workers in Fifteen Countries,* pp. 13–33.
25. Lapidus, pp. 182, 307; Lovenduski, pp. 285–286 in *The Politics of the Second Electorate;* Norton T. Dodge: "Women in the Professions" in *Women in Russia,* Atkinson, Dallin & Lapidus, eds., Harvester Press, Hassocks, England, 1978, pp. 208–209.
26. *Women's Work and Wages in the Soviet Union,* p. 46.
27. M.P. Sachs in *Women in Russia,* p. 202.
28. *Women in Soviet Society,* pp. 186–191.
29. *Women's Work and Wages in the Soviet Union,* p. 48.
30. *Ibid.,* p. 96.
31. *Women and European Politics,* U. of Mass. Press, Amherst, 1986, p. 237.
32. June 6, 1988, pp. 35, 37.
33. *Ibid.,* p. 37.
34. *Ibid.,* pp. 35, 37.
35. Mary Buckley, "Soviet Interpretations of the Woman Question," in *Soviet Sisterhood,* p. 48.
36. *Ibid.,* p. 46.
37. *Time,* June 6, 1988, pp. 30, 35.
38. Willis, p. 182.
39. *The Atlanta Constitution,* January 24, 1988, p. A4.
40. Willis, pp. 168–172.
41. Pantheon Books, New York, 1983.
42. *Moscow Women,* pp. 188–191.
43. Pp. 335–340.
44. *Women in Soviet Society,* p. 7.
45. *Ibid.,* p. 109.
46. *Ibid.,* p. 338.

47. *Ibid.*, pp. 147–151.
48. International Labour Organization, *Women in Economic Activity*, pp. 141–143.
49. Pp. 392–393.
50. *The Politics of the Second Electorate*, pp. 296–297.
51. "Soviet Women Losing Fight for Equality," *The Atlanta Constitution*, February 1, 1987.
52. *The New York Times*, February 4, 1984, I.23.1.
53. United States State Department.
54. Alix Holt, "The First Soviet Feminists," in *Soviet Sisterhood*, p. 262.
55. *Soviet Sisterhood*, p. 49.
56. *Moscow Women*, Introduction, pp. 10–15.
57. Harper and Row, New York, 1987.
58. *U.S. News and World Report*, November 9, 1987, p. 79.
59. *U.S. News and World Report*, December 14, 1987, p. 10.
60. Buckley in *Soviet Sisterhood*, p. 40.
61. *U.S. News and World Report*, December 14, 1987, p. 10.
62. *The Atlanta Journal and Constitution*, March 9, 1989, p. 3A.

Chapter 19. General Survey

1. United Nations, *Five Studies on the Situation of Women in Latin America*, New York, 1983, p. 170.
2. *Women of the World*, WID1-4, United States Agency for International Development, United States Department of Commerce, Washington DC, 1984 and 1985, Table 4.7, p. 63.
3. United Nations Document A/CONF/116/10, report of the Secretary General of the United Nations to the conference in Nairobi.
4. *Five Studies*, E.82.11.G.10.
5. *Economic Commission for Latin America and the Caribbean, The Decade for Women in Latin America and the Caribbean*, Santiago, Chile, 1985, p. 145.
6. *Ibid.*, p. 105.
7. *Ibid.*, p. 143.
8. *Five Studies*, p. 170.
9. C.D. Deere and M. Leon del Leal, *Women in Andean Agriculture*, International Labour Organization, Geneva, 1982; and Center for Policy Studies, Population Council, *The Impact of Agrarian Reform on Different Members of the Family*, New York, 1983.
10. Economic Commission for Latin America, *Rural Women in Latin America*, 1975–1984.
11. *The State of the World's Women*, New International Publications, New York, 1985, p. 7.
12. Daphne Patai, *Brazilian Women Speak*, Rutgers University Press, New Brunswick NJ, 1988, reveals the restraints under which women still live in Latin America's most populous state.
13. *The State of the World's Women*, p. 7.
14. *Ibid.*, p. 33.
15. *Women of the World*, p. 4.
16. United Nations, *World Survey on the Role of Women in Development*, E.86.IV.3, New York, 1986, pp. 92–93.
17. *Five Studies*, p. 89.
18. See International Labour Organization, *Conditions of Work, Vocational Training and Employment of Women*, Report III, Geneva, 1979, Eleventh Conference of American States Members of the International Labour Organization.

19. See *Five Studies on the Situation of Women in Latin America,* p. 89.

20. S.S. Maccan and M. Bamberger, "Employment and the Status of Women in Venezuela," *Development Digest,* Vol. 13, No. 3, July 1975.

21. *Five Studies,* p. 93.

22. *Five Studies,* pp. 132–134.

23. "Population, Development and Latin American Women," *INSTRAW News,* No. 7, 1986, p. 29.

24. *Mujeres Jovenes en America Latín: Aportes para una Discusión,* ECLAC, Foro Juvenil, Montevideo, 1985.

25. *Women of the World,* p. 4.

26. See Mayra Buvinic, et al., *Integrating Women into Development Programs,* International Center for Research on Women, Washington DC, May 1986.

27. P. Chandhuri and N. Till, *Participation of Women in Co-operatives and Productive Groups in Honduras,* World Bank, Washington DC, 1986, p. iii.

28. Asuncion Lavrin, "Women, the Family and Social Change in Latin America," *World Affairs,* Washington DC, Vol. 150, No. 2, 1987, pp. 117–120.

29. Ana Maria Portugal, "Not Even with a Rose Petal," in *Sisterhood Is Global,* p. 552.

Chapter 20. Brief Case Studies of Colombia, Bolivia, Brazil and Peru

1. Bolivia has had 191 governments in its 158-year history.

2. Bolivia's gross national product is a modest $600 per capita.

3. Article 1 of the Law of October 11, 1911. It states: "—The law only recognizes civil marriage, which must be instituted as prescribed below."

4. Article 10 of the Law of October 11, 1911. It states: "—The marriage will be performed before the Official of the Civil Register, in his office or in a private home, and before two qualified witnesses, with the contracting parties appearing personally or by legal proxy."

5. Article 2 of the Law of October 11, 1911. It states: "—After the ceremony of the civil marriage, the canonical or religious marriage may be performed, but only the civil marriage will yield effects. The religious marriage will only be verified in consequence of the certificate of the civil marriage." But see Article 2 of the Supreme Decree of March 2, 1937, which states: "For superior reasons of justice, marriages of the indigenous elements performed in the Church are declared valid in accordance with this Decree, and are to produce the same legal effects as do civil marriages."

6. Article 159 of the 1972 Code of the Family. It states: "—Free or *de facto* unions that are stable and monogamous produce effects similar to those of marriage, in the personal as well as the patrimonial relations of the cohabitants. The norms that regulate the effects of matrimony can be applied to such unions . . . without prejudice to the existing particular rules."

7. Article 160 of the 1972 Code of the Family. It states: "—Understood to be included in the above provision are pre-marital indigenous forms such as 'tantanacu' or 'sirvinacu,' *de facto* unions of aborigines, and other unions in urban, industrial, or rural centers."

8. Article 131.

9. This was the Civil Code promulgated by Marshall Andres de Santa Cruz on August 27, 1861.

10. In fact, the 1972 Code of the Family establishes the following rights for women: Article 34. "—The administration of the family patrimony is the right of both spouses or only one if the other is absent or disabled." // Article 96. "—In the interest of the family and in accordance with the personal condition of each one, the spouses have equal rights and duties in the direction and management of the affairs of their marriage, such as the raising and education of the children."

11. The Constitution of 1967.

12. Article 6.

13. See footnote 10 above. What the law gives, the law can take away. Note the following provisions from the 1972 Code of the Family: Article 98. "—The woman fulfills in the home a societal and economically useful function that is to be under the protection of legal regulation." // Article 99. "—The husband can restrain or prohibit the wife from exercising a certain profession or office for moral reasons or when the function of marriage would be harmfully affected."

14. The Law of the Civil Register of November 26, 1898, promulgated by President Severo Fernandez Alonso first declared the right of a Bolivian woman to bear the name of her husband.

15. Article 34 of the 1972 Code of the Family.

16. Article 969 of the 1861 Santa Cruz Code stated that "only the husband can administer the dowry property during the marriage; and upon its devolution, this property will by law be mortgaged."

17. Article 980 of the 1861 laws on dowry. Also see the following provisions from the 1861 Code: Article 983. "—All the property of the woman not a part of the dowry is paraphernalia (goods brought by the wife into the marriage other than the dowry, and which are at her disposal)." // Article 984. "—The wife has the right to administer and make use of the paraphernalia, but she cannot alienate this property or appear in court with respect to it without the permission of the husband or at his refusal, the permission of the judge." // Article 985. "—If the wife gives the husband the power to administer her (goods of) paraphernalia under the condition that he return to her the profits on this property, he will be obligated to her like any mandatory agent."

18. Article 61 of the 1943 Labor Law.

19. Article 56 of the 1943 Labor Law.

20. As well as a rich local literature based on the tragedies suffered by miners.

21. As well as minors.

22. Article 213 of the 1967 Constitution reads as follows: "Every Bolivian is obligated to render military service in accordance with the law."

23. Without children.

24. Article 421 of the Penal Code of 1972. The problem with making such distinctions between "notorious" and "vulgar" women is that in many cases a woman's status is the result of men's misconduct.

25. Previously, women and peasants were excluded from electoral participation.

26. See Title Nine, Chapter I—Articles 219 through 221 of the Constitution of 1967.

27. See Title Nine, Chapter II—Articles 222 through 224 of the Constitution of 1967.

Chapter 21. General Survey

1. *The Atlanta Constitution.* The flogging took place in the town of Liagapur. The widow was 35 years old. Normally 100 lashes are applied.

2. See Kathleen Barry, *Female Sexual Slavery,* Prentice Hall, Englewood Cliffs NJ, 1979; and Lillian Sanderson, *Against the Mutilation of Women,* Ithaca Press, London, 1981.

3. See *Time,* May 19, 1986.

4. *The New York Times,* February 18, 1985, p. A7.

5. Jane Lewis, "A Western Woman in Saudi Arabia," in *International Living,* Vol. 3, No. 4, 1983, p. 1. Cf. N.J. Coulson, "The State and the Individual in Islamic Law," *International and Comparative Law Quarterly,* 6/49, 1957, and *Arab Women,* Minority Rights Group Reports, Benjamin Franklin House, London, No. 27.

6. *International Herald Tribune,* February 22, 1983.

7. *The Qur'an,* 4-S, 35-V.

8. Clement Ameluxen, "Marriage and Women in Islamic Countries" in *Case Studies on Human Rights,* Vol. II, pp. 94–95.

9. *The Qur'an,* 2.228-237; 5.288 and 65.1-6.

10. *Ibid.,* 4.12-13.

11. *Surah,* 53-V-29.

12. Egyptian Marriage Law, Article 67; cf. Joseph P. O'Kane, "Islam in the New Egyptian Constitution," *Middle East Journal,* 16.137, 1972.

13. *Encyclopedia Biblica,* Vol. III, p. 2942.

14. Kurt Glaser and Stefan Possony, editors: *Victims of Politics,* Columbia University Press, New York, 1979, pp. 458–9.

15. Jane Alford in *The Atlanta Journal and Constitution,* November 6, 1983, p. 37-A.

16. Rounaq Jahan, "Women in Bangladesh" in *Case Studies on Human Rights,* Vol. V, p. 558.

17. Marielouise Jannsen-Jurreit, *Sexism,* McGraw-Hill, New York, 1982, p. 237.

18. Jannsen-Jurreit, pp. 264–265.

19. See Nadia Youssef, "Women in the Muslim World," in *Women in the World: A Comparative Study,* Lynn Iglitzin and Ruth Ross, eds., ABC–CLIO, Santa Barbara CA, 1976; and *Women Employment and Development in the Arab World,* Nasr J. Abu and N. Khoury (eds.), Institute for Women's Studies in the Arab World, Beirut University College, Mouton, Berlin, 1985.

20. *Time,* April 21, 1986.

21. International Labour Organization, *Women in Economic Activity,* Geneva, 1986, pp. 57, 61–62.

22. United Nations, *World Survey of the Role of Women in Development,* New York, 1986, pp. 39–40.

23. F. Kirwan, "Labour Exporting in the Middle East: The Jordanian Experience," *Development and Change,* Vol. 14, 1982, pp. 63–89; and United Nations, *World Survey on the Role of Women in Development,* p. 47.

24. International Labour Organization, *Women in Economic Activity,* pp. 66–67.

25. *Women of the World,* WID-3, Office of Women in Development, United States Agency for International Development, United States Department of Commerce, Washington DC, 1984 and 1985, p. 73.

26. *Ibid.,* pp. 36–37.

27. "Political Activism and Islamic Identity in Iran," pp. 210–211.

28. Article 179.

29. Retribution Law, 1981, Articles 157–162.

30. "The Position of Women in Shi'a Iran," in *Women and the Family in the Middle East,* Elizabeth Fernea, ed., University of Texas Press, Austin, 1985, pp. 264–265.

31. "The Family," p. 32.

32. "The Social and Political Implications of Female Circumcision," pp. 149, 154–155.

33. John L. Esposito, *Women in Muslim Family Law,* Syracuse University Press, Syracuse NY, 1982, p. 130.

34. "Women, Work and Ideology in the Islamic Republic," *International Journal of Middle East Studies,* Vol. 20, 1988, pp. 221, 234, 238.

Chapter 22. Case Study: Egypt

1. *Sisterhood Is Global,* Robin Morgan, ed., Anchor Press/Doubleday, Garden City NY, 1984, p. 194.

2. Audrey Chapman Smock and Nadia Hagga Youssef, "Egypt: From Seclusion to Limited Participation," in *Women, Roles and Status in Eight Countries,* Janet Zollinger Fiele and Audrey Chapman Smock, eds., John Wiley & Sons, New York, 1977, p. 67.

3. *Ibid.*, p. 68.
4. *Ibid.*, p. 70.
5. *Sisterhood Is Global,* p. 194.
6. Naila Minai, *Women in Islam,* Seaview Books, New York, 1981, p. 78.
7. Charles Greenfield, "A Widow Fights On," *Macleans,* Vol. 97, No. 26, June 25, 1984, p. 69.
8. Smock and Youssef, p. 69.
9. *Ibid.*, pp. 69–70.
10. Minai, pp. 69–70.
11. Morgan, p. 194.
12. Smock and Youssef, p. 45.
13. Morgan, p. 195.
14. *Ibid.*
15. Minai, p. 70.
16. *Ibid.*
17. Smock and Youssef, p. 47.
18. Barbara Freyer Stowasser, "The Status of Women in Early Islam," in *Muslim Women,* Freda Hussai, ed., Croom Helm, Kent, England, 1984, p. 17.
19. Morgan, p. 195.
20. *Ibid.*
21. *Ibid.*
22. *Ibid.*
23. Nawal El Saadawi, "Egypt: When a Woman Rebels," Sherif Hetata, trans., in *Sisterhood Is Global,* p. 203.
24. Aziza Hussein, "Recent Amendments to Egypt's Personal Status Law," in *Women and the Family in the Middle East,* Elizabeth Warnock Fernea, ed., University of Texas Press, Austin, 1985, p. 231.
25. *Ibid.*
26. *Ibid.*
27. Minai, p. 178.
28. Morgan, p. 195.
29. Hussein, p. 231.
30. Morgan, p. 195.
31. *Ibid.*
32. *Ibid.*
33. *Ibid.*
34. Hussein, p. 231.
35. Morgan, p. 195.
36. Saadawi, p. 203.
37. Robin Morgan, "Good News from 18 Countries," *Ms.,* September 1985, p. 14.
38. Hussein, p. 232.
39. Morgan, "Good News . . . ," p. 14.
40. Audrey Chapman Smock, "Bangladesh: A Struggle with Tradition and Poverty" in *Women, Roles and Status in Eight Countries,* Janet Zollinger Giele and Audrey Chapman Smock, eds., John Wiley & Sons, New York, 1977, p. 89.
41. Smock and Youssef, p. 47.
42. *Ibid.*
43. Morgan, p. 195.
44. *Ibid.*
45. *Ibid.*, pp. 195–196.
46. Smock and Youssef, p. 73.
47. *Ibid.*, pp. 57–58.
48. Hussein, p. 232.
49. Nadia H. Youssef, "Women in the Muslim World," in *Women in the World,*

Lynn B. Iglitzen and Ruth Ross, eds., ABC-CLIO, Santa Barbara CA, 1976, p. 209.

50. Smock and Youssef, p. 61.
51. Morgan, p. 194.
52. Smock and Youssef, p. 61.
53. Saadawi, p. 204.
54. *Ibid.,* p. 203.
55. Morgan, p. 195.
56. Smock and Youssef, p. 45.
57. *Ibid.,* p. 39.
58. *Ibid.,* p. 45.
59. *Ibid.,* p. 60.
60. Morgan, p. 195.
61. Minai, p. 96.
62. Morgan, p. 196.
63. *Ibid.*
64. *Ibid.*
65. Minai, p. 164.
66. Morgan, p. 197.
67. Mohammed Shallan, Ahmed Shawki El-Akaboui, and Sayed El-Kott, "Rape Victimology in Egypt," *Victimology: An International Journal,* Vol. 8, 1983, p. 288.
68. Morgan, p. 197.

Chapter 23. Case Study: Tunisia

1. Naila Minai, *Women in Islam,* Seaview Books, New York, 1981, p. 68.
2. *Tunisia: A Country Study,* Harold D. Nelson, ed., The American University, Washington DC, 1979, p. 202.
3. Clement Henry Moore, *Tunisia Since Independence,* University of California Press, Berkeley and Los Angeles, 1965, p. 56.
4. *Ibid.*
5. *Ibid.*
6. *Ibid.,* pp. 145–146.
7. Lorna Hawker Durrani, "Employment of Women and Social Change," in *Change in Tunisia,* eds. Russell A. Stone and John Simmons, Albany: State University of New York Press, 1976, p. 57.
8. Minai, pp. 68–69.
9. "The Tunisian Code of Personal Status," trans. George N. Sfeir, *The Middle East Journal,* Vol. 11, Summer 1957, p. 309.
10. *Ibid.*
11. *Ibid.*
12. *Tunisia: A Country Study,* p. 86.
13. Moore, p. 51.
14. Howard C. Reese, et al., *Area Handbook for the Republic of Tunisia,* United States Government Printing Office, Washington DC, 1970, p. 86.
15. "Tunisian Code...," p. 309.
16. Reese et al., p. 86.
17. Minai, p. 172.
18. "Tunisian Code...," p. 310.
19. Nelson, p. 86.
20. "Tunisian Code...," p. 310.
21. Reese, pp. 84–85.
22. Nelson, p. 88.
23. Reese, p. 360.

24. *Ibid.*, p. 86.
25. *Ibid.*, p. 87.
26. "Tunisian Code...," p. 310.
27. Reese, p. 87.
28. "Tunisian Code...," p. 310.
29. *Ibid.*, p. 309.
30. *Ibid.*
31. *Ibid.*, p. 311.
32. *Ibid.*, p. 310.
33. Reese, p. 87.
34. "Tunisian Code...," p. 310.
35. Minai, p. 179.
36. "Tunisian Code...," p. 310.
37. *Ibid.*
38. *Ibid.*, p. 311.
39. *Ibid.*
40. *Ibid.*
41. *Ibid.*
42. *Ibid.*
43. *Ibid.*
44. "Tunisian Code...," p. 310; Personal Status Code, Article 28.
45. "Tunisian Code...," p. 310.
46. Nelson, p. 86.
47. "Tunisian Code...," p. 312.
48. Nelson, p. 86.
49. "Tunisian Code...," p. 312; Personal Status Code, Article 56.
50. Nelson, p. 86.
51. "Tunisian Code...," p. 312; Personal Status Code, Article 67.
52. "Tunisian Code...," p. 309.
53. Reese, p. 86.
54. "Tunisian Code...," p. 310.
55. "Tunisian Code...," p. 310; Personal Status Code, Articles 101, 102.
56. Durrani, p. 57.
57. "Tunisian Code...," p. 314; Personal Status Code, Articles 101, 102.
58. "Tunisian Code...," p. 314; Personal Status Code, Articles 101, 102.
59. "Tunisian Code...," p. 315; Personal Status Code, Articles 103(1), 103(2).
60. "Tunisian Code...," p. 310; Personal Status Code, Article 103(3).
61. Durrani, p. 57.
62. Reese, pp. 107–108.
63. Durrani, p. 57.
64. *Ibid.*, p. 63.
65. Nelson, pp. 88–89.
66. *Ibid.*
67. Durrani, p. 63.
68. *Ibid.*
69. *Ibid.*
70. Reese, p. 295.
71. *Ibid.*, p. 293.
72. *Ibid.*
73. Durrani, p. 63.
74. Reese, pp. 294–295.
75. Durrani, p. 58.
76. Nelson, p. 42.
77. Durrani, p. 67.

78. *Ibid.*
79. Minai, p. 68.
80. Reese, p. 157.
81. Nelson, p. 52.
82. *Ibid.,* p. 99.
83. *Ibid.,* p. 89.
84. Reese, p. 50.
85. Durrani, p. 202.
86. Durrani, p. 202.
87. Nelson, p. 89.
88. Reese, p. 50.
89. Reese, p. 50.
90. Youssef, Nadia H.: "Women in the Muslim World," in *Women in the World,* eds. Lynne B. Iglitzin and Ruth Ross, Santa Barbara: Clio Books, 1976, p. 213.
91. Minai, p. 68.
92. Minai, p. 68.

Chapter 24. Case Study: Iran

1. *Sisterhood Is Global,* Robin Morgan, ed., Anchor Press/Doubleday, Garden City NY, 1984, p. 325.
2. Badr ol-Moluk Bamdad, *From Darkness into Light,* F.R.C. Bagley, trans. and ed., Hicksville NY, Exposition Press, 1977, p. 116.
3. Bamdad, pp. 119–120.
4. *Sisterhood Is Global,* p. 335.
5. *Ibid.,* p. 324.
6. Farah Azari, "The Post-Revolutionary Women's Movement in Iran," in *Women of Iran,* Farah Azari, ed., Ithaca Press, London, 1983, p. 201.
7. Barbara Freyer Stowasser, "The Status of Women in Early Islam," in *Muslim Women,* Freda Hussain, ed., Croom Helm, Kent, England, 1984, p. 19.
8. Guity Nashat, "Women in the Ideology of the Islamic Republic," in *Women and Revolution in Iran,* Guity Nashat, ed., Westview Press, Boulder CO, 1983, p. 195.
9. *Ibid.,* p. 201.
10. Stowasser, p. 25.
11. *Ibid.,* p. 32.
12. S. Kaveh Mirani, "Social and Economic Change in the Role of Women, 1956–1978," in *Women and Revolution in Iran,* Guity Nashat, ed., Westview Press, Boulder CO, 1983, pp. 74–75.
13. *Ibid.,* p. 74.
14. Nashat, p. 197.
15. Farah Azari, "Islam's Appeal to Women in Iran: Illusions and Reality," in *Women of Iran,* Farah Azari, ed., Ithaca Press, London, 1983, p. 15.
16. *Ibid.,* p. 10.
17. *Ibid.,* p. 11.
18. Naila Minai, *Women in Islam,* Seaview Books, New York, 1981, pp. 9–10.
19. Stowasser, p. 19.
20. Azari, "Islam's Appeal," p. 12.
21. *Ibid.*
22. Stowasser, p. 17. Surah 4 (Women) verses 4, 24.
23. Morgan, p. 325.
24. Farah Azari, "Sexuality and Women's Oppression in Iran," in *Women of Iran,* Farah Azari, ed., Ithaca Press, London, 1983, p. 108.
25. Mahnaz Afkhami, "Iran: A Future in the Past," in *Sisterhood Is Global,* Robin Morgan, ed., Anchor Press/Doubleday, Garden City NY, 1984, p. 333.

26. *Ibid.*
27. Stowasser, p. 21.
28. Afkhami, p. 336.
29. Stowasser, p. 16.
30. Minai, p. 68.
31. Hamideh Sedghi, "Women in Iran," in *Women in the World,* Lynn B. Iglitzen and Ruth Ross, eds., ABC–CLIO, Santa Barbara CA, 1976, p. 221.
32. Azari, "Islam's Appeal," p. 12.
33. Stowasser, p. 19; Surah 4 (Women), verse 34.
34. Stowasser, p. 18; Surah 4 (Women), verse 34.
35. Azari, "Islam's Appeal," p. 11.
36. *Sisterhood Is Global,* p. 326.
37. Azari, "Islam's Appeal," p. 11.
38. *Sisterhood Is Global,* p. 326.
39. Azari, "Islam's Appeal," p. 15.
40. *Sisterhood Is Global,* p. 326.
41. Azari, "Post-Revolutionary," p. 213.
42. Fazlur Rahman, "Status of Women in the Qur'an," in *Women and Revolution in Iran,* Guity Nashat, ed., Westview Press, Boulder CO, 1983, p. 49.
43. *Ibid.,* p. 51.
44. Nashat, p. 198.
45. Stowasser, p. 18; Surah 2 (The Cow), verse 228.
46. Minai, p. 175.
47. *Ibid.*
48. Stowasser, p. 17.
49. *Ibid.,* p. 16.
50. *Sisterhood Is Global,* p. 325.
51. Stowasser, p. 19.
52. *Sisterhood Is Global,* p. 325.
53. *Ibid.*
54. *Ibid.*
55. *Ibid.,* p. 326.
56. *Ibid.,* p. 327.
57. *Ibid.,* p. 324.
58. *Ibid.,* p. 761.
59. *Ibid.,* p. 324.
60. "A Dressing Down," *New York Daily News,* June 8, 1986, p. 16, col. 1.
61. *Sisterhood Is Global,* p. 324.
62. Minai, p. 226.
63. Erika Friedl, "State Ideology and Village Women," in *Women and Revolution in Iran,* Guity Nashat, ed., Westview Press, Boulder CO, 1983, p. 223.
64. *Sisterhood Is Global,* p. 325.
65. *Ibid.,* p. 324.
66. Azari, "Post-Revolutionary," p. 220.
67. *Sisterhood Is Global,* p. 324.
68. Mary E. Hegland, "Aliabad Women: Revolution as Religious Activity," in *Women and Revolution in Iran,* Guity Nashat, ed., Westview Press, Boulder CO, 1983, p. 188.
69. Azari, "Post-Revolutionary," pp. 219–220.
70. *Sisterhood Is Global,* p. 325.
71. *Ibid.*
72. Minai, p. 233.
73. *Sisterhood Is Global,* p. 326.
74. Azari, "Sexuality," p. 135.

75. *Sisterhood Is Global,* p. 327.
76. *Ibid.*
77. *Ibid.*
78. *Ibid.*
79. Nashat, p. 196.
80. *Ibid.,* p. 197.
81. *Sisterhood Is Global,* p. 325.
82. Afkhami, p. 335.
83. Nashat, p. 195.
84. Nashat, pp. 207–208.
85. Azari, "Post-Revolutionary," p. 200.
86. Janet Bauer, "Poor Women and Social Consciousness in Revolutionary Iran," in *Women and Revolution in Iran,* Guity Nashat, ed., Westview Press, Boulder CO, 1983, p. 148.
87. Nashat, p. 209.
88. *Ibid.,* p. 204.
89. *Ibid.,* p. 206.
90. *Sisterhood Is Global,* p. 324.
91. *Ibid.,* p. 325.
92. *Ibid.*
93. *Ibid.,* p. 326.
94. *Ibid.*
95. Bauer, p. 147.

Chapter 25. General Survey

1. International Labour Organization, *Women in Economic Activity 1950–2000,* Geneva, 1986, table 1, p. 18.
2. *Women of the World,* WID1-4, United States Agency for International Development, United States Department of Commerce, Washington DC, 1984 and 1985, p. 72; International Labor Organization, *Yearbook of Labour Statistics,* Geneva, 1983, table 2B; and International Labor Organization, *Women at Work,* Vol. 2, 1987, p. 13.
3. *Women in Economic Activity 1950–2000,* pp. 57–61.
4. *Women in Rural Development. The Republic of China,* E. Croll, Ed., International Labor Organization, Geneva, 1979; and *Changing Patterns of Rural Women's Employment, Production and Reproduction in China,* International Labor Organization, Geneva, 1986.
5. United Nations, *World Survey of the Role of Women in Development,* E.86.IV.3, New York, 1986, table 3, p. 73.
6. United Nations Economic Commission for Asia and the Pacific, *Women's Economic Participation in Asia and the Pacific,* Bangkok, 1987.
7. See F.J. Frobel, et al., *Die Neue Internationale Arbeitseiung,* Reinbek Publishers, Hamburg, 1977.
8. *Working Women in South East Asia,* Open University Press, Philadelphia, 1986, p. 110.
9. *Ibid.,* p. 49.
10. International Labor Organization, *Women in Economic Activity,* Geneva, 1985, p. 25; and cf. M. Mies, *Indian Women in Subsistence and Agricultural Labour,* International Labor Organization, Geneva, 1986.
11. New Internationalist Publications, Oxford, 1985, p. 7. Cf. P. Harrison, *Inside the Third World,* Penguin Books, London, 1981, and R. Chambers, L. Longhurst, and A. Pacey, *Seasonal Dimensions to Rural Power,* Frances Pinter, London, 1981.
12. *Women in Economic Activity,* p. 62.
13. *World Survey on the Role of Women in Development,* p. 39.

14. M. Acharya and L. Benett, "The Rural Women of Nepal," in *The Status of Women in Nepal,* Center for Economic Development and Administration, Tribhuvan University, Katmandu, 1981.

15. See Chapter 27 of this work. See also M. Buvinic, M.A. Lycette, and W. McGreevey, *Women and Poverty in the Third World,* Johns Hopkins University Press, Baltimore, 1983.

16. *Women of the World,* p. 55.

17. *Ibid.*

18. "South Korea: A Nation Trapped by Its Male Dominant Ethic," *Atlanta Journal and Constitution,* December 25, 1983, p. A24.

19. *Sisterhood Is Global,* Robin Morgan, ed., Doubleday, Garden City NY, 1984, p. 310.

20. *Ibid.,* p. 311.

21. *Ibid.,* p. 311.

22. "Multiple Roles and Double Burdens," p. 318.

23. *Sisterhood Is Global,* p. 313.

24. Article 27 of the 1945 Constitution as amplified by the Guidelines of State Policy, 1978.

25. A. Ramanamma and Usha Bumbawale, "The Mania for Sons in South Asia," *Social Science and Medicine,* Vol. 14B, 1980.

26. *Women of the World,* p. 97.

27. *Ibid.,* p. 33.

28. *For the Record,* Caroline Pezzullo, ed., International Women's Tribune Center, New York, 1985.

29. International Labor Organization, *Resources, Power and Women,* Geneva, 1985, p. 30.

Chapter 26. Case Study: India

1. United Nations Economic and Social Commission for Asia and the Pacific, *Population of India,* Bangkok, 1982, Country Series No. 10.

2. In *Women of the World,* WID1-4, United States Agency for International Development, United States Department of Commerce, Washington DC, 1984 and 1985, p. 365. Cf. A. Ramanamma and Usha Bumbawale, "The Mania for Sons in South Asia," *Social Science and Medicine,* Vol. 14B, 1980.

3. *India Today,* October 31, 1988, pp. 22–23.

4. "Practice of Aborting Female Fetuses in India Coming Under Fire," *The Atlanta Constitution,* March 28, 1988, pp. B1, B4.

5. *India Today,* January 31, 1988, p. 68.

6. *Sisterhood Is Global,* Robin Morgan, ed., Doubleday, Garden City NY, 1984, p. 295; cf. T. Dyson and M. Moore, "On Kinship Structure, Female Autonomy and Demographic Behavior in India," *Population and Development Review,* Vol. 9, No. 1, 1983.

7. *Sisterhood Is Global,* p. 294.

8. Margot Duley and Mary Edwards, eds., Feminist Press, New York, 1986.

9. Ministry of Education and Social Welfare, *Towards Equality. Report of the Committee on the Status of Women,* Government Printer, New Delhi, 1975.

10. Center for Women's Development Studies, B-43 Panchsheel Enclave, New Delhi, 110017, India.

11. See J. Minattur, "Women and the Law," in *Women in Contemporary India and South Asia,* Alfred de Souza, ed., 2nd edition, Manohar Publications, New Delhi, 1980; Manju Kumar, *Social Equality—The Constitutional Experiment in India,* Chand & Co., New Delhi, 1982; and *The Cross Cultural Study of Women,* Margot Duley and Mary Edwards, eds., Feminist Press, New York, 1986, p. 200.

12. *Sisterhood Is Global,* p. 295.

13. See M. Menon, *Indu: Status of Muslim Women in India,* Uppal Publication House, New Delhi, 1981; also J. Brijbhushan, *Muslim Women. In Purdah and Out of It,* Vikas Publications, New Delhi, 1980.

14. *The New York Times,* March 17, 1984, I.24.1.

15. *The Atlanta Constitution,* October 14, 1987, pp. B1, B4.

16. "Bride Burning, the Horror Spreads," June 30, 1988, pp. 58–59.

17. Lyung Sook Bae, *Women and the Law in Korea,* League of Women Voters, Seoul, 1973; Irene R. Cortes, "Women's Rights under the 1973 Philippine Constitution," *Philippine Law Journal,* Vol. 50, No. 1, 1975; Katie Curtin, *Women in China,* Pathfinder Press, New York, 1975; M.S. McDougall, H.D. Laswell and Lung-Chu Chen, "Human Rights for Women and World Public Order: The Outlawing of Sex Based Discrimination," *American Journal of International Law,* Vol. 69, No. 497, 1975; M.P. Tandon, "Constitutionality of the Hindu Marriage Act," *Allahabad Law Review,* Vol. 5, No. 75, 1973; United Nations, "Law and the Status of Women: International Symposium," *Human Rights Law Review,* Vol. 8, No. 1, 1977; and cf. Magda Cordell and John McHale, *Women in World Terms, Facts and Trends,* Center for Integrative Studies, State University of New York, 1975.

18. Articles 14, 15 respectively.

19. Phiroza Ankleseria in *Comparative Law Yearbook,* Vol. 8, p. 19.

20. *Indian Bar Council Review,* Vol. 10, No. 4, 1983, p. 553.

21. *Comparative Law Journal,* Vol. 8, pp. 17–20.

22. October 31, 1988, p. 39.

23. *India Today,* June 30, 1988, pp. 58–59.

24. *The Cross Cultural Study of Women,* pp. 207–211.

25. Census of India, 1981.

26. "Women in India: The Reality," p. 367.

27. *Women in the World,* p. 376.

28. "A Condition Across Caste and Class," pp. 305–306.

29. *The Cross Cultural Study of Women,* p. 206.

30. "False Specialization and the Purdah of Scholarship," *Journal of Asian Studies,* Vol. 44, No. 1, 1984, p. 131.

31. International supplement, *Women's Studies Quarterly,* January 1982.

Chapter 27. Case Study: Japan

1. Machiko Osawa, "Working Mothers, Changing Patterns of Employment and Fertility in Japan," *Economic Development and Cultural Change,* University of Chicago, Vol. 36, No. 4, July 1988, p. 631, Table 3.

2. Article 14. It also forbids discrimination on grounds of social status or family origin.

3. Dorothy Robins-Mowry, *The Hidden Sun, Women of Modern Japan,* Westview Press, Boulder CO, 1983, p. 319.

4. *Sisterhood Is Global,* Robin Morgan, ed., Anchor/Doubleday, Garden City NY, 1984, p. 384.

5. *The Economic Emergence of Women,* Basic Books, New York, 1986, p. 15.

6. Jane Condon, *Japanese Women of the Eighties,* Dodd, Mead, New York, 1985, pp. 4–5. Cf. Japanese Ministry of Labor, *Labour Force Survey,* Tokyo, 1984.

7. *Sisterhood Is Global,* p. 376.

8. *The Hidden Sun, Women of Modern Japan,* p. 189.

9. Osawa, p. 630 and Table 3, p. 631.

10. *The Hidden Sun, Women of Modern Japan,* pp. 168–169.

11. *Time,* December 12, 1983, p. 46; Bernard Krishner, "How the Japanese

Discriminate Against Women," *Parade,* June 9, 1985; and "Japanese Women in a Male Society," *Christian Science Monitor,* January 10, 1985, p. 16.

12. See *Christian Science Monitor,* January 10, 1985, p. 16-1, and September 4, 1985, p. 32; and *The New York Times,* September 7, 1986.

13. *The Atlanta Journal and Constitution,* October 16, 1983, p. A36.

14. "Japanese Women in a Male Society."

15. *Ibid.;* and Krishner.

16. Hiroko Hayashi, "Japan," in *Working Women in Fifteen Countries,* p. 58; and *The Hidden Sun, Women of Modern Japan,* p. 169.

17. Krishner.

18. Office of the Prime Minister, Present Status of Women and Politics, Tokyo, April 1983.

19. Ministry of Labor, *Labor Force Survey,* Tokyo, 1984.

20. Ministry of Labor, *Survey on Corporate Hiring Plans,* 1981.

21. *Working Women in Japan,* New York State School of Industrial and Labor Relations, Cornell University, Ithaca NY, 1980, p. 8.

22. *The Hidden Sun, Women of Modern Japan,* pp. 171.

23. *Japanese Women of the Eighties,* p. 195.

24. *Sisterhood Is Global,* p. 377.

25. *Working Women in Japan,* p. 26.

26. Pp. 58–59.

27. *Working Women in Japan,* pp. 84–85.

28. *Sisterhood Is Global,* p. 377.

29. Pp. 7–8.

30. *Japanese Women of the Eighties,* pp. 295–298.

31. *Ibid.,* p. 300.

32. *Sisterhood Is Global,* p. 377.

33. *Japanese Women of the Eighties,* pp. 288–289.

34. Joni Lovenduski and Jill Hills, eds., Routledge and Kegan Paul, London, 1981, p. 313.

35. University of California Press, Berkeley, 1981.

36. *Ibid.,* pp. 3–5.

37. *The Hidden Sun, Women of Modern Japan,* p. 319.

38. *The Politics of the Second Electorate,* Joni Lovenduski and Jill Hills, eds., Routledge and Kegan Paul, London, 1981, p. 308, Table 14.1.

39. *The Atlanta Journal and Constitution,* September 7, 1986, p. 20.

40. *Political Women in Japan,* University of California Press, Berkeley, 1981, p. 184.

41. *Japanese Women of the Eighties,* Introduction.

42. *Ibid.,* Frontispiece and pp. 20, 26–27.

43. *Tokyo Newsletter,* January 1983, p. 10.

44. *Sisterhood Is Global,* p. 378.

45. Office of the Prime Minister, *Present Status of Women and Politics,* 3rd Report, Tokyo, April 1983, p. 9.

46. *Japanese Women of the Eighties,* pp. 47–48.

47. *Ibid.,* p. 85.

48. Ministry of Health and Welfare, *Population Vital Statistics,* Tokyo, 1984.

49. Kyodo News Service, *Japan Times,* April 23, 1983.

50. "Teen-Age Abortions Jump," *Asahi Evening News,* June 3, 1983.

51. Ministry of Education, *Basic Survey of Schools,* March 1984, p. 160.

52. *The Hidden Sun, Women of Modern Japan,* p. 140.

53. "Higher Education May Not Lead to Higher Income," *Japan Times,* September 28, 1984, p. 3.

54. Tokyo Metropolitan Government, *Stride by Stride. Women's Issues in Tokyo,* December 1983, p. 23.

55. *Basic Survey of Schools,* July 1983, p. 26.
56. *Japanese Women of the Eighties,* p. 145, and cf. pp. 121–140.
57. *Working Women in Japan,* pp. 14–15.
58. *The Politics of the Second Electorate,* pp. 302–303.
59. *Working Women in Japan,* p. 15.
60. *Ibid.,* p. 17.
61. *Ibid.,* p. 21.
62. *The Hidden Sun, Women of Modern Japan.*
63. *The Atlanta Constitution,* March 25, 1989, p. A26.
64. *The Hidden Sun, Women of Modern Japan,* p. 62.
65. *Ibid.,* p. 235.
66. *Ibid.,* pp. 308–309.
67. Takie S. Lebra, *Japanese Women,* University of Hawaii Press, Honolulu, 1984, Preface.
68. *Ibid.,* pp. 301–313.
69. "From the Moon to the Sun: Women's Liberation in Japan," in *Women in the World,* Lynn Iglitzin and Ruth Ross, eds., 2nd edition, ABC–CLIO, Santa Barbara CA, 1986, p. 124.

Chapter 28. Case Study: China

1. See, for example, Karen T. Wei, *Women in China: A Selected Bibliography,* Greenwood Press, Westport CT, 1984.
2. *Women in the World,* Lynn Iglitzin and Ruth Ross, eds., 2nd edition, ABC–CLIO, Santa Barbara CA, 1986, p. 77.
3. *The Unfinished Liberation of Chinese Women,* Indiana University Press, Bloomington, 1983, p. 45; and cf. Esther Lee Yao, *Chinese Women Past and Present,* Ide House, Chapters 4 and 5.
4. The Marriage Law, adopted April 13, 1950, promulgated May 1, 1950, Article 1.
5. See Wolfram Ebernard, *A History of China,* University of California Press, Los Angeles, 1977.
6. United Nations, *World Population Politics,* New York, 1987, p. 129.
7. Article 48.
8. Article 49.
9. *Chinese Women Since Mao,* Sharpe Inc., New York, 1983, p. 128.
10. Robin Morgan, ed., Doubleday, Garden City NY, 1984, p. 142 and p. 152.
11. Xiao Lu, "Feudal Attitudes, Party Control and Half the Sky," in *Sisterhood Is Global,* Robin Morgan, ed., Doubleday, Garden City NY, 1984, p. 152.
12. "Women's Rights in China," *Christian Science Monitor,* April 8, 1985; and "Women's Rights in China," *The New York Times,* March 5, 1986.
13. Jingji Yanjiu, June 20, 1982.
14. *Chinese Women Since Mao,* p. 46.
15. "Women, Fighting Discrimination in Jobs and Schooling," *China Reconstructs,* March 1986, pp. 34–35.
16. *Chinese Women Past and Present,* p. 170.
17. *Ibid.,* p. 176.
18. Article 34.
19. *The Unfinished Liberation of Chinese Women,* p. 45.
20. Wan Shanping, "The Emergence of Women's Studies in China," *Women's Studies International Forum,* Vol. 11, No. 5, 1988, p. 456.
21. *Ibid.*
22. *Chinese Women Past and Present,* p. 158.
23. *Revolution Postponed, Women in Contemporary China,* Stanford University Press, Stanford CA, 1985, p. 261.

24. See A.S. Chin, "Mainland China," in *Women in the Modern World,* Raphael Patai, ed., Free Press, New York, 1967.
25. *Women in the World,* p. 154.
26. Shanping, p. 455.
27. *Women at Work,* Vol. 1, International Labor Organization, Geneva, 1988, p. 45.
28. Tan Manni, "Women, Fighting Discrimination in Jobs and Schooling," *China Reconstructs,* March 1986, p. 35.
29. *Chinese Women Past and Present,* pp. 170–171.
30. Jennie Farley, ed., ILR Press, Cornell University, Ithaca NY, 1985, pp. 35–38.
31. *Ibid.,* pp. 38–40.
32. *Chinese Women Since Mao,* p. 56.
33. *The New Yorker,* January 19, 1987, pp. 25–26.
34. "Women's Rights, Family Reform and Population Control in the People's Republic of China," in *Women in the World,* p. 450.
35. Esther Yao, *Chinese Women Past and Present,* pp. 159–160.
36. *Ibid.,* p. 453.
37. "The People's Republic of China," in *Women Workers in Fifteen Countries,* pp. 33–48.
38. *Revolution Postponed: Women in Contemporary China,* p. 270.
39. P. 98.
40. Peking, March 3, 1983.
41. Margery Wolf, *Revolution Postponed: Women in Contemporary China,* p. 270.
42. "Women's Rights, Family Reform and Population Control in the People's Republic of China," p. 454.
43. *Women, the Family and Peasant Revolution in China,* University of Chicago Press, Chicago, 1983, p. 215.
44. United Nations, *World Population Policies,* Vol. 1, New York, 1987, p. 129.
45. Jerome Cohen, *The New Yorker,* January 19, 1987, pp. 25–26.
46. P. 70 and p. 149. Cf. "The Four Modernizations and the Chinese Policy on Women," *Bulletin of Concerned Asian Scholars,* Vol. 13, No. 2, 1981, pp. 44–56.
47. *Revolution Postponed: Women in Contemporary China,* p. 261.
48. *Ibid.,* pp. 26–27.
49. *INSTRAW News,* Santo Domingo CA, No. 11, Winter, 1988, p. 20.

Chapter 29. General Conclusions

1. Margot Duley and Mary Edwards, eds., Feminist Press, New York, 1986, p. 375.
2. *Women and European Politics,* University of Massachusetts Press, Amherst, 1986, p. 248.
3. *Ibid.,* p. 293.
4. *Ibid.,* p. 259.
5. *Women in the World,* Lynn Iglitzin and Ruth Ross, eds., 2d edition, ABC-CLIO, Santa Barbara CA, 1986, p. 399.
6. P. 412.
7. Muhammad Abdul-Rauf, *The Islamic View of Women and the Family,* Speller Publications, New York, 1977; and Michael J. Fischer, "On Changing the Concept and Position of Persian Women," in *Women and the Muslim World,* Louis Beck and Nikki Keddie, eds., Harvard University Press, Cambridge MA, 1978.
8. Translation from Mohammed Pickthall, *The Meaning of the Glorious Koran,* Mentor Books, New York, 1953.
9. Louis Beck, "The Religious Lives of Muslim Women," in *Women in Contem-*

porary Muslim Societies, Jane Smith, ed., Bucknell University Press, East Brunswick NJ, 1980, pp. 27–60.

10. Nadia Youssef; *Women and Work in Developing Societies,* Greenwood Press, New York, 1976, p. 100.

11. This example is based on the case of Shah Bano Begum, the woman, against her husband, Mohammed Ahmed Khan, in the town of Indore, Madhya Pradesh, 1978.

12. An excellent article on the problems facing India in respect of its Muslim community can be found in *The New Yorker,* January 19, 1987.

13. Free Press, New York, 1985, p. 40.

14. *The Atlanta Constitution,* September 4, 1986, p. 3.

15. *The Divorce Revolution,* Free Press, New York, 1985, p. 360.

16. *The Atlanta Constitution,* April 18, 1987.

17. *A Lesser Life: The Myth of Women's Liberation in the U.S.A.,* Warner Books, New York, 1986.

18. *Policy Review,* pp. 46–52.

19. *The Atlanta Constitution,* September 25, 1986, p. B1.

20. Reprinted in *The Atlanta Constitution,* December 2, 1986.

21. Tatyana Mamonova, ed., Beacon Press, Boston, 1984.

22. Virago Press, London, 1987.

23. Simon & Schuster, New York, 1988.

24. *The Equality Trap,* Simon & Schuster, New York, 1988, pp. 23–25, 30–31.

25. *Ibid.,* p. 45.

26. *Time,* August 18, 1986, p. 64.

27. *The Atlanta Constitution,* June 9, 1986, p. B1, and July 28, 1986, p. B1.

28. John Wiley & Sons, New York, 1986.

29. *A Lesser Life,* p. 402.

30. *Ibid.,* pp. 51, 52.

31. *Ibid.,* pp. 138, 141–143, 173.

32. *Gender Politics,* Harvard University Press, Cambridge MA, 1984, p. 167.

33. *Ibid.,* pp. 169–172.

34. *The Economic Emergence of Women,* Basic Books, New York, 1986, p. 200.

35. On abortion and child care, see *Newsweek,* February 29, 1988, pp. 60–61; *Newsweek,* March 28, 1988, p. 73; *Newsweek,* June 27, 1988, p. 45; *The Atlanta Constitution,* March 22, 1988; p. A23; *U.S. News and World Report,* June 20, 1988, pp. 69–70; *U.S. News and World Report,* August 22, 1988, pp. 33–36; *U.S. News and World Report,* September 19, 1988, pp. 43–45; and *U.S. News and World Report,* October 31, 1988, p. 13.

Chapter 30. Recommendations

1. Margot Duley and Mary Edwards, eds., Feminist Press, New York, 1986, 112. Cf. *Women in World Religions,* Arvind Sharma, ed., State University of New York Press, 1987.

2. Margaret Schuler, OEF International, Washington DC, 1986, pp. 30–31.

3. *The Politics of the Second Electorate,* Joni Lovenduski and Jill Hills, eds., Routledge and Kegan Paul, London, 1981, p. 328.

4. *For the Record Forum 1985,* Caroline Pezzullo, ed., International Women's Tribune Center, New York, 1986.

5. July 14, 1986, II.5.2.

6. *The New York Times,* October 17, 1986, I.28.5.

7. Michele Matterlat, *Woman and the Cultural Industries,* Documentary Dossier 23, U.N.E.S.C.O., Paris, 1981, p. 41.

8. Report of the Expert Group Meeting on Women and the Media, Vienna, Austria, November 1981, p. 1.

9. World Health Organization, *Women, Health and Development,* p. 12, Table 2.
10. *Ibid.,* p. 11 and table, annexure I, p. 40.
11. *For the Record Forum 1985,* p. 22.
12. *Ibid.,* p. 26.
13. *Ibid.,* pp. 10–11.
14. Cf. International Political Science Association, 4000 Cathedral Avenue, Washington DC 20016, United States.
15. Center on Women and Public Policy, H.H. Humphrey Institute of Public Affairs, University of Minnesota.
16. Third World Forum on Women, Law and Development, OEF International, Washington DC. Cf. *Empowerment and the Law,* Margaret Schuler, ed., published by OEF in 1986.
17. International Federation of Agricultural Producers, Rome, Italy.
18. *Women: A World Survey,* World Priority Publications, Washington DC, 1986, pp. 20–21. Cf. *For the Record Forum, 1985,* p. 26.
19. Similar to a proposal by editor Robin Morgan in *Sisterhood Is Global,* Doubleday, Garden City NY, 1984, Introduction, p. 35.
20. Vedam Books, New Delhi, India, 1985.
21. R.C. Rabin, "Israeli Women Protest Divorce Laws," *The New York Times,* February 8, 1987, p. E8.
22. P. 155.
23. *The Unfinished Liberation of Chinese Women,* Indiana University Press, Bloomington, 1983, p. 169.
24. *Population Growth and Policies in Sub-Saharan Africa,* International Bank for Reconstruction and Development, Washington DC, 1986, p. 21.
25. *Ibid.,* p. 5.
26. In *Women and the Family in the Middle East,* Elisabeth Fernea, ed., University of Texas Press, Austin, 1985, p. 146.
27. International Labor Organization, *Resources, Power and Women,* Geneva, 1985, p. 47.
28. United Nations, *World Survey of the Role of Women in Development,* E.86.IV.3, New York, 1986, p. 38.
29. *Population Growth and Policies in Sub-Saharan Africa.*
30. See Eschel Rhoodie, *Power and the Presidency,* Strydom Publishers, Pretoria, 1989, Chapters 7 and 8.
31. *The Star,* Johannesburg.
32. Sylvia Hewlett, *A Lesser Life: The Myth of Women's Liberation in the U.S.A.,* Warner Books, New York, 1986, p. 91.
33. *Ibid.,* p. 398.
34. See Chapter 17.
35. Joni Lovenduski, *Women and European Politics,* University of Massachusetts Press, Amherst, 1986, pp. 270–271.
36. P. 411.
37. *The Economic Emergence of Women,* Basic Books, New York, 1986, p. 5.
38. Hewlett, pp. 90–94, 100, 133, 138, 175, 374, 411–412.
39. *Gender Politics,* Harvard University Press, Cambridge MA, p. 166.
40. Hewlett, pp. 344–349, 354–365.
41. P. 168.
42. *Resources, Power and Women,* Geneva, 1985, p. 7.
43. "The Equality Principle and the Section Division of Labour," *Women's Studies International Forum,* Vol. 9, No. 1, 1986, pp. 13–18.
44. P. 146.
45. *Economic Emergence of Women,* p. 162.
46. *Ibid.,* p. 163.

47. *Ibid.,* p. 164.
48. *Ibid.,* p. 171.
49. Gilda Berger, *Women, Work and Wages,* Franklin Watts, New York, 1986, p. 34.
50. *Ibid.,* p. 40.
51. *Gender Politics,* p. 168.
52. National Academy Press, 1985, p. 30.
53. Temple University Press, Philadelphia, 1984, Preface.
54. *Ibid.*
55. *Ibid.*
56. Section II, Appendix I.
57. "Canada's Equal Pay for Work of Equal Value Law," pp. 173–187.
58. *Ibid.*
59. A tax-exempt educational foundation formed in 1983 to engage in research on the development of policy and law designed to eliminate all aspects of employment discrimination, including gender discrimination. Its purpose is to supply objective explanations of the background, controlling factors, applicable law and practical considerations in dealing with these issues. Results are published in monographs, books and other publications. The foundation is an outgrowth of the Equal Employment Advisory Council.
60. *A Closer Look at Comparable Worth,* Robert Williams and Lorence Kessler, eds., National Foundation for the Study of Equal Employment, Washington DC, 1984, pp. 10–12, 82–83.
61. *Ibid.,* pp. 13–14.
62. For further data on the general subject of comparable worth, see *Sex Segregation in the Workplace: Trends, Explanations and Remedies,* Barbara Reskin, ed., Committee on Women's Employment and Related Social Issues, National Academy Press, Washington DC, 1984; and Women's Bureau of National Affairs, *Pay Equity and Comparable Worth,* Washington DC, 1984.

Chapter 32. Research Proposals

Employment References, Africa

1. "Equal access to all jobs with the government and organizations falling under its jurisdiction is guaranteed to all citizens without other requirements than those of merit and aptitudes." Constitution, Article 44 (1976).
2. "Work shall be the right and duty of all citizens, each of whom must produce according to his ability and be remunerated according to his work." Constitution, Article 26, (1980).
3. "Citizens . . . shall have the right to work . . ." Constitution, Article 127 (1979).
4. "In the area of production, women will be invited to redouble their efforts to contribute to the socio-economic improvement of the country." Constitution (Declaration Concerning the Fundamental Objectives of the Movement), Union of Barundikani Women (1976).
5. "Everyone has the right and duty to work." Constitution, Preamble (1972).
6. "All citizens shall be equal in work. No one may be jeopardized in his work or employment by reasons of . . . sex . . ." Constitution, Article 10 (1981).
7. "In the People's Republic of the Congo, work is an honor, a right and a sacred duty . . ." Constitution, Article 20 (1979).
8. "Work is a right, a duty and an honor guaranteed by the state." Constitution, Article 13 (1971).

9. "Work ... is a right, a duty ... for every citizen." Constitution, Article 27 (1973).

10. "Every Ethiopian subject shall have the right to work according to capacity." Constitution, Article 47 (1977).

11. "Parliament shall enact such laws as will ensure (a) that all citizens, without discrimination on any grounds have the opportunity for securing adequate means of livelihood as well as adequate opportunities to secure suitable employment..." Constitution, 9(2) (1979).

12. "All citizens of the Republic of Guinea shall enjoy the same right to work..." Constitution, Article 44 (1958).

13. "The State considers that work and education are fundamental rights and duties of all citizens." Constitution, Article 14 (1973).

14. "Work is an honor and a firm duty for every citizen..." Constitution, Article 21 (1975). "Access to public office, professions, positions, and employment shall be open to all citizens without any conditions other than ability and aptitude." Constitution, Article 26 (1975).

15. "The Republic of Mali guarantees to its citizens, within the framework of the law: the right to work; equality in employment..." Constitution, Article 13 (1974).

16. "All citizens shall have equal access to public employment and office." Constitution, Article 12 (1972). "All citizens shall have an equal right to education and employment," Constitution, Article 13 (1972).

17. "In the People's Republic of Mozambique work is esteemed and protected.... Work is the right and duty of every citizen of either sex, and it is the criterion for the distribution of national wealth." Constitution, Article 7 (1975). "In the People's Republic of Mozambique work and education are the right and duty of every citizen..." Constitution, Article 31 (1975).

18. "The State shall direct its policy towards ensuring that—all citizens without discrimination on any ground whatsoever have the opportunity for securing adequate means of livelihood as well as adequate opportunities to secure suitable employment." Constitution, Article 17(3) (1979).

19. "Everyone has the right to work, to choose his work freely..." Constitution, Article 30 (1978).

20. "Everyone has the right to work and to seek employment." Constitution, Article 20 (1963).

21. "Every citizen shall be entitled to work." Constitution, Article 21(1) (1979).

22. "Work is a right, a duty, and an honour..." Constitution, Article 36 (1973). "The State shall ensure equality of opportunities for all Sudanese and prohibit any discrimination in work opportunities or conditions ... on the grounds of ... sex...." Constitution, Article 56 (1973).

23. "...Every community has the duty—to ensure that in the State every man able to work does work, the meaning of work being any sort of lawful activity by which a man acquires the necessities of life...." Constitution, Foreword C (1977).

24. "The Togolese Republic shall assure to each citizen ... economic ... rights." Constitution, Article 6 (1979).

25. "The Republic shall guarantee to all citizens within the framework of the laws: —equality in employment..." Constitution, Article 15 (1977). "Freedom of enterprise is guaranteed...." Constitution, Article 19 (1977).

26. "Every Zairian shall have the right and the duty to contribute, through his work, to the construction and prosperity of the Nation. No one may be jeopardized in his work because of his origins, sex, or beliefs." Constitution, Article 27 (1978).

27. "The State guarantees the coordination between the woman's duties to the family and her career in society, and equality with men in the fields of ... economic life without any violation of the rules of Islamic Shari'a." Constitution, Article 11 (1971).

28. Public Service Regulation No. 6, Articles 5, 6 (1962)—the only conditions of eligibility for public service are Ethiopian nationality, attainment of majority and nonexistence of disqualifying factors such as prior dismissal from public service or criminal conviction. Public Employment Order No. 18, Article 10 (1962) provides that in the private sector, the main objective of the Public Employment Administration is to facilitate the employment desires, and capabilities, adhering to the principle of non-discrimination against any person.

29. "The remunerations, founded on the principle of 'equal pay for equal work,' are determined as a function of the quality and quantity of work effectively completed." Constitution, Article 59 (1976).

30. "Work shall be the right and duty of all citizens, each of whom must produce according to his ability and be remunerated according to his work." Constitution, Article 26 (1980).

31. "To provide equal employment, women have the right to salaries equal to those of men." Constitution, Article 17 (1979). "Every citizen has the right to be remunerated according to his work and his capacity." Constitution, Article 20 (1979).

32. "Every worker is entitled to appropriate remuneration for the work he performs, according to its quantity and quality." Constitution, Article 29 (1973).

33. "All employees shall be entitled to equal pay for equal work irrespective of sex or any other reason not related to the work condition." Constitution, Article 48 (1977).

34. "Parliament shall enact such laws as will ensure . . . that there is equal pay for equal work without discrimination on account of sex. . . ." Constitution, Article 9(2)(f) (1979).

35. Article 31 of the Personal Status Act specified that equality in wages shall be maintained when the circumstances and nature of the work are similar. (Act. No. 976 of 1972.) In addition, the Basic People's Congresses decided in their third regular session for 1980 to issue the necessary legislation concerning citizens' wages in order to emphasize the principle of equal pay for equal work and responsibilities.

36. ". . . Everyone shall be remunerated according to the quality and quantity of his work." Constitution, Article 21 (1972).

37. "The State shall direct its policy towards ensuring that— . . . there is equal pay for equal work without discrimination on account of sex, or any other ground whatsoever. . . ." Constitution, Article 17(3)e (1979).

38. "Everyone has the right to work, to choose his work freely, and to equitable and satisfying terms of labor." Constitution, Article 30 (1978).

39. "The workers shall be entitled to receive without discrimination a remuneration equal to the amount and value of work done." Constitution, Article 57(3) (1979).

40. "The State shall ensure equality of opportunities for all Sudanese and prohibit any discrimination in work opportunities or conditions or pay on the grounds of . . . sex. . . ." Constitution, Article 56 (1973).

41. Constitution, Article 36 (1973).

42. "The State shall direct its policy towards ensuring that—(c) the health, safety and welfare of all persons in employment are safeguarded and not endangered or abused. . . ." Constitution, Article 17(3) (1979).

43. Labor Decree §54 (1974) states that no woman shall be employed on night work in a public or private industrial undertaking or in any agricultural undertaking (some categories of women, mainly professionals and top management staff, are excluded from this prohibition). Labor Decree §56 (1974) empowers the Commissioner to make regulations restricting or prohibiting the employment of women in any particular type or types of industrial or other undertakings.

44. Employment Act, No. 2/1976, §7 (1976). No woman or juvenile can be employed in any industrial capacity between the hours of 6:30 p.m. and 6:30 a.m. There are several exceptions to this rule. Women or young men may be employed in cases of unforeseen emergencies which interfere with normal undertakings and which are not of

a recurring nature. Women may also be employed where they work with raw materials which are subject to rapid deterioration. Women may also be employed where they hold responsible positions of a managerial or technical nature or are employed in the medical or paramedical professions. Women are prohibited from working in mines. (See R. Maina, "Law and the Status of Women in Kenya," *Col. Human Rights L. Rev.* 8:185-206 [1976].)

45. Labor Standards Proclamation, *Negarit Gazetta,* 25th year, No. 13, Article 10(A) (1966)—requires an employer to provide special care and protection to avoid injuries to minors, women and disabled persons employed by him. Labor Proclamation, *Negarit Gazetta,* 35th year, No. 11 (1975), Article 30(3)—treats men and women identically as far as safety and working conditions are concerned; however, a pregnant woman may not work after 10 P.M. or engage in dangerous trades. (See D. Haile, "Law and the Status of Women in Ethiopia," *U.N. Research Series* [1980].)

46. "The state shall promote the requisite measures to ensure the right of citizens to . . . assistance in . . . motherhood . . . and any other form of incapacity for work." Constitution, Article 27 (1980).

47. "The state shall guarantee to the working woman the right to maternity leave before and after childbirth, with a continuation of her salary." Constitution, Article 125 (1979). "The State shall . . . assure the development of . . . nursery schools, and kindergartens." Constitution, Article 126 (1979).

48. "The State guarantees the coordination between the woman's duties to the family and her career in society. . . ." Constitution, Article 11 (1971). "The State guarantees maternal and child care, looks after the young and provides suitable conditions for the development of their faculties." Constitution, Article 10 (1971).

49. "The State, within its possibilities, shall guarantee to everyone, especially to children, to mothers and to older workers, health protection, material security, rest and leisure." Constitution, Article 1(5) (1975).

50. "Where assistance, special care and facilities necessary for the maintenance, safety and development of a woman as a mother are provided by or at the expense of the State, such assistance, special care and facilities shall be available to all mothers without discrimination." Constitution, Article 32(1) (1979).

51. Constitutional Declaration, December 11, 1969, Article 43 prohibits women's work for 30 days after delivery; labor legislation provides maternity leave of 50 days at half pay. See Report of the Secretary-General, U.N. General Assembly, U.N. Decade for Women, *Equality, Development and Peace: Promotion of Full Equality of Women and Men in All Spheres of Life in Accordance with International Standards and the Declaration on the Elimination of Discrimination against Women,* October 3, 1977, p. 33.

52. Labor Decree 60-124, Articles 24, 25 provide for two months' maternity leave.

53. "The state shall promote child care homes. . . ." Constitution, Article 53 (1979). "The state . . . shall protect the family and shall assist the mother and child." Constitution, Article 56(1) (1979).

54. ". . . The state shall ensure adequate guarantees for mothers and the working women," Constitution, Article 55 (1973).

55. Labor Proclamation, Article 30(3) (1975)—a pregnant woman is to be paid for checkups upon certification of a medical doctor, and is to be paid for 45 consecutive days of maternity leave.

56. Labor Decree, N.L.C.D. 157 §42(1) (1967)—industrial and commercial employers were required by statute to provide certain minimal benefits to pregnant female employees who were also allowed to take a maximum 12 weeks' leave. Collective bargaining contracts authorized by statute may also confer maternity benefits upon female employees, enforceable in the courts. (See Y. Luckham, "Law and the Status of Women in Ghana," *Col. Human Rights L. Rev.* 8:69-94 [1976].)

57. Employment Act (1976)—working mothers are entitled to two months' paid

maternity leave, although it comes at the expense of their annual leave for the year. As of 1975, there were 5,000 day care centers in Kenya.

58. Labor Code Article 112 provides for a maternity leave of 14 weeks for the pregnant working woman. Labor Code Article 113 provides that where the mother who has resumed her work after birth is nursing her child, she has the right to two hour rest periods a day for which no deduction may be made from her paycheck. (See V. Dagadzi, "Law and the Status of Women in Togo: Discrimination against Women in Togo," *Col. Human Rights Rev.* 8: 295-310 [1976].)

Employment References, Middle East/Arabian Gulf

1. "...Every citizen shall have the right to work and to choose his type of work in accordance with public order and moral standards. The State shall ensure that work is made available to the citizen and that its terms are equitable..." Constitution, Article 13 (1973).

2. "Work is a right, a duty and an honor guaranteed by the State." Constitution, Article 13 (1971). "The State guarantees the coordination between the woman's duties to the family and her career in society, and equality with man in the fields of ... economic life without any violation of the rules of Islamic Sharia." Constitution, Article 11 (1971).

3. "Every person has the right to choose the profession he wishes, provided it is not contrary to the principles of Islam, to the public interest or to the rights of others." Constitution, Article 28, (1979).

4. "Equal opportunities are guaranteed to all citizens, according to the law." Constitution, Article 19(2) (1970). "Work is a right, which is ensured to be available for every able citizen." Constitution, Article 32 (1970).

5. "...The Government shall ensure work and education." Constitution, Article 6(2) (1952). "It is the right of every citizen to work.... The State shall protect labor and enact a legislation therefore...." Constitution, Article 23 (1952).

6. "The State ... ensures ... equal opportunities for citizens." Constitution, Article 8 (1962). "Every Kuwaiti has the right to work and to choose the type of his work. Work is a duty of every citizen necessitated by personal dignity and public good. The State shall endeavour to make it available to citizens...." Constitution, Article 41 (1962).

7. "Every Lebanese shall have the right to public employment without distinction except on the basis of merit and competence according to the conditions established by law." Constitution, Article 12 (1926).

8. "The State shall endeavor to provide equal opportunities for all citizens, and to make it possible for them to exercise the right to work under laws that will ensure social justice." Constitution, Article 7(4) (1970).

9. "The state insures the principle of equal opportunities for citizens." Constitution, Article 25(4) (1973). "Work is a rght and duty of every citizen...." Constitution, Article 36(1) (1973). "The state shall guarantee for women all opportunities enabling them to fully and effectively participate in the ... economic life. The State must remove the restrictions that prevent women's development and participation in building the socialist Arab society." Constitution, Article 45 (1973).

10. "Every individual is entitled to carry on business activities, and to enter into contracts in the field of his choice." Constitution, Article 40 (1974). "It is the right and duty of every individual to work...." Constitution, Article 42 (1974). "No individual can be employed at a job that does not suit his age, capacity and sex." Constitution, Article 43 (1974).

11. "Every citizen shall be free to choose his occupation, trade or profession...." Constitution, Article 34 (1971).

12. "Every citizen has the right to work. Work is the duty of every able person....

No citizen shall be barred from practicing his profession, job or work in all parts of the Republic." Constitution, Article 35 (1970). ". . . Special care shall be given to working women for professional competence." Constitution, Article 36 (1970).

13. "Every citizen has the right to undertake work chosen by him and in accordance with the law." Constitution, Article 36 (1970).

14. Under the Civil Code Article 1117, a husband could prevent his wife from working simply by notifying her employer that she did not have his permission to work. The wife then had to go to court and prove that her occupation was not "repugnant to the honor" of the family. Under the Family Protection Law, Article 15 (1967), however, the husband could no longer prevent his wife from working merely by going to her employer. He was required to go to court and prove that her job was against the interests of the family. Family Protection Law Article 18 (1967) accorded the wife full independence to choose her profession or occupation. It also authorized her to remove her husband from his employment by proving to the court that his job was "against the interests and honor of the family." (See F. Mirvahal, "The Status of Women in Iran," *J. Family Law* 14:383-404 [1975/76].)

15. Employment Service Law 5719, §42 (1959)—in referring employees, the labor exchange shall not discriminate against a person on account of his sex (among other grounds) and a person requiring an employee shall not refuse to engage a person for work on such account. . . . It shall not be considered discrimination if the character or nature of the task . . . prevents reference or hiring of a person for some particular work. Outside the scope of the Employment Service Law discrimination against women is not forbidden except in specific fields, and the employer may seek either men or women at his discretion. (See P. Albeck, "The Status of Women in Israel," *Am. J. Comp. L.* Vol. 20, No. 4, 693ff. [Fall, 1972].)

16. See note 3.

17. "No individual can be employed at a job that does not suit his age, capacity and sex. . . ." Constitution, Article 43 (1974).

18. ". . . The State shall ensure that work is made available to the citizens and that its terms are equitable. . . ." Constitution, Article 13(b) (1973).

19. ". . . Every workman shall receive wages commensurate with the quantity and quality of his work. . . ." Constitution, Article 23(2)(a).

20. ". . . The State shall endeavour to make (work) available to citizens and to make its terms equitable." Constitution, Article 41 (1962).

21. ". . . Every citizen has the right to earn his wage according to the nature and yield of his work." Constitution, Article 36(2) (1973).

22. "The State shall adopt the necessary measures so that workers may earn decent wages commensurate with the work they perform. . . ." Constitution, Article 45 (1974).

23. Labor Code Article 23 recognizes the principle of equal pay for men and women for doing the same job.

24. Male and Female Workers (Equal Pay) Law, 5724, §1 (1964) provides "An employer shall pay to a female worker a wage equal to the wage paid to a male worker at that place of employment for the same work." This was amended by the 1974 amendment of the Labor Law to reinforce equal pay provisions previously subject to practical abuses. (See P. Albeck; Report of the Secretary-General, U.N. General Assembly, U.N. Decade for Women: *Equality, Development and Peace: Promotion of Full Equality of Women and Men in All Spheres of Life in Accordance with International Standards and the Declaration on the Elimination of Discrimination against Women,* p. 30, October 3, 1977 (hereinafter cited as Report of the Secretary General).

25. Decree-Law No. 29, §3 (May 12, 1943).

26. ". . . Special conditions shall be made for the employment of women and juveniles," Constitution, Article 23(2)(d) (1952).

27. "No individual can be employed at a job that does not suit his age, capacity and

sex. Children, young people, and women shall be accorded special protection in terms of conditions of work," Constitution, Article 43 (1974).

28. Labor Code prohibits women from heavy or dangerous work.

29. Employment of Women Law 5714, §1 (1954) empowers the Minister of Labor to issue rules forbidding or restricting employment of women in jobs, production processes or work places especially apt to endanger their health. The Law precludes employment of women at night, generally from midnight until 6:00 in the morning. There are a number of exceptions, e.g., it does not apply to hospitals and other facilities for care of sick people, child care facilities, hotels and restaurants. Women working in executive capacities are not subject to the night work restriction." (See P. Albeck.)

30. Labor Law of 1946, §26—it is forbidden to employ women on night work. Certain other forms of employment are also forbidden to women. (See H. Nemer, "The Status of Women in the World of Today: Lebanon," *Rev. Contemp. L.* 7 No. 1:134-43 (1960).

31. "The State guarantees maternal and child care, looks after the young and provides suitable conditions for the development of their faculties." Constitution, Article 10 (1971).

32. ". . . The State shall provide special protection for women, particularly working women and children, by the grant of leave with pay to pregnant women as set out by law. The State shall establish nurseries and kindergartens and other means of care as prescribed by law." Constitution, Article 36 (1970).

33. Labor Code provides pregnant women with 12 weeks' maternity leave (six weeks before, and six weeks after, birth). Employers of working mothers are required to give them a half-hour break every three hours if they breast-feed their babies. Employers also provide a day care center in every factory or mill in which the number of babies is ten or more. Women enjoy the same social security rights and medical insurance benefits as men. (See F. Mirvahali; S. Sadaji, "Law and the Status of Women in Iran," *Columbia Human Rights L. Rev.* 8:141-164 [1976].)

34. Employment of Women Law—an employee in the fifth month of pregnancy is obliged to inform her employer; once so informed, the employer may not employ her overtime or during the weekly rest period. During pregnancy a woman is entitled to be absent from work on account of that condition for any period prescribed in writing by a doctor. Every woman who gives birth is entitled to 12 weeks' maternity leave. A working mother who is breast-feeding her baby is entitled to an hour's absence from work daily, either consecutively or divided into two intervals, in addition to any other rest periods. Maternity allowances include childbirth grant, and childbirth pay or payment to an adoptive mother. (See P. Albeck; Report of the U.N. Secretary General, p. 33.)

35. Labor Law of 1946, §26—women are entitled to maternity leave both before and after confinement with full pay. (See H. Nemer.)

Employment References, Far East

1. "Citizens have the right to work. . . ." Constitution, Article 48 (1978). "Women enjoy equal rights with men in all spheres of . . . economic . . . life." Constitution, Article 53 (1978).

2. "Every person shall have freedom to . . . choose his occupation to the extent that it doesn't interfere with the public welfare." Constitution, Article 22 (1947). "All people shall have the right and the obligation to work." Constitution, Article 27 (1947).

3. "Women hold equal social status and rights with men. . . . The State frees women from the heavy burdens of household chores and provides every condition for them to participate in public life." Constitution, Article 62 (1972).

4. "All citizens shall enjoy freedom of occupation." Constitution, Article 14 (1980). "All citizens shall have the right to work. . . . Constitution, Article 30(1) (1980).

5. "Citizens . . . have the right to work. . . ." Constitution, Article 77 (1960).

"Women in the MPR are accorded the same rights as men in all spheres of economic . . . life. The realization of these rights is ensured by according women the same conditions of work . . . as men. . . ." Constitution, Article 84 (1960).

6. ". . . The right of work . . . shall be guaranteed to the people." Constitution, Article 15 (1947). "The State shall provide suitable opportunity for work to people who are able to work." Constitution, Article 152 (1947).

7. ". . . Men and women enjoy equal pay for equal work." Constitution, Article 53 (1978). In the people's communes, the wages paid to individual workers are based on the accumulation of work points. The principle of allocating work points is "equal pay for equal work among men and women." In practice, there are problems in the execution of this policy (e.g., men are placed on a higher wage-point scale). More recently, however, there has been reevaluation of the work point assessment methods. In the urban areas, the principle is also equal pay for equal work. However, women are involved in the highest-paying jobs less than men. (See J. Slade Tien, "Unbound: The Women of New China," *Intellect,* Vol. 109, No. 37, August 1977.)

8. Labor Standard Law—guarantees the right to equal pay for equal work (yet there have been many instances of inequality of wages as between men and women). (See C. Kaji, "The Status of Women in the World of Today: Japan," *Rev. Contemp. L.* No. 1:129-133 [1960].)

9. ". . . The State shall endeavor to guarantee optimum wages." Constitution, Article 30(1) (1980). Labor Standards Law (1953) provides for equal treatment of all workers in setting terms and conditions of employment regardless of sex, creed, social status, nationality. Nevertheless, in every occupational field and education level, women's pay is lower than the male counterpart. (See *Women at Work 1/1980,* Special/World Conf. of the U.N. Decade for Women: Equality, Development and Peace, 1980, 16–21.)

10. "Citizens . . . have the right to work and to payment for their work in accordance with its quantity and quality." Constitution, Article 77 (1960).

11. "Special protection shall be accorded to working women and children." Constitution, Article 30(4) (1980).

12. ". . . Women and children engaged in labor shall, according to their age and physical condition, be accorded special protection." Constitution, Article 153 (1957).

13. ". . . The State affords special protections to Mothers and children through maternity leave, shortened working hours for mothers of large families, an expanding network of maternity hospitals, nurseries and kindgergartens and other measures. The State frees women from the heavy burdens of household chores and provides every condition for them to participate in public life." Constitution, Article 62 (1972).

14. "Women . . . are accorded the same rights as men in all spheres of economic . . . life. The realization of these rights is ensured by . . . the state promotion of mother and child welfare, state assistance for mothers of large families, leave of absence from work before and after confinement with full pay and the extension of the network of maternity hospitals, nurseries and kindergartens.' Constitution, Article 84 (1960).

15. "Working women who become pregnant are sustained by a number of provisions which, measured in strictly economic terms, give them a privileged position in the work force." There are maternity leave provisions (56 days), with full pay. Also, after returning to work, day care is available and nursing time is arranged. (See J. Slade Tien, p. 41.)

16. Labor Standards Law provides that women must be allowed maternity leave for six weeks before and six weeks after delivery of a child. Also, a mother who is rearing a child under one year of age is entitled to a nursing time of 30 minutes twice a day in addition to regular rest periods. Due to a paucity of creches, however, wives are often obliged to give up their jobs when they bear a child. (See C. Kaji.)

Employment References, Indochina/Southeast Asia

1. "Every citizen shall have the right to work and to expect a reasonable standard of living." Constitution, Article 27(2) (1945).

2. ". . . Every Cambodian is guaranteed a living. . . ." Constitution, Article 12 (1976).

3. "It shall be the duty of every citizen to engage in gainful work to assure himself and his family a life worthy of human dignity." Constitution, Section 3 (1973).

4. "The State should support the people of working age to obtain suitable employments, ensure the fair protection of labor, and provide for the system of labor relations including the settlement of fair wages." Constitution, Section 72 (1978).

5. "Work is the primary right, obligation and privilege of citizens. Citizens have the right to work." Constitution, Article 58 (1980).

6. Article 2, §9 of 1973 Constitution emphasizes equality of treatment, the announced policy being, "to afford protection to labor, promote full employment and equality in opportunities, regardless of sex. . . ." This equality principle was codified by the 1973 Labor Code, and by Pres. decree No. 442 (1974).

7. Law No. 14, Article 2 (1969) prohibits sex discrimination in the implementation of the general labor laws.

8. ". . . Women and men receive equal pay for equal work. . . ." Constitution, Article 63 (1980).

9. Law No. 68 (1958) ratifies Convention No. 100 of the International Labor Organization regarding "Equal Remuneration for Men and Women Workers for Work of Equal Value."

10. Labor Code, Article 135 – "No employer shall discriminate against any woman with respect to terms and conditions of employment on account of her sex. Equal remuneration shall be paid to both men and women for work of equal value."

11. "The state establishes work conditions suited to women's needs. . . ." Constitution, Article 63 (1980).

12. Decree No. 29 of March 12, 1947, Article 130, forbids employment of women of any age in underground mines, in dangerous work, or in work detrimental to their health in industrial establishments. Decree No. 29, Article 107, forbids night work between 9 P.M. and 5 A.M. In the Dem. Rep. of Vietnam, minors and women had to have a minimum night rest period of 11 consecutive hours, except with regard to industrial enterprises handling materials susceptible to rapid spoilage or in case of extreme emergency. Girls under 15 could not be employed as singers and dancers. (See G. Ginsburgs, "The Role of the Law in the Emancipation of Women in the Democratic Republic of Vietnam," *Am. J. Comp. L.* Vol. 23, No. 4: 613 (Fall, 1975); Nguyen Van Huong, "The Status of Women in the World of Today: Democratic Republic of Vietnam," *Rev. Contemp. L.* No. 1:210-23 [1963].)

13. Labor Law No. 12 (1948), Jo. Law No. 1, Articles 7–9 (1951) – women are prohibited from working during night hours (6 P.M. to 6 A.M.), from working in mines, or from engaging in any kind of work which endangers their health, safety and morals.

14. Labor Code (1973) – "Working Conditions for Special Groups of Employees" (Title III, Articles 130–55). The title includes provisions concerning the employment of women in prohibited kinds of night work (Article 130), facilities to ensure a working woman's health and safety (Article 132). A new provision brings women who work in night clubs, bars and similar kinds of establishments within the provisions of the Labor Code (Article 138). Industrial home workers are also placed under the regulatory powers of the Secretary of Labor (Articles 153–55).

15. ". . . Women are entitled to pre- and post-natal paid leave if they are workers or office employees, or to maternity allowances if they are cooperative members. The state and society ensure the development of maternity homes, creches, kindergartens, community dining halls . . . to create favourable conditions for women to produce, work, study and rest." Constitution, Article 63 (1980).

16. Decree No. 29—pregnant women, whether workers or in the civil service, are entitled to three pre-natal visits to doctors; the first during the first days of pregnancy, the second in the fifth month, and the third in the eighth month; to a daily rest hour at work during the seventh and eighth months; and to maternity benefits in money and kind at the period of confinement. Decree No. 29, Article 121 forbids factory management to dismiss women workers on account of pregnancy, to allow them to take arduous work, or to transfer them to other work without their consent. Upon confinement women workers are entitled to two months' paid maternity leave, one month before and one month after confinement. Women taking the eight-week maternity leave receive half their salaries plus subsidies. For the first year of the child's life, breast-feeding mothers had to be given time on the job for nursing purposes—30 minutes in the morning and in the afternoon. Every enterprise which employed more than 100 women was obliged to maintain a creche for nursing children. (See G. Ginsburgs and Nguyen Van Huong.)

17. Labor Law, Article 13—women have the right to paid leave 1½ months before childbirth as well as 1½ months after birth or miscarriage, and after return to work, a woman has the right to time to breast-feed her infant.

18. Labor Code, Article 133 provides maternity leave benefits; Article 134 directs the Secretary of Labor to develop incentive bonus schemes to encourage family planning among female workers. The Labor Code also provides for free family planning services.

19. See Report of the U.N. Secretary General, U.N. Decade for Women, *Equality, Development and Peace: Promotion of Full Equality of Women and Men in All Spheres of Life in Accordance with International Standards and the Declaration on the Elimination of Discrimination Against Women,* U.N. General Assembly, October 3, 1977, p. 33.

Employment References, South Pacific

1. "Every person has the right to freedom of choice of employment in any calling for which he has the qualifications (if any) lawfully required." Constitution, Article 48(1) (1975).

2. Everyone has the duty to "work according to his talents in socially useful employment." Constitution, Article 7(e) (1980).

3. "It shall be unlawful for any person who is an employer . . . to refuse or omit to employ any person . . . to refuse or omit to offer or afford any person the same terms of employment, conditions of work . . . and opportunities for training, promotion, and transfer as are made available for persons of the same or substantially similar qualifications employed in the same or substantially similar circumstances on work of that description; or to dismiss any person . . . by reasons of the sex . . . of that person. . . ." Human Rights Commission Act, Article 15(1) (1977). (Articles 16–17, 19–25 have similar, more specific, provisions.)

4. There are no legal restrictions either in the Australian Public Service or any of six State Public Services on the appointment of women to paid public service posts, except in Tasmania, where women can be prevented from holding certain posts. (Also in Tasmania, there is Public Service Act, Sec. 54 [1967] which provides that if a male is appointed to a job advertised as specifically suitable for males, a woman cannot appeal, but if a woman is appointed to such a job, a man may appeal.) In Australian and State Public Services, there are no distinctive legal restrictions relating to women's retirement except in three states where women, but not men, are required to retire at 60. Under income tax provisions, it is more attractive financially for a married woman to take a job outside the home than for the husband to improve his income. Under Widow's Pension provisions, in 1968 a government training scheme was set up to help widow pensioners acquire vocational skills, along with their pension and training allowance. A married woman with an unemployed husband is ineligible for unemployment benefits. (See Manpower and Social Affairs Committee, Organization for Economic Cooperation and

Development, *The Role of Women in the Economy—National Report: Australia* [Note by the Secretariat], Paris, April 22, 1973, pp. 220, 239–40.)

5. Id. at 246, 248–49.

6. Id. at 248–49.

7. See note 3.

8. See *Women at Work 1/1980,* Special/World Conf. of U.N. Decade for Women: Equality, Development and Peace (July, 1980), p. 24.

9. While some restrictions have been repealed, existing ones include work on dangerous machinery, in underground mines and in processes harmful to health or where high accident rates exist. Also, there have been established by law for women maximum permissible weights to be carried and maximum hours of work. (See *The Role of Women in the Economy—National Report: Australia,* 231–35.)

10. Human Rights Commission Act, Article 3 (1977).

11. Sec. 51 (xxiiiA) of the Commonwealth Constitution enables legislation to be introduced concerning "the provision of maternity allowances, widow's pensions, child endowment, unemployment. . . ." The Maternity Allowance is a lump sum payment designed to help mothers meet expenses associated with the births of their children (there is no means requirement). Child Endowment is a continuing payment to people with a child under 16 or 21. Again, there is no means test—rates depend on the number of children under the mother's care. There is also a Supporting Mother's Benefit for unmarried mothers and mothers who are deserted, separated, or wives of prisoners. There are four State Acts concerning Maternity Leave, but they are of a limited nature. In 1973, only 10 percent of private employers granted maternity leave and only one in five granted paid leave. The Maternity Leave (Australian Government Employees) Act, 1973 provides maternity leave on full pay to all Australian Government employees in accord with the I.L.O. Convention on minimum maternity leave. However, provisions for medical benefits, nursing breaks, etc., are not available. (See *The Role of Women in the Economy—National Report: Australia,* pp. 216, 218–19, 221, 229–30.)

Employment References, Caribbean

1. "Every person has the obligation to engage in work of his own choice in order to provide fittingly for the maintenance of himself and his family, to achieve the broadest possible improvement of his personality, and to contribute to the well-being and progress of society." Constitution, Article 9(f) (1966).

2. ". . . In the administration of government services, the appointment of personnel, and the terms and conditions of their employment, must be free of privileges, favors, and discrimination." Constitution, Article 16 (1964).

3. "Nothing contained in any law shall be held to be inconsistent with or in contravention of subsection (1) of this section (prohibiting discriminatory laws) to the extent that it makes provision with respect to standards or qualifications (not being standards or qualifications specifically relating to sex. . .) to be required of any person who is appointed to or to act in any office or employment." Constitution, Article 13(5) (1978).

4. "The socialist state . . . guarantees—that every man or woman who is able to work have the opportunity to have a job with which to contribute to the good of society and to the satisfaction of individual needs." Constitution, Article 8(b) (1976). "The state consecrates the right achieved by the Revolution that all citizens, regardless of race, color or national origin: —have access, in keeping with their merits and abilities, to all positions and state and administrative jobs. . . ." Constitution, Article 42 (1976). "Women have the same rights as men in the economic . . . fields. . . . In order to assure the exercise of these rights and especially the incorporation of women into socially organized work, the state sees to it that they are given jobs in keeping with their physical makeup. . . ." Constitution, Article 43 (1976). "Work in a socialist society is a right and duty. . . ." Constitution, Article 44 (1976).

5. "Every citizen has the right to work and its free selection in accordance with social requirements and personal qualifications. . . ." Constitution, Article 22(1) (1980). "The exercise of women's rights is ensured by according women equal access with men to academic, vocational and professional training, equal opportunities in employment, remuneration and promotion. . . ." Constitution, Article 29(2) (1980).

6. ". . . Every person shall have the right to practice any profession or to carry on any occupation, trade or business." Constitution, Article 13 (1976). "Every person . . . has the following fundamental duties—to work according to his capacity in useful employment . . . to respect the rights and freedoms of other persons without regard to . . . sex . . . and to cooperate fully with them in order to achieve national progress. . . ." Constitution, Article 29(d) (1976).

7. See note 2.

8. "The state consecrates the right achieved by the Revolution that all citizens . . . be given equal pay for equal work. . . ." Constitution, Article 42 (1976). ". . . Work is remunerated according to its quality and quantity. . . ." Constitution, Article 44 (1976).

9. "Every citizen . . . has the right to be awarded according to the nature, quality and quantity of his work. Women and men have the right to equal pay for equal work." Constitution, Article 22(1). "The exercise of women's rights is ensured by according women . . . equal opportunities in . . . remuneration. . . ." Constitution, Article 29(2) (1980).

10. The Women (Employment of) Law, Statutes of Jamaica, Cap. 417 restricts the employment of women in night work, specifying how long and in what occupations such work is allowed. It also empowers the Minister of Labor to make regulations prohibiting altogether the employment of women in any specified industry or undertaking; to restrict, prohibit or regulate employment of women before or after childbirth; and to prescribe the hours of work and the general conditions under which women may be employed.

11. See note 4, Constitution, Article 43 (1976).

12. "The exercise of women's rights is ensured by . . . special labor and health protection measures for women. . . ." Constitution, Article 29(2) (1980).

13. See Report of the U.N. Secretary General, U.N. General Assembly, U.N. Decade for Women, *Equality, Development and Peace: Promotion of Full Equality of Women and Men in All Spheres of Life in Accordance with International Standards and the Declaration on the Elimination of Discrimination Against Women,* October 3, 1977, p. 32.

14. "In order to assure the exercise of these rights and especially the incorporation of women into socially organized work . . . women are given paid maternity leave before and after giving birth; the state organizes such institutions as children's day care centers, semiboarding schools and boarding schools; and (the state) strives to create all the conditions which help to make real the principle of equality." Constitution, Article 43 (1976).

15. "The exercise of women's rights is ensured by . . . providing conditions enabling mothers to work, and by legal protection and material and moral support for mothers and children including paid leave and other benefits for mothers and expectant mothers." Constitution, Article 29(2) (1980).

Employment References, North America

1. Title VII of the 1964 Civil Rights Act (amended in 1972) prohibits sex discrimination by public or private employers with more than 15 workers in all classification, assignment, promotion and training. (A plaintiff must first exhaust all appeals through the Equal Employment Opportunity Commission, created to enforce Title VII.) In 1981, the U.S. Supreme Court extended Title VII to "comparable worth" instances. The United States Civil Service Commission has also issued guidelines pursuant to an Executive Order, requiring Federal agencies to develop and implement affirmative action

plans for hiring minorities and women. Title IX of the 1972 Education Amendments was held in a 1982 United States Supreme Court decision to proscribe sex-based employment discrimination in federally funded education programs. (See *Child Care and Equal Opportunity for Women,* U.S. Commission on Civil Rights, Clearinghouse Publication No. 67 [June, 1981]; J.M. Picker, "Law and the Status of Women in the United States," *Colum. Human Rights L. Rev.* 8:311 [1976].)

2. See S. Alexander, *State-by-State Guide to Women's Legal Rights* (1975), pp. 166–75.

3. The 1963 Equal Pay Act (amending Fair Labor Standards Act) also calls for equal wages for work requiring similar or equal skill, effort and responsibility and performed under similar conditions (comparable worth doctrine). (See *Child Care and Equal Opportunity for Women;* J.M. Picker.)

4. See S. Alexander.

5. Canadian Human Rights Act (1977) states that it is discriminatory not to pay equal wages to men and women employed in the same establishment who are performing work of equal value. All provinces contain similar legislative provisions. (See *Women at Work,* I.L.O. News Bulletin, World Conference of the U.N. Decade for Women [July, 1980], p. 16.)

6. See P. Francis, *Legal Status of Women,* 2d ed. (1978), pp. 82–84; S. Alexander.

7. See S. Alexander.

Voting Rights References, Africa

1. "All citizens and persons under the jurisdiction of the Republic of Guinea, without distinction as to . . . sex . . . shall be entitled to elect and be elected in the manner prescribed by law." Constitution, Article 39 (1968).

2. "Suffrage shall be universal, equal and secret. All Ivory Coast nationals of both sexes . . . shall be eligible to vote within the conditions determined by law." Constitution, Article 5 (1959).

3. "All elections shall be by ballot, and every citizen (Male and Female) of 21 years of age possessing real estate shall have the right of suffrage." Constitution Article 11 (1955) now suspended. ("Male and Female" added after "citizen" and "male" deleted before "citizen" by amend. proposed L. 1945–46, ch. III, declared adopted L. 1946–47, ch. VI.) Constitution now suspended.

4. "All citizens, regardless of . . . sex . . . are electors and shall be eligible to vote in accordance with the conditions determined by law." Constitution, Article 16 (1974).

5. "Men and women shall enjoy equality of political rights. All citizens of the Republic having attained their majority and possessing civil and political rights shall be electors, including both sexes." Constitution, Article 10 (1978). [Suspended]

6. "Men and women shall enjoy equal political rights. All citizens of either sex, of age . . . shall be eligible to vote." Constitution, Article 8 (1972).

7. "Suffrage shall be universal, equal and secret. All nationals . . . of both sexes, having attained their majority and possessing their civil and political rights, shall be eligible to vote, within the conditions determined by law." Constitution, Article 5 (1960).

8. ". . . All Senegalese nationals of either sex, who have attained their majority and enjoy civil and political rights, shall be eligible to vote. . . ." Constitution, Article 2 (1963).

9. "Suffrage shall always be universal, equal and secret. All Togolese citizens, of both sexes, having attained their majority and enjoying civil and political rights, shall be electors. . . ." Constitution, Article 3 (1979).

10. "All Voltan men and women, 21 years of age or older who possess their civil and political rights shall be electors, under conditions to be determined by law." Constitution, Article 6 (1977).

11. "All citizens are equal in rights and duties. Any discrimination based on

prejudice relating to sex . . . is abolished." Constitution, Article 39 (1976). "All political . . . rights of the Algerian woman are guaranteed by the Constitution." Constitution, Article 42 (1976). "Any citizen meeting the legal requirements is a voter and eligible for elective office." Constitution, Article 58 (1976).

12. "All citizens shall be equal before the law and enjoy the same rights. They shall be subject to the same duties, without any distinction based on . . . sex. . . ." Constitution, Article 18 (1980). "All citizens aged over 18 . . . shall have the right and the duty . . . to vote and be elected." Constitution, Article 20 (1980). [Suspended.]

13. "All citizens . . . are equal before the law." Constitution, Article 121 (1979). "All citizens . . . who are 18 years of age shall have the right to vote and to hold office." Constitution, Article 122 (1979). "Women . . . shall have equal rights with men in politics. . . ." Constitution, Article 124 (1979).

14. ". . . Every person . . . is entitled to the fundamental rights and freedoms of the individual . . . whatever his . . . sex. . . ." Constitution, Article 3 (1966). "A person who (a) is a citizen . . . and (b) has attained the age of 21 years . . . shall . . . be entitled . . . to be registered as a voter for the purpose of elections of Elected Members of the National Assembly." *Constitution,* Article 68(1) (1966).

15. "All human beings shall be equal before the law without distinction as to . . . sex. . . ." *Constitution,* Article 3 (1981). "Suffrage shall be universal, equal and secret." Constitution, Article 13 (1981).

16. "All . . . citizens have equal rights," Constitution, Article 11 (1979). "All . . . citizens of at least 18 years of age have judicial and political capacity and should take part in the elections." Constitution, Article 12 (1979). "Women have rights equal to men in the domains of . . . political . . . life." Constitution, Article 17, (1979).

17. "This community shall consist of all persons who are recognized as members and who accept its duties, without distinction as to . . . sex. . . ." Constitution, Article 2(1) (1977). "Popular legitimacy, expressed by secret, equal, and universal suffrage, shall be the basis and source of all power." Constitution, Article 2(2) (1977).

18. "Citizens are equal before the law. They have equal public rights and duties without discrimination between them on the basis of sex. . . ." Constitution, Article 40 (1971). "A citizen has the right to elect and to be nominated. . . ." Constitution, Article 62 (1971).

19. "All citizens . . . irrespective of sex, shall have equal rights and the same duties." Constitution, Article 23 (1973). "Any form of discrimination on grounds of . . . sex . . . is prohibited." Constitution, Article 24 (1973). "All citizens . . . 18 years of age or over shall have the right to vote." Constitution, Article 25 (1973).

20. "All people shall have equal protection of the law," Constitution, Article 21 (1971). "There shall be no discrimination among Ethiopian subjects on the basis of . . . sex. . . ." Constitution, Article 22 (1977). "Ethiopian subjects shall have the right to elect and be elected in accordance with this Constitution." Constitution, Article 46 (1977).

21. ". . . Every person . . . is entitled to the fundamental rights and freedoms whatever his . . . sex. . . ." Constitution, Article 13 (1970). "Every citizen who has attained the age of 21 years shall . . . be entitled to be registered as . . . a voter. . . ." Constitution, Article 60 (1970).

22. "Every person in Ghana, whatever his . . . sex, shall be entitled to the fundamental rights and freedoms of the individual. . . ." Constitution, Article 19 (1979). "A citizen of Ghana not being less than 18 years of age and of sound mind shall have the right to vote. . . ." Constitution, Article 36 (1979). (Constitution now suspended.)

23. "Citizens shall be equal before the law, without distinction as to . . . sex. . . ." Constitution, Article 13 (1973). "Men and women shall have equal rights . . . in public life." Constitution, Article 16 (1973). "The right to elect organs representative of the people shall be universal and equal and shall be exercised by direct and secret suffrage. All citizens over the age of 18 who satisfy the other conditions prescribed in the electoral shall enjoy this right." Constitution, Article 25 (1973).

24. "Ever person who is registered in a constituency as a voter in elections ... shall ... be entitled so to vote in that constituency in accordance with the law...." Constitution, Article 32(2) (1969). "...A person shall be qualified to be registered as a voter in elections ... if ... at the date of his application to be registered he—(a) is a citizen of Kenya who has attained the age of 18 years...." Constitution, Article 43 (1969). "...Every person in Kenya is entitled to the fundamental rights and freedoms of the individual ... whatever his ... sex." Constitution, Article 70 (1969).

25. "The State shall insure the equality of all its citizens by: prohibiting all discrimination based on ... sex." *Constitution,* Article 12(3) (1975). "All citizens who fulfill the legal requirements shall have the right to vote and to be elected." Constitution, Article 40 (1975).

26. "The emancipation of women is one of the State's essential tasks," Constitution, Article 17 (1975). "All citizens ... enjoy the same rights, and are subject to the same duties, irrespective of ... sex...." Constitution, Article 26 (1975). "All citizens ... over 18 years of age are entitled to vote and be elected...." 28 (1975). "...Women and men enjoy the same rights and are subject to the same duties." Constitution, Article 29 (1975).

27. "...Discrimination on the grounds of ... sex ... shall be prohibited...." Constitution, Article 15 (1979). "Every citizen of Nigeria, who has attained the age of 18 years ... shall be entitled to be registered as a voter...." Constitution, Article 71(2) (1979). Electoral Decree No. 77 of 1977, §1(1) entitled all adults of 18 years and above to vote. [Constitution is now suspended.]

28. "All citizens are equal before the law without distinction of ... sex...." Constitution, Article 16 (1978). "All ... citizens of majority age not excluded by law may vote, in the conditions set out by law." Constitution, Article 9 (1978).

29. "...Every person ... is entitled to the fundamental rights and freedoms of the individual ... whatever his ... sex...." Constitution, Sec. 5 (1978). "Every citizen ... being 21 years of age and of sound mind shall have the right to vote...." Constitution, Sec. 33 (1978). [Suspended.]

30. "All citizens regardless of sex, ... shall be entitled to equal rights and duties before the law." Constitution, Article 6 (1979). "Every citizen who fulfills the conditions prescribed by the law shall be entitled to elect and be elected." Constitution, Article 22 (1979). [Suspended.]

31. "All persons ... have equal rights and duties, irrespective of ... sex...." Constitution, Article 38 (1973). "Every citizen shall have the right to participate in elections and referendums when he attains 18 years of age and fulfills conditions of eligibility as prescribed by law." Constitution, Article 45 (1973). [Suspended.]

32. "Every citizen of Tanzania who has attained the age of 18 years is entitled to vote in an election performed in Tanzania by the people." Constitution, Article 4(1) (1977). "...Every community has the duty—To ensure that Government and all National Institutions give the same opportunities to all the people, women and men...." Constitution, Foreword, C(6) (1977). [Constitution now suspended.]

33. "All Zairians are equal before the law ... no Zairian may be subject to discriminatory measures ... by reason of his ... sex...." Constitution, Article 12 (1978). "Every Zairian shall be an elector at 18 years of age." Constitution, Article 29 (1978).

34. "...Every person ... has been and shall continue to be entitled to the fundamental rights and freedoms of the individual ... whatever his ... sex...." Constitution, Article 13 (1973). "Every citizen ... who has attained the age of 18 years shall ... be entitled to be registered as ... a voter.... Every person who is registered ... as a voter ... shall ... be entitled ... to vote...." Constitution, Article 72 (1973).

35. "...Every person is entitled to the fundamental rights and freedoms of the individual regardless of ... sex...." Constitution, Article 11 (1979). "...Any citizen ... who has attained the age of 18 years shall be qualified for registration as a voter." Constitution, Schedule 3, 3(1) (1979).

36. "Lack of interest in political life, which has characterized the Murundikaza woman, must disappear from our political scene. . . . We will work for their emancipation and their political training, and we will foster their participation in the political life of the country." Constitution, Provision: The Union of Barundikazi Women (1976).

37. "All persons . . . should enjoy equal rights and freedoms." Constitution, Article 2(1)(v) (1966). ". . . Every citizen . . . who has attained the age of 21 years shall be entitled to be registered . . . as a voter . . . a person shall be qualified to be registered as a voter . . . if . . . he—is a citizen of the Republic [and] . . . has attained the age of 21 years." Constitution, Article 29 (1966).

38. "All citizens have the same rights and the same duties. They are equal before the law." Constitution, Article 6 (1959). "An elector is every citizen . . . having attained at least 20 years of age." Constitution, Article 20 (1959).

Voting Rights References, Middle East/Arabian Gulf

1. "Citizens . . . have equal public rights and duties without discrimination between them on the basis of sex. . . ." Constitution, Article 40 (1971). "A citizen has the right to elect and to be nominated. . . ." Constitution, Article 62 (1971). Women were first granted the right to vote in Egypt in 1956.

2. "All citizens of the nation, whether men or women, are equally protected by the law. They also enjoy . . . political . . . rights according to Islamic standards." Constitution, Article 20 (1979). Women were first granted the right to vote in Iran in 1963 by declaration of the Shah.

3. "A man and a woman shall have equal status with regard to any legal proceeding. . . ." Women's Equal Rights Law, Article 1 (1951). Under the Basic Law, every citizen who has reached the age of 18 is entitled to vote. See P. Albeck, "The Status of Women in Israel," *Am. J. Comp. L.,* Vol. 20, No. 4, p. 693 (Fall, 1972).

4. "All Lebanese are equal before the law. They enjoy civil and political rights and shall be liable to public charges and obligations without any distinction." Constitution, Article 7 (1947). Women in Lebanon generally enjoy the same political rights as men, including the vote. See H. Nemer, "The Status of Women in the World Today: Lebanon," *Rev. Contemp. L.,* Vol. 7, No. 1, 134–43 (1960). [Suspended.]

5. "All individuals are equal before the law irrespective of . . . sex. . . ." Constitution, Article 12 (1974). "All citizens are entitled to elect and be elected. . . . Elections shall be free and secret, and shall be conducted on the basis of equality, direct suffrage, open counting and classification." Constitution, Article 55 (1974).

6. "Every citizen being 18 years old on elections day, shall have the right to vote," Constitution, Article 10 (1970). "All thc citizens are equal in their rights and duties. . . ." Constitution, Article 34 (1970). "The State shall ensure equal rights for men and women in all fields of political . . . life. . . ." Constitution, Article 36 (1970).

7. "Citizens are equal before the law, without discrimination because of . . . sex. . . ." Constitution, Article 19(1) (1970).

8. "All persons shall enjoy equal public rights and shall be subject to equal public duties without distinction on grounds of . . . sex. . . ." Constitution, Article 9 (1970).

9. "All Yemenis are equal in (terms of) public rights and obligations." Constitution, Article 19 (1970). "Women are the sisters of men. They have their mandatory rights and obligations as stipulated in the Shari'ah and in accordance with the law." Constitution, Article 34 (1970). "The State has no right to impose distinction in human rights due to . . . sex. . . ." Constitution, Article 43 (1970).

10. "Jordanians shall be equal before the law. There shall be no discrimination between them as regards their rights and duties, on grounds of race, language or religion." Constitution, Article 6(1) (1952). [Suspended.]

11. "The citizens are equal before the law in their rights and duties." Constitution,

Article 25(3) (1973). "Every citizen has the right to participate in the political ... life." Constitution, Article 26 (1973).

12. "All persons shall be equal before the law. No discrimination shall be practiced between citizens of the Union by reason of race, nationality, religious belief or social position." Constitution, Article 25 (1971).

Voting Rights References, Far East

1. "All citizens aged 17 and above have the right to elect and be elected, irrespective of sex. . . ." Constitution, Article 52 (1972).

2. "All citizens who have reached the age of 18 have the right to vote and to stand for election. . . ." Constitution, Article 44 (1978). "Women enjoy equal rights with men in all spheres of political ... life. . . ." Constitution, Article 53 (1978).

3. "All of the people are equal under the law and there shall be no discrimination in political ... relations because of ... sex. . . ." Constitution, Article 14 (1947). ". . . Universal adult suffrage is guaranteed with regard to the election of public officials." Constitution, Article 15 (1947). Women were first given the right to vote on November 3, 1946, when the new Constitution came into force.

4. "Citizens ... enjoy equal rights irrespective of sex. . . ." Constitution, Article 76 (1960). "All citizens ... who have attained the age of 18 ... are granted the right to vote in elections. . . ." Constitution, Article 81 (1960). ". . . The infringement, in any form whatsoever, of the equal rights of men and women is forbidden by law." Constitution, Article 84 (1960).

5. "All citizens shall be equal before the law, and there shall be no discrimination in political ... life on account of sex. . . ." Constitution, Article 10(1) (1980). "All citizens who have attained to the age of 20 shall have the right to vote. . . ." Constitution, Article 23 (1980).

6. "All citizens ... irrespective of sex ... shall be equal before the law." Constitution, Article 7 (1947). "Any citizen ... who has attained the age of 20 years shall have the right of election in accordance with law." Constitution, Article 130 (1947).

7. Electoral Law. See M. Tsao, "The Status of Women in the World of Today, China," *Rev. Contemp. L.* Vol. 7, No. 1: 54–60 (1960).

Voting Rights References, Indochina/Southeast Asia

1. "All citizens, regardless of their ... sex ... have the right to vote upon reaching the age of 18, and to stand for election." Constitution, Article 57 (1980). In addition, Decrees No. 14 of September 8, 1945 and No. 51 of October 17, 1945 (Dem. Rep. of Vietnam) specified that men and women over 18 are entitled to vote and stand for election in elections to the National Assembly.

2. "All citizens shall have the same status in law and in the government." Constitution, Article 27 (1945).

3. "All persons are equal before the law and entitled to the equal protection of the law. . . ." Constitution, Article 8(1) (1963).

4. "All persons are equal before the law and entitled to the equal protection of the law." Constitution, Article 12(1) (1963).

5. "All persons are equal before the law and shall enjoy equal protection under the law." Constitution, Article 23 (1978). "All persons shall enjoy political rights." Constitution, Article 23 (1978).

6. "Every citizen who ... [is 21] ... is entitled to vote. . . ." Constitution, Article 119 (1963).

7. Law No. 15 (1969), as amended by Law No. 4, Article 9 (1975).

8. "It shall be the obligation of every citizen qualified to vote to register and cast his vote." Constitution, Article 4 (1973).

9. The Philippine legislature granted the right of suffrage to women by Act No. 4112 (1933). (Women did not actually exercise this right until 1937.) See I.R. Cortes, "Philippine Law and the Status of Women," *Col. Human Rights Rev.* Vol. 8: 229–61 (1976).

10. "...Men and women are fully equal in every respect...." Constitution, Article 13 (1972).

Voting Rights References, South Pacific

1. Constitution, Article 3 (1970); Constitution, Article 41 (1970).
2. Constitution, Article 3 (1979); Constitution, Article 64(1) (1979).
3. Constitution, Article 3 (1968); Constitution, Article 29 (1968).
4. Constitution, Articles 2, 5, 55 (1975); Constitution, Article 50 (1975).
5. Constitution, Article 3 (1978); Constitution, Article 56 (1978).
6. Constitution, Article 3 (1978); Constitution, Article 54 (1978).
7. Constitution, Article 5 (1980); Constitution, Article 17(1) (1978).
8. "All persons are equal before the law and entitled to equal protection under the law ... (No) law and no ... action of the State shall ... subject any person ... to any disability or restriction or confer ... any privilege or advantage on grounds only of ... sex...." Constitution, Article 15 (1960). "Subject to the Provisions of this Constitution, the mode of electing members of the Legislative Assembly ... the qualifications of electors, and the manner in which the roll for each territorial constituency and the individual voters' rolls shall be established and kept shall be prescribed by law." Constitution, Article 44(3) (1960).
9. Constitution, Article 30 (1901).
10. 1893 Electoral Act. See R. Clark, "Introduction to New Zealand," *Constitutions of the Countries of the World.*

Voting Rights References, the Caribbean

1. Constitution, Article 3, 14 (1981); Constitution, Article 40(2) (1981).
2. Constitution, Article 15 (1973); Constitution, Article 47, 48 (1973).
3. Constitution, Article 11 (1966); Constitution, Article 42(1) (1966).
4. Constitution, Article 3 (1981); Constitution, Article 92 (1981).
5. Constitution, Article 1, 13 (1978); Constitution, Article 33(2) (1973).
6. Constitution, Article 1, 13 (1973); Constitution, Article 32(2) (1978).
7. Constitution, Article 29(1), 40(1) (1980); Constitution, Article 32(2) (1973).
8. Constitution, Article 13 (1962); Constitution, Article 37(2) (1962).
9. Constitution, Article 1, 13 (1978); Constitution, Article 33(2) (1978).
10. Constitution, Article 1, 13 (1979); Constitution, Article 27(2) (1979).
11. Constitution, Article 1, 14 (1976); Constitution, Article 82(2) (1976).
12. Representation of the People Law, Cap. 342 (1955), provides that all persons who have attained the age of 18 are entitled to vote.
13. "All Dominicans of either sex over 18 years of age, and those who are or who have been married, although under that age, are citizens." Constitution, Article 12 (1966). "The rights of citizenship are: (1) the right to vote...." Constitution, Article 13 (1966). "Voting is compulsory for all citizens. Voting shall be personal, free and secret." Constitution, Article 88 (1966).
14. "All Haitians, regardless of sex, who have attained 18 years of age may exercise their political and civil rights...." Constitution, Article 8 (1964). "Haitians shall be equal before the law.... Every Haitian may take an active part in his country's government ... without distinction as to ... sex...." Constitution, Article 16 (1964). "For the citizen, voting is not only a right but an obligation imposed by his civic duty." Constitution, Article 40 (1964). [Constitution now suspended.]

15. "Considering the equality before the law of all citizens without distinction as to . . . sex. . . ." Constitution, Preamble (1975). ". . . No one may be given any advantage or placed at any disadvantage because of his . . . sex. . . ." Constitution, Article 1(2) (1975). "The members of Parliament shall be directly elected, by universal suffrage, by the inhabitants who are of Suriname nationality and who have reached the age of 21 years." Article 53 (1975).

16. "All Cubans 16 years of age and over, men and women alike, have the right to vote." Constitution, Article 135 (1976).

Voting Rights References, North America

1. Every citizen . . . has, without unreasonable distinction or limitation, the right to vote in an election of members of the House of Commons or of a legislative assembly. . . ." Constitution Act, pt. 1, Article 3 (1980).

2. Constitution (1789), Article 19 (added in 1920).

Bibliography

Books written by several contributors are listed alphabetically by title indicating the name(s) of the editor(s).

Abdul-Rauf, Muhammad: *The Islamic View of Women and the Family.* New York: Speller, 1977.

Abortion Law and Public Policy. Dennis Campbell, editor. The Hague: Martinus Nijhof, 1984.

Access to Birth Control: A World Assessment. Population Briefing Paper No. 19. Washington DC: Population Crisis Committee, 1987.

Adei, Christopher. *African Law South of the Sahara.* Missouri: International Institute for Advanced Studies, 1981.

African Problems and Challenges. C.F. de Villiers, editor. Johannesburg: Valiant, 1976.

African Women and the Law. Margaret Hay and Marcia Wright, editors. Boston: Boston University African Studies Center, 1982.

African Women South of the Sahara. Margaret Hay and Sharon Stichter, editors. New York: Longmans, 1984.

Akande, J.O. *Introduction to the Nigerian Constitution.* London: Sweet and Maxwell, 1981.

Alic, Margaret. *Hypatia's Heritage: A History of Women in Science.* Boston: Beacon, 1986.

The American Woman 1988–1989: A Status Report. Sara Rix, editor. New York: Norton, 1988.

Andors, Phylis. *The Unfinished Liberation of Chinese Women.* Bloomington: Indiana University Press, 1983.

Annual Summary of Births, Marriages, Divorces and Deaths 1986. Washington DC: United States National Center for Health Statistics.

Ardagh, John. *France in the 1980s.* London: Penguin, 1984.

Area Handbooks. Washington DC: United States State Department.

Bae, L.S. *Women and the Law in Korea.* Seoul: League of Women Voters, 1973.

Bamdad, Badr. *From Darkness into Light.* F.R. Bagley, translator. Hicksville NY: Exposition, 1977.

Barry, Kathleen. *Female Sexual Slavery.* Englewood Cliffs NJ: Prentice Hall, 1979.

Basic Survey of Schools 1984. Tokyo: Japanese Ministry of Education.

Berger, Gilda. *Women, Work and Wages.* New York: Franklin Watts, 1986.

Bergmann, Barbara. *The Economic Emergence of Women.* New York: Basic, 1986.

Bernard, Jessie. *The Female World from a Global Perspective.* Bloomington: Indiana University Press, 1987.

Behind the Green Revolution. Washington DC: World Watch Institute, 1986.

Bielby, W.T., and Baron, J.N. *Women's Place Is with Other Women: Sex Segregation in the Workplace.* Berkeley: University of California Press, 1983.

Birnbaum, Leslie. *Feminism in Italy.* Middletown CT: Wesleyan University Press, 1987.

Blaustein, Albert, and Gisbert, F. *Constitutions of the Countries of the World.* Dobbs Ferry NY: Oceana, 1986.

Brijbhushan, J. *Muslim Women: In Purdah and Out of It.* New Delhi: Vikas, 1980.

Buvinic, M.; Lycette, M.; and McGreevey, W. *Women and Poverty in the Third World.* Baltimore: Johns Hopkins University Press, 1983.

Case Studies of Human Rights. Willem Veenhoven, editor. The Hague: Martinus Nijhof, 1975.

Chambers, R.; Longhurst, L.; and Pacey, A. *Seasonal Dimensions to Rural Power.* London: Pinter, 1981.

Change in Tunisia. Russel Stone and John Simmons, editors. State University of New York Press, 1976.

Changing Patterns of Rural Women's Employment, Production, and Reproduction in China. Geneva: International Labor Organization, 1986.

Child Care and Equality of Opportunities 1988. Strasbourg: European Commission.

China Reconstructs. Beijing: Chinese Government.

Citoyennes à part entière 1986. Paris: French Government.

A Closer Look at Comparable Worth. Robert Williams and Lorence Kessler, editors. Washington DC: National Foundation for the Study of Equal Employment, 1984.

Cohen, Marcia. *The Sisterhood.* New York: Simon & Schuster, 1988.

Comparable Worth. Heidi Hartmann, editor. Washington DC: National Academy Press, 1985.

Comparable Worth and Wage Discrimination. Helen Remick, editor. Philadelphia: Temple University Press, 1984.

Comparative Human Rights. Richard Claude, editor. Baltimore: Johns Hopkins University Press, 1976.

Comparative Perspectives of Third World Women. Beverly Lindsy, editor. New York: Praeger, 1980.

Comparative Perspectives of Third World Women. Geneva: International Labor Organization, 1985.

Conditions of Work: Vocational Training and Employment of Women. Geneva: International Labor Organization, 1979.

Condon, J. *Japanese Women of the Eighties.* New York: Dodd, Mead, 1985.

Cook, A., and Hayashi, H. *Working Women in Japan.* Ithaca NY: Cornell University Press, 1980.

Croll, Elisabeth. *Chinese Women Since Mao.* New York: Sharpe, 1983.

The Cross Cultural Study of Women. Margot Duley and Mary Edwards, editors. New York: Feminist, 1986.

Curtin, K. *Women in China.* New York: Pathfinder, 1975.

The Decade for Women in Latin America and the Caribbean. Santiago: Economic Commission for Latin America and the Caribbean, 1988.

A Decade of Women and the Law. Margaret Rogers, editor. London: Commonwealth Secretariat Legal Division, 1985.

Development Forum. New York: United Nations, 1985.

Die Neue Internationale Arbeidseiung. Frobel, F.J., et al. Hamburg: Reinbek, 1977.

Digest of Educational Statistics. Washington DC: United States Department of Education, 1987.

The Economic Role of Women in the E.C.E. Region. Geneva: International Labor Organization, 1985.

Economic Report of the President 1987. Washington DC: United States Government Printing Office.

Education and Manpower Development Study. Bloemfontein, South Africa: University of the Orange Free State Research Institute for Educational Planning, 1988.

Egalité(e) 1981 les droits des femmes vers l'an 1000. Paris: French Ministry of Women's Affairs.

Eisenhardt, G. *Deutsche Rechtsgeschichte.* West Germany: Beck Verlag, 1984.

Employment and Earnings. Washington DC: United States Bureau of Labor Statistics, 1987.

Employment Gazette. London: Government of Great Britain.

Employment Trends. Washington DC: O.E.C.D., 1986.

Equal Opportunity for Women. Spain: Spanish Ministry of Social Welfare, 1987.

Equal Rights for Women in the German Democratic Republic. East Berlin: G.D.R. Committee for Human Rights, 1973.

Equality Between Men and Women 1984. Strasbourg: Council of Europe.

Esposito, John L. *Women in Muslim Family Law.* Syracuse NY: Syracuse University Press, 1982.

Estimates of the Population of the United States 1987. Washington DC: United States Bureau of Census.

Export Processing Zones. Geneva: International Labor Organization, 1983.

Factory and Family: The Divided Lives of South African Women. Fatima Meer, editor. Durban: Institute of Black Research, 1985.

Fakten zur Emanzipation von Frau und Mann 1983. Bern: Swiss Commission on Women's Questions.

Female and Male in West Africa. Christine Oppong, editor. London: Allen & Unwin, 1983.

Female Power, Autonomy and Demographic Change in the Third World. Richard Anker, editor. London: Croom Helm, 1982.

Fertility of American Women 1984. Washington DC: United States Bureau of the Census.

Fisher, John. *The Afrikaners.* London: Cassell, 1969.

Five Studies on the Situation of Women in Latin America. New York: United Nations, 1982.

Flanz, Gisbert. *Comparative Women's Rights and Political Participation in Europe.* Dobbs Ferry NY: Transitional, 1983.

For the Record. Caroline Pezzullo, editor. New York: International Women's Tribune Center, 1985.

A Fourteen Country Alternative Asian Report on the Impact of the U.N. Decade for Women. Philippines: Asian Women's Research and Action Network, 1985.

Frau, Realitat and Utopie. Lili Nabholz-Haidegger, et al. Switzerland: Christa Koppel, 1984.

Frauen Europas. Brussels: European Commission.

Frauen in der Bundesrepublik Deutschland 1984. Bonn: German Ministry for Youth, Health and Family.

Frauenfragen, 1985 and 1986. Bern: Swiss Commission on Women's Questions.

Gates, A., and Shelley, K. *Fringe Benefits.* New York: Fine, 1986.

Gazette. Prague: Czechoslovakian Government.

Glazer, Nathan. *Affirmative Discrimination.* New York: Basic, 1975.

Gold, M. *A Dialogue on Comparable Worth.* Ithaca NY: I.L.R. Press, 1983.

Goldstein, Leslie. *The Constitutional Rights of Women.* Madison: University of Wisconsin Press, 1988.

Government Gazette. Pretoria: South African Government Printer.

Grieve, N., and Grimshaw, P. *Australian Women.* Melbourne, Australia: Oxford University Press, 1981.

Growing Up in a Divided Society. Eleanor Whyte and Jennifer Louw, editors. Johannesburg: Ravan, 1986.

Guide des droits des femmes 1986. Paris: French National Center for Information on the Status of Women.

Handbuch zur beruflichen Forderung von Frauen. H. Daubler-Gmelin, et al. West Germany: VSA Verlag, 1985.

Hansonn, C., and Liden, K. *Moscow Women.* New York: Pantheon, 1983.

Harrison, David. *The White Tribe of Africa.* London: Macmillan, 1981.

Harrison, P. *Inside the Third World.* London: Penguin, 1981.

Hay, M.J., and Bay, E.G. *African Women South of the Sahara.* New York: Longmans, 1984.

Hazelton, Leslie. *Israeli Women: The Reality Behind the Myths.* New York: Simon & Schuster, 1987.

Heitlinger, Alena. *Women and State Socialism.* Montreal, Canada: McGill-Queens State University Press, 1979.

Hewlett, Sylvia. *A Lesser Life: The Myth of Women's Liberation in the U.S.A.* New York: Warner, 1986.

Heyzer, Noeleen. *Working Women in South East Asia.* Philadelphia: Open University Press, 1986.

Hogg, Peter W. *Constitutional Law of Canada.* Toronto: Carswell, 1985.

Hough, J. *The Soviet Union and Social Science Theory.* Princeton NJ: Princeton University Press, 1977.

Hoyrup, E. *Women of Science, Technology and Medicine.* Denmark: Roskilde University Press, 1987.

Hubbs, Joanna. *Mother Russia*. Bloomington: Indiana University Press, 1988.
Human Rights: International Instruments. New York: United Nations, 1982.
Indian Women in Subsistence and Agricultural Labour. Geneva: International Labor Organization, 1986.
Industrialization, Trade and Female Employment in Developing Countries. Susan Joekes, editor. Santo Domingo: INSTRAW, 1986.
INSTRAW News: Women and Development. Santo Domingo.
Integrating Women into Development Programs. Mayra Buvinic, et al. Washington DC: International Center for Research on Women, 1986.
Israel Yearbook of Human Rights 1973. Jerusalem: Israeli Government.
Jancar, Barbara. *Women Under Communism*. Baltimore: Johns Hopkins University Press, 1978.
Jannsen-Jurreit, M. *Sexism*. New York: McGraw-Hill, 1982.
Johnson, Kay. *Women, the Family and Peasant Revolution in China*. Chicago: University of Chicago Press, 1983.
Klein, Ethel. *Gender Politics*. Cambridge MA: Harvard University Press, 1984.
Kome, Penney. *Women of Influence*. Toronto: Doubleday, 1985.
Kumar, M. *Social Equality—The Constitutional Experiment in India*. New Delhi: Chand, 1982.
Labor Force Survey 1984. Tokyo: Japanese Ministry of Labor.
Lacour-Gayet, Robert. *A History of South Africa*. London: Cassell, 1977.
Lapidus, Gail. *Women in Soviet Society*. Berkeley: University of California Press, 1978.
Lebra, T.S. *Japanese Women*. Honolulu: University of Hawaii Press, 1984.
The Legal Status of Rural Women. Rome: F.A.O., 1979.
le Riche, W. Harding. *Why Africa Is Poor*. Toronto: Citizens for Foreign Aid Reform, 1987.
Lerner, Gerda. *The Creation of Patriarchy*. New York: Oxford University Press, 1986.
List of Ratifications of Conventions. Geneva: United Nations, 1986.
Lovenduski, Joni. *Women and European Politics*. Amherst: University of Massachusetts Press, 1986.
McCauley, A. *Women's Work and Wages in the Soviet Union*. London: Allen & Unwin, 1981.
Male-Female Differences in Work Experience, Occupations and Earnings 1987. Washington DC: United States Bureau of the Census.
Markowitz, I.L. *Studies in Power and Class in Africa*. New York: Oxford University Press, 1987.
Mason, Mary Anne. *The Equality Trap*. New York: Simon & Schuster, 1988.
Menon, M. *Indu: Status of Muslim Women in India*. New Delhi: Uppal, 1981.
Milburn, Josephine. *Women as Citizens*. London: Sage, 1976.
Minai, Naila. *Women in Islam*. New York: Seaview, 1981.
The Modern Employment Market in Selected African Countries. Geneva: International Labor Organization, 1984.
Money Income of Households, Family and Persons in the United States of America 1987. Washington DC: United States Bureau of the Census.

Monthly Labor Review. United States Government.

Moore, C.H. *Tunisia Since Independence.* Los Angeles: University of California Press, 1965.

Morello, Karen. *The Invisible Bar.* Boston: Beacon, 1986.

Mother Was Not a Person. Margret Andersen, editor. Toronto: Content, 1972.

Muslim Peoples. Richard Weekes, editor. Westport CT: Greenwood, 1984.

Muslim Women. Freda Hussain, editor. Kent: Croom Helm, England, 1984.

Mutterkreutz and Arbeitsbuch. West Germany: Fischer Taschenbuch Verlag, 1980.

New Earnings Survey. Government of Great Britain.

Obi, S.N. Chinwuba. *Modern Family Law in Southern Nigeria.* London: Sweet & Maxwell, 1966.

Official Yearbook 1985. Pretoria: South African Government.

Participation of Women in Co-operatives and Productive Groups in Honduras. P. Chanduri and N. Till, editors. Washington DC: International Bank for Reconstruction and Development, 1986.

Patai, Daphne. *Brazilian Women Speak.* Rutgers University Press, 1988.

Patriarchy in a Welfare Society. H. Holter, editor. Oslo University Press, 1984.

Pay Equity and Comparable Worth. Washington DC: Women's Bureau of National Affairs, 1984.

Perspectives on Power: Women in Africa, Asia and Latin America. Jean O'Barr, editor. Durham NC: Duke University Center for International Studies, 1982.

Pharr, Susan. *Political Women in Japan.* Berkeley: University of California Press, 1981.

Pickthall, Mohammed. *The Meaning of the Glorious Koran.* Translation. New York: Mentor, 1953.

The Politics of Law: A Progressive Critique. New York: Pantheon, 1982.

The Politics of the Second Electorate. Joni Lovenduski and Jill Hills, editors. London: Routledge & Kegan Paul, 1981.

Population Briefing Paper No. 20. Washington DC: Population Crisis Committee, 1988.

Population Growth and Policies in Sub-Saharan Africa. Washington DC: International Bank for Reconstruction and Development, 1986.

Population of India. Bangkok: Economic Commission for Asia and the Pacific, 1982.

Population Vital Statistics 1984. Tokyo: Japanese Ministry of Health and Welfare.

Positive Action for the Benefit of Women 1986. Strasbourg: Council of Europe.

Present Status of Women and Politics 1983. Tokyo: Japanese Office of the Prime Minister.

Prinsloo, E. *Ek, My Kind of My Werk.* Pretoria: HAUM, 1987.

The Profile of Working Women. Washington DC: National Association of Working Women, 1987.

Putnam, R.D. *The Comparative Study of Political Elites.* Englewood Cliffs NJ: Prentice Hall, 1978.

Rakusen, M.L., and Hunt, D.P. *Distribution of Matrimonial Assets on Divorce*. London: Butterworth, 1982.

Recruitment, Training and Career Development in the Public Service. Geneva: International Labor Organization, Report 11, 1983.

Report on the Situation of Women in Europe 1984. Strasbourg: European Parliament.

Resources, Power and Women. Geneva: International Labor Organization, 1985.

Reversing Africa's Decline. Washington DC: World Watch Institute, 1985.

Rhoodie, Eschel. *Discrimination in the Constitutions of the World*. Columbus GA: Brentwood, 1984.

Robins-Mowry, Dorothy. *The Hidden Sun: Women of Modern Japan*. Boulder CO: Westview, 1983.

Rogers, Barbara. *The Domestication of Women: Discrimination in Development Societies*. New York: St. Martin's, 1979.

The Role of A.C.A.S. Conciliation in Equal Pay and Sex Discrimination Cases. C. Graham and N. Lewis, editors. London: Equal Opportunities Commissioin, 1985.

Ross, Susan, and Barcher, Ann. *The Rights of Women*. New York: Bantam, rev. ed., 1983.

Rover, Constance. *Women's Suffrage and Party Politics in Britain 1866–1914*. London: Routledge & Kegan Paul, 1967.

Rural Development and Women in Africa. Geneva: International Labor Organization, 1985.

Rural Labour Markets and Employment Opportunities. Geneva: International Labor Organization, ACRDX/1983/111.

Rural Women in Latin America 1975–1984. Santiago: Economic Commission for Latin America, 1985.

Sachs, Albie, and Wilson, John. *Sexism and the Law*. New York: Free Press, 1979.

Sanasarian, Elisabeth. *The Women's Rights Movement in Iran*. New York: Praeger, 1982.

Sanderson, Lillian. *Against the Mutilation of Women*. London: Ithaca, 1981.

Saunders, C., and Marsden, D. *Pay Inequalities in the European Community*. London: Butterworth, 1981.

Schuler, Margaret. *Empowerment and the Law*. OEF International, Washington, 1986.

Scientific-Technological Change and the Role of Women in Development. P. D'Onofrio-Fores and Sheila Pfafflin, editors. Boulder CO: Westview, 1982.

Seager, Joni, and Ollson, Ann. *Women in the World, an International Atlas*. New York: Simon & Schuster, 1986.

Segal, Lynne. *Is the Future Female?* London: Virago, 1987.

Sex and Class in Latin America. June Nash and Helen Safa, editors. Brooklyn NY: Bergin, 1980.

Sex Inequalities in Urban Employment in Third World Countries. Richard Anker and Catherine Hein, editors. Geneva: International Labor Organization, 1986.

Sex Segregation in the Workplace: Trends, Explanations and Remedies. Barbara Reskin, editor. Washington DC: National Academy Press, 1984.

Simeone, Angela. *Academic Women.* New York; 1987.

Sisterhood Is Global. Robin Morgan, editor. Garden City NY: Doubleday, 1984.

Sivard, Ruth. *Women: A World Survey.* Washington DC: World Priority, 1986.

South Africa: The Road Ahead. G.F. Jacobs, editor. Johannesburg: Jonathan Ball, 1986.

South African Digest. Pretoria: South African Government.

Soviet Sisterhood. Barbara Holland, editor. Bloomington: Indiana University Press, 1985.

State by State Guide to Women's Rights. Washington DC: National Organization of Women, 1986 and 1987.

The State of the World's Women. New York: New Internationalist Publications, 1985.

Statistiches Jahrbuch der Schweiz 1985. Bern: Swiss Government.

The Status of Women in Nepal. Katmandu: Center for Economic Development and Administration, Tribhuvan University, 1981.

Steiner, Shari. *The Female Factor: Women in Western Europe.* Chicago: Intercultural, 1977.

Stride by Stride: Women's Issues in Tokyo 1983. Tokyo: Metropolitan Government.

Survey on Corporate Hiring Plans 1981. Tokyo: Japanese Ministry of Labor.

Tamarin, G.R. *The Israeli Dilemma.* Rotterdam University Press, 1973.

Thibault, Giselle. *The Dissenting Feminist Academy.* New York: American University Studies, 1987.

Timberlake, L. *Africa in Crisis.* Washington DC: International Institute for Environment and Development, 1985.

Tokyo Newsletter. Japanese Government.

Towards Equality. Report of the Committee on the Status of Women. New Delhi: Government Printer, 1975.

Treiman, D., and Hartman, H. *Women, Work and Wages: Equal Pay for Jobs of Equal Value.* Washington DC: National Academy Press, 1981.

Tunisia: A Country Study. Harold Nelson, editor. The American University, 1979

The Unfinished Democracy—Women in Nordic Politics. Elina Haavio-Mannila, editor. Oxford: Pergammon, 1985.

The United Nations and the Status of Women. New York: United Nations, 1964.

Van der Walt, S. *Die Vrou in die Werksituasie in die RSA: 'n Verwysingsraamwerk.* Pretoria: Human Sciences Research Council, 1986.

Vestnik Statistiki 1984. Moscow: Census Ministry.

Victims of Politics. Kurt Glaser and Stefan Possony, editors. New York: Columbia University Press, 1979.

Wei, Karen T. *Women in China: A Select Bibliography.* Westport CT: Greenwood, 1984.

Weitzman, L. *The Divorce Revolution.* New York: Free Press, 1985.
White, S. *Political Culture and Soviet Politics.* London: Macmillan, 1979.
Wiehahn Commission Report. Pretoria: South African Government.
Willis, D. *Klass.* New York: St. Martin's, 1985.
Wolf, Margery. *Revolution Postponed, Women in Contemporary China.* Stanford CA: Stanford University Press, 1985.
Wolfram, E. *A History of China.* Los Angeles: University of California Press, 1977.
Women: A World Report. Debbie Taylor, editor. New York: Oxford University Press, 1985.
Women and Development: Perspectives from South and South East Asia. Rounaq Jahan and Hanna Papanek, editors. Dacca, Bangladesh: Institute of Law, 1979.
Women and Revolution in Iran. Guity Nashat, editor. Boulder CO: Westview, 1983.
Women and Russia. Tatyana Mamonova, editor. Boston: Beacon, 1984.
Women and Technological Change in Developing Countries. Rosslyn Dauber and Melinda Cain, editors. Boulder CO: Westview, 1981.
Women and the Constitution in Canada. Audrey Doerr and Micheline Carrier, editors. Ottowa: Canadian Advisory Council on the Status of Women, 1981.
Women and the Cultural Industries. Michele Matterlat, editor. Paris: U.N.E.S.C.O., 1981.
Women and the Equal Rights Amendment. Catherine Simpson, editor. New York: Bowker, 1972.
Women and the Family in the Middle East. Elisabeth Fernea, editor. Austin: University of Texas Press, 1985.
Women and the Law. Flerida Romero, editor. University of the Philippines Law Center.
Women at Work. Geneva: International Labor Organization, Vols. 1 and 2, 1988.
Women, Employment and Development in the Arab World. Nasr J. Abu and N. Khoury, editors. Institute for Women's Studies in the Arab World, Beirut University. Berlin: Mouton, 1985.
Women, Health and Development. Geneva: World Health Organization, 1985.
Women in Africa: Studies in Social and Economic Change. N.J. Hafkin and E.G. Bay, editors. Stanford CA: Stanford University Press, 1975.
Women in Andean Agriculture. C.D. Deere and M. del Leal, editors. Geneva: International Labor Organization, 1982.
Women in Contemporary India and South Asia. Minnatur J., editor. New Delhi: Manohar, 1980.
Women in Contemporary Muslim Societies. Jane Smith, editor. New Jersey: Bucknell University Press, 1980.
Women in Developing Countries. Kathleen Staudt and Jane Jacquette, editors. New York: Naworth, 1983.
Women in Economic Activity. Geneva: International Labor Organization, 1985.
Women in Economic Activity, 1950–2000. Geneva: International Labor Organization, 1986.

Women in Law. Julia Brophy and Carol Smart, editors. London: Routledge & Kegan Paul, 1985.

Women in Rural Development: The Republic of China. E. Croll, editor. Geneva: International Labor Organization, 1979.

Women in Russia. Atkinson, Dallin and Lapidus, editors. Hassocks, England: Harvester, 1978.

Women in Russia. Sachs and Atkinson, et al., editors. Hassocks, England: Harvester, 1978.

Women in the Modern World. Raphael Patai, ed. New York: Free Press, 1967.

Women in the Muslim World. Louis Beck and Nikki Keddie, editors. Cambridge MA: Harvard University Press, 1978.

Women in the Political World in Europe 1984. Strasbourg: European Commission.

Women in the World Economy. Susan Joekes, editor. New York: Oxford University Press, 1986.

Women in the World. Lynn Iglitzin and Ruth Ross, editors. Santa Barbara CA: ABC–CLIO, 2nd ed., 1986.

Women in World Religions. Arvind Sharma, editor. State University of New York Press, 1987.

Women in World Terms, Facts and Trends. Center for Integrative Studies, State University of New York, 1975.

Women of Europe. Strasbourg: European Commission, 1984.

Women of Iran. Farah Azari, editor. London: Ithaca, 1983.

Women of the World. WID1-4. Washington DC: United States Agency for International Development, United States Department of Commerce, 1984 and 1985.

Women, Roles and Status in Eight Countries. Janet Fiele and Audrey Smock, editors. New York: Wiley, 1977.

Women: The Quiet Revolution. Johannesburg: J. Walter Thompson Agency, 1985.

Women Workers in Fifteen Countries. Jennie Farley, editor. Ithaca NY: I.L.R. Press, 1985.

Women's Changing Role. Wylie TX: Information Aids, 1988.

Women's Economic Participation in Asia and the Pacific. Bangkok: Economic Commission for Asia and the Pacific, 1987.

Women's Education in the Third World. Gail Kelly and Carolyn Elliot, editors. Albany: State University of New York, 1982.

Women's Rights and the Law. Brown, Freedman, Katz, Price, et al. New York: Praeger, 1977.

Women's Work, Men's Work: Sex Segregation on the Job. Barbara Reskin and Heidi Hartmann, editors. Washington DC: National Academy Press, 1986.

Written Constitutions. Henk van Marseveen and Ger van der Tang, editors. New York: Oceana, 1978.

The Work Situation of South African Women. Ros Hirschowitz and Gerri Cilliers, editors. Pretoria: Human Sciences Research Council, 1987.

World Economic Survey 1988: Current Trends and Policies in the World Economy. New York: United Nations, 1988.

World Population Policies. New York: United Nations, 1988.
World Population Trends and Politics. New York: United Nations, 1988.
World Survey: Women in Agriculture. A/Conf/116/4. New York: United Nations, 1985.
World Survey on the Role of Women in Development. E.86.IV.3. New York: United Nations, 1986.
World Watch Paper No. 37. Washington DC: World Watch Institute, 1980.
Yao, Esther Lee. *Chinese Women Past and Present.* Ide House, 1983.
Yearbook. Geneva: U.N.E.S.C.O., 1982.
Yearbook of Human Rights. New York: United Nations, annual.
Yearbook of Labour Statistics. Geneva: International Labor Organization, 1982, 1983, 1986.
Ziskind, David. *Labor Provisions in Asian Constitutions.* Los Angeles: Litlaw Foundation, 1984.
________. *Labor Provisions in the Constitutions of Europe.* Los Angeles: Litlaw Foundation, 1985.

Newspapers, Journals and Other Periodicals

(Published and distributed in the United States unless otherwise indicated.)

African Law Studies Review
African Studies Review
Allahabad Law Review [India]
American Anthropologist
American Economic Review
American Journal of Comparative Law
American Journal of International Law
American University Law Review
Annals of the American Academy of Political and Social Science
The Atlanta Constitution
The Atlanta Journal and Constitution
Bulletin [Africa Institute, Pretoria]
Bulletin [New Delhi, India]
Bulletin of Concerned Asian Scholars
Business Day [Johannesburg]
Business Week
Canadian Journal of African Studies
Catalyst
The Cape Times [Cape Town]
Ceres
Christian Science Monitor
Chronicle of Higher Education
The Citizen [Johannesburg]
City Press [Johannesburg]
Columbia Human Rights Law Review
Columbia Journal of Law and Social Problems
Columbia Journal of Transnational Law
Common Market Law Review
Common Market Law Review [London]
Commonwealth Law Bulletin [London]
Comparative and International Law Journal [Pretoria]
Comparative Labor Law
Comparative Law Yearbook
Comparative Politics
Comparative Studies in Society and History
Creative Loafing
Current Magazine

Development and Change
Development Digest
The Economist [London]
Economic Development and Cultural Change
Encyclopedia Biblica
Europe
Evening News [Asahi, Japan]
Fair Lady [Johannesburg]
First Class [I.A.P.A.]
Focus [Johannesburg]
The Herald [Port Elizabeth, South Africa]
The Houston Post
Human Rights Law Review
Human Rights Journal
Hypatia
INC. Magazine
India Today
Indian Bar Council Review [New Delhi]
Industry Week
Insight
International and Comparative Law Review
International Herald Tribune [Paris]
International Journal of Middle East Studies
International Journal of Sociology of Law
International Journal of Women's Studies
International Labour Review
International Studies Quarterly
International Yearbook 1987 [London]
IR Journal [Pretoria]
Japan Times [Tokyo]
Journal About Women and Society [New Delhi]
Journal of African Law [London]
Journal of Asian Studies
Journal of College Science Teaching
Journal of Economic Issues
Journal of Inter American Studies and World Affairs
Journal of Law and Society [London]
Journal of Modern African Studies [London]
Journal of Social History
Journal of Southern African Studies [London]
Journal of Women and Law [Canada]
Latin American Perspectives
Latin American Research Review
Le Nouvelle Observateur [Paris]
Louisiana Law Review
Macleans [Canada]
Metropolitan Digest [Johannesburg]
Middle East Journal
The Minneapolis Star and Tribune
Modern Law Review [London]
Mosaic
Ms.
National Georgraphic
Neue Juristiche Wochenzeitschrift [West Germany]
New Scientist [London]
Newsweek
Nederlands Juristenblad [The Hague]
New York State Journal of Medicine
The New York Times
The New Yorker
Parade
Philippine Law Journal [Manila]
Population and Development Review
Populi
The Pretoria News [South Africa]
Rapport [Johannesburg]
Relations Industrielle [University Laval, Canada]
Révue des Droits de l'Homme [Strasbourg]
Rooi Rose [Johannesburg]
St. Louis Post-Dispatch
Savvy Women

Scientific American
Signs: Journal of Women in Culture and Science
Slavic Review
Social Science and Medicine
Social Science Research
South African Yearbook of International Law [Pretoria]
Southern Africa Today [Johannesburg]
The Star [Johannesburg, airmail edition]
The Sunday Telegraph [London]
The Sunday Times [Johannesburg]
The Sunday Times [London]
Texas International Law Review
Time
U.S. News and World Report
Die Vaderland [Johannesburg]
Virginia International Law Review
Voice of Women [Sri Lanka]
The Wall Street Journal
The Washington Post
Women and Politics
Women's International Network News
Women's Studies Abstracts
Women's Studies International Forum
Working Woman
World Affairs
Yale Law Journal

Index

Subjects in this index not otherwise noted are women-specific.

A

Alexandria 13

B

C

D

G

H

I

J

K

L

M

T

U

V

W

X

Y

Z